THE CRIMINAL RESPONSIBILITY OF SENIOR POLITICAL AND MILITARY PRINCIPALS TO INTERNATIONAL CRIMES

ONE WEEK

As shown by the recent trials of Slobodan Milosevic, Charles Taylor and Saddam Hussein, the large-scale and systematic commission of international crimes is usually planned and set in motion by senior political and military leaders. Nevertheless, the application of traditional forms of criminal liability leads to the conclusion that they are mere accessories to such crimes. This does not reflect their central role and often results in a punishment which is inappropriately low in view of the impact of their actions and omissions. For these reasons, international criminal law has placed special emphasis on the development of the concepts of joint criminal enterprise (also known as the common purpose doctrine) and control of the crime, which aim to better reflect the central role played by senior political and military leaders in campaigns of large scale and systematic commission of international crimes. The Rome Statute of the International Criminal Court and the case law of the ICTY and the ICTR have, in recent years, played a unique role in achieving this goal.

Studies in International and Comparative Criminal Law: Volume 4

Studies in International and Comparative Criminal Law

General Editor: Michael Bohlander

Criminal law had long been regarded as the preserve of national legal systems, and comparative research in criminal law for a long time had something of an academic ivory tower quality. However, in the past 15 years it has been transformed into an increasingly, and moreover practically, relevant subject of study for international and comparative lawyers. This can be attributed to numerous factors, such as the establishment of ad hoc international criminal tribunals and the International Criminal Court, as well as to developments within the EU, the UN and other international organisations. There is a myriad of initiatives related to tackling terrorism, money laundering, organised crime, people trafficking and the drugs trade, and the international 'war' on terror. Criminal law is being used to address global or regional problems, often across the borders of fundamentally different legal systems, only one of which is the traditional divide between common and civil law approaches. It is therefore no longer solely a matter for domestic lawyers. The need exists for a global approach which encompasses comparative and international law.

Responding to this development this new series will include books on a wide range of topics, including studies of international law, EU law, the work of specific international tribunals, and comparative studies of national systems of criminal law. Given that the different systems to a large extent operate based on the idiosyncracies of the peoples and states that have created them, the series will also welcome pertinent historical, criminological and socio-legal research into these issues.

Editorial Committee:

Mohammed Ayat (ICTR, Kigali)
Robert Cryer (Birmingham)
Caroline Fournet (Exeter)
Kaiyan Kaikobad (Brunel)
Alex Obote-Odora (ICTR, Arusha)
Dawn Rothe (Old Dominion University, VA)
Silvia Tellenbach (Freiburg)
Helen Xanthaki (IALS, London)
Liling Yue (Beijing)

Volume 1: The German Criminal Code: A Modern English Translation
Michael Bohlander

Volume 2: Principles of German Criminal Law
Michael Bohlander

Volume 3: Crime, Procedure and Evidence in a Comparative and International Context: Essays in Honour of Professor Mirjan Damaška
Edited by John Jackson, Máximo Langer and Peter Tillers

Volume 4: The Criminal Responsibility of Senior Political and Military Leaders as Principals to International Crimes
Héctor Olásolo, with a Foreword by Judge Sir Adrian Fulford and an Introduction by Judge Ekaterina Trendafilova and an Epilogue by Professor Dr. Kai Ambos

The Criminal Responsibility of Senior Political and Military Leaders as Principals to International Crimes

Héctor Olásolo

with a Foreword by
Judge Sir Adrian Fulford

an Introduction by
Judge Ekaterina Trendafilova

and an Epilogue by
Professor Dr Kai Ambos

·H A R T·
PUBLISHING

OXFORD AND PORTLAND, OREGON
2010

Published in North America (US and Canada) by
Hart Publishing
c/o International Specialized Book Services
920 NE 58th Avenue, Suite 300
Portland, OR 97213-3786
USA
Tel: +1 503 287 3093 or toll-free: (1) 800 944 6190
Fax: +1 503 280 8832
E-mail: orders@isbs.com
Website: http://www.isbs.com

Hart Publishing Ltd, 16C Worcester Place, Oxford, OX1 2JW
Telephone: +44 (0)1865 517530 Fax: +44 (0)1865 510710
E-mail: mail@hartpub.co.uk
Website: http://www.hartpub.co.uk

British Library Cataloguing in Publication Data
Data Available

ISBN: 978-1-84113-695-0 (hardback)
ISBN: 978-1-84946-090-3 (paperback)

Typeset by Hope Services, Abingdon
Printed and bound in Great Britain by
CPI Antony Rowe, Chippenham, Wiltshire

FOREWORD

This book provides a hugely important contribution to a complex and vital area of international criminal law. For the courts and tribunals which are charged with the responsibility of trying the most serious cases in the criminal calendar, there can be few subjects of greater concern than the approach that should be taken when dealing with the alleged responsibility of those who are seemingly 'in control' when the worst international crimes are committed. The author, who brings to bear his distinguished academic and practical experience in this area, has subjected the issue to painstaking research and, in the event, he has provided with his personal views a penetrating analysis of the extensive materials which relate to this subject, as found in the academic writing and the leading jurisprudence.

The issue of practical and serial concern is, very often, not whether crimes of real magnitude have been committed by someone, but rather whether blame can properly be attached to those who, although at some distance from the event, were seemingly responsible for strategy and controlling the immediate perpetrators. The evidence-trail leading to the General at his headquarters and the politician in his office is often imperfect: identifying what a figure in authority did or did not know, or did or did not order, is frequently hard to establish for the prosecution and the defence.

Given the current trend of concentrating the limited time and resources that are available for these often lengthy and expensive trials on those believed to be the most culpable perpetrators, this becomes a subject of heightened importance. For a court to arrive at a valid judgment on the true position in these circumstances, evidence of the crimes themselves can, almost perversely, become of lesser importance. Instead, different kinds of evidence—often at some remove from the core events—take on a high degree of significance, such as meetings, telephone calls, letters and the movement of funds. This emphasis can have a critical effect on the content of trials and their focus, and to the public and the victims it may lead to a sense that the court has lost sight of the true nature of what happened.

To meet at least the legal aspect of these dilemmas and difficulties, international criminal law has adopted some necessary principles so as to address the role of these particular co-perpetrators, for instance those of 'joint criminal enterprise' (or the 'common purpose doctrine') and 'control of crime'. However, for prosecutors much of the debate has revolved around the need to find safe mechanisms that, within a juridical setting, will reflect the true role of senior political and military leaders, who often are not in the 'lower' position (as they are often understood) of accessories or aiders and abettors. The goal, therefore, has been to enable the court to address the 'leader's' true position—that of an indirect participant who is also a principal.

v

This book provides the practitioner with fascinating and highly useful historical, national and international insights into how these problems have been addressed and how the law has emerged in this area. The developments are traced with skill, and although there is for the most understandable of reasons a strong focus on the jurisprudence of the ad hoc tribunals, academic writing and the important contributions by national systems are nevertheless generously included. In the event, a text has been produced that should be in the Chambers of every judge and in the office of every lawyer and academic who practices or writes in this field.

In short, I suspect this will rapidly become the *locus classicus* on this subject.

Judge Sir Adrian Fulford
Den Haag
24 April 2008

ACKNOWLEDGEMENTS

'all men make mistakes, but a good man yields when he knows his course is wrong, and repairs the evil. The only crime is pride.'

Sophocles

To Judge Sylvia Steiner, who stood up for me in the most difficult moments; Ana Isabel Perez Cepeda and Aleksandra Bojovic for their invaluable help in so many aspects, including the references in German; my former colleagues at the legal advisory and appeals sections of the ICTY Office of the Prosecutor, in particular Barbara Goy, Norman Farrel, Helen Brady and William Fenrick, from whom I learnt so much; my truly dedicated colleagues Josyanne Pierrat and Leila Bourguiba without whose support this book would not have been possible; and Enrique Carnero Rojo whom I wish a thorough recovery after the countless hours spent at the ICC.

The views expressed herein are those of the author alone and do not necessarily reflect the views of the ICC, the ICTY, the United Nations or the Spanish Government.

SUMMARY CONTENTS

CONTENTS

Contents

Contents

xiv

Contents

TABLE OF ABBREVIATIONS

ABiH	Army of the Republic of Bosnia and Herzegovina (also referred to as Bosnian-Muslim Armed Forces)
AFRC/RUF	Armed Forces Revolutionary Council / Revolutionary United Front
ARK	Serb Autonomous Region of Krajina
AP I	First Additional Protocol to the Geneva Conventions
AP II	Second Additional Protocol to the Geneva Conventions
art/arts	Article/s
BGH	Bundesgerichtshof (German Federal Supreme Court)
BGHSt	Entscheidungen des Bundesgerichtshofs in Strafsachen (Decisions of the German Federal Supreme Court in criminal matters)
BiH	Bosnia and Herzegovina
CAR	Central African Republic
DRC	Democratic Republic of Congo
EC	Elements of the Crimes
ed/eds	Editor/s
et al	And others
et seq	And the following
FAR	Rwandan Armed Forces
FNI	Front National Integrationniste
FPLC	*Les Forces Populaires pour la Liberation du Congo*
FRG	Federal Republic of Germany
FRPI	Forces de Résistance Patriotique d'Ituri
FRY	Federal Republic of Yugoslavia
GC I	First Geneva Convention
GC II	Second Geneva Convention
GC III	Third Geneva Convention
GC IV	Fourth Geneva Convention
GDR	German Democratic Republic
Gestapo	*Die Geheime Staatspolizei*
HVO	Croatian Defence Council (also referred to as Bosnian Croat Armed Forces)
HDZ-BiH	Croatian Democratic Union of Bosnia and Herzegovina
IACHR	Inter-American Commission on Human Rights
ICC	International Criminal Court
ICJ	International Court of Justice
ICRC	International Committee of the Red Cross
ICTR	International Criminal Tribunal for Rwanda

ICTRS	Statute of the International Criminal Tribunal for Rwanda
ICTY	International Criminal Tribunal for the former Yugoslavia
ICTY OTP	Office of the Prosecutor of the International Criminal Tribunal for the former Yugoslavia
ICTYS	Statute of the International Criminal Tribunal for the former Yugoslavia
IMT	International Military Tribunal (also referred to as Nuremberg Tribunal)
IMTFE	International Military Tribunal for the Far East (also referred to as Tokyo Tribunal)
KLA	Kosovo Liberation Army
JCE	Joint Criminal Enterprise
JNA	Former SFRY Armed Forces (also referred to as Yugoslav People's Army)
LRA	Lord's Resistance Army
MLC	Mouvement pour la Liberation du Congo
mm	Millimetres
Mtbr	Motorized Brigade
MUP	Special Police Forces of Serb Ministry of Interior
n	Footnote
NATO	North Atlantic Treaty Organization
No	Number
OSP	Organised Structure of Power
p/pp	Page/s
ICC PTC	Pre-Trial Chamber of the International Criminal Court
ICC TC	Trial Chamber of the International Criminal Court
PUSIC	*Le Parti pour l'Unite et la Sauvegarde de'l Integrite du Congo*
RPE	Rules of Procedure and Evidence
RPF	Rwandan Patriotic Front
RPP	Relevant Physical Perpetrators
RS	Rome Statute
SD	*Sicherheitsdients des Reichsfuehrer SS*
SDS	Serbian Democratic Party
SFRY	Socialist Federal Republic of Yugoslavia
SpCC	Spanish Criminal Code
SRT	Serb Radio Television
SRK	Sarajevo Romanija Korps (part of the VRS)
SS	*Die Schutzstaffeln Der Nationalsocialistischen Deutschen Arbeiterpartei*
TO	Territorial Defence Unit
UN	United Nations
UNESCO	United Nations Educational, Scientific and Cultural Organization
UNTAET	United Nationsl Transitional Administration for East Timor
UNMO	United Nations Military Observer

UNPROFOR	United Nations Protection Force
UPC/RP	*L'Union Populaire Congolaise/Rasemblement pour la Democracie*
UPDF	Ugandan People Defence Forces
US	United States of America
VJ	Armed Forces of the Federal Republic of Yugoslavia
VRS	Bosnian-Serb Armed Forces
WW II	Second World War

TABLE OF CASES

European Court of Human Rights

Streletz Case:
Streletz, Kessler and Krenz v Germany (App Nos 340044/96 and 44801/98) ECHR 22 March 2001.

International Court of Justice

Asylum Case:
Colombian-Peruvian Asylum Case (*Colombia v Peru*) [1950] ICJ Rep 266.

Continental Shelf Case:
North Sea Continental Shelf Cases (*Federal Republic of Germany v Denmark; Federal Republic of Germany v Netherlands*) [1969] ICJ Rep 4.

Nicaragua Case:
Case Concerning Military and Paramilitary Activities in and against Nicaragua (*Nicaragua v United States of America*) [1986] ICJ Rep 14.

International Criminal Court

Bemba Case:
Bemba Case (Pre-Trial Chamber III Decision on the Prosecutor's Application for a Warrant of Arrest against Jean-Pierre Bemba Gombo) ICC-01/05-01/08-14-TEn (10 Jun 2008).

Katanga and Ngudjolo Case:
Katanga and Ngudjolo Case (Pre-Trial Chamber I Decision on the Applications for Leave to Appeal the Decision on the Admission of the Evidence of Witnesses 132 and 287 and on the Leave to Appeal on the Decision on the Confirmation of Charges) ICC-01/04-01/07 (24 Oct 2008).
Katanga and Ngudjolo Case (Pre-Trial Chamber I Decision on the Confirmation of Charges) ICC-01/04-01/07 (1 Oct 2008).
Katanga and Ngudjolo Case Confirmation of Charges, (Partially Dissenting Opinion of Judge Anita Usascka) ICC-01/04-01/07 (1 Oct 2008).
Katanga and Ngudjolo Case (Pre-Trial Chamber I Decision on the Three Defence's Requests Regarding the Prosecution's Amended Charging Document) ICC-01/04-01/07 (25 June 2008).

International Criminal Tribunal for Rwanda

Akayesu Case:
The Prosecutor v Jean-Paul Akayesu (Appeals Chamber Judgment)
   ICTR-96-4-A (1 June 2001).
The Prosecutor v Jean Paul Akayesu (Judgment) ICTR-96-4-T
   (2 September 1998).

Bagilishema Case:
The Prosecutor v Ignace Bagilishema (Appeals Chamber Judgment)
   ICTR-95-01A-A (3 July 2002).
The Prosecutor v Ignace Bagilishema (Judgment) ICTR-95-01A-T (7 June 2001).

Bisengimana Case:
The Prosecutor v Paul Bisengimana (Judgment) ICTR-00-60-T (13 April 2006).

Gacumbitsi Case:
Sylvestre Gacumbitsi v The Prosecutor (Appeals Chamber Judgment)
   ICTR-01-64-A (7 July 2006).
Sylvestre Gacumbitsi v The Prosecutor (Appeals Chamber Judgment, Separate
   Opinion of Judge Schomburg on the Criminal Responsibility of the
   Appellant for Committing Genocide) ICTR-01-64-A (7 July 2006).
The Prosecutor v Sylvestre Gacumbitsi (Judgment) ICTR-01-64-T (17 June 2004).

Kajelijeli Case:
Juvenal Kajelijeli v The Prosecutor (Appeals Chamber Judgment)
   ICTR-98-44A-A (23 May 2005).
The Prosecutor v Juvenal Kajelijeli (Judgment) ICTR-98-44A-T (1 December 2003).

Kambanda Case:
Jean Kambanda v The Prosecutor (Appeals Chamber Judgement) ICTR-97-23-A
   (19 October 2000).
The Prosecutor v Jean Kambanda (Judgment) ICTR-97-23-S (4 September 1998).

Kamuhanda Case:
Jean de Dieu Kamuhanda v The Prosecutor (Appeals Chamber Judgment)
   ICTR-99-54A-A (19 September 2005).
The Prosecutor v Jean de Dieu Kamuhanda (Judgment) ICTR-95-54A-T
   (22 January 2004).

Karemera Case:
Edouard Karemera v The Prosecutor (Appeals Chamber Decision on
   Jurisdictional Appeals: Joint Criminal Enterprise) ICTR-98-44-AR72.5
   (12 April 2006).

Kayishema Case:
The Prosecutor v Clement Kayishema and Obed Ruzindana (Appeals Chamber
   Judgment) ICTR-95-1-A (1 June 2001).

International Military Tribunal

International Military Tribunal for the Far East

Post War II Cases under Control Council Law No. 10

National Cases

Argentina

Judgment of the Camara Nacional en lo Criminal y Correccional Federal de la
  Capital Federal, 'Sala 4a' (22 May 2002).
Judgment of the Tribunal Nacional Oral Criminal 'No 7' (3 Nov 1998).
Judgment of the Camara Nacional en lo Criminal y Correccional Federal de la
  Capital Federal, 'Sala 1a' (31 October 1988).
Judgment of Penal Chamber of Parana, 'Section 1a' (10 November 1987).
Juntas Trial Case, Judgment of the Camara Federal de Apelaciones en lo
  Criminal de la Capital Federal (9 December 1985).

Australia

Clarkson [1971] 3 All ER 344.
R v Johns [1978] 1 NSWLR 282, 290.
R v McAuliffe (1995) 69 ALJR 621.
The Queen v Crabbe [1985] 156 CLR 464.

Chile

Prosecutor v Generals Contreras and Espinoza (Orlando Letelier Case), Judgment
  of 12 November 1993.

Colombia

La Gabarra Case (Case No 24448), Judgment of the Supreme Court of Colombia,
  Penal Chamber, 12 September 2007.
Machuca Case (Case No 23825), Judgment of the Supreme Court of Colombia,
  Penal Chamber, 7 Marc 2007.
Yamid Amat Case (Case No 25974), Judgment of the Supreme Court of
  Colombia, Penal Chamber, 8 August 2008.

England and Wales

Wilcox v Jeffery [1951] 1 All ER 464.
R v Anderson, R v Morris [1966] 2 QB 110.
Regina v Cogan and Leak [1976] QB 217.
Metropolitan Police Commissioner v Caldwell [1982] AC 341.
R v Hyde [1991] 1 QB 134.
Stringer [1991] 94 Cr. App. R. 13.
DPP v K & B [1997] 1 Cr App R 36
R v Powell, R v English [1997] 4 All ER 545.

TABLE OF LEGISLATION

Italy

Kenya

Malawi

Paraguay

Poland

Spain

INTRODUCTION

I was very pleased to be asked to write a brief introduction to Hector Olasolo's new book on criminal liability of political and military leaders as principals to international crimes. After all, this book is the result of many years of study and teaching in several universities in countries with very different approaches to substantive criminal law and procedure, such as the United States, the Netherlands, Spain and several Latin American States. It is also the result of the author's involvement in the negotiations of substantive and procedural matters during the Preparatory Commission for the International Criminal Court and of his practical experience at the Prosecutor's Office and Chambers in the ICTY and the ICC since 2002.

The book is comprised of five chapters. In the first chapter, the book addresses the specific features of crime and criminal liability in international criminal law and stresses the central role played by senior political and military leaders in campaigns of large scale and systematic commission of international crimes. As the author explains, senior political and military leaders are usually geographically remote from the scene of the crime when the crime takes place and have no contact with the low level members of their organisations who physically carry out the crimes.

As a result, the gravity of their actions or omissions is not well reflected by the traditional modes of liability in national criminal law because they never amount to an objective element of a crime. Consequently, international criminal law has put a particular emphasis on the development of certain notions, such as control of the crime and joint criminal enterprise, which aim at better reflecting the central role played by senior political and military leaders. However, as the author highlights, such notions have not been created by international criminal law. They have emerged in national criminal law, although they have since been developed and adjusted to be applicable to the special circumstances in which international crimes take place.

The second chapter addresses the distinction between principal and accessorial liability. As the author explains, perpetrators or principals to a crime are those whose liability can be established independently of all other parties to the crime, whereas accessories or secondary parties are those whose liability derives from the principal liability of the perpetrators. Subsequently, the book focuses on whether international criminal law has adopted such a distinction. After answering this question in the affirmative on the basis of the evolution of international criminal law since World War II, the book goes on to address the different approaches to the distinction between principal and accessorial liability.

The author places particular emphasis on the differences between the notion of joint criminal enterprise, which is based on a subjective approach to the distinction between principal and accessorial liability, and the notion of control of the crime which is based on a materially objective approach to such a distinction. Finally, the author explores the customary status of both approaches under international law and concludes that, in spite of the findings of the ICTY Appeals Chamber in the *Tadic* case, customary international law has not embraced to date any given approach to the distinction between principal and accessorial liability, although it is progressively moving towards a wider acceptance of the notion of control of the crime.

The third chapter addresses the notions of direct and indirect perpetration. With regard to direct perpetration, it places particular emphasis on the concept of commission by omission, and on the distinction between this type of omission and those other omissions that give rise to either accessorial liability or to liability under the doctrine of superior responsibility.

Subsequently, the book focuses on the notion of indirect perpetration, defined in article 25(3)(a) of the Rome Statute as the commission of a crime through another person, regardless of whether that other person is criminally liable. The author analyses, in particular, the characteristics that an organised structure of power must have in order for the notion of indirect perpetration to be applicable. As a result, it reaches the conclusion that indirect perpetration is not applicable in cases of crimes committed by small paramilitary groups or terrorists cells, where the limited number of members prevents them from being qualified as interchangeable, or by organisations—such as enterprises in the context of economic crime—with a horizontal as opposed to a vertical structure. The chapter finishes with an analysis of several forms of accessorial liability, such as ordering, instigation and planning, which are related to the notion of indirect perpetration and can be applied when the latter is not applicable.

The last two chapters analyse the notion of co-perpetration, which must be consistent with the general approach adopted for the distinction between principal and accessorial liability. Chapter four addresses in great detail the doctrine of joint criminal enterprise. It analyses the three variants of joint criminal enterprise found by the ICTY Appeals Chamber in the *Tadic* case and its relationship with the notion of aiding and abetting as a mode of accessorial liability.

The author places particular attention on the latest developments of the doctrine in cases against high level perpetrators such as Radoslav Brdjanin and Moncilo Krajisnik. As a result, the author distinguishes between two different models of joint criminal enterprise. The first, referred to as 'the traditional joint criminal enterprise', in which the senior political and military leaders who mastermind the crimes and the low level perpetrators who materially commit the crimes are all members of the same criminal enterprise. The second, referred to as 'joint criminal enterprise at the leadership level', in which only the senior political and military leaders who at the highest level plan and set into motion the execution of the criminal campaign are members of the criminal enterprise, whereas the low level executers are mere tools through which the former secure the commission of the crimes. After analysing these two models, the author discusses how this second model is the result of the attempt to make the best of a bad choice, that is to say, the initial adoption by the *ad hoc* Tribunals of a subjective approach to the distinction between principal and accessorial liability.

The fifth chapter analyses the notion of co-perpetration based on joint control of the crime and, in particular, the essential character of the task entrusted to each of the co-perpetrators—which gives them the power to disrupt the execution of the common plan by not performing it. The book focuses on those situations of indirect co-perpetration in which the co-perpetrators (high level political and military leaders) carry out their essential tasks through the organised structures of power (military units, police forces and/or political parties) that they control. It concludes that the shortcomings of the model of 'joint criminal enterprise at the leadership level' can be overcome by resorting to the notion of indirect co-perpetration.

I would like to highlight that Hector Olasolo's new book is particularly useful because it is based on a profound knowledge of different national systems and international criminal law. Furthermore, it combines a deep theoretical analysis of the relevant issues with numerous practical examples that facilitate the reader's understanding of the *contours* of the various notions addressed in the book, as well as of the problems posed by their application.

Last but not least, I would like to congratulate the author and the publisher on the book. I highly recommend this new and relevant work. I dare to make a prediction that it will serve as a key reference in the coming years for practitioners and scholars of international criminal law. It is a valuable contribution to the knowledge of everyone inspired by international justice.

Judge Ekaterina Trendafilova
Den Haag
19 May 2008

1

First Approach to the Criminal Liability of Political and Military Leaders for International Crimes

Trials for genocide, crimes against humanity and war crimes have a number of distinctive features. These crimes typically take place in situations of large scale or widespread criminality. By simply looking at situation reports—such as UN reports indicating that half of the population in Bosnia and Herzegovina became internally displaced persons during the conflict that took place in Bosnia-Herzegovina between 1992 and 1995,[1] or that between half a million and eight hundred thousand civilians were murdered in Rwanda between April and June 1994[2]—one realizes that, unless the underlying facts of an indictment are extremely narrow, shortage of evidence concerning the crimes charged will not be the main problem faced by the Prosecution at trial. This is particularly true when senior political and military leaders are subject to prosecution because the higher the rank of the defendant, the broader the factual basis of the indictment usually becomes.[3]

For instance, the indictment against the former president of Liberia Charles Taylor before the Special Court of Sierra Leone charges him with a series of unlawful attacks throughout the territory of the Republic of Sierra Leone, including, but

---

[1] United Nations Security Council (UNSC) 'Final Report of the Commission of Experts established pursuant to Security Council Resolution 780 (1992)' (27 May 1994) UN Doc S/1994/674; UNSC 'Annexes to the Final Report of the Commission of Experts established pursuant to Security Council Resolution 780 (1992)' (28 Dec 1994) UN Doc S/1994/674/Add 2 (Vol II); See also MC Bassiouni, 'The United Nations Commission of Experts Established pursuant to Security Council Resolution 780' (1994) 88 *AJIL* 784.

[2] UNSC 'Preliminary Report of the Independent Commission of Experts in accordance with Security Council Resolution 935 (1994)' (4 Oct 1994) UN Doc S/1994/1125; UNSC 'Final Report of the Commission of Experts Established pursuant to Security Council Resolution 935 (1994)' (9 Dec 1994) UN Doc S/1994/1405.

[3] Nevertheless, this is not an absolute rule, as shown by the 3 charging instruments against the former President of Iraq, Sadam Hussein, issued in the course of the proceedings before the Iraqi Supreme Court. In such charging instruments, the charges against him were confined to (i) the deaths of 9 people who were killed in the first days of the crackdown on the town of Dujail in 1982; (ii) the unlawful arrest of 399 townspeople; (iii) the torture of women and children, and ordering the razing of farmlands in retaliation for the assassination attempt against him; and (iv) the deaths of the 148 who were sentenced to death by his Revolutionary Court. Saddam Hussein was subsequently convicted and sentenced to death by the judgment of the Iraqi Supreme Court of 11 Nov 2006.

not limited to, Bo, Kono, Kenema, Bombali and Kailahun Districts and Freetown conducted between 1997 and 1999 by Armed Forces Revolutionary Council/Revolutionary United Front (AFRC/RUF) forces 'acting in concert with and/or subordinate' to him.[4] These attacks, which targeted civilians as well as peacekeepers of the United Nations Mission in Sierra Leone, included unlawful killings, physical and sexual violence against civilian men, women and children, mutilation of hands or feet, abductions, looting and destruction of civilian property, and were carried out to primarily terrorise the civilian population as well as to punish the population for failing to provide sufficient support to the AFRC/RUF or for allegedly providing support to forces supporting the Kabbah government.[5] Moreover, as part of this campaign of terror and punishment, many abducted girls and boys were given combat training and used in active fighting.[6]

As a result, after having heard testimony for weeks on how civilians were murdered, injured or expelled from their homes, and how prisoners of war were mistreated in several detention camps, it is often the case that during the trials of senior political and military leaders the court must ask the question: what did the defendant have to do with the crimes charged in the indictment? Furthermore, as these trials progress and when the Prosecution is already halfway through presenting its case, it is not unusual for the bench to ask the Prosecution whether it could focus on the evidence relating to the defendant's alleged actions and omissions which are related to the commission of the crimes charged in the indictment, and whether the Prosecution could be more precise as to the exact nature of the link between the defendant's actions and omissions and the said crimes.

In other words, the single most important issue during the trials of senior political and military leaders is the determination of the specific mode of liability the respective leader has incurred in criminal liability for the crimes charged in the indictment.[7] Other important issues raised during the trials against senior political and military leaders include the problems relating to the need to prove a broad range of criminal activities, as shown by the unfinished four-year-long trial against Slobodan Milosevic, and the specific defences raised by the defendants.

---

[4] *Charles Ghankay Taylor* (Indictment) SCSL-03-01-I (3 Mar 2003) para 29.

[5] *Ibid* at para 30.

[6] *Ibid* at para 31.

[7] WA Schabas, *An Introduction to the International Criminal Court* (2nd edn, Cambridge, Cambridge University Press, 2004) 105. Schabas refers to this phenomenon as 'one of the dilemmas of war crimes prosecutions'. According to him, the difficulty of linking commanders to the crimes committed by their subordinates, particularly in the absence of actual proof that orders were given:

'probably explains why Louise Arbour, Prosecutor of the Yugoslav Tribunal, waited for many weeks before indicting President Milosevic for crimes against humanity. She was unsatisfied with the circumstantial evidence of atrocities in Kosovo for which he had been condemned in the international press and was awaiting more concrete evidence that he had ordered them before proceeding'.

See also Y Kang and T Wu, 'Criminal Liability for the Actions of Subordinates: The Doctrine of Command Responsibility and its Analogues in United States Law' (1997) 38 *Harvard International Law Journal* 272–97. Kang and Wu have said: 'The further away a superior is from the actual "smoking gun" the more difficult he is to prosecute'.

Senior political and military leaders are usually geographically remote from the scene of the crime when the crimes take place and have no contact whatsoever with the low level members of their organisations who physically carry out the crimes ('the physical perpetrators').[8] As a result, the gravity of their actions or omissions is not well reflected by the traditional modes of liability in national criminal law because they never amount to an objective element of a crime. As the District Court of Jerusalem said in the Eichmann Trial:

> In such an enormous and complicated crime as the one we are now considering, wherein many people participated at various levels and in various modes of activity—the planners, the organizers and those executing the acts, according to their various ranks—there is not much point in using the ordinary concepts of counselling and soliciting to commit a crime. For these crimes were committed en masse, not only in regard to the number of the victims, but also in regard to the numbers of those who perpetrated the crime, and the extent to which any one of the many criminals were close to, or remote from, the actual killer of the victim, means nothing as far as the measure of his responsibility is concerned. On the contrary, in general, the degree of responsibility increases as we draw further away from the man who uses the fatal instrument with his own hands and reach the higher ranks of command, the 'counsellors' in the language of our Law. As regards the victims who did not die but were placed in living conditions calculated to bring about their physical destruction, it is especially difficult to define in technical terms who abetted whom: he who hunted down the victims and deported them to a concentration camp, or he who forced them to work there.[9]

Indeed, despite the fact that senior political and military leaders are usually the individuals who plan and set into motion campaigns of large-scale and systematic commission of international crimes (or at least have the power to prevent or stop them), the application of the traditional modes of liability in national criminal law leads to the conclusion that they are mere participants in the crimes committed by others (accessories to the crimes), as opposed to perpetrators of the crimes (principals to the crimes). This does not reflect the central role that they usually play in the commission of international crimes, and often results in a punishment, which is inappropriately low considering the wrongdoing of their actions and omissions. As the ICTY Appeals Chamber has highlighted in the *Tadic* case:

> Under these circumstances, to hold criminally liable as a perpetrator only the person who materially performs the criminal act would disregard the role as co-perpetrators of all those who in some way made it possible for the perpetrator physically to carry out that criminal

---

[8] Those individuals who physically carry out the objective elements of the crimes have been referred to with different expressions such as 'direct perpetrators', 'principal perpetrators', 'material perpetrators', 'physical perpetrators', 'relevant physical perpetrators' or 'perpetrators behind the direct perpetrators/actors'. See also *Prosecutor v Brdanin* (Appeals Chamber Judgment) ICTY-99-36-A (3 Apr 2007) para 362 [hereinafter *Brdanin Case* Appeals Judgment]. In this book they are referred to as 'physical perpetrators' because, regardless of their mental state, what is common to all of them is that they physically perform ,at least, one objective element of the crime.

[9] *Attorney General v Adolf Eichmann* (1968) 36 ILR 18 para 197.

act. At the same time, depending upon the circumstances, to hold the latter liable only as aidors and abettors might understate the degree of their criminal responsibility.[10]

For these reasons, international criminal law has put a particular emphasis in the development of a set of notions, and in particular the notion of joint criminal enterprise[11] (also known as the common purpose doctrine)[12] and the notion of control of the crime,[13] which aim at better reflecting the central role played by senior political and military leaders in campaigns of large scale and systematic commission of international crimes.[14] However, international criminal law has not created these notions; it has just developed them to be applied to the special circumstances in which international crimes take place.

In this regard, it is important to highlight that joint criminal enterprise and control of the crime are notions, which have been long resorted to at the national level in the context of ordinary crimes. They are closely related to the various criteria that have been traditionally used in national criminal law to distinguish between the concepts of perpetration, which gives rise to principal liability, and participation in the commission of a crime by a third person, which gives rise to accessorial liability.[15] According to the formal-objective approach, perpetrators are only those persons who carry out an objective element of the crime, whereas participants are those other persons who contribute in any other way to the crime. For the subjective approach, no matter the nature and scope of the contribution, perpetrators are those persons who make a contribution to the commission of the

---

[10] *Prosecutor v Tadic* (Appeals Chamber Judgment) ICTY-94-1-A (15 July 1999) para 192 [hereinafter *Tadic Case* Appeals Judgment].

[11] *Ibid* at paras 227–8.

[12] *Prosecutor v Milutinovic* (Decision on Dragoljub Ojdanic's Motion Challenging Jurisdiction—Joint Criminal Enterprise) ICTY-99-37-AR72 (21 May 2003). As this Tribunal held at para 36: 'The phrases "common purpose" doctrine on the one hand, and "joint criminal enterprise" on the other, have been used interchangeably and they refer to one and the same thing. The latter term joint criminal enterprise is preferred, but it refers to the same form of liability as that known as the common purpose doctrine'.

[13] Rome Statute of the International Criminal Court' UN Diplomatic Conference of Plenipotentiaries on the Establishment of an International Criminal Court (Rome 15 Jun–17 Jul 1998) (17 Jul 1998) UN Doc A/Conf. 183/9 [hereinafter RS]. Art 25(3)(a) RS explicitly refers to those who commit such a crime, 'whether as an individual, jointly with another or through another person, regardless of whether that other person is criminally responsible'.

[14] The emphasis placed by international criminal law on this matter is, to an important extent, the result of the particular focus that international prosecutions have placed on senior political and military leaders. See ICC Office of the Prosecutor, 'Paper on Some Policy Issues before the Office of the Prosecutor' (Sep 2003) p 7, http://www.icc-cpi.int/library/organs/otp/030905_Policy_Paper.pdf> accessed 18 Jan 2008. See also MC Bassiouni, *International Criminal Law: A Draft International Criminal Code* (2nd edn, Ardsley, New York, Transnational Publishers, 1999) 22–3; H Olasolo, *The Triggering Procedure of the International Criminal Court* (Leiden, Brill, 2005) 165, 182–93 [hereinafter Olasolo, *Triggering Procedure*].

[15] Only a few national systems (usually referred to as 'unitary systems'), such as those of Denmark and Italy, do not endorse this distinction and consider anyone who contributes to the commission of the crime as a perpetrator no matter the nature and context of his contribution. See Danish Penal Code art 23 and Italian Penal Code art 110. See also K Ambos, *La Parte General del Derecho Penal Internacional: Bases para una Elaboracion Dogmatica* (Uruguay, Konrad-Adenauer-Stiftung, 2005) 272–3; G Quintero Olivares, *Manual de Derecho Penal: Parte General* (3rd edn, Pamplona, Aranzadi, 2002) 613.

crime with the intent of becoming principals to the crime. Finally, from a material-objective approach, perpetrators are those who have the control of the crime, meaning that they have the last word on its commission.[16]

The notion of joint criminal enterprise, or the common purpose doctrine, is a manifestation of the subjective approach because in cases where a crime is committed by a plurality of persons acting together in pursuance of a common criminal purpose, every member of the group becomes a principal to the crime (a co-perpetrator), no matter the importance of his contribution. What matters is that any given participant makes his contribution with the purpose of implementing the common criminal plan because the essence of the wrongdoing lies in the shared intent by all the participants to have the crimes encompassed by the enterprise committed.[17]

The notion of control of the crime is a manifestation of the material-objective approach because it is rooted in the idea that principals to the crime ((co)-perpetrators) are those who dominate its commission insofar as they decide whether the crime will be committed and how it will be carried out.[18] And this, regardless of whether they are geographically and/or structurally remote from the scene of the crime when the crime is committed.

The notion of joint criminal enterprise was originally conceived in common law jurisdictions to deal with 'mob-crimes' as well as other crimes, such as bank

---

[16] F Munoz Conde and M Garcia Aran, *Derecho Penal: Parte General* (5th edn, Valencia, Tirant lo Blanch, 2002) 448–9.

[17] According to the *Tadic Case* Appeals Judgment (Above n 10), at para 229, the following four features distinguish the notion of joint criminal enterprise (or common purpose doctrine) and the notion of aiding and abetting:

(i) The aidor and abettor is always an accessory to a crime perpetrated by another person, *the principal.*

(ii) In the case of aiding and abetting no proof is required of the existence of a *common concerted plan*, let alone of the pre-existence of such a plan. No plan or agreement is required: indeed, the principal may not even know about the accomplice's contribution.

(iii) The aidor and abettor carries out acts specifically directed to assist, encourage or lend moral support to the perpetration of a certain specific crime (murder, extermination, rape, torture, wanton destruction of civilian property, etc.), and this support has a substantial effect upon the perpetration of the crime. By contrast, in the case of acting in pursuance of a common purpose or design, *it is sufficient for the participant to perform acts that in some way are directed to the furthering of the common plan or purpose.*

(iv) In the case of aiding and abetting, the requisite mental element is knowledge that the acts performed by the aidor and abettor assist the commission of a specific crime by the principal. By contrast, *in the case of common purpose or design more is required (i.e., either intent to perpetrate the crime* or intent to pursue the common criminal design plus foresight that those crimes outside the criminal common purpose were likely to be committed), as stated above'. (Emphasis added).

[18] C Roxin, 'Sobre la autoria y la participacion en el derecho Penal' in *Problemas actuales de las ciencias Penales y de la filosofia del Derecho* (Buenos Aires, Ediciones Pannedille, 1970) 60; A Eser, 'Individual Criminal Responsibility' in A Cassese, P Gaeta, and JRWD Jones (eds), *The Rome Statute of the International Criminal Court: A Commentary* (Oxford, Oxford University Press, 2002) 793 [hereinafter Eser]; K Ambos, 'Article 25. Individual Criminal Responsibility' in O Triffterer (ed), *Commentary on the Rome Statute of the International Criminal Court* (Baden-Baden, Nomos, 1999) 479 [hereinafter Ambos, *Article 25*]; A Perez Cepeda, *La responsabilidad de los administradores de sociedades: criterios de atribucion* (Barcelona, Cedecs Editorial, 1997) 369.

robberies, which were committed by a plurality of persons acting in a concerted manner to implement a common criminal purpose.[19] Likewise, the notion of control of the crime was first utilised at the national level to address situations where a person uses an innocent agent, such as a child or a mentally disabled person, to commit a crime.[20] Subsequently, both notions have been used at the national level in relation to organised crime, such as drug-trafficking, economic crime or even terrorism, where the number of persons involved is higher than in ordinary crimes, but is still limited.[21]

Although the notions of joint criminal enterprise and control of the crime have not been created by international criminal law, the latter has not merely borrowed them from national law. Quite the contrary, international criminal law has developed them to comprehensively reflect the wrongdoing and culpability of senior political and military leaders as principals to the widespread and systematic commission of international crimes. In this regard, it must be highlighted that, although a few post WW II cases (in particular the Justice[22] and the RuSHA[23] cases under Control Council Law No 10) have often been portrayed as establishing the first precedents in the development of these notions,[24] the fact of the matter is that

---

[19] See generally (i) Australia: *R v Johns* [1978] 1 NSWLR 282, 290; *R v McAuliffe* (1995) 69 ALJR 621; Western Australian Criminal Code Act § 8(1) (1913); Queensland Criminal Code Act § 8 (1899); (ii) England and Wales: *R v Powell, R v English* [1997] 4 All ER 545; *R v Hyde* [1991] 1 QB 134.; *R v Anderson, R v Morris* [1966] 2 QB 110; and (iii) The United States of America: *Pinkerton v United States*, 328 US 640 (1946); *State of Connecticut v Diaz*, 679 A.2d 902 (1996); Iowa Code § 703.2 (1997); Kan Stat Ann § 21-3205 (1997); 17 Me Crim Code § 57 (1997); Minn Stat § 609.05 (1998); Wis Stat § 939.05 (1995); *State v Walton*, 630 A.2d 990 (1993). Civil law jurisdictions have also resorted to theories of criminal liability similar to the notion of joint criminal enterprise or the common purpose doctrine. For instance the Spanish Supreme Court followed for the most part the 'doctrine of the previous agreement' (*doctrina del acuerdo previo*) until the approval of new Spanish Criminal Code of 1995. See generally the Judgments of the Spanish Supreme Court of 22 Feb 1985; 31 May 1985 and 13 May 1986.

[20] In relation to common law jurisdictions, see generally (i) Australia: P Rush and S Yeah, *Criminal Law Sourcebook* (Sydney, Butterworths, 2000) 662; L Waller and C Williams, *Criminal Law Text and Cases* (Sydney, Butterworths, 2001) 560; (ii) England: *Regina v Cogan and Leak* [1976] QB 217; (iii) South Africa: CR Snyman, *Criminal Law* (Durban, Butterworths, 1995) 246–7; and (iv) United States: Model Penal Code §2.06(1)-(4); *State v Ward*, 396 A.2d 1041, 1046 (1978). In relation to civil law jurisdictions, see generally (i) Argentina: C Fontan Balestra, *Tratado de Derecho Penal: Parte General* (Albany, Lexis Publishing, 1995) Lexis No 1503/001660; (ii) France: Cour de Cassation, Chambre Criminelle Dalloz (6 Mars 1964) 562; (iii) Germany: Bundesgerichtshof, Entscheidungen des Bundesgerichtshofs in Strafsachen 32, 35, 41, 351; (iv) Spain: J Gonzalez Rus, 'Autoria Unica Inmediata, Autoria Mediata y Coautoria' in *Cuadernos de Derecho Judicial, No XXXIX Ed Consejo General del Poder Judicial* (1994); and (v) Switzerland: Entscheidungen des Schweizerischen Bundesgerichts 101 IV 310; Entscheidungen des Schweizerischen Bundesgerichts 85 IV 23.

[21] *Prosecutor v Stakic* (Judgment) ICTY-97-24-T (31 Jul 2003) para 439, fn 942, explicitly refers to the use of the notions in the context of white collar crime or other forms of organised crime.

[22] *US v Altstoetter* (1947) in Trial of the Major War Criminals before the International Military Tribunal under Control Council Law No 10, Vol III (US Government Printing Office, 1951) 954.

[23] *United States v Greifelt et al* (1948) in Trial of the Major War Criminals before the International Military Tribunal under Control Council Law No 10, Vols IV and V (US Government Printing Office, 1951).

[24] See *Rwamakuba Case* (Appeals Chamber Decision) ICTR-98-44-AR72.4 (23 Jul 2004) para 25; *Karemera v Prosecutor* (Appeals Chamber Decision on Jurisdictional Appeals: Joint Criminal Enterprise) ICTR-98-44-AR72.5 (12 Apr 2006) para 14; *Brdanin Case* Appeals Judgment (Above n 8) at paras 195–404; *Prosecutor v Milutinovic* (Decision On Ojdanic's Motion Challenging Jurisdiction: Indirect Co-Perpetration, Separate Opinion of Judge Bonomy) ICTY-05-87-PT (22 Mar 2006) paras 18–22.

after the *Tadic* Appeal Judgement of 15 July 1999, the case law of the ICTY and the ICTR (the '*Ad hoc* Tribunals'), and the nascent case law of the ICC, have played a unique role in the achievement of this goal.

The important evolution experienced by international criminal law in the last few years to better reflect the criminal responsibility of senior political and military leaders as principals to the large scale and systematic commission of international crimes can be observed by reading the latest indictments produced by the ICTY and ICTR Offices of the Prosecutor. For instance, the 21 June 2006 Third Amended Joinder Indictment against Milan Milutinovic (former President of Serbia), Nikola Sainovic (former Deputy Prime Minister of the FRY) and Colonel General Dragoljub Ojdanic (former Chief of Staff of the VJ) and other close aides of Slobodan Milosevic,[25] charges the defendants with the commission of the following crimes between January and June 1999[26]:

(i)   the deportation and forcible transfer of approximately 800,000 Kosovo Albanian civilians[27];

(ii) the systematic murder of hundreds of Kosovo Albanian civilians (men, women and children)[28]; and

(iii) the execution of a persecutorial campaign against the Kosovo Albanian civilian population through forcible transfer, deportation, murder, sexual assault

---

[25] On 11 March 2006, Slobodan Milosevic died in the ICTY detention centre.

[26] *Prosecutor v Milutinovic* (Third Amended Joinder Indictment) ICTY-05-87-PT (21 Jun 2006) paras 18–19 [hereinafter *Milutinovic Amended Indictment*].

[27] The deportation and forcible transfer of the Kosovo Albanian population took place in the following municipalities: Orahovac/Rahovec, Prizren, Srbica/Skenderaj, Suva Reka/Suhareke, Pec/Peje, Kosovska Mitrovica/Mitrovice, Pristina/Prishtine, Dakovica/Gjakove, Gnjilane/Gjilan, Urosevac/Ferizaj, Kacanik, Decani/Deçan and Vucitrn/Vushtrri. In order to facilitate these expulsions and displacements, forces of the former Federal Republic of Yugoslavia (FRY) and Serbia deliberately created an atmosphere of fear and oppression through the use of force, threats of force and acts of violence including the systematic shelling of towns and villages, the burning of homes and farms, the damage and destruction of Kosovo Albanian cultural and religious institutions, the murder of Kosovo Albanian civilians and the sexual assault of Kosovo Albanian women. See *Milutinovic Amended Indictment* (*Ibid*) at para 72.

[28] This included the following mass killing incidents: (i) on 15 January 1999 in the village of Racak (Stimlje/Shtime municipality); (ii) on or about 25 March 1999 in the village of Bela Crkva/Bellacerke (Orahovac/Rahovec municipality); (iii) on or about 25 March 1999 in the villages of Mala Krusa/Kruse e Vogel and Velika Krusa/Krushe Mahde (Orahovac/Rahovec municipality); (iv) on or about 26 March 1999 in the town of Suva Reka/Suhareke (Suva Reka/ Suhareke municipality); (v) on or about the 26 March 1999 in the town of Dakovica/Gjakove; (vi) on or about 26 March 1999 in the village of Padaliste/Padalishte (Istok/Istog municipality); (vii) on or about 27 March 1999 in the village of Izbica/Izbice (Srbica/Skenderaj municipality); (vii) on or about 1–2 April 1999 in the Qerim district of Dakovica/Gjakove; (viii) on or about the early morning hours of 27 April 1999, in the Carragojs, Erenik and Trava Valleys (Dakovica/Gjakove municipality); (ix) on or about 2 May 1999 in several villages north-east of the town of Vucitrn/Vushtrri including Skrovna/Skrome, Slakovce/Sllakofc, Ceceli/Cecelija and Gornja Sudimlja/Studime Eperme; (x) on or about 22 May 1999 in the Dubrava/Dubrave Prison complex (Istok/Istog municipality); (xi) on or about 24 March 1999, the village of Kotlina/Kotline (municipality of Kacanik/Kacanik); (xii) on or about 13 April 1999, forces of the FRY and Serbia surrounded the village of Slatina/Sllatine and the hamlet of Vata/Vata (municipality of Kacanik/Kacanik); (xiii) on or about 21 May 1999, the village of Stagovo/Stagove (municipality of Kacanik/Kacanik); and (xiv) on or about 25 May 1999 in the village of Dubrava/Lisnaje (municipality of Kacanik/Kacanik). See *Milutinovic Amended Indictment* (*Ibid*) at para 75.

and wanton destruction or damage of Kosovo Albanian religious sites during and after attacks on towns and villages.[29]

According to the Third Amended Joinder Indictment, the numerous crimes were physically committed by the defendants' subordinates in the forces of the FRY and Serbia—including members of the FRY army ('VJ'), the special police of the Serbian Ministry of the Interior ('MUP'), military-territorial units, civil defence units and other armed groups operating under the authority, or with the knowledge, of the defendants or their subordinates.[30] Nevertheless, the Third Amended Joinder Indictment alleges that the defendants were principals, as opposed to the accessories, because they were (i) co-perpetrators as participants in a joint criminal enterprise to ensure Serbian control over the province of Kosovo through the commission of the above-mentioned crimes, or alternatively, (ii) indirect co-perpetrators based on their joint control over such crimes. As the Third Amended Joinder Indictment puts it:

> A number of individuals participated in this joint criminal enterprise during the entire duration of its existence, or, alternatively, at different times during the duration of its existence, including Milan Milutinovic, Nikola Sainovic, Dragoljub Ojdanic, Nebojsa Pavkovic, Vladimir Lazarevic, Vlastimir Djordevic, Sreten Lukic, Slobodan Milosevic and Vlajko Stojiljkovic. Other members included Radomir Markovic, Obrad Stevanovic, Dragan Ilic and unidentified persons who were members of command and coordinating bodies and members of the forces of FRY and Serbia who shared the intent to effect the purpose of the joint criminal enterprise. In addition, and/or in the alternative, Milan Milutinovic, Nikola Sainovic, Dragoljub Ojdanic, Nebojsa Pavkovic, Vladimir Lazarevic, Vlastimir Djordevic, Sreten Lukic, Slobodan Milosevic and Vlajko Stojiljkovic, Radomir, Markovic, Obrad Stevanovic and Dragan Ilic implemented the objectives of the joint criminal enterprise through members of the forces of the FRY and Serbia, whom they controlled, to carry out the crimes charged in this indictment.[31]
>
> The crimes enumerated in Counts 1 to 5 of this Indictment were within the object of the joint criminal enterprise and the accused shared the intent with the other co-perpetrators that these crimes be perpetrated. Alternatively, the crimes enumerated in Counts 3 to 5 were natural and foreseeable consequences of the joint criminal enterprise and the accused were aware that such crimes were the possible consequence of the execution of that enterprise.[32]
>
> In the alternative, the accused are also charged as indirect co-perpetrators, based on their joint control over the criminal conduct of forces of the FRY and Serbia. The accused had the mens rea for the specific crimes charged in this indictment, acted with the mutual awareness of the substantial likelihood that crimes would occur as a direct consequence of the pursuit of the common goal, and were aware of the importance of their own roles.[33]

---

[29] This included the destruction of Mosques in Vucitrn/Vushtrii, Suva Reka/Suhareke, Celina/Celine, Rogovo/Rogove, Bela Crkva/Bellacerke, Cirez/Qirez, Kotlina/Kotline, Ivaja/Ivaje, Brestovac/Brestovc, Velika Krusa/Krushe Mahde, Kosovska, Mitrivica/Mitrovice, Vlastica/Vlastica, Landovica/Landovice and Dakovica/Gjakove. See *Milutinovic Amended Indictment* (*Ibid*) at para 77.

[30] *Milutinovic Amended Indictment. Ibid* at para 20.

[31] *Ibid.*

[32] *Ibid* at para 21.

[33] *Ibid* at para 22.

Each of the accused participated in the joint criminal enterprise in the ways set out (for each accused) in the paragraphs below. Alternatively, each of the accused contributed, as a co-perpetrator based on joint control, to the common goal in the ways set out in those paragraphs.[34]

However, the language of the Third Amended Joinder Indictment is not as clear as would be desired, and in some of the excerpts quoted above it is rather 'cryptic'. For instance, it is not clear who are the other participants in the joint criminal enterprise in which Milutinovic, Sainovic, Ojdanic and the other defendants participated. In addition to naming some individuals, the Third Amended Joinder Indictment also includes among the participants in the enterprise a number of:

[U]nidentified persons who were members of command and coordinating bodies and members of the forces of FRY and Serbia who shared the intent to effect the purpose of the joint criminal enterprise.[35]

The question arises as to whether the hundreds (or even thousands) of defendants' subordinates in the FRY and Serbian forces who physically committed the crimes were also part of the enterprise. If the answer is affirmative, and given the fact that the defendants in this case are structurally and geographically remote from the physical perpetrators and that the enterprise includes a broad range of criminal activities, it will be difficult to prove that there was a common criminal plan and a shared intent to commit the crimes encompassed by such a plan among all participants in the enterprise.[36] Indeed, one might find that the Prosecution is resorting to a sort of legal fiction which can hardly correspond to reality, coming closer to a form of collective criminal liability, and risking an unacceptable extension of criminal liability for low and mid level members of the enterprise.[37]

Nevertheless, it is also possible to read the Third Amended Joinder Indictment as excluding the physical perpetrators from the joint criminal enterprise in which Milutinovic, Sainovic, Ojdanic and the other defendants participated. Indeed, those other unidentified persons could be limited to those mid level members of the FRY and Serbian forces who, acting on instructions of their superiors, prepared logistically and operationally the commission of the crimes by their subordinates. If this is the case, the question arises as to whether the notion of joint criminal enterprise or the common purpose doctrine can be applied when the physical perpetrators of the crimes are not part of the enterprise in light of the fact that the cornerstone of such a notion is the existence of an express or implicit agreement among a group of people who share the criminal intent to carry out a crime. Or to put it in different words, whether—in addition to the 'traditional notion of joint criminal enterprise' that would require the participation in the

---

[34] *Ibid* at para 34.

[35] *Ibid* at para 22.

[36] H Olasolo, 'Reflections on the Treatment of the Notions of Control of the Crime and Joint Criminal Enterprise in the Stakic Appeal Judgment' (2007) 7 *International Criminal Law Review* 157.

[37] M Elewa Badar, 'Just Convict Everyone!—Joint Perpetration from Tadic to Stakic and Back Again' (2006) 6 *International Criminal Law Review* 302.

enterprise of the small group of senior political and military leaders who designed and set into motion the persecutory campaign, the mid-level superiors who prepare its implementation and the thousands of low perpetrators who physically implement it—it is also possible to have a 'joint criminal enterprise at the leadership level' in which only the core group of senior political and military leaders (and eventually certain mid level superiors) participate.

Additionally, the Third Amended Joinder Indictment does not specify what it means when it alleges that the Milutinovic, Sainovic, Ojdanic and the other defendants are, in the alternative, 'indirect co-perpetrators, based on their joint control over the criminal conduct of forces of the FRY and Serbia'. It appears as if the Prosecution is relying on the combined application of two of the manifestations of the notion of control of the crime (indirect perpetration and co-perpetration based on functional control), that the Stakic Trial Judgement referred to as 'co-perpetratorship'.[38]

If this is the case, the question arises as to whether the notion of control of the crime, which has been explicitly embraced by article 25(3)(a) RS,[39] is also applicable before the ICTY and the ICTR. And, if so, how the specific problems posed by the application of this notion to senior political and military leaders who are involved in the widespread and systematic commission of international crimes have been dealt with. In particular, those relating to:

(i)   the minimum requirements for the organisations through which senior political and military leaders operate to plan and set into motion the commission of international crimes to be considered 'organized structures of power' controlled by them; and

(ii) the necessary adjustments to the notions of indirect perpetration (which reflects a hierarchical or vertical relationship between senior political and military leaders and mid and low level members of their organisations) and functional control (which reflects a horizontal relationship between individuals who are at the same level; in our case high ranking political and military leaders), in light of the fact that the magnitude of the crimes often requires a machinery which combines a horizontal relationship between a core group of senior political and military leaders, and hierarchical relationships between the latter on the one hand, and mid level superiors and physical perpetrators on the other hand.

Moreover, if the notion of control of the crime is also applicable before the *Ad hoc* Tribunals, as it is before the ICC, the question arises as to whether, as the Prosecution alleges in the Third Amended Joinder Indictment in the Milutinovic case, the notions of joint criminal enterprise and control of the crime are to be seen

---

[38] *Prosecutor v Stakic* (Appeals Chamber Judgment) ICTY-97-24-A (22 Mar 2006) para 468.

[39] *Lubanga Case* (Pre-Trial Chamber I Decision on the Confirmation of Charges) ICC-01/04-01/06 (29 Jan 2007) para 338 [hereinafter *Lubanga Case* Confirmation of Charges]. The same view is held by Ambos, *Article 25* (Above n 18), at 479; Eser (Above n 18), at 795.

as two alternative theories of co-perpetration or principal liability[40]; or whether, on the contrary, as ICC Pre-Trial Chamber I has affirmed in relation to article 25(3) (a) and (d) RS, only the notion of control of the crime is a theory of co-perpetration whereas notions akin to joint criminal enterprise are a 'residual form of accessorial liability'.[41]

In answering these questions, one has to keep in mind that the case law of the *Ad hoc* Tribunals and the drafters of the RS might have made different choices concerning the approach to the distinction between principals and accessories to the crime and the role to be played by the notions of joint criminal enterprise and control of the crime to comprehensively reflect the wrongdoing and culpability of senior political and military leaders as principals to the widespread and systematic commission of international crimes. In this regard, it must be underscored that the choice of the drafters of the RS is, in principle, confined to the ICC system and does not affect necessarily the evolution of other ambits of international criminal law as shown by the evolving jurisprudence of the *Ad hoc* Tribunals. Indeed, articles 10, 21 and 22(3) RS explicitly safeguard the autonomy of the ICC system vis-à-vis other ambits of international criminal law with regard to the content of their respective substantive provisions[42].

---

[40] *Milutinovic Amended Indictment* (Above n 26), at paras 22, 34.
[41] *Lubanga Case* Confirmation of Charges (Above n 39), at para 337.
[42] Olasolo, *Triggering Procedure* (Above n 14), at 19, 23–5.

2

Perpetration of a Crime and Participation in a Crime Committed by a Third Person: Principal versus Accessorial Liability

I Introduction

The Nuremberg and Tokyo military tribunals and the courts acting in subsequent proceedings in relation to WW II cases, particularly under Control Council Law No 10, provided an initial set of rules on the punishable forms of intervention in the commission of a crime in international criminal law.[1] The Statutes of the ICTY and the ICTR and the 1991 and 1996 Draft Codes of Crimes against Peace and Security of Mankind of the International Law Commission constituted a first attempt to refine such rules.[2] A further attempt was carried out by the case law of the ICTY and the ICTR, which contains extensive discussions on the nature and scope of the punishable forms of intervention in the commission of a crime.[3]

Part III of the Rome Statute establishes the general principles of criminal law (general part of substantive criminal law)—including the set of rules provided for in article 25(3) RS on the punishable forms of intervention in the commission of a crime—which are applicable at the ICC. For some writers, this set of rules 'reflects the development of the concept of individual criminal responsibility in international law as it has taken place since Nuremberg'.[4] For others, this set of rules is, almost in its entirety, part of customary international law.[5] However, as will be shown in the following sections, the differences between the rules

---

[1] G Werle, *Tratado de Derecho Penal Internacional* (Valencia, Tirant lo Blanch, 2005) 211 [hereinafter Werle]; E Van Sliedregt, *The Criminal Responsibility of Individuals for Violations of International Humanitarian Law* (The Hague, TMC Asser Press, 2003) 41 [hereinafter Van Sliedregt].

[2] Werle (*Ibid*) at 211.

[3] According to Van Sliedregt (Above n 1) at 41, the ICTY and the ICTR, '[b]y expanding on some parts and leaving out others, they construed a more refined and coherent concept of criminal responsibility, reflecting principles of national criminal law, but retaining its international origin'. For Werle (*Ibid*) at 211, the case law of the ICTY gave the final step towards the creation of a theoretical framework concerning the punishable forms of intervention in the commission of a crime in international criminal law.

[4] Van Sliedregt (Above n 1), at 41.

[5] Werle (Above n 1), at 211.

contained in article 25(3) RS and those rules provided for in the Statutes and case law of the *Ad hoc* Tribunals are substantial.[6]

Despite the above-mentioned developments, the provisions on the punishable forms of intervention in the commission of a crime in international criminal law are not different from the provisions regulating other aspects of the general part of international criminal law in terms of their rudimentary and fragmented character.[7] Hence as Van Sliedregt has rightly pointed out:

> While the Nuremberg and Tokyo Judgments and the subsequent proceedings are important sources of law and indispensable in developing a theory of individual responsibility in international criminal law, they do not provide us with a system of criminal law and doctrine. For that, we need to turn to municipal law. National law and doctrine not only serve as guidance and inspiration in developing a theory of individual responsibility in international criminal law, they also assist in understanding and describing current international criminal law concepts. It is clear from the jurisprudence emanating from the *Ad hoc* Tribunals that the judges have recourse to, and draw inspiration from national law and doctrine in forming and founding their judgement, and in interpreting certain notions and concepts.[8]

II First Approach to the Problem: Principal versus Accessorial Liability in National Law

The distinction between perpetration of a crime, which gives rise to principal liability, and participation in a crime committed by a third person, which gives rise to accessorial liability, responds to the distinction between those who are directly liable for the violation of a penal norm (perpetrators or principals to a crime) and those others who are derivatively liable (accessories to a crime or secondary parties).[9] Perpetrators or principals to a crime are those whose liability can be established independently of all other parties to the crime, whereas accessories or secondary parties are those others whose liability derives from the principal liability of the perpetrators.[10]

---

[6] These differences have been pointed out by K Kittichaisaree, *International Criminal Law* (Oxford, Oxford University Press, 2001) 235; Compare H Olasolo and A Perez Cepeda, 'The Notion of Control of the Crime in the Jurisprudence of the ICTY: The Stakic Case' (2004) 4 *International Criminal Law Review* 474, 476.

[7] Werle (Above n 1), at 210; A Clapham 'On Complicity' in M Henzelin and R Roth (eds), *Le droit penal à l'epreuve de l'internationalisation* (Paris, LGDJ, 2002) 241–75; A Eser, 'Individual Criminal Responsibility' in A Cassese, P Gaeta, and JRWD Jones (eds.), *The Rome Statute of the International Criminal Court: A Commentary* (Oxford, Oxford University Press, 2002) 784; K Ambos, *La Parte General del Derecho Penal Internacional: Bases para una Elaboracion Dogmatica* (Uruguay, Konrad-Adenauer-Stiftung, 2005) 243 [hereinafter Ambos];Van Sliedregt (Above n 1) at 41

[8] Van Sliedregt (Above n 1) at 41

[9] GP Fletcher, *Rethinking Criminal Law* (2nd edn, Oxford, Oxford University Press, 2000) 636 [hereinafter Fletcher].

[10] JC Smith and B Hogan, *Criminal Law* (11th edn, London, Butterworths, 2005) 165 [hereinafter Smith and Hogan].

The notions of perpetration and participation must be distinguished from the category of complicity (giving rise to the so-called 'accomplice' liability). While the category of complicity is used in a number of national systems (such as the German,[11] French,[12] Spanish[13] or Latin-American systems)[14] to refer to contributions in a crime committed by a third person that only give rise to accessorial liability, in common law jurisdictions the category of complicity is relied on to generally refer to partnership in crime.[15] Furthermore, the ICTY Appeal Judgment in the *Tadic* case has followed the common law approach to complicity,[16] according to which the category of complicity does not distinguish per se between principals and accessories to the crime insofar as it encompasses cases in which all partners are co-perpetrators (joint principals to the crime), and those other cases in which one or some of the partners are principals to the crime and the others are accessories.[17] It is for this reason that, according to Fletcher:

> The central question in any system of complicity is distinguishing between co-perpetrators and accessories. The former are punished as full perpetrators, regardless of the liability of anyone else.[18]

The distinction between perpetrators or principals to the crime on the one side, and accessories to the crime or secondary parties on the other, is embraced by most national criminal law systems.[19] The main reason justifying this distinction is the derivative nature of any punishable form of participation in the commission of a crime by a third person. As Gillies has put it:

---

[11] K Hamdorf, 'The Concept of a Joint Criminal Enterprise and Domestic Modes of Liability for Parties to a Crime: A Comparison of German and English Law' (2007) 1 *Journal of International Criminal Justice* 210–14 [hereinafter Hamdorf].

[12] F Desportes and F Le Gunehec, *Droit Penal General* (12th edn, Paris, Economica, 2005) 491 [hereinafter Desportes and Gunehec].

[13] JM Zugaldia Espinar (ed), *Derecho Penal: Parte General* (Valencia, Tirant lo Blanch, 2002) 727–8 [hereinafter Zugaldia Espinar].

[14] J Bustos Ramirez, *Obras Completas, Vol I Derecho Penal: Parte General* (Lima, ARA Editores EIRL, 2004) 660 [hereinafter Bustos Ramirez]; E Magalhaes Noronha, *Direito Penal, Vol 1: Introducao e Parte Geral* (37th Edition, Saraiva, Sao Paulo, 2003) 221 [hereinafter Magalhaes Noronha]; S Politoff, JP Matus and MC Ramirez, *Lecciones de Derecho Penal Chileno: Parte General* (Santiago de Chile, Editorial Juridica de Chile, 2003) 391 [hereinafter Politoff, Matus and Ramirez]; F Velasquez, *Manual de Derecho Penal: Parte General* (2nd edn, Bogota, Comlibros, 2004) 447 [hereinafter Velasquez]; ER Zaffaroni, *Manual de Derecho Penal: Parte General* (6th edn, Buenos Aires, Editor SA, 2003) 565 [hereinafter Zaffaroni].

[15] Fletcher (Above n 9), at 636; P Gillies, *Criminal Law* (4th edn, North Ryde, LBC Information Services, 1997), at 155 [hereinafter Gillies].

[16] *Prosecutor v Tadic* (Appeals Chamber Judgment) ICTY-94-1-A (15 July 1999) para 220 [hereinafter *Tadic Case* Appeals Judgment]. In this regard, *Prosecutor v Krnojelac* (Appeals Chamber Judgment) ICTY-97-25-A (17 September 2003) para 70 [hereinafter *Krnojelac Case* Appeals Judgment] has stated in relation to the meaning given by the Tadic Appeal Judgment to the term 'accomplice' as follows: 'The Appeals Chamber notes first of all that, in the case-law of the Tribunal, even within a single judgment, this term has different meanings depending on the context and may refer to a *co-perpetrator* or an *aidor and abettor*'.

[17] Fletcher (Above n 9), at 636; Gillies (Above n 15), at 155; *Tadic Case* Appeals Judgment (*Ibid*) at paras 220, 228.

[18] Fletcher (*Ibid*), at 659.

[19] Ambos (Above n 7), at 171; Van Sliedregt (Above n 1), at 59.

15

Accessoryship is not a crime in itself. Rather, it is simply a mode of participation in another's crime—an alternative route to liability. Because accessoryship is not an independent head of liability in the criminal law, there can be no accessory without a principal.[20]

Hence, no matter whether an accessory or a secondary party to a crime may deserve the same punishment as the perpetrator, his criminal liability is always dependant on the existence of a perpetrator who commits a crime. In common law jurisdictions this principle is reflected in the theory of 'derivative liability'[21]; under French law this is encapsulated in the expression *'l'emprunt de criminalité'*[22]; Spanish and Latino-American systems embrace this idea under the principle of *'accesoriedad de la participación'*,[23] and German law refers to it with the expression *'Akzessorietät'*.[24]

In addition to the derivative nature of participation,[25] there are other reasons which call for the distinction between perpetration of a crime giving rise to

---

[20] Gillies (Above n 15), at 154.

[21] SH Kadish, 'Complicity, Cause and Blame: A Study in the Interpretation of Doctrine' (1985) 73 *California law Review* 337–42; Smith and Hogan (Above n 10); Gillies (*Ibid*), at 154–157; Fletcher (Above n 9), at 636–7.

[22] H Angevin and A Chavanne, *Editions du Juris-Classeur Penal* (Paris, LexisNexis, 1998), Complicite: art 121–6 et 121–7.

[23] F Munoz Conde and M Garcia Aran, *Derecho Penal: Parte General* (5th edn, Valencia, Tirant lo Blanch, 2002) 455 [hereinafter Munoz Conde and Garcia Aran]; G Quintero Olivares, *Manual de Derecho Penal: Parte General* (3rd edn, Pamplona, Aranzadi, 2002) 611, 626 [hereinafter Quintero Olivares]; A Bruno, *Direito Penal, Vol II* (3rd edn, Rio de Janeiro, Forense, 1967) 257; Bustos Ramirez (Above n 14), at 660; Velasquez (Above n 14), at 447; Zaffaroni (Above n 14), at 565.

[24] HH Jescheck and T Weigend, *Lehrbuch des Strafrechts* (5th edn, Berlin, Duncker and Humblot, 1996) 655–61 [hereinafter Jescheck and Weigend].

[25] Although the principle of accessoryship is embraced by most national systems of criminal justice, its content varies from one to another. For instance, in some national systems, advising, encouraging or assisting an accessory does not give rise to criminal liability, so that the advisor of a planner, the instigator of an instigator or the person who assists an aidor or an abettor is not criminally liable. This is justified as a consequence of the derivative nature of those punishable forms of participation in a crime committed by a third person, so that the accessory of an accessory is not criminally liable (Quintero Olivares (Above n 23), at 626.). For instance, under Spanish law 'indirect instigation', also known as 'chain of instigation', is not criminally relevant and therefore no criminal liability arises for the instigator of the instigator (Zugaldia Espinar (Above n 13), at 763.). However, in other national systems the principle of accessory-ship does include this limitation. For instance, as Desportes and Gunehec (Above n 12), at 523, have pointed out, under French law, the instigator of the instigator is criminally liable as an accessory to the crime (the same goes for other modes of participation in the commission of a crime by a third person who gives rise to criminal liability, that is to say *'le complice du complice'* is criminally liable).
  The different scope of the principle of accessoryship in those national systems that embrace it is also reflected in the definition of its quantitative and qualitative dimensions. The quantitative dimension of the principle of accessoryship refers to the stage of the *iter criminis* that must be reached for acts of participation to give rise to accessory liability. For instance, under Spanish law, acts of participation are only punishable if the preparatory stage is completed and the stage of execution of the crime is reached, no matter whether the offence is finally completed. See Zugaldia Espinar (Above n 13), at 757. The qualitative dimension of the principle of accessoryship refers to whether conduct amounting to the execution, or attempted execution, of the objective elements of the crime suffices for participation to give rise to criminal liability, or whether it is also necessary that conduct, besides fulfilling the objective elements of the crime, be also unlawful and culpable. For instance, under Spanish law, the relevant conduct must amount to the execution, or attempted execution, of the objective elements of the crime and must be unlawful. Nevertheless, the relevant conduct does not need to be culpable. See Zugaldia

principal liability and participation in a crime committed by a third person giving rise to accessorial liability. As Smith & Hogan have put it with respect to common law jurisdictions, such a distinction is also necessary because (i) while no mens rea is required from perpetrators or principals in offences of strict liability, accessories to this type of offences must always have mens rea; (ii) while in some offences vicarious liability can be imposed for the acts of another who does the act of a principal, no vicarious liability can be imposed for the act of an accessory to the crime; and (iii) some offences require that perpetrators or principals be members of a specified class or possess an specific status.[26] Moreover, in those jurisdictions belonging to the Romano-Germanic tradition, such as the German,[27] the Spanish[28] or the Latino-Americans,[29] the principle of mitigation for accessorial liability constitutes an important additional reason for the distinction between principals and accessories to the crime.

Concerning this fast principle, it must be highlighted that the distinction between perpetration and participation does not necessarily mean that punishment for accessories must always be less severe than punishment for perpetrators or principals. Only in those national systems belonging to the Romano-Germanic tradition, the principle of mitigation for accessorial liability is, in one way or another, explicitly recognised.[30] This distinction on the level of punishment is based on the premise that punishment should be inflicted in proportion to the blameworthiness of the conduct of each person involved in the commission of a crime.[31] As a result, each

---

Espinar (Above n 13), at 757. As a result, if the objective elements of the crime have not been carried out by the perpetrator with the required mental element, or if the perpetrator's conduct was not unlawful because he acted under a cause of justification such as self defence, any form of advice, encouragement or assistance to the perpetrator will not give rise to criminal liability (Quintero Olivares (Above n 23), at 627.). There is no reason to punish those persons who in one way or another contribute to an action or omission, which is criminally irrelevant, or does not give rise to criminal liability because it is justified (Munoz Conde and Garcia Aran (Above n 23), at 455.). Therefore, aiding a military commander to pillage enemy houses in a village by telling him where the enemy houses are located does not give rise to criminal liability unless the military commander directs his troops to pillage them. However, the same does not hold true if the perpetrator carries out the objective elements of the crime with the required mental element, but he ends up not being criminally liable because of a ground for excuse, such as duress, mental illness or intoxication. The reason is that grounds for excuse change neither the nature nor the unlawfulness of the conduct of the perpetrator (Quintero Olivares (Above n 23), at 627.). Indeed, grounds for excuse are individual and are only related to the level of culpability of the perpetrator and of any other person who participates in the commission of the crime. Hence, those soldiers who direct prisoners of war under their custody to pillage enemy houses will be criminally liable as accessories to the crime even if those physically committing the pillage may not be criminally liable because they act under duress.

[26] Smith and Hogan (Above n 10), at 165–6.

[27] Hamdorf (Above n 11), at 210; See also German Criminal Code § 27(2).

[28] Zugaldia Espinar (Above n 13), at 934. See also Spanish Criminal Code arts 28 and 63.

[29] Magalhaes Noronha (Above n 14), at 221; Politoff, Matus and Ramirez (Above n 14), at 391; Velasquez (Above n 14), at 447; Zaffaroni (Above n 14), at 565. See also Argentinean Criminal Code arts 45 and 46; Colombian Criminal Code arts 29 and 30.

[30] See Hamdorf (Above n 11); Zugaldia Espinar (Above n 13); Magalhaes Noronha (*Ibid*).

[31] Fletcher (Above n 9), at 651. See also Hamdorf (*Ibid*), at 210, who is of the view that, due to the fact that punishment for accessorial liability is to be mitigated pursuant to German Criminal Code § 27(2), 'a lot of attention has been paid by German courts and scholars to the line between principals and accessories'.

person involved should be punished according to his or her individual culpability. Moreover, although the wrongdoing of the perpetrator sets the maximum level of permissible punishment, the wrongdoing of the accessory is less than that of the perpetrator and therefore should be subject to a lesser level of punishment. In other national systems, such as the French[32] and the Common Law systems,[33] the principle of mitigation is not officially recognised, although punishment for accessories can be informally mitigated through prosecutorial and judicial discretion.[34]

There are a few national systems—usually referred to as 'unitary systems', such as those of Denmark[35] and Italy,[36] which do not endorse the distinction between perpetration of a crime giving rise to principal liability, and participation in a crime committed by a third person giving rise to accessorial liability.[37] For these

[32] Desportes and Gunehec (Above n 12), at 541.

[33] Hamdorf (Above n 11), at 218; Fletcher (Above n 9), at 636.

[34] According to Fletcher, this would explain why the systems that are part of the Romano-Germanic tradition have given a lot of attention to the distinction between principal and accessory liability, while the English speaking world has shown an 'extraordinary disinterest' for this field. (Fletcher (Above n 9), at 637, fn 4.). It is also from this perspective that Judge Iain Bonomy has affirmed that that '[i]n countries with a common law tradition, the distinction between "principals" and "accessories" is more nominal than real'. (*Prosecutor v Milutinovic* (Decision On Ojdanic's Motion Challenging Jurisdiction: Indirect Co-Perpetration, Separate Opinion of Judge Bonomy) ICTY-05-87-PT (22 March 2006) para 29 [hereinafter *Prosecutor v Milutinovic*, Bonomy Opinion].) For Hamdorf, 'under English criminal law, the distinction between principals and accessories is not as important as under German law because the punishment for both modes of liability is identical and accessory liability is—unlike in German law—as a rule not restricted to the intentional acts of the principal and the accessory'. (Hamdorf (Above n 11), at 218.); Desportes and Gunehec (Above n 12), at 541 also point out the limited interest for this field in French Law.

[35] Danish Penal Code art 23(1). See also K Cornils and V Greve, *Das Danische Strafgesetz-Straffeloven, Zweisprachige Ausgabe* (2nd edn, Friburg, Max-Planck-Institut, 2001); K Hamdorf, *Beteiligungsmodelle im Strafrecht: Ein Vergleich von Teilnahme –und Einheitstatersystemen in Skandinavien, Osterreich und Deutschland* (Friburg, Max-Planck-Institut, 2002) 66, 233. As Ambos (Above n 7), at 173, has pointed out, Denmark has adopted the purest variant of the unitary system because it does not even embrace a purely formal distinction between perpetration and participation.

[36] Italian Penal Code art 110 states: 'When a plurality of persons participate in the crime, each of them will be imposed the sentence attached to such crime, unless the following articles provide otherwise'. See also R Dell'Andro, *La fattispecie plurisoggettiva in Diritto penale* (Milan, Giuffre, 1957) 77; A Pagliaro, *Principi di Diritto Penale: Parte Generale* (8th edn, Milan Giuffre, 2003) 540.

[37] Austria and Poland have adopted a so-called 'functional unitary system', as opposed to the pure unitary system adopted in Denmark and Italy. Austrian Penal Code § 12 and Polish Penal Code art 18 formally distinguish between perpetration and participation. Nevertheless, the Austrian and Polish systems do not recognise the derivative nature of participation. In relation to Austria, see O Triffterer, *Die Osterreichische Beteiligungslehre: Eine Regelung Zwischen Einheitstater und Teilnahmesystem?* (Vienna, MANZ'sche Wien, 1983) 33; D Kienapfel, *Erscheinungsformen der Einheitstaterschaft* in Strafrechtsdogmatik und Kriminalpolitik (Cologne, Muller-Dietz, 1971) 25. In relation to Poland see, A Zoll, 'Alleinhandeln und Zusammenwirken aus Polnischer Sicht' in K Cornils, A Eser and B Huber (eds), *Einzelverantwortung und Mitverantwortung im Strafrecth* (Friburg, Max-Planck-Institut, 1998) 57–60. In relation to the distinction between pure unitary systems, which do not even embrace a formal distinction between perpetration and participation, and functional unitary systems, which do not recognise the derivative nature of participation despite formally embracing the distinction between perpetration and participation, see Ambos (Above n 7), at 172–3; M Diaz y Garcia Conlledo, *La Autoria en Derecho Penal* (Barcelona, Universidad de Leon, 1991) 47, 200 [hereinafter Diaz y Garcia Conlledo]; MJ Lopez Peregrin, *La Complicidad en el Delito* (Valencia, Tirant Lo Branch, 1997) 29 [hereinafter Lopez Peregrin]; R Bloy, *Die Beteiligungsform als Zurechnungstypus im Strafrecth* (Berlin, Duncker and Humblot, 1985) 149 [hereinafter Bloy]; J Renzikowski, *Restriktiver Taterbegriff und Fahrlassige Beteiligung* (Tubinga, Mohr Siebeck, 1997) 10.

systems, perpetrators are all those persons who contribute to the commission of a crime with the subjective element required by the crime in question.[38] As a result, these systems affirm the autonomous criminal liability as a perpetrator of any person who contributes to the commission of the crime.[39]

For the unitary systems, the nature of one's contribution to the commission of the crime and the role of the other persons involved in the crime are irrelevant for the determination of a person as a perpetrator. As a consequence, irrespective of who physically carries out the objective elements of the crime, all senior political and military leaders involved in its planning, preparation and execution will be criminally liable as perpetrators of the crime. Indeed, the main advantage of the unitary systems is that they do not have to deal with the problems arising from the determination of the principal or derivative nature of the liability of those who intervene in the commission of a crime by a plurality of persons.[40]

However, at the same time, unitary systems present a number of disadvantages. First, instead of referring to the contribution to the execution of the crime and to distinguish between the wrongdoing of participating in the crime and the wrongdoing of executing the objective elements of the crime, unitary systems consider causalities in isolation, which alone do not determine criminal behaviour.[41] Second, unitary systems bring about unfair legal consequences for those who have a rather limited intervention in the commission of the crime insofar as they are qualified as perpetrators of the crime.[42]

Third, unitary systems are also problematic from the perspective of the principle of legality.[43] In this regard, it is important to highlight that in those systems in which there is a distinction between principal and accessorial liability, the different forms of participation in a crime committed by a third person give rise to accessorial liability only if it is explicitly stated in the law, otherwise there is no criminal liability attached to them.[44] This is due to the fact that penal norms, when defining a crime, only refer to the conduct of the perpetrator.

Fourth, unitary systems may also present problems from the perspective of the principle of minimal intervention of criminal law.[45] This is particularly true with

---

[38] By doing so, these systems adopt a purely causal approach to the notion of perpetration.

[39] The unitary approach to perpetration and participation has lately also been adopted in other national jurisdictions. For example, it has been introduced in Spanish law for crimes, which often take the form of organised crimes (ie money-laundering, trafficking in human beings and drug trafficking; Spanish Penal Code arts 301, 318 *bis* and 368). In relation to these crimes it is not necessary to distinguish between perpetrators or principals and accessories to the crime. However, this approach is controversial among writers, who have highlighted concerns regarding the principles of legality and minimum intervention (see Munoz Conde and Garcia Aran (Above n 23), at 447–8).

[40] For this reason, some writers support the adoption of the unitary system at the European level. See CE Paliero, 'Grunderfordenisse des Allgemeinen Teils fur ein europaisches Sanktionenrecht. Landesbericht Italien' (1998) 100 *ZSTW* 438.

[41] G Jakobs, *Strafrecht Allgemeiner Teil* (2nd edn, Berlin, Gruyter, 1991) para 21/6 [hereinafter Jakobs].

[42] Diaz y Garcia Conlledo (Above n 37), at 47; Lopez Peregrin (Above n 37), at 29.

[43] F Munoz Conde, 'Problemas de Autoria y Participacion en la Criminalidad Organizada' in C Ferre Olive and E Anarte Borrallo (eds), *Delincuencia Organizada: Aspectos Penales, Procesales y Criminologicos* (Universidad de Huelva, 1999) 159 [hereinafter Munoz Conde].

[44] Quintero Olivares (Above n 23), at 626.

[45] Munoz Conde (Above n 43), at 159.

regard to those systems in which the principle of accessoryship is defined in such a way as to prevent criminal liability from arising as a result of advising, encouraging or assisting an accessory to the crime to carry out his contribution. Hence, according to such systems, the advisor of a planner, the instigator of an instigator and the person who assists an aidor or an abettor are not criminally liable.[46]

Finally, unitary systems do not solve the problems of distinguishing between different forms of involvement in the commission of a crime; rather, this becomes a question for sentencing.[47]

III Principal versus Accessorial Liability in International Criminal Law

As the ICTY Appeal Judgment in the *Tadic* case has explicitly stated, crimes under international criminal law 'do not result from the criminal propensity of single individuals but constitute manifestations of collective criminality: the crimes are often carried out by groups of individuals acting in pursuance of a common criminal design'.[48] Moreover, as is shown by the case of Adolf Eichmann (who organised the transportation of thousands of persons to Nazi detention camps in which they were subsequently exterminated), these crimes are also characterised by the fact that the level of criminal responsibility does not diminish as a result of being away from the scene of the crime. In fact, the individual's level of criminal responsibility usually increases.[49] As a result, there is an even more pressing need in international criminal law than in national law to provide the necessary tools to properly assess the part of the crime attributable to the relevant senior political and military leaders. The rules on the punishable forms of contribution to the commission of a crime constitute the main tool through which this assessment can be made.

The IMT and IMTFE charters set out the first rules on the punishable forms of intervention in international criminal law. These rules were scattered throughout the text because certain punishable forms of intervention were directly introduced as part of the definition of the crimes,[50] whereas others were included after the

---

[46] These national systems, in particular those belonging to the Romano-Germanic tradition, see the general rule that the accessory of an accessory is not criminally liable as an important safeguard for individuals, which is derived from the derivative nature of those punishable forms of participation in a crime committed by a third person. See Quintero Olivares (Above n 23), at 626.

[47] C Roxin, *Taterschaft und Tatherrschaft* (7th edn, Berlin, Gruyter, 2000) 451 [hereinafter Roxin].

[48] *Tadic Case* Appeals Judgment (Above n 16), at para 191.

[49] Werle (Above n 1), at 209. See also *Tadic Case* Appeals Judgment (*Ibid*), at para. 16.

[50] Charter of the International Military Tribunal at Nuremberg, in Trial of the Major War Criminals before the International Military Tribunal under Control Council Law No 10, Vol I (US Government Printing Office, 1951) [hereinafter IMT Charter]. Art 6(a) IMT Charter and art 5(a) IMFTE Charter defined crimes against peace as 'namely, planning, preparation, initiation or waging of a war of aggression, or a war in violation of international treaties, agreements or assurances, or participation in a common plan or conspiracy for the accomplishment of any of the foregoing'.

definition of crimes against humanity in the last paragraph of articles 6(c) IMT Charter and 5(c) IMTFE Charter.[51] Furthermore, they did not distinguish between principal and accessorial liability. In this regard, as Ambos has pointed out, the IMT and the IMTFE embraced a unitary model which did not distinguish between the perpetration of a crime (which gives rise to principal liability) and participation in a crime committed by a third person (which gives rise to accessorial liability).[52] According to the case law of these bodies, any type of material or legal support or assistance to the crime was simply considered as a punishable form of intervention in the commission of the crime.[53]

The rules on the punishable forms of intervention in the commission of crimes included in the Allied Control Council Law No 10 were somewhat more systematised than in the Nuremberg and Tokyo Charters. Although some rules were still introduced as part of the definition of crimes against peace,[54] there was a specific provision on the punishable forms of intervention, which, for the first time, introduced the distinction between principal and accessorial liability in international criminal law.[55] Nevertheless, despite these developments, US military tribunals acting under Allied Control Council Law No. 10 embraced a unitary model, which did not distinguish between perpetration (principal liability) and participation (accessorial liability).[56]

One has to wait until the elaboration of the Statutes of the ICTY and the ICTR[57] and the 1991 and 1996 Draft Codes of Crimes against Peace and Security of Mankind of the International Law Commission[58] to find a real attempt to refine

---

[51] According to art 6(c) IMT Charter and art 5(c) IMFTE Charter '[l]eaders, organizers, instigators and accomplices participating in the formulation or execution of a common plan or conspiracy to commit any of the foregoing crimes are responsible for all acts performed by any persons in execution of such plan'.

[52] Ambos (Above n 7), at 75.

[53] Werle (Above n 1), at 211, fn 636.

[54] According to art II(1)(a) of Allied Control Council Law No 10, crimes against peace were defined as follows: 'Initiation of invasions of other countries and wars of aggression in violation of international laws and treaties, including but not limited to planning, preparation, initiation or waging a war of aggression, or a war of violation of international treaties, agreements or assurances, or participation in a common plan or conspiracy for the accomplishment of any of the foregoing'.

[55] Art II(2) of Allied Control Council Law No. 10, which followed the provisions on the definition of the crimes, established that: 'Any person without regard to nationality or the capacity in which he acted, is deemed to have committed a crime as defined in paragraph 1 of this Article, if he was (a) a principal or (b) was an accessory to the commission of any such crime or ordered or abetted the same or (c) took a consenting part therein or (d) was connected with plans or enterprises involving its commission or (e) was a member of any organization or group connected with the commission of any such crime or (f) with reference to paragraph 1 (a) if he held a high political, civil or military (including General Staff) position in Germany or in one of its Allies, co-belligerents or satellites or held high position in the financial, industrial or economic life of any such country'.

[56] Ambos (Above n 7), at 75; Werle (Above n 1), at 211, fn 636.

[57] In particular, arts 7(1) ICTYS and 6(1) ICTRS.

[58] ILC, 'Report of the International Law Commission on the Work of its 48th Session' (6 May–26 July 1996) UN Doc A/51/10, Draft Code of Crimes against Peace and Security of Mankind, art 2(3) states: 'An individual shall be responsible for a crime set out in article 17, 18, 19 or 20 if that individual: (*a*) Intentionally commits such a crime; (*b*) Orders the commission of such a crime which in fact occurs or is attempted; (*c*) Fails to prevent or repress the commission of such a crime in the circumstances set out in article 6; (*d*) Knowingly aids, abets or otherwise assists, directly and substantially, in

the rules on the punishable forms of intervention in the commission of crimes provided for in the Nuremberg and Tokyo Charters and in the Allied Control Council Law No. 10.[59]

At the ICTY, the issue of whether article 7(1) ICTYS embraces the distinction between perpetration of a crime giving rise to principal liability and participation in a crime committed by a third person giving rise to accessorial liability came up in the context of the discussion about the nature of the notion of joint criminal enterprise or the common purpose doctrine.

According to article 7(1) ICTYS:

> A person who planned, instigated, ordered, committed or otherwise aided and abetted in the planning, preparation or execution of a crime referred to in articles 2 to 5 of the present Statute, shall be individually responsible for the crime.

As no explicit reference to the notion of joint criminal enterprise or the common purpose doctrine is made in this provision, the question arose as to whether such a notion was included in article 7(1) ICTYS.[60] The ICTY Appeal Judgment in the *Tadic* case answered this question in the affirmative as a result of a systematic and teleological interpretation of article 7(1) ICTYS[61] in light of article 1 ICTYS, the report of the UN Secretary General on the establishment of the ICTY,[62] and the 'inherent characteristics of many crimes perpetrated in wartime'.[63] It was only then that a second issue arose as to whether the notion of joint criminal enterprise or the common purpose doctrine was included in one of the five modes of criminal liability explicitly referred to in article 7(1) ICTYS, or whether it was an additional mode of liability falling within the general scope of application of article 7(1) ICTYS.[64]

In order to answer this last question, it was necessary to determine whether those individuals participating in a joint criminal enterprise (or acting in the execution of a common criminal purpose), and who did not physically carry out the objective elements of the crimes, were:

the commission of such a crime, including providing the means for its commission; (*e*) Directly participates in planning or conspiring to commit such a crime which in fact occurs; (*f*) Directly and publicly incites another individual to commit such a crime which in fact occurs; (*g*) Attempts to commit such a crime by taking action commencing the execution of a crime which does not in fact occur because of circumstances independent of his intentions'.

---

[59] Werle (Above n 1), at 211.

[60] *Tadic Case* Appeals Judgment (Above n 16), at para 186. See also K Gustafson, 'The Requirements of an "Express Agreement" for Joint Criminal Enterprise Liability: A Critique of Brdanin' (2007) 5 *Journal of International Criminal Justice* 134–58, 136 [hereinafter Gustafson].

[61] *Tadic Case* Appeals Judgment (*Ibid*), at paras 187–93.

[62] United Nations Security Council (UNSC) 'Report of the Secretary-General pursuant to Paragraph 2 of Security Council Resolution 808 (1993)' (3 May 1993) UN Doc S/25704, para 53 [hereinafter Report of the Secretary-General].

[63] *Tadic Case* Appeals Judgment (Above n 16), at para 193. See also A Cassese, 'The Proper Limits of Individual Responsibility under the Doctrine of Joint Criminal Enterprise' (2007) 5 *Journal of International Criminal Justice* 110–14 [hereinafter Cassese]; E Van Sliedregt, 'Joint Criminal Enterprise as a Pathway to Convicting Individuals for Genocide' (2007) 5 *Journal of International Criminal Justice* 184–207, 185–7 [hereinafter Van Sliedregt, Joint Criminal Enterprise].

[64] *Tadic Case* Appeals Judgment (*Ibid*), at para 186.

i)   Always principals to the crimes as co-perpetrators[65];
ii) Always accessories to the crimes as participants in a crime committed by others[66];
iii) Sometimes principals and other times accessories to the crimes, depending on their level of contribution to the implementation of the common criminal plan or on their state of mind in carrying out such contribution[67];
iv) Neither principals nor accessories to the crimes—but just criminally liable for the crimes—because article 7(1) ICTYS did not embrace the distinction between principal (perpetration) and accessorial or derivative (participation) liability.

It was in this context that the ICTY case law addressed the issue of whether article 7(1) ICTYS established a unitary system, which did not embrace the distinction between perpetration of a crime giving rise to principal liability, and participation in a crime committed by a third person giving rise to accessorial liability; or whether, on the contrary, art 7(1) ICTYS endorsed the distinction between perpetration and participation. Only if the ICTY case law concluded that article 7(1) ICTYS departed from the unitary systems because it embraced the distinction between perpetration and participation, would it then have to address the issue of whether the notion of joint criminal enterprise was (i) a theory of co-perpetration giving rise to principal liability, (ii) a form of accessorial or derivative liability, or (iii) a theory of partnership in crime ('accomplice' liability) which could give rise to principal or accessorial liability depending on the level of the individual's contribution or state of mind.

In spite of the uncertainty that the ICTY Appeal Judgment in the *Tadic* case created in relation to the nature of the notion of joint criminal enterprise or the common purpose doctrine,[68] the distinction between principal (perpetration) and accessorial liability (participation) in article 7(1) ICTYS has been consistently embraced by ICTY case law. In this regard, it is important to highlight that in the *Tadic* case, the Appeals Chamber expressly affirmed on 15 July 1999 that the first feature which distinguishes the notions of 'acting in pursuance of a common purpose or design to commit a crime' and aiding and abetting is that the '[t]he aidor and abettor is always an accessory to a crime perpetrated by another person, the principal'.[69] Subsequently, ICTY Trial Chamber I in its 26 February 2001 Judgment in the *Kordic* case stated that '[t]he various forms of participation listed

---

[65] In this case, the notion of joint criminal enterprise or the common purpose doctrine would fall under the heading 'committed' in art 7(1) ICTYS.

[66] In this case, the notion of joint criminal enterprise or the common purpose doctrine would fall under the heading 'aided and abetted' in art 7(1) ICTYS or would constitute an autonomous form of accessorial liability within the scope of such provision.

[67] In this case, the notion of joint criminal enterprise or the common purpose doctrine would be a theory of accomplice liability or partnership in crime (as seen above, this is the sense of accomplice liability in common law jurisdictions) amounting to an autonomous mode of liability within the scope of art 7(1) ICTYS.

[68] Van Sliedregt, Joint Criminal Enterprise (Above n 63), at 189. See also Ch 2, s VII.B.

[69] *Tadic Case* Appeals Judgment (Above n 16), at para 229.

in Article 7(1) may be divided between principal perpetrators and accomplices',[70] whereas in its 2 August 2001 Judgment in the *Krstic* case, it affirmed that:

> It seems clear that 'accomplice liability' denotes a secondary form of participation which stands in contrast to the responsibility of the direct or principal perpetrators.[71]

In its 21 May 2003 *Ojdanic* SCE Appeals Decision, the ICTY Appeals Chamber expressly affirmed that 'joint criminal enterprise is to be regarded, not as a form of accomplice liability, but as a form of commission'.[72] Subsequent ICTY case law, such as the *Krnojelac*,[73] *Vasiljevic*,[74] *Blaskic*,[75] *Krstic*,[76] *Kvocka*,[77] *Simic*,[78] and the *Brdanin* Appeal Judgments[79] or the *Krajisnik*[80] and *Martic*[81] Trial Judgments, have affirmed that article 7(1) ICTYS does not establish a unitary system and has consistently embraced the distinction between perpetration of a crime giving rise to principal liability and participation in a crime committed by a third person giving rise to accessorial liability.

---

[70] *Prosecutor v Kordic* (Judgment) ICTY-95-14/2-T (26 Feb 2001) para 373 [hereinafter *Kordic Case* Trial Judgment].

[71] *Prosecutor v Krstic* (Trial Judgment) ICTY-98-33-T (2 Aug 2001) para 642 [hereinafter *Krstic Case* Trial Judgment]. This distinction was also embraced in *Prosecutor v Kvocka et al* (Trial Judgment) ICTY-98-30/1-T (2 Nov 2001) paras 249, 273 [hereinafter *Kvocka Case* Trial Judgment]. There, the Trial Chamber pointed out that those participating in a joint criminal enterprise who did not physically carry out the objective elements of the crime could be (i) either principals to the crime (co-perpetrator) if they made their contribution sharing the common criminal purpose; or (ii) accessories to the crime (aidors or abettors) if they made their contribution knowing (but not sharing) the common criminal purpose.

[72] *Prosecutor v Milutinovic* (Decision on Dragoljub Ojdanic's Motion Challenging Jurisdiction—Joint Criminal Enterprise) ICTY-99-37-AR72 (21 May 2003) para 20, 31 [hereinafter *Ojdanic* JCE Appeals Decision].

[73] *Krnojelac Case* Appeals Judgment (Above n 16), at paras 30, 73.

[74] *Prosecutor v Vasiljevic* (Appeals Chamber Judgment) ICTY-98-32-A (25 Feb 2004) paras 95, 102, 111 [hereinafter *Vasiljevic Case* Appeals Judgment].

[75] *Prosecutor v Blaskic* (Appeals Chamber Judgment) ICTY-95-14-A (29 Jul 2004) para 33 [hereinafter *Blaskic Case* Appeals Judgment] .

[76] *Prosecutor v Krstic* (Appeals Chamber Judgment) ICTY-98-33-A (19 Apr 2004) paras 134, 137, 266–9 [hereinafter *Krstic Case* Appeals Judgment].

[77] *Prosecutor v Kvocka et al* (Appeals Chamber Judgment) ICTY-98-30/1-A (28 Feb 2005) paras 79, 91 [hereinafter *Kvocka Case* Appeals Judgment].

[78] Implicitly in *Prosecutor v Simic et al* (Appeals Chamber Judgment) ICTY-95-9-A (28 Nov 2006) para 243, fn 265.

[79] Implicitly in *Prosecutor v Brdanin* (Appeals Chamber Judgment) ICTY-99-36-A (3 Apr 2007) paras 431, 434, 444–50 [hereinafter *Brdanin Case* Appeals Judgment]. The *Prosecutor v Stakic* (Appeals Chamber Judgment) ICTY-97-24-A (22 Mar 2006) para 62 [hereinafter *Stakic Case* Appeals Judgment], affirms the customary nature of the notion of joint criminal enterprise and its applicability before the ICTY. Moreover, given the limited adjustments made in the sentence imposed on the defendant Stakic after substituting his conviction under the notion of joint criminal enterprise for his conviction as a co-perpetrator based on the notion of control of the crime ('co-perpetratorship'), it seems that in this case, the Appeals Chamber also accepted that the notion of joint criminal enterprise or common purpose doctrine gives rises to principal liability.

[80] *Prosecutor v Krajisnik* (Judgment) ICTY-00-39-T (27 Sep 2006) paras 79–81 [hereinafter *Krajisnik Case* Trial Judgment].

[81] *Prosecutor v Martic* (Judgment) ICTY-95-11-T (12 Jun 2007) paras 435–40.

It is important to highlight that there are a few decisions that have unsuccessfully tried to reject the distinction between principal (perpetration) and accessorial liability (participation) in article 7(1) ICTYS. In this regard, the Trial Judgment in the *Krnojelac* case, issued on 15 February 2002 by ICTY Trial Chamber II (Judge Hunt Presiding), affirmed that the distinction between principal and accessorial or derivative liability was not only alien to the ICTYS but it was also unnecessary.[82] Subsequently, Judge Hunt explained in his Separate Opinion to the *Ojdanic* SCE Appeals Decision that:

> No such distinction exists in relation to sentencing in this Tribunal, and I believe that it is unwise for this Tribunal to attempt to categorise different types of offenders in this way when it is unnecessary to do so for sentencing purposes. The Appeals Chamber has made it clear elsewhere that a convicted person must be punished for the seriousness of the acts which he has done, whatever their categorisation.[83]

Nevertheless, in the view of the author, these are exceptional instances of disagreement and the approach overwhelmingly adopted by the ICTY case law does not justify the statement by Van Sliedregt that '[t]he courts have neither consistently applied or disregarded the distinction between types of offenders'.[84] Quite the contrary, the ICTY has consistently rejected the unitary system and embraced the distinction between perpetration and participation in article 7(1) ICTYS.

At the ICTR, like at the ICTY, the issue of whether article 6(1) ICTRS (which mirrors article 7(1) ICTYS) embraces the distinction between perpetration of a crime giving rise to principal liability and participation in a crime committed by a third person giving rise to accessorial liability has also been dealt with in the context of the nature of the notion of joint criminal enterprise or the common purpose doctrine. Nevertheless, the discussion of this issue at the ICTR has been far more limited than at the ICTY.

On 13 December 2004, the ICTR Appeals Chamber in the *Ntakirutimana* case explained that the ICTY Appeal Judgment in the *Tadic* case had already held that participation in a joint criminal enterprise or common criminal purpose is a form of 'commission' under article 7(1) ICTYS, and hence gives rise to principal, as opposed to accessorial or derivative, liability.[85] Subsequently, on 13 December 2005, the ICTR Trial Judgment in the *Simba* case explicitly affirmed that:

> If the Prosecution intends to rely on the theory of joint criminal enterprise to hold an accused criminally responsible as a principal perpetrator of the underlying crimes rather

---

[82] *Prosecutor v Krnojelac* (Judgment) ICTY-97-25-T (15 Mar 2002) paras 75–7 [hereinafter *Krnojelac Case* Trial Judgment].

[83] *Prosecutor v Milutinovic* (Decision on Dragoljub Ojdanic's Motion Challenging Jurisdiction—Joint Criminal Enterprise, Separate Opinion of Judge Hunt) ICTY-99-37-AR72 (21 May 2003) para 31.

[84] Van Sliedregt, Joint Criminal Enterprise (Above n 63), at 190.

[85] *Prosecutor v Ntakirutimana* (Appeals Chamber Judgment) ICTR-96-10-A (13 Dec 2004) para 462 [hereinafter *Ntakirutimana Case* Appeals Judgment].

than as an accomplice, the indictment should plead this in an unambiguous manner and specify on which form of joint criminal enterprise the Prosecution will rely.[86]

Likewise, in the *Gacumbitsi* case of 7 July 2006, the ICTR Appeals Chamber expressly stated that:

> The Appeals Chamber, following ICTY precedent, has recognized that an accused before this Tribunal may be found individually responsible for 'committing' a crime within the meaning of article 6 (1) of the Statute under one of the three categories of 'joint criminal enterprise' ("JCE") liability.[87]

Hence, it can be concluded that, according to the ICTR case law, article 6(1) ICTRS embraces the distinction between perpetration of a crime giving rise to principal liability and participation in a crime committed by a third person giving rise to accessorial or derivative liability.

Article 25(3) RS contains a systematised set of rules on the publishable forms of intervention in the commission of crimes, which are part of the general principles of criminal law applicable at the ICC. This provision explicitly embraces the distinction between perpetration of a crime giving rise to principal liability, and participation in a crime committed by a third person giving rise to accessory liability.[88] Paragraph (3)(a) of article 25 RS introduces the notion of perpetration by using the expression 'commits such a crime' to refer to the 'commission *stricto sensu* of a crime'.[89] Paragraphs (3)(b) to (3)(d) of article 25 RS use the expressions 'orders', 'solicits', 'induces', 'aids', 'abets', 'assists' and 'in any other way contributes' to provide for several forms of participation which give rise to accessorial, as opposed to principal, liability.[90]

As ICC Pre-Trial Chamber I Decision on the Confirmation of the Charges in the *Lubanga* case has explained:

> The Chamber recalls that in the decision concerning the issuance of a warrant of arrest, it distinguished between (i) the commission stricto sensu of a crime by a person as an individual, jointly with another or through another person within the meaning of article 25 (3) (a) of the Statute, and (ii) the responsibility of superiors under article 28 of the

---

[86] *Prosecutor v Simba* (Judgment) ICTR-01-76-T (13 Dec 2005) para 389 [hereinafter *Simba Case* Trial Judgment].

[87] *Prosecutor v Gacumbitsi* (Appeals Chamber Judgment) ICTR-2001-64-A (7 Jul 2006) para 158 [hereinafter *Gacumbitsi Case* Appeals Judgment].

[88] See also K Ambos, 'Article 25. Individual Criminal Responsibility' in O Triffterer (ed), *Commentary on the Rome Statute of the International Criminal Court* (Baden-Baden, Nomos, 1999) 478–80 [hereinafter Ambos, Article 25]; Werle (Above n 1), at 212–13.

[89] *Lubanga Case* (Pre-Trial Chamber I Decision on Prosecution's Application for Warrant of Arrest) ICC-01/04-01/06 (10 Feb 2006) para 78 [*Lubanga Case* Warrant of Arrest]; *Lubanga Case* (Pre-Trial Chamber I Decision on the Confirmation of Charges) ICC-01/04-01/06 (29 Jan 2007) para 320 [*Lubanga Case* Confirmation of Charges]; *Katanga and Ngudjolo Case* (Pre-Trial Chamber I Decision on the Confirmation of Charges) ICC-01/04-01/07 (1 Oct 2008) paras 466 and 467 [*Katanga and Ngudjolo Case* Confirmation of Charges].

[90] *Lubanga Case* Warrant of Arrest (*Ibid*), at para 78; *Lubanga Case* Confirmation of Charges (*Ibid*), at para 320; *Katanga and Ngudjolo Case* Confirmation of Charges (*Ibid*), at paras 466 and 467.

Statute and "any other forms of accessory, as opposed to principal, liability provided for in article 25 (3) (b) to (d) of the Statute.[91]

IV Differences between the ICC and the *Ad hoc* Tribunals with regard to the Notion of Accessorial Liability

Although the ICTY, the ICTR and the ICC all embrace the distinction between principal and accessorial liability, certain differences in their approach to the principle of accessoryship must be highlighted. The first difference relates to the role played by the principle of mitigation in relation to accessorial liability. At the ICC, rule 145(1)(c) RPE implicitly recognises the principle of mitigation for accessorial liability insofar as it imposes upon the Chambers of the ICC the duty to 'give consideration' to the 'degree of participation of the convicted person' in their determination of the sentence pursuant to article 78(1) RS. Nevertheless, neither the RS nor the RPE explicitly provide for the mitigation of punishment in relation to any specific form of participation which gives rise to accessorial liability under subparagraphs (b) to (d) of article 25(3) RS. As a result, the manner in which the principle of mitigation, implicitly recognised in rule 145(1)(c) RPE, is going to operate vis-à-vis each punishable form of participation provided for in article 25(3) (b) to (d) RS is left up to the discretion of the ICC Chambers.

At the ICTY and the ICTR, no implicit or explicit recognition of the principle of mitigation for accessorial liability can be found in their Statutes and Rules of Procedure and Evidence. This does not mean, however, that punishment for accessories cannot be informally mitigated through judicial discretion. On the contrary, the ICTY and ICTR Appeals Chambers have consistently stated that a person must be punished for the seriousness of the acts which he has done.[92]

The second difference refers to the issue of whether participation in the attempt by a third person to commit a crime gives also rise to criminal liability. To answer this question, one has to go back to the concept of *iter criminis,* understood as the

---

[91] *Lubanga Case* Confirmation of Charges (*Ibid*), at para 320.

[92] See also *Prosecutor v Delalic et al* (Appeals Chamber Judgment) ICTY-96-21-A (20 Feb 2001) paras 429–30 [hereinafter *Celebici Case* Appeals Judgment]; *Prosecutor v Aleksovski* (Appeals Chamber Judgment) ICTY-95-14/1-A (24 Mar 2000) para 180 [hereinafter *Aleksovski* Case Appeals Judgment]; *Gacumbitsi Case* Appeals Judgment (Above n 87), at para 204. In this regard, *Krnojelac Case* Appeals Judgment (Above n 16), at para 75 affirmed that: '[T]he acts of a participant in a joint criminal enterprise are more serious than those of an aidor and abettor since a participant in a joint criminal enterprise shares the intent of the principal offender whereas an aidor and abettor need only be aware of that intent'. Furthermore, the *Kvocka Case* Appeals Judgment (Above n 77), at para 92, in explaining the reasons of the importance of the distinction between the notions of joint criminal enterprise and aiding and abetting, stated: 'The Appeals Chamber notes that the distinction between these two forms of participation is important, both to accurately describe the crime and to fix an appropriate sentence. Aiding and abetting generally involves a lesser degree of individual criminal responsibility than co-perpetration in a joint criminal enterprise'. See also *Vasiljevic Case* Appeals Judgment (Above n 74), at para 102.

process starting with the adoption of the decision by one or more persons to commit a crime and continuing until such crime is completed. In this process, a distinction can be drawn between the preparatory acts and the execution stage.

The expression 'preparatory acts' refers to a set of activities that give rise to criminal liability although they take place before the commencement of the execution stage. The mere adoption of a decision to commit a crime does not usually give rise to criminal liability unless such a decision is manifested by conduct that aims at implementing it,[93] although, in some national systems, when the decision is taken by a plurality of persons, criminal liability may arise from the mere agreement to commit the crime pursuant to the notion of conspiracy.[94] The determination of which specific acts undertaken after deciding to commit a crime and before the commencement of the execution stage give rise to criminal liability is a matter of policy and it is closely linked to the safeguard of fundamental freedoms.[95] Furthermore, in some national systems there is a general clause criminalising certain preparatory acts of any crime,[96] whereas in others, only certain preparatory acts of specific crimes are criminalised.[97]

According to the RS and the Statutes of the *Ad hoc* Tribunals, no criminal liability arises from the preparatory acts of crimes against humanity or war crimes.[98] The

---

[93] Quintero Olivares (Above n 23), at 581.

[94] According to the notion of conspiracy, the mere meeting of the minds to commit a crime gives rise to criminal liability, regardless of whether the common criminal plan is subsequently implemented. As a result, conspiracy has been defined as 'a partnership for criminal purposes'. (*United States v Kissel*, 218 US 601, 608 (1910)). Some national jurisdictions also require the performance of an overt act indicating the existence of the common criminal purpose in order for criminal liability to arise. See GP Fletcher, 'Is Conspiracy Unique to the Common Law?' (1995) 43 *American Journal of Comparative Law* 171. The notion of conspiracy has been particularly developed in the United States after the Pinkerton case (*Pinkerton v United States*, 328 US 640 (1946)). According to the so-called 'Pinkerton rule', an individual who enters into an agreement with other persons to commit a crime becomes party to a conspiracy and may be held liable for all the crimes that comprise the common criminal purpose even if he does not participate at all in its implementation. See A Fichtelberg, 'Conspiracy and International Criminal Justice' (2006) 17 *Criminal Law Forum* 149–76, 156 [hereinafter Fichtelberg]; J Winograd, 'Federal Criminal Conspiracy' (2004) 41 *American Criminal Law Review* 611, 639–40; GP Fletcher, 'The Handam Case and Conspiracy as a War Crime. A new Beginning for International Law in the US' (2006) 4 *Journal of International Criminal Justice* 442. Concerning the development of the notion of conspiracy at the international level in post WW II case law, see E O'Brien, 'The Nuremberg Principles, Command Responsibility and the Defence of Captain Rockwood' (1985) 149 *Minnesota Law Review* 275, 281; T Taylor, *The Anatomy of the Nuremberg Trials: A Personal Memoir* (Boston, Little Brown and Company,1992) 284; A Cassese, *International Criminal Law* (Oxford, Oxford University Press 2003) 197 [hereinafter Cassese, *International Criminal Law*].

[95] Quintero Olivares (Above n 23), at 581.

[96] This is the case of conspiracy to commit a crime in common law jurisdictions.

[97] For instance, Spanish Penal Code arts 17 and 18 define conspiracy to commit a crime, soliciting the commission of a crime and inducement to commit a crime. Immediately after the definition of these preparatory acts, the same provision explicitly states that they will only be punishable in those instances in which the Spanish Penal Code provides.

[98] Although the use of the term 'solicits' in art 25(3)(b) RS could give the impression that criminal responsibility arises from the mere invitation to commit a crime provided for in the RS, regardless of whether the invitee subsequently attempted to commit the crime. See JL Rodriguez-Villasante y Prieto, 'Los Principios Generales del Derecho Penal en el Estatuto de Roma de la Corte Penal Internacional' (Jan-Jun 2000) 75 *Revista Espanola de Derecho Militar* 406. Art 25(3)(b) RS explicitly requires that, after the act of soliciting, the crime 'in fact occurs or is attempted'.

common approach of the RS, the ICTYS and the ICTRS is the result of only focus-ing on conduct that most severely undermines the highest values of the inter-national community.[99] However, due to the unique characteristics of the crime of genocide—which is usually referred to as 'the crime of the crimes' because it aims at destroying a people as opposed to harming individuals—[100] criminal responsi-bility arises from undertaking certain preparatory acts as provided for in articles 25(3) RS, 4(3) ICTYS and 2(3) ICTRS. Moreover, while the last two provisions grant the ICTY and the ICTR jurisdiction over those preparatory acts of genocide that have already been criminalised by article 3 of the 1948 Genocide Convention, article 25(3) RS takes a more restrictive approach because it only attributes crimi-nal liability to the public and direct incitement to commit genocide.[101] Therefore, no criminal liability arises under the RS for conspiracy to commit genocide.[102] This results in the exclusion of the notion of 'conspiracy' from the RS—and this no matter how often it is resorted to at the national level or at the *Ad hoc* Tribunals.[103]

---

[99] The exclusion of preparatory acts from the realm of art 25(3) RS is a natural consequence of the ultimate goal of the RS to focus the activities of the ICC on those behaviours which, in addition to giv-ing rise to individual criminal responsibility according to customary international law, undermine more acutely the highest values of the international community (Preamble and Arts 1 and 5 RS). See also H Von Hebel and D Robinson, 'Crimes within the Jurisdiction of the Court' in RS Lee (ed), *The International Criminal Court: The Making of the Rome Statute* (The Hague, Kluwer, 1999) 103–104.

[100] *Prosecutor v Kambanda* (Judgment) ICTR-97-23-S (4 Sep 1998), para 16; *Serushago Case* (Trial Sentence) ICTR-98-39-S (5 Feb 1999), para 15; *Prosecutor v Jelisic* (Judgment, Partial and Dissenting Opinion of Judge Wald) ICTY-95-10-T (14 Dec 1999), para 1; *Prosecutor v Stakic* (Decision on the Defence Rule 98 *bis* Motion for Judgment of Acquittal) ICTY-97-24-T (31 Oct 2002), para 22. See also WA Schabas, *An Introduction to the International Criminal Court* (2nd edn, Cambridge, Cambridge University Press, 2004) 37.

[101] Ambos, Article 25 (Above n 88), at 486–7. On the content of the notion of 'public and direct incite-ment to commit genocide' see Cassese, *International Criminal Law* (Above n 94), at 196–8; WA Schabas, *Genocide in International Law* (Cambridge, Cambridge University Press, 2001) 266–80 [hereinafter Schabas *Genocide*]. In relation to the development of this notion in the *Nahimana* case before the ICTR, see G Della Morte, 'De-Mediatizing the Media Case: Elements of a Critical Approach' (2005) 3 *Journal of International Criminal Justice* 1019–33; A Zahar, 'The ICTR's Media Judgment and the Reinvention of Direct and Public Incitement to Commit Genocide' (2005) 16 *Criminal Law Forum* 33–48.

[102] On the content of the notion of 'conspiracy to commit genocide', see Cassese, *International Criminal Law* (Above n 94), at 196–8; Schabas *Genocide* (*Ibid* n 101), at 259–66; Fichtelberg (Above n 94), at 164–5. In relation to the development of this notion in the *Musema* and *Kambanda* cases at the ICTR, see A Obote-Odora, 'Conspiracy to Commit Genocide: Prosecutor v Jean Kambanda and Prosecutor v Alfred Musema' (2001) 8 *Murdoch University Electronic Journal of Law*.

[103] Some writers have highlighted that the exclusion of conspiracy from the Rome Statute is not in line with international customary law (Cassese, *International Criminal Law* (Above n 94), at 347). Moreover, for LN Sadat, *The International Criminal Court, and the Transformation of International Law* (Ardsley, New York, Transnational Publishers, 2002) 175–80, and for Fichtelberg (Above n 94), at 166, the notion of conspiracy could still be applicable under art 21(1)(b) or (c) RS because it is part of the 'principles and rules of international law' as well as of the 'general principles of law' that the Court may derive from the main legal systems of the world. Nevertheless, the author considers that this inter-pretation disregards the role to be played in the interpretation of the forms of liability provided for in the RS by the principle *nullum crimen sine lege* pursuant to art 22 RS. The application of this principle to modes of liability (in addition to crimes) has been repeatedly affirmed by the ICTY Appeals Chamber (See *Ojdanic* JCE Appeals Decision (Above n 72), at paras 9, 21; *Prosecutor v Hadzihasanovic* (Decision on Interlocutory Appeal Challenging Jurisdiction in Relation to Command Responsibility) ICTY-01-47-AR72 (23 Jul 2003) para 32 [hereinafter *Hadzihasanovic Case* Decision on Jurisdiction]. As a result, as provided for in art 22(2) RS, the definition of modes of liability must be 'strictly

Nevertheless, despite the restrictive approach taken by the RS with respect to the criminalisation of preparatory acts, it is important to highlight that article 25(3)(f) RS embraces a broad interpretation of the doctrine of unity of action between the execution of the objective elements of the crime and the performance of those other acts which immediately prepare for it.[104] As a result, the execution stage starts by carrying out any action or omission that constitutes a 'substantial step' for the execution of any crime contained in the RS.[105]

Furthermore, while articles 4(3) and 7(1) ICTYS and 2(3) and 6(1) ICTRS do not attribute to the *Ad hoc* Tribunals jurisdiction over the attempt to commit any of the crimes provided for in the ICTYS or ICTRS (except for the attempt to commit genocide), according to article 25(3)(f) RS, the attempt to commit any of the crimes provided for in the RS—that is to say, the non-completion of the offence after reaching the execution stage due to circumstances other than the voluntary abandonment of the perpetrator—gives rise to criminal liability. Thus, once the execution stage of any crime provided for in the RS has been reached, criminal liability arises both in cases of completion of the offence and in cases of attempt where some of the objective elements of the crime are not fulfilled 'because of circumstances independent of the person's intentions'. Moreover, paragraphs (3)(b) to (3)(d) of article 25 RS, unlike articles 7(1) ICTYS and 6(1) ICTRS, explicitly establish that participation in the attempt by a third person to commit any of the crimes provided for in the Rome Statute also gives rise to criminal liability.

V Different Approaches to the Distinction between Principal and Accessorial Liability

Those systems which distinguish between perpetration (principal liability) and participation (accessorial or derivative liability) rely on different criteria to define the notion of perpetration and to differentiate it from the notion of participation. When a plurality of persons intervenes in the commission of a crime, the consideration of each of them as a principal or as an accessory to the crime depends on the criterion chosen to define the notion of perpetration. The different approaches to the notion of perpetration can be placed into three main groups: (i) the formal-objective approach; (ii) the subjective approach; and (iii) the material-objective approach.

---

construed' and cannot be extended by analogy. In addition, 'in case of ambiguity, the definition shall be interpreted in favour of the person being investigated, prosecuted or convicted'. In the author's view, this is not compatible with resorting to subsidiary sources of law in order to bring back forms of criminal responsibility, such as the notion of conspiracy, which have not been explicitly provided for in the RS.

[104] C Roxin, *Autoria y Dominio del Hecho en Derecho Penal* (6th edn, Madrid, Marcial Pons, 1998) 334 [hereinafter Roxin *Autoria*].

[105] Art 25(3)(f) RS.

According to the formal-objective approach, perpetrators or principals to the crime are only those persons who carry out one or more objective elements of the crime, whereas participants or accessories to the crime are those others who contribute in any other way to the commission of the crime.[106] Supporters of this approach claim that (i) those individuals who physically carry out an objective element of the crime show a higher degree of dangerousness and wrongdoing; and (ii) this approach fits better with the definitions of the crimes and with the common meaning that an average person would give to the language used in such definitions.[107]

Nevertheless, this approach has been exposed to substantial criticism. For instance, this approach has been considered inadequate in explaining those cases of indirect perpetration or perpetration by means, where the person who carries out the objective elements of a crime is a mere tool of somebody else (for instance, the observer of an artillery platoon makes the other members of the platoon believe that the new coordinates for the attack correspond to the enemy's headquarters when in fact the observer knows that such coordinates correspond to civilian houses). Additionally, this approach does not explain the commission of crimes by senior political and military leaders through the use of the organisations led by them.[108]

The subjective approach to the notion of perpetration finds it impossible to rely on an objective approach to the distinction between principals and accessories to the crime because the contribution of every person who is involved in a crime is causally connected with its commission.[109] As a result, the subjective approach looks at the distinction between perpetration and participation in the personal attitude vis-à-vis the crime of each person involved in its commission. According to this approach, no matter the nature and scope of the contribution to the commission of the crime, principals to the crime are only those who make their contribution with the intent to have the crime as their own deed. Those persons who contribute to the commission of the crime with the intent not to have the crime as

---

[106] E Mezger, *Tratado de Derecho Penal* Vol II (Madrid, Editorial Revista de Derecho Privado, 1957) 339–40 [hereinafter Mezger]; A Gimbernat Ordeig, *Autor y Complice en Derecho Penal* (Madrid, Universidad de Madrid, 1966) 19–22 [hereinafter Gimbernat Ordeig]; Zugaldia Espinar (Above n 13), at 733–4.

[107] The formally-objective approach to the notion of perpetration is the approach adopted by Common Law jurisdictions. See Gillies (Above n 15), at 157–8; Smith and Hogan (Above n 10), at 166–8. The formally objective approach is also supported certain authors in countries of a Roman-Germanic tradition. For instance, in Spain, see T Vives Anton, *Libertad de Prensa y Responsabilidad Penal (La regulacion de la autoria en los delitos cometidos por medio de la imprenta)* (Madrid, 1977) 151; G Rodriguez Mourullo, *Comentarios al Codigo Penal* (Civitas Ediciones, 1997) 800–802. For Germany, see Mezger (Above n 106), at 339–40. As Gimbernat Ordeig (Above n 106), at 21–2, points out, a number of other German authors, including Mittermaier, Finger, Thomsen, Wachenfeld, Liszt, Liepmann, Sauer, Meyer/Allfeld, Mayer, Engelsing, Von Hippel, Merkel, Zimmerl, Frank, Hegler, zu Dohna and Wegner, have also embraced the formally-objective approach.

[108] Munoz Conde and Garcia Aran (Above n 23), at 448.

[109] Roxin *Autoria* (Above n 104), at 71; Gimbernat Ordeig (Above n 106), at 42–4; Zugaldia Espinar (Above n 13), at 732–3.

their own deed and subordinating their will to that of the perpetrator(s) are to be considered accessories to the crime.[110]

The subjective approach to the notion of perpetration solves the problems encountered by the formal-objective approach in relation to indirect perpetration because it is the personal attitude of the relevant senior political and military leaders, as opposed to their nearness to the scene of the crime, that marks the distinction between perpetration and participation. However, it has faced strong criticism because if the distinction between principals and accessories to the crime is exclusively based on the will of the relevant senior political and military leaders, the latter would be deciding on the nature of their contribution to the crime. Moreover, a distinction between perpetration and participation solely based on a subjective criterion would make the definitions of the crimes wholly irrelevant for the purpose of such a distinction and the safeguards provided for by such definitions would be lost.[111]

The subjective approach has traditionally had two variants: (i) the 'theory of the interest'; and (ii) the 'theory of the *dolus*'. The first variant relies on the interest in the crime of the persons involved in its commission as evidence of their intent. As a result, those who intervene in the commission of the crime because its completion will satisfy their personal interest are considered perpetrators or principals to the crime. Those who simply assist in the satisfaction of the interest of third persons are considered participants or accessories to the crime because they only have an *animus socii* in the offence.[112]

The theory of the interest has been put into question because it does not rely on any material criterion in addition to the will of the persons involved in the commission of the crime. This has resulted in (i) convictions as (co)perpetrators or principals to the crime of persons with a personal interest in the crime who have not intervened during the execution of the objective elements of the crime; (ii) convictions as participants or accessories to the crime of persons who have carried out all objective elements of the crime with the aim to assist a third person.[113]

According to the theory of the *dolus*, principals to the crime are those persons who intervene in the commission of a crime and believe that they are the 'owners of the crime' because no other will is above theirs concerning its commission. Accessories to the crime are those others whose will is subordinated to the will of

---

[110] Prior to the approval of the 1995 Criminal Code, the Spanish Supreme Court embraced the subjective approach to the notion of perpetration as reflected in the so-called doctrine of the *acuerdo previo*. For instance, see the Judgments of the Spanish Supreme Court of 22 February 1985, 31 May 1985 and 13 May 1986. However, since the end of the 1980s, the Spanish Supreme Court steadily abandoned the subjective approach and embraced the notion of control of the crime. With the approval of the 1995 Spanish Criminal Code, the Spanish Supreme Court definitively abandoned the subjective approach to the notion of perpetration. Likewise, in the last 25 years, German jurisprudence has gone back and forth from a subjective approach to the notion of perpetration to an approach based on the notion of control of the crime.

[111] Munoz Conde and Garcia Aran (Above n 23), at 448.

[112] Zugaldia Espinar (Above n 13), at 732.

[113] Roxin *Autoria* (Above n 104), at 71; Gimbernat Ordeig (Above n 106), at 44–8; Bloy (Above n 37), at 78.

the principal(s), and their *animus socii* is characterised by leaving the decision of whether to commit the crime to the principal(s).[114] The theory of the *dolus*, in addition to the evidentiary problems posed by it, has also been the subject of a number of criticisms. In particular, it has been pointed out that it opens the door to cases in which there is no perpetrator or principal to the crime because those who carried out the objective elements of the crime believed that they left the decision whether to commit the crime to others.[115]

The material-objective approach to the notion of perpetration is an attempt to solve the problems presented by the other two above-mentioned approaches. According to this approach, perpetration and participation are distinguished on the basis of the level and intensity of the contribution to the execution of the objective elements of the crime. Perpetration requires that the contribution be essential for the completion of the crime in the sense that without it the crime would not have been committed. Those favouring this approach justify it on the higher dangerousness of principals to the crime in comparison with accessories due to the different level and intensity of their respective contributions to the commission of the crime.[116]

This approach has been criticised because any attempt to differentiate between indispensable or primary contributions and dispensable or secondary contributions is unfeasible unless one resorts to hypothetical and abstract value judgements. This would entail the use of vague and imprecise criteria such as 'more objective importance' or 'higher dangerousness for the protected societal value', which would leave aside the reality of the criminal plan and create great legal uncertainty.[117]

VI First Approach to the Notion of Joint Criminal Enterprise as Elaborated by the Case Law of the *Ad hoc* Tribunals and to the Notion of Control of the Crime

The notion of joint criminal enterprise as elaborated by the case law of the *Ad hoc* Tribunals, and in particular by the case law of the ICTY, is built on the idea of a group of individuals, who do not need to belong to any administrative, military, economic or political structure, freely agreeing to jointly carry out one or more crimes.[118]

---

[114] Zugaldia Espinar (Above n 13), at 732.

[115] Roxin *Autoria* (Above n 104), at 71; Gimbernat Ordeig (Above n 106), at 44–8; Bloy (Above n 37), at 149.

[116] Roxin *Autoria* (*Ibid*), at 58; Gimbernat Ordeig (*Ibid*), at 115–17; Munoz Conde and Garcia Aran (Above n 23), at 448–9; Zugaldia Espinar (Above n 13), at 734–5.

[117] Gimbernat Ordeig (*Ibid*), at 117–21.

[118] *Tadic Case* Appeals Judgment (Above n 16), at para 227; *Krnojelac Case* Appeals Judgment (Above n 16), at para 31; *Vasiljevic Case* Appeals Judgment (Above n 74), at 100; *Kvocka Case* Appeals Judgment (Above n 77), at para 81; *Stakic Case* Appeals Judgment (Above n 79), at para 64; *Brdanin Case* Appeals Judgment (Above n 79), at para 364; *Prosecutor v. Simic* (Judgment) ICTY-95-9-T (17 Oct 2003) para 158 [hereinafter *Simic Case* Trial Judgment]; *Krajisnik Case* Trial Judgment (Above n 80), at para 883. See also Ch 4, s III.A.i and s III.A.ii.

Nevertheless, unlike in cases of conspiracy, the mere agreement to carry out one or more crimes is not sufficient for criminal liability to arise under the notion of joint criminal enterprise. On the contrary, it requires the subsequent implementation of the common criminal purpose.[119]

In order to become a participant in a joint criminal enterprise it is not sufficient to agree with the common criminal purpose; it is also necessary to make a contribution to its implementation with a view to commit the crimes that are either the ultimate goal of the enterprise or the means through which the goal of the enterprise is to be achieved.[120] This intent must be shared by all participants in a joint criminal enterprise, no matter whether they are physical perpetrators or senior political and military leaders.[121]

The level of contribution of those participating in a joint criminal enterprise to the achievement of the common criminal purpose is secondary.[122] What really matters is that they make their contributions with the aim of furthering the common criminal purpose.[123] Hence, minor contributions, including further planning and preparation of the actual commission of the crimes, may suffice as

---

[119] In this regard, the *Ojdanic* JCE Appeals Decision (Above n 72), at paras 23 to 26 has explained that the notions of 'conspiracy' and 'membership in a criminal organisation' differ from the notion of joint criminal enterprise or the common purpose doctrine in that the latter is 'a form of liability concerned with the participation in the commission of a crime as part of a joint criminal enterprise'. According to the ICTY Appeals Chamber, 'mere agreement is sufficient in the case of conspiracy' no matter whether or not the crime is subsequently committed, whereas for membership in a criminal organisation it is sufficient 'a knowing and voluntary membership of organisations which did in fact commit crimes'. See also *Prosecutor v Martic* (Appeals Chamber Judgment) ICTY-95-11-A (8 Oct 2008) para 82 [hereinafter Martic Case Appeals Judgment]. A different view is held by RP Barret and LE Little, 'Lessons of Yugoslav Rape Trials: A Role for Conspiracy Law in International Criminal Tribunals' (2003) 88 *Minnesota Law Review* 30. According to these writers, the ICTY case law has developed a notion of 'collective criminal enterprise', which is 'difficult to distinguish from the crime of conspiracy'. See also Fichtelberg (Above n 94), at 165; *Prosecutor v Martic* (Appeals Chamber Judgment, Separate Opinion of Judge Schomburg on the individual criminal responsibility of Milan Martic) ICTY-95-11-A (8 Oct 2008) paras 5–7.

[120] *Tadic Case* Appeals Judgment (Above n 16), at para 227; *Krnojelac Case* Appeals Judgment (Above n 16), at para 31; *Vasiljevic Case* Appeals Judgment (Above n 74), at para 100; *Kvocka Case* Appeals Judgment (Above n 77), at para 96; *Stakic Case* Appeals Judgment (Above n 79), at para 64; *Brdanin Case* Appeals Judgment (Above n 79), at para 364; *Krajisnik Case* Trial Judgment (Above n 80), at para 883. See also Ch 4, s III.A.iii.

[121] *Tadic Case* Appeals Judgment (*Ibid*) at para 228; *Krnojelac Case* Appeals Judgment (*Ibid*) at paras 32–3; *Vasiljevic Case* Appeals Judgment (*Ibid*) at para 101; *Kvocka Case* Appeals Judgment (*Ibid*) at paras 82, 83, 89; *Stakic Case* Appeals Judgment (*Ibid*) at para 65; *Brdanin Case* Appeals Judgment (*Ibid*) at para 365; *Simic Case* Trial Judgment (Above n 118), at para 158; *Krajisnik Case* Trial Judgment (*Ibid*) at paras 879, 883. See also Ch 4, s III.B.i.

[122] *Tadic Case* Appeals Judgment (*Ibid*) at paras 227, 229; *Kvocka Case* Appeals Judgment (*Ibid*) at paras 97–8; *Vasiljevic Case* Appeals Judgment (*Ibid*) at para 100; *Brdanin Case* Appeals Judgment (*Ibid*) at para 263; *Krajisnik Case* Trial Judgment (*Ibid*) at para 883. See also Ch 4, s III.A.iii.

[123] *Tadic Case* Appeals Judgment (*Ibid*) at para 228; *Krnojelac Case* Appeals Judgment (Above n 16), at para 84; *Kvocka Case* Appeals Judgment (*Ibid*) at para 82; *Vasiljevic Case* Appeals Judgment (*Ibid*) at para 97; *Stakic Case* Appeals Judgment (Above n 79), at para 65; *Brdanin Case* Appeals Judgment (*Ibid*) at para 365; *Simic Case* Trial Judgment (Above n 118), at para 157; *Krajisnik Case* Trial Judgment (*Ibid*), at para 79. See also A Bogdan, 'Individual Criminal Responsibility in the Execution of a "Joint Criminal Enterprise" in the Jurisprudence of the *Ad hoc* International Tribunal for the Former Yugoslavia' (2006) 6 *International Criminal Law Review* 63–120, 82 [hereinafter Bogdan]. See Ch 4, s III.B.i.

long as the common criminal purpose is shared.[124] Likewise, major contributions with knowledge of the common criminal purpose, but without sharing it, will not suffice for criminal liability to arise under the notion of joint criminal enterprise.[125]

As a result, for the notion of joint criminal enterprise or the common purpose doctrine, the essence of the wrongdoing lies in the shared intent by all the participants in the enterprise to have the crimes encompassed by the common criminal purpose committed.[126] When the crimes are committed within a system of ill treatment (systematic form of joint criminal enterprise), the shared intent to commit the core crimes carried out through such a system is inherent to the awareness of its nature and the intent to further it.[127] Criminal responsibility for the commission by other members of the criminal enterprise of foreseeable crimes which are not part of the common criminal plan only arises as long as there is a shared intent by all participants in the enterprise to have the core crimes of the enterprise committed.[128]

Hence, the notion of joint criminal enterprise is grounded in a subjective criterion consisting of the sharing of the wish to have the common criminal purpose of the enterprise implemented. As a result, one would have to conclude that the case law of the *Ad hoc* Tribunals has chosen a subjective approach to the notion of perpetration and to the distinction between principal (perpetration) and accessorial or derivative liability (participation) if it is shown that:

(i) the case law of the *Ad hoc* Tribunals has configured the notion of joint criminal enterprise as a theory of co-perpetration giving rise to principal liability and falling under the heading 'committed' in articles 7(1) ICTYS and 6(1) ICTRS; and, consequently,

---

[124] Gustafson (Above n 60), at 141. The need for the interpretation of the notion of joint criminal enterprise as requiring a significant level of contribution to implementation of the common criminal purpose has been emphasised by: AM Danner and JS Martinez, 'Guilty Associations: Joint Criminal Enterprise, Command Responsibility and the Development of International Criminal Law' (2005) 93 *California Law Review* 75–169, 150–51 [hereinafter Danner and Martinez]; JD Ohlin, 'Three Conceptual Problems with the Doctrine of Joint Criminal Enterprise' (2007) 5 *Journal of International Criminal Justice* 69–90, 89.

[125] This has been made clear in particular in the context of the distinction between the notions of joint criminal enterprise and aiding and abetting. See *Tadic Case* Appeals Judgment (Above n 16), at para 229; *Vasiljevic Case* Appeals Judgment (Above n 74), at para 102; *Ojdanic* JCE Appeal Decision (Above n 72), at para 20; *Krajisnik Case* Trial Judgment (Above n 80), at para 885.

[126] *Ojdanic* JCE Appeal Decision (*Ibid*) at para 20. See also Ch 4, s III.B.i.

[127] As Van Sliedregt, Joint Criminal Enterprise (Above n 63), at 186, has pointed out: 'With regard to the *mens rea*, the First and Second Category of JCE require "an intention to participate in and further the criminal activity or purpose of the group", thus suggesting that all participants possess the same intent'. See also *Tadic Case* Appeals Judgment (Above n 16), at para 228; *Krnojelac Case* Appeals Judgment (Above n 16), at paras 93-4; *Kvocka Case* Appeals Judgment (Above n 77), at para 82; *Brdanin Case* Appeals Judgment (Above n 79), at para 365.

[128] *Tadic Case* Appeals Judgment (*Ibid*), at para 228; *Vasiljevic Case* Appeals Judgment (Above n 74), at para 101; *Blaskic Case* Appeals Judgment (Above n 75), at para 33. See also H Van der Wilt, 'Joint Criminal Enterprise: Possibilities and Limitations' (2007) 5 *Journal of International Criminal Justice* 96 [hereinafter Van der Wilt]; Van Sliedregt, Joint Criminal Enterprise (*Ibid*) at 186. See Ch 4, s III.B.iii.

(ii) in cases where the crimes are committed by a plurality of persons acting together, it distinguishes between principals and accessories to the crimes on the basis of the notion of joint criminal enterprise.

The notion of control of the crime reflects a material-objective approach to the notion of perpetration, and to the distinction between principal (perpetration) and accessorial or derivative liability (participation). As ICC Pre-Trial Chamber I has repeatedly stated, according to this notion, perpetrators or principals to the crime are those who dominate the commission of the crime in the sense that they decide whether the crime will be carried out and how it will be performed.[129]

The majority of the writers who support the theory of control of the crime affirm that it combines: (i) an objective element consisting of the factual circumstances that lead to control of the crime and (ii) a subjective element consisting of the awareness of the factual circumstances, which lead to such control. In this regard, ICC Pre-Trial Chamber I has recently stated in the *Katanga and Ngudjolo* case that the theory of control of the crime is one that synthesises both objective and subjective components since:

> [. . .] the doctrine of control over the crime corresponds to an evolution of subjective and objective approaches, such that it effectively represents a synthesis of previously opposed views and doubtless owes its broad acceptance to this reconciliation of contrary positions[130]

Although the theory of control of the crime was first put forward by Welzel,[131] it was elaborated and redefined by Roxin. According to him, such a notion is an open concept that,[132] when analysing the different forms of perpetration, develops in three different ways: (i) in the direct or immediate perpetration as 'control of the action'; (ii) in the indirect perpetration as 'control of the will'; and (iii) in co-perpetration as 'functional control'.[133]

---

[129] As *Lubanga Case* Confirmation of Charges (Above n 89), at para 330, has put it: 'The concept of control over the crime constitutes a third approach for distinguishing between principals and accessories which, contrary to the Defence claim, is applied in numerous legal systems. The notion underpinning this third approach is that principals to a crime are not limited to those who physically carry out the objective elements of the offence, but also include those who, in spite of being removed from the scene of the crime, control or mastermind its commission because they decide whether and how the offence will be committed'. A similar language is used by *Katanga and Ngudjolo Case* Confirmation of Charges (Above n 89), at para 485. For a more detailed analysis and critique of such a theory, see A Perez Cepeda, *La Responsabilidad de los Administradores de Sociedades: Criterios de Atribucion* (Barcelona, Cedecs Editorial, 1997) 369 [hereinafter Perez Cepeda]

[130] *Katanga and Ngudjolo Case* Confirmation of Charges (Above n 89), at para 484. Against considering the subjective element, Gimbernat Ordeig (Above n 106), at 124; Diaz y Garcia Conlledo (Above n 37), at 573.

[131] See H Welzel, 'Studien zum System des Strafrechts' 58 (1939) *ZSTW* 491–566.

[132] Roxin was of the opinion that it was not possible to have a fixed concept of perpetration which encompasses all interventions in the crime which deserve to be qualified as perpetration (principal liability) as opposed to mere participation in the crime (accessorial liability). As a consequence, he gave to the notion of control of the crime a material content, which is sufficiently general and abstract as to encompass all such interventions in the crime, and, at the same time, gives clear criteria to decide in specific cases whether there is a case of perpetration or mere participation in the crime. See Roxin (Above n 47), at 122.

[133] See also *Lubanga Case* Confirmation of Charges (Above n 89), at para 332; *Katanga and Ngudjolo Case* Confirmation of Charges (Above n 89) at para 488.

The direct perpetrator is the person who physically carries out the objective elements of the crime with the subjective elements required by the crime in question. He has the control of the crime because he controls the action as he physically carries out its objective elements. Thus, the physical execution of the objective elements of the crime is the criterion of objective attribution, which entails the qualification of a given contribution to the crime as perpetration.[134]

In the case of indirect perpetration, someone, who does not physically carry out the objective elements of the crime, indirectly commits the crime by using the physical perpetrator as an 'instrument' or a 'tool' who is controlled by his dominant will. As a result, he has power to decide whether the crime will be carried out and how it will be performed. In these cases, the notion of control of the crime is referred to as 'control of the will' because, unlike in those cases of 'control of the action', the indirect perpetrator commits the crime although he does not physically carry out its objective elements. Thus, the indirect perpetrator's control of the crime is not derived from the physical execution of the objective elements of the crime, but it is derived from the power of his dominant will.[135]

In accordance with the notion of joint or functional control, the contribution of several persons to the commission of a crime amounts to the co-performance on the basis of the principle of divisions of tasks. As a result, the sum of the individual contributions considered as a whole amounts to the completion of the objective elements of the crime. The control of each co-perpetrator over the crime is based on the division of functions without which it would be impossible to complete the objective elements of the crime. The co-perpetrators can only implement the common plan insofar as they act jointly, and each co-perpetrator may ruin the implementation of the common plan by withholding his contribution to the crime.[136] This key position of each co-perpetrator is the basis of their shared control of the crime.[137]

---

[134] Roxin (Above n 47), at 127. See also *Lubanga Case* Confirmation of Charges (*Ibid*) at para 332 (i); *Katanga and Ngudjolo Case* Confirmation of Charges (Above n 89) at para 488 (a).

[135] Roxin (*Ibid*) at 141 et *seq.* See also *Lubanga Case* Confirmation of Charges (*Ibid*) at para 332 (ii); *Katanga and Ngudjolo Case* Confirmation of Charges (Above n 89) at para 488 (c).

[136] Roxin (*Ibid*). See also *Lubanga Case* Confirmation of Charges (*Ibid*) at para 332 (iii); *Katanga and Ngudjolo Case* Confirmation of Charges (Above n 89) at para 488 (b). A number of German authors mainly base co-perpetration on joint or functional control. See Jescheck and Weigend (Above n 24), at 674; H Otto, *Strafrecht Allgemeiner Teil* (6th edn, 2000) No 57 (gemeinsames Innehaben der *Tatherrschaft*). See also Jakobs (Above n 41), at para 21/35, fn 86, who uses a different terminology, but following the distinction between control of the act, control of the will and joint or functional control. The majority of Spanish authors base co-perpetration on joint or functional control. See S Mir Puig, *Derecho Penal: Parte General* (6th edn, Barcelona, Edisofer Libros Juridicos, 2002) 385 [hereinafter Mir Puig]; Munoz Conde and Garcia Aran (Above n 23), at 452–4; Perez Cepeda (Above n 129), at 417.

[137] Mir Puig (*Ibid*), at 385; Munoz Conde and Garcia Aran (*Ibid*) at 452–453; K Kuhl, *Strafrecht Allgemeiner Teil* (4th edn, Munich, Vahlen Franz GMBH, 2002) No 99; H Trondle and T Fischer, *Strafgesetzbuch Kommentar* (51st edn, Munich, 2003) § 25 No 6 [hereinafter Trondle and Fischer]; J Wessels and W Beulke, *Strafrecht Allgemeiner Teil* (31st edn, Heidelberg, Muller, 2001) No 526.

VII Are the Notions of Joint Criminal Enterprise and Control of the Crime Part of Customary International Law?

The issue of whether the notion of joint criminal enterprise or the common purpose doctrine is part of customary international law is closely related to the possible customary status of the notion of control of the crime because this last notion may constitute a competing approach to the distinction between principals and accessories to the crime. This issue has been dealt with at length by the ICTY case law and, to a lesser extent, by the ICTR case law. Nevertheless, it is important to highlight that the treatment of this question by the case law of the *Ad hoc* Tribunals has been made in the context of its interpretation of the principle *nullum crimen sine lege*. For this reason, one should pay attention to the changes experienced in the interpretation of this principle in the ICTY case law.

A The Backdrop against which the Analysis of the Customary Status of the Notion of Joint Criminal Enterprise has taken Place in the Case Law of the *Ad hoc* Tribunals: The Interpretation of the Principle *Nullum Crimen Sine Lege*

Unlike the ICC, the ICTY and the ICTR were established after the commission of most of the crimes over which they have been granted jurisdiction.[138] As a result, their respective statutes do not contain provisions of a penal nature, which criminalise conduct, but only provisions of a procedural nature granting the *Ad hoc* Tribunals material jurisdiction over crimes already existing under international criminal law.[139] Against this backdrop, compliance with the demands of the legality principle becomes a particularly important issue.[140] However, despite

---

[138] See UNSC Res 827 (25 May 1993) UN Doc S/RES/827, whereby the ICTY is established and its Statute is approved, and UNSC Res 855 (8 Nov 1994) UN Doc S/RES/855 whereby the ICTR is established and its Statute is approved.

[139] H Olasolo, 'A Note on the Evolution of the Principle of Legality in International Criminal Law' (2007) 2 *Criminal Law Forum, 301.*

[140] According to this principle, the exercise of the *ius puniendi* of the State—or of the international community—is subject to the principle of legal certainty as an essential component of the fundamental rights of any person. As a result, the State or the International Community must exercise their *ius puniendi* on the basis of previous criminal norms (*lex praevia*) defining the prohibited acts and the attached penalties (*lex certa*), which cannot be interpreted by analogy *in malam partem* (*lex stricta*). Hence, neither States nor the International Community can exercise their *ius puniendi* beyond what they are allowed to by criminal norms. See *Lubanga Case* Confirmation of Charges (Above n 89), at para 303. See also K Ambos, 'Nulla Poena Sine Lege in International Criminal Law' in R Haveman and O Olusanya (eds), *Sentencing and Sanctioning in Supranational Criminal Law* (Antwerp, Intersentia, 2006) 20–3; Quintero Olivares (Above n 23), at 68; Munoz Conde and Garcia Aran (Above n 23), at 98–9.

its importance, the statutes of the *Ad hoc* Tribunals do not contain any express reference to the legality principle.[141] Moreover, the interpretation of this principle by the Appeals Chambers of the *Ad hoc* Tribunals (particularly the ICTY Appeals Chamber), which have so far only acknowledged two of the dimensions of the legality principle (those conveyed in the maxim *nullum crimen sine lege* and the principle of non-retroactivity), are still far from being settled due to changes in recent years.

The most important problem faced by the *Ad hoc* Tribunals regarding the legality principle pertains to the determination of the sources of international criminal law that are relevant to decide whether the requirements of the principle *nullum crimen sine lege* are complied with. In the final analysis, this issue is limited to determining if, in addition to international customary law, conventional international law must also be taken into account when carrying out such analysis.

The report of the UN Secretary General on the establishment of the ICTY serves as the basis for answering this question. In this report, the Secretary General pointed out that the statute of ICTY does not purport to create new crimes and that the ICTY must apply existing international humanitarian law,[142] including both customary and conventional law.[143] However, in the same report, the Secretary General also said that in order to avoid any problem derived from the adherence of some—but not all—States to specific conventions, the principle *nullum crimen sine lege* would require the ICTY to apply those rules of international humanitarian law which are, beyond any doubt, part of customary law.[144]

In its decision on jurisdiction in the *Tadic* case, the ICTY Appeals Chamber defined the content of the principle *nullum crimen sine lege* for the first time. In this decision, the issue was to determine whether the ICTY has jurisdiction over violations of international humanitarian law other than grave breaches of the Geneva Conventions on the basis of article 3 ICTYS, which refers generally to violations of the laws and customs of war.[145]

The ICTY Appeals Chamber answered this question in the affirmative, stating that both international custom and conventional law are sources of international criminal law relevant to any analysis of the compliance with the principle *nullum crimen sine lege*. When justifying the relevance of conventional law, the Appeals Chamber pointed out that the only reason why the drafters of the ICTYS emphasised the application of customary law was to avoid any violation of the principle *nullum crimen sine lege* in those cases where any of the parties to the conflict was not a party to the relevant international treaty.[146]

---

[141] S Lamb, 'Nullum Crimen sine Lege' in A Cassese, P Gaeta, and JRWD Jones (eds.), *The Rome Statute of the International Criminal Court: A Commentary* (Oxford, Oxford University Press, 2002) 742 [hereinafter Lamb].

[142] Report of the Secretary-General (Above n 62), at para 29.

[143] *Ibid* at para 33.

[144] *Ibid* at para 34.

[145] The grave breaches of the Geneva Conventions are provided for in art 2 ICTYS.

[146] *Tadic Case* Appeals Judgment (Above n 16), at para 143.

As a consequence, the ICTY Appeals Chamber concluded that conventional law is also applicable when the two following conditions are met: (i) the adherence of all parties to the conflict to the relevant international treaty at the moment when the alleged criminal conduct takes place; and (ii) the consistency between the content of the conventional norms at hand and international norms of *jus cogens,* which include most of the laws and customs of war.[147]

In the same decision, the Appeals Chamber established four requirements that must be met for the ICTY to have jurisdiction over violations of international humanitarian law other than grave breaches of the Geneva Conventions. First, the violation must constitute an infringement of a rule of international humanitarian law. Second, the rule must be customary in nature or, if it belongs to treaty law, the two conditions indicated above must be met. Third, the violation must be 'serious', in that, it must constitute a breach of a rule protecting important values, and the breach must involve grave consequences for the victim. Finally, the violation of the rule must entail, under customary or conventional law, the individual criminal responsibility of the person breaching the rule.[148]

The case law of the ICTY Appeals Chamber on this subject has, nevertheless, experienced important changes in recent years. For example, the ICTY Appeals Chamber has lately adopted a more restrictive interpretation of the principle *nullum crimen sine lege* that excludes the application of conventional law. This change in the case law first appeared in the ICTY Appeals Chamber Interlocutory Decision in the *Strugar* case in relation to attacks directed against civilian objects and civilian persons,[149] and was stated more clearly in the *Ojdanic* JCE Appeals Decision.[150] Accordingly, in this decision, the Appeals Chamber established four preconditions that any form of liability must fulfil in order to be part of the applicable law before the ICTY: (i) it must be provided for in the Statute; (ii) it must have existed under customary international law at the time when the allegedly criminal conduct took place; (iii) the law providing for that form of liability must have been sufficiently accessible at the relevant time to anyone who acted in such a way; and (iv) any such person must have been able to foresee that he or she could be held criminally liable for his conduct if apprehended.[151]

Subsequently, this new approach has been ratified in the ICTY Appeal Decision on Jurisdiction concerning Command Responsibility in the *Hadzihasanovic* case,[152] and in the ICTY Appeal Judgment in the *Stakic* case, in which the mode of liability of 'co-perpetratorship' was considered not to be part of customary international law at the time the crimes charged in the indictment took place in 1992.[153]

---

[147] *Ibid.* See also Lamb (Above n 141), at 742.

[148] *Tadic Case* Appeals Judgment (Above n 16), at para 94.

[149] *Prosecutor v Strugar* (Decision on Interlocutory Appeal) ICTY-01-42-AR72 (22 Nov 2002) paras 9, 10, 13.

[150] *Ojdanic* JCE Appeals Decision (Above n 72), at para 9.

[151] *Ibid* at para 21.

[152] *Hadzihasanovic Case* Decision on Jurisdiction (Above n 103), at para 32.

[153] *Stakic Case* Appeals Judgment (Above n 79), at para 62.

This new interpretation of the principle *nullum crimen sine lege* is based on the report by the UN Secretary General, which, according to the ICTY Appeals Chamber, clearly states that the ICTY can only apply those rules of international humanitarian law which are, beyond any doubt, a part of customary law. Accordingly, for the ICTY Appeals Chamber, the scope of the material jurisdiction of the Tribunal is determined by its Statute and by customary law. As a consequence, the ICTY can only deal with conduct, which at the moment of its commission was criminal pursuant to customary international law.[154]

The 15 July 1999 ICTY Appeal Judgment in the *Tadic* case was confronted with the issue of:

[W]hether the acts of one person can give rise to the criminal culpability of another where both participate in the execution of a common criminal plan.[155]

In order to answer this question, the Appeals Chamber had to ascertain 'whether criminal responsibility for participating in a common criminal purpose falls within the ambit of Article 7(1) of the Statute'.[156] It was in this context that the Appeals Chamber first dealt with the issue of whether the notion of joint criminal enterprise or the common purpose doctrine was part of international customary international law.[157] In so doing, it interchangeably used the expressions 'common purpose', 'joint criminal enterprise' and 'criminal enterprise'.[158]

---

[154] *Prosecutor v. Galic* (Appeals Chamber Judgment) ICTY-98-29-A (30 Nov 2006) para 85, seems prima facie to depart from this new interpretation of the principle *nullum crimen sine lege* insofar as it affirms that 'binding conventional law that prohibits conduct and provides for individual criminal responsibility could provide the basis for the International Tribunals jurisdiction'. However, such a departure is more formalistic than material because at the same paragraph the ICTY Appeals Chamber emphasises that 'in practice the International Tribunal always ascertains that the treaty provision in question is also declaratory of custom'.

[155] *Tadic Case* Appeals Judgment (Above n 16), at para 185(i).

[156] *Ibid* at para 187.

[157] The *Tadic Case* Appeals Judgment (*Ibid*) reversed the Trial Chamber acquittal of Dusko Tadic for the killing of five non-Serb men from the village of Jaskici on 14 June 1992. It convicted him as a co-perpetrator for such killings pursuant to an extended form of joint criminal enterprise and increased his sentence from 7 to 20 years. According to the ICTY Appeals Chamber, from May 1992 onwards, the common criminal purpose to rid the Prijedor region of the non-Serb population by committing inhumane acts against them started being implemented. The common criminal purpose did not include the killing of non-Serb men. Nevertheless killings frequently occurred in the effort to rid the Prijedor region of the non-Serb population. The attack to Jaskici on 14 June 1992 took place in furtherance of this common criminal purpose. During this attack, 5 non-Serb men were killed (4 of them were shot in their heads). The fact that non-Serbs could be killed was a foreseeable consequence of the implementation of the common criminal purpose through the attack on Jaskici. Dusko Tadic was a member of the armed group, which attacked the village of Jaskici. During the attack he rounded up and severely beat some of the non-Serb men from Jaskici, although he did not kill any of them. He participated in the attack with the intent to further the common criminal purpose to rid the Prijedor region of the non-Serb population by committing inhumane acts against them. He was also aware that the actions of his armed group were likely to lead to such killings and willingly took that risk by participating in the attack. See *Tadic Case* Appeals Judgment (Above n 16), at paras 230–32; *Prosecutor v Tadic* (Judgment in Sentencing Appeals) ICTY-94-1-A (26 Jan 2000) para 76.

[158] See the explanation contained in *Ntakirutimana Case* Appeals Judgment (Above n 85), at fn 73 in relation to the interchangeable manner in which the *Tadic Case* Appeals Judgment (*Ibid*) used the expressions 'common purpose', 'joint criminal enterprise' and 'criminal enterprise'.

B The Analysis by the *Ad hoc* Tribunals of the Customary Status of the Notion of Joint Criminal Enterprise

The analysis conducted by the 15 July 1999 ICTY Appeals Judgment in the *Tadic* case did not stop at finding that under customary international law, and thus under article 7(1) ICTYS, criminal liability arises for those acting pursuant to a joint criminal enterprise or a common criminal purpose.[159] On the contrary, the ICTY Appeals Chamber went further and also found that, according to international customary law (and thus under article 7(1) ICTYS), there are three different forms of joint criminal enterprise, each of them with their own objective and subjective elements.[160] For the ICTY Appeals Chamber, these findings were warranted by:

> [C]onsistency and cogency of the case law and the treaties referred to above, as well as their consonance with the general principles on criminal responsibility laid down both in the Statute and general international criminal law and in national legislation.[161]

The ICTY Appeals Chamber relied on the above reasoning to support its finding that the notion of joint criminal enterprise or the common purpose doctrine gives rise to principal (as opposed to accessorial or derivative) liability.[162] In coming to the conclusion that the first feature which distinguishes the notions of joint criminal enterprise and aiding and abetting is that the '[t]he aidor and abettor is always an accessory to a crime perpetrated by another person, the principal',[163] the ICTY Appeals Chamber explained:

> The above interpretation is not only dictated by the object and purpose of the Statute but is also warranted by the very nature of many international crimes, which are committed most commonly in wartime situations. Most of the time these crimes do not result from the criminal propensity of single individuals but constitute manifestations of collective criminality: the crimes are often carried out by groups of individuals acting in pursuance of a common criminal design. Although only some members of the group may physically perpetrate the criminal act (murder, extermination, wanton destruction of cities, towns or villages, etc.), the participation and contribution of the other members of the group is often vital in facilitating the commission of the offence in question. It follows that the moral gravity of such participation is often no less—or indeed no different—from that of those actually carrying out the acts in question.[164]
>
> Under these circumstances, to hold criminally liable as a perpetrator only the person who materially performs the criminal act would disregard the role as co-perpetrators of all those who in some way made it possible for the perpetrator physically to carry out that criminal act. At the same time, depending upon the circumstances, to hold the latter liable only as aidors and abettors might understate the degree of their criminal responsibility.[165]

---

[159] *Tadic Case* Appeals Judgment (Above n 16), at paras 190, 220, 226.
[160] *Ibid* at paras 220, 226–8.
[161] *Ibid* at para 226.
[162] *Ibid* at paras 192, 229, read along with paras 190, 220, 226.
[163] *Ibid* at para 229.
[164] *Ibid* at para 191.
[165] *Ibid* at para 192.

Nevertheless, as Van Sliedregt has pointed out,[166] the ICTY Appeals Chamber introduced an element of uncertainty in relation to its interpretation that the notion of joint criminal enterprise is, under customary international law, a theory of co-perpetration which gives rise to principal liability (and thus falls under the heading 'committed' in article 7(1) ICTYS). It introduced this uncertainty by explicitly stating that the ICTY Statute:

[It] does not exclude those modes of participating in the commission of crimes which occur where several persons having a common purpose embark on criminal activity that is then carried out either jointly or by some members of this plurality of persons,[167]

and that:

[T]he notion of common design as a form of accomplice liability is firmly established in customary international law and in addition is upheld, albeit implicitly, in the Statute of the International Tribunal.[168]

As a result of this uncertainty, ICTY Trial Chamber I, in its 26 February 2001 Judgment in the *Kordic* case, after stating that 'the various forms of participation listed in Article 7(1) may be divided between principal perpetrators and accomplices',[169] dealt with the notion of joint criminal enterprise or common purpose doctrine in a common subsection with the notion of aiding and abetting, which came after the subsections on 'committing' and on 'planning, instigating and ordering'.[170] A month afterwards, ICTY Trial Chamber II, in its 28 March 2001 Decision on Provisional Release in the *Brdanin* case, stated that the Tadic Appeal Judgment referred to the notion of joint criminal enterprise as a 'form of accomplice liability', which is not covered by the expression 'committed' in article 7(1) ICTYS because the meaning of this expression is limited to the physical perpetration of the crime.[171] According to ICTY Trial Chamber II:

Common purpose as a 'form of accomplice liability' is more naturally comprehended within the words 'otherwise aided and abetted in the planning, preparation or execution' in Article 7.1.[172]

[166] Van Sliedregt, Joint Criminal Enterprise (Above n 63), at 189–90.

[167] *Tadic Case* Appeals Judgment (Above n 16), at para 190.

[168] *Ibid* at para 220. These statements generated uncertainty as to whether the ICTY Appeals Chamber really saw the notion of joint criminal enterprise or the common purpose doctrine as a theory of co-perpetration giving rise to principal liability and falling under the heading 'committed' in art 7 (1) ICTYS. This is reflected in the following passage of the *Kvocka Case* Trial Judgment (Above n 71), at para 273: 'It must be conceded that the *Tadic* formula for joint criminal enterprise responsibility appears to contain an inherent contradiction. On the one hand, it expressly allows for contribution to the commission of the crime through aiding or abetting which, as we have discussed, require only knowledge, not shared intent. At other times, *Tadic* defines participation in terms of shared intent and it is not clear that this is limited to co-perpetrators'.

[169] *Kordic Case* (Above n 70), at para 373.

[170] In its brief subsection on 'committing', the *Kordic Case* (*Ibid*), at para 376, simply states that 'any finding of direct commission requires the direct personal or physical participation of the accused in the actual acts which constitute a crime under the International Tribunal's Statute with the requisite knowledge'.

[171] *Prosecutor v Brdanin* (Decision on Motion by Momir Talic for Provisional Release) ICTY-99-36-T (28 Mar2001) paras 40–45.

[172] *Ibid* at para 43.

Subsequently, ICTY Trial Chamber I, in its 2 August 2001 Trial Judgment in the *Krstic* case, emphasised that:

> It seems clear that 'accomplice liability' denotes a secondary form of participation which stands in contrast to the responsibility of the direct or principal perpetrators,[173]

ICTY Trial Chamber 1 went on to embrace the view that the notion of joint criminal enterprise constituted an autonomous mode of liability under article 7(1) ICTYS.[174] Furthermore, it found that those individuals participating in a joint criminal enterprise (or acting in execution of a common criminal purpose), who did not physically carry out the objective elements of the crime, could be either principals to the crime (co-perpetrators) or accessories to the crime (aidors or abettors) depending on the level of their contribution to the implementation of the common criminal purpose.[175]

Nevertheless, the best example of the consequences of the uncertainty generated by the *Tadic* Appeal Judgment in relation to the nature of the notion of joint criminal enterprise is to be found in the important divergences on this point between the ICTY Trial Judgments in the *Kvocka* and the *Krnojelac* cases—both issued within three months and both dealing with crimes committed in Bosnian/Serb detention camps. On 2 November 2001, ICTY Trial Chamber I, in its Trial Judgment in the *Kvocka* case, adopted the position that the notion of joint criminal enterprise was a theory of accomplice liability, understood as partnership in crime, which constituted an autonomous mode of liability under article 7(1) ICTYS.[176] Furthermore, it considered that those individuals participating in a

---

[173] *Krstic Case* Trial Judgment (Above n 71), at para 643.

[174] *Ibid* at para 601.

[175] *Ibid* at paras 642, 643. As the Trial Chamber put it: 'In the *Tadic* Appeal Judgment, the Appeals Chamber referred to "the notion of common design *as a form of accomplice liability*", a phrase upon which Trial Chamber II subsequently relied to distinguish "committing " from "common purpose liability" under Article 7(1). However, this Trial Chamber views the comment in the *Tadic* Appeal Judgment as not part of the *ratio decidendi* of that Judgment and does not believe that *Tadic* characterisation means that any involvement in a joint criminal enterprise automatically relegates the liability of an accused to that of "complicity in genocide" in Article 4(3)(e). In the *Celebici* Appeal Judgment, the Appeals Chamber reaffirmed the meaning of the plain language of Article 7 (1) that "liability under Article 7(1) applies to direct perpetrators of crimes and to accomplices", and the *Kordic and Cerkez* Trial Chamber stated that '[t]he various forms of participation listed in Article 7(1) may be divided between principal perpetrators and accomplices'. In short, the Trial Chamber sees no basis for refusing to accord the status of a co-perpetrator to a member of a joint genocidal enterprise whose participation is of an extremely significant nature and at the leadership level. It seems clear that "accomplice liability" denotes a secondary form of participation, which stands in contrast to the responsibility of the direct or principal perpetrators. The Trial Chamber is of the view that this distinction coincides with that between "genocide" and "complicity in genocide" in Article 4(3). The question comes down to whether, on the face of the case, a participant in the criminal enterprise may be most accurately characterised as a direct or principal perpetrator or as a secondary figure in the traditional role of an accomplice'.

[176] The *Kvocka Case* Trial Judgment (Above n 71), at para 249, treated the notion of joint criminal enterprise or common purpose doctrine as an autonomous mode of liability which differed from the categories of 'committing' and 'aiding and abetting' under art 7(1) ICTYS. For the *Kvocka Case* Trial Judgment at para 250, 'committing' under art 7(1) ICTYS 'covers first and foremost the physical perpetration of a crime by the offender himself, or the culpable omission of an act that was mandated by a rule of criminal law'. As a result, according to the *Kvocka Case* Trial Judgment, at para 251, cases of 'committing' were only those of physical or otherwise direct participation in the objective elements of

joint criminal enterprise (or acting in execution of a common criminal purpose), who did not physically carry out the objective elements of the crime, could be (i) either principals to the crime (co-perpetrators) if they made their contribution sharing the common criminal purpose; or (ii) accessories to the crime (aidors and abettors) if they made their contribution knowing (but not sharing) the common criminal purpose.[177] Moreover, according to ICTY Trial Chamber I, in those cases in which their contribution lasted for an extensive period or became more directly involved in maintaining the functioning of the enterprise, an intent to further the efforts of the joint criminal enterprise so as to rise to the level of co-perpetration could also be inferred from their knowledge of the commission of crimes in the camp and their continuous participation which enables the camp's functioning.[178]

On 15 February 2002, ICTY Trial Chamber II issued its Judgment in the *Krnojelac* case, stating that the distinction between principal and accessorial liability was alien to the ICTYS and thus unnecessary.[179] This Judgment also embraced the position that the notion of joint criminal enterprise was a theory of accomplice liability in which the alleged distinction between principal and accessorial liability played no role.[180] As a result, those individuals participating in a joint criminal enterprise (or acting in execution of a common criminal purpose), who did not physically carry out the objective elements of the crime, were neither principals nor accessories to the crime, but they were criminally liable for the crime.[181]

These differences in the interpretation of the notion of joint criminal enterprise were not clarified until the 21 May 2003 ICTY *Ojdanic* JCE Appeals Decision. This ICTY Appeals Chamber Decision provided a new clear ruling on the notion of joint criminal enterprise under customary international law. In this decision, the ICTY Appeals Chamber reaffirmed that, according to customary international law: (i) criminal liability arises for those acting pursuant to a joint criminal enterprise or a common criminal purpose[182]; (ii) there are three different forms of joint criminal enterprise, each with their own objective and subjective elements[183]; and (iii) the notion of joint criminal enterprise or the common purpose doctrine constitutes a theory of co-perpetration which gives rise to principal (as opposed to accessorial or derivative) liability (and thus it falls under the heading 'committed' in article 7(1) ICTYS).[184]

---

the crime through positive acts or omissions whether individually or jointly with others. On the other hand, for the *Kvocka Case* Trial Judgment at para 253, 'aiding and abetting were forms of accessory or accomplice liability', which required providing practical assistance, encouragement, or moral support that has a substantial effect on the perpetration of the crime with the knowledge that these acts assist or facilitate the commission of the offence.

[177] *Kvocka Case* Trial Judgment (Above n 71), at paras 249, 273.
[178] *Ibid* at paras 278 and 284.
[179] *Krnojelac Case* Trial Judgment (Above n 82), at paras 75–7.
[180] *Ibid* at para 77.
[181] *Ibid* at paras 73–77.
[182] *Ojdanic* JCE Appeals Decision (Above n 72), at paras 21, 29.
[183] *Ibid* at paras 21, 29.
[184] *Ibid* at paras 20, 31.

In reaching these three findings, the ICTY Appeals Chamber rejected the Defence's claim that the statement of the customary status of the notion of joint criminal enterprise in the *Tadic* Appeal Judgment was obiter dictum.[185] On the contrary, it considered that such a finding was ratio decidendi binding upon the Trial Chamber because:

> [I]t is every Chamber's duty to ascertain that a crime or a form of liability charged in the indictment is both provided for under the Statute and that it existed at the relevant time under customary law.[186]

Subsequently, the ICTY Appeals Chamber rejected the Defence's claim that the customary status of the notion of joint criminal enterprise was inconsistent with existing customary law because state practice was too weak to give rise to such a rule. As it explained:

> The Appeals Chamber does not propose to revisit its findings in *Tadic* concerning the customary status of this form of liability. It is satisfied that the state practice and *opinio iuris* reviewed in that decision was sufficient to permit the conclusion that such a norm existed under customary international law in 1992 when Tadic committed the crimes for which he had been charged and for which he was eventually convicted.[187]

Finally, in concluding that the notion of joint criminal enterprise or the common purpose doctrine is a theory of co-perpetration which gives rise to principal liability, the Appeals Chamber did not refer to any source other than those provided in the *Tadic* Appeal Judgment. The Appeals Chamber justified its finding as follows:

> Leaving aside the appropriateness of the use of the expression 'co-perpetration' in such a context, it would seem therefore that the Prosecution charges co-perpetration in a joint criminal enterprise as a form of 'commission' pursuant to Article 7 (1) of the Statute, rather than as a form of accomplice liability. The Prosecution's approach is correct to the extent that, insofar as a participant shares the purpose of the joint criminal enterprise (as he or she must do) as opposed to merely knowing about it, he or she cannot be regarded as a mere aidor or abettor to the crime which is contemplated. The Appeals Chamber therefore regards joint criminal enterprise as a form of 'commission' pursuant to Article 7 (1) of the Statute.[188]

The subsequent case law of the ICTY Appeals Chamber on the notion of joint criminal enterprise has systematically relied on the *Tadic* Appeal Judgment and on the *Ojdanic* JCE Appeals Decision—without providing any additional sources—to restate that under customary international law: (i) criminal liability arises for those acting pursuant to a joint criminal enterprise or a common criminal purpose; and (ii) the notion of joint criminal enterprise constitutes a theory of co-perpetration which gives rise to principal (as opposed to accessorial or deriva-

---

[185] *Ibid* at para 17.
[186] *Ibid.*
[187] *Ibid* at para 29.
[188] *Ibid* at para 20.

tive) liability (and it thus falls under the heading 'committed' in article 7(1) ICTYS).[189] Indeed, the ICTY Appeals Judgments in the *Vasiljevic, Kvocka, Krnojelac, Krstic, Stakic,* and *Brdanin* cases only analyse specific aspects of the objective and/or subjective elements of some of the three forms of joint criminal enterprise in depth.

As a result, it can be stated that the ICTY Appeals Chamber has never reanalysed the sources relied upon in the ICTY Appeal Judgment in the *Tadic* case in order to support the findings that the notion of joint criminal enterprise or the common purpose doctrine (i) is part of customary international law; and (ii) gives rise to principal liability according to customary international law. Moreover, in the view of the author, and contrary to what has been recently pointed out by Van Sliedriegt,[190] the case law of the ICTY Appeals Chamber, after *Tadic*, rejects the consideration of the notion of joint criminal enterprise as a theory of either accessorial or accomplice liability, despite the fact that a few decisions at the trial level have declined to apply such notion to their respective cases[191] For instance, one can refer to (i) the *Krnojelac* Trial Judgment which found that the second variant of joint criminal enterprise as described by the *Tadic* Appeal Judgment did not comply with the principle of individual criminal responsibility,[192] and (ii) the *Stakic* Trial Judgment which warned against an extensive interpretation of the notion of joint criminal enterprise because it could lead to a 'flagrant infringement of the principle *nullum crime sine lege*'.[193] Nevertheless, in the view of the author, these are exceptional instances of disagreement with the position consistently adopted by the case law of the ICTY Appeals Chamber since the *Ojdanic* JCE Appeals Decision, which has put an end to any uncertainty that joint criminal enterprise is a theory of co-perpetration that gives rise to principal liability.

Against this new backdrop, one seriously doubts that Judge Per-Joham Lindholm, who in October 2003 dissociated himself from the notion of joint criminal enterprise[194]—which for many probably constitutes the 'harshest critique of the concept'—[195] would still, today, maintain the same approach to this notion. One would especially doubt that Judge Per-Joham Lindholm would express the same opinion today that he expressed in 2003 after carefully analysing the reasons

---

[189] *Vasiljevic Case* Appeals Judgment (Above n 74), at para 95; *Kvocka Case* Appeals Judgment (Above n 77), at para 79; *Krnojelac Case* Appeals Judgment (Above n 16), at paras 29–30; *Krstic Case* Appeals Judgment (Above n 76), at para 134. Please note that in these cases, the ICTY Appeals Chamber refers to a participant in a joint criminal enterprise as a 'principal perpetrator'.

[190] Compare Van Sliedregt, Joint Criminal Enterprise (Above n 63), at 202.

[191] V Haan, 'The Development of the Concept of Joint Criminal Enterprise at the International Criminal Tribunal for the Former Yugoslavia'(2005) 5 *International Criminal Law Review* 175 [hereinafter Haan].

[192] *Krnojelac Case* Trial Judgment (Above n 82), at para 78.

[193] *Prosecutor v Stakic* (Judgment) ICTY-97-24-T (31 Jul 2003) para 433 [hereinafter *Stakic Case* Trial Judgment].

[194] *Prosecutor v Simic* (Judgment, Separate and Partly Dissenting Opinion of Judge Per-Johan Lindholm) ICTY-95-9-T (17 Oct 2003) paras 2, 5 [hereinafter *Simic Case* Dissenting Opinion].

[195] Haan (Above n 191), at 175.

why, in his view, the notion had caused 'confusion and a waste of time'[196] and was of 'no benefit to the work of the Tribunal or the development of international criminal law'[197]:

> The so-called basic form of joint criminal enterprise does not, in my opinion, have any substance of its own. It is nothing more than a new label affixed to a since long well known concept or doctrine in most jurisdictions as well as in international criminal law, namely co-perpetration. What the basic form of a joint criminal enterprise comprises is very clearly exemplified by Judge David Hunt in his Separate Opinion in *Milutinovic, Sainovic and Ojdanic*. The reasoning in the *Kupreskic* Trial Judgment is also illustrative. The acts of—and the furtherance of the crime by—the co-perpetrators may of course differ in various ways. If something else than participation as co perpetrator is intended to be covered by the concept of joint criminal enterprise, there seems to arise a conflict between the concept and the word 'committed' in Article 7(1) of the Statute.[198]
>
> The so-called extended form of joint criminal enterprise is also in a clear manner exemplified in the Separate Opinion in *Ojdanic* by Judge Hunt. This form of joint criminal enterprise contains neither anything new. It defines the kind of *mens rea* regarded as sufficient to hold co-perpetrator A liable for a crime committed by co-perpetrator B going beyond their common plan. The *mens rea* according to the extended form of joint criminal enterprise is known in Civil Law countries as *dolus eventualis* and in several Common Law countries as (*advertent*) *recklessness*. Whether especially the latter form of *mens rea* was foreseen in the Statute and laid down in customary international law, as stated in the *Tadic* Appeal Judgement, is a question I leave aside.[199]

The ICTR case law relies almost exclusively on the ICTY Appeal Judgment in the *Tadic* case to affirm the customary nature of the notion of joint criminal enterprise or the common purpose doctrine and the fact that, under customary international law and under article 6(1) ICTRS, participation in a joint criminal enterprise or common purpose gives rise to principal (as opposed to accessorial or derivative) liability.

In this regard, the 13 December 2004 ICTR Appeal Judgment in the *Ntakirutimana* case[200] explained that the ICTY Appeal Judgment in the *Tadic* case

---

[196] *Simic Case* Dissenting Opinion (Above n 194), at para 5.

[197] *Ibid.*

[198] *Ibid* at para 2.

[199] *Ibid* at para 3.

[200] A month and a half before, the *Rwamakuba v Prosecutor* (Appeals Chamber Decision on Interlocutory Appeal Regarding Application of Joint Criminal Enterprise to the Crime of Genocide) ICTR-98-44-AR72.4 (22 Oct 2004) paras 6, 7, had described the scope of the Appellant's challenge as follows: 'The Appellant contends in this Appeal that the International Tribunal does not have subject-matter jurisdiction to try an accused for genocide on a theory of joint criminal enterprise because, he asserts, such a mode of liability for genocide was not recognized by customary international law in 1994, the year in which the events charged in the Indictment allegedly occurred. In this regard, it is important to recognize what the Appellant does not dispute. He does not contend that conviction for genocide on a theory of joint criminal enterprise would result in a genocide conviction on an improper *mens rea* standard, an argument recently rejected by the Appeals Chamber of the International Criminal Tribunal for the former Yugoslavia (ICTY). Nor does he contend that the doctrine of joint criminal enterprise is completely alien to customary international law or to the Statute of the International Tribunal; rather, he acknowledges that the ICTY Appeals Chamber's judgment in *Tadic* ("*Tadic* Appeals Judgment") recognized the doctrine of "common purpose" or joint criminal

had already held that under customary international law and under article 7(1) ICTYS: (i) criminal liability arises for those acting pursuant to a joint criminal enterprise or a common criminal purpose;[201] (ii) participation in a joint criminal enterprise or in a common criminal purpose is a form of 'commission', and hence gives rise to principal (as opposed to accessorial or derivative) liability;[202] and (iii) there are three different forms of joint criminal enterprise, each of them with their own objective and subjective elements.[203] It concluded that, given the fact that articles 6(1) ICTRS and 7(1) ICTRS are 'mirror provisions', ICTY case law should be applied to the interpretation of article 6(1) ICTRS.[204]

More recently, the 12 April 2006 ICTR Appeal Decision on Joint Criminal Enterprise in the *Karemera* case explicitly stated that the extended form of joint criminal enterprise is firmly accepted in customary international law as shown by the *Tadic* Appeal Judgment.[205] And the 7 July 2006 ICTR Appeal Judgment in the *Gacumbitsi* case highlighted that:

> The Appeals Chamber, following ICTY precedent, has recognized that an accused before this Tribunal may be found individually responsible for 'committing' a crime within the meaning of article 6 (1) of the Statute under one of the three categories of 'joint criminal enterprise' ('JCE') liability.[206]

From the analysis conducted above, it can be concluded that the ICTY Appeal Judgment in the *Tadic* case is still, today, the cornerstone of the ICTY and ICTR case law on the notion of joint criminal enterprise or the common purpose doctrine.[207] After the *Tadic* case, the ICTY and ICTR Appeals Chambers have, for the most part, discussed only issues such as the specific content of some of the elements of the three forms of joint criminal enterprise and the degree of specificity required for their pleading. However, these Appeals Chambers have never reviewed the merits of the analysis undertaken by the *Tadic* Appeal Judgment.

enterprise as established in customary international law and that it was an applicable mode of liability under Article 7(1) of the Statute of the ICTY. Furthermore, the Appellant does not dispute that Article 6(1) of the Statute of the International Tribunal—identical in all relevant respects to Article 7(1) of the Statute of the ICTY—incorporates the doctrine of joint criminal enterprise and that that article applies to all crimes within the jurisdiction of the International Tribunal. Rather, the Appellant argues that the application of the doctrine of joint criminal enterprise to genocide, as mentioned in Article 2 of the Statute, would extend the crime to situations not covered by customary international law; the extension would therefore be outside of the jurisdiction of the International Tribunal. For this reason, he argues, Article 6(1) of the Statute cannot be read as applying that doctrine to genocide'.

[201] *Ntakirutimana Case* Appeals Judgment (Above n 85), at para 462.

[202] *Ibid* at para 462.

[203] *Ibid* at para 463. See also paras 464–7.

[204] *Ibid* at para 468.

[205] *Karemera v Prosecutor* (Appeals Chamber Decision on Jurisdictional Appeals: Joint Criminal Enterprise) ICTR-98-44-AR72.5 (12 April 2006) para 13.

[206] *Gacumbitsi Case* Appeals Judgment (Above n 87), at para 158.

[207] As K Ambos, 'Joint Criminal Enterprise and Command Responsibility' (2007) 5 *Journal of International Criminal Justice* 159 and 161 has pointed out, 'the joint criminal enterprise doctrine (hereinafter: JCE) can be traced back to the Tadic Appeal Judgment', and 'the subsequent case law basically followed the Tadic ruling'. See also Danner and Martinez (Above n 124), at 104; Cassese (Above n 63), at 110–11; Van Sliedregt, Joint Criminal Enterprise (Above n 63), at 185–7; Van der Wilt (Above n 128), at 96; Gustafson (Above n 60), at 136–9.

C Revisiting the Analysis of the Customary Status of the Notion of Joint Criminal Enterprise by the ICTY Appeals Chamber in the *Tadic* Case

Regardless of the reasons why the ICTY and ICTR Appeals Chambers have never revisited the analysis of the customary status of the notion of joint criminal enterprise carried out by the *Tadic* Appeal Judgment, recent events call for a careful review of the merits of this analysis. First, the 29 January 2007 ICC Pre-Trial Chamber I Decision on the Confirmation of the Charges in the *Lubanga* case has:

(i)   rejected the conclusion of the Tadic Appeal Judgment[208] that article 25(3) RS embraces a subjective approach to the distinction between principal (perpetration) and accessorial (participation) liability as a result of the consideration of the notion joint criminal enterprise as a theory of co-perpetration;

(ii) based the distinction between principal and accessorial liability on the notion of control of the crime;

(iii) defined the form of liability provided for in article 25(3)(d) RS, which according to ICC Pre-Trial Chamber I 'is closely akin to the concept of joint criminal enterprise or the common purpose doctrine adopted by the jurisprudence of the ICTY', as 'a residual form of accessory liability'.[209]

Second, on 3 April 2007, the ICTY Appeals Chamber, in its Appeal Judgment in the *Brdanin* case, has relied upon the notion of control of the crime in its variant of indirect perpetration in an attempt to address the problems posed by the traditional notion of joint criminal enterprise to prosecute senior political and military leaders.[210] According to the ICTY Appeals Chamber, those individuals who physically commit the crimes do not need to be members of the joint criminal enterprise because those senior political and military leaders participating in such an enterprise may use them as mere 'tools' to carry out the crimes.[211]

Third, in its Separate Opinion to the 7 July 2006 ICTR Appeal Judgment in the *Gacumbitsi* case, Judge Schomburg cited a variety of national and international case law and doctrine in which the different manifestations of the notion of control of the crime have been applied[212] in order to support the following claim:

---

[208] *Tadic Case* Appeals Judgment (Above n 16), at para 223.
[209] *Lubanga Case* Confirmation of Charges (Above n 89), at paras 333–8; *Katanga and Ngudjolo Case* Confirmation of Charges (Above n 89) at para 483.
[210] *Brdanin Case* Appeals Judgment (Above n 79), at paras 410–14.
[211] *Ibid* at para 412.
[212] As jurisprudential precedents of the application of the notion of perpetration by means, Judge Schomburg referred to the Colombian Penal Code art 29, Paraguay Penal Code Art 29(1), Spanish Penal Code art 28, United States: Model Penal Code §2.06(2), German Penal Code §25(1), Finish Penal Code §4, and Corpus Iuris art 11. He also cites Fletcher (Above n 9), at 639; G Werle, *Principles of International Criminal Law* (Cambridge, TMC Asser Press, 2005) 354; Roxin (Above n 47), at 142–274; Ambos, Article 25 (Above n 88) at marginal 9. Furthermore, as jurisprudential precedents of the notion of co-perpetration based on joint control of the crime, Judge Schomburg refers to the Penal Code of Colombia art 29, Paraguay Penal Code art 29(2), German Penal Code §25(2), Finish Penal Code §3 and certain additional precedents from Argentina, France, Spain and Switzerland. He also refers to Roxin

The concept of joint criminal enterprise is not expressly included in the Statute and it is only one possibility to interpret 'committing' in relation to the crimes under the ICTR and ICTY Statutes. In various legal systems, however, 'committing' is interpreted differently. Since Nuremberg and Tokyo, national as well as international criminal law has come to accept, in particular, co-perpetratorship and indirect perpetratorship (perpetration by means) as a form of 'committing'.[213]

As provided for in article 38 ICJ Statute, 'international custom, as evidence of a general practice accepted as law' is one of the four sources of international law. The ICJ Decision in the *Colombian-Peruvian Asylum* case held that, in accordance with article 38 ICJ Statute, the constitutive elements of international custom are general practice by States and *opinio iuris*.[214] Subsequently, the ICJ has highlighted in the *North Sea Continental Shelf* cases the need for a 'settled practice' and the:

[E]vidence of a belief that this practice is rendered obligatory by the existence of a rule of law requiring it.[215]

Moreover, the ICJ has held in the Military and Paramilitary Activities in and against *Nicaragua* case that it must satisfy itself 'that the existence of the rule in *opinio iuris* of States is confirmed by practice'.[216] Hence, norms of customary international law are developed by the general practice of states, which is accepted and observed as a legal obligation.[217]

Leaving aside for the time being any question concerning the specific elements of the different forms of joint criminal enterprise, the author is of the view that the analysis undertaken by the *Tadic* Appeal Judgment only supports, at best, the conclusion that:

[W]here multiple persons participate in a common purpose or common design, all are responsible for the ensuing criminal conduct, whatever their degree or form of participation, provided all had the intent to perpetrate the crime envisaged in the common purpose.[218]

In other words, the ICTY Appeals Chamber analysis shows, at best, that, if the notion of accomplice liability is understood (following the common law

---

at 275–305 and Ambos, Article 25 at marginal 8. See *Gacumbitsi v Prosecutor* (Appeals Chamber Judgment, Separate Opinion of Judge Schomburg on the Criminal Responsibility of the Appellant for Committing Genocide) ICTR-2001-64-A (7 Jul 2006) paras 16–18, fns 29–33 [hereinafter *Gacumbitsi Case* Appeals Judgment Separate Opinion].

[213] *Gacumbitsi Case* Appeals Judgment Separate Opinion (*Ibid*), at para 16.

[214] *Colombian-Peruvian Asylum Case* (*Colombia v Peru*) [1950] ICJ Rep 266, para 276. See also I Brownlie, *Principles of Public International Law* (5th edn, Oxford, Oxford University Press, 1998) 4–11 [hereinafter Brownlie]; M Akehurst, 'Custom as a Source of International Law' (1974) 47 *British Yearbook of International Law* 1 [hereinafter Akehurst].

[215] *North Sea Continental Shelf Cases* (*Federal Republic of Germany v Denmark; Federal Republic of Germany v Netherlands*) [1969] ICJ Rep 4, para 44.

[216] *Case Concerning Military and Paramilitary Activities in and against Nicaragua* (*Nicaragua v United States of America*) [1986] ICJ Rep 14, para 98.

[217] MC Bassiouni, *Introduction to International Criminal Law* (Ardsley, New York, Transnational Publishers, 2003) 222. See also Brownlie (Above n 214), at 4–11; Akehurst (Above n 214), at 1.

[218] *Tadic Case* Appeals Judgment (Above n 16), at para 224.

approach) as referring generally to partnership in crime (no matter whether such partners are joint principals or accessories to the crime):[219]

> [T]he notion of common design as a form of accomplice liability is firmly established in customary international law and in addition is upheld, albeit implicitly, in the Statute of the International Tribunal.[220]

Nevertheless, for the reasons spelled out below, there is no consistency and cogency in the case law and treaty law referred to by the *Tadic* Appeal Judgment to support the conclusion that, according to international customary law, participation in a joint criminal enterprise or common criminal purpose gives rise to principal (as opposed to accessorial or derivative) liability and, hence, that the distinction between principal and accessorial liability (or between perpetration and participation) is based on the subjective approach that lies at the heart of the notion of joint criminal enterprise. Furthermore, this conclusion is not necessarily consistent with those general principles on criminal responsibility laid down both in the ICTYS and in general international criminal law. Although this conclusion finds some support in some national systems of criminal law, it is contrary to the practice in other national systems of criminal law.

i The Rome Statute, the International Convention for the Suppression of Terrorist Bombing and other International and Regional Conventions

The *Tadic* Appeal Judgment cites certain provisions of two international treaties in support of its conclusion that customary international law embraces a subjective approach to the distinction between principals and accessories to the crime, so that participation in a joint criminal enterprise gives rise to principal liability.[221] These provisions are article 25(3)(d) of the Rome Statute,[222] and article 2(3)(c) of the International Convention for the Suppression of Terrorist Bombing of 15 December 1997.[223] According to the *Tadic* Appeal Judgment, these two provisions not only explicitly embrace the notion of joint criminal enterprise, but they also possess a 'significant legal value' insofar as the former was adopted by an overwhelming majority of States attending the Rome Diplomatic Conference[224], and the latter 'was adopted by consensus by all the members of the General Assembly'.[225]

---

[219] Fletcher (Above n 9), at 636; Gillies (Above n 15) at 155.
[220] *Tadic Case* Appeals Judgment (Above n 16), at para 220.
[221] *Ibid* at paras 222–3.
[222] Adopted by the Rome Diplomatic Conference on 17 July 1998, with 120 votes in favour, 7 against and 21 abstentions. It entered into force on 1 July 2002. It has been signed to date by 139 States and there are currently 105 States Parties.
[223] Adopted by General Assembly Resolution 52/164. It entered into force on 22 May 2001. There are currently 145 States Parties.
[224] *Tadic Case* Appeals Judgment (Above n 16), at para 223.
[225] *Ibid* at para 221.

The language used in these two provisions is quite similar. On the one hand, article 25(3)(d) RS—after having referred to committing a crime (as an individual, with others or through another person) and to ordering, inducing, procuring, aiding and abetting, and assisting in the commission of a crime—provides for the criminal liability of any person who:

(d) In any other way contributes to the commission or attempted commission of such a crime by a group of persons acting with a common purpose. Such contribution shall be intentional and shall either:

  i. Be made with the aim of furthering the criminal activity or criminal purpose of the group, where such activity or purpose involves the commission of a crime within the jurisdiction of the Court; or
  ii. Be made in the knowledge of the intention of the group to commit the crime.

On the other hand, article 2(3)(c) of the International Convention for the Suppression of Terrorist Bombing—after having referred to committing a crime, to participating as an accomplice, and to organising or directing the commission of a crime—provides for the criminal liability of any person who:

In any other way contributes to the commission of one or more offences as set forth in paragraph 1 or 2 by a group of persons acting with a common purpose; such contribution shall be intentional and either be made with the aim of furthering the general criminal activity or purpose of the group or be made in the knowledge of the intention of the group to commit the offence or offences concerned.

As seen above, the 29 January 2007 ICC Pre-Trial Chamber I Decision on the Confirmation of the Charges in the *Lubanga* case has explained that:

Not having accepted the objective and subjective approaches for distinguishing between principals and accessories to a crime, the Chamber considers, as does the Prosecution and, unlike the jurisprudence of the *Ad hoc* tribunals, that the Statute embraces the third approach, which is based on the concept of control of the crime.[226]

Moreover, in the view of ICC Pre-Trial Chamber I:

Article 25 (3) (d) of the Statute provides for a residual form of accessory liability which makes it possible to criminalise those contributions to a crime which cannot be characterised as ordering, soliciting, inducing, aiding, abetting or assisting within the meaning of article 25 (3) (b) or article 25 (3) (c) of the Statute, by reason of the state of mind in which the contributions were made.[227]

Hence, the author considers that the *Tadic* Appeal Judgment was inaccurate in portraying articles 25(3)(d) RS and 2(3)(c) of the International Convention for the Suppression of Terrorist Bombing as endorsing a subjective approach to the

---

[226] *Lubanga Case* Confirmation of Charges (Above n 89), at para 338. See also *Katanga and Ngudjolo Case* Confirmation of Charges (Above n 89) at paras. 484–486.

[227] *Lubanga Case* Confirmation of Charges (Above n 89), at para 337. See also *Katanga and Ngudjolo Case* Confirmation of Charges (Above n 89) at paras. 483; Ambos, Article 25 (Above n 88), at 478–80; Werle (Above n 1), at 212–13.

distinction between principals and accessories to the crime, so that participation in a joint criminal enterprise gives rise to principal liability. On the contrary, these two provisions support quite a different approach because (i) they embrace the notion of control of the crime as the criterion to distinguish between principals and accessories to the crime; and (ii) they, at best, rely on the notion of joint criminal enterprise or common purpose doctrine as a residual form of accessorial liability for those cases in which the objective contribution to the commission of the crime does not even reach to the level required for aiding and abetting.[228] In this regard, it is important to highlight that, in setting out the principles of individual criminal liability, section 14 (3) of UNTAET Regulation 2000/15 on the Establishment of the Panels with Exclusive Jurisdiction over Serious Offences (East Timor) and article 15(b) of the Statute of the Iraqi Special Tribunal use the very same language as article 25(3)(d) RS.

Moreover, international and regional conventions generally refer to the notion of perpetration (principal liability) by using the term 'to commit', and only sometimes include explicit references to the concept of co-perpetration.[229] Nevertheless, as it is the case with article 7(1) ICTYS and article 6(1) ICTRS, they, for the most part, do not develop the notions of perpetration and co-perpetration, nor do they specify the approach taken with respect to the distinction between principals and accessories to the crime. As a result, the question of whether international and regional conventions adopt a subjective approach to this distinction or whether they base this distinction on other criterion (such as on the notion of control of the crime) is left, to a very important extent, to be answered by case law.

Further, with regard to most international and regional conventions, case law will be developed by national courts applying such conventions. In doing so, national courts will most likely apply the notions of perpetration and co-perpetration, and the distinction between principals and accessories to the crime that they have developed at the national level. As a result, those States that have adopted a subjective approach to such a distinction will consider those participating in a joint criminal enterprise as principals to the crime, whereas those States that base such a distinction on a formal-objective approach or on the notion of control of the crime, will look at the notion of joint criminal enterprise as a theory of accessorial liability. It is unlikely that another result will be reached

---

[228] The same inaccuracies in the interpretation of the RS can be found in *Prosecutor v Furundzija* (Judgment) ICTY-95-17/1-T (10 Dec 1998) para 216 and *Prosecutor v Furundzija* (Appeals Chamber Judgment) ICTY-95-17/1-A (21 Jul 2000) para 117, which interpreted this provision as supporting the conclusion that 'two separate categories of liability for criminal participation appear to have crystallised in international law—co-perpetrators who participate in a joint criminal enterprise, on the one hand, and aidors and abettors, on the other'.

[229] For instance, by using the formula 'participating in [the commission of a crime]'. See International Convention on the Suppression and Punishment of the Crime of Apartheid, General Assembly Res AG/Res 3068 (XXVIII) (Washington DC 30 Nov 1973) art II(a). See United Nations Convention Against Illicit Traffic in Narcotic Drugs and Psychotropic Substances (1998) art 3(c)(iv); art 11 of the 2000 Corpus Iuris; art 25(3)(a) RS, which uses the formula: '[committing a crime] jointly with others'.

through the application of the criteria of interpretation contained in the Vienna Convention on the Law of the Treaties.

ii *Post WW II Case Law*

The *Tadic* Appeal Judgment also cited two groups of post WW II cases in support of its conclusion that customary international law embraces a subjective approach to the distinction between principals and accessories to the crime, so that participation in a joint criminal enterprise gives rise to principal liability. The first group includes (i) the *Georg Otto Sandrock et al* case (also known as the *Almelo Trial*),[230] the *Jepsen and others* case,[231] the *Schonfeld et al* case,[232] the *Ponzano* case,[233] the *Belsen* case,[234] and the *Essen Lynching* (also called *Essen West*) case,[235] all tried before British Courts sitting in Germany; (ii) the *Einsatzgruppen* case,[236] the *Dachau Concentration Camp*,[237] and the *Kurt Goebell et al* case (also called the *Borkum Island* case),[238] all tried before US Courts sitting in Germany; and (iii) the *Hoelzer et al* case tried before a Canadian Military Court sitting in Germany.[239]

The *Tadic* Appeal Judgment did not explain, however, whether the defendants were convicted as principals or as accessories to the crimes in these cases. This is particularly relevant considering that, in most common law jurisdictions, participation in a joint criminal enterprise or common criminal purpose gives rise to accessorial liability, unless the accused physically commits the crime—and this applies to both the foundational crimes and any foreseeable incidental crime committed in the execution of the common criminal plan. In this regard, as Gillies has

---

[230] *Tadic Case* Appeals Judgment (Above n 16), at para 197. See also *Trial of Otto Sandrock and three others* (1945) British Military Court for the Trial of War Criminals, held at the Court House, Almelo, Holland, in UNWCC, Vol I, p 35.

[231] *Tadic Case* Appeals Judgment (*Ibid*) at para 198. See also *Trial of Gustav Alfred Jepsen and others* (1946) Proceedings of a War Crimes Trial, held at Luneberg, Germany (Judgment of 24 Aug 1946).

[232] *Tadic Case* Appeals Judgment (*Ibid*), at para 198. See also *Trial of Franz Schonfeld and others* (1946) British Military Court for the Trial of War Criminals, held at the Court House, Almelo, Holland, in UNWCC, Vol XI.

[233] *Tadic Case* Appeals Judgment (*Ibid*) at para 199. See also *Trial of Feurstein and others* (1948) Proceedings of a War Crimes Trial, held at Hamburg, Germany (Judgment of 24 Aug 1948).

[234] *Tadic Case* Appeals Judgment (*Ibid*) at para 202. See also *Trial of Josef Kramer and 44 others* (1954) British Military Court for the Trial of War Criminals, held at Luneberg, Germany, UNWCC, Vol II, p 1.

[235] *Tadic Case* Appeals Judgment (*Ibid*) at paras 205–207. See also *Trial of Erich Heyer and six others* (1945) British Military Court for the Trial of War Criminals, held at Essen, Germany, UNWCC, Vol I, p 88.

[236] *Tadic Case* Appeals Judgment (*Ibid*) at para 200. See also *United States v Otto Ohlenforf et al* in Trial of the Major War Criminals before the International Military Tribunal under Control Council Law No 10, Vol I (US Government Printing Office, 1951) Vol IV, p 3.

[237] *Tadic Case* Appeals Judgment (*Ibid*) at para 202. See also *Trial of Martin Gottfried Weiss and thirty-nine others* (1945) General Military Government Court of the United States Zone, held at Dachau, Germany, UNWCC, Vol XI, p 5.

[238] *Tadic Case* Appeals Judgment (*Ibid*), at paras 210–13.

[239] *Ibid* at para 197. *Hoelzer et al* (1946) Canadian Military Court, Aurich, Germany, Vol I, pp 341, 347, 349 (RCAF Binder 181.009/D2474).

pointed out, in common law jurisdictions 'pursuant to the doctrine of common purpose, a person becomes liable as an accessory to any crime committed by another person in that circumstance where the two of them are currently party to an agreement for the commission of this crime';[240] and hence this doctrine 'does not represent a substantive addition to, or supplanting of, the general principles of accessorial liability'.[241] The main exception to this general approach is Australia where all participants in a joint criminal enterprise or all persons acting with a common criminal purpose are considered as principals.[242] However, as Smith & Hogan have pointed out, this approach 'is contrary to all English authority'.[243]

The second group of post WW II cases cited by the *Tadic* Appeal Judgment are the *D'Ottavio et al* case,[244] the *Aratano et al* case,[245] the *Tosani* case,[246] the *Bonati et al* case,[247] the *Peveri* case,[248] the *Manneli* case,[249] the *PM v Minafo* case,[250] the *Montagnino* case,[251] the *Solesio et al* case,[252] the *Minapo el al* case[253] and the *Antonino et al* case,[254] all tried before Italian Courts.[255] The *Tadic* Appeal Judgment resorted to these cases to justify the application of the concept of *dolus eventualis* in the extended form of joint criminal enterprise.[256] Nevertheless, it did not rely on these cases to justify its conclusion that customary international law embraces a subjective approach to the distinction between principals and acces-

---

[240] Gillies (Above n 15), at 173.

[241] *Ibid* at 175.

[242] Smith and Hogan (Above n 10), at 168.

[243] Smith and Hogan (*Ibid*) at 169. See also Hamdorf (Above n 11), at 208, 221–3; Van Sliedregt, Joint Criminal Enterprise (Above n 63), at 197.

[244] Italian Court of Cassation, Judgment of 12 Mar 1947. This case is referred to in the *Tadic Case* Appeals Judgment (Above n 16), at para 215.

[245] Italian Court of Cassation, Judgment of 27 Aug 1947. This case is referred to in the *Tadic Case* Appeals Judgment (*Ibid*) at para 216.

[246] Italian Court of Cassation, Judgment of 12 Sep 1946. This case is referred to in the *Tadic Case* Appeals Judgment (*Ibid*) at para 217.

[247] Italian Court of Cassation, Judgment of 25 Jul 1946. This case is referred to in the *Tadic Case* Appeals Judgment (*Ibid*) at para 217.

[248] Italian Court of Cassation, Judgment of 15 Mar 1948. This case is referred to in the *Tadic Case* Appeals Judgment (*Ibid*) at para 219, fn 277.

[249] Italian Court of Cassation, Judgment of 27 Oct 1949. This case is referred to in the *Tadic Case* Appeals Judgment (*Ibid*) at para 219, fn 277.

[250] Italian Court of Cassation, Judgment of 24 Feb 1950. This case is referred to in the *Tadic Case* Appeals Judgment (*Ibid*) at para 219, fn 277.

[251] Italian Court of Cassation, Judgment of 19 Apr 1950. This case is referred to in the *Tadic Case* Appeals Judgment (*Ibid*) at para 219, fn 277.

[252] Italian Court of Cassation (1950). This case is referred to in the *Tadic Case* Appeals Judgment (*Ibid*) at para 219, fn 277.

[253] Italian Court of Cassation, Judgment of 23 Oct 1946. This case is referred to in the *Tadic Case* Appeals Judgment (*Ibid*) at para 219, fn 277.

[254] Italian Court of Cassation, Judgment of 29 Mar 1949. This case is referred to in the *Tadic Case* Appeals Judgment (*Ibid*) at para 219, fn 278.

[255] They all deal with war crimes committed either by civilians or by military personnel belonging to the armed forces of the so-called '*Repubblica Sociale Italiana*' ('RSI'), a *de facto* government under German control established by the Fascist leadership in central and northern Italy, following the declaration of war by Italy against Germany on 13 Oct 1943.

[256] *Tadic Case* Appeals Judgment (Above n 16), at para 214–19.

sories to the crime so that participation in a joint criminal enterprise gives rise to principal liability. Indeed, the *Tadic* Appeal Judgment could not have found support for this conclusion in post WW II cases tried before Italian Courts because Italy is one of the few jurisdictions which have rejected the distinction between perpetration (principal liability) and participation (accessorial or derivative liability) and have adopted a unitary system whereby any person who intervenes in the commission of the crime is criminally liable as a perpetrator.[257]

In conclusion, those post WW II cases tried before British, US and Canadian Courts on which the *Tadic* Appeal Judgment relied upon are not examples of a subjective approach to the distinction between principals and accessories to the crime, nor do they affirm that participation in a joint criminal enterprise or a common criminal purpose gives rise to principal liability. The post WW II cases tried before Italian Courts do not support such an approach either. In this regard, it must be highlighted that even the *Tadic* Appeal Judgment had to acknowledge that:

> It should be noted that in many post-World War II trials held in other countries, courts took the same approach to instances of crimes in which two or more persons participated with a different degree of involvement. However, they did not rely upon the notion of common purpose or common design, preferring to refer instead to the notion of co-perpetration. This applies in particular to Italian and German cases.[258]

iii General Principles on Criminal Responsibility in the ICTYS and in General International Criminal Law

The *Tadic* Appeal Judgment highlighted that its conclusion that customary international law embraces a subjective approach to the distinction between principals and accessories to the crime so that participation in a joint criminal enterprise gives rise to principal liability is in consonance with the general principles of criminal responsibility laid down both in the ICTY and in general international criminal law. In this regard, the *Tadic* Appeal Judgment stated that, according to the Secretary General's Report:

> [A]ll those who have engaged in serious violations of international humanitarian law, whatever the manner in which they may have perpetrated, or participated in the perpetration of those violations, must be brought to justice. If this is so, it is fair to conclude that the Statute does not confine itself to providing for jurisdiction over those persons who plan, instigate, order, physically perpetrate a crime or otherwise aid and abet in its planning, preparation or execution. The Statute does not stop there. It does not exclude those modes of participating in the commission of crimes, which occur where several persons having a common purpose embark on criminal activity that is then carried out either jointly or by some members of this plurality of persons. Whoever contributes to the commission of crimes by the group of persons or some members of the group, in

---

[257] See Ch 2, s II.
[258] *Tadic Case* Appeals Judgment (Above n 16), at para 201.

execution of a common criminal purpose, may be held to be criminally liable, subject to certain conditions, which are specified below.[259]

Furthermore, the *Tadic* Appeal Judgment highlighted that this interpretation was also warranted by the very nature of many international crimes committed in wartime situations because (i) they are often committed by a plurality of persons acting in pursuance of a common criminal design, (ii) the contribution of those members of the group who do not carry out physically the objective elements of the crimes is often vital and (iii) 'the moral gravity of such participation is often no less—or indeed no different—from that of those actually carrying out the acts in question'.[260]

The arguments of the *Tadic* Appeal Judgment explain why nothing in article 7(1) ICTYS prevents the application of the notion of joint criminal enterprise as a theory of accomplice liability. Nevertheless, such arguments do not grant any support to its conclusion that article 7(1) ICTYS embraces a subjective approach to the distinction between principals and accessories so that participation in a joint criminal enterprise gives rise to principal liability. Quite the contrary, stating, on the one hand, that the justification for the consideration as principals of those members of a joint criminal enterprise who do not carry out the objective elements of the crime is the 'vital' nature of their contribution and the moral gravity of their conduct (which is not less than that of the physical perpetrators), is not consistent with saying, on the other hand, that when a plurality of persons participate in a joint criminal enterprise, all are responsible for the ensuing criminal conduct as principals:

> [W]hatever their degree or form of participation, provided all had the intent to perpetrate the crime envisaged in the common purpose.

Indeed, in the view of the author, the arguments put forward by the *Tadic* Appeal Judgment support (i) the adoption of the notion of control of the crime as the criterion to distinguish between principals and accessories to the crime and (ii) the consideration of the notion of joint criminal enterprise or common purpose doctrine as a theory of accessorial liability. In this regard, one has to underscore that the notion of control of the crime considers as principals to the crime those individuals who dominate its commission in the sense that they decide whether the crime will be carried out and how it will be performed, that is to say, those whose contributions are vital and whose conduct has a moral gravity which is not less than that of the physical perpetrators.

---

[259] *Ibid* at para 190.
[260] *Ibid* at para 191.

iv The Notions of Joint Criminal Enterprise and Control of the Crime in National Legislations

The *Tadic* Appeal Judgment affirmed in its conclusion that, under customary international law, the distinction between principal and accessorial liability is based on a subjective approach, in that participation in a joint criminal enterprise gives rise to principal liability, was consistent with national legislation. In this regard, the ICTY Appeals Chamber explained that the notion of joint criminal enterprise or the common purpose doctrine is accepted in many national systems of criminal justice,[261] although the scope and nature of such notion varies from system to system.[262] The *Tadic* Appeal Judgment stated that Germany, the Netherlands, Italy, France, England and Wales, Canada, the United States, Australia and Zambia are examples of nations which have accepted the notion of joint criminal enterprise.[263]

In the view of the author, the ICTY Appeals Chamber rightly pointed out that joint criminal enterprise, common purpose or similar notions, which are all based on the concept of the 'meeting of the minds' to carry out a crime, are theories of accomplice liability or partnership in crime in most national systems of the world. Nevertheless, jumping from this conclusion to the finding that a subjective approach to the distinction between principals and accessories to the crime (according to which joint criminal enterprise is a theory of principal liability) is consonant with national legislation is unsupported by the sources put forward by the ICTY Tadic Judgment. Indeed, except for Australia, most common law jurisdictions—including England and Wales, Canada, the United States, and Zambia—consider the notion of joint criminal enterprise or the common purpose doctrine as a theory of accessorial liability because, for these jurisdictions, principals to the crime are only: (i) those who carry out all or part of the objective elements of the crime; and (ii) those others who exceptionally can be considered principals through the doctrines of 'vicarious liability' or 'innocent agency'.[264]

Furthermore, out of the four civil law jurisdictions cited by the *Tadic* Appeal Judgment in support of its finding, Italy has adopted a unitary system which rejects any distinction between principal (perpetration) and accessorial (participation) liability, and in the last 25 years, German jurisprudence has gone back and forth from a subjective approach to the notion of control of the crime as the controlling criterion to distinguish between principals and accessories to the

---

[261] *Ibid* at paras 224–5.

[262] *Ibid* at para 225.

[263] *Ibid*.

[264] Gillies (Above n 15), at 157–8; Smith and Hogan (Above n 10), at 167–168; Fletcher (Above n 9), at 638–9. See also Hamdorf (Above n 11), at 221–3; Van Sliedregt, Joint Criminal Enterprise (Above n 63), at 197.

crime[265]. This phenomenon has also taken place in Spain since the end of the 1980s, long before the approval of the current Spanish Penal Code in 1995,[266] because the Spanish Supreme Court steadily abandoned the subjective approach to the above-mentioned distinction (as reflected in the so-called doctrine of the *acuerdo previo*)[267] and embraced the notion of control of the crime[268].

Moreover, the Appeals Chamber did not analyse the abundant national case law, which distinguishes between principals and accessories to the crime on the basis of approaches other than the subjective one. For instance, common law jurisdictions base the distinction between principals and accessories to the crime on a formal-objective approach, according to which only those who carry out all or part of the objective elements of the crime are considered principals to the crime—the only exceptions are the doctrines of vicarious liability and innocent agency, none of which is based on the state of mind of the persons involved in the commission of the crime.[269]

More importantly, it must be underscored that, even though the degree of development of the notion of control of the crime varies among national jurisdictions, such a notion has, for a long time, been embraced by both common and civil law jurisdictions. As the *Katanga and Ngdujolo* Case Confirmation of Charges has recently held at paras 484 and 485:

> By adopting the final approach of control of the crime, the Chamber embraces a leading principle for distinguishing between principals and accessories to a crime [. . .] The control of over the crime approach has been applied in a number of legal systems, and is widely recognised in legal doctrine.

[265] German jurisprudence has often applied the notion of control of the crime. See, for instance, the judgment of the German Federal Supreme Court in the German Border Case (Entscheidungen des Bundesgerichtshofs in Strafsachen 40 p 218). See also Entscheidungen des Bundesgerichtshofs in Strafsachen 2 p 151, 9 p 393, 19 p 138. Moreover, apart from Roxin, a number of German authors have also embraced (though with certain particularities) the notion of control of the crime. Gallas, *Taterschaft und Teilnahme, Materialin zum Strafrechtsreform, Teil 1, Gutachten der Strafrechtslehrer* (1954) 152; Lange, *Der moderne Taterbergriff und der deutsche Strafgesetzentwurf* (1935) 32; See Niese, *Die finale Handlungslehre und ihre praktische Bedeutung, Deutsche Richterzeitung* (1952) 21–4; Sax, *Dogmatische Streifzuge durch den Entwurf des Allgemeinen Teils eines Strafgesetzbuches nach den Beschlussen der Groben Strafrechtskommission, Zeitschrift fur die gesamte Strafrechtswissenschaft* 69 (1957) 412; Von Weber, *Der strafrechtliche Schutz des Urheberrechts* (1976) 65; Jescheck and Weigend (Above n 24), at 897; Bockelmann, *Strafrechtliche Untersuchungen* (1957) 31; Baumann, 'Mittelbare Taterschaft oder Anstiftung bei Fehlvorstellungen uber den Tatmittler?' (1958) *Juristenzeitung* 230; Jakobs (Above n 41), at 611; R Maurach, KH Gossel and H Zipf, *Strafrecht Allgemeiner Teil, Teil II* (6th edn, Munich, 1984) 208. Compare S Hoyer in HJ Rudolphi, H Eckard and E Samson, *Systematischer Kommentar zum Strafgesetzbuch* (Munich, Luchterhand Fachb, 2003) § 25 No 10.

[266] Art 28 of the Spanish Penal Code of 1995 defines perpetration as committing a crime as an individual, jointly with others or through another person. Besides, the instigators and the so-called necessary (as opposed to unnecessary) aidors and abettors shall also be considered perpetrators for the purpose of punishment.

[267] This approach is taken, for instance, in the Judgments of the Spanish Supreme Court of 22 Feb 1985, 31 May 1985 and 13 May 1986.

[268] See Judgments of the Spanish Supreme Court of 24 Feb 1989 and 4 Oct 1994. For additional jurisprudence of the Spanish Supreme Court applying the notion of control of the crime, see Diaz y Garcia Conlledo (Above n 37), at 564.

[269] Gillies (Above n 15), at 157–8; Smith and Hogan (Above n 10), at 167–8; Fletcher (Above n 9), at 638–9.

Common law jurisdictions, such as Australia,[270] Canada,[271] South Africa,[272] England and Wales,[273] and the United States,[274] have traditionally applied the notion of control of the crime to convict, as a perpetrator, the person who uses an innocent agent as a tool to commit a crime. In these cases, the person 'behind the scenes' is said to have control of the crime because he controls the will of the person who physically commits the crime.

Civil law jurisdictions, such as Argentina,[275] France,[276] Germany,[277]

---

[270] P Rush and S Yeah, *Criminal Law Sourcebook* (Sydney, Butterworths, 2000) 560.

[271] The phrase 'actually commits it' in Canadian Criminal Code § 21(1)(a) includes a case in which the defendant causes the offence to be committed by an innocent agent under his or her direction. See Tremeear's Criminal Code, Statutes of Canada Annotated (2003, Carswell) 61.

[272] CR Snyman, *Criminal Law* (Durban, Butterworths, 1995) 246–7.

[273] *Regina v Cogan and Leak* [1976] QB 217; *Stringer* [1991] 94 Cr. App. R. 13, cited by A Reed, B Fitzpatrick and P Seago, *Criminal Law* (Andover, Sweet and Maxwell Publishing, 1999) 123, fn 17; *DPP v K & B* [1997], cited by Smith and Hogan (Above n 10), at 167, fn 29.

[274] Model Penal Code §2.06(1)-(4). See also *State v Ward*, 396 A.2d 1041, 1046 (1978); J Dressler, *Understanding Criminal Law* (2nd edn, Albany, Lexis Publishing, 1995) §30.03[A].

[275] The notion of control of the crime has been applied to convict as a perpetrator the person who uses an innocent agent to commit a crime by, inter alia, Penal Chamber of Parana, 'Section 1a' (10 Nov 1987); JA 1988-III-299; Tribunal Nacional Oral Criminal, 'No 7' (3 Nov 1998); JA 2002-I-sintesis. See also C Fontan Balestra, *Tratado de Derecho Penal: Parte General* (Albany, Lexis Publishing, 1995) Lexis No 1503/001660, § 49. E Cuello Calon, *Derecho Penal* (9th edn, Barcelona, Libreria Bosch, 1926) 5. The notion of control of the crime has been applied to convict as a perpetrator the person who uses a fully responsible person as an instrument to commit a crime by the Judgment of the Camara Federal de Apelaciones en lo Criminal de la Capital Federal (9 December 1985) in the case against the members of the three Juntas that governed Argentina from 1976 to 1983. This notion has also been used by the Argentine jurisprudence to characterise the conduct of the main executives of an enterprise that had committed crimes against the environment. See Judgment of the Camara Nacional en lo Criminal y Correccional Federal de la Capital Federal, 'Sala 4a' (22 May 2002). See also MA Sancinetti and M Ferrante, *El Derecho Penal en la Proteccion de los Derechos Humanos, La Proteccion de los Derechos Humanos mediante el Derecho Penal en las Transiciones Democraticas* (Buenos Aires, Hammurabi, 1999) 204–212; E Malarino, 'El Caso Argentino', in K Ambos (ed), *Imputacion de Crimenes de Subordinados al Dirigente: Un Estudio Comparado* (Bogotá, Temis 2008) 37–68.

[276] French jurisprudence has also applied the notion of control of the crime to convict as a perpetrator the person who uses an innocent agent to commit a crime. See Cour de Cassation, Chambre Criminelle Dalloz (6 Mach 1964) 562. See also ML Rassat, *Droit Penal General* (2nd edn, Paris, Presses Universitaires France, 1999) No 325. When defining genocide, French Penal Code Art 211(1) refers to a similar notion with the expression '*faire commettre*'. But even regarding offences for which '*faire commettre*' is not foreseen, the jurisprudence has held liable as a perpetrator of the offence the employer who gave the order to his employees to commit a certain offence. See Larguier, *Chronique de jurisprudence, Droit penal general* (1976) Revue des Sciences Criminelles 410. Finally, in order to determine whether a person is a co-perpetrator or an accomplice, French jurisprudence also relies on the importance of the role played during the commission of the crime. See Cour de Cassation, Chambre Criminelle Dalloz (25 Jan 1962) No 68; Salvage, *Editions du Juris-Classeur Penal* (Paris, LexisNexis, 1998) Complicite: Arts 121–6 to 121–7.

[277] German jurisprudence has applied the notion of control of the crime to convict, as a perpetrator, the person who uses an innocent agent to commit a crime. See Bundesgerichtshof, Entscheidungen des Bundesgerichtshofs in Strafsachen 32 p 41, 35, p 351.The German Supreme Court has also applied the notion of control of the crime to convict as a perpetrator the person who uses a fully responsible person as an instrument to commit a crime. See the German Border Case, Bundesgerichtshof, Neue Juristische Wochenschrift (1994) 2307 and in other subsequent cases, Bundesgerichtshof 5 StR 98/94 (26 July 1997) and Bundesgerichtshof 5 StR 176/98 (28 Oct 1998). See also K Kuhl, *Strafrecht Allgemeiner Teil* (4th edn, Munich, Vahlen Franz GMBH, 2002) § 20, No 73b; Trondle and Fischer (Above n 137), at § 25 No 3c. Finally, German jurisprudence has also occasionally embraced the notion of co-perpetration based on joint or functional control. See Entscheidungen des Bundesgerichtshofs in Strafsachen 37 p 291, 38 p 319; Bundesgerichtshof, Strafverteidiger (1994) p 241.

Spain[278] and Switzerland,[279] have also embraced several manifestations of the notion of control of the crime.[280] They have applied this notion to convict (i) as a perpetrator or principal, the person who uses another, be him an innocent agent or a fully responsible person, to commit a crime; and (ii) as a co-perpetrator or co-principal, anyone who plays an essential role in the commission of a crime by a plurality of people.

As a result, as Fletcher has pointed out referring to perpetration-by-means (use of a person as a tool to commit a crime), '[v]irtually all legal systems, it should be noted, recognize the principle of perpetration-by-means'.[281] The importance of this national practice is evident if one considers that, as seen above, most of international and regional conventions do not elaborate upon the distinction between principals and accessories to the crime, and that such distinction will be developed by national courts applying such conventions.

---

[278] Art 28 of the Spanish Penal Code has embraced the notion of control of the crime, to hold responsible, as a perpetrator, the person who uses an innocent agent to commit a crime ('*Son autores quienes realizan el hecho por si solos, conjuntamente or por medio de otro del que se sirven como instrumento*'). See also Diaz y Garcia Conlledo (Above n 37); J Gonzalez Rus, 'Autoria Unica Inmediata, Autoria Mediata y Coautoria' in *Cuadernos de Derecho Judicial, No XXXIX Ed Consejo General del Poder Judicial* (1994). Spanish Jurisprudence has also applied the notion of control of the crime to convict the person, who uses a fully responsible person as an instrument to commit a crime, as a perpetrator. For Spain, the judgment of the Spanish Supreme Court of 14 Oct 1999, with Judge Joaquin Martin Canivell presiding, is especially important. In this judgment, control of the crime via an organised structure of power was applied to convict some leaders of the terrorist organisation ETA. Co-perpetration based on joint or functional control has also been applied by the Spanish Supreme Court. See the judgments of the Spanish Supreme Court of 13 Dec 2002. See also A Gil y Gil, 'El Caso Español', in K Ambos (ed), *Imputación de Crimenes de los Subordinados al Dirigente: Un Estudio Comparado* (Bogotá, Temis 2008) 87–128.

[279] Swiss jurisprudence has applied the notion of control of the crime to hold responsible, as a perpetrator, the person who uses an innocent agent to commit a crime. See Entscheidungen des Schweizerischen Bundesgerichts 101 IV 310; Entscheidungen des Schweizerischen Bundesgerichts 85 IV 23; S Trechsel and P Noll, *Schweizerisches Strafrecht, Allgemeiner Teil I, Allgemeine Voraussetzungen der Strafbarkeit* (5th edn, Zurich, Schulthess, 1998) 199. The Swiss Supreme Court has also applied co-perpetration based on joint or functional control. See Entscheidungen des Schweizerischen Bundesgerichts 118 IV 399, 120 IV 142; Entscheidungen des Schweizerischen Bundesgerichts 120 IV 272.

[280] Other civil law jurisdictions have also embraced some of the manifestations of the notion of control of the crime. For instance, Chilean Courts have applied this notion to convict Generals Contreras and Espinoza for the murdering of the former Chilean Minister of Foreign Affairs, Orlando Letelier. Published in Fallos del Mes, Year XXXV, Nov 1993, Suplementaria, p 154. Furthermore, Penal Code of Colombia Art 29(1) also embraces this notion. See Law 599 of 24 Jul 2000: '*Es autor quien realice la conducta punible por si mismo o utilizando a otro como instrumento*'. See also, K Ambos (ed), *Imputación de Crimenes de los Subordinados al Dirigente: Un Estudia Comparado* (Bogotá, Temis 2008), where the application of some of the manifestations of the notion of control of the crime in Chile, Peru and Colombia are analysed.

[281] Fletcher (Above n 9), at 639; See also *Prosecutor v Milutinovic*, Bonomy Opinion (Above n 34), at paras 28–30.

v Conclusion

In the view of the author, from the above-mentioned analysis, a number of conclusions can be drawn. First, as the *Tadic* Appeal Judgment found, there are numerous sources supporting the principle that, under customary international law (and hence under articles 7(1) ICTYS and 6(1) ICTRS as well), criminal liability arises for those acting pursuant to a joint criminal enterprise or common criminal purpose. As a result, as the ICTY Appeals Chamber explained:

> [W]here multiple persons participate in a common purpose or common design, all are responsible for the ensuing criminal conduct, whatever their degree or form of participation, provided all had the intent to perpetrate the crime envisaged in the common purpose.[282]

Second, international treaties, post WW II case law, general principles of international criminal law and national legislation and case law analysed by the *Tadic* Appeal Judgment do not support the conclusion that customary international law (and hence articles 7(1) ICTYS and 6(1) ICTRS) embraces a subjective approach to the distinction between principals and accessories to the crime, so that participation in a joint criminal enterprise or common criminal purpose gives rise to principal (as opposed to accessorial or derivative) liability.[283] Quite the contrary, these sources grant support, to an important extent, to (i) the choice of the notion of control of the crime as the controlling criterion to distinguish between principals and accessories to the crime, and (ii) the definition of the notion of joint criminal enterprise or common purpose doctrine as a theory of accessorial liability. Furthermore, there are a number of additional sources not analysed by the *Tadic* Appeal Judgment (such as a number of international and regional conventions, the latest ICC case law, and the legislation and case law of most national systems of criminal justice), which: (i) support either the formal-objective approach, or the approach based on the notion of control of the crime, to the distinction between principal (perpetration) and accessorial (participation) liability; and (ii) rely on the notion of joint criminal enterprise or common purpose doctrine as a theory of accessorial liability.

---

[282] *Tadic Case* Appeals Judgment (Above n 16), at para 224.

[283] The same conclusion, but from a different perspective, is reached by Bogdan (Above n 123), at 109–111. According to this writer: 'The methodology employed by the Appeals Chamber, therefore, fails to follow established rules that can be utilized in determining rules of customary international law. Rather th[a]n engaging in a rigorous examination similar to the one performed by the International Court of Justice in the *North Sea Continental Shelf Cases*, the Appeals Chamber judgment provides only a cursory examination of general state practice in regards to "joint criminal enterprise", and fails to altogether examine opinio iuris with respect to this issue. As will be recalled, the focus in trying to determine the existence of a "custom" is on evidence of intent by states to be bound by a certain rule and to establish reliance by other states on such a rule (which is demonstrated by consistent practice). In other words, for customary rules the primary focus is on the examination of executive branch action by various states'.

Third, although national legislation and case law (in particular in common law jurisdictions) applying the formal-objective approach to the distinction between principals and accessories to the crime do not make such an approach part of customary international law (especially in light of the essential role played by senior political and military leaders in the commission of international crimes in spite of being far away from the scene of the crime), it cannot simply be disregarded.

Fourth, the increasing instances of application of the notion of control of the crime at the national and international levels—and the fact that this notion best suits the characteristics of international crimes by considering as principals those senior political and military leaders who play a vital role in the commission of the crimes and whose moral gravity is by no means less than that of the physical perpetrators—do not necessarily lead to the conclusion that the different manifestations of such a notion are currently part of customary international law or were part of it at the time the armed conflict in the former Yugoslavia broke out in 1991 or the crisis situation in Rwanda started in 1994.

D Final Remarks on the Lack of Customary Status of the Notions of Joint Criminal Enterprise and Control of the Crime

In the view of the author, the variety of approaches to the distinction between principal (perpetration) and accessorial (participation) liability at the international and national levels is such, that one cannot conclude that any of these approaches (be it the formal-objective, the subjective or the one based on the notion of control of the crime) have reached customary status in international law, despite the fact that the above-mentioned case law and legislation shows an increasing application of the notion of control of the crime.

In order to better explain this situation, it is worth taking a look at the essential divergences between the 10 February 2006 ICC Pre-Trial Chamber I Decision on the Issuance of a Warrant of Arrest in the *Lubanga* case and the 22 March 2006 ICTY Appeal Judgment in the *Stakic* case. The former explicitly endorsed the notion of control of the crime by stating that:

> In the Chamber views there are reasonable grounds to believe that, given the alleged hierarchical relationship between Mr. Thomas Lubanga Dyilo and the other members of the UPC and the FPLC, the concept of indirect perpetration, which along with that of co-perpetration based on joint control of the crime referred to in the Prosecution's Application, is provided for in article 25 (3) (a), could be applicable to Mr. Thomas Lubanga Dyilo's alleged role in the commission of the crimes set out in the Prosecution's Application.[284]

---

[284] *Lubanga Case* Warrant of Arrest (Above n 89), at para 96.

A month afterwards, the ICTY Appeal Judgment in the *Stakic* case dismissed the possible customary status of the notion of control of the crime without further explanation:

> Upon a careful and thorough review of the relevant sections of the Trial Judgement, the Appeals Chamber finds that the Trial Chamber erred in conducting its analysis of the responsibility of the Appellant within the framework of 'co-perpetratorship'. This mode of liability, as defined and applied by the Trial Chamber, does not have support in customary international law or in the settled jurisprudence of this Tribunal, which is binding on the Trial Chambers. By way of contrast, joint criminal enterprise is a mode of liability, which is 'firmly established in customary international law' and is routinely applied in the Tribunal's jurisprudence. Furthermore, joint criminal enterprise is the mode of liability under which the Appellant was charged in the Indictment, and to which he responded at trial. In view of these reasons, it appears that the Trial Chamber erred in employing a mode of liability, which is not valid law within the jurisdiction of this Tribunal. This invalidates the decision of the Trial Chamber as to the mode of liability it employed in the Trial Judgement.[285]

Subsequently, the 1 October 2008 ICC Pre Trial Chamber Decision on the Confirmation of the Charges in the *Katanga and Ngudjolo* case held the following in relation to the treatment of the notion of control of the crime by the ICTY Appeal Judgment in the *Stakic* case:

> The Appeals Chamber rejected this mode of liability by stating that it did not form part of customary international law. However, under article 21(1)(a) of the Statute, the first source of applicable law is the Statute. Principles and rules of international law constitute a secondary source applicable only when the statutory material fails to prescribe a legal solution. Therefore, and since the Rome Statute expressly provides for this specific mode of liability, the question as to whether customary law admits or discards the 'joint commission through another person' is not relevant for this Court. This is a good example of the need not to transfer the *ad hoc* tribunals' case law mechanically to the system of the Court[286].

As is illustrated above, the ICTY and the ICTR have relied, for almost a decade, on the analysis of the ICTY Appeal Judgment in the *Tadic* case to justify a subjective approach to the distinction between principals and accessories to the crime, and a definition of the notion of joint criminal enterprise or common purpose doctrine as a theory of principal liability. Nevertheless, one cannot obviate the ad hoc nature of the ICTY and the ICTR and the fact that jurisprudential shifts, such as the one put forward by the *Stakic* Trial Judgment, at this stage may undermine

---

[285] *Stakic Case* Appeals Judgment (Above n 79), at para 62. As seen in further detail in Ch 5, s VI.C below, the notion of 'co-perpetratorship' resorted to by the *Stakic Case* Trial Judgment (Above n 193), at para 468 was an attempt to use the notion of control of the crime to overcome some of the problems posed by the traditional notion of joint criminal enterprise in cases where the accused is a senior political or military leader. This constituted a shift from the subjective approach to the distinction between principals and accessories to the crime that had been previously embraced by the ICTY Appeals Chamber.

[286] *Katanga and Ngudjolo Case* Confirmation of Charges (Above n 89) para. 509.

the legal certainty offered by the ICTY and ICTR settled case law.[287] Hence, the reversal of the jurisprudential shift carried out by the Trial Chamber in the *Stakic* case, although debatable, is not per se unreasonable, particularly in light of the facts that at the ICTY (i) principals to the crime are not automatically given higher sentences than accessories[288]; and (ii) one of the factors that has systematically been given greater weight in sentencing is the nature of the contribution to the commission of the crimes by the convicted person.[289] Indeed, in the author's view, the main problem of the ICTY Appeal Judgment in the *Stakic* case—apart from the lack of any reasoning in dismissing the customary status and the application at the ICTY of the notion of control of the crime—is that the ICTY Appeals Chamber did not explicitly address the matter which prompted the Trial Chamber to resort to the notion of control of the crime: the multiple problems posed by the traditional notion of joint criminal enterprise when applied to senior political and military leaders.

Remarkably, when the ICTY Appeals Chamber finally decided to address these problems in the *Brdanin* case, it resorted to the notion of indirect perpetration (a manifestation of the notion of control of the crime) to justify the existence of a joint criminal enterprise at the leadership level in which the physical perpetrators are not included. Although the Appeals Chamber did not explicitly acknowledge its reliance on the very same notion that it had dismissed without further explanation a year before, the explicit reference in the following excerpt to the use of the physical perpetrators by the members of the joint criminal enterprise as mere tools to commit the crimes eliminates any doubt concerning its reliance on the notion of control of the crime:

> In light of the above discussion of relevant jurisprudence, persuasive as to the ascertainment of the contours of joint criminal enterprise liability in customary international law, the Appeals Chamber is of the view that what matters in a first category JCE is not whether the person who carried out the *actus reus* of a particular crime is a member of the JCE, but whether the crime in question forms part of the common purpose [. . .] As the Prosecution recognizes, for it to be possible to hold an accused responsible for the criminal conduct of another person, there must be a link between the accused and the

---

[287] This shift is nothing new at the national level. For instance, since the end of the 1980s, long before the approval of the current Spanish Penal Code in 1995, the Spanish Supreme Court steadily abandoned the subjective approach to the distinction between principals and accessories to the crime (as reflected in the so-called doctrine of the *acuerdo previo*) and embraced the notion of control of the crime. See in this regard the differences between the subjective approach to the distinction between principals and accessories taken in the Judgments of the Spanish Supreme Court of 22 February 1985, 31 May 1985 and 13 May 1986, and the subsequent approach based on notion of the crime taken by the Judgments of the Spanish Supreme Court of 24 February 1989 and 4 October 1994. See also Diaz y Garcia Conlledo (Above n 37), at 564. Likewise, as seen above, in the last 25 years, German jurisprudence has gone back and forth from a subjective approach to the notion of control of the crime. For the application of the notion of control of the crime by the German Federal Court, see the German Border Case (Entscheidungen des Bundesgerichtshofs in Strafsachen 40 p 218). See also Entscheidungen des Bundesgerichtshofs in Strafsachen 2 p 151, 9 p 393, 19, p 138.

[288] See Ch 2, s IV.

[289] See *Celebici Case* Appeals Judgment (Above n 92), at paras 429, 430; *Aleksovski* Appeals Judgment (Above n 92), at para 182; *Gacumbitsi Case* Appeals Judgment (Above n 87), at para 204.

crime as legal basis for the imputation of criminal liability. According to the Prosecution, this link is to be found in the fact that the members of the joint criminal enterprise use the principal perpetrators as "tools" to carry out the crime [. . .] the Appeals Chamber finds that, to hold a member of a JCE responsible for crimes committed by non-members of the enterprise, it has to be shown that the crime can be imputed to one member of the joint criminal enterprise, and that this member—when using a principal perpetrator— acted in accordance with the common plan. The existence of this link is a matter to be assessed on a case-by-case basis.[290]

---

[290] *Brdanin Case* Appeals Judgment (Above n 79), at paras 410, 412–13.

3

Direct Perpetration and Indirect Perpetration

I Direct Perpetration

A Concept

Direct perpetration takes place when an individual physically carries out the objective elements of a crime with the mental state required by the crime in question.[1] It is referred to as committing a crime 'as an individual' in article 25(3)(a) RS,[2] and it constitutes the most straightforward form of 'committing' a crime under articles 7(1) ICTYS and 6(1) ICTRS. Indeed, when the Prosecution alleges that a senior political or military leader is a principal to the crime despite having no involvement in its physical commission, the following language is usually introduced in the indictment:

> By using the word committed in this indictment the Prosecutor does not intend to suggest that the accused physically committed any of the crimes charged personally. Committing in this indictment refers to participation in a joint criminal enterprise as co-perpetrator.[3]

---

[1] A Cassese, *International Criminal* Law (Oxford, Oxford University Press 2003) 180 [hereinafter Cassese, *International Criminal Law*]. As the *Prosecutor v Delalic et al* (Appeals Chamber Judgment) ICTY-96-21-A (20 Feb 2001) para 345 [hereinafter *Celebici Case* Appeals Judgment] has emphasised, in the case of 'primary or direct responsibility, where the accused himself commits the relevant act or omission, the qualification that his participation must "directly and substantially affect the commission of the offence" is an unnecessary one'.

[2] K Ambos, *La Parte General del Derecho Penal Internacional: Bases para una Elaboracion Dogmatica* (Uruguay, Konrad-Adenauer-Stiftung, 2005) 174 [hereinafter Ambos, *La Parte General del Derecho Penal Internacional*] has pointed out that it would have been preferable to define the notion of direct perpetration with the expression 'committed by his own conduct' used in s 2.06(1) of the US Model Penal Code. According to Ambos, the language of the US Model Penal Code better expresses that the essence of 'direct perpetration' lies in the fact that the perpetrator physically commits the crime.

[3] *Prosecutor v Milosevic* (Croatia: Second Amended Indictment) ICTY-02-54-T (28 Jul 2004) para 5.

Direct perpetration is normally used as the starting point for the definition of the crimes and the description of their elements.[4] No matter which approach one takes with respect to the distinction between principals and accessories to the crime, the person who physically carries out the objective elements of a crime with the state of mind required for the crime in question becomes a perpetrator or principal to the crime. For the formal-objective approach, he is a perpetrator because he carries out the objective elements of the crime. For the subjective approach, he is a principal to the crime because he intends the crime as his own deed. Finally, for the material-objective approach based on the notion of control of the crime, he is also a perpetrator or principal to the crime because he has the control over the action insofar as he himself carries out the objective elements of the crime.[5]

B Fulfilling the Objective Elements of the Crime

The definition of any crime, including international crimes, is comprised of a set of contextual and specific objective elements and certain subjective elements.[6] The objective elements of the crimes within the jurisdiction of the ICC and the *Ad hoc* Tribunals can be classified into: (i) material contextual elements, which are common to a number of crimes provided for in the RS, ICTYS and ICTRS (particularly to crimes against humanity and war crimes); and (ii) the specific elements of any of the crimes provided for in those instruments. The material contextual elements, which must be met for any conduct to amount to a crime under the RS, the ICTYS or the ICTRS, must be distinguished from those other circumstances (known as 'jurisdictional contextual elements') which do not affect the qualification of a conduct as a crime and are only required for the exercise by the ICC, the ICTY or the ICTR of its subject matter jurisdiction. As a result, direct perpetration does not require awareness of the factual circumstances that establish the existence of the jurisdictional contextual elements.

---

[4] For instance, if one takes the war crime of using protected persons as shields ('Rome Statute of the International Criminal Court' UN Diplomatic Conference of Plenipotentiaries on the Establishment of an International Criminal Court (Rome 15 Jun–17 Jul 1998) (17 Jul 1998) UN Doc A/Conf. 183/9 [hereinafter RS]), art 8(2)(b)(xiii) RS defines it as 'utilizing the presence of a civilian or other protected person to render certain points, areas or military forces immune from military operations'. Furthermore, the EC describe the elements of this offence as follows: '(i) the perpetrator moved or otherwise took advantage of the location of one or more civilians or other persons protected under the international law of armed conflict; (ii) the perpetrator intended to shield a military objective from attack or shield, favour or impede military operations; (iii) the conduct took place in the context of and was associated with an international armed conflict; and (iv) the perpetrator was aware of factual circumstances that established the existence of an armed conflict'. The case law of the *Ad hoc* Tribunals operates in the same way. For instance, the *Celebici Case* Appeals Judgment (Above n 1), at para 422 described the elements of the war crime of wilful killing as a grave breach of the Geneva Conventions under art (2) (a) ICTYS as '(a) death of the victim as the result of the action(s) of the accused, (b) who intended to cause death or serious bodily injury which, as it is reasonable to assume, he had to understand was likely to lead to death, and (c) which he committed against a protected person'.

[5] See Ch 2, s VI.

[6] GP Fletcher, *Rethinking Criminal Law* (2nd edn, Oxford, Oxford University Press, 2000) 575–6 [hereinafter Fletcher].

The case law of the *Ad hoc* Tribunals has considered that the existence of an armed conflict and its link with the forbidden conduct, as well as the protected status of persons or objects subject to the forbidden conduct, are jurisdictional contextual elements (as opposed to material contextual elements).[7] The author disagrees with this approach because both elements are objective elements of the crime; if they are not met there is no crime. For instance, in the context of an armed conflict, wilful killing is only prohibited if the person killed is a protected person. However, if the person killed is an enemy combatant, then that action is considered lawful according to international humanitarian law, and hence it does not give rise to criminal responsibility. Likewise, using the presence of civilians to render certain points, areas or military forces immune from military operations only gives rise to criminal responsibility if it is carried out in connection with an armed conflict. Absent this connection, the action of placing civilians around a military objective does not give rise to criminal liability.

The RS and the EC have corrected the approach of the case law of the *Ad hoc* Tribunals by treating the existence of an armed conflict, its link with the forbidden conduct and the protected status of the persons or objects subject to the forbidden conduct as material contextual elements. They have done so by explicitly requiring for the direct perpetration of the crimes the awareness of factual circumstances that: (i) establish the existence of an armed conflict; and (ii) underlie the protected status of the victim (for instance, the fact that he was in the hands of an adverse party to the conflict).

The case law of the *Ad hoc* Tribunals and the EC have taken the same approach in relation to the jurisdictional nature of the international character of the armed conflict because neither require the awareness of the factual circumstances that establish the international character of the armed conflict in order to find direct perpetration.

Nevertheless, the author considers that this approach is also incorrect, particularly in the context of the RS. As Von Hebel and Robinson have pointed out, the reason why paragraphs (2)(a) and (b) of article 8 RS contain more war crimes than paragraphs (2)(c) and (e) of article 8 RS is because the drafters decided to criminalise, for the purposes of the ICC system, a broader range of conduct in relation to international armed conflicts given the higher degree of protection that international humanitarian law grants in these types of conflicts.[8] As a result,

---

[7] See *Prosecutor v Tadic* (Appeals Chamber Decision on the Defence Motion for Interlocutory Appeal on Jurisdiction) ICTY-94-1-A (2 Oct 1995) paras 79–84; *Prosecutor v Tadic* (Appeals Chamber Judgment) ICTY-94-1-A (15 Jul 1999) para 80 [hereinafter *Tadic Case* Appeals Judgment].

[8] According to H Von Hebel and D Robinson, 'Crimes within the Jurisdiction of the Court' in RS Lee (ed), *The International Criminal Court: The Making of the Rome Statute* (The Hague, Kluwer, 1999) 125, 'In general, one may conclude that the definition of war crimes is consistent with two important trends of the last few years, namely, the gradual blurring of the fundamental differences between international and internal armed conflicts, and the recognition of individual criminal responsibility for violations of fundamental provisions of relevant international humanitarian law instruments. As described above, many of the provisions relating to internal armed conflicts were drawn from provisions relating to international armed conflicts. This result is consistent with the view that differences in the regulation of the two forms of conflict must be reduced. Although it was suggested that the Conference should do away completely with that distinction, that suggestion clearly was a 'bridge too far' for most of delegations'.

the very same conduct (for instance, directing an attack against civilian objects or launching a disproportionate attack) gives rise to criminal liability if it takes place in connection with an international armed conflict, but not when it takes place in connection with a non international armed conflict. This leads to the conclusion that the international character of an armed conflict is an objective element of the crime (material contextual element) because, depending on how it is labelled, the very same conduct may or may not amount to a war crime under the RS. Hence, as it has already been highlighted:

> [R]egardless of what is set out in the introduction to the war crimes section of the EC, the perpetrator should, at the very least, be aware of the factual circumstances that establish the character of the conflict as international or non-international.[9]

This approach has already been implicitly followed by ICC Pre-Trial Chamber I Decision on the Confirmation of the Charges in the *Lubanga* case.[10]

In this regard, it is important to highlight that the temptation to circumvent the requirement of the awareness of the factual circumstances that establish the existence of the material contextual elements of the crimes should be avoided[11].

C Fulfilling the Subjective Elements of the Crime

i General Subjective Element and Additional Subjective Elements

The subjective elements contained in the definition of any crime, including international crimes, can be classified into: (i) a general subjective element consisting of the state of mind that must drive the execution of the objective elements of the crime;[12] and (ii) additional subjective elements—normally referred to as ulterior

---

[9] H Olasolo, *Unlawful Attacks in Combat Operations* (Leiden, Brill, 2007) at 248 [hereinafter Olasolo, *Unlawful Attacks*]; Ambos, *La Parte General del Derecho Penal Internacional* (Above n 2), at 410–11. In this regard, it is important to highlight that, according to art 9 RS, the EC 'shall assist the Court in the interpretation and application of articles 6, 7 and 8' but are not binding on the Chambers of the Court.

[10] At para 406 of this decision, ICC Pre-Trial Chamber I explicitly found that Thomas Lubanga Dyilo was aware of the factual circumstances establishing the international (from the beginning of Sep 2002 until 2 Jun 2003) and the non-international (from 2 Jun 2003 until the end of 2003) character of the armed conflict that took place in the territory of Ituri.

[11] In the author's view, in the context of the RS, only the gravity threshold provided for in arts 8(1) and 17(1)(d) RS should be qualified as a true jurisdictional contextual element. This gravity threshold constitutes a true objective requisite to proceed insofar as it is a circumstance that, without affecting the existence of the crimes in any given situation or case, must be met for their investigation and prosecution. Otherwise, the Court cannot exercise its jurisdiction over them.

[12] Fletcher (Above n 6), at 575–6; See also JC Smith and B Hogan, *Criminal Law* (11th edn, London, Butterworths, 2005) 113 [hereinafter Smith and Hogan], who conclude that 'the best we can do by way of a general definition of mens rea is as follow: "Intention, knowledge or recklessness with respect to all the elements of the offence together with any ulterior intent which the definition of the crime requires"'.

intent or *dolus specialis*—which consist of specific purposes that must motivate the commission of the crime.[13]

The subjective elements are far more vague and difficult to prove than the objective elements of the crime because they consist of a state of mind as opposed to actions or omissions. Therefore, the subjective elements cannot be observed; they can only be deduced.[14]

The general subjective element usually varies from crime to crime. Sometimes criminal law only criminalises certain conduct when the perpetrator's purpose is to achieve the forbidden result.[15] Other times, criminal law criminalises the means used to achieve a lawful goal. In this last scenario, it may very well happen that, due to lack of due diligence, an individual is unaware of the likelihood that his conduct may undermine the societal value protected by the penal norm. As the RS and the case law of the *Ad hoc* Tribunals reject the notions of strict liability and liability for the result, all objective elements of the crime (specific and contextual) must be covered by the general subjective element.

Nevertheless, in relation to normative elements, it is not necessary to make the value judgement inherent to their legal qualification; it is sufficient to be aware of the factual circumstances establishing their existence. This is particularly relevant for the contextual elements insofar as most of them are normative elements: whether a given crisis situation legally amounts to an armed conflict, whether an armed conflict can be legally qualified as international or non-international, or whether the persons or objects subject to the forbidden conduct have been granted a protected status by international humanitarian law.

ii The Subjective Elements of the Crimes in the RS

According to ICC Pre-Trial Chamber I, article 30 RS sets out the general subjective element for all crimes within the ICC jurisdiction by specifying that:

> Unless otherwise provided, a person shall be criminally responsible and liable for punishment for a crime within the jurisdiction of the Court only if the material elements are committed with intent and knowledge.[16]

---

[13] See the excellent explanation of the notion of ulterior intent given by Smith and Hogan (*Ibid*), at 112–13. Particular attention must be paid not to confuse the common law notions of specific intent (which refers to the general subjective element and is equivalent to the civil law notion of *dolus directus* in the first degree) and ulterior intent (which refers to an additional subjective element consisting of a specific purpose that must motivate the commission of the crime and its equivalent to the civil law notion of *dolus specialis*).

[14] Smith and Hogan (*Ibid*), at 112–13.

[15] This scenario has been referred to as a conscious rebellion against the societal value protected by the penal norm.

See F Munoz Conde and M Garcia Aran, *Derecho Penal: Parte General* (5th edn, Valencia, Tirant lo Blanch, 2002) 455 [hereinafter Munoz Conde and Garcia Aran].

[16] *Lubanga Case* (Pre-Trial Chamber I Decision on the Confirmation of Charges) ICC-01/04-01/06 (29 Jan 2007) para 350 [hereinafter *Lubanga Case* Confirmation of Charges].

Moreover, in the *Lubanga* case, ICC Pre-Trial Chamber I held that article 30 RS embraces the notion of *dolus* as the general subjective element of the crimes, which includes *dolus directus* in the first degree, *dolus directus* in the second degree and *dolus eventualis*.[17]

As ICC Pre-Trial Chamber I has explained in the *Lubanga* case:

> The cumulative reference to 'intent' and 'knowledge' requires the existence of a volitional element on the part of the suspect. This volitional element encompasses, first and foremost, those situations in which the suspect (i) know that his or her actions or omissions will bring about the objective elements of the crime, and (ii) undertakes such actions and omissions with the concrete intent to bring about the objective elements of the crime (also known as *dolus directus* of the first degree). The above-mentioned volitional elements also encompasses other forms of the concept of *dolus* which have already been resorted to by the jurisprudence of the *Ad hoc* tribunals, that is: (i) situations in which the suspect, without having the concrete intent to bring about the objective elements of the crime, is aware that such elements will be the necessary outcome of his actions or omissions (also known as *dolus directus* of the second degree), and (ii) situations in which the suspect (a) is aware of the risk that the objective elements of the crime may result from his actions or omissions, and (b) accepts such an outcome by reconciling himself or herself with it or consenting to it (also know as *dolus eventualis*).[18]

In the *Lubanga* case ICC Pre-Trial Chamber I has also explained that the notion of *dolus eventualis* is applicable in two different kinds of scenarios:

> First, if the risk of bringing about the objective elements of the crime is substantial (that is, there is a risk of the substantial likelihood that 'it will occur in the ordinary course of events') the fact that the suspect accepts the idea of bringing about the objective elements of the crime can be inferred from: (i) the awareness by the suspect of the substantial likelihood that his or her actions or omissions would result in the realisation of the objective elements of the crime; and (ii) the decision by the suspect to carry out his or her actions or omissions despite such awareness. Secondly, if the risk of bringing about the objective elements of the crime is low, the suspect must have clearly or expressly accepted the idea that such objective elements may results from his or her actions or omissions.[19]

In the *Katanga and Ngudjolo* case, ICC Pre Trial Chamber I has, to a large extent, adopted the definition of *dolus directus* of the first degree, *dolus directus* of the second degree and *dolus eventualis* provided for in the Lubanga case. It has also confirmed that *dolus directus* of the first degree and *dolus directus* of the second degree are part of the general subjective element provided for in article 20 RS.[20]

---

[17] *Lubanga Case* Confirmation of Charges (*Ibid*), at paras 351–2.

[18] *Ibid.*

[19] *Ibid* at paras 352–3. In the same sense, see the definition of *dolus eventualis* provided for in the *Prosecutor v Stakic* (Judgment) ICTY-97-24-T (31 Jul 2003) para 287 [hereinafter *Stakic Case* Trial Judgment].

[20] Katanga and Ngudjolo Case (Pre-Trial Chamber I Decision on the Confirmation of Charges) ICC-01/04-01/07 (1 Oct 2008) paras 529, 530 [*Katanga and Ngudjolo Case* Confirmation of Charges]. See also Katanga and Ngudjolo Case (Pre Trial Chamber 1 Decision on the Applications for Leave to

Concerning whether *dolus eventualis* is also part of the general subjective element provided for in article 30 RS, ICC Pre Trial Chamber I made no finding for the following reasons:

> In the Lubanga Decision, the Chamber found that article 30(1) of the Statute encompasses also dolus eventualis. The majority of the Chamber endorses this previous finding. For the purpose of the present charges in the present Decision, it is not necessary to determine whether situations of dolus eventualis could also be covered by this offence, since, as shown later, there are substantial grounds to believe that the crimes were committed with dolus directus. Judge Anita Uaacka disagrees with the position of the majority with respect to the application of dolus eventualis. Judge Anita Uaacka finds that, at this time, it is unnecessary for her to provide reasons, since the issue of whether article 30 of the Statute also encompasses cases of dolus eventualis is not addressed in the present Decision.[21]

ICC Pre-Trial Chamber I has also underscored in the Lubanga case that *dolus eventualis* and advertent recklessness are different notions insofar as (advertent) recklessness is limited to the following situations:

> The concept of recklessness requires only that the perpetrator be aware of the existence of a risk that the objective elements of the crime may result from his or her actions or omissions, but does not require that he or she reconcile himself or herself with the result. In so far as recklessness does not require the suspect to reconcile himself or herself with the causation of the objective elements of the crime as a result of his or her actions or omissions, it is not part of the concept of intention. According to Fletcher, 'Recklessness is a form of *culpa*—equivalent to what German Scholars call "conscious negligence". The problem of distinguishing "intention" and "recklessness" arises because in both cases the actor is aware that his conduct may generate a specific result'.[22]

Situations of advertent recklessness are those where a person is aware of the likelihood—although the required level of risk varies between national systems, and it goes from mere 'possibility' to 'probability'—that the objective elements of the crime would occur as a result of his actions or omissions, and in spite of that, takes the risk (taking the risk is usually considered to be inherent to the decision to proceed with one's conduct) in the belief that his expertise will suffice in preventing the realisation of the objective elements of the crime[23]. This would be the case if

---

Appeal the Decision on the Admission of the Evidence of Witnesses 132 and 287 and on the Leave to Appeal on the Decision on the Confirmation of Charges) ICC-01/04-01/07 (24 Oct 2008) pp 15–16 [hereinafter Katanga and Ngudjolo Case Leave to Appeal].

[21] *Katanga and Ngudjolo Case* Confirmation of Charges (*Ibid*), para 251, fn 329. See also para 531.

[22] *Lubanga Case* Confirmation of Charges (Above n 16), at para 355, fn 438. See also Fletcher (Above n 6), at 443.

[23] The perpetrator's awareness of the mere possibility of causing the forbidden result is sufficient, at least in relation to the crime of homicide, in countries such as South Africa. See CR Snyman, *Criminal Law* (Durban, Butterworths, 1995) 169. The perpetrator's awareness of the likelihood of causing the forbidden result is required, at least with regard to the crime of homicide, in Australia. See *The Queen v Crabbe* [1985] 156 CLR 464; B Fisse, *Howard's Criminal Law* (5th edn, Sydney, Law Book Company Limited, 1990) 59. See also The Bahamas Penal Code of 1987, SS 311 and 11(2). See also Kenya Penal Code of 1985, SS 203 and 206(b); Malawi Penal Code, SS 209 and 212(b); Zambia Penal Code, SS 200 and 204(b); B Thompson, *The Criminal Law of Sierra Leone* (Lanham, University Press of America, 1999) 61.

an artillery officer, in spite of being aware of the likelihood of hitting an apartment building occupied only by civilians due to the lack of precision of his mortar, carries out the attack because he is confident that his skills will allow him to ensure that the projectile hits the small munitions warehouse located next to the apartment building. This would also be the case if a taxi driver takes the risk of driving at a very high speed on a local road, trusting that nothing would happen on account of his or her driving expertise.

As a result, according to ICC Pre-Trial Chamber I in the *Lubanga* case, while *dolus eventualis* is part of the broader notion of *dolus* and meets the 'intent and knowledge' requirement of article 30 RS, advertent recklessness does not meet such requirement because:

> Where the state of mind falls short of accepting that the objective elements of the crime may result from his or her actions or omissions, such a state of mind cannot qualify as a truly intentional realisation of the objective elements, and hence would not meet the 'intent and knowledge' requirement embodied in article 30 of the Statute.[24]

Advertent or subjective recklessness can be distinguished from inadvertent or objective recklessness. The latter usually takes place when a person, without being aware of the risk that is inherent to his conduct, proceeds with his conduct and, in so doing, unconsciously creates an objectively high risk which exceeds what is socially acceptable (advertent recklessness, thus, is closely related to the civil law category of gross negligence which in civil law systems is included within the notion of negligence).[25] Finally, both advertent and inadvertent recklessness can, in principle, be distinguished from the broader category of negligence which would include the breach of the duty to conduct oneself with due diligence in performing the conduct that brings about the objective elements of the crime.[26] According to Pre-Trial Chamber I, inadvertent recklessness and negligence do not meet either the 'intent and knowledge' requirement provided for in article 30 RS.[27]

The general subjective element provided for in article 30 RS is not applicable to a handful of crimes within the ICC jurisdiction, which include in their definition their own general subjective element. In particular, the definitions of several war crimes appear to require *dolus directus* of the first degree because of the use of expressions such as 'intentionally' or 'wilfully'. However, this is not always the

---

[24] *Lubanga Case* Confirmation of Charges (Above n 16), at para 355; See also JL Rodriguez-Villasante y Prieto, 'Los Principios Generales del Derecho Penal en el Estatuto de Roma de la Corte Penal Internacional' (Jan-Jun 2000) 75 *Revista Espanola de Derecho Militar* 417 [hereinafter Rodriguez-Villasante y Prieto]; DK Piragoff, 'Article 30: Mental Element' in O Triffterer (ed), *Commentary on the Rome Statute of the International Criminal Court* (Baden-Baden, Nomos, 1999) 534. Compare E Van Sliedregt, *The Criminal Responsibility of Individuals for Violations of International Humanitarian Law* (The Hague, TMC Asser Press, 2003) 87 [hereinafter Van Sliedregt].

[25] The judgment of the House of Lords in *Metropolitan Police Commissioner v Caldwell* [1982] AC 341 established the inadvertent, objective or Caldwell recklessness as opposed to the advertent, subjective or Cunningham recklessness.

[26] See G Quintero Olivares, *Manual de Derecho Penal: Parte General* (3rd edn, Pamplona, Aranzadi, 2002) 354–5 [hereinafter Quintero Olivares].

[27] *Lubanga Case* Confirmation of Charges (Above n 16), at para 355, fn 438.

case, as shown by the fact that the expression 'intentionally' appears to have a broader meaning than *dolus directus* of the first degree in the crime of:

> Intentionally directing attacks against buildings dedicated to religion, education, arts, science or charitable purposes, historic monuments, hospitals and places where the sick and wounded are collected[28]

This leads to the conclusion that in order to determine the meaning of these expressions in the definition of a particular crime, one needs to analyse them in the context of the other elements of the definition.

Exceptionally, under the RS, mere negligence is the general subjective element of a few war crimes. This is the case with the crimes of conscripting, enlisting and using to actively participate in hostilities children under the age of 15 years, where it is sufficient that the perpetrator 'should have known that such person or persons were under the age of 15 years'.[29] As ICC Pre-Trial Chamber I has affirmed, this 'should have known' standard falls within the notion of negligence because it is met when a person:

(i)   did not know that the victims were under the age of fifteen years at the time they were enlisted, conscripted or used to actively participate in hostilities; and

(ii) lacked such knowledge because he or she did not act with due diligence in the relevant circumstances (one can only say that the suspect 'should have known' if his or her lack of knowledge results from his or her failure to comply with his or her duty to act with due diligence).[30]

Finally, in addition to the general subjective element, the definition of certain crimes within the ICC jurisdiction, such as, inter alia, genocide, hostage taking, torture, pillaging, enforced prostitution or the use of human shields, requires an ulterior intent or *dolus specialis*. This additional subjective element, which consists of a specific purpose that must motivate the commission of the crime, is normally introduced by using expressions such as 'with intent to', 'for the purpose of' and 'by reason of'.

iii The Subjective Elements of the Crimes in the Case Law of the Ad hoc Tribunals

The Statutes and case law of the *Ad hoc* tribunals have used a number of different expressions to define the general subjective element of the crimes within their jurisdiction, including 'wilful', 'intentional', 'awareness of substantial likelihood', 'reasonable knowledge of the likelihood', 'reckless disregard for human life', and '*dolus eventualis*'. Hence, the question arises as to whether each crime has a

---

[28] See art 8(2)(b)(ix) and (e)(iv) RS and the respective EC.

[29] Art 8(2)(b)(xxvi) and (e)(vii) RS and the respective EC of conscripting, enlisting or using children under the age of 15.

[30] *Lubanga Case* Confirmation of Charges (Above n 16), at para 358.

different general subjective element; or whether, on the contrary, it can be stated that there is a general subjective element, which applies to most crimes within the jurisdiction of the *Ad hoc* tribunals.

Although the case law of the *Ad hoc* Tribunals has employed various expressions to define the general subjective element of the crimes within their jurisdiction, the fact of the matter is that its main concern has been to cope with the gap between the civil law notion of *dolus eventualis* and the common law notion of advertent recklessness. As a result, in its early years, it has often gone back and forth between these two notions.[31] However, over time, it can be stated that the case law of the *Ad hoc* Tribunals has progressively moved towards a common general subjective element, which is applicable to most crimes within their jurisdiction. This is the 'awareness of substantial likelihood' standard, which requires: (i) the awareness of the substantial likelihood that one's conduct will generate the objective elements of the crime, and (ii) the acceptance of such risk (which is considered to be implicit in the decision to proceed with one's conduct in spite of knowing the likely consequences of it).[32]

---

[31] This dynamic was highlighted in the Prosecution Closing Brief in the *Kordic* case, Annex IV, paras 40–41. See *Prosecutor v Kordic* (Judgment) ICTY-95-14/2-T (26 Feb 2001) para 375 [hereinafter *Kordic Case* Trial Judgment].

[32] In the *Kordic Case* Trial Judgment (*Ibid*), at para 375, the Trial Chamber explains that the Prosecution proposed the standard 'awareness of substantial likelihood' as a common general subjective element. As the Trial Chamber highlighted when describing the submissions of the parties in relation to the legal elements of 'committing' as a mode of liability: 'The *mens rea* required is that the accused acted with the requisite intent for the crime under customary international law. The Prosecution is of the view that this requirement is satisfied when the accused acted in the awareness of the substantial likelihood that a criminal act or omission would occur as a consequence of his conduct'.

Subsequently, this standard has been embraced to define the general subjective element of numerous crimes within the jurisdiction of the *Ad hoc* Tribunals. Indeed, according to the ICTY and ICTR case law, most crimes within the jurisdiction of the *Ad hoc* Tribunals can be committed by either 'direct' or 'indirect' intent. And the standard 'awareness of substantial likelihood' is, to a very important extent, used to define the notion of 'indirect intent'. For instance, the ICTY Trial Judgment in *Prosecutor v Martic* (Judgment) ICTY-95-11-T (12 June 2007) para 58 [hereinafter *Martic Case* Trial Judgment] has defined the general subjective element of the crime of murder as a war crime and as a crime against humanity in the following manner: 'The act or omission was committed with intent to kill, or in the knowledge that death was a probable consequence of the act or omission'. Furthermore, at para 60, it has added that: 'The *mens rea* of murder is the intent to kill, including indirect intent, that is the knowledge that the death of the victim was a probable consequence of the act or omission. This Trial Chamber does not consider it to be sufficient that the perpetrator knew that death would be a *possible* consequence of his act or omission'. This definition has also been embraced inter alia in *Prosecutor v Kvocka et al* (Appeals Chamber Judgment) ICTY-98-30/1-A (28 Feb 2005) para 261 [hereinafter *Kvocka Case* Appeals Judgment], *Prosecutor v Strugar* (Judgment) ICTY-01-42-T (31 Jan 2005) paras 235–6 [hereinafter *Strugar Case* Trial Judgment], *Prosecutor v Limaj* (Judgment) ICTY-03-66-T (30 Nov 2005) para 241 [herinafter *Limaj Case* Trial Judgment], and *Prosecutor v Oric* (Judgment) ICTY-03-68-T (30 Jun 2006) para 348 [herinafter *Oric Case* Trial Judgment].

Likewise, *Prosecutor v Ntakirutimana* (Appeals Chamber Judgment) ICTR-96-10-A (13 Dec 2004) para 522 [hereinafter *Ntakirutimana Case* Appeals Judgment], *Prosecutor v Stakic* (Appeals Chamber Judgment) ICTY-97-24-A (22 Mar 2006) para 259 [hereinafter *Stakic Case* Appeals Judgment], and *Martic Case* Trial Judgment (*Ibid*), at para 65, have defined the general subjective element of the crime of extermination as a crime against humanity in the following manner: 'The *mens rea* element of extermination requires that the act or omission was committed with the intent to kill persons on a large scale or in the knowledge that the deaths of a large number of people were a probable consequence of the act or omission'.

In the 8 October 2008 *Martic Case* Appeals Judgment, the ICTY Appeals Chamber, when dealing with the mode of liability of 'ordering' at paragraphs 222 and 223, defined this common general subjective element in the following manner:

> From the outset, the Appeals Chamber recalls its discussion in the *Blaskic* Appeal Judgement of the requisite subjective element for 'ordering' a crime under the Statute. The Appeals Chamber in that case had to address the question of 'whether a standard of *mens rea* that is lower than direct intent may apply in relation to ordering under Article 7(1) of the Statute, and if so, how it should be defined.' After an extensive analysis, the Appeals Chamber concluded as follows: 'The Appeals Chamber therefore holds that a person who orders an act or omission with the awareness of the substantial likelihood that a crime will be committed in the execution of that order, has the requisite *mens rea* for establishing liability under Article 7(1) pursuant to ordering. Ordering with such awareness has to be regarded as accepting the crime.'
>
> The Appeals Chamber explained that there is indeed a lower form of intent than direct intent. It specified, however, that the 'knowledge of any kind of risk, however low, does not suffice' to impose criminal responsibility under the Statute. It considered that 'an awareness of a higher likelihood of risk and a volitional element must be incorporated in the legal standard.' Hence, it reached its conclusion that the person giving the order must act with the awareness of the *substantial* likelihood that a crime will be committed in the execution of the order. This reasoning was confirmed in the *Kordic and Cerkez* and *Galic* Appeal Judgments.

In the view of the author, the emergence of this standard is due to the fact that it constitutes the best attempt to fill the gap between the civil law notion of *dolus eventualis* and the common law notion of advertent recklessness.[33] On the one hand, the 'awareness of substantial likelihood' standard meets the requirements of advertent recklessness.

The standard 'awareness of substantial likelihood' has also been resorted to in the context of the definition of the subjective elements of modes of liability, such as planning, instigating and ordering, under arts 7(1) ICTYS and 6(1) ICTRS. See *Prosecutor v Blaskic* (Appeals Chamber Judgment) ICTY-95-14-A (29 Jul 2004) para 42 [hereinafter *Blaskic Case* Appeals Judgment]; *Prosecutor v Kordic* (Appeals Chamber Judgment) ICTY-95-14/2-A (17 Dec 2004) paras 30–32 [hereinafter *Kordic Case* Appeals Judgment]; *Prosecutor v Martic* (Appeals Chamber Judgment) ICTY-95-11-A (8 Oct 2008) para 222 [hereinafter *Martic* Case Appeals Judgment].

[33] Other standards proposed by the Prosecution in relation to specific crimes have not found the same level of general acceptance. For instance, in relation to the crime of extermination, the Prosecution proposed the following general subjective element during the appeal in the Stakic case: awareness of the possibility of causing death in a massive scale coupled with the wilful taking of the risk. See *Stakic Case* Appeals Judgment (Above n 32), at para 255, referring to s 5.16 of the Prosecution Appeals Brief. However, this standard does not meet the requirements of advertent recklessness in those common law jurisdictions in which the required level of risk is higher than a mere possibility. Moreover, it does not meet the requirements of *dolus eventualis* because as ICC Pre-Trial Chamber I has affirmed, 'if the risk of bringing about the objective elements of the crime is low, the suspect must have clearly or expressly accepted the idea that such objective elements may results from his or her actions or omissions'. See *Lubanga Case* Confirmation of Charges (Above n 16), at para 353. In the same sense, see the definition of *dolus eventualis* provided for in the *Stakic Case* Trial Judgment (Above n 19), at para 287.

On the other hand, one can argue that the 'awareness of substantial likelihood' standard also meets the requirements of *dolus eventualis* because in those situations in which the risk of causing the crime is high, the only reasonable inference from the decision to go ahead with one's conduct is the acceptance of the causation of the crime. As seen above, ICC Pre-Trial Chamber I has explicitly endorsed this idea in the *Lubanga* case by stating that in high risk situations:

> [T]he fact that the suspect accepts the idea of bringing about the objective elements of the crime can be inferred from: (i) the awareness by the suspect of the substantial likelihood that his or her actions or omissions would result in the realisation of the objective elements of the crime; and (ii) the decision by the suspect to carry out his or her actions or omissions despite such awareness.[34]

However, there are certain crimes within the jurisdiction of the *Ad hoc* tribunals for which the case law has established a different general subjective element. For instance, according to the case law of the *Ad hoc* Tribunals, the general subjective element of the crime of directing an attack against civilians or civilian objects includes *dolus directus* in the first and second degrees, *dolus eventualis*, advertent recklessness and objective recklessness. Nevertheless, it does not include mere negligence (understood as the breach of the duty to conduct oneself with due diligence in performing the conduct that brings about the objective elements of the crime) because the case law of the *Ad hoc* Tribunals has consistently excluded it from the realm of the general subjective element of any of the crimes within their jurisdiction.[35]

The reason for this exception is that the case law of the *Ad hoc* Tribunals has interpreted the expression 'wilful' in article 85(3) of AP I so as to include advertent (subjective) and inadvertent (objective) recklessness. As the ICTY Appeals Chamber has recently held in the *Strugar* case:

> The Appeals Chamber has previously ruled that the perpetrator of the crime of attack on civilians must undertake the attack 'wilfully' and that the latter incorporates 'wrongful intent, or recklessness, [but] not 'mere negligence'. In other words, the mens rea requirement is met if it has been shown that the acts of violence which constitute this crime were wilfully directed against civilians, that is, either deliberately against them or through recklessness. The Appeals Chamber considers that this definition encompasses both the notions of 'direct intent' and 'indirect intent' mentioned by the Trial Chamber, and referred to by Strugar, as the mens rea element of an attack against civilians [] As specified by the Trial Chamber in the Galic case, 'For the mens rea recognized by Additional Protocol I to be proven, the Prosecution must show that the perpetrator was aware or should have been aware of the civilian status of the persons attacked. In case of doubt as

---

[34] *Lubanga Case* Confirmation of Charges (*Ibid*), at para 353. In the same sense, see the definition of *dolus eventualis* provided for in the *Stakic Case* Trial Judgment (*Ibid*), at para. 287.

[35] *Stakic Case* Trial Judgment (*Ibid*), at para 587; *Prosecutor v Galic* (Judgment) ICTY-98-29-T (5 Dec 2003) paras 54–5 [hereinafter *Galic Case* Trial Judgment]; *Prosecutor v Brdanin* (Judgment) ICTY-99-36-T (1 Sep 2004) para 386 [hereinafter *Brdanin Case* Trial Judgment]; *Oric Case* Trial Judgment (Above n 32), at para 348; *Martic Case* Trial Judgment (Above n 32), at para 60.

to the status of a person, that person shall be considered to be a civilian.' However, in such cases, the Prosecution must show that in the given circumstances a reasonable person could not have believed that the individual he or she attacked was a combatant.

The intent to target civilians can be proved through inferences from direct or circumstantial evidence. There is no requirement of the intent to attack particular civilians; rather it is prohibited to make the civilian population as such, as well as individual civilians, the object of an attack. The determination of whether civilians were targeted is a case-by-case analysis, based on a variety of factors, including the means and method used in the course of the attack, the distance between the victims and the source of fire, the ongoing combat activity at the time and location of the incident, the presence of military activities or facilities in the vicinity of the incident, the status of the victims as well as their appearance, and the nature of the crimes committed in the course of the attack.[36]

As a result, even in those cases in which a sniper did not intend to attack civilian persons, he would be criminally liable if he recklessly (with conscious culpability or gross negligence) disregarded the possible civilian status of the persons against whom his attack was directed. Hence, the sniper is punished for a manifest lack of due diligence in verifying the factual circumstances underlying the civilian status of the persons against whom his attack was directed. In this context, the sniper's mistake regarding the civilian status of the persons and objects targeted by his attack does not per se exclude his criminal liability unless it is shown that he could not have overcome his mistake if he had acted without a manifest lack of due diligence.

The ICTY Trial Judgment in the *Galic* case gives several examples of the reckless (with conscious culpability or gross negligence) commission of the crime of directing attacks against a civilian population or civilian persons. For instance, in relation to sniping incident Num 8, the Majority found that—although there is usually sunlight at six o'clock in the morning in the month of July in Sarajevo—given the lack of evidence regarding the amount of sunlight at the time the victim was shot at, it could not exclude the possibility that the perpetrator was unaware of the fact that the victim was a middle-aged women carrying wood. Nevertheless, for the Majority, the absence of a military presence in the area where the victim was hit (it was an open space with only three houses in the vicinity) should have put the perpetrator on notice of the need to further verify whether the victim had a military status before shooting at her. As a result, the Majority concluded that the

---

[36] *Prosecutor v Strugar* (Appeals Chamber Judgment) ICTY-01-42-A (17 July 2008) paras 270–1 [hereinafter *Strugar Case* Appeals Judgment]. According to the *Galic Case* Trial Judgment (*Ibid*), at paras 54–5: [T]he notion of "wilfully" incorporates the concept of recklessness, whilst excluding mere negligence. The perpetrator who recklessly attacks civilians acts "wilfully". For the *mental element* recognized by Additional Protocol I to be proven, the Prosecution must show that the perpetrator was aware or should have been aware of the civilian status of the persons attacked. In case of doubt as to the status of a person, that person shall be considered to be a civilian. However, in such cases, the Prosecution must show that in the given circumstances a reasonable person could not have believed that the individual he or she attacked was a combatant'. This finding has been upheld by the *The Prosecutor v Galic* (Judgment) ICTY-98-29-A (30 Nov 2006) para 140 [hereinafter *Galic Case* Appeals Judgment] and the Strugar Case Appeals Judgment, at para 271.

victim had been shot at without any consideration being given by the perpetrator to her possible civilian status.[37]

Finally, the Statutes and case law of the *Ad hoc* Tribunals, like the RS, have affirmed that the definition of a handful of crimes, such, as inter alia, genocide, torture, terrorising civilians or hostage taking, use the expressions 'with intent to', 'for the purpose of' and 'by reason of' to require, in addition to the general subjective element, an ulterior intent or *dolus specialis*.

II Principal Liability of Senior Political and Military Leaders for Commission by Omission

A Concept

Omissions are one fact of human conduct[38] and thus, can give rise to individual criminal responsibility.[39] As a result, criminal law is not only comprised of norms which prohibit certain actions, but is also comprised of norms which mandate performing certain actions—for instance, preventing subordinates from committing crimes against humanity or war crimes or punishing subordinates for having committed such crimes.[40] Nevertheless, for an omission to give rise to individual criminal responsibility, it is necessary that the person who fails to carry out the required action is in a position that enables him to undertake such action. Furthermore, such a person must have a duty to carry out the required action, so that the action is expected from him.[41]

In criminal law, there are two types of offences of omission.[42] Offences of mere omission are those consisting of a breach of the duty to undertake a certain action—for instance, the duty to assist a person whose life is at risk. The structure of these offences is similar to that of the offences of mere action in which—as

---

[37] *Galic Case* Appeals Judgment (*Ibid*), paras 522–3.

[38] M Moore, *Act and Crime: The Philosophy of Action and its Implications for Criminal Law* (Oxford, Oxford University Press, 1993) 28.

[39] As Cassese, *International Criminal Law* (Above n 1), at 200, has explained: 'International Criminal Liability may arise not only as a result of a positive act or conduct (killing an enemy civilian, unlawfully destroying works of art, etc.) but also from an omission, that is, failure to take action'. See also WR LaFave and AW Scott, *Substantive Criminal Law* (St Paul, West Publishers, 1986) 282.

[40] Fletcher (Above n 6), at 421; P Gillies, *Criminal Law* (4th edn, North Ryde, LBC Information Services, 1997) 37–8.

[41] Munoz Conde and Garcia Aran (Above n 15), at 238; I Kugler, 'Two Concepts of Omission' (2003) 14 *Criminal Law Forum* 421–2.

[42] See inter alia Ambos, *La Parte General del Derecho Penal Internacional* (Above n 2), at 295–302; GP Fletcher, *Basic Concepts of Criminal Law* (New York/Oxford, Oxford University Press, 1998) 47; J Pradel, *Droit Penale Compare* (Paris, Dalloz, 2002) 267; S. Mir Puig, *Derecho Penal: Parte General* (6th edn, Barcelona, Edisofer Libros Juridicos, 2002) 306 [hereinafter Mir Puig].

opposed to those offences requiring a specific result—criminal liability arises from carrying out the forbidden action. In the offences of mere omission, criminal responsibility arises from omitting an expected action in a situation in which the duty to undertake such an action has been triggered.[43]

However, in the offences of omission requiring a specific result, an omission only gives rise to individual criminal liability if it is causally linked to the forbidden result.[44] In this second type of offences of omission, one can distinguish between those cases in which the expected action and the forbidden result are expressly described in the relevant penal norm—such as the norm mandating a record keeper to take all action within his power to prevent third parties from accessing confidential documents—and those other cases (traditionally referred to as 'commission by omission') in which the expected action and the forbidden result are not described by the relevant penal norm—for instance the norm criminalising the killing of a person does not expressly refer to the specific scenario in which a mother causes the death of a newborn by not feeding him.[45]

In cases of 'commission by omission', criminal liability only arises if (i) the person failing to take action has a duty to act in order to prevent the forbidden result because he is in charge of safeguarding the societal value undermined by such result (for instance, the mother has a duty to take care of the newborn, including by feeding him, in order to prevent his death because she is in charge of safeguarding the life of the newborn), and (ii) there is a causal link between the omission of the expected action and the generation of the forbidden result consisting of the fact that the expected action would have likely avoided the forbidden result.[46]

Some national penal codes, such as section 13 of the German Penal Code or article 11 of the Spanish Penal Code explicitly elaborate on the notion of 'commission by omission'.[47] This is not the case with articles 7(1) ICTYS and 6(1) ICTRS,

---

[43] Smith and Hogan (Above n 12), at 76. See also Munoz Conde and Garcia Aran (Above n 15), at 241. Duttwiler refers to this type of offences of omission as 'proper crimes of omission'. See M Duttwiler, 'Liability for Omissions in International Criminal Law' (2006) 6 *International Criminal Law Review* 4 [hereinafter Duttwiler].

[44] Smith and Hogan (Above n 12), at 77.

[45] PH Robinson, 'Criminal Liability for Omissions: A Brief Summary and Critique of the Law of the United States' (1984) 55 *Revue Internationale de Droit Penal* 634. Actions to prevent a forbidden result are a normative equivalent under certain conditions because such failures can be as blameworthy as causing the forbidden result. However, as HH Jescheck and T Weigend, *Lehrbuch des Strafrechts* (5th edn, Berlin, Duncker and Humblot, 1996) 600 have stated, the question arises as to what the conditions are that justify this approach. See also Fletcher (Above n 6), at 611, 628–31, in particular the arguments in favour and against the notion of 'commission by omission'.

[46] J Silva Sanchez, *El Nuevo Codigo Penal: Cinco Cuestiones Fundamentales* (Barcelona, 1997) 51. See also Smith and Hogan (Above n 12), at 77, concerning the necessary causal link between the omission of the expected action and the generation of the forbidden result.

[47] S Cramer and Sternberg-Lieben in Schonke and Schroder (eds), *Kommentar zum Strafgesetzbuch* (26th edn, Munich, CH Beck, 2001) § 15, No 177 [hereinafter Cramer and Sternberg-Lieben]. See also Munoz Conde and Garcia Aran (Above n 15), at 242–3; Mir Puig, (Above n 42), at 311–24; Quintero Olivares (Above n 26), at 376–8; J Wessels and W Beulke, *Strafrecht Allgemeiner Teil* (31st edn, Heidelberg, Muller, 2001) No 711. See also the judgment of the Spanish Supreme Court of 13 Dec 1988; BGH and BGHSt 43, p 397.

which only explicitly refer to the general notion of 'committing' a crime. Likewise, article 25(3)(a) RS, in spite of elaborating on the notion of 'committing' a crime by distinguishing among direct perpetration, indirect perpetration and co-perpetration, does not include any explicit reference to the notion of 'commission by omission'. Nevertheless, the case law of the *Ad hoc* Tribunals has repeatedly stated that 'committing by omission' is possible.[48]

In this regard, the ICTY Appeal Judgment in the *Tadic* case has stated in relation to article 7(1) ICTYS:

> This provision covers first and foremost the physical perpetration of a crime by the offender himself, or the culpable omission of an act that was mandated by a rule of criminal law. However, the commission of one of the crimes envisaged in Articles 2, 3, 4 or 5 of the Statute might also occur through participation in the realisation of a common design or purpose.[49]

In light of the above-mentioned, the author considers that this notion is particularly well suited for reflecting the criminal liability of senior political and military leaders as principals to the crimes provided for in the RS, ICTYS and ICTRS because: (i) they are under a legal obligation to prevent their commission

---

[48] As Van Sliedregt (Above n 24), at 54, has stated, 'the judges of the *Ad hoc* Tribunals have held that most of the offences listed in the Statutes can be committed by both, actions and omissions'. For instance, in *Prosecutor v Kambanda* (Judgment) ICTR-97-23-S (4 Sep 1998) para 40 [hereinafter *Kambanda Case* Trial Judgment], the ICTR Trial Chamber held that all acts of genocide could be committed by omission. This position has been also taken by WA Schabas, *Genocide in International Law* (Cambridge, Cambridge University Press, 2001) 156 [hereinafter Schabas *Genocide*]. Likewise, the ICTY Trial Judgments in *Prosecutor v Delalic et al* (Judgment) ICTY-96-21-T (16 Nov 1998) paras 424, 494, 511 [hereinafter *Celebici Case* Trial Judgment], *Kordic Case* Trial Judgment (Above n 31), at para 236 and *Prosecutor v Blaskic* (Judgment) ICTY-95-14-T (3 Mar 2000) paras 154, 186 [hereinafter *Blaskic Case* Trial Judgment] have equated actions with omissions for the purpose of the commission of the war crimes of murder, torture, wilfully causing great suffering, inhuman treatment and cruel treatment. The *Prosecutor v Oric* (Appeals Chamber Judgment) ICTY-03-68-A (3 July 2008) para 41 [hereinafter *Oric Case* Appeals Judgment] and the Blaskic Appeals Judgment (Above n 664) have also held that 'committing by omission' is possible under article 7 (1) ICTYS.

[49] *Tadic Case* Appeals Judgment (Above n 7), para 188. Likewise, *Prosecutor v Simic* (Judgment) ICTY-95-9-T (17 Oct 2003) para 137 [hereinafter *Simic Case* Trial Judgment] held: 'The meaning to be attached to "committed", the highest degree of participation in a crime, is not controversial. Any finding of commission requires the personal or physical, direct or indirect, participation of the accused in the relevant criminal act, or a finding that the accused engendered a culpable omission to the same effect, where it is established that he had a duty to act, with the requisite knowledge'.

It is important to highlight that the language used by the ICTY case law to refer to the notion of 'commission by omission' varies considerably. For instance, the *Stakic Case* Trial Judgment (Above n 19), at para 439, and *Galic Case* Trial Judgment (Above n 35), at para 179, refer to it as a failure of a 'duty to act', whereas the ICTY Trial Judgments in *Prosecutor v Kunarac* (Judgment) ICTY-96-23-T and ICTY-96-23/1-T (22 Feb 2001) para 390 [hereinafter *Kunarac Case* Trial Judgment], *Prosecutor v Kvocka et al* (Trial Judgment) ICTY-98-30/1-T (2 Nov 2001) paras 243 [hereinafter *Kvocka Case* Trial Judgment], *Prosecutor v Vasiljevic* (Judgment) ICTY-98-32-T (29 Nov 2002) para 62, *Prosecutor v Krstic* (Trial Judgment) ICTY-98-33-T (2 Aug 2001) para 601 [hereinafter *Krstic Case* Trial Judgment] use the following expressions respectively: 'culpable omission in violation of a rule of criminal law', 'culpable omission in violation of criminal law', 'personally omitted to something in violation of international humanitarian law' and 'culpable omission in violation of criminal law'.

by their subordinates, and (ii) they usually have available to them those measures that can prevent their commission by their subordinates.[50]

Furthermore, although, as the *Oric* and *Blaskic Cases* Appeals Judgments have recently acknowledged at paragraphs 43 and 47, the ICC, the ICTY and the ICTR have not developed in detail the elements of the notion of 'commission by omission', in order to hold a senior political or military leader criminally liable as a principal to a crime as a result of having committed it by omission, it will be necessary that (i) he breaches his duty to act by failing to carry out an expected action that was available to him and that would have likely prevented the criminal result (the *Oric* and *Blaskic Cases* Appeals Judgment at paragraphs 41 and 664 require an 'elevated degree of concrete influence'); (ii) he has the subjective elements required by the crime in question, including any ulterior intent or *dolus specialis*; and (iii) he is aware of the factual circumstances on which his duty to act is based (for instance his position of authority).

Finally, before concluding this section it is important to highlight that the ICTY Appeals Chamber has also repeatedly affirmed that the omissions of senior political and military leaders may also entail their criminal responsibility as principals to the crimes (co-perpetrators) when this is the manner in which they participate in a joint criminal enterprise or common criminal purpose.[51]

B Distinguishing Cases of Commission by Omission from Other Cases of Punishable Omissions

According to the ICRC Commentary to Additional Protocol I,[52] cases of omission that give rise to principal liability of senior political and military leaders pursuant to the notions of 'commission by omission' and co-perpetration—they are part of

---

[50] See also G Werle, *Tratado de Derecho Penal Internacional* (Valencia, Tirant lo Blanch, 2005) 283–4 [hereinafter Werle]. In this regard, Duttwiler (Above n 43), at 60–61, has argued that the ICC is in a position to apply the notion of commission by omission because there is a general principle of law equating the human conduct of omission with action whenever a legal duty to act exists. And this, despite acknowledging that treaty law contains only provisions of a very limited scope on omissions, that there is no general provision on 'commission by omission' in the RS and that no customary rule on commission by omission exists due to the lack of *opinion iuris*.

[51] *Tadic Case* Appeals Judgment (Above n 7), at para 192; *Prosecutor v Krnojelac* (Appeals Chamber Judgment) ICTY-97-25-A (17 Sep 2003) para 81 [hereinafter *Krnojelac Case* Appeals Judgment]; *Kvocka Case* Appeals Judgment (Above n 32), at para 112; *Simic Case* Trial Judgment (above n 49), at para 137; See also V Haan, 'The Development of the Concept of Joint Criminal Enterprise at the International Criminal Tribunal for the Former Yugoslavia' (2005) 5 *International Criminal Law Review* 137.

[52] According to the ICRC, one has to distinguish between cases of superiors' principal liability for the commission of crimes by omission, superiors' accessorial liability for participation in the commission of crimes by third persons, and superior's responsibility under the art 28 RS, art 7(3) ICTYS and art 6(3) ICTRS for the deliberate or negligent breach of their duties to supervise and discipline their subordinates. See Y Sandoz, C Swinarski, and B Zimmermann (eds), *ICRC Commentary on the Additional Protocols of 8 June 1977* (Geneva, Martinus Nijhoff Publishers, 1987) 1011 [hereinafter Sandoz, Swinarski and Zimmermann].

the broader notion of 'committing' under articles 25(3)(a) RS, 7(1) ICTYS and 6(1) ICTRS)—must be distinguished from:

(i)   cases of omission that give rise to accessorial liability for participation in the commission of a crime by a third person—they are not part of the notion of 'committing', but they fall within the scope of application of other modes of liability provided for in articles 25(3)(b) to (d) RS, 7(1) ICTYS and 6(1) ICTRS;

(ii) cases of omission that give rise to criminal responsibility pursuant to the notion of 'superior responsibility' provided for in articles 28 RS, 7(3) ICTYS and 6(3) ICTRS.

i Accessorial Liability of Senior Political and Military Leaders for their Participation by Omission in Crimes Committed by Third Persons

When the omissions of senior political and military leaders do not give rise to principal liability for international crimes, they can still give rise to accessorial liability pursuant to articles 25(3)(b) to (d) RS, 7(1) ICTYS and 6(1) ICTRS. In this regard, the ICTY Appeals Chamber has recently emphasised in the *Oric* case that:

> The Appeals Chamber recalls that omission proper may lead to individual criminal responsibility under Article 7 (1) of the Statute where there is a legal duty to act. The Appeals Chamber has never set out the requirements for a conviction for omission in detail. However, at a minimum, the offender's conduct would have to meet the basic elements of aiding and abetting. Thus his omission must be directed to assist, encourage or lend moral support to the perpetration of a crime and have a substantial effect upon the perpetration of the crime (*actus reus*). The aider and abettor must know that his omission assists in the commission of the crime of the principal perpetrator and must be aware of the essential elements of the crime which was ultimately committed by the principal.[53]

---

[53]   *Oric Case* Appeals Judgment (Above n 48), at para 43. The possibility of aiding and abetting by mere presence of a person of authority at the scene of the crime has also been highlighted in *Prosecutor v Kayishema* (Appeals Chamber Judgment) ICTR-95-1-A (1 Jun 2001) para 201; *Blaskic Case* Appeals Judgment (Above n 32), at para 47; *Prosecutor v Mpambara* (Judgment) ICTR-01-65-T (11 Sep 2006) para 22; *Prosecutor v Bisengimana* (Judgment) ICTR-00-60-T (13 Apr 2006) para 34; *Prosecutor v Ndindabahizi* (Judgment) ICTR-2001-71-I (15 Jul 2004) para 457; *Prosecutor v Semanza* (Judgment) ICTR-97-20-T (15 May 2003) para 386 [hereinafter *Semanza Case* Trial Judgment]; *Limaj Case* Trial Judgment (Above n 32), at para 517; *Blaskic Case* Trial Judgment (Above n 48), at para 284; *Prosecutor v Krnojelac* (Judgment) ICTY-97-25-T (15 Mar 2002) para 89 [hereinafter *Krnojelac Case* Trial Judgment]; *Oric Case* Trial Judgment (Above n 32), at para 281. Moreover, the *Blaskic Case* Appeals Judgment (Above n 32), at para 47, has left open the possibility of aiding and abetting by omission in other scenarios. See also *Prosecutor v Akayesu* (Judgment) ICTR-96-4-T (2 Sep 1998) para 548 [hereinafter *Akayesu Case* Trial Judgment]; *Blaskic Case* Trial Judgment (Above n 48), at para 284.

Although those cases of aiding and abetting by omission are the most common manifestation of this phenomenon, the case law of the *Ad hoc* Tribunals also admits cases of instigation by omission.[54]

Repeated failures to prevent subordinates from committing crimes or to punish subordinates for the commission of crimes may attach criminal liability to senior political and military leaders for instigating or aiding and abetting future crimes by their subordinates. In this regard, the ICTY Appeals Chamber has recently stressed that:

[A] superior's failure to punish a crime of which he has actual knowledge is likely to be understood by his subordinates at least as acceptance, if not encouragement, of such conduct with the effect of increasing the risk of new crimes being committed.[55]

Likewise, the mere presence of a senior political or military leader at the scene of the crime without preventing its commission may have an encouraging or approving effect on the physical perpetrators that, depending on the circumstances, may also amount to instigating or aiding and abetting.[56]

The distinction between instigation by omission and aiding and abetting by omission in these types of situations has been explained as follows:

Second, with regard to 'instigation', which shares common features with 'aiding and abetting' particularly in cases of encouragement, a line may be drawn along the strength of inducement and the motivation of the principal perpetrator. Indeed, as long as the principal perpetrator is not finally determined to commit the crime, any acts of demanding, convincing, encouraging or morally assuring him to commit the crime may constitute instigation, and even qualify as ordering if a superior-subordinate relationship exists. As soon as the principal perpetrator is already prepared to commit the crime, but may still need or appreciate some moral support to pursue it or some assistance in performing the crime, any contributions making the planning, preparation or execution of the crime possible or at least easier may constitute aiding and abetting.[57]

---

[54] *Prosecutor v Kamuhanda* (Judgment) ICTR-95-54A-T (22 Jan 2004) para 593 [hereinafter *Kamuhanda Case* Trial Judgment]; *Prosecutor v Kajelijeli* (Judgment) ICTR-98-44A-T (1 Dec 2003) para 762 [hereinafter *Kajelijeli Case* Trial Judgment]; *Blaskic Case* Trial Judgment (Above n 48), at paras 270, 280; *Kordic Case* Trial Judgment (Above n 31), at para 387; *Prosecutor v Mladen Naletilic and Vinko Martinovic* (Judgment) ICTY-98-34-T (31 Mar 2003) para 60 [hereinafter Tuta and Stela Trial Judgment]; *Brdanin Case* Trial Judgment (Above n 35), at para 269; *Limaj Case* Trial Judgment (Above n 32), at para 514; *Oric Case* Trial Judgment (Above n 32), at para 273.

[55] *Prosecutor v Hadzihasanovic and Kubura* (Appeals Chamber Judgment) ICTY-01-47-A (22 Apr 2008) para 30 [hereinafter *Hadzihasanovic Case* Appeals Judgment]. According to the *Blaskic Case* Trial Judgment (Above n 48), at paras 337–9, 'the failure to punish past crimes, which entails the commander's responsibility under Article 7(3), may, pursuant to Article 7(1) and subject to the fulfilment of the respective *mens rea* and *actus reus* requirements, also be the basis for his liability for either aiding and abetting or instigating the commission of further crimes'. See also A Reggio, 'Aiding and Abetting in International Criminal Law: The Responsibility of Corporate Agents and Business for "Trading with the Enemy" of Mankind' (2005) 5 *International Criminal Law Review* 639.

[56] *Oric Case* Trial Judgment (Above n 32), at para 281.

[57] *Oric Case* Trial Judgment (Above n 32), at para 281.

The ICTY Trial Judgment in the *Galic* case has also endorsed the possibility of being criminally liable for ordering by omission.[58] However, the ICTY Appeals Chamber rejected it because instructing a physical perpetrator to commit a crime always requires a positive action.[59] As it has explained:

> The Appeals Chamber finds that the very notion of 'instructing' requires a positive action by the person in a position of authority. The failure to act of a person in a position of authority, who is a in a superior-subordinate relationship, may give rise to another mode of responsibility under Article 7(1) of the Statute or superior responsibility under Article 7(3) of the Statute. However, the Appeals Chamber cannot conceive of a situation in which an order would be given by an omission, in the absence of a prior positive act. The Appeals Chamber concludes that the omission of an act cannot equate to the mode of liability of ordering under Art 7(1) of the Statute.[60]

The ICTY Appeals Chamber has also highlighted that the fact that it is not possible to incur criminal liability for ordering by omission does not mean that a senior political or military leader cannot incur criminal liability for ordering an omission. In this regard, the ICTY Appeals Chamber has pointed out that a person incurs criminal liability if he:

> [O]rders an act or omission with the awareness of the substantial likelihood that a crime will be committed in the execution of that order.[61]

Furthermore, the fact that 'ordering' requires a positive action does not mean that it cannot be proven by taking into account the omissions of the defendant. Quite the contrary, criminal liability for ordering:

> [C]an be proven, like any other mode of liability, by circumstantial or direct evidence, taking into account evidence of acts or omissions of the accused.[62]

In this regard, the lack of any action by a superior who is at the scene of the crime while the crime is being committed, or immediately afterwards, may be a relevant factor to infer that the superior ordered the commission of such crime –otherwise, if his approving presence is a clear and contributing factor to, or has a substantial effect in, the commission of the crime, he could be held liable for instigating or aiding and abetting.

Moreover, in those cases in which an unlawful order is handed down through the chain of command, those intermediate superiors who, in spite of not endorsing the order, take no action to oppose it, can be considered to have silently consented to the order. In these cases, if the silent approval of the intermediate

---

[58] *Galic Case* Trial Judgment (Above n 35), at paras 169–170.

[59] *Blaskic Case* Appeals Judgment (Above n 32), at para 660; *Galic Case* Appeals Judgment (Above n 37), at para 176.

[60] *Galic Case* Appeals Judgment (*Ibid*), at para 176.

[61] *Blaskic Case* Appeals Judgment (Above n 32), at para 42; *Kordic Case* Appeals Judgment (Above n 32), at para 30; *Galic Case* Appeals Judgment (*Ibid*), at para 176.

[62] *Galic Case* Appeals Judgment (*Ibid*), at para 176.

superiors resulting from their inaction substantially facilitates the implementation of the unlawful order because it is a sign, if not of encouragement, at least of official tolerance of the crimes, they could be held liable for aiding and abetting.[63]

ii Superior Responsibility for Failures to Prevent or Punish Crimes Committed by Subordinates

Articles 28 RS, 7(3) ICTYS and 6(3) ICTRS describe those omissions of senior political and military leaders that give rise to criminal liability pursuant to the notion of superior responsibility: failures to take all necessary and reasonable measures within their power to prevent or punish the commission by subordinates of genocide, crimes against humanity and war crimes. As the ICTY Appeals Chamber has recently held in the *Oric* case:

> For a superior to incur in responsibility under Article 7 (3), in addition to establishing beyond reasonable doubt that his subordinate is criminally responsible, the following elements must be established beyond reasonable doubt: (i) the existence of a superior-subordinate relationship; (b) that the superior knew or had reason to know that his subordinate was about to commit a crime or had done so; and (iii) that the superior failed to take the necessary and reasonable measures to prevent his subordinate's criminal conduct or punish his subordinate.[64]

The notion of superior responsibility is rooted in the idea that:

> By virtue of the authority vested in them, commanders are qualified to exercise control over troops and the weapons they use; more than anyone else, they can prevent breaches by creating the appropriate frame of mind, ensuring the rational use of the means of combat, and by maintaining discipline.[65]

---

[63] *Akayesu Case* Trial Judgment (Above n 53), at paras 693–4. In this regard, the duty of every intermediate military superior to oppose unlawful orders is particularly relevant. Concerning this duty, the second requisite of the defence of 'superior orders' provided for in art 33 RS requires that the physical perpetrators do not know that the order is unlawful. As a consequence, from the moment the physical perpetrators discover the unlawfulness of the order, they cannot execute it without being criminally liable. This leads to the conclusion that the RS imposes a duty on every subordinate (including intermediate superiors receiving orders from senior military leaders) to disobey any order requiring him to carry out a war crime provided for in the RS. The same view is held by Rodriguez-Villasante y Prieto (Above n 24), at 437. See also *United States v Wilhelm von Leeb* (1948) in Trial of the Major War Criminals before the International Military Tribunal under Control Council Law No 10, Vol XI (US Government Printing Office, 1951) 513.

[64] *Oric Case* Appeals Judgment (Above n 48), at para 18. Some writers see responsibility for superiors' omissions ('passive superior responsibility') and responsibility for superiors' orders ('active superior responsibility') as different sides of the same coin. See LC Green, 'Superior Orders and Command Responsibility' (1989) 27 *Canadian Yearbook of International Law* 167; WG Eckhardt, 'Command Criminal Responsibility: A Plea for a Workable Standard' (1982) 97 *Military Law Review* 4–5 [hereinafter Eckhardt].

[65] *Prosecutor v Hadzihasanovic* (Judgment) ICTY-01-47-T (15 Mar 2006) para 66 [hereinafter *Hadzihasanovic Case* Trial Judgment]. See also *Prosecutor v Hadzihasanovic* (Decision on Interlocutory Appeal Challenging Jurisdiction in Relation to Command Responsibility) ICTY-01-47-AR72 (23 Jul 2003) paras 22–3 [hereinafter *Hadzihasanovic Case* Decision on Jurisdiction]; *Prosecutor v Halilovic* (Judgment) ICTY-01-48-T (16 Nov 2005) para 85 [hereinafter *Halilovic Case* Trial Judgment].

All political and military superiors, at all levels (from the commander-in-chief to the soldier who takes over as platoon commander), have the legal obligation to prevent and punish the commission by subordinates of crimes within the jurisdiction of the ICC, the ICTY and ICTR.[66] As a result, criminal responsibility for failures to prevent or punish is not limited to the immediate superior of the physical perpetrators. In fact, criminal responsibility can be attributed to several superiors, following the chain of command up to its highest echelons.

Furthermore, according to the latest case law of the Appeals Chambers of the *Ad hoc* Tribunals, which has not been endorsed yet by the ICC:

> [S]uperior responsibility encompasses criminal conduct by subordinates under all modes of participation under Article 7(1) of the Statute. It follows that a superior can be held criminally responsible for his subordinates' planning, instigating, ordering, committing or otherwise aiding and abetting a crime.[67]

The duty to prevent and the duty to punish are two distinct legal obligations. The duty to prevent arises prior to the commission of offences by subordinates and can only be complied with before the completion of the crimes.[68] The so-called 'duty to suppress', which arises when an offence is in the process of being committed, is also part of the duty to prevent because it aims at preventing further offences.[69] The duty to punish only arises after the completion of the offences and it also includes the duty to report the crimes to the competent investigating and/or prosecuting authorities.[70] Breaches of the duty to prevent cannot be 'compensated' by subsequently punishing those subordinates who physically committed the crimes.[71]

---

[66] For the general requirements of the notion of superior responsibility, see Cassese, *International Criminal Law* (Above n 1), at 208–209 and Ambos, *La Parte General del Derecho Penal Internacional* (Above n 2), at 333–4.

[67] *Oric Case* Appeals Judgment (Above n 48), at para 21. See also *Prosecutor v Blagojevic* (Appeals Chamber Judgment) ICTY-02-60-A (9 May 2007) para 280, 282 [hereinafter *Blagojevic Case* Appeals Judgment]; *Prosecutor v Nahimana et al.* (Appeals Chamber Judgment) ICTR-99-52-A (28 Nov 2007) paras 485–6 [hereinafter *Nahimana Case* Appeals Judgment].

[68] *Strugar Case* Trial Judgment (Above n 32), at para 373; *Hadzihasanovic Case* Trial Judgment (Above n 65), at para 125.

[69] *Kajelijeli Case* Trial Judgment (Above n 54), at para 740; *Halilovic Case* Trial Judgment (Above n 65), at para 87; *Hadzihasanovic Case* Trial Judgment (Above n 65), at para 127. In the Kajelijeli case, the Trial Chamber found that the defendant 'failed to prevent or stop the killings of early to mid April 1994 in Mukingo, Nkli and Kigombe communes', whereas in the *Strugar Case* Trial Judgment (Above n 32), at para 373, the Trial Chamber found that the defendant 'did not take necessary and reasonable measures to ensure at least that the unlawful shelling of the Old Town be stopped'.

[70] *Strugar Case* Trial Judgment (*Ibid*); *Hadzihasanovic Case* Trial Judgment (*Ibid*), at para 125.

[71] *Prosecutor v Kayishema* (Judgment) ICTR-95-1-T (21 May 1999) para 315 [hereinafter *Kayishema Case* Trial Judgment]; *Blaskic Case* Trial Judgment (Above n 48), at para 515; *Hadzihasanovic Case* Trial Judgment (Above n 65), at para 126. See also S Boelaert-Suominen, 'Prosecuting Superiors for Crimes Committed by Subordinates: A Discussion of the First Significant Case Law' (2001) 41 *Virginia Journal of International Law* 783, 785 [hereinafter Boelaert-Suominen].

a Superior-Subordinate Relationship

Senior political and military leaders are only criminally liable under articles 28 RS, 7(3) ICTYS and 6(3) ICTRS if there is a superior-subordinate relationship between them and the physical perpetrators of the crimes. In other words, the relevant senior political or military leader must be, 'by virtue of his position in the formal or informal hierarchy', a superior to the physical perpetrators of the crimes.[72] If the physical perpetrators cannot be identified, it is sufficient to specify to which group the perpetrators belonged at the time he committed the crimes and to show the existence of a superior-subordinate relationship vis-à-vis that group.[73]

Only those senior political and military leaders who are superiors of the physical perpetrators at the time in which the crimes are committed can be held liable pursuant to the notion of 'superior responsibility'. No criminal liability arises under this notion for those who become superiors of the physical perpetrators after the commission of the crimes and decide not to take the measures within their power to punish their new subordinates for previous crimes.[74] Nevertheless, whenever possible, these cases will be treated as cases of assistance to the concealment of the crimes (aiding and abetting), or as cases of failure to prevent, or even instigating, the commission of future similar crimes by subordinates.[75]

For instance, suppose that Military Unit X is well known for resorting to armed violence against enemy civilians who do not take active part in the hostilities in order to secure control of recently seized areas. General Y, former superior of Military Unit X, never opened an inquiry about war crimes allegedly committed by members of Military Unit X after the successful execution of assault operations on enemy towns and villages. Due to its military achievements, General Y was promoted to the post of Deputy Chief of Staff of the Army and General Z was appointed to replace him as military superior of Military Unit X. After taking office, General Z soon learns about the allegations made by different sources concerning war crimes allegedly committed in the past by members of Military Unit X that have gone unpunished to date. Due to the fact that those crimes were mostly committed when General Y was in charge of Military Unit X, and considering that General Y has been promoted to the position of Deputy Chief of Staff of the Army, General Z decides not to open an inquiry into such allegations nor to report them to the competent authorities in order to avoid problems with General Y.

---

[72] *Celebici Case* Appeals Judgment (Above n 1), at para 303.

[73] *Blaskic Case* Appeals Judgment (Above n 32), at para 217; *Prosecutor v Krnojelac* (Decision on Form of Second Amended Indictment) ICTY-97-25 (11 May 2000) para 46; *Hadzihasanovic Case* Trial Judgment (Above n 65), at para 90; *Oric Case* Appeals Judgment (Above n 48), at para 35.

[74] See art 28(a)(i) and (b)(i) RS See also *Hadzihasanovic Case* Decision on Jurisdiction (Above n 65), at para 51; *Hadzihasanovic Case* Trial Judgment (Above n 65), at para 76.

[75] See Ch 3, s II.B.i.

A few weeks afterwards, General Z orders an assault on town A, which is a military target because it oversees the only road linking both sides of the main valley of the region where Military Unit X is deployed and is defended by some 200 enemy combatants. In spite of being aware of the allegations against Military Unit X, and despite the fact that town A is populated by around 1,000 enemy civilians who do not take active part in the hostilities, General Z decides to entrust the assault on town A to Military Unit X. The assault on town A is performed by Military Unit X with the same degree of success as previous assault operations, and the town falls into the hands of Military Unit X in a few hours. Nevertheless, after the seizure of the town, Military Unit X resorts once again to armed violence against enemy civilians who do not take active part in the hostilities in order to secure the control of the town. As a result, in a few days, new allegations of war crimes allegedly committed by Military Unit X (this time under the command of General Z) are spread over by a number of different sources.

In light of these facts, General Z could not be held liable pursuant to the notion of superior responsibility for failing to punish members of Military Unit X for crimes allegedly committed by them before he was appointed commander of the unit. Nevertheless, insofar as, according to the case law of the Ad hoc Tribunals, aiding and abetting can arise from assistance provided for before, during or after the commission of the crimes,[76] General Z's decision not to open an inquiry nor to report the crimes once he learnt about them could be considered as a way to provide assistance to the physical perpetrators. The case law of the Ad hoc Tribunals has also held that accessorial liability for aiding and abetting only arises if the assistance reaches the level of a substantial contribution to the commission of the crimes.[77] However, as the commission of the crimes had already been completed by the time General Z learnt about them, General Z's decision not to open an inquiry nor to report the crimes aimed primarily to ensuring impunity for the physical perpetrators (in this particular case, the aim of General Z is not to secure the enjoyment of the proceeds of the crime by members of Military Unit X). As a result, if one follows the case law of the Ad hoc Tribunals, General 2 could only be held liable for aiding and abetting as long as his decision not to open an inquiry

---

[76] *Prosecutor v Ntagerura* (Appeals Chamber Judgment) ICTR-99-46-A (7 Jul 2006) para 372 [hereinafter *Ntagerura Case* Appeals Judgment]; *Blaskic Case* Appeals Judgment (Above n 32), at para 48; *Prosecutor v Simic* (Appeals Chamber Judgment) ICTY-95-9-A (28 Nov 2006) para 85 [hereinafter *Simic Case* Appeals Judgment]; *Blagojevic Case* Appeals Judgment (above n 67) at para 172. See also Ch 4, s VII.A.

[77] *Ntagerura Case* Appeals Judgment (*Ibid*), at para 370; *Blaskic Case* Appeals Judgment (*Ibid*), at paras 45–6; *Prosecutor v Vasiljevic* (Appeals Chamber Judgment) ICTY-98-32-A (25 Feb 2004) para 102 [hereinafter *Vasiljevic Case* Appeals Judgment]; *Simic Case* Appeals Judgment (*Ibid*), at para 85; *Blagojevic Case* Appeals Judgment (*Ibid*), at para 127; *Prosecutor v Bagilishema* (Judgment) ICTR-95-01A-T (7 Jun 2001) para 33 [hereinafter *Bagilishema Case* Trial Judgment]; *Kajelijeli Case* Trial Judgment (Above n 54), at para 766; *Kamuhanda Case* Trial Judgment (Above n 54), at para 597; *Prosecutor v Furundzija* (Judgment) ICTY-95-17/1-T (10 Dec 1998) para 249; *Prosecutor v Aleksovski* (Judgment) ICTY-95-14/1-T (25 Jun 1999) para 61 [hereinafter *Aleksovski Case* Trial Judgment]; *Kunarac Case* Trial Judgment (Above n 49), at para 391; *Krnojelac Case* Trial Judgment (Above n 53), at para 88; *Oric Case* Trial Judgment (Above n 32), at para 282. See also Ch 4, s VII.A.

nor to report the crimes had a substantial effect in securing the impunity of members of Military Unit X.[78]

Furthermore, opening an inquiry into these crimes or reporting them to the competent authorities for their investigation could be considered a necessary and reasonable measure within the power of General Z to prevent the repetition of these crimes by members of Military Unit X in the assault on town A. As a result, General Z could be held liable pursuant to the notion of superior responsibility for failing to prevent the crimes committed by his new subordinates in the assault on town A.

General Z could also be held liable for instigating the crimes committed by his new subordinates from Military Unit X if, by failing to open an inquiry or to report them to the competent authorities, he prompted them to commit crimes in the assault on town A.[79] In this last scenario, it will be necessary that General Z's omission amounts to a substantially contributing factor in the commission of the crimes.[80] In the view of the author, this would particularly be the case if General Z addresses Military Unit X before launching the assault operation against town A in the following manner:

(i)   First, he emphasises the important military achievements obtained by Military Unit X under the command of General Y;
(ii) Second, he highlights the great admiration in the army for the manner in which Military Unit X has conducted its assault operations and has secured the control of seized areas in the past;
(iii) Third, he expresses his belief that in this new stage of Military Unit X under his command, which starts with the assault on town A, all members of the unit will fulfil their tasks with the same patriotism and courage shown in the past.

---

[78] *Ntagerura Case* Appeals Judgment (*Ibid*), at para 372; *Blaskic Case* Appeals Judgment (*Ibid*), at para 48; *Simic Case* Appeals Judgment (*Ibid*), at para 85; *Blagojevic Case* Appeals Judgment (*Ibid*), at para 127. According to Fletcher (Above n 6), at 645: 'Having knowledge of the illegal purposes of the action, and of the crimes which accompanied it, [the accused's] active participation *even in the after-phases* of the Action make him *participes criminis* in the whole affair'. See *United States v Oswald Pohl et al* (1947–48) in United Nations War Crimes Commission, Law Reports of Trial of War Criminals, Vol V, 53. See also Ch 4, s VII.A.

[79] O Triffterer, 'Causality, A Separate Element of the Doctrine of Superior Responsibility as Expressed in Article 28 Rome Statute?' (2002) 15 *Leiden Journal of International Law* 187 [hereinafter Triffterer, *Causality*] highlights that superiors' failures to punish may have an encouraging effect upon subordinates for the commission of future crimes.

[80] *Kordic Case* Appeals Judgment (Above n 32), at para 27; *Blaskic Case* Trial Judgment (Above n 48), at para 278; *Kvocka Case* Trial Judgment (Above n 49), at para 252; Tuta and Stela Trial Judgment (Above n 54), at para 60; *Limaj Case* Trial Judgment (Above n 32), at para 514; *Oric Case* Trial Judgment (Above n 32), at para 274; *Bagilishema Case* Trial Judgment (Above n 77), at para 30; *Kamuhanda Case* Trial Judgment (Above n 54), at para 590. See also Ch 3, s III.D.ii.

Regardless of the specific term used to describe a superior-subordinate relationship—be it 'command', be it 'authority'—[81] senior political and military leaders must have 'effective control' over the physical perpetrators of the crime in order to be liable under the notion of superior responsibility. Furthermore, as the *Oric Case* Appeals Judgment has emphasised:

> Whether the effective control descends from the superior to the subordinate culpable of the crime though intermediary subordinates is immaterial as a matter of law; instead what matters is whether the superior has the material ability to prevent or punish the criminally responsible subordinate. The separate question of whether—due to proximity or remoteness of control—the superior indeed possessed effective control is a matter of evidence, not of substantive law.[82]

Whenever senior political and military leaders exercise powers of influence, as opposed to effective control, over the physical perpetrators of the crimes, they are not criminally liable pursuant to this notion. In this regard, as the ICTY Appeals Chamber has highlighted in the *Oric* case:

> It is well established that the Prosecution must prove effective control beyond reasonable doubt in establishing a superior-subordinate relationship within the meaning of Article 7(3) of the Statute. For that purpose, *de jure* authority is not synomous with effective control. Whereas the possession of *de jure* powers may certainly suggest a material ability to prevent or punish criminal acts of subordinates, it may be neither necessary nor sufficient to prove such ability. If *de jure* power always results in a presumption of effective control, then the Prosecution would be exempted from its burden to prove effective

---

[81] Art 28(a) RS refers to 'forces under his or her effective command and control, or effective authority and control'. Moreover, it is important to highlight that art 28(b)(ii) RS adds an additional clause in relation to non-military superiors, according to which the crimes committed by their subordinates must concern 'activities that were within the effective responsibility and control of the superior'. For Van Sliedregt (Above n 24), at 185, this clause only states the differences between the control exercised by military superiors and non-military superiors. However, GR Vetter, 'Command Responsibility of Non-Military Superiors in the ICC' (2000) 25 *Yale Journal of International Law* 89–144 [hereinafter Vetter] disagrees because, although the content of the clause provided for in art 28(b)(ii) RS is not clear, it cannot just be a mere statement of the difference between civilian control and military control. Concerning this difference, K Ambos, 'Superior Responsibility' in A Cassese, P Gaeta, and JRWD Jones (eds), *The Rome Statute of the International Criminal Court: A Commentary* (Oxford, Oxford University Press, 2002) 857 [hereinafter Ambos, *Superior Responsibility*] has highlighted that in a non-military context, control is more limited because military superiors act within a structure of hierarchy and a system of obedience. Y Kang and T Wu, 'Criminal Liability for the Actions of Subordinates: The Doctrine of Command Responsibility and its Analogues in United States Law' (1997) 38 *Harvard International Law Journal* 295, explains that the differences between a military and a non-military superior stem from the fact that the former can order his subordinates to take certain activities which put their lives at great risk. For instance, in a military context, there exists a specific disciplinary system and military code, and, during military operations, superiors have control over the activities of their subordinates 24 hours a day.

[82] *Oric Case* Appeals Judgment (Above n 68), para 20. On the effective control test, see also *Celebici Case* Appeals Judgment (Above n 1), at paras 197, 256; *Blaskic Case* Appeals Judgment (Above n 32), at para 67; *Halilovic Case* Trial Judgment (Above n 65), at para 58; *Hadzihasanovic Case* Trial Judgment (Above n 65), at para 76; *Semanza Case* Trial Judgment (Above n 53), at para 402; *Prosecutor v Ntagerura* (Judgment) ICTR-99-46-T (25 Feb 2004) para 628 [hereinafter *Ntagerura Case* Trial Judgment]. The formal appointment to a position of authority (*de iure* position) is neither required nor sufficient to entail superior responsibility.

control beyond reasonable doubt. The Appeals Chamber is therefore unable to agree with the Prosecution's proposed legal presumption [] The Appeals Chamber acknowledges that its jurisprudence might have suggested otherwise, using the terms "presume" or "*prima facie* evidence of effective control". The import of such language has not always been clear. Although in some common law jurisdiction "*prima facie* evidence" leads to by definition to a burden-shifting presumption, the Appeals Chamber underscores that before the International Tribunal the Prosecution still bears the burden of proving beyond reasonable doubt that the accused had effective control over his subordinates. The possession of *de jure* authority, without more, provides only some evidence of such effective control. Before the International Tribunal there is no such presumption to the detriment of an accused.[83]

Effective control has been defined as the material ability to prevent the commission of crimes by subordinates—which is derived from operational control over subordinates as a result of the capacity to issue orders and to have them implemented—[84] or to punish subordinates for the commission of crimes (which would include the power to open an investigation, to suspend suspects from official functions during the investigation, and to eventually impose sanctions).[85] Nevertheless, according to the ICTY Appeal Judgments in the *Celebici*, *Blaskic* and *Halilovic* cases,[86] partial control of an operational or a disciplinary nature

---

[83] *Oric Case* Appeals Judgment (Above n 48), at paras 90 and 91. *Hadzihasanovic Case* Appeals Judgment (Above n 55), para 21. See also Oric Case Appeals Judgment (Above n 48), at paras 91 and 92; *Prosecutor v Halilovic* (Appeals Chamber Judgment) ICTY-01-48-A (16 Oct 2007) paras 59 and 60 [hereinafter Halilovic Case Appeals Judgment]; *Celebici Case* Appeals Judgment (*Ibid*), at para 266; *Kordic Case* Appeals Judgment (Above n 32), at paras 842, 849.

[84] See WH Parks, 'Command Responsibility for War Crimes' (1973) 62 *Military Law Review* 84 in reference to *Yamashita v Styer*, 327 US 1, 15 (1946).

[85] *Celebici Case* Appeals Judgment (Above n 1), at para 198; *Blaskic Case* Appeals Judgment (Above n 32), at para 67–9; *Semanza Case* Trial Judgment (Above n 53), at para 203; *Prosecutor v Ntakirutimana* (Judgment) ICTR-96-10 (21 Feb 2003) para 819. The degree of control required for a finding of the existence of a superior-subordinate relationship is similar in cases of military superiors and in cases of non-military superiors. Nevertheless, the hierarchical structure of the organisations through which non-military superiors operate does not need to mirror that of military organisations. See *Kayishema Case* Trial Judgment (Above n 71), at para 217, in relation to a *prefect*, *Kambanda Case* Trial Judgment (Above n 48), at para 39, in relation to a *Prime Minister*, *Prosecutor v Musema* (Judgment) ICTR-96-13-A (27 Jan 2000) para 868 in relation to the director of a tea factory, and *Prosecutor v Nahimana* (Judgment) ICTR-99-52-T (3 Dec 2003) para 970 in relation to the director of a radio station. Moreover, art 28(b) RS requires in cases of non-military superiors that the crimes committed by their subordinates be related to 'activities that were within the effective responsibility and control of the superior'. See also WJ Fenrick, 'Article 28. Responsibility of Commanders and Other Superiors' in O Triffterer (ed), *Commentary on the Rome Statute of the International Criminal Court* (Baden-Baden, Nomos, 1999) 520–22 [hereinafter Fenrick]; Ambos, *Superior Responsibility* (Above n 81), at 870–71. According to K Kittichaisaree, *International Criminal Law* (Oxford, Oxford University Press, 2001) 252, in addition to the army, effective control can, in particular, exist within some State organisations (members of the government, majors, police chiefs). See also Boelaert-Suominen (Above n 71), at 748; Vetter (Above n 81), at 95.

[86] As the *Celebici Case* Appeals Judgment (*Ibid*), at para 198, states: 'As long as a superior has effective control over subordinates, to the extent that he can prevent them from committing crimes or punish them after they committed the crimes, he would be held responsible for the commission of the crimes if he failed to exercise such abilities of control'. See also *Blaskic Case* Appeals Judgment (Above n 32), at paras 67–9; *Halilovic Case* Appeals Judgment (Above n 83), para 66. In particular, in the *Halilovic Case* Appeals Judgment (Above n 83), at para 182, the ICTY Appeals Chamber underlined

(such as, the power to report the crimes to the competent authorities, no matter whether they are military or ordinary prosecutors or investigative judges) may suffice.[87]

Other indicators of effective control are, inter alia, the power to give orders and have them executed, the conduct of combat operations involving the forces in question, the authority to apply disciplinary measures, the authority to promote or remove soldiers, and the participation in negotiations regarding the troops in question.[88]

In particular, in relation to the power to give orders as an indicator of effective control, the ICTY Appeals Chamber has underscored in the *Strugar* case:

> The Appeals Chamber recalls that a superior's authority to issue orders does not automatically establish that a superior had effective control over his subordinates, but is one of the indicators to be taken into account when establishing the effective control. As the Appeals Chamber held in Halilovic, in relation to such capacity, "the orders in question will rather have to be carefully assessed in light of the rest of the evidence in order to ascertain the degree of control over the perpetrators". For instance, in Blaskic, the Appeals Chamber found that "the issuing of humanitarian orders does not by itself establish that the Appellant had effective control over the troops that received the orders" [] Indeed, as held by the Appeals Chamber in Blaskic, "the indicators of effective control are more a matter of evidence than of substantive law, and those indicators are limited to showing that the accused had the power to prevent, punish, or initiate measures leading to proceedings against the alleged perpetrators where appropriate". Therefore, whether a given form of authority possessed by a superior amounts to an indicator of effective control depends on the circumstances of the case. For example, with respect to the

that in the case at hand the issue of the defendant's material ability to punish the perpetrators in order to establish his effective control over them was solely based on his alleged capacity to initiate investigations leading to the criminal prosecution of the perpetrators. Moreover, according to the *Halilovic Case* Appeals Judgment, paras 177–9, a conclusion of lack of material ability to punish can not be exclusively derived from the fact that the evidence shows that the defendants did not initiate or take any action to carry forward an investigation.

[87] This interpretation could also find some support in arts 28(a)(ii) and (b)(iii) RS according to which, a superior is responsible for the crimes committed by his subordinates if he did not adopt all necessary and reasonable measures within his power to report the crimes to the competent investigating and/or prosecuting authorities. As a result, the effective control of senior political and military leaders over the physical perpetrators would be based on their material ability to take such reporting measures and they would incur a criminal liability if they failed to take them. Nevertheless, in the author's view, this sets too low of a threshold for a finding of a superior-subordinate relationship, and makes it extremely difficult to distinguish those cases of effective control from those other cases of power to influence the physical perpetrators.

[88] *Celebici Case* Trial Judgment (Above n 48), at para 767; *Kordic Case* Trial Judgment (Above n 31), at para 421; *Strugar Case* Trial Judgment (Above n 32), at paras 404–13; *Hadzihasanovic Case* Trial Judgment (Above n 65), at para 83. The fact that the only measure available to a superior to prevent the commission of the crime is the use of force does not prevent a finding of effective control. See *Hadzihasanovic Case* Trial Judgment, at paras 85–8. Furthermore, if a superior uses combat troops knowing, or having reasons to know, that such troops have previously committed crimes, he may be held liable for the crimes subsequently committed by them even if at the time of the commission of the crimes he does not have the material ability to control them. See *Hadzihasanovic Case* Trial Judgment, at para 89. Finally, in cases of joint action of different units in combat, the cooperation among the different units is not per se sufficient to find that the superior of each unit exercises effective control over all troops involved in combat. See *Hadzihasanovic Case* Trial Judgment, at para 84.

capacity to issue orders, the nature of the orders which the superior has the capacity to issue, the nature of his capacity to do so as well as whether or not his orders are actually followed would be relevant to the assessment of whether a superior had the material ability to prevent or punish.[89]

b Failure to take all Reasonable and Necessary Measures within a Superior's Power

Once a superior-subordinate relationship between a senior political or military leader and the physical perpetrators is shown, article 28(a)(ii) and (b)(iii) RS and the case law of the *Ad hoc* Tribunals establish that the former will only be criminally liable, pursuant to the notion of superior responsibility, if he failed to take all necessary and reasonable measures within his power to: (i) prevent subordinates from committing crimes; or (ii) to punish those subordinates who physically committed the crimes.[90]

A superior is not obliged to perform the impossible, and can only be held liable for failing to take measures within his material ability.[91] Nevertheless, as long as a superior had the material ability to take a given measure and failed to do so, he will be held liable regardless of whether he had the 'formal legal competence' to take it.[92] The determination of which measures were available to a superior is a question of evidence that must be assessed on a case-by-case basis.[93] It requires the examination of national law because national law sets out the duties and powers of civilian and military representatives of the State.[94]

Concerning the duty to prevent, a distinction must be drawn between: (i) general measures to secure the control of the troops, and (ii) those specific measures which aim at preventing subordinates from committing specific crimes that the superior knows they could carry out.[95] Among the former, one can refer to the setting up of a monitoring system, ensuring proper instruction and a rational use of

---

[89] Strugar Case Appeals Judgment (Above n 41), at paras 253–4.

[90] See M Nybondas, 'Civilian Superior Responsibility in the Kordic Case' (2003) 50 *Netherlands International Law Review* 68; JA Williamson, 'Command Responsibility in the Case Law of the International Criminal Tribunal for Rwanda' (2003) 13 *Criminal Law Forum* 380.

[91] ICTY Trial Judgments in *Celebici Case* Trial Judgment (Above n 48), at para 395; *Strugar Case* Trial Judgment (Above n 32), at para 73; *Hadzihasanovic Case* Trial Judgment (Above n 65), at para 122; and *Kayishema Case* Trial Judgment (Above n 71), at para 217.

[92] The *Kamuhanda Case* Trial Judgment (Above n 54), at para 601, puts particular emphasis on the necessity and reasonableness of the measures available to the superior.

[93] *Blaskic Case* Appeals Judgment (Above n 32), at para 72; *Celebici Case* Trial Judgment (Above n 48), at para 394; *Strugar Case* Trial Judgment (Above n 32), at para 73; *Hadzihasanovic Case* Trial Judgment (Above n 65), at para 124.

[94] Sandoz, Swinarski and Zimmermann (Above n 52), at para 3537. For instance, the *Blaskic Case* Appeals Judgment (Above n 32), at para 414, relied on the Regulations concerning the Application of International Law to the Armed Forces of the Socialist Federal Republic of Yugoslavia (SFRY) to establish the superior's duty to report offences to the competent authorities. Likewise, the *Aleksovski Case* Trial Judgment (Above n 77), at paras 91, 136, took into consideration the fact that the law of Bosnia and Herzegovina imposed a civic duty on all its citizens to report any offence to the judicial authorities.

[95] *Halilovic Case* Trial Judgment (Above n 65), at para 81; *Hadzihasanovic Case* Trial Judgment (Above n 65), at para 144. See also Sandoz, Swinarski and Zimmermann (*Ibid*), at paras 3557–60.

the weaponry and ammunition, the maintenance of discipline and the creation of the appropriate frame of mind.[96] Failing to take general measures increases the risk that subordinates may commit offences, but it does not entail criminal responsibility per se, whereas failures to take specific measures give rise to criminal liability.[97] Furthermore, the adoption of general measures does not release a superior from criminal liability,[98] although they will be taken into consideration when assessing the efforts made by a superior to comply with his duty to prevent.[99]

The necessary and reasonable specific measures available to a superior to prevent subordinates from committing crimes must be assessed on a case-by-case basis,[100] and they may include: (i) opening an inquiry whenever there is information indicating that subordinates may be about to commit crimes; (ii) suspending (or excluding from assault operations and reducing to the greatest extent possible exposure to enemy civilians and prisoners of war) those subordinates who are allegedly planning the commission of offences or who have a violent criminal record; (iii) transmitting reports to the competent authorities which warn of the risk that war crimes might be committed in the execution of certain military operations and proposing measures to advert such risks; (iv) reporting allegations of prior commission of war crimes to the competent authorities; and (v) delaying the execution of certain military operations.[101]

According to the ICTR Trial Judgment in the *Bagilishema* case:

> In the case of failure to punish, a superior's responsibility may arise from his or her failure to create or sustain among the persons under his or her control, an environment of discipline and respect for the law.[102]

---

[96] *Celebici Case* Appeals Judgment (Above n 1), at para 226; *Strugar Case* Trial Judgment (Above n 32), at para 420; *Halilovic Case* Trial Judgment (*Ibid*), at paras 85–8; *Hadzihasanovic Case* Trial Judgment (*Ibid*), at paras 146–8. As Sandoz, Swinarski and Zimmermann (*Ibid*), at para 3558, have highlighted, these measures can be taken periodically; they can also be taken before a military operation to draw the attention of subordinates to the type of conduct that should be avoided.

[97] *Celebici Case* Appeals Judgment (*Ibid*), at para 226; *Halilovic Case* Trial Judgment (*Ibid*), at para 88; *Strugar Case* Trial Judgment (*Ibid*), at para 420; *Hadzihasanovic Case* Trial Judgment (*Ibid*), at para 144.

[98] In this regard, the *Strugar Case* Trial Judgment (*Ibid*), at para 375, highlighted that the International Military Tribunal for the Far East held that the issuance of 'routine' orders is not sufficient to discharge a superior's duty and that more active steps must be taken.

[99] *Halilovic Case* Trial Judgment (Above n 65), at para 88; *Hadzihasanovic Case* Trial Judgment (Above n 65), at para 151.

[100] Sandoz, Swinarski and Zimmermann (Above n 52), at para 3561. See also *Hadzihasanovic Case* Appeals Judgment (Above n 55), at para. 33; *Bagilishema Case* Trial Judgment (Above n 77), at para 48; *Strugar Case* Trial Judgment (Above n 32), at para 375.

[101] *Blaskic Case* Trial Judgment (Above n 48), at para 285; *Stakic Case* Trial Judgment (Above n 19), at para 461; *Halilovic Case* Trial Judgment (Above n 65), at para 89. Moreover, the *Strugar Case* Trial Judgment (*Ibid*), at para 374, found that post WW II case law took into account the superiors' failures to (i) secure reports that military actions have been carried out in accordance with international law; (ii) issue orders aimed at bringing the relevant practices into accord with the rules of war; (iii) protest against or criticise criminal action; and (iv) insist before a superior authority that immediate action be taken.

[102] *Bagilishema Case* Trial Judgment (Above n 77), at para 50.

However, a superior is not responsible for failing to punish crimes committed by his new subordinates before he assumes command over them.[103]

Whenever a superior does not have the power to sanction himself, he has, at least, the obligation to start an investigation to establish the facts and to report them to the competent authorities.[104] In other words, if a superior does not have the power of punishment, he must at least take an important step in the disciplinary process.[105] Hence, the fact that the measures available to a superior may be insufficient to punish certain offences[106] does not eliminate the duty of the superior to take them.[107]

c Causal Link

Neither article 28 RS nor the case law of the *Ad hoc* Tribunals require any kind of causal link between the superior's failure to punish and the commission of the crimes by the subordinates. This is justified by the fact that no such causal link can exist because a superior's duty to punish is only triggered as a result of the prior commission of crimes by his subordinates.[108]

However, article 28 RS and the case law of the *Ad hoc* Tribunals have taken different approaches in relation to the need for a causal link between the superior's failure to prevent and the commission of crimes by subordinates. According to the ICTY Appeals Chamber, no such causal link is required to hold a superior liable

---

[103] *Hadzihasanovic Case* Decision on Jurisdiction (Above n 65), at para 50. This case law is consistent with the use of the language 'the forces were committing or about to be commit' in arts 28(a)(i) and (b)(i) RS. Nevertheless, the *Hadzihasanovic Case* Trial Judgment, at paras 196, 199, has explained that in situations where crimes are committed shortly before a superior is replaced, the reports on the commission of the crimes may not reach the superior who was in command at the time the crime was committed and may be received only by the new superior who has taken up duties.

[104] *Blaskic Case* Appeals Judgment (Above n 32), at para 72; *Halilovic Case* Appeals Judgment (Above n 83), at paras 66 and 182; *Kordic Case* Trial Judgment (Above n 32), at para 446; *Kvocka Case* Trial Judgment (Above n 49), at para 316; *Halilovic Case* Trial Judgment (Above n 65), at para 100; *Hadzihasanovic Case* Trial Judgment (*Ibid*), at paras 173–4.

[105] For Sandoz, Swinarski and Zimmermann (Above n 52), at para 3562, art 87(2) API imposes upon superiors the duty to inform their own superiors of the situation by drawing up a report. Furthermore, they also have the duty to propose a sanction to a superior who has disciplinary power, or—in the case of someone who holds such power himself—to exercise it within the limits of his competence. Moreover, where necessary, due to the gravity of the case, they must also remit the case to the judicial authority with such factual evidence as it was possible to find. The *Strugar Case* Trial Judgment (Above n 32), at para 376, also found that post WW II case law put particular emphasis on whether the superior was called for a report on the incident as well as whether the investigation was thorough.

[106] For instance, in the Kayishema case before the ICTR, the defendant only had the power to detain the physical perpetrators of the massacre of Tutsis at the Mubuga church for up to 30 days. *Kayishema Case* Trial Judgment (Above n 71), at para 315.

[107] *Kayishema Case* Trial Judgment (*Ibid*), at para 514; *Hadzihasanovic Case* Trial Judgment (Above n 65), at para 178.

[108] *Krnojelac Case* Appeals Judgment (Above n 51), at paras 170–72; *Blaskic Case* Appeals Judgment (Above n 32), at para 77; *Kordic Case* Appeals Judgment (Above n 32), at para 832; *Hadzihasanovic Case* Appeals Judgment (Above n 55), at paras 38–42; *Celebici Case* Trial Judgment (Above n 48), at para 400; *Halilovic Case* Trial Judgment (Above n 65), at paras 75–8.

for breaches of his duty to prevent the commission of crimes by subordinates.[109] However, article 28(a) and (b) RS explicitly requires the existence of a causal link between the superior's failure to prevent the commission of crimes by subordinates by providing that military and non-military superiors shall be criminally liable for those crimes committed by his subordinates' as a result of his or her failure to exercise proper control over them.[110]

The exact nature of this causal link would depend on whether a superior's failure to prevent gives rise to principal liability for the subordinate's crimes because they are considered cases of 'commission by omission'; or whether, on the contrary, they give rise to accessorial or derivative liability because they are considered cases of participation in the crimes committed by the subordinates. The first scenario would require showing that those measures available to the relevant superior would have likely prevented his subordinates from committing the crimes,[111] whereas the second scenario would require a less stringent causal link.[112]

d Subjective Requirements: The 'Should Have Known' Standard versus the 'Had Reasons to Know' Standard

From a subjective perspective, article 28(a)(i) RS establishes that criminal liability arises when military superiors:

---

[109] The *Blaskic Case* Appeals Judgment reversed the finding of the ICTY Trial Judgment in the Celebici case that required the existence of a causal link between the superior's failure to prevent and the commission of crimes by subordinates. As the *Blaskic Case* Appeals Judgment (*Ibid*), at para 77, explained: 'The Appeals Chamber is therefore not persuaded by the Appellant's submission that the existence of causality between a commander's failure to prevent subordinates' crimes and the occurrence of these crimes, is an element of command responsibility that requires proof by the Prosecution in all circumstances of a case. Once again, it is more a question of fact to be established on a case-by-case basis, than a question of law in general'.

This position was already hinted by the *Krnojelac Case* Appeals Judgment (*Ibid*), at paras 170–72, where the defendant (the warden of the KP Dom prison facility) was convicted for his failure to prevent the commission of torture by his subordinates without discussing the potential causal link between the defendant's omission and the acts of torture for which he was convicted (the Appeals Chamber did not discuss the need for the Prosecution to adduce evidence of this causal link). This position has been ratified in the *Hadzihasanovic Case* Appeals Judgment (Above n 55), at paras 38–40. This is also the solution adopted in national systems with such different legal traditions, such as Germany and the United States. Concerning Germany see, German Code of Crimes against International Law § 13(a) and (b). In relation to the United States, see *Ford v. Garcia*, 289 F.3d 1283 (11th Cir. 2002), specifically rejecting the argument that proximate cause is a required element of the doctrine of command responsibility. The same decision was also held in *Hilao v Estate of Marcos*, 103 F.3d 767 (9th Cir 1996).

[110] Triffterer, *Causality* (Above n 79), at 179; C Meloni, 'Command Responsibility: Mode of Liability for the Crimes of Subordinates or Separate Offence of the Superior?' (2007) 5 *Journal of International Criminal Justice* 636 [hereinafter Meloni].

[111] See Ch 3, s II.A.

[112] For instance, refer to the 'substantial effect' requirement for aiding and abetting, or the 'clear contributing factor' requirement for instigation. Logically, due to the fact that in this scenario the superiors' failures to prevent would constitute a distinct theory of accessorial or derivative liability, it is not necessary to adopt the same causal link of other forms of accessorial liability such as aiding and abetting or instigation.

[E]ither knew or, owing to the circumstances at the time, should have known that the forces were committing or about to commit such crimes.[113]

According to this provision, military superiors' failures to prevent or punish give rise to criminal liability no matter whether such failures are intentional or negligent.[114] The inclusion of negligence through the 'should have known' standard is surprising given that, according to article 30 RS, negligence is excluded from the realm of the general subjective element of most crimes provided for in the RS. Moreover, this is also in contrast with the general subjective element provided for in article 28(2) RS for non-military superiors, according to which, criminal liability only arises when they:

[E]ither knew or consciously disregarded information which clearly indicated, that the subordinates were committing or about to commit such crimes.[115]

---

[113] Art 28(a) RS applies to both military superiors and to persons effectively acting as military superiors. As P Saland, 'International Criminal Law Principles' in RS Lee (ed), *The International Criminal Court: The Making of the Rome Statute* (The Hague, Kluwer, 1999) 203, has explained, the delegates at the Rome Conference considered it unacceptable to have less stringent requirements for de facto military superiors than for *de iure* military superiors in regular armed forces.

[114] In relation to their duty to prevent, the 'should have known' standard used in this provision makes military superiors criminally liable if they do not act with the diligence required from an average military superior in the same circumstances to: (i) obtain information about the fact that subordinates were about to commit crimes within the ICC jurisdiction (negligence in learning about the situation that activates their duty to prevent); (ii) assess the measures within their power to prevent subordinates from committing crimes (negligence in the appreciation of the extent of their power to intervene); and (iii) apply the measures available to them. With regard to their duty to punish, the 'should have known' standard used in this provision makes military superiors criminally liable if they do not act with the diligence required from an average military superior in the same circumstances to: (i) obtain information about the fact that subordinates were committing, or had committed, crimes within the ICC jurisdiction (negligence in learning about the situation that activates their duty to prevent punish); (ii) assess the measures within their power to punish his subordinates (negligence in the appreciation of the extent of their power to intervene); and (iii) apply the measures available to them. A negligence standard was already applied in relation to the notion of superior responsibility in certain post WW II cases, such as in the case of *United States v Wilhelm List et al* (1948) in Trial of the Major War Criminals? before the International Military Tribunal under Control Council Law No 10, Vol XI (US Government Printing Office, 1951) 957, 1236. The interpretation of the expression 'should have known' in Art 28(a)(i) RS as setting out a negligence standard would be consistent with the view held by a number of writers that the notion of superior responsibility creates criminal liability for negligence. See WA Schabas, 'General Principles of Criminal Law in the International Criminal Court Statute, Part III' (1998) 6 *European Journal of Crime, Criminal Law and Criminal Justice* 417 [hereinafter Schabas, *General Principles*]; I Bantekas, 'The Contemporary Law of Superior Responsibility' (1999) 93 *American Journal of International Law* 590; KMF Keith, 'The Mens Rea of Superior Responsibility as Developed by ICTY Jurisprudence' (2001) 14 *Leiden Journal of International Law* 632. However, for Van Sliedregt (Above n 24), at 186, the expression 'should have known' in art 28(a)(i) RS introduces a recklessness standard. The same view is also held by BD Landrum, 'The Yamashita War Crimes Trial: Command Responsibility Then and Now' (1995) 149 *Military Law Review* 300, where he affirms that there is no distinction between the 'should have known' standard and the 'had reasons to know' standard. As a result, the only point of agreement among writers is that the 'should have known' standard is not a strict liability standard. See BB Jia, 'The Doctrine of Command Responsibility: Current Problems' (2000) 3 *Yearbook of International Humanitarian Law* 161–2.

[115] See Fenrick (Above n 85), at 520–22; Ambos, *Superior Responsibility* (Above n 81), at 870–71. This standard was also originally followed in relation to non-military superiors by the *Kayishema Case* Trial Judgment (Above n 71), at paras 227–8. Van Sliedregt (Above n 24), at 164, and A Zahar, 'Command Responsibility for Civilian Superiors for Genocide' (2001) 14 *Leiden Journal of International Law* 613–16, refer to this finding as 'erroneous'.

In this regard, it is worth noting that not even the case law of the *Ad hoc* Tribunals, which in general has enlarged the scope of responsibility of military superiors provided for in articles 86 and 87 AP I, supports the choice made by the drafters of the RS. Indeed, the ICTR and ICTY Appeals Chambers in the *Celebici, Bagilishema, Krnojelac, Blaskic, Halilovic, Oric and Strugar* cases rejected the attempt of the Trial Chamber in the *Blaskic* case to give the same meaning to the expressions 'had reason to know' and 'should have known'.[116] The Appeals Chambers of the *Ad hoc* Tribunals have held that 'had reasons to know' is a higher standard than 'should have known' because it does not criminalise the superiors' mere lack of due diligence in complying with their duty to be informed of their subordinates' activities.[117] According to the ICTR and ICTY Appeals Chambers, the 'had reason to know' standard provided for in article 7(3) ICTYS and 6(3) ICTRS requires superiors to, at the very minimum, have had information of a general nature available to them that should have put them on notice of the risk of offences by their subordinates and of the consequent need to set in motion an inquiry to determine whether crimes were about to be or had been committed.[118]

---

[116] The reasons given by the *Blaskic Case* Trial Judgment (Above n 48), at para 332, for giving the same meaning to the standards 'should have known' and 'had reason to know' are the following: 'If a commander has exercised due diligence in the fulfilment of his duties yet lacks knowledge that crimes are about to be or have been committed, such lack of knowledge cannot be held against him. However, taking into account his particular position of command and the circumstances prevailing at the time, such ignorance cannot be a defence where the absence of knowledge is the result of negligence in the discharge of his duties: this commander had reason to know within the meaning of the Statute'. According to MR Lippman, 'The Evolution and Scope of Command Responsibility' (2000) 13 *Leiden Journal of International Law* 157, the 'should have known' test, providing for a negligence standard for superior responsibility, was introduced by the findings of the Kahan Commission in 1983, which was subsequently relied on by the Trial Chamber in the Blaskic case. See also N Keijzer and E Van Sliedregt, 'Commentary to Blaskic Judgment' in A Klip and G Sluiter, *Annotated Leading Cases of International Criminal Tribunals* (Vol 4, Oxford, Hart Publishing, 2001) 656–7; MF Tinta, 'Commanders on Trial: The Blaskic Case and the Doctrine of Command Responsibility' (2000) 47 *Netherlands International Law Review* 293–322.

[117] *Celebici Case* Appeals Judgment (Above n 1), at para 226. From this perspective, *Prosecutor v Bagilishema* (Appeals Chamber Judgment) ICTR-95-01A-A (3 Jul 2002) para 35 [hereinafter *Bagilishema Case* Appeals Judgment] has highlighted that '[r]eferences to negligence in the context of superior responsibility are likely to lead to confusion of thought'.

[118] *Bagilishema Case* Appeals Judgment (*Ibid*), at paras 35–42; *Celebici Case* Appeals Judgment (Above n 1), at para 241; *Krnojelac Case* Appeals Judgment (Above n 51), at para 62; *Blaskic Case* Appeals Judgment (Above n 32), at para 62; *Galic Case* Appeals Judgment (Above n 37), at para 184; *Hadzihasanovic Case* Appeals Judgment (Above n 55), at paras. 26–29; *Oric Case* Appeals Judgment (Above n 48), at para 51; Strugar Case Appeals Judgment (Above n 41), at para 297; *Hadzihasanovic Case* Trial Judgment (Above n 65), at para 95; *Strugar Case* Trial Judgment (Above n 32), at para 399; See also E Carnero Rojo and F Lagos Polas, 'The Strugar Case before the International Criminal Tribunal for the Former Yugoslavia' (2005) 2 *Journal of International Law of Peace and Armed Conflict* 140–142; S Hinek, 'The Judgment of the International Criminal Tribunal for the Former Yugoslavia in Prosecutor v. Pavle Strugar' (2006) 19 *Leiden Journal of International Law* 477–90.

It is important to highlight the emphasis placed by the recent *Oric Case* Appeals Judgment (Above n 48), at para 55, on the fact that the accused's knowledge or reasons to know of his subordinate's criminal conduct constitutes a 'crucial element of the accused's criminal liability under Article 7 (3)'. In applying this principle to the facts of the case, the ICTY Appeals Chamber held: '[T]he Appeals Chamber considers that, read in context, the finding on Oric's "prior notice" relates to his knowledge that "Serb detainees kept at the Srebrenica Police Station were cruelly treated, and that one of them had been killed." Thus the finding did not concern Oric's rreason to know of his subordinate's conduct,

In applying the 'had reasons to know' standard, the *Strugar Case* Appeals Judgment has recently held:

The Trial Chamber erred in finding that Strugar's knowledge of the risk that his forces might unlawfully shell the Old Town was not sufficient to meet the mens rea element under Article 7(3) and that only knowledge of the 'substantial likelihood' or the 'clear and strong risk' that his forces would do so fulfilled this requirement. In so finding, the Trial Chamber erroneously read into the mens rea element of Article 7(3) the requirement that the superior be on notice of a strong risk that his subordinates would commit offences. In this respect, the Appeals Chamber recalls that under the correct legal standard, sufficiently alarming information putting a superior on notice of the risk that crimes might subsequently be carried out by his subordinates and justifying further inquiry is sufficient to hold a superior liable under Article 7(3) of the Statute.[119]

The information available to superiors needs not be of a nature such that it alone establishes that crimes were about to take place or had already taken place, and needs not contain specific details about the offences that were about to be committed or had been committed.[120] Furthermore, the awareness of a superior that his subordinates have previously committed offences could be, depending on the circumstances of the case, sufficient to alert him that other crimes of a similar nature might be committed by the same 'identifiable group of subordinates' who operate in the same geographical area. In this regard, the ICTY Appeals Chamber has recently explained:

In Krnojelac, the Trial Chamber found that '[t]he fact that the Accused witnessed the beating of [a detainee, inflicted by one of his subordinates], ostensibly for the prohibited purpose of punishing him for his failed escape, is not sufficient, in itself, to conclude that the Accused knew or [. . .] had reason to know that, other than in that particular instance, beatings were inflicted for any of the prohibited purposes'. The Appeals Chamber rejected this finding and held that 'while this fact is indeed insufficient, in itself, to

---

but, instead, his notice of the crimes committed by others at the Srebrenica Police Station.' See Oric Case Appeals Judgment (Above n 48), at paras 55 and 174.

[119] Strugar Case Appeals Judgment (Above n 41), at para 304.

[120] *Bagilishema Case* Appeals Judgment (Above n 118), at para 28; *Celebici Case* Appeals Judgment (Above n 1), at para 238; *Krnojelac Case* Appeals Judgment (Above n 51), at paras 154–5; *Galic Case* Appeals Judgment (*Above n 37*), at para 184; Strugar Case Appeals Judgment (*Ibid*), at para 298; *Kordic Case* Trial Judgment (Above n 31), at paras 436–7; *Strugar Case* Trial Judgment (Above n 32), at paras 360–70; *Hadzihasanovic Case* Trial Judgment (Above n 65), at para 97. Information of a general nature which meets the 'had reason to know' standard in relation to the fact that subordinates were about to commit a crime exists, for instance, when: (i) a superior has been informed that some soldiers under his command were drinking prior to being sent on a mission or have a violent or unstable character (*Celebici Case* Appeals Judgment (Above n 1), at para 228); or (ii) a superior has been informed of the low level of training, the character traits or habits of some of his subordinates (*Kordic Case* Trial Judgment (Above n 31), at para 247). Issuing orders to comply with international humanitarian law is not per se sufficient to show that a superior knew or had reason to know that subordinates were about to commit crimes. See *Celebici Case* Appeals Judgment (Above n 1), at para 238; *Hadzihasanovic Case* Trial Judgment (Above n 65), at para 100, fn 199. Moreover, such orders are only relevant to the issue of whether a superior is criminally liable under the notion of superior responsibility if they have been issued because the superior knew or had reason know that subordinates were about to commit crimes. See *Blaskic Case* Appeals Judgment (Above n 32), at para 486.

conclude that Krnojelac knew that acts of torture were being inflicted on the detainees, as indicated by the Trial Chamber, it may nevertheless constitute sufficiently alarming information such as to alert him to the risk of other acts of torture being committed, meaning that Krnojelac had reason to know that his subordinates were committing or were about to commit acts of torture' [] In Hadzihasanovic and Kubura, the Trial Chamber found that 'the Accused Kubura, owing to his knowledge of the plunder committed by his subordinates in June 1993 and his failure to take punitive measures, could not ignore that the members of the 7th Brigade were likely to repeat such acts. The Appeals Chamber in that case found that the Trial Chamber had erred in making this finding as it implied that the Trial Chamber considered Kubura's knowledge of and past failure to punish his subordinates' acts of plunder in the Ovnak area as automatically entailing that he had reason to know of their future acts of plunder in Vares'. The Appeals Chamber thus applied the correct legal standard to the evidence on the trial record: 'While Kubura's knowledge of his subordinates' past plunder in Ovnak and his failure to punish them did not, in itself, amount to actual knowledge of the acts of plunder in Vares, the Appeals Chamber concurs with the Trial Chamber that the orders he received on 4 November 1993 constituted, at the very least, sufficiently alarming information justifying further inquiry.'[121]

Furthermore, in the particular situation of multiple offences of a similar nature, a superior's awareness that his subordinates have committed a crime is sufficient to alert him to the fact that other similar offences might have been previously committed by the same identifiable group of subordinates.[122]

Concerning those crimes requiring an ulterior intent or a *dolus specialis*, such as genocide or torture, the superior himself does not need be motivated by such an ulterior intent. On the contrary, as the ICTY Appeal Judgment in the *Krnojelac* case indicated, it is sufficient if the superior had available to him information of a general nature which should have put him on notice that subordinates might have

---

[121] *Strugar Case* Appeals Judgment (Above n 41), at paras 299 and 300. According to the *Hadzihasanovic Case* Appeals Judgment (Above n 55), at para. 30: 'While a superior's knowledge of and failure to punish his subordinates' past offences is insufficient, in itself, to conclude that the superior knew that similar future offences would be committed by the same group of subordinates, this may, depending on the circumstances of the case, nevertheless constitute sufficiently alarming information to justify further inquiry'. In this regard, the *Hadzihasanovic Case* Trial Judgment (Above n 65), at paras 115–16, rejected the Prosecution's argument that this rule should be extended to all subordinates, regardless of whether they belong to the same group. As the Trial Chamber explained: 'To adopt such a position misconstrues the reasoning of the *Krnojelac* Appeals Chamber, in that it is silent about taking into account one same group of subordinates and the geographical aspects related to that group (for example, the location of a subordinate unit), which fall within the scope of Krnojelac's prior knowledge'. As a result, the Trial Chamber, in light of the structure and operations of the 3rd Corps of the ABiH, limited the 'identifiable group of subordinates' to a brigade battalion, and this assuming that a battalion 'has a geographical location different from that of the other units of the brigade to which it belongs'. See *Hadzihasanovic Case* Trial Judgment (*Ibid*), at para 117. See also on this matter *Krnojelac Case* Appeals Judgment (Above n 51), at para 155; *Strugar Case* Appeals Judgment (*Ibid*), para 301.

[122] *Hadzihasanovic Case* Trial Judgment (Above n 65), at para 185 referring to the treatment of this issue in the *Krnojelac Case* Appeals Judgment (Above n 51), at paras 156–69.

been motivated by the required ulterior intent.[123] Following the same rationale, article 28(a)(i) RS would only require that military superiors either knew or, owing to the circumstances at the time, should have known that their subordinates had the required ulterior intent. In the case of non-military superiors, it would be sufficient if they either knew or consciously disregarded information, which clearly indicated that their subordinates had the requisite ulterior intent.

e Nature of Criminal Liability under the Notion of Superior Responsibility

The most salient feature of the notion of superior responsibility in the ICTY and ICTR case law is the absence of any causal connection between a superior's failure to prevent or punish, and the commission of crimes by his subordinates. As a result, as the ICTY Appeals Chamber in the *Krnojelac* case has explained:

> [W]here superior responsibility is concerned, an accused is not charged with the crimes of his subordinates but with his failure to carry out his duty as a superior to exercise control.

---

[123] The question as to whether criminal liability for superiors' failures to prevent the commission by subordinates of offences requiring an ulterior intent (such as genocide or torture) only arises if the superiors' omissions are also motivated by such ulterior intent was dealt with by *Prosecutor v Stakic* (Decision on the Defence Rule 98 *bis* Motion for Judgment of Acquittal) ICTY-97-24-T (31 Oct 2002) para 92 [hereinafter *Stakic Case* Rule 98 *bis* Decision]. The Trial Chamber stated: 'It follows from Article 4 and the unique nature of genocide that the *dolus specialis* is required for responsibility under Article 7(3) as well'. This question was not further elaborated upon in the *Stakic* Trial and Appeals Judgments. Subsequently, in the *Krnojelac* case, the Prosecution argued in the appeal that a superior could be found guilty of an ulterior intent crime even if the superior did not posses the requisite ulterior intent. According to the Prosecution, Krnojelac (the warden of the KPDom detention camp at the relevant time) was informed that prisoners were beaten in the camp by his subordinates, and this information amounted to putting him on notice of the risk that subordinates were mistreating prisoners for one of the specific purposes required by the crime of torture (Prosecution Appeals Brief in the *Krnojelac* case, third and fifth grounds of appeal; this position had already been advanced by the Prosecution in an implicit manner in the *Bagilishema* appeal). The ICTY Appeals Chamber accepted the argument of the Prosecution and stated that in the case of torture, the information available to the superior must put him on notice not only of the beatings committed or about to be committed by his subordinates, but also of the ulterior intent which must motivate this treatment by his subordinates. See *Krnojelac Case* Appeals Judgment (*Ibid*), at para 155.

In applying this standard to the facts of the case, the Appeals Chamber came to the conclusion that: 'Krnojelac had a certain amount of general information putting him on notice that his subordinates might be committing abuses constituting acts of torture. Accordingly, he must incur responsibility pursuant to Article 7(3) of the Statute. It cannot be overemphasised that, where superior responsibility is concerned, an accused is not charged with the crimes of his subordinates but with his failure to carry out his duty as a superior to exercise control. There is no doubt that, given the information available to him, Krnojelac was in a position to exercise such control, that is, to investigate whether acts of torture were being committed, especially since the Trial Chamber considered he had the power to prevent the beatings and punish the perpetrators. In holding that no reasonable trier of fact could have made the same findings of fact as the Trial Chamber, the Appeals Chamber takes the view that the Trial Chamber committed an error of fact'. See *Krnojelac Case* Appeals Judgment, at para 171.

As a result, it can be affirmed that the *Krnojelac Case* Appeals Judgment took the approach that in cases of ulterior intent crimes, such as torture, a superior can be found liable for having failed to prevent subordinates from committing such crimes even though his omission was not motivated by the requisite ulterior intent. It is sufficient for the superior to have had information available to him that should have put him on notice that subordinates might be acting with the requisite ulterior intent.

The Trial Chambers in the *Halilovic* and *Hadzihasanovic* cases have subsequently justified this approach because of the '*sui generis* nature' of the notion of superior responsibility. But what do they mean by '*sui generis* nature'? The Trial Chamber in the *Halilovic* case explained it as follows:

> The Chamber finds that under Article 7(3) command responsibility is responsibility for an omission. The commander is responsible for the failure to perform an act required by international law. This omission is culpable because international law imposes an affirmative duty on superiors to prevent and punish crimes committed by their subordinates. Thus 'for the acts of his subordinates' as generally referred to in the jurisprudence of the Tribunal does not mean that the commander shares the same responsibility as the subordinates who committed the crimes, but rather that because of the crimes committed by his subordinates, the commander should bear responsibility for his failure to act. The imposition of responsibility upon a commander for breach of his duty is to be weighed against the crimes of his subordinates; a commander is responsible not as though he had committed the crime himself, but his responsibility is considered in proportion to the gravity of the offences committed. The Chamber considers that this is still in keeping with the logic of the weight which international humanitarian law places on protection values.[124]
>
> The Trial Chamber further notes that the nature of command responsibility itself, as a *sui generis* form of liability, which is distinct from the modes of individual responsibility set out in Article 7(1), does not require a causal link. Command responsibility is responsibility for omission, which is culpable due to the duty imposed by international law upon a commander. If a causal link were required this would change the basis of command responsibility for failure to prevent or punish to the extent that it would practically require involvement on the part of the commander in the crime his subordinates committed, thus altering the very nature of the liability imposed under Article 7(3).[125]

This explanation has been recently endorsed by ICTY Appeals Judgment in the *Hadzihasanovic case* Appeals Judgment. In the author's view, the Trial Chambers in the *Halilovic* and *Hadzihasanovic* cases used the expression '*sui generis* nature' to emphasise that the notion of superior responsibility is an offence of mere omis-

---

[124] *Halilovic Case* Trial Judgment (Above n 65), at para 54. The *Hadzihasanovic Case* Trial Judgment (Above n 65), at para 75, explicitly endorsed this position.

[125] *Halilovic Case* Trial Judgment (*Ibid*), at para 78, quoted with approval by the *Hadzihasanovic Case* Appeals Judgment (Above n 55), at para 39. The *Hadzihasanovic Case* Trial Judgment (*Ibid*), at paras 191–2, also agreed with this position. However, it added that: 'The Chamber would, however, note that command responsibility may be imposed only when there is a relevant and significant nexus between the crime and the responsibility of the superior accused of having failed in his duty to prevent. Such a nexus is implicitly part of the usual conditions, which must be met to establish command responsibility. [...] Considering the foregoing, the Chamber makes the following findings as regards a superior's failure to prevent his subordinates from committing crimes. Firstly, a superior who exercises effective control over his subordinates and has reason to know that they are about to commit crimes, but fails to take the necessary and reasonable measures to prevent those crimes, incurs responsibility, both because his omission created or heightened a real and reasonably foreseeable risk that those crimes would be committed, a risk he accepted willingly, and because that risk materialised in the commission of those crimes. In that sense, the superior has substantially played a part in the commission of those crimes. Secondly, it is presumed that there is such a nexus between the superior's omission and those crimes. The Prosecution therefore has no duty to establish evidence of that nexus. Instead, the Accused must disprove it'.

sion consisting of a breach of the duty imposed by international law on superiors to take the necessary and reasonable measures at their disposal to prevent and punish subordinates' offences (expected action).[126] As a result, a superior's criminal liability does not result from subordinates' crimes. On the contrary, it arises from not taking the above-mentioned measures (omission of the expected action) in a situation in which the duty to take them has been triggered.[127] Subordinates' crimes are only relevant insofar as they constitute an objective requirement for punishment in relation to a superior's failures to prevent[128] and a necessary prerequisite for the triggering of a superior's duty to punish.[129]

The configuration of the notion of superior responsibility as a crime of pure omission excludes any superiors' liability for those specific crimes committed by their subordinates.[130] As a result, the author considers that, given the gravity of the crimes within the jurisdiction of the *Ad hoc* Tribunals, the application of the principle of culpability—which requires the careful determination of the specific wrongdoing and the adjustment of punishment in light of it—should normally result in lower sentences for those superiors who breach their duties to prevent and punish, than for subordinates who commit genocide, crimes against humanity or war crimes.[131]

The nature of the notion of superior responsibility under article 28 RS is different for a superior's failure to punish than for superior's failure to prevent. According to article 28 RS, a superior's failure to punish does not require any

---

[126] Smith and Hogan (Above n 12), at 76.

[127] Munoz Conde and Garcia Aran (Above n 15), at 240–41. According to the *Strugar Case* Trial Judgment (Above n 32), at para 373, and the *Hadzihasanovic Case* Trial Judgment (Above n 65), at para 125: 'The duty to prevent arises for a superior from the moment he acquires knowledge or has reasonable grounds to suspect that a crime is being or is about to be committed, while the duty to punish arises after the commission of the crime'.

[128] There is no necessity of punishment when, despite the superiors' failures to prevent, subordinates do not commit any crime. As Olasolo, *Unlawful Attacks* (Above n 9), at 248, has pointed out: 'The category of necessity of punishment includes a number of heterogeneous elements that the drafters, for purely utilitarian reasons, configured as requisites for punishment or grounds for exemption of punishment. These elements are not part of the objective or subjective elements of the crime and do not fall into the categories of either unlawfulness or culpability. As a result, they do not need to be included in the subjective elements of the crime and thus mistakes over their existence are wholly irrelevant'.

[129] Considering the 'triggering' function of subordinates' crimes, Van Sliedregt (Above n 24), at 219, has pointed out: 'Under modern doctrine of superior responsibility, the superior is criminally liable for his failure to supervise properly. His responsibility is mainly "triggered" by subordinates' crimes'.

[130] Compare Eckhardt (Above n 64), at 4.

[131] It is for this reason that the German Code of Crimes against International Law §§ 13 and 14 has established lower penalty-ranges for infringement of superiors' duties to prevent and punish. In relation to breaches of superiors' duty to punish, the German Code of Crimes against International Law §14(1) states that: 'A military commander or a civilian superior who omits immediately to draw the attention of the agency responsible for the investigation or prosecution of any offence pursuant to this Act, to such an offence committed by a subordinate, shall be punished with imprisonment for not more than five years'. The breach of superiors' duty to prevent the commission of crimes by subordinates is also considered by the German Code of Crimes against International Law § 13(a) and (b) as a crime of pure omission. According to § 13(d): 'Intentional violation of the duty of supervision shall be punished with imprisonment for not more than five years, and negligent violation of the duty of supervision shall be punished with imprisonment for not more than three years'.

causal link with his subordinates' crimes, and therefore, like in the case law of the *Ad hoc* Tribunals, it constitutes an offence of mere omission.[132] However, paragraphs (a) and (b) of article 28 RS require the existence of a causal connection between a superior's failure to prevent and the commission of crimes by subordinates, so that a superior's breach of his duty to prevent does not entail criminal liability unless his subordinates' offences are 'the result of' the superior's failure 'to exercise control properly over such subordinates'. As a consequence, the author considers that, according to article 28 RS, superiors are liable for the crimes committed by their subordinates due to the effect that their failure to prevent has on the commission of such crimes.

The question arises as to whether article 28 RS holds superiors liable as principals or as accessories to the offences committed by their subordinates. The expression 'the result of' used in article 28(a) and (b) RS gives prima facie the impression that superiors are held liable as principals for the 'commission by omission' of their subordinates' offences. However, this would require that superiors possess the subjective elements of the crimes in question, including any ulterior intent required by such crimes.[133] And, as seen above, article 28(a)(i) RS does not establish that military superiors must fulfil the 'knowledge and intent' requirement provided for in article 30 RS; quite the contrary, it only requires the far lower 'should have known' standard (a negligence standard). Moreover, superiors need not themselves have any ulterior intent required by the crimes in question; it is sufficient if they should have known that those subordinates who physically committed the crimes were going to act with such ulterior intent.

As a result, and despite the use of the words 'the result of' in article 28(a) and (b) RS, one can only conclude that the superiors' failures to prevent give rise to accessorial or derivative liability for facilitating with their omissions the commission of crimes by their subordinates.[134] Furthermore, even if this conclusion leads to the application of a less stringent causal connection and to accessorial (as opposed to principal) liability, the author still considers that, given that negligence has been, as a general rule, excluded from the RS,[135] the adoption in article 28(a)(i) RS of a negligence standard for military superiors can hardly be justified.[136]

---

[132] Meloni (Above n 110), at 637.

[133] See Ch 3, s II.A.

[134] Otherwise it will be particularly striking that art 28(a)(i) RS provides for the military superiors' negligent commission by omission of any of the crimes contained in the RS as a result of their negligent failure to prevent subordinates from committing such crimes, when, as a general rule, art 30 RS excludes negligence from the realm of the general subjective element of any crime provided for in the RS. In other words, how can a negligent failure to prevent a crime turn a superior into a perpetrator (or principal) to such a crime if the physical perpetrators must act with at least *dolus eventualis* in order to incur criminal liability? The same conclusion is reached by Meloni (Above n 110), at 636–7.

[135] As seen above in Ch 3, s I.C.ii, the exceptions to this general rule are very limited.

[136] The contradiction between the negligent conduct of superiors and subordinates' intentional conduct has been pointed out by Ambos, *Superior Responsibility* (Above n 81), at 852; M Damaska, 'The Shadow Side of Command Responsibility' (2001) 49 *The American Journal of Comparative Law* 463–4; Schabas, *General Principles* (Above n 114), at 417.

C Final Remarks: Concurrent Application of Commission by Omission, Instigation, Aiding and Abetting and Superior Liability

When in a case relating to omissions by senior political or military leaders, the notions of commission by omission, instigation by omission, aiding and abetting by omission and superior responsibility are all applicable, the author considers that one should look at their respective nature in order to determine the manner in which they should be applied.

In this regard, the author considers that, although the case law of the *Ad hoc* Tribunals has not been consistent on this point, theories of principal liability, such as commission by omission, must have preference over forms of accessorial or derivative liability such as instigation or aiding and abetting (or superior responsibility for the superiors' failures to prevent in the context of the Rome Statute).

Furthermore, in those cases in which no theory of principal liability is applicable, but there is more than one form of accessorial or derivative liability that can be applied, one should choose the form of accessorial liability that better suits the role of the omissions of senior political and military leaders in the commission of the crimes.

Finally, when a senior political or military leader has committed an offence of mere omission for his failure to prevent or punish, and has also participated as a principal, or as an accessory, in the commission of his subordinates' crimes, he should be convicted for both offences; and, subsequently, the rules of *concursus delictorum* should be applied in sentencing, to individualise the appropriate sentence.

III Indirect Perpetration

A Concept and Treatment in the Rome Statute and in the Case Law of the *Ad hoc* Tribunals

While articles 7(1) ICTYS and 6(1) ICTRS refer generally to 'committing' a crime,[137] article 25(3)(a) RS explicitly provides for the commission of a crime 'through another person, regardless of whether that other person is criminally responsible'. According to this last provision, for a senior political or military leader to 'commit' a crime (and thus become a perpetrator or principal to the crime), he does not need to physically carry out the objective elements of the crime; it is sufficient if they are physically carried out by the person that he uses as a tool to have the crime committed.[138]

---

[137] Van Sliedregt (Above n 24), at 68.

[138] A Eser, 'Individual Criminal Responsibility' in A Cassese, P Gaeta, and JRWD Jones (eds), *The Rome Statute of the International Criminal Court: A Commentary* (Oxford, Oxford University Press, 2002) 791 [hereinafter Eser]; Werle (Above n 50), at 217; Ambos, *La Parte General del Derecho Penal Internacional* (Above n 2), at 196.

As ICC Pre-Trial Chamber I has highlighted in the *Katanga and Ngudjolo* case, as long as the senior political or military leader controls the will of the person who physically carries out the objective elements of the crime (and thus has the power to decide whether the crime will be committed and how it will be committed), he is considered to have in fact committed the crime—the person who physically carries out the objective elements of the crime is only used by the senior political or military leader as a tool through which his decision to commit the crime is physically implemented.[139]

In the *Katanga and Ngudjolo* case, ICC Pre-Trial Chamber I has also explained that, according to the legality principle, in order for a senior political or military leader to be held liable as an indirect perpetrator, it is necessary that the objective elements of the crime be, indeed, physically executed by the person that he uses as a tool. Furthermore, senior political and military leaders, in spite of the fact that they do not physically carry out the objective elements of the crime, must fulfil all specific objective requisites provided for in the definition of the crime in question—for instance, if the crime can only be committed by a specific category of individuals, such as civil servants or military personnel, they must have that status in order to become indirect perpetrators; otherwise, they will be liable only as accessories to the crime for ordering or instigating it. Moreover, they must also fulfil all subjective elements of the crime, including any requisite ulterior intent or *dolus specialis*.[140]

Werle has affirmed that the notion of indirect perpetration has neither been explicitly regulated by international criminal law, nor has it been applied by international case law before the Rome Statute. Likewise, Van Sliedregt has pointed out that:

> Rather than adopting the terms of direct and indirect perpetration, the *Ad hoc* Tribunals use the verb 'commit' to express the nature of the various contributions to a crime. 'Committing' at the *Ad hoc* Tribunals covers direct perpetration and joint participation as in the common purpose doctrine, leaving aiding and abetting outside it. Perpetration by means is not recognised as such.[141]

Nevertheless, the ICTY Appeals Chamber has recently stated in the Brdanin case that, in light of some post WW II cases, such as the *Justice* and the *RuSHA* cases,[142] a member of a joint criminal enterprise may use the physical perpetrators as 'tools' to have the crimes committed.[143] In particular, it held in the *Brdanin* case that:

---

[139] *Katanga and Ngudjolo Case* Confirmation of Charges (Above n 20) at para 495; *Lubanga Case* Confirmation of Charges (Above n 16), at paras 332(ii) and 333. See also C Roxin, *Taterschaft und Tatherrschaft* (7th edn, Berlin, Gruyter, 2000) 141 *et seq* [hereinafter Roxin].

[140] *Katanga and Ngudjolo Case* Confirmation of Charges (Above n 20) at para 497.

[141] Van Sliedregt (Above n 24), at 68. See also Werle (Above n 50), at 218.

[142] *Prosecutor v Brdanin* (Appeals Chamber Judgment) ICTY-99-36-A (3 Apr 2007) para 414. See also the discussion of the Justice and RuSHA cases at paras 395–404.

[143] *Ibid* at paras 410–14.

[I]t appears that the fact that the RPPs [Relevant Physical Perpetrators] were used as mere 'tools' by their superiors was, actually, the most likely explanation for what happened in the territory of the ARK during the indictment period.[144]

Moreover, before the *Brdanin* Appeals Judgment, the exclusion of the physical perpetrators from the group of participants in a joint criminal enterprise on account that they have been used as mere tools by the members of the enterprise had already been explicitly or implicitly accepted by the ICTY Trial Judgments in the *Kordic*,[145] *Krstic*[146] and *Krajisnik*[147] cases and by the ICTY Appeal Judgment in the *Stakic* case.[148]

B Indirect Perpetration by Using Persons Who are not Fully Criminally Liable

The most common application of the notion of indirect perpetration is the use of a person, who is not fully criminally liable, as a tool to have the crimes committed.[149]

---

[144] *Ibid* at para 448.

[145] See Ch 4, sV.D.i.

[146] See Ch 4, s V.D.ii.

[147] See Ch 4, s V.D.v.

[148] See Ch 4, s III.D.iii.

[149] In these cases, it is broadly accepted that the persons who use an innocent agent should be considered principals to the crimes insofar as they are indirect perpetrators. See *Katanga and Ngudjolo Case* Confirmation of Charges (Above n 20), at para 495. See also Ambos, *La Parte General del Derecho Penal Internacional* (Above n 2), at 195–6; Werle (Above n 50), at 217; Van Sliedregt (Above n 24), at 69–70. Even common law jurisdictions, such as Australia, Canada, South Africa, England, or the United States, which have a narrower approach to the notion of control of the crime as the basis for perpetration, have traditionally applied the notion of indirect perpetration to convict as a principal to the crime the person who uses an innocent agent to commit the crime. In these cases, the person behind is said to have control of the crime because he controls the will of the person who physically carries out the objective elements of the crime. For Australia, see P Rush and S Yeah, *Criminal Law Sourcebook* (Sydney, Butterworths, 2000) 662; L Waller and C Williams, *Criminal Law Text and Cases* (Sydney, Butterworths, 2001) 560. The phrase 'actually commits it' in the Canadian Criminal Code § 21(1)(a) includes a case where the defendant causes the offence to be committed by an innocent agent under his or her direction. See Tremeear's Criminal Code, Statutes of Canada Annotated (2003, Carswell) 61. For South Africa, see CR Snyman, *Criminal Law* (Durban, Butterworths, 1995) 246–7. For the United States, see Model Penal Code §2.06(1)-(4); *State v Ward*, 396 A.2d 1041, 1046 (1978); J Dressler, *Understanding Criminal Law* (2nd edn, Albany, Lexis Publishing, 1995) §30.03[A]; 18 USCS §2. For England, see *Regina v Cogan and Leak* [1976] QB 217; *Stringer* [1991] 94 Cr App R 13, cited by A Reed, B Fitzpatrick and P Seago, *Criminal Law* (Andover, Sweet and Maxwell Publishing, 1999) 123, fn 17; *DPP v K and B* [1997], cited by Smith and Hogan (Above n 12), at 167, fn 29. Civil law jurisdictions, which for the most part have a broader approach to the notion of control of the crime as the basis for perpetration, have also applied the notion of indirect perpetration to convict as a principal to the crime the person who uses an innocent agent to commit the crime. For Argentina see Penal Chamber of Parana, § 1a 10/11/1987C; C Fontan Balestra, *Tratado de Derecho Penal: Parte General* (Albany, Lexis Publishing, 1995) Lexis No 1503/001660; JA 1988-III-299; Tribunal Nacional Oral Criminal, No 7, 3/11/1998; JA 2002-I-Sintesis; E Cuello Calon, *Derecho Penal* (9th edn, Barcelona, Libreria Bosch, 1926) 5. Art 29.1 of the Penal Code of Colombia also embraces this notion in Law 599 of 24 Jul 2000, '*Es autor quien realice la conducta punible por si mismo o utilizando a otro como instrumento*'. For France, see Cour de Cassation, Chambre Criminelle Dalloz (6 Mars 1964) 562; ML Rassat, *Droit Penal General* (2nd edn, Paris, Presses Universitaires France, 1999) No 325. For Germany, see Bundesgerichtshof, Entscheidungen des Bundesgerichtshofs in Strafsachen 32, 35, 41, 351. Art 28 of the Spanish Penal

As ICC Pre-Trial Chamber I has highlighted in the *Katanga and Ngudjolo* case, in this situation the person who physically carries out the objective elements of the crime acts under mistake, duress, or has no capacity of culpability.[150] Werle considers that this situation includes cases in which the physical perpetrator is not criminally liable because he is under the age required for criminal liability to arise[151] or he benefits from other grounds for excluding his criminal liability.[152] In turn, Van Sliedregt explicitly refers to cases in which the person used as a tool is a minor, acted with a mental defect or acted under mistake.[153] In the view of the author, among all those cases in which the persons used as tools are not fully criminally liable, those in which they act under either mistake or duress are, as shown by the *Erdemovic* case before the ICTY, the most relevant for the indirect perpetration of international crimes by senior political and military leaders.

In situations where the physical perpetrator is mistaken about the factual circumstances on which an objective element of the crime is based, or about a cause of justification, it is irrelevant whether the mistake was actively caused by the person behind, or whether the latter just took advantage of the mistake of the physical perpetrator to have him commit the crime.[154] This is the case when a senior military leader directs his subordinates to shell an undefended village by misleading them about the location of the enemy's artillery in that area.[155] In this particular scenario, subordinates follow the instructions of their superior because they believe the shelling is a lawful action based on what they believe is a lawful order; subordinates are not motivated by fear resulting from the threat of sanctions if they disobey the order of their superior.

According to Ambos, in this scenario, the superior dominates the will of his subordinates because the latter do not know that the shelling is unlawful, and he uses his 'superior knowledge' to secure the execution of the shelling.[156] Moreover,

---

Code has also embraced this notion, '*Son autores quienes realizan el hecho por si solos, conjuntamente or por medio de otro del que se sirven como instrumento*'. See also M Diaz y Garcia Conlledo, *La Autoria en Derecho Penal* (Barcelona, Universidad de Leon, 1991) 47 and 200; J Gonzalez Rus, 'Autoria Unica Inmediata, Autoria Mediata y Coautoria' in *Cuadernos de Derecho Judicial, No XXXIX Ed Consejo General del Poder Judicial* (1994). Swiss jurisprudence has also applied this notion. See Entscheidungen des Schweizerischen Bundesgerichts 101 IV 310; Entscheidungen des Schweizerischen Bundesgerichts 85 IV 23; S Trechsel and P Noll, *Schweizerisches Strafrecht, Allgemeiner Teil I, Allgemeine Voraussetzungen der Strafbarkeit* (5th edn, Zurich, Schulthess, 1998) 199.

[150] *Katanga and Ngudjolo Case* Confirmation of Charges (Above n 20), at para 495. See also Werle (*Ibid*), at 218.

[151] According to art 26 RS, '[t]he Court shall have no jurisdiction over any person who was under the age of 18 at the time of the alleged commission of a crime'.

[152] See arts 31, 32 and 33 RS. See also, Werle (Above n 50), at 218.

[153] Van Sliedregt (Above n 24), at 71.

[154] Ambos, *La Parte General del Derecho Penal Internacional* (Above n 2), at 215.

[155] Van Sliedregt (Above n 24), at 71, puts the example of a bomber pilot who drops poisoned bombs without being aware of their poisonous content. In this case, the superior of the pilot will be considered an indirect perpetrator or a perpetrator by means if it can be shown that he manipulated the pilot in that he knew that that the bombs contained poison, but assured his subordinate that they were 'clean' in order to have the poisoned bombs dropped.

[156] Ambos, *La Parte General del Derecho Penal Internacional* (Above n 2), at 216.

according to article 25(3)(a) RS, even if subordinates are not excused pursuant to articles 32[157] and 33 RS[158] because the order was manifestly unlawful and their mistake about the unlawfulness of the order was due to their lack of due diligence, the superior will be a principal to the crime as an indirect perpetrator as long as he profited from his superior knowledge and from the error of his subordinates to secure the execution of the shelling.[159]

---

[157] Art 32(1) RS establishes that mistakes of fact are only relevant if they negate the general subjective element (mental element) required by the crime in question, which, as a general rule, is comprised of *dolus* (which includes *dolus directus* in the first degree, *dolus directus* in the second degree and *dolus eventualis*). See *Lubanga Case* Confirmation of Charges (Above n 16), at paras 150–55. As a result, only those mistakes over the existence of the objective elements of the crime, which negate the perpetrator's *dolus*, are relevant under the RS; mistakes concerning the existence of factual circumstances for the application of a ground for justification or a ground for excuse are irrelevant. As, as a general rule, criminal liability does not arise from negligent behaviour under the RS, any mistake of fact by the perpetrator negates his *dolus* regardless of whether the mistake was due to his lack of due diligence or any other reason. As provided for in art 32(2) RS, mistakes of law only exclude the perpetrator's criminal liability if they negate the general subjective element of the crime; mistakes of law as to whether a given circumstance constitutes a ground for justification are excluded from the scope of application of art 32(2) RS. Moreover, according to art 32(1) RS, 'a mistake of law as to whether a particular type of conduct is a crime within the jurisdiction of the Court shall not be a ground for excluding criminal responsibility'. As a result, the scope of application of this ground for excuse is limited to mistakes over the social meaning for an average person (or, in the case of members of the armed forces, for an average soldier or an average commander) of the factual circumstances that establish the normative elements of the crime. See *Lubanga Case* Confirmation of Charges (Above n 16), at paras 315–16; A Eser, 'Mental Element-Mistake of Fact and Mistake of Law' in A Cassese, P Gaeta, and JRWD Jones (eds), *The Rome Statute of the International Criminal Court: A Commentary* (Oxford, Oxford University Press, 2002) 941.

[158] The ground for excuse provided for in art 33 RS is an exception to the general rule according to which 'the fact that a crime within the jurisdiction of the Court has been committed by a person pursuant to an order of a Government or of a superior, whether military or civilian, shall not relieve that person of criminal responsibility'. Moreover, it never excludes the perpetrator's criminal liability for genocide and crimes against humanity because, 'for the purpose of this article, orders to commit genocide or crimes against humanity are manifestly unlawful. See O Triffterer, 'Article 33: Superior Orders and Prescription of Law' in O Triffterer (ed), *Commentary on the Rome Statute of the International Criminal Court* (Baden-Baden, Nomos, 1999) 586; F Bueno Arus, 'Perspectivas de la Teoria General del Delito en el Estatuto de Roma de la Corte Penal Internacional de 17 de Julio de 1998' in FJ Quel Lopez (ed), *Creacion de una Jurisdiccion Penal Internacional, Coleccion Escuela Diplomatica* (4th edn, Madrid, 2000) 123–4. It only excludes the perpetrator's criminal liability for war crimes when the following three requisites set forth in art 33 RS are met. The first requisite requires that the physical perpetrator carries out the objective elements of the crime (in the example above, the shelling of the undefended village) in compliance with 'a legal obligation to obey orders of the Government or the superior in question'. The crime must take place in execution of a clear mandate (not just mere advice) to carry out a specific activity (in the example above, to shell certain coordinates) issued by the Government or a military or civilian superior acting within their respective spheres of competence. The second requisite requires that the physical perpetrator does not know that the order is unlawful. As a consequence, from the moment the perpetrator discovers the unlawfulness of the order, he cannot execute it without being criminally liable. The third requisite requires that, in addition to the perpetrator's unawareness of the unlawfulness of the order, the order is not manifestly unlawful. This third requisite seems to limit the scope of application of this ground for excuse to those mistakes over the unlawfulness of the order which are not due to the perpetrator's lack of due diligence.

[159] In this regard, it is important to highlight that art 25(3)(a) RS *in fine* embraces the notion of indirect perpetration regardless of whether the person used as a tool is criminally liable. See also Van Sliedregt (Above n 24), at 71. According to Van Sliedregt, in the above-mentioned example of the pilot who is manipulated by his superior to drop poisoned bombs without being aware of their poisonous content, if the pilot cannot avail himself of a defence pursuant to arts 32 and 33 RS, the superior can still be held liable as an indirect perpetrator pursuant to art 25(3)(a) RS.

Another situation of indirect perpetration through the use of a person who is not fully criminally liable takes place when the physical perpetrator acts under duress because he carries out the objective elements of the crime due to fear resulting from an imminent threat against his life or his relatives' lives. This is the case when a detention camp warden directs those police officers providing security to the camp to deport a number of camp prisoners and the police officers carry out his instructions because they are motivated by the fear of a summary execution if they refuse to do so. Another example of this type of situation is illustrated by the *Erdemovic* case before the ICTY.

i The Erdemovic *Case before the ICTY*

In the *Erdemovic* case, the defendant Drazen Erdemovic, a member of the 10th Sabotage Detachment of the Bosnian Serb army, entered a guilty plea after consenting to the following version of the facts set forth by the Prosecution:

> On 16 July 1995, he was sent with other members of his unit to the Branjevo collective farm near Pilica, northwest of Zvornik. Once there, they were informed that later that day Muslim men from 17 to 60 years of age would be brought to the farm in buses. The men were unarmed civilians who had surrendered to the members of the Bosnian Serb army or police after the fall of the United Nations 'safe area' at Srebrenica. Members of the military police took the civilians off the buses in groups of ten and escorted them to a field next to the farm buildings, where they were lined up with their backs to a firing squad. The men were then killed by Drazen Erdemovic and other members of his unit with the help of soldiers from another brigade.[160]

In his guilty plea, Erdemovic added the following to the version of the facts presented by the Prosecution:

> Your honour, I had to do this. If I had refused, I would have been killed together with the victims. When I refused, they told me: 'If you are sorry for them, stand up, line up with them and we will kill you too'. I am not sorry for myself but for my family, my wife and son who then had nine months, and I could not refuse because then they would have killed me.[161]

The first thing that must be underscored in this case is that physical perpetrators like Erdemovic keep their capacity of action because, although they act out of fear, they are not physically forced to carry out the objective elements of the crime. For this reason, one should distinguish these cases from those other cases where the person who carries out the objective elements of the crimes acts subject to a *vis absoluta*—for instance, when a subordinate is pushed by his superior against the special envoy of the enemy who is standing next to a railway when the train is approaching, and, as a result, the special envoy of the enemy falls on the railway and is mortally wounded by the train. In cases of *vis absoluta*, it is not necessary to

---

[160] *Prosecutor v Erdemovic* (Judgment) ICTY-96-22-T (29 Nov 1996) para 2.
[161] *Ibid* at para 10.

resort to the notion of indirect perpetration because the person behind (the superior in our example) is considered a direct perpetrator who uses his subordinate as he could have used any other non-human tool, such as a hammer or pistol.[162]

In the Erdemovic scenario—where the physical perpetrator acts out of fear for his life and/or his relatives' lives based on an imminent threat—the question arises as to whether the level of pressure over the physical perpetrator (the subordinate) is such that the physical perpetrator's control over the action turns into a control over his will by the person behind (the superior), which is used by the latter to secure the commission of the crime.

According to Roxin, the notion of control of the will in this scenario is a normative concept because only when the legal requirements for the exclusion of the criminal liability of the subordinate are met, his control over the action turns into a control over his will by the superior.[163] For Kuper, however, although the legislative exoneration of the subordinate is important to formally consider a superior as an indirect perpetrator, the essence of the superior's control of the subordinate's will lies on the use by the superior of an intense pressure over the subordinate in order to motivate him, and essentially undermine his freedom to decide whether to physically carry out the objective elements of the crime.[164]

In the author's view, a strict application of the approach proposed by Roxin, which makes the existence of a superior's control over the subordinate's will subject to the exoneration of the subordinate, would preclude the application of the notion of indirect perpetration in this type of cases before the *Ad hoc* Tribunals because, according to the ICTY Appeals Chamber:

> [D]uress does not afford a complete defence to a soldier charged with a crime against humanity and/or a war crime involving the killing of innocent human beings.[165]

The situation is somewhat different in the system of the RS because, under article 31(1)(d) RS, duress constitutes a ground for excluding criminal liability.[166]

---

[162] JL Hernandez Plasencia, *La Autoria Mediata en Derecho Penal* (Granada, Comares, 1996) 93 [hereinafter Hernandez Plasencia]; Ambos, *La Parte General del Derecho Penal Internacional* (Above n 2), at 202–203.

[163] Roxin (Above n 140), at 144–8.

[164] W Kuper, *Mittelbare Taterschaft, Verbotsirrtum des Tatmittlers und Verantwortungsprinzip* in Juristenzeitung (1989) 946.

[165] Accordingly, the ICTY Appeals Chamber held that in this type of case, duress could only be used in mitigation of punishment. See *Prosecutor v Erdemovic* (Appeals Chamber Judgment) ICTY-96-22-A (7 Oct 1997) para 19; See also Cassese, *International Criminal Law* (Above n 1), at 248.

[166] For Rodriguez-Villasante y Prieto (Above n 24), at 429–30, the inclusion in art 31(1)(d) RS of this ground for excluding criminal responsibility (which is in fact a ground for excuse) corrects the controversial approach taken by the *Erdemovic Case* Appeals Judgment, according to which duress is not a ground for excuse in the case of crimes against humanity. It requires the existence of threat of imminent death or of continuing or imminent serious bodily harm against the physical perpetrator or another person. The threat must come from a third person or from circumstances beyond the control of the physical perpetrator (such as natural forces) and must bring about a real, imminent and serious risk—unlike self-defence, it is irrelevant whether the risk results from the lawful or unlawful use of force. The key element is that the physical perpetrator must commit the crime as a result of giving in to the psychological pressure to avoid the threat of harm. The psychological pressure must be strong enough to overcome the resistance of an average person (or, in the case of members of the armed

Nevertheless, considering that the notion of indirect perpetration under article 25(3)(a) RS does not require that the physical perpetrator be fully exonerated of criminal liability, it is advisable to move somewhat away from an exclusively normative approach, and give particular weight to the intensity of the pressure and the intention of the superior in exercising such pressure.

The Erdemovic situation must also be distinguished from those other cases where the physical perpetrators act solely out of fear of disobeying the orders of their superiors. In these cases, the pressure comes exclusively from a legal duty to obey because the physical perpetrators know that the orders of their superiors are unlawful and there is no additional threat to their lives or to their relatives' lives if they fail to comply with them. In other words, while in the Erdemovic situation, the physical perpetrators face death or the loss of a close relative if they do not commit the offence, in this second category of cases, the physical perpetrators only face a disciplinary sanction. Due to the fact that, in principle, law can require an individual to bear a disciplinary sanction, but it cannot require him to bear death, those physical perpetrators who commit crimes because they are fearful of disobeying their superiors' unlawful orders are considered to have made this choice freely.[167] As a result, as Ambos has pointed out, one cannot say that those superiors who issue the unlawful orders are indirect perpetrators because they do not really control the will of the physical perpetrators.[168] They could only be considered indirect perpetrators if they accompany their unlawful orders with imminent death threats.[169]

C Indirect Perpetration by Using Persons Who are Fully Criminally Liable: Commission of Crimes through Organised Structures of Power

i Concept: Superiors' Control of the Subordinates' Will within Organised Structures of Power

When crimes are committed through organised structures of power (ie state structures or Mafia-like organisations), the decisions to carry out such crimes are

---

forces, of an average soldier or military superior). Art 31(1)(d) RS also requires that the response (the commission of the objective elements of the crime) be objectively suitable and necessary to avoid the threatened harm. Moreover, the response must not be wholly disproportionate to the threatened harm, although there is no express requirement that the damage caused be lesser than the threatened harm. From a subjective perspective, art 31 (1)(d) RS requires that the physical perpetrator (i) be aware that his conduct constitutes a suitable, necessary and not wholly disproportionate response to the threatened harm; and (ii) does not intend to cause a greater harm than the one he seeks to avoid. Finally, it will be up to the ICC case law to decide whether it is also necessary for the main goal of the physical perpetrator to be the avoidance of the threatened harm.

[167] Ambos, *La Parte General del Derecho Penal Internacional* (Above n 2), at 208–209.
[168] *Ibid* at 209.
[169] FC Schroeder, *Der Täter hinter dem Täter: Ein Beitrag zur Lehre von der mittelbaren Täterschaft* (Berlin, Duncker and Humblot, 1965) 136.

frequently made before the execution of the crimes by senior political and military leaders who are located far away from the scene of the crimes,[170] which complicates the investigation and identification of the main protagonists of the crimes. The people who physically carry out the objective elements of the crimes are not the main protagonists of the crimes because they neither participate in the initial decision to commit the crimes, nor in the subsequent planning and preparation at the different levels of the organised structure of power. In fact, they are simply given the 'order' to physically carry out the objective elements of the crime in a certain way.[171]

In these kinds of cases, the main protagonists of the crimes can be said to be the senior political and military leaders who plan out the commission of the crimes, direct the organised structures of power that they control to implement the plan, and supervise how mid-level superiors define, in further detail, the criminal plan and how the lowest echelons of their organisation physically carry out the objective elements of the crimes.[172] As a result, the question arises whether those superiors are criminally liable as perpetrators or principals to the crimes or whether they can only be considered as mere participants or accessories to the crimes.

The problem in these cases is that the persons who have physically carried out the objective elements of the crimes are fully criminal liable. Hence, the question is whether senior political and military leaders can be considered indirect perpetrators (principals to the crime) despite the fact that the direct perpetrators are fully criminally liable.

Apart from the consequences of the solution given to this problem for sentencing purposes, such a solution is important because planning, instigating, ordering or aiding and abetting are modes of participation in crimes committed by third persons and therefore they are subject to the principles of accessoryship and unity of attribution. Hence, only if these cases are treated as cases of indirect perpetration, would these principles not be applicable. Moreover, adopting this last approach would entail that, when crimes are committed through organised structures of power, the criminal liability of the persons who physically commit the crimes is irrelevant for the purposes of determining the criminal liability of those senior political and military leaders who plan and direct the commission of the crimes.

According to one approach to this problem,[173] when the crimes are physically committed by subordinates as a consequence of implementing the orders given by

---

[170] K Ambos, *Dominio del Hecho por Dominio de la Voluntad en virtud de Aparatos Organizados de Poder* (Bogota, Universidad Externado de Colombia, 1998) 12.

[171] See Roxin (Above n 139), at 247.

[172] F Munoz Conde, '¿Como Imputar a Titulo de Autores a las Personas que sin Realizar Acciones Ejecutivas, Deciden la Realizacion de un Delito en el Ambito de la Delincuencia Economica Empresarial?' in Donna (dir), *Revista de Derecho Penal* (9th edn, Buenos Aires, 2002) 62.

[173] See T Rotsch, 'Tatherrschaft Kraft Organisationsherrschaft' (2000) 112 *Zeitschrift fir die gesamte Strafrechtswissenschaft* 561; H Kohler, *Strafrecht Allgemeiner Teil* (Berlin, 1997) 509 [hereinafter Kohler]; J Renzikowski, *Restriktiver Taterbegriff und fahrlassige Beteiligung* (Tubingen, Mohr Siebeck, 1997) 87.

their superiors, or when subordinates have, at least, been provoked or assisted by their superiors, one can resort to a mode of liability other than perpetration, to which some national criminal laws attach the same penalty as the one attached to perpetration.[174] According to this approach, in the context of an organised structure of power, those who give the orders would simply be liable for ordering or instigating the crimes because they psychologically influence their subordinates, convince them to commit the crime, and have no further relation with the crime at the execution stage. For this approach, when the subordinates are not mere innocent agents, but fully criminally responsible for their free decision to carry out the objective elements of the crime, the criminal liability of the person instructing the commission of the crime can only amount to ordering or instigating because of the lack of control of the crime.[175] This is because the person behind the crime can never be sure of whether his decision will be carried out by his subordinates.

However, unlike other kinds of organisations, organised structures of power, such as organised state structures or Mafia-like organisations, are hierarchically organised, their members are interchangeable and there is a high degree of automatism in its functioning.[176] In these situations, senior political and military leaders who control organised structures of power only need to give an order to secure the commission of the crimes, without having to carry out any further act of provocation or assistance to the physical perpetrators of the crimes. In addition, for Ambos, instigating or ordering requires a more direct relationship between the instigator and the person instigated regarding a specific case. In cases where an organised structure of power is used, the person behind the crime does not, in general, even know who is going to carry out his order.[177]

Moreover, some legal writers, such as Munoz Conde, have stated that considering the hierarchical structure of the said organisations and the division of functions and competence within them, it seems strange to attribute criminal liability as mere participants (accessories) in the crime to senior political and military leaders for the crimes committed by their subordinates.[178] For these writers, this solution does not adequately reflect the nature of the contributions made by senior political and military leaders because it relegates these leaders to a secondary role, which does not correspond to their real level of relevance when the crimes are committed through organised structures of power. In this regard, Silva Sanchez considers that it is surprising that senior political and military leaders who control

---

[174] See arts 28 and 29 of the Spanish Penal Code, which attach the same penalty to the instigator and the necessary contributor as to the perpetrator or principal to the crime.

[175] See Mir Puig (Above n 47), at 372; Quintero Olivares (Above n 26), at 625–6.

[176] See Kohler (Above n 173), at 510, who prefers to characterise the contribution of the superiors as instigation even in those cases of interchangeability of the subordinates because, for him, the fact that the physical perpetrator is criminally liable prevents any other person behind him being considered as a perpetrator of the crime.

[177] See K Ambos and C Grammer, 'Dominio del Hecho por Organizacion. La Responsabilidad de la Conduccion Militar Argentina por la Muerte de Elisabeth Kasemann' (2003) 12 *Revista Penal* 28 [hereinafter Ambos and Grammer].

[178] F Munoz Conde, *El delito de alzamiento de bienes* (2nd edn, Barcelona, Libreria Bosch, 1999) 180.

the crime by planning it and controlling the means and tools through which the criminal activity is carried out are not considered perpetrators (principals), but mere participants or accessories to the crime.[179]

A second approach to this problem is rooted in the idea that the notion of perpetration is not limited to those who physically carry out the objective elements of the crime, but it also covers those who, despite being far away from the scene of the crime, control the commission of the crime. This approach was originally put forward by Roxin[180] and it consists of a variant of the notion of control of the crime which, as seen above, defines perpetrators as the persons who dominate the commission of the crime in the sense that they decide whether the crime will be carried out and how it will be performed.[181] In these cases, the notion of control of the crime is denominated 'control of the will' because the indirect perpetrator's control of the crime is not derived from the physical execution of the objective elements of the crime, but it is derived from the power of his dominant will.[182]

As ICC Pre Trial Chamber I has pointed out in the *Katanga and Ngudjolo* case, this approach is based on the consideration that an organised structure of power has a life of its own, irrespective of the identity of its replaceable members.[183] Therefore, the person who controls it can, in general, be certain that his wishes will be carried out by his subordinates, and does not need to bother about who will carry them out. In addition, the person who controls an organised structure of power does not need to resort to coercion or deception of the physical perpetrators because he knows that should a member of his organisation refuse to carry out his instructions, someone else would replace him and carry them out.[184]

Thus, from the perspective of the senior political or military leader who controls an organised structure of power, subordinates are not perceived as free responsible individuals, but they are actually perceived as anonymous and replaceable members of the organisation. The indirect perpetrator keeps control of the crime because the commission of the crime cannot be stopped by the opposition or resistance of his subordinates due to the fact that they are fungible and should they refuse to implement the superior's decision, they would be replaced by other members of the organisation. The replaceable character of the physical perpetrator is the key factor, which sustains the superior's control of the will of the subordinates, in the sense that the superior's dominant will has ultimate control of the

---

[179] JM Silva Sanchez, 'Responsabilidad Penal de las Empresas y de sus Organos en Derecho Espanol' in *Fundamentos del sistema europeo de derecho Penal. Libro homenaje a Claus Roxin* (Barcelona, JM Bosch, 1995) 369.

[180] Roxin (Above n 139), at 242; C Roxin, 'Sobre la autoria y la participacion en el derecho Penal' in *Problemas actuales de las ciencias Penales y de la filosofia del Derecho* (Buenos Aires, Ediciones Pannedille, 1970) 60. The term originally used by Roxin to refer to this notion is *Tatherrschaft*.

[181] For a more detailed analysis and critique of such a theory, see A Perez Cepeda, *La responsabilidad de los administradores de sociedades: criterios de atribucion* (Barcelona, Cedecs Editorial, 1997) 369 [hereinafter Perez Cepeda].

[182] Roxin (Above n 139), at 141 et seq.

[183] *Katanga and Ngudjolo Case* Confirmation of Charges (Above n 20), at paras 515 and 516. See also Roxin (Above n 139), at 245.

[184] Roxin (Above n 139), at 245.

crime. Therefore, the superior does not leave the decision on whether or not to commit the crime up to the persons who physically carry out its objective elements.[185] From this perspective, the superior appears as the main perpetrator.[186]

As ICC Pre Trial Chamber I has held in the *Katanga and Ngdujolo* case:

> In addition, particular characteristics of the organised and hierarchical apparatus enable the leader to actually secure the commission of crimes. In essence, the leader's control over the apparatus allows him to utilise his subordinates as 'a mere gear in a giant machine' in order to produce the criminal result 'automatically' [. . .]Above all, this 'mechanisation' seeks to ensure that the successful execution of the plan will not be compromised by any particular subordinate's failure to comply with an order. Any one subordinate who does not comply may simply be replaced by another who will; the actual executor of the order is merely a fungible individual. As such, the organisation also must be large enough to provide a sufficient suppy of subordinates. [] The main attribute of this kind of organisation is a mechanism that enables its highest authorities to ensure automatic compliance with their orders. Thus, '[s]uch Organisation develops namely a life that is independent of the changing composition of its members. It functions, without depending on the individual identity of the executant, as if it were automatic.' An authority who issues an order within such an organisation therefore assumes a different kind of responsibility than ordinary cases of criminal ordering. In the latter cases, article 25 (3)(b) of the Statute provides that a leader or commander who orders the commission of a crime may be regarded as an accessory.[187]

Roxin requires that the organised structure of power must act outside the law in more than just exceptional circumstances.[188] According to him, when an organised structure of power (ie a state army) usually acts in accordance with the law, a criminal order from its top or mid-level leaders may not be sufficient to set in motion such an organised structure of power. In fact, the physical perpetrators would have to be carefully selected and individually enrolled in the common plan because they are not replaceable. Very few people within the organisation would be willing to carry out the criminal order, especially considering that such an order would have to be issued and carried out evading the regular mode of functioning of the organisation, and it would have to be carefully hidden from the rest of the members of the organisation. Thus, in these cases, it can be said that the crimes are committed 'against the organised structure of power' as opposed to 'through the organised structure of power', and they cannot be attributed to the organisation, but to particular individuals within it.

---

[185] Roxin (Above n 139), at 245.

[186] *Ibid.*

[187] *Katanga and Ngudjolo Case* Confirmation of Charges (Above n 20), at paras 515–517. See also Roxin (Above n 139), at 245.

[188] Roxin (Above n 139), at 249. See also T Rotsch, 'Die Rechtsfigur des Taters hinter dem Tater bei der Begehung von Straftaten im Rahmen organisatorischer Machtapparate und ihre Ubertragbarkeit auf wirtschaftliche Organisationsstrukturen' (1998) *Neue Zeitschrift fur Strafrecht* 495 [hereinafter Rotsch, *Die Rechtsfigur*]. Compare K Kuhl, *Strafrecht Allgemeiner Teil* (4th edn, Munich, Vahlen Franz GMBH, 2002) § 20, No 73b [hereinafter Kuhl].

Nevertheless, for Bottke, this requirement is not necessary because subordinates have a diminished capacity to autonomously decide whether or not to carry out the objective elements of the crime and to impose their refusals on their superiors. Thus, due to the power derived from the institutional connection, subordination and power of direction, the superior can use the subordinate as an instrument, who does not have the capacity for autonomous action.[189]

ICC Pre-Trial Chamber I has not addressed this matter in the *Katanga and Ngudjolo* case. As a result, when defining, at paragraphs 500 to 518 of its Confirmation of the Charges Decision, the objective elements of the notion of indirect perpetration through the use of an organised structure of powers (also referred to by ICC Pre-Trial Chamber I as 'control over an organisation' or 'control over an organised apparatus of power'), it does not require that the relevant organised structure of power must act outside the law in more than just exceptional circumstances.

Unlike in cases of indirect perpetration through coercion or deception of somebody else, when using an organised structure of power to carry out an offence, the members of the organised structure of power who physically carry out the objective elements of the crime may: (a) have full knowledge of its underlying circumstances; and (b) act under no coercion when they decide whether or not to perform the crime. Therefore, from their perspective, they may retain ultimate control of the criminal action, and, thus, they may be criminally liable as direct perpetrators.[190]

Although direct and indirect perpetration results from different conditions (the physical execution of the objective elements of the crime and the control of an

---

[189] S Bottke, 'Criminalidad Economica y Derecho Criminal Economico en la Republica Federal de Alemania' (1999) 4 *Revista Penal* 25 [hereinafter Bottke]. In addition, for this author, even though the notion of OSP is based on pre-juridical criteria, such as the alleged dominion of an organised structure of power and the alleged use of an instrument to commit a crime, its use is justified when the situation constitutes an egregious violation of the most important values upon which an international community is built. See Bottke (*Ibid*), at 26. See also Bundesgerichtshof wistra (1998) 150; S Cramer and Sternberg-Lieben (Above n 47), at § 25, No 25; A Ransiek, *Unternehmensstrafrecht. Strafrecht, Verfassungsrecht, Regelungsalternativen* (Munich, Muller Jur Vlg CF, 1996) 46–9; K Lackner and K Kuhl, *Strafgesetzbuch mit Erlauterungen* (24th edn, Munich, CH Beck, 2001) § 25, No 2. Compare Kuhl (*Ibid*), at § 20 No 73b.

As Judge Iain Bonomy has explained, the German Supreme Court has embraced the notion of OSP: 'In Germany an accused may be held responsible as a perpetrator (*Tater*) for using another as an instrument or tool (*Werkzeug*) to physically perpetrate a crime, regardless of whether the physical perpetrator is himself culpable or is an "innocent agent", that is, not responsible for the criminal act because, for example, he is a minor or lacks the *mens rea* required for the crime'. See *Prosecutor v Milutinovic* (Decision On Ojdanic's Motion Challenging Jurisdiction: Indirect Co-Perpetration, Separate Opinion of Judge Iain Bonomy) ICTY-05-87-PT (22 Mar 2006). However, the German Supreme Court has not upheld the requirement that the organised structure of power must not only exceptionally act outside the law. See Bundesgerichtshof, Entscheidungen des Bundesgerichtshofs in Strafsachen 40 at p 237, 43 at p 219. See also Zeitschrift fur Wirtschafts-und Steuerstrafrecht (1998) 150.

[190] Roxin (Above n 139), at 245. See also *Katanga and Ngudjolo Case* Confirmation of Charges (Above n 20), at para. 499, in particular fn 660.

organised structure of power), they can logically and teleologically exist at the same time.[191]

Nevertheless even in this last scenario, from the perspective of the senior political or military leader behind the crime, the direct perpetrator is just an anonymous and interchangeable person, and his decision does not affect the implementation of the superior's decision to commit the crime. As a result, when the person carrying out the objective elements of the crime is criminally liable, the person behind has been referred to as the 'perpetrator behind the perpetrator'.[192] However, if the person physically carrying out the objective elements of the crime is not fully criminally liable, the person behind has been referred to as the 'perpetrator behind the actor'.[193] As for the purposes of ascertaining the criminal responsibility of the senior political or military leader behind the crime, it is irrelevant whether the physical perpetrator is criminally liable or not,[194] the former have been referred to by the ICTY Trial Judgment in the *Stakic* case by using the expression 'perpetrator behind the perpetrator/actor'.[195]

For Roxin, indirect perpetrators are not only those senior political and military leaders at the very top of organised structures of power who, without carrying out any objective element of the crime, decide the commission of the crime. For him, those at the intermediate echelons of the organised structures of power who can give 'orders' to their subordinates are also principals to the crime due to their control of the will, in case they use their power for the execution of criminal activities.[196]

Regarding intermediate superiors, Ambos has also pointed out that crimes are committed through an organised structure of power because its members, at different levels, direct the part of the organisation that is under their control at securing the commission of the crimes.[197] From the perspective of the senior political and military leaders, members of the organised structure of power at the intermediate level are replaceable links within the organisation. Nevertheless, from the perspective of such intermediate superiors, they retain ultimate control of the criminal actions of their subordinates because: (a) they have full knowledge of the underlying factual circumstances of the objective elements of the crime;

---

[191] C Roxin, *Strafrecht Allgemeiner Teil* (Vol II, Munich, Beck Juristischer Verlag, 2003) § 25, No 107.

[192] Kuhl (Above n 188), at § 20, No 72; Rotsch, *Die Rechtsfigur* (Above n 188), at 491. This is also the expression used by ICC Pre-Trial Chamber I in *Katanga and Ngudjolo Case* Confirmation of Charges (Above n 20), paras 496 and 497.

[193] *Stakic Case* Trial Judgment (Above n 19), at para 741.

[194] Entscheidungen des Bundesgerichtshofs in Strafsachen 40, p 218.

[195] *Stakic Case* Trial Judgment (Above n 19), at paras 741–3.

[196] Roxin (Above n 139), at 248.

[197] In this regard, Ambos and Grammer (Above n 177), at 31, have pointed out that the traditional formula to distinguish between perpetrators (principals) and other participants (accessories) in the crime has been replaced by three levels. The first level, the highest, is comprised of the indirect perpetrators who plan and organise the crimes, that is, those who control and put in motion the organisation. The second level is comprised by the intermediate superiors who control a part of the organisation and direct it towards the implementation of the plan. They can, thus, also be considered indirect perpetrators. The third level, the lowest, is comprised of the physical perpetrators who play only an auxiliary role in the global criminal event.

(b) they act under no coercion when deciding whether to direct the part of the organised structure of power under their control at securing the commission of the crimes; and (c) they perceive the members of the part of the organisation under their control as anonymous and replaceable, and, thus, do not leave up to the autonomous decision of the physical perpetrators whether the objective elements of the crimes will be performed.[198]

In sum, the basis for the control of the crime in these cases is the control of the will of the physical perpetrators as a result of the control of the organised structure of power to which they belong. This presupposes an extensive notion of 'instrument' or 'tool' based on the interchangeable character of those who physically commit the crime and who are members of the lowest echelons of the organisation, and on the automatism in the functioning of the organisation. It is for this reason that this variant of the broader notion of indirect perpetration is referred to in this book as 'OSP'[199].

Moreover, as ICC Pre-Trial Chamber I has highlighted at paragraphs 498 and 499 of the *Katanga and Ngudjolo* Case Confirmation of the Charges:

> Several groups of cases have been presented as examples for the perpetrator behind the perpetrator's being assigned principal responsibility despite the existence of a responsible, direct perpetrator (i.e., one whose actions are not exculpated by mistake, duress, or the lack of capacity for blameworthiness). This notwithstanding, the cases most relevant to international criminal law are those in which the perpetrator commits the crime through another by means of 'control over an organisation'(*Organisationsherrschaft*). []
> Despite some criticism of this doctrine, the Chamber notes that the drafters of the Rome Statute sought to establish a mode of commission in article 25 (3)(a) of the Statute which encompasses the commission of a crime through a non-innocent individual (i.e. responsible) acting as an instrument. Accordingly, contrary to the suggestions of Germain Katanga's Defence at the hearing on 11 July 2008, assigning the highest degree of responsibility for commission of a crime—that is, considering him a principal—to a person who uses another, individually responsible person to commit a crime, is no merely a theoretical possibility in scarce legal literature, but has been codified in article 25 (3)(a) of the Statute.

---

[198] Roxin (Above n 139), at 245.

[199] The notion of OSP has been supported in relation to State criminality by inter alia P Faraldo Cabana, *Responsabilidad Penal del Dirigente en Estructuras Jerarquicas* (Valencia, Tirant lo Blanch, 2004); J Figueiredo Dias, 'Autoria y Participacion en el dominio de la Criminalidad Organizada: El Dominio de la Organizacion' in C Ferre Olive and E Anarte Borrallo (eds), *Delincuencia Organizada: Aspectos Penales, Procesales y Criminologicos* (Universidad de Huelva, 1999) 99–107; G Kupper, 'Zur Abgrenzung der Taterschaftsformen' (1998) 3 *Goldammer's Archiv* 523; G Heine, Taterschaft und Teilnahme in staatlichen Machtapparaten (2000) *JZ* 924; F Munoz Conde, 'Problemas de Autoria y Participacion en la Criminalidad Organizada' in C Ferre Olive and E Anarte Borrallo (eds), *Delincuencia Organizada: Aspectos Penales, Procesales y Criminologicos* (Universidad de Huelva, 1999) 151–9 [hereinafter Munoz Conde]; H Olasolo and A Perez Cepeda, 'The Notion of Control of the Crime in the Jurisprudence of the ICTY: The Stakic Case' (2004) 4 *International Criminal Law Review* 506–508 [hereinafter Olasolo and Perez Cepeda]; Hernandez Plasencia (Above n 162), at 273; K Rogall, 'Bewaltigung von Systemkriminalitat' in C Roxin and G Widmaier (eds), *50 Jahre Bundesgerichtshof, Festgabe aus der Wissenschaft, Band IV* (Munich, 2000) 424; J Schlosser, *Mittelbare Individuelle Verantwortlichkeit im Volkerstrafrecht* (Berlin, 2004); H Vest, 'Humanitatsverbrechen—Herausforderung fur das Individualstrafrecht?' (2001) 113 *Zeitschrift fir die gesamte Strafrechtswissenschaft* 457–98.

ii Objective and Subjective Elements of the Notion of OSP

According to ICC Pre Trial Chamber I, a number of requirements have to be met for the application of the notion of OSP. First, the physical perpetrators must be members of an organisation or group organised into a hierarchy ('organised and hierarchical apparatus of power').[200]

Second, the execution of the crimes must be secured by 'almost automatic compliance with the orders'.[201] This requirement is fulfilled when the physical perpetrators are replaceable, which requires that the group or organisation to which they belong have a certain size—Roxin also requires that such group or organisation must act outside the law in more than just exceptional circumstances.[202] However, according to ICC Pre-Trial Chamber I, this is not the only manner in which this requirement can be fulfilled. On the contrary, as it pointed out in the *Katanga and Ngudjolo* case:

> Attributes to the organisation—other than the replaceability of subordinates—may also enable automatic compliance with the senior authority's orders. An alternative means by which a leader secures automatic compliance via his control of the apparatus may be through intensive, strict, and violent training regimes. For example, abducting minors and subjecting them to punishing training regimes in which they are taught to shoot, pillage, rape, and kill, may be an effective means for ensuring automatic compliance with leaders' orders to commit such acts.[203]

Third, the relevant senior political or military leader must use the organised structure of power, or part thereof, that he controls to secure the commission of the crimes. In this regard, ICC Pre-Trial Chamber I has explained that:

> The leader's ability to secure this automatic compliance with his orders is the basis for his principal—rather than accesorial—liability. The highest authority does not merely order the commission of a crime, but through his control over the organisation, essentially decides whether and how the crime would be committed.[204]

As a result, any activity which neither puts in motion, nor propels the organised structure of power towards the performance of the objective elements of the crime, can, at the most, only give rise to liability as an accessory to the crime[205] (ie advising to undertake a campaign of persecution without having any executive power, planning a mass deportation without having any executive power, recruiting volunteers to join an organised structure of power who subsequently will be employed as physical perpetrators, or providing the necessary information for the performance of the objective elements of the offence). Hence, one can only

---

[200] *Katanga and Ngudjolo Case* Confirmation of Charges (Above n 20), at paras. 511–514.

[201] *Ibid*, at paras. 515–518.

[202] *Ibid*, at paras. 515–517.

[203] *Ibid*, at para. 518.

[204] *Ibid*, at para. 518. See also See also *Stakic Case* Trial Judgment (Above n 19), at paras. 497 and 498.

[205] Roxin (Above n 139), at 249.

consider those persons who act as advisors, who contribute to the implementation of plans or orders without the power to give new orders or who simply provide the means to commit the crime as accessories to the crime.[206]

From a subjective perspective, the notion of OSP requires that the senior political or military leader who uses the organised structure of power that he controls to secure the commission of the crimes fulfils all the subjective elements required by the crimes in question, including any requisite ulterior intent or *dolus specialis*.[207] In addition, the defendant must also be aware of his control over the commission of the crime, which includes the defendant's awareness of the hierarchical structure of his organisation, his position within such a hierarchical structure and the replaceable character of the physical perpetrators.[208]

iii Applications of the Notion of OSP: The Juntas Trial and the German Border Case

As ICC Pre-Trial Chamber I has pointed out in the *Katanga and Ngudjolo* case, the notion of OSP, in addition to being accepted by modern legal doctrine, has been explicitly applied in a number of national jurisdictions to date,[209] as well as in the *Stakic* Trial Judgment at the ICTY and in the jurisprudence of ICC Pre-Trial Chambers I and III in the *Katanga and Ngudjolo* and *Bemba* cases.[210] Moreover, as

---

[206] *Ibid.*

[207] *Katanga and Ngudjolo Case* Confirmation of Charges (Above n 20), at para. 527. See also *Stakic Case* Trial Judgment (Above n 19), at paras 495, 587 (in relation to the crime of murder) and 818 (in relation to the crime of persecution); Roxin (*Ibid*), at 550; Olasolo and Perez Cepeda (Above n 199), at 523–4.

[208] *Katanga and Ngudjolo Case* Confirmation of Charges (*Ibid*), at 538–539. See also *Stakic Case* Trial Judgment (*Ibid*), at para 498, in connection with paras 493–4; Roxin (*Ibid*), at 550; Olasolo and Perez Cepeda (*Ibid*), at 524-5.

[209] *Katanga and Ngudjolo Case* Confirmation of Charges (*Ibid*), at 510. For Argentina, see the Judgment of the Camara Federal de Apelaciones en lo Criminal de la Capital Federal (13 December 1985) in the case against the members of the three Juntas that governed Argentina from 1976 to 1983. This notion has also been used by the Argentine jurisprudence to characterise the conduct of the main executives of an enterprise that had committed crimes against the environment. See Judgment of the Camara Nacional en lo Criminal y Correccional Federal de la Capital Federal, 'Sala 4a' (22 May 2002). See also MA Sancinetti and M Ferrante, *El Derecho Penal en la Proteccion de los Derechos Humanos, La Proteccion de los Derechos Humanos mediante el Derecho Penal en las Transiciones Democraticas* (Buenos Aires, Hammurabi, 1999) 204–12. Chilean Courts have applied the notion of OSP in the case against Generals Contreras and Espinoza for the murdering of the former Chilean Minister of Foreign Affairs, Orlando Letelier. The judgment is published in Fallos del Mes, Year XXXV, Nov 1993, Suplementaria, p 154. The Peruvian Supreme Court has applied the notion of OSP in the case against Abimael Guzman (former leader of *Sendero Luminso*). Judgment of 14 December 2007, Case Num. 5385-200. The German Supreme Court has applied the notion of OSP in the German Border Case, Bundesgerichtshof, Neue Juristische Wochenschrift (1994) 2307 and in other subsequent cases, Bundesgerichtshof 5 StR 98/94 (26 Jul 1997) and Bundesgerichtshof 5 StR 176/98 (28 Oct 1998). See also Kuhl (Above n 188), at § 20 No 73; H Trondle and T Fischer, *Strafgesetzbuch Kommentar* (51st edn, Munich, 2003) § 25 No 3c. For Spain, the judgment of the Spanish Supreme Court of 14 Oct 1999 with Judge Joaquin Martin Canivell presiding is especially important as the notion of OSP was applied to convict some leaders of the terrorist organisation ETA. See also the judgments of the Spanish Supreme Court of 13 Dec 2002 and 17 July 2008.

[210] *Katanga and Ngudjolo Case* Confirmation of Charges (Above n 20), at 510.

will be seen in the next chapter, OSP is also part of the notion of 'joint criminal enterprise at the leadership level' that has been applied in a number of cases before the ICTY.[211]

The *Stakic, Katanga and Ngudjolo* and *Bemba* cases will be dealt with in Chapter 5 of this book, as they are all cases in which the notion of OSP has been applied jointly with the notion of co-perpetration based on joint control of the crime. Nevertheless, it is worth-mentioning at this moment that, in relation to the apli-cation of the notion of OSP in the *Bemba* case, ICC Pre-Trial Chamber I has found that:

> Finally, most recently, the Pre-Trial Chamber III of the Court also endorsed this notion of individual criminal responsibility in the case of *The Prosecutor v. Jean Pierre Bemba Gombo*. Having established the suspect's position as the leader of thte organisation and described the functioning of the militia, the Pre-Trial Chamber III stated: 'In light of the foregoing, the Chamber considers that there are reasonable grounds to believe that, as a result of his authority over his military organisation, Mr. [. . .] had the means to exercise control over the crime committed by MLC troops deployed in the CAR'.[212]

The *Juntas* Trial carried out in Argentina and the *German Border* case constitute hallmarks in the application of the notion of OSP. In the *Juntas* Trial, the defen-dants were members of the three consecutive military Juntas, which governed Argentina from 1976 to 1983. In the *German Border* case, the defendants were some of the members of the National Defence Council (*Nationaler Verteidigungsrat*) responsible for the direction of defence and security measures in East Germany. In both cases, the notion of OSP was applied to convict the accused for the crimes committed by their subordinates.

The value of the national case law arising out of these two cases has been recently dealt with by ICC Pre-Trial Chamber I in the *Katanga and Ngudjolo* case as a result of a challenge made by the Defence for Germain Katanga. According to ICC Pre-Trial Chamber I:

> The Defence for Germain Katanga submitted that, although this notion was applied by the Appeals Chamber in the Argentine Junta Trial, the decision was overturned by the National Supreme Court. According to the Defence for Germain Katanga, the Supreme Court rejected the theory on the ground that it had not been applied in Germany (its country of origin), and also because it could lead to inequitable results. [] Rejection by an Argentine court can hardly be said to preclude the International Criminal Court from resorting to this notion of criminal responsibility if it finds compelling reasons to do so. Nevertheless, German jurisprudence was in fact applied to this notion in the East German Border Trials. Moreover, while the present Decision will not discuss the Argentine Supreme Court's reasons for rejecting liability based upon 'control over an organised apparatus of power' in the aforementioned case, it is worth noting that the

---

[211] See Ch 4, s V.B.
[212] *Katanga and Ngudjolo Case* Confirmation of Charges (Above n 20), at 509, quoting from *Bemba Case* (Pre-Trial Chamber III Decision on the Prosecutor's Application for a Warrant of Arrest against Jean-Pierre Bemba Gombo) ICC-01/05-01/08-14-TEn (10 Jun 2008) para 78 [hereinafter Bemba *Case* Warrant of Arrest].

concept was impugned in part because it created a 'contradiction' in its simultaneous incorporation, as principals, of an indirect perpetrator and a direct perpetrator. As already stated, article 25 (3)(a) of the Statute has criminalised precisely the kind of responsibility that embodies such an apparent contradiction.[213]

a The Juntas Trial

Upon seizing power in 1976, the Argentine armed forces began an unprecedented attack aimed at left-wing terrorist groups. These gangs killed and maimed not only government and police officials, but civilians as well. The military backlash affected a substantial sector of the population, who suffered unjust and indiscriminate punishment. Between 1976 and 1983, the military established an elaborate network of clandestine detention centres, where kidnapped victims or disappeared persons (*desaparecidos*) underwent interrogation and torture. The country was divided into a number of military zones, within which a regional commander was given complete autonomy over clandestine operations. Within each zone, middle-ranking officers of the three services of the armed forces co-operated in the abduction of suspected subversives. While some of the disappeared persons were eventually released, many others still remain unaccounted for.

During this period, Argentine courts were unable to secure justice. At the height of the campaign against subversion, the Supreme Court, whose members had been appointed by the military, repeatedly urged the commanders to clarify the fate of the disappeared persons in a consolidated action on some 400 petitions for habeas corpus. Despite the many civilians who had been kidnapped, murdered and tortured, not a single person was successfully prosecuted in either military or civilian courts. The military government at the time constantly denied that such crimes had ever taken place.

The Federal Court of Appeals insisted on the responsibility as indirect perpetrators under the notion of OSP of any given member of the three consecutive Military Juntas (each Military Junta was comprised of the Commander-in-Chief of the Army, the Navy and the Air Forces) for the crimes committed by those members of the military service that each of them commanded, citing a variety of arguments for that conclusion. While the members of the three Military Juntas did not themselves, as individuals, abduct, murder or torture anyone, the charges against them assumed their responsibility for the acts of others. They issued general instructions calling for extraordinary measures to be used not only against terrorists but 'subversive elements' in general.[214] Publicity within Argentina and diplomatic inquiries from abroad, the Federal Court of Appeals reasoned, left the members of the three Military Juntas in no doubt about how those general directives were implemented by their subordinates.

---

[213] *Katanga and Ngudjolo Case* Confirmation of Charges (*Ibid*), at 504–505.

[214] See for instance, Dir 504/77 issued in April 1977 by General Roberto Eduardo Viola, then head of the First Army Corps and later head of the Second Military Junta, concerning the industrial front of the anti-subversive campaign, La Prensa, on 23 Jul 1984, p 5.

The Federal Court of Appeals considered that the defendants were in control of those acts because the machinery of people and property that made the commission of the crimes possible was under their command. The events in question were not the result of the erratic, solitary and individual decisions of those who carried them out; they were part of an overall strategy devised by the members of the three consecutive Military Juntas in order to fight subversion. The acts were performed throughout a complex group of elements (men, orders, places, arms, vehicles, food, etc) that took part in every military operation.

The Federal Court of Appeals also pointed out that the defendants not only commanded their own forces, but also the security forces, which were in charge of preventing crimes. The defendants had installed themselves, through an act of force, as the only source of power in the Republic, so that there was no authority capable of exercising an effective control over what went on. Under these circumstances, the Federal Court of Appeals affirmed that it was not so important who actually perpetrated the crimes. The control of those who headed the system was absolute. Even if a subordinate refused to obey, he would automatically be replaced by another who would conform to the directives. Thus, the plan conceived by the defendants could not have been upset by the will of the physical perpetrators of the crimes, who simply performed a minor function within a gigantic machine. As the Federal Court of Appeals affirmed, this case did not concern the usual case of control of the will through indirect participation. The instrument operated by the man behind the scene is the system itself, which he manipulates at his discretion, a system composed of interchangeable men. Thus, the control was not so much over a specific will but over an undetermined will. Regardless of who the subordinate officers happened to be, the criminal acts would have taken place anyway.

As a result, the Federal Court of Appeals affirmed that the physical perpetrators were not that significant, since they play only a secondary role in committing the crimes. The individual who controls the system, controls the will of the men who are part of that system. In fact, the defendants' lack of knowledge of the existence of each criminal act in particular and of the victims' identities is not relevant in determining their criminal responsibility. The orders referred generally to all 'subversive people', allowing ample freedom for the subordinates to determine who fell in that category and to act accordingly. The members of the three consecutive Juntas, however, always retained the power to stop the crimes that were being committed. In fact, the Federal Court of Appeals considered that there is ample evidence showing that when the defendants deemed it necessary, they suddenly stopped all irregular operations and announced to the population that 'the war had ended'. After that time, there was no further kidnapping, torture or disappearances.

Further, the Federal Court of Appeals considered that the intervention of the defendants from the very top of the power structure was not limited to ordering an unlawful activity. They also contributed actively to the commission of the crimes. As the Federal Court of Appeals pointed out, the detention centres had to be financed and staffed centrally, and it was impossible for the commanders not to have been aware of their existence and activities. As a result, the physical perpetrators of the crimes would not have been able to commit those crimes unless they had the necessary means. These means were made available to them by order of the defendants: clothes, vehicles, fuel, weapons and ammunition, detention centres, food, etc., were indispensable factors.

Finally, the Federal Court of Appeals found that there was still another circumstance which made success of the illegal plans possible and which only the defendants could have made available: impunity. In this regard, the Federal Court of Appeals found that, while the above-mentioned criminal system was implemented, society was still governed by the traditional legal order. The constitution (with the limitations imposed by a de facto government) was still in force, the police continued to arrest criminals and courts continued to render judgments. Such a legal system was incompatible with the one applied to fight against the guerrillas. The stunning co-existence of a legal and extra-legal systems during such a prolonged time was only possible with the presence of the defendants at the summit of power. From there, an attempt was made to hide the facts by lying to judges, to the victims' relatives, to national and foreign organisations, and to foreign governments. They orchestrated fake investigations, gave misleading assurances of hope and childish explanations.

The Federal Court of Appeals rejected the defence counsel's argument that the crimes were acts committed in excess by individual servicemen, for which their superiors could not be held responsible. According to the Federal Court of Appeals, the sustained pattern of abduction, torture, and murder could not possibly be explained as the acts of a few deranged officers. Many of the abductions had been carried out after the police in the district had been ordered not to interfere, and this would have been impossible without an established system of impunity.[215]

b The German Border Case

Between 1949 and 1961 approximately two and a half million Germans fled from the German Democratic Republic ('GDR') to the Federal Republic of Germany ('FRG'). In 1961, due to the political situation, the number of people who tried to flee increased. Therefore, on 12 August 1961, the Council of Ministers (*Ministerrat*) of the GDR decided to close the border between East and West Germany. On 13 August 1961, the GDR started building the Berlin Wall and reinforced security measures along the inner German border. Anti-personnel mines and automatic-fire systems were installed. Many people lost their lives when trying to cross the border.

---

[215] For a complete report and translation of the judgment, see American Society of International Law, (1987) 26 *International Legal Materials* 2. The Introductory Note and English translation were prepared for International Legal Materials by E Dahl, Visiting Professor of Law, Southern Methodist University School of Law, and AM Garro, Lecturer in Law, Columbia University.

The organisation of the security at the border was as follows: The first organ of power in Eastern Germany was the '*Volkskammer*'. In between the meetings of the *Volkskammer*, the Council of State (*Staatsrat*) held its powers. This Council of State laid down principles to be followed in the matters of national defence and security, and organised the defence of the state with assistance of the National Defence Council (*Nationaler Verteidigungsrat*). The National Defence Council was the central state organ, responsible for the direction of defence and security measures of the GDR. It consisted of approximately 14 members. The president of the National Defence Council was elected by the members of the *Volkskammer*, the other members of the National Defence Council were appointed by the State Council. The National Defence Council met in general twice a year and took important decisions about the establishment and consolidation of the border-policing regime and about the orders to open fire. The army of the German Democratic Republic (*Nationale Volksarmee, NVA*) and the GDR border guards (*Grenztruppen, DDR*) were under the authority of the Minister of National Defence (*Minister fur Nationale Verteidigung*). Every order to the border guards, including the installation of mines and automatic shooting mechanism as well as the orders to shoot, was based on the yearly order (*Jahresbefehl*) of the Minister of National Defence. This yearly order was based on decisions of the National Defence Council.

The crossing of the border from East to West Germany had to be prevented in any case and by any means. For instance, in a decision of 14 September 1962, the National Defence Council made it clear that the orders and service instructions laid down by the Minister of Defence should point out to the border guards that they were fully responsible for the preservation of the inviolability of the State border in their section and that border violators should in all cases be arrested as adversaries or, if necessary, annihilated. The death of fleeing persons was accepted, if it was not possible to stop them by another means. The border guards were told that in case of a successful crossing of the border, the guards on duty could expect to be the subject of an investigation conducted by the military prosecutor. Those who had stopped a person trying to flee were rewarded, even if that person was killed.

In addition to important functions in the SED (*Sozialistische Einheitspartei Deutschlands*) and in the State, the three defendants were members of the National Defence Council. The first defendant was a member of the SED's Central Committee from 1946 onwards, Chief of Staff of the NVA, a member of the National Defence Council from 1967 onwards and Minister of Defence from 1985 to 1989. The second defendant was a member of the National Defence Council from 1971 onwards, a member the SED's Central Committee from 1981 onwards and Deputy Defence Minister from 1979 to 1989. The third defendant was a member of the SED's Central Committee since 1963, who in 1971 became member of the *Volkskammer* and from 1972 to 1989 was a member of the National Defence Council. The situation described above had existed before the defendants joined the National Defence Council, but with the co-operation of the defendants the Council decided to uphold or strengthen the measures at the border, especially concerning the mines. The defendants were also aware of the consequences caused by those mines. As a consequence of the 'security-measures' along the border, many people, who tried to flee, were killed. Seven killings were the subject of this trial. Five people were killed due to injuries caused by mines and two were shot by soldiers when they tried to cross the border.

The German Federal Supreme Court held the defendants criminally liable for homicide as indirect perpetrators by using an organised structure of power. They applied the criminal law of the FRG, partly because it was the law of the place where the result of the offences had occurred, since one of the fugitives had died inside FRG territory, and partly because the criminal law of the FRG was more lenient than that of the GDR.

The German Supreme Federal Court discussed the question whether indirect perpetration is possible in cases where the person physically carrying out the crimes is fully criminally liable (culpable), and reached two conclusions. First, in general, the person behind cannot be considered as an indirect perpetrator if the person physically carrying out the crimes does not act under mistake and therefore is fully culpable. In these cases, the indirect perpetrator lacks the required control over the commission of the offence.

Second, exceptionally, indirect perpetration is possible even if the person physically carrying out the crimes is fully criminally liable. This is the case when the person behind makes use of an organised structure of power (*Befehlshierarchie*). In these cases, the contribution of the person behind leads almost automatically to the commission of the objective elements of the crime. If in these cases the person behind is aware of the circumstances and makes use of the unconditional willingness of the person physically carrying out the objective elements of the crime, and if the person behind wants the result as being the effect of his contribution, he is considered an indirect perpetrator. In these cases, the person behind has the necessary control over the commission of the offence and the will to control the offence, if he knows that due to the circumstances, the decision to be taken by the person physically carrying out the objective elements of the crimes will not be an obstacle for the accomplishment of the result. To not consider the person behind as a perpetrator would not take the objective weight of his contribution correctly into account, because in these cases, the higher the responsibility, the further away the person behind is from the scene of the crime. The question of whether the persons physically carrying out the objective elements of the crimes are fully criminally liable does not need to be decided in these cases.

As a result, the defendants were held liable as indirect perpetrators under OSP due to their membership in the National Defence Council, as the decisions of this Committee was a prerequisite for the orders on the border. Furthermore, the German Federal Supreme Court took into account that the defendants did not have a completely subordinate position with regard to Honecker (who was president of the National Defence Council, president of the Council of State and Secretary-General of the Central Committee of the SED) because, in addition to their membership in the National Defence Council, each defendant had important functions in the SED and in the State. Furthermore, according to the German Federal Supreme Court, they knew that the orders based on their decisions would be obeyed and that fugitives had died at the border as a result of acts of violence. All in all, the German Federal Supreme Court considered that the border guards, carrying out the objective elements of the crimes, acted as subordinates in a military hierarchy and thus their role was predetermined.[216]

iv Final Remarks: Suitability of the Notion of OSP for Reflecting the Criminal Liability of Senior Political and Military Leaders as Principals to International Crimes

There are two types of organisations that have the features required by the notion of OSP. On the one hand, as seen in the *Juntas* Trial and the *German Border* case, state structures and state-related organisations are used de facto or are expressly created for criminal purposes by senior political and military leaders. On the other hand, there are secret organisations, criminal gangs or terrorist groups whose ultimate goals violate the criminal law of the States in which they operate. This second type of organisation needs to have a rigid hierarchy, so that their members do not act on their own but at the request of their top leaders. In addition, their structure needs to be such that the decision of one of its members not to contribute to the execution of the objective elements of the crime does not stop its commission.[217] When a criminal gang only consists of half a dozen members, no organised structure of power can be said to exist because the gang is based on the personal relationships of its members and, thus, it has no independent existence.[218]

The special features required of the relevant organisations by the notion of OSP makes this theory particularly suitable to reflect the criminal liability of senior political and military leaders as principals to genocide, crimes against humanity and war crimes. Indeed, senior political and military leaders usually require the support of sizable organisations organised into a hierarchy to carry out a widespread or systematic attack against a civilian population,[219] to implement a plan, policy or large scale campaign of war crimes,[220] to set into motion a manifest

---

[216] See also, concerning the *German Border* case, *Streletz, Kessler and Krenz v Germany* (App Nos 340044/96 and 44801/98) ECHR 22 Mar 2001.

[217] This is the case when the murder of a selected target is attempted several times until the goal is achieved. The failure of previous attempts due to the lack of co-operation of individual members of the organisation did not stop the actual execution of the murder.

[218] Although Roxin does not say it explicitly, the criteria given for secret organisations, criminal gangs or armed groups appear to be, for the most part, also applicable to state-related organisations.

[219] Art 7 RS, 5 ICTYS and 4 ICTRS.

[220] Art 8 RS. Nevertheless, the ICTYS and the ICTRS do not contain this gravity threshold with regard to war crimes. See H Olasolo, *The Triggering Procedure of the International Criminal Court* (Leiden, Brill, 2005) 183–4 [hereinafter Olasolo, *Triggering Procedure*].

pattern of genocidal acts[221] or to carry out acts of such a magnitude that can cause in and of themselves the destruction of a targeted group in whole or in part.[222]

This is shown by post WW II cases. For instance, the IMT Judgment declared pursuant to article 9 IMT Charter that the Leadership Corps of the Nazi Party, the Gestapo,[223] the SD[224] and SS[225] were criminal organisations.[226] This is also shown by those trials for genocide, war crimes and crimes against humanity held before national Courts after post WW II cases and prior to the establishment of the *Ad hoc* Tribunals, such as the *Juntas* Trial,[227] the *German Border* case[228] or the *Eichmann* Trial.[229] Likewise, those trials for genocide, crimes against humanity and war crimes brought to date before the ICC, the ICTY and the ICTR, concern, inter alia, political parties (such as the SDS or the HDZ-BiH), armies (such as the VRS, the VS, the HVO or the ABiH), military or civil police units and political movements and their militias (such as *L'Union Populaire Congolaise/ Rasemblement pour la Democracie* (UPC/RP) and its military branch *Les Forces Popularies pour la Liberation du Congo* (FPLC), the Interahamwe militia or the Lord's Resistance Army).

Against this backdrop, the expression 'regardless of whether the other person is criminally liable' at the end of article 25(3)(a) RS makes clear that the notion of indirect perpetration in the RS does not require for the physical perpetrators to be fully exonerated of criminal liability.[230] Accordingly, this provision also includes those situations in which (i) senior military and political leaders use those organised structures of power that they control to secure the commission of the crimes, and (ii) those low level members of the organisation who physically carry out the objective elements of the crimes are also criminally liable.[231] From this perspective, Van Sliedregt has pointed out:

Article 25 (3) (a) introduces to the international level a new form of perpetration: perpetration by means. As this perpetration by means concept includes both innocent

---

[221] Elements of the crime of genocide pursuant to art 9 RS. Nevertheless, the ICTYS and the ICTRS do not require this contextual element for the crime of genocide. See Olasolo, *Triggering Procedure* (*Ibid*), paras 183–4.

[222] *Ibid.*

[223] *Die Geheime Staatspolizei.*

[224] *Sicherheitsdienst des Reichsfuehrers.*

[225] *Die Schutzstaffeln der Nationalsocialistischen Deutsche Arbeiterpartei.*

[226] According to art 9 of the IMT Charter: 'At the trial of any individual member of any group or organization the Tribunal may declare (in connection with any act of which the individual may be convicted) that the group or organization of which the individual was a member was a criminal organization'.

[227] See Ch 3, s III.C.iii.a.

[228] See Ch 3, s III.C.iii.b.

[229] *Attorney General v Adolf Eichmann* (1968) 36 ILR 18, concerning crimes committed by Adoft Eichmann, who was a high functionaire of the SS Race and Resettlement Main Office (RuSHA).

[230] *Lubanga Case* Confirmation of Charges (Above n 16), at para 334.

[231] See also K Ambos, 'Article 25. Individual Criminal Responsibility' in O Triffterer (ed), *Commentary on the Rome Statute of the International Criminal Court* (Baden-Baden, Nomos, 1999) 480 [hereinafter Ambos, *Article 25*]. See also Eser (Above n 138), at 794. Compare Werle (Above n 50), at 218, which shows certain doubts in this regard.

agents and culpable agents, it is likely to cover a wide range of situations than does the classic concept of perpetration through innocent agents developed in national law. Bearing in mind the systemic and widespread nature of the crimes within the jurisdiction of the ICC, it makes senses to equate concepts such as hegemony-over-the-act and functional perpetration, which are well-equipped to deal with that type of crime, with perpetration by means.[232]

Those crimes committed in the context of economic activities in enterprises share a common feature with the above mentioned crimes in that those individuals who are members of the board of directors, plan and decide the commission of the crimes and they are also far away from the scene of the crime when the offences are physically committed. Hence, in the ambit of economic crimes, one also faces problems relating to the distinction between principals (perpetration) and accessories to the crime (participation).

In those situations in which the members of the board of directors of a company direct subordinates who act under duress or mistake (and thus are not fully criminally liable) to commit the crimes, they can be considered as indirect co-perpetrators who act together to commit the crimes through a tool (their subordinates) that is not fully liable. However, the problem arises when the physical perpetrators are fully liable for the crimes.

The author considers that there are three major problems in applying the notion of OSP to these cases. First, most of the activities undertaken by companies are usually in accordance with the law. Therefore, an average subordinate will not be willing to accept a criminal assignment. As a result, those subordinates who could accept unlawful assignments are not fungible (in the sense of being easily replaceable by other subordinates).

Second, companies are usually comprised of a limited number of members and their hierarchical structure is not as rigid as it can be in the armed forces, secret services or certain organised armed groups because superior-subordinate relationships within a company are based on the division of tasks to maximise its productivity and not in a culture of obedience to the superior.[233] As a result, those companies involved in the commission of economic crimes do not usually have the special features required by the notion of OSP to be qualified as organised structures of power.[234]

Finally, according to Bottke, the notion of OSP would only be acceptable for crimes that affect the common values of civilized nations (such as committing genocide, crimes against humanity or war crimes through State structures) because it is based on pre-juridical criteria, such as the control over an organised structure of power or the use of an OSP to have the crimes committed.[235]

---

[232] Van Sliedregt (Above n 24), at 71.

[233] Perez Cepeda (Above n 181), at 369; Munoz Conde (Above n 199), at 151–9.

[234] However, on occasions, German courts have considered business companies as organised structures of power and have applied, in this context, the notion of OSP. See BGH (Bundesgerichtshof) and NJW (Neue Juristische Wochenschrift) (1994) 2703.

[235] Bottke (Above n 189), at 25.

D Distinction between the Notion of Indirect Perpetration and Ordering, Instigating and Planning as Forms of Accessorial Liability

i Ordering

According to Ambos, 'ordering' under articles 25(3)(b) RS, 7(1) ICTYS and 6(1) ICTRS is more related to the notion of indirect perpetration (principal liability) than to the concept of participation in the crimes committed by third persons (accessorial liability) because it is based on the use of a hierarchical structure to secure the commission of the crimes.[236] In this regard, it has been suggested that, in the context of article 25(3) RS, ordering could be considered a way of indirect perpetration.[237]

Nevertheless, articles 25(3)(a) and (b) RS, 7(1) ICTYS and 6(1) ICTRS explicitly distinguish between ordering and committing a crime. Hence, it is important to analyse which are the boundaries between the notion of indirect perpetration, which gives rise to principal liability and ordering as a form of accessorial or derivative liability.[238]

According to the case law of the *Ad hoc* Tribunals, ordering consists of using a position of authority to instruct another person to carry out the objective elements of a crime.[239] For this reason, as Del Ponte has pointed out:

> In circumstances in which persons jointly decide to commit a crime and are not in a hierarchical relationship or not acting pursuant to a hierarchical relationship, ordering will not be the appropriate mode to correctly capture their joint criminal participation.[240]

---

[236] Ambos, *La Parte General del Derecho Penal Internacional* (Above n 2), at 196.

[237] Ambos, *Article 25* (Above n 231), at 491; Van Sliedregt (Above n 24), at 76.

[238] According to Cassese, *International Criminal Law* (Above n 1), at 194, 'ordering' as form of criminal liability is also recognised by customary international law. The same view is held by Werle (Above n 50), at 219; Ambos, *La Parte General del Derecho Penal Internacional* (*Ibid*), at 274; Eser (Above n 138), at 796. Nevertheless, for Cassese, *International Criminal Law*, the nature of 'ordering' is not that of a form of accessorial liability; quite the contrary, he understands 'ordering' as a preparatory act, which gives rise to criminal liability regardless of whether the unlawful order is executed. Nevertheless, in the view of the author, the ICTR and the ICTY case law do not support this interpretation because it requires that the crimes ordered be committed, and that they be committed in execution or furtherance of the order. See *Kamuhanda v Prosecutor* (Appeals Chamber Judgment) ICTR-99-54A-A (19 Sep 2005) para 75 [hereinafter *Kamuhanda Case* Appeals Judgment]; *Gacumbitsi v Prosecutor* (Appeals Chamber Judgment) ICTR-2001-64-A (7 Jul 2006) para 185 [hereinafter *Gacumbitsi Case* Appeals Judgment]; *Semanza Case* Trial Judgment (Above n 53), at para 61; See *Blaskic Case* Trial Judgment (Above n 48), at para 278; *Stakic Case* Trial Judgment (Above n 19), at para 445; *Tuta and Stela* Trial Judgment (Above n 54), at para 61.

[239] *Semanza v Prosecutor* (Appeals Chamber Judgment) ICTR-97-20-A (20 May 2005) para 361 [hereinafter *Semanza Case* Appeals Judgment]; *Gacumbitsi Case* Appeals Judgment (*Ibid*), at para 182; *Kordic Case* Appeals Judgment (Above n 32), at para 28; *Galic Case* Appeals Judgment (Above n 37), at para 176.

[240] C Del Ponte, 'Investigation and Prosecution of Large-Scale Crimes at the International Level. The Experience of the ICTY' (2006) 4 *Journal of International Criminal Justice* 549 [hereinafter Del Ponte].

As long as the relevant senior political or military leader has the authority to instruct the physical perpetrator to commit the crimes, no superior-subordinate relationship is necessary.[241] As the ICTR Appeals Chamber has explained in the *Gacumbitsi* case:

> The Appeals Chamber notes that this element of 'ordering' is distinct from that required for liability under Article 6(3) of the Statute, which does require a superior-subordinate relationship (albeit not a formal one but rather one characterized by effective control). Ordering requires no such relationship—it requires merely authority to order, a more subjective criterion that depends on the circumstances and the perceptions of the listener.[242]

Senior political and military leaders can also be said to have a position of authority in those situations in which they have a significant influence upon the physical perpetrators, which would prompt the latter to obey their instructions.[243] Hence, in addition to the military superiors of regular army units, superiors of irregular forces, such as paramilitary groups, and leaders of political parties organised into a hierarchy may also incur criminal liability for ordering. For instance, the ICTR Appeals Chamber in the *Semanza* case convicted the defendant (former mayor of Bicumbi in the Kigali rural province) for ordering because he directed the attackers, including soldiers and Interahamwe, to kill Tutsi refugees who had been separated from Hutu refugees, and the attackers 'regarded him as speaking with authority'.[244] According to the ICTR Appeals Chamber, such authority:

> [C]reated a superior-subordinate relationship which was real, however informal or temporary, and sufficient to find the Appellant responsible for ordering under Article 6(1) of the Statute.[245]

Furthermore, in the *Kamuhanda*[246] and *Gacumbitsi*[247] cases, the ICTR Appeals Chamber also convicted the defendants (the former Rwandan Minister of Higher Education and Scientific Research, and the former mayor of the Commune of Rusomo in Rwanda) for ordering under similar circumstances.

In order to be held liable for ordering, senior political and military leader must 'instruct' the physical perpetrators to commit a crime. This requires a positive

---

[241] *Kamuhanda Case* Appeals Judgment (Above n 238), at para 75; *Semanza Case* Appeals Judgment (Above n 239), at para 361; *Gacumbitsi Case* Appeals Judgment (Above n 238), at para 181; *Kordic Case* Appeals Judgment (Above n 32), at para 28; *Galic Case* Appeals Judgment (Above n 37), at para 176. The same view is held by Cassese, *International Criminal Law* (Above n 1), at 193. Nevertheless, for Werle (Above n 50), at 219, a superior-subordinate relationship in the military sense is required, whereas for Ambos, *La Parte General del Derecho Penal Internacional* (Above n 2), at 274, the issue of whether a superior-subordinate relationship is required is still a controversial question.

[242] *Gacumbitsi Case* Appeals Judgment (*Ibid*), at para 182. See also Del Ponte (Above n 240), at 548.

[243] *Semanza Case* Appeals Judgment (Above n 239), at para 361. See also VL Hamilton and H Kelman, *Crimes of Obedience: Toward a Social Psychology of Authority and Responsibility* (Binghamton, Yale University Press, 1989) 77.

[244] *Semanza Case* Appeals Judgment (Above n 239), at para 363.

[245] *Ibid.*

[246] *Kamuhanda Case* Appeals Judgment (Above n 238), at para 76.

[247] *Gacumbitsi Case* Appeals Judgment (Above n 238), at para 187.

action.[248] In other words, they must give an order. However, the order does not have to take any particular form: it can be oral or in writing; it can be express or implicit.[249] Moreover, an express order to carry out a lawful military operation may be accompanied by an implicit order to commit a crime.[250]

As the ICTY Appeals Chamber has held in the *Galic* case, the existence of an order does not need to be proven by direct evidence because it can be also proven by circumstantial evidence.[251] This is consistent with post WW II case law. For instance, in the *Abbaye Ardenne* case, a US military Tribunal held:

> There is no evidence that anyone heard any particular words uttered by the accused which would constitute an order, but it is not essential that such evidence be adduced. The giving of the order may be proved circumstantially; that is to say, you may consider the facts you find to be proved bearing upon the question whether the alleged order was given, and if you find that the only reasonable inference is that an order that the prisoners be killed was given by the accused at the time and place alleged, and that the prisoners were killed as a result of that order, you may properly find the accused guilty.[252]

In this regard, the approving presence of a superior at the scene of the crime while the crimes are being committed, or immediately afterwards, can be a relevant factor to infer that the superior ordered the commission of the crimes.[253] In this regard, the ICTY Appeals Chamber in the *Kupreskic* case gave the following reasons to hold defendant Santic guilty for ordering the crimes committed during the initial assault to Ahmici on 16 April 1993:

> The Appeals Chamber is of the view that there was ample reliable evidence before the Trial Chamber to conclude that, on 16 April 1993, Santic was both Commander of the 1st Company of the 4th Battalion of the Military Police and the Jokers. There was also evidence from Witness EE, that Santic was present in Ahmici with the attacking forces on 16 April 1993. From this, it was reasonable for the Trial Chamber to infer that on 16 April 1993 Santic was in Ahmici and, given his position in the hierarchy of the units involved in the attack, that he must have been carrying out a command role during that attack. Similarly, the Appeals Chamber can find no error in the Trial.[254]

---

[248] *Blaskic Case* Appeals Judgment (Above n 32), at para 660; *Galic Case* Appeals Judgment (Above n 37), at para 176.

[249] *Blaskic Case* Trial Judgment (Above n 48), at para 281; *Brdanin Case* Trial Judgment (Above n 35), at para 270.

[250] See the example discussed in Ch 3, s III.D.ii.

[251] *Galic Case* Appeals Judgment (Above n 37), at para 178. See also *Blaskic Case* Trial Judgment (Above n 48), at para 281; *Brdanin Case* Trial Judgment (Above n 35), at para 270; *Limaj Case* Trial Judgment (Above n 32), at para 515; *Martic Case Trial* Judgment (Above n 32), at para 442.

[252] *Canada v Brigadefuhrer Kurt Meyer* (1950) in United Nations War Crimes Commission, Law Reports of Trial of War Criminals, Vol IV, 108.

[253] According to the United Nations Security Council (UNSC) 'Final Report of the Commission of Experts established pursuant to Security Council Resolution 780 (1992)' (27 May 1994) UN Doc S/1994/674, para 17, other relevant factors to infer the existence of an order to commit the crimes are the number of illegal acts, the number, identity and type of troops involved, the logistics involved, the widespread occurrence of the acts, the tactical tempo of operations, the modus operandi of similar illegal acts, the officers and staff involved and the location of the superior at the time.

[254] *Prosecutor v Kupreskic* (Appeals Chamber Judgment) ICTY-95-16 (23 Oct 2001) para 365.

Senior political and military leaders do not need to give the order directly to the physical perpetrators[255] because the order to commit the crimes can be handed down to the physical perpetrators through several levels of the chain of command.[256] Each intermediate commander who passes the order is considered to be reissuing the order, and can be held liable for ordering the commission of the crimes.[257] Moreover, in those cases in which an unlawful order is handed down through the chain of command, those intermediate superiors who silently consent to the order by taking no action to oppose it can be held liable for aiding and abetting.[258]

In order to hold a senior political or military leader liable for ordering, the physical perpetrators must commit the crimes in execution or furtherance of his order,[259] although, according to article 25(3)(b) RS, it is sufficient if the physical perpetrators attempt to commit the crimes in execution or furtherance of the order. This causal connection between the order of the senior political or military leader and the commission of the crime is essential; without it there is no responsibility for ordering pursuant to articles 25(3)(b) RS, 7(1) ICTYS and 6(1) ICTRS. The ICTR Appeals Chamber has repeatedly defined this causal connection as 'direct and substantial effect on the commission of the crimes'.[260]

Concerning the subjective elements, a senior political or military leader will only be held liable for ordering the commission of the crimes if he is, at least, aware of the substantial likelihood (i) that the objective elements of the crime will be carried out as a result of implementing his order, (ii) that the physical perpetrators

---

[255] *Blaskic Case* Trial Judgment (Above n 48), at para 282; *Brdanin Case* Trial Judgment (Above n 35), at para 270.

[256] *Blaskic Case* Trial Judgment (*Ibid*), at para 282. The same view is expressed in the ILC, 'Report of the International Law Commission on the Work of its 48th Session' (6 May–26 Jul 1996) UN Doc A/51/10, Draft Code of Crimes against Peace and Security of Mankind, Art 2, commentary para 14 [hereinafter ILC, *Draft Code of Crimes against Peace and Security of Mankind*]. See also Ambos, *Article 25* (Above n 231), at 480.

[257] *Prosecutor v Kupreskic* (Judgment) ICTY-95-16 (14 Jan 2000) paras 827, 862.

[258] *Akayesu Case* Trial Judgment (Above n 53), at paras 693–4.

[259] *Blaskic Case* Trial Judgment (Above n 48), at para 278, uses the expression 'in furtherance of', whereas the *Stakic Case* Trial Judgment (Above n 19), at para 445, uses the expression 'executing or otherwise furthering the implementation of the order'. The *Semanza Case* Trial Judgment (Above n 53), at para 382, and the Tuta and Stela Trial Judgment (Above n 54), at para 61, also use the expression 'to execute' but not in the context of the causal connection between the order to commit the crimes and the actual commission of the crimes.

[260] *Kamuhanda Case* Appeals Judgment (Above n 238), at para 75; *Gacumbitsi Case* Appeals Judgment (Above n 238), at para 185. The importance of this causal connection is reflected in the fact that a senior political and military leader may be held liable for ordering the crimes even if he does not have *stricto sensu* authority vis-à-vis the physical perpetrator, as long as the crimes are committed in furtherance of his order. This is the case, for instance, where: (i) a brigade commander orders to make sure that enemy civilians of Village X leave the village forever; (ii) the order goes down through the chain of command to a battalion commander, who decides to entrust the task to a paramilitary group operating in the area and headed by a person with whom he works closely on a regular basis; (iii) the head of the paramilitary group gives instructions to the members of his group to expel enemy civilians from Village X and burn down their houses; and (iv) the members of the paramilitary group physically commit the crimes in execution of the instructions received from their leader. In this scenario, although the brigade commander did not have authority to instruct the physical perpetrators, he could be held liable for ordering the commission of the crimes.

will act with the state of mind required by the crime in question; and (iii) that the physical perpetrators will act motivated by any requisite ulterior intent or *dolus specialis.*[261] In this regard, the ICTY Appeals Chamber has pointed out the following in the *Blaskic* case:

> The knowledge of any kind of risk, however low, does not suffice for the imposition of criminal responsibility for serious violations of international humanitarian law. The Trial Chamber does not specify what degree of risk must be proven. Indeed, it appears that under the Trial Chamber's standard, any military commander who issues an order would be criminally responsible, because there is always a possibility that violations could occur. The Appeals Chamber considers that an awareness of a higher likelihood of risk and a volitional element must be incorporated in the legal standard. The Appeals Chamber therefore holds that a person, who orders an act or omission with the awareness of the substantial likelihood that a crime will be committed in the execution of that order, has the requisite mens rea for establishing liability under Article 7(1) pursuant to ordering. Ordering with such awareness has to be regarded as accepting that crime.[262]

Hence, if a senior military leader orders that after the take over of a village, enemy houses be burnt down and enemy civilians be gathered in the main square and be forced to walk across the front line to enemy territory, and in execution of his order a number of civilians are killed when crossing the front-line, he will be liable for the deaths of enemy civilians as long as, at the time he issued his order, he was aware of the substantial likelihood that civilians would be killed as a result of the execution of his order by his subordinates.

The ICTY Trial Judgments in the *Blaskic* and *Stakic* cases have held that '[t]he person "ordering" must have the required *mens rea* for the crime with which he is charged'.[263] Based on these findings, and in light of the fact that the crimes must be carried out in execution or furtherance of the order, the Prosecution has argued that, pursuant to articles 7(1) ICTYS and 6(1) ICTRS, ordering gives rise to principal, as opposed to accessorial, liability.[264] It is precisely from this perspective that one has to asses the comment by Ambos that ordering under articles 25(3)(b) RS, 7(1) ICTYS and 6(1) ICTRS is more related to the notion of indirect perpetration (principal liability) than to the concept of participation in crimes committed by third persons (accessorial liability).[265]

Nevertheless, as seen above, the ICTY Appeals Chamber in the *Blaskic* and *Kordic* cases has not required that those senior political and military leaders who issue the orders must themselves fulfil the subjective elements of the crimes in

---

[261] *Blaskic Case* Appeals Judgment (Above n 32), at para 42; *Kordic Case* Appeals Judgment (Above n 32), at para 30; *Martic Case* Appeals Judgment (Above 32), at paras 222–3. As seen above in Ch 3, s I.C.ii, this standard could be sufficient to infer the existence of *dolus eventualis*, and hence to meet the 'intent and knowledge' requirement of art 30 RS.

[262] *Blaskic Case* Appeals Judgment (Above n 32), at para 42.

[263] *Blaskic Case* Trial Judgment (Above n 48), at paras 278, 282; *Stakic Case* Trial Judgment (Above n 19), at para 445.

[264] *Semanza Case* Appeals Judgment (Above n 239), at para 352, referring to paras 3.53–3.69 of the Prosecution Appeals Brief.

[265] Ambos, *La Parte General del Derecho Penal Internacional* (Above n 2), at 196.

question, including any requisite ulterior intent. Quite the contrary, according to the ICTY Appeals Chamber, it is sufficient if such leaders are aware of the substantial likelihood that the physical perpetrators will act with the mental state required by the crimes. As a consequence, if those senior political and military leaders who issue the orders need not fulfil the subjective elements of the crimes, they cannot become principals to the crimes (and the state of mind of the physical perpetrators becomes relevant to the determination of the existence of the crimes to which such leaders are accessories). In this regard, it is important to highlight that the notion of indirect perpetration always requires that the person behind personally fulfils all subjective elements of the crimes in question, including any requisite ulterior intent.[266]

In other words, according to the ICTY Trial Judgments in the *Blaskic* and *Stakic* cases, in those situations in which a military superior orders the shelling of a primary school under the false pretext that it is being used by the enemy as a weapons warehouse, and the artillery platoon executes such an order in the belief that the superior's explanation is correct and that the order is thus legitimate, the military superior could be held liable for ordering pursuant to article 7(1) ICTYS.[267] Theoretically, this would only be acceptable if one considers that the notion of ordering under article 7(1) ICTYS gives rise to principal (as opposed to accessorial or derivative) liability. The problem is that if one considers that the notion of ordering gives rise to principal liability, it becomes de facto a form of indirect perpetration where the military superior is a principal to the crime because he controls the will of the physical perpetrators due to his superior knowledge. In this scenario, the distinction between ordering and 'committing' in articles 25(3)(a) and (b) RS, 7(1) ICTYS and 6(1) ICTRS would be meaningless.

It is for this reason that the ICTY Appeals Chamber followed a different approach in the *Blaskic* and *Kordic* cases. According to the approach of the ICTY Appeals Chamber, in situations in which the physical perpetrators act under mistake, and considering that as a general rule mere negligence is not sufficient to fulfil the subjective elements of the crimes provided for in the ICTYS, the notion of ordering as a form of accessorial liability under article 7(1) ICTYS would not be applicable. As a result, either one considers that the military superior who gave the order to shell the primary school 'committed' the crime because he is an indirect perpetrator who used his superior knowledge to secure the commission of the crime; or the absence of a perpetrator who fulfils the objective and subjective elements of the crime leads to the conclusion that there is no crime, and thus no form of accessorial or derivative liability (including ordering) is applicable.

Particularly relevant is the distinction between the notions of OSP (a form of indirect perpetration which gives rise to principal liability) and ordering as a form of accessorial liability. In the view of the author, there are certain scenarios in

---

[266] See Ch 3, s III.C.ii.
[267] See *Blaskic Case* Trial Judgment (Above n 48), at para 282. See also *Stakic Case* Trial Judgment (Above n 19), at para 445.

which political and military leaders cannot be considered principals to the crime pursuant to the notion of OSP, and thus they can only be considered accessories to the crime pursuant to ordering.

A first scenario takes place when, in spite of the fact that the physical perpetrators do not belong to the organisation controlled by the senior political or military leader who issues the order, the latter is found to have authority to order over the former. In this regard, one has to keep in mind that the notion of OSP always requires the physical perpetrators to be members of the organised structure of power controlled by the senior political or military leader who uses it to commit the crimes.

A second scenario takes place when, despite the fact that the senior political or military leader who issues the order and the physical perpetrators belong to the same organisation, such organisation has a very limited membership and its members are not interchangeable. This is the situation when crimes are committed by paramilitary groups. This scenario also takes place when crimes are committed by terrorist organisations organised in small squads with a high degree of autonomy in their operations. Indeed some terrorist groups prefer to have a 'loose' organisation to avoid police and army pressure. They are organised in small squads which operate with a great level of autonomy and which have a relationship of coordination (horizontal), as opposed to one based on hierarchy (vertical) with the other squads of the organisation. The leaders of these terrorist groups are geographically remote from the areas in which the squads of the group operate and they posses, at best, authority to order over the squad leaders.

Nevertheless, according to ICC Pre-Trial Chamber I, in these cases of limited membership in the relevant organisation or group, it would still be possible to apply the notion of OSP if the relevant leader has secured automatic compliance with his orders via altenative means, such as through intensive, strict and violent training regimes.[268] In the view of ICC Pre-Trial Chamber I, under these conditions, the application of the notion of OSP in situations where the members of the relevant group or oganization are not interchangeable is still possible because the basis for the principal—rather than accessorial—liability of the senior political or military leader who issues the order is his ability to secure automatic compliance with it. If automatic compliance is secured, the senior political or military leader, in issuing the order, is not merely ordering the commission of a crime, but is essentially deciding whether and how the crime would be committed.[269]

Moreover, in the event one follows Roxin's approach to OSP,[270] a third scenario takes place when the organisation through which the crimes are committed does not usually act outside the law. In these cases, the physical perpetrators are not

---

[268] *Katanga and Ngudjolo Case* Confirmation of Charges (Above n 20), at para 518.
[269] *Ibid.*
[270] Roxin (Above n 139), at 249. See also Rotsch, *Die Rechtsfigur* (Above n 188), at 495. Contrary to Roxin's approach on this point, see *inter alia* Ambos, *La Parte General del Derecho Penal Internacional* (Above n 2), at 234–9.

interchangeable and the political or military leader who issues the order cannot be said to have indirectly committed the crime because he does not have the control over the will of the physical perpetrators. This scenario takes place when political and military leaders at the top of state structures that usually act in accordance with the law orders a specific subordinate to commit a crime (for instance, the head of a regular unit of the civil police orders a subordinate on whom he has particular trust to torture a specific terrorist suspect who has just been detained).

Finally, it is important to highlight that ordering as a form of accessorial liability, like indirect perpetration as form of principal liability, do not appropriately reflect the criminal liability of a group of senior political and military leaders who work together to achieve a common criminal purpose. As Del Ponte has highlighted:

> [O]rdering as a mode of liability may capture those crimes directly committed as a result of orders but fails to recognize full liability where the authority or superior acts jointly with others intent on committing a broader crime and his contribution is the ordering of his subordinates to carry out part of it. If the person ordering has the shared intent for the broader crime, takes steps to achieve the crime and his contribution is to order those under his authority to commit component parts of the crime, it would compartmentalize and limit his liability to only hold him responsible for those crimes he ordered.[271]

ii Instigating

Articles 7(1) ICTYS and 6(1) ICTRS explicitly refer to 'instigating' as a distinct form of accessorial liability, which differs from the notions of ordering and committing. In turn, article 25(3)(b) RS refers to the person who 'solicits or induces the commission of such a crime which in fact occurs or is attempted'. In relation to this last provision Eser[272] and Van Sliedregt[273] have pointed out that it appears appropriate to use 'instigation' as a common denominator in describing liability for prompting a person to commit a crime.

The case law of the *Ad hoc* Tribunals has accepted the definition of instigation given by the ICTR Trial Judgment in the *Akayesu* case.[274] According to this definition, instigation consists of 'prompting another person to commit an offence'.[275]

As in cases of indirect perpetration and ordering, in situations of instigation, the senior political or military leader involved does not himself carry out any of the

---

[271] Del Ponte (Above n 240), at 149.

[272] Eser (Above n 138), at 795. See also Ambos, *La Parte General del Derecho Penal Internacional* (Above 2, at 275).

[273] Van Sliedregt (Above n 24), at 77.

[274] *Kordic Case* Appeals Judgment (Above n 32), at para 27; *Blaskic Case* Trial Judgment (Above n 48), at para 280; *Krstic Case* Trial Judgment (Above n 49), at para 601; *Kvocka Case* Trial Judgment (Above n 49), at paras 243,252; Tuta and Stela Trial Judgment (Above n 54), at para 60; *Limaj Case* Trial Judgment (Above n 32), at para 514; *Kajelijeli Case* Trial Judgment (Above n 54), at para 762; *Kamuhanda Case* Trial Judgment (Above n 54), at para 593; *Prosecutor v Gacumbitsi* (Judgment) ICTR-2001-64-T (17 Jun 2004) para 279 [hereinafter *Gacumbitsi Case* Trial Judgment].

[275] *Akayesu Case* Trial Judgment (Above n 53), at para 482.

objective elements of the crime.[276] Indeed, if he physically carries some of the objective elements of the crime and prompts others to carry out the other objective elements of the crime, he will be considered a principal to the crime as a co-perpetrator.[277] Nevertheless, instigation can be distinguished from indirect perpetration (particularly OSP) and ordering because in situations of instigation, the influence exercised by the relevant senior political or military leader on the physical perpetrator is due to factors other than a superior-subordinate relationship or an authority to order.[278] These factors would include inter alia family links, friendship, professional trust, ideological affinity or religious links. As the ICTY Trial Judgment in the *Oric* case has explicitly stated:

> On the other hand, although the exertion of influence would hardly function without a certain capability to impress others, instigation, different from 'ordering', which implies at least a factual superior-subordinate relationship, does not presuppose any kind of superiority.[279]

This would be the case if the ideologist of a political movement who is currently in power in State X prompts the president of such a movement (who is also the president of State X) to carry out a persecutorial campaign against the members of an opposing political group through the joint action of the intelligence services and 'elite units' of the civil police.

Instigation can take place in many different ways, including by omission.[280] It can consist of threats or menaces, bribery or financial promises; it can also consist of persuasion by appealing to family links, friendship, group ideology or even patriotism.[281] Moreover, the act of instigation can be implicit or explicit,[282] which causes some problems to factually distinguish situations of instigation from situations of ordering. For instance, suppose that a military superior orders one of his units, which has a record of pillaging and burning down 'enemy houses', to assault an enemy village. At the time of issuing the order, the superior (i) emphasises that the unit has been selected for this operation due to the 'scrupulous' manner in which it has carried out in the past similar military operations; and (ii) manifests its confidence in that the unit will carry out the military operation with the

---

[276] See *Blaskic Case* Trial Judgment (Above n 48), at para 282; *Kordic Case* Trial Judgment (Above n 31), at para 388.

[277] *Stakic Case* Rule 98 *bis* Decision (Above n 123), at para 107.

[278] Cassese, *International Criminal Law* (Above n 1), at 189.

[279] *Oric Case* Trial Judgment (Above n 32), at para 272.

[280] *Kamuhanda Case* Trial Judgment (Above n 54), at para 593; *Kajelijeli Case* Trial Judgment (Above n 54), at para 762; *Blaskic Case* Trial Judgment (Above n 48), at paras 270, 280; *Kordic Case* Trial Judgment (Above n 31), at para 387; *Tuta and Stela* Trial Judgment (Above n 54), at para 60; *Brdanin Case* Trial Judgment (Above n 35), at para 269; *Limaj Case* Trial Judgment (Above n 32), at para 514; *Oric Case* Trial Judgment (Above n 32), at para 273.

[281] As the *Oric Case* Trial Judgment (*Ibid*), at para 273, states '[i]nstigation can be performed by any means'. See also *Blaskic Case* Trial Judgment (*Ibid*), at paras 270, 277, 280; *Brdanin Case* Trial Judgment (*Ibid*), at para 269; *Limaj Case* Trial Judgment (*Ibid*), at para 514. According to A Ashworth, *Principles of Criminal Law* (3rd edn, Oxford, Oxford University Press, 1999) 481, threats or other forms of pressure can also constitute an act of incitement.

[282] *Blaskic Case* Trial Judgment (*Ibid*), at paras 270, 277, 280; *Brdanin Case* Trial Judgment (*Ibid*), at para 269; *Limaj Case* Trial Judgment (*Ibid*), at para 514; *Oric Case* Trial Judgment (*Ibid*), at para 273.

'scrupulousness' required by the situation. In this scenario, one could argue that an express order to carry out a lawful military operation (the assault to a village defended by enemy forces) may be accompanied by an implicit order to commit a crime. Nevertheless, if the speech of the superior is not considered to amount to an implicit unlawful order, he could still be liable for prompting his subordinates to commit the war crimes of pillage and extensive destruction of property not justified by military necessity.

The act of instigation need not be 'public'[283]—instigation and 'direct and public incitement to commit genocide' under articles 25(3)(e) RS, 4(3)(c) ICTYS and 2(3)(c) ICTRS have a different nature because the latter gives rise to criminal liability since the moment in which the act of public and direct incitement takes place and regardless of whether genocide is finally committed or even attempted.[284]

Furthermore, consistent ICTR case law has held that the act of instigation need not be 'direct' either.[285] As a result, instigation:

> [C]an be generated both face to face and by intermediaries as well as exerted over a smaller or larger audience, provided that the instigator has the corresponding intent.[286]

Hence, according to this case law, senior political and military leaders who prompt persons of trust to prompt the physical perpetrators to commit the crimes will be criminally liable for instigation. Likewise, the head of a religious group will be liable for instigation if he prompts the main political advisor of the president of State X (who belongs to the same religious group) to provoke the latter to use special units of the civil police to carry out an ethnic cleansing campaign against the members of an opposing religious group.

Some national systems, such as the Spanish system,[287] require that the act of instigation be direct. If, unlike the case law of the *Ad hoc* Tribunals, the ICC case

---

[283] See *Prosecutor v Akayesu* (Appeals Chamber Judgment) ICTR-96-4 (1 Jun 2001) paras 474–83, which reverses the Trial Chamber's legal finding requiring that any act of instigation be public and direct. See also *Akayesu Case* Trial Judgment (Above n 53), at paras 481–2. The *Kajelijeli Case* Trial Judgment (Above n 54), at para 762, *Kamuhanda Case* Trial Judgment (Above n 54), at para 593, and *Gacumbitsi Case* Trial Judgment (Above n 274), at para 279, follow the position taken by the Appeals Chamber in the *Akayesu Case* Appeals Judgment.

[284] Cassese, *International Criminal Law* (Above n 1), at 189, has pointed out that instigation (also referred to as 'incitement' by this writer) 'is not punished *per se*, but only if it leads to the commission of a crime. As we shall see, international criminal law provides for an exception to this rule, in the case of genocide'. On the distinction between the notions of public and direct incitement to commit genocide and instigation, see Ambos, *La Parte General del Derecho Penal Internacional* (Above n 2), at 279–82. On the content of the notion of 'public and direct incitement to commit genocide' see Cassese, *International Criminal Law* (Above n 1), at 196–8; Schabas *Genocide* (Above n 48), at 266–80. In relation to the development of this notion in the Nahimana Case before the ICTR, see G Della Morte, 'De-Mediatizing the Media Case: Elements of a Critical Approach' (2005) 3 *Journal of International Criminal Justice* 1019–33; A Zahar, 'The ICTR's Media Judgment and the Reinvention of Direct and Public Incitement to Commit Genocide' (2005) 16 *Criminal Law Forum* 33–48.

[285] *Kayishema Case* Trial Judgment (Above n 71), at para 200; *Semanza Case* Trial Judgment (Above n 53), at para 381; *Kajelijeli Case* Trial Judgment (Above n 54), at para 762; *Kamuhanda Case* Trial Judgment (Above n 54), at para 593; *Gacumbitsi Case* Trial Judgment (Above n 274), at para 279.

[286] *Oric Case* Trial Judgment (Above n 32), at para 273; See also Eser (Above n 138), at 796.

[287] For instance, art 28(a) of the Spanish Penal Code explicitly requires to directly prompt the physical perpetrators to carry out the crimes.

law embraces this approach, the requirement of direct instigation will be an important feature to distinguish instigation from the notions of OSP under article 25(3)(a) RS and ordering under article 25(3)(b) RS. Indeed, as seen above, according to the notions of OSP and ordering, criminal liability arises in the likely situation where the orders of senior political and military leaders are reissued by intermediate superiors before reaching the physical perpetrators. Nevertheless, in the view of the author, the requirement of direct instigation would substantially reduce the scope of application of this form of accessorial liability in relation to senior political and military leaders who are geographically and structurally remote from the physical perpetrators.[288]

Instigation, like ordering, requires a causal connection between the act of provocation by the relevant senior political or military leader and the commission of the crime by the physical perpetrator,[289] although, according to article 25(3)(b) RS, it is sufficient if there is a causal connection between the act of provocation and the attempt to commit the crime by the physical perpetrator. Nevertheless, the nature of the required causal connection differs between ordering and instigation. While ordering requires that the crimes be committed in execution or furtherance of an order, the content of the causal connection for instigation seems to have changed over time. Initially, some ICTY Trial Chambers used the 'clear and contributing factor' test. According to this test, the act of instigation does not need to generate, in the physical perpetrator, the intention to commit the crime because it is sufficient if it strengthens his will to commit the offence by providing an additional motive or purpose.[290]

This standard creates some overlap between instigation and aiding and abetting in those cases where senior political and military leaders give further encouragement to the physical perpetrators before starting with the execution of the objective elements of the crime. This overlap does not extend, however, to those cases of encouragement at the scene of the crime while the offence is being committed (these have always been cases of aiding and abetting because the fact that the encouragement is simultaneous to the commission of the crime makes it difficult to qualify it as strengthening the will of the physical perpetrator to commit an offence that is already taking place).

Subsequently, the ICTY Appeals Chamber in the *Kordic* case defined the causal connection for instigation as follows:

---

[288] Van Sliedregt (Above n 24), at 83, also favours the possibility of 'indirect instigation', although, for her, cases of indirect instigation 'would come close to the participation mode of "planning"'. Indirect instigation is also supported by Eser (Above n 138), at 796; Werle (Above n 50), at 220.

[289] *Blaskic Case* Trial Judgment (Above n 48), at para 280, *Kordic Case* Trial Judgment (Above n 31), at para 387, *Brdanin Case* Trial Judgment (Above n 35), at para 269, and *Oric Case* Trial Judgment (Above n 32), at para 274, refer to 'causal relationship', whereas the *Bagilishema Case* Trial Judgment (Above n 77), at para 30, *Semanza Case* Trial Judgment (Above n 53), at para 381, *Kajelijeli Case* Trial Judgment (Above n 54), at para 762, *Kamuhanda Case* Trial Judgment (Above n 54), at para 593, and *Gacumbitsi Case* Trial Judgment (Above n 274), at para 279, use the language 'causal connection'.

[290] *Blaskic Case* Trial Judgment (*Ibid*), at paras 270, 277; *Kvocka Case* Trial Judgment (Above n 49), at para 252; Tuta and Stela Trial Judgment (Above n 54), at para 60; *Brdanin Case* Trial Judgment (*Ibid*) at para 269.

While it is not necessary to prove that the crime would not have been perpetrated without the involvement of the accused, it is sufficient to demonstrate that the instigation was a factor substantially contributing to the conduct of another person committing the crime.[291]

As a result, it introduced the 'substantially contributing factor' test,[292] which has been recently defined in the following manner:

This does not necessarily presuppose that the original idea or plan to commit the crime was generated by the instigator. Even if the principal perpetrator was already pondering on committing a crime, the final determination to do so can still be brought about by persuasion or strong encouragement of the instigator. However, if the principal perpetrator is an '*omnimodo facturus*' meaning that he has definitely decided to commit the crime, further encouragement or moral support may merely, though still, qualify as aiding and abetting.[293]

In other words, the 'substantially contributing factor' test requires that the 'concrete person or group of persons prompted has not already, and independently from the instigator, formed an intent to commit the crime in question'.[294] This reduces, to an important extent, the above-mentioned overlap between instigating and aiding and abetting.[295]

Concerning the subjective elements, a senior political or military leader will only be liable for instigation if he is, at least, aware of the substantial likelihood (i) that the objective elements of the crime will be carried out as a result of his act of instigation; (ii) that the physical perpetrators will act with the state of mind required by the crime in question; and (iii) that the physical perpetrators will act motivated by any requisite ulterior intent or *dolus specialis*.[296] As the ICTY Appeals Chamber has explained in the *Kordic* case:

---

[291] *Kordic Case* Appeals Judgment (Above n 32), at para 27; *Blaskic Case* Trial Judgment (*Ibid*), at para 278; *Kvocka Case* Trial Judgment (*Ibid*), at para 252; *Tuta and Stela* Trial Judgment (*Ibid*), at para 60; *Limaj Case* Trial Judgment (Above n 32), at para 514; *Oric Case* Trial Judgment (Above n 32), at para 274; *Bagilishema Case* Trial Judgment (Above n 77), at para 30; *Kamuhanda Case* Trial Judgment (Above n 54), at para 590.

[292] The 'substantially contributing factor' test has been also applied by the *Bagilishema Case* Trial Judgment (*Ibid*), at para 30, *Kamuhanda Case* Trial Judgment (*Ibid*), at para 590, *Limaj Case* Trial Judgment (*Ibid*), at para 514 and *Oric Case* Trial Judgment (*Ibid*), at paras 271, 274.

[293] *Oric Case* Trial Judgment (*Ibid*), at para 271.

[294] This position was advanced for the first time by the *Stakic Case* Rule 98 *bis* Decision (Above n 123), at para 107.

[295] The *Kamuhanda Case* Appeals Judgment (Above n 238), at paras 58–66, implicitly applied the 'substantially contributing factor' test as a result of the Prosecution acknowledgement that the defendant's actions 'must substantially contribute' to the commission of the crimes. In applying this test, the ICTR Appeals Chamber stated that the fact that former Rwandan Minister of Higher Education and Scientific Research (Jean de Dieu Kamuhanda) enjoyed 'a certain influence' in the Gikomero community was not sufficient to hold him liable for instigating the crimes occurred during the massacre of Tutsis at the Gikomero Commune Parish.

[296] *Kordic Case* Appeals Judgment (Above n 32), at para 32. See also Werle (Above n 50), at 220. As seen above in Ch 3, s I.C.ii, this standard could be sufficient to infer the existence of *dolus eventualis*, and hence to meet the 'intent and knowledge' requirement of RS.

With respect to 'instigating', a person who instigates another person to commit an act or omission with the awareness of the substantial likelihood that a crime will be committed in the execution of that instigation, has the requisite *mens rea* for establishing responsibility under Article 7(1) of the Statute pursuant to instigating. Instigating with such awareness has to be regarded as accepting that crime.[297]

Hence, when the main political advisor of the president of State X prompts him to carry out a campaign of unlawful arrest and detention of members of an opposing political group, and in the implementation of such a campaign some members of the group are beaten up while resisting their arrest by elite police units, the political advisor will be criminally liable for instigating the mistreatment of the members of the targeted group as long as he was aware of the substantial likelihood that such mistreatment would take place in the execution of the campaign of unlawful arrest and detention.

Those senior political and military leaders who carry out acts of instigation do not need to act motivated by any ulterior intent or *dolus specialis* required by the crime in question.[298] On the contrary, as the ICTY Trial Chamber in the *Martic* case has explicitly stated, the subjective element of instigation:

> [D]oes not mean, however, that the instigator would also have to share a 'special intent' as it may be required for the commission of certain crimes, such as genocide with regard to 'destroying, in whole or in part, an ethnical group' (Article 4 (1) of the Statute).[299]

Therefore, if senior political and military leaders who carry out acts of instigation need not fulfil the subjective elements of the offences, they cannot be considered principals to the crimes (and the state of mind of the physical perpetrators becomes relevant to the determination of the existence of the crimes to which such leaders are accessories). In this regard, the notion of instigation, like the notion of ordering, as forms of accessorial or derivate liability, differ from the notion of indirect perpetration, which establishes as a requisite for principal liability that those senior political or military leaders, who use other persons as tools to commit the crimes, personally fulfil all subjective elements of the offences in question, and thus act motivated by any requisite ulterior intent or *dolus specialis*.[300]

iii Planning

Articles 7(1) ICTYS and 6(1) ICTRS, unlike article 25(3) RS, explicitly refers to 'planning' as a distinct form of accessorial liability, which differs from the notions of instigating, ordering and committing.[301] For Van Sliedregt, cases of planning

---

[297] *Kordic Case* Appeals Judgment (*Ibid*), at para 32.

[298] See *Ntakirutimana Case* Appeals Judgment (Above n 32), at para 494; *Semanza Case* Trial Judgment (Above n 53), at para 388.

[299] *Oric Case* Trial Judgment (Above n 32), at para 279, fn 772.

[300] See Ch 3, s III.C.ii.

[301] As V Morris and MP Scharf, *The International Criminal Tribunals for Rwanda* (Ardsley, New York, Transnational Publishers, 1998) 236 have affirmed, the expression 'planning' refers to the first stage of a crime.

are implicitly provided for in article 25(3)(b) RS, which explicitly refers to 'orders, solicits or induces'.[302]

A senior political or military leader is criminally liable for planning if he designs by himself or together with others 'the criminal conduct constituting one or more statutory crimes that are later perpetrated'.[303] Hence, the objective elements of the crimes included in the criminal plan must be subsequently committed— although, according to article 25(3)(b) RS, it is sufficient if the crimes contained in the plan are attempted. In this regard, 'planning', as a form of accessorial liability, differs from 'conspiracy to commit genocide' under articles 4(3)(b) ICTYS and 2(3)(b) ICTRS, which, unlike article 25(3) RS, attaches criminal liability for merely agreeing to commit genocide, regardless of whether the crime is subsequently committed or even attempted.[304] Furthermore, while 'planning' also includes cases where the criminal design is elaborated by only one person, 'conspiracy to commit genocide' requires that at least two persons agree to commit genocide.[305]

In order to be held criminally liable for 'planning', senior political and military leaders do not need to participate in the implementation of the criminal plan. Criminal liability arises as a result of their participation in the formulation of the criminal plan or as a result of embracing the formulation proposed by another person.[306] From this perspective, the International Law Commission has affirmed that 'planning':

> [I]s intended to ensure that high-level government officials or military commanders who formulate a criminal plan or policy, as individuals or as co-conspirators, are held accountable for the major role that they play which is often a decisive factor in the commission of the crimes covered by the Code.[307]

However, the author does not fully agree with this view because 'planning' is a form of accessorial, as opposed to principal liability, which is only applicable when those senior political and military leaders involved in the formulation of the criminal plan do not participate subsequently in its implementation. Whenever such leaders also participate in the implementation of the common criminal plan they

---

[302] Van Sliedregt (Above n 24), at 78.

[303] *Kordic Case* Appeals Judgment (Above n 32), at para 26.

[304] See Ch 2, s IV; See also Van Sliedregt (Above n 24), at 79.

[305] *Akayesu Case* Trial Judgment (Above n 53), at para 480. See also *Blaskic Case* Trial Judgment (Above n 48), at para 279; *Kordic Case* Trial Judgment (Above n 31), at para 386; *Krstic Case* Trial Judgment (Above n 49), at para 601.

[306] Bagilishema Case Trial Judgment (Above n 77), at para 30.

[307] ILC, *Draft Code of Crimes against Peace and Security of Mankind* (Above n 256). This view, which is also endorsed by Van Sliedregt (Above n 24), at 80, finds some support in some post WW II cases under Control Council Law No 10. For instance, in the *Justice Case*, the defendants were found guilty, inter alia, for their participation in the design of the *Nacht und Nebel* plan, which was subsequently mainly executed by the Gestapo. See *US v Altstoetter* (1947) in Trial of the Major War Criminals before the International Military Tribunal under Control Council Law No 10, Vol III (US Government Printing Office, 1951) 954 [hereinafter *Justice Case*]. See also *Trial of Dr Joseph Buhler* (1948) in United Nations War Crimes Commission, Law Reports of Trial of War Criminals, Vol XIV, 23.

will become principals to the crime (co-perpetrators).[308] Furthermore, whenever the criminal plan is designed by only one senior political or military leader, if he also uses his subordinates as tools to commit the crime, he will become a principal to the crime as an indirect perpetrator.[309] As a consequence, the author considers that 'planning', as a form of accessorial liability, will only be applied whenever the role played by the senior political and military leaders is not that 'major' because it is limited to the formulation of the criminal plan.

The ICTY Rule 98 Decision in the *Stakic* case extended the scope of application of 'planning' to some instances in which those formulating the common criminal plan also intervene during its implementation. As the Trial Chamber explained:

> An accused will only be convicted for planning a crime where his contribution during the planning stage *is of greater weight* than at the execution stage.[310]

Thus, according to this decision, the key criterion to distinguish between accessorial liability for 'planning' and principal liability for indirect perpetration or co-perpetration (regardless of whether co-perpetration is based on the notion of joint criminal enterprise or on the notion of control of the crime) is the importance of the contribution of a senior political or military leader at the planning stage vis-à-vis his contribution at the execution stage.[311]

This criterion has not been subsequently followed by the case law of the *Ad hoc* Tribunals, which has consistently held that principal liability arises for those participating in a joint criminal enterprise (co-perpetrators) even if their contribution to the implementation of the common criminal plan is not significant.[312] But, even if one applies the criterion set forth by the Trial Chamber in the *Stakic* case, a senior political or military leader would be liable as a principal for indirect perpetration (or for indirect co-perpetration, in case he does so together with other senior political and military leaders) if he, in addition to being primarily responsible for formulating the criminal plan, directs his subordinates to implement it.[313]

There might be different levels of design of the criminal plan, each of them taking place at a different level of command. For instance, senior political leaders and top members of the Main Staff of the army may work together to formulate an overall plan to carry out a persecutorial campaign against the members of an opposing religious group. Subsequently, mid-level military superiors and field commanders will still have to further elaborate the plan in light of the logistical and operational capabilities of the military units which are going to physically implement it. For this reason, the case law of the *Ad hoc* Tribunals do not require

---

[308] See Ch 4, s III.A.iii and Ch 5, s III.A.ii; See also Stakic Case Rule 98 bis Decision (Above n 123), at para 104.

[309] See Ch 3, s III.C.i.

[310] Stakic Case Rule 98 bis Decision (Above n 123), at para 104.

[311] Ibid.

[312] See Ch 4, s III.A.iii.

[313] The same view is held by K Ambos, Der Allgemeine Teil des Volkerstrafrechts: Ansatze einer Dogmatisierung (Berlin, Duncker und Humblot, 2002) 566.

a 'direct' connection between the planners and the physical perpetrators[314]—as seen above, a direct connection is not required for either instigation or ordering;[315] otherwise, the scope of the application of planning, instigation and ordering, as forms of accessorial liability, to senior political and military leaders would be very limited.

Although some early case law of the *Ad hoc* Tribunals might have given the impression that no causal connection between the formulation of the criminal plan and the commission of the crimes by the physical perpetrators was necessary, the ICTY Appeals Chamber in the *Kordic* case has made it clear that a causal link is required.[316] Moreover, although the ICTY Appeals Chamber has not required *stricto sensu* that the crimes be committed in furtherance of the plan,[317] it has held that the planning must be 'a factor substantially contributing to such criminal conduct'.[318]

Concerning the subjective elements, a senior political or military leader will only be liable for planning if he is, at least, aware of the substantial likelihood (i) that the objective elements of the crime will be carried out as a result of implementing the plan that he formulates; (ii) that the physical perpetrators will act with the state of mind required by the crime in question; and (iii) that the physical perpetrators will act motivated by any requisite ulterior intent or *dolus specialis*.[319] As, the ICTY Appeals Chamber has explained in the *Kordic* case:

> The Appeals Chamber similarly holds that in relation to "planning", a person who plans an act or omission with the awareness of the substantial likelihood that a crime will be committed in the execution of that plan, has the requisite *mens rea* for establishing responsibility under Article 7(1) of the Statute pursuant to planning. Planning with such awareness has to be regarded as accepting that crime.[320]

Hence, where the Chief of Staff, who lacks operational powers over subordinate brigades, formulates a plan for the unlawful arrest and detention of enemy civilians, and in the execution of such a plan some civilians are beaten up while resisting their arrest, he will be held liable for planning the mistreatment as long as he was aware of the substantial likelihood that civilians would be mistreated in the implementation of his plan.

Like in instigation and ordering', senior political and military leaders who formulate a criminal plan do not need to act motivated by any ulterior intent or *dolus specialis* required by the crimes in question.[321] Therefore, if senior political and military leaders formulating criminal plans need not fulfil the subjective elements of the crimes, they cannot be considered principals to the crimes (and the state of

---

[314] Van Sliedregt (Above n 24), at 80.
[315] See Ch 3, s III.D.i and s III.D.ii.
[316] Kordic Case Appeals Judgment (Above n 32), at para 26.
[317] This had been previously required by the Blaskic Case Trial Judgment (Above n 48), at para 278.
[318] Kordic Case Appeals Judgment (Above n 32), at para 26.
[319] Ibid at para 31. As seen above in Ch 3, s I.C.ii, this standard could be sufficient to infer the existence of dolus eventualis, and hence to meet the 'intent and knowledge' requirement of art 30 RS.
[320] Kordic Case Appeals Judgment (Ibid), at para 31.
[321] *Ibid.*

mind of the physical perpetrators becomes relevant to the determination of the existence of the offences to which such leaders are accessories). From this perspective, the notion of planning, like the notions of instigation and ordering, as forms of accessorial or derivate liability, differ from the notion of indirect perpetration as a form of principal liability, which, as seen above, requires that the indirect perpetrator personally fulfils all subjective elements of the offences in question (including any requisite ulterior intent).[322]

Finally, it is important to address the confusion in which the ICTY Appeals Chamber seems to have incurred in the *Krnojelac* case when discussing whether the physical perpetrators of the crimes must be participants in a joint criminal enterprise together with the defendant. According to the ICTY Appeals Chamber, the following example given by the Prosecution 'appears more relevant to the planning of a crime under Article 7(1) of the Statute than to a joint criminal enterprise'[323]:

> The Prosecution adds that such an approach could render the notion of joint criminal enterprise redundant in the context of State criminality. It gives as an illustration the example of high-level political and military leaders who, from a distant location, plan the widespread destruction of civilian buildings (hospitals and schools) in a particular area in order to demoralise the enemy without the soldiers responsible for carrying out the attacks sharing the objective in question or even knowing the nature of the relevant targets. The Prosecution argues that, in that context, the Trial Chamber's criterion would make it impossible to implement the concept of joint enterprise.[324]

The author disagrees with the comment of the ICTY Appeals Chamber because this is a case of indirect co-perpetration (principal liability) as opposed to a case of 'planning' (accessorial liability). Indeed, in this particular case, a group of senior political and military leaders are acting together not only to formulate a criminal plan but also to secure its implementation—'planning' would require them to stop their contribution after formulating the criminal plan. Furthermore, they are profiting from their superior knowledge to use their subordinates as tools to secure the commission of the crimes. As a result, they are in control of the crimes because, due to their superior knowledge, they control the will of their subordinates who physically carry out the unlawful shelling in the belief that they are shelling a lawful target—'planning' would require that the subordinates fulfil the subjective elements of the crimes, but this is not the case because they are acting under mistake (however, for indirect perpetration, the state of mind of the subordinates is irrelevant as long as the senior political and military leaders directing the unlawful shelling fulfil themselves the subjective elements of the crimes). Finally, in the scenario described by the ICTY Appeals Chamber, the central role played by the senior political and military leaders in the commission of the crimes is better reflected by a notion of principal liability (indirect co-perpetration) than by a notion of accessorial liability ('planning').

[322] See Ch 3, s III.C.ii.
[323] *Krnojelac* Case Appeals Judgment (Above n 51), at para 84.
[324] *Ibid* at para 83.

4

Co-perpetration Based on Joint Criminal Enterprise

I Joint Criminal Enterprise and Joint Control as Two Competing Definitional Criteria of the Concept of Co-perpetration

The notion of perpetration giving rise to principal liability is not limited to those cases in which a person physically carries out all the objective elements of the crime (direct perpetration) or uses another person as a tool to carry them out (indirect perpetration). It also includes cases of co-perpetration, where the objective elements of the crime are carried out by a plurality of persons acting in furtherance of a common criminal plan. In these cases, senior political and military leaders can be held liable as principals to a crime as a whole, even though they have not physically carried out, or used another person to carry out, all the objective elements of the crime. This is only possible because they, together with other individuals, agree to jointly implement a common criminal plan that results in the execution of all objective elements of the crime.[1]

As ICC Pre-Trial Chamber I has recently explained:

> The concept of co-perpetration is originally rooted on the idea that when the sum of the co-ordinated individual contributions of a plurality of persons results in the realisation of all objective elements of a crime, any person making a contribution can be held vicariously responsible for the contributions of all the others and, as a result can be considered as a principal to the whole crime.[2]

---

[1] GP Fletcher, *Rethinking Criminal Law* (2nd edn, Oxford, Oxford University Press, 2000) 659 [hereinafter Fletcher]; F Munoz Conde and M Garcia Aran, *Derecho Penal: Parte General* (5th edn, Valencia, Tirant lo Blanch, 2002) 451–4 [hereinafter Munoz Conde and Garcia Aran]; K Ambos, *La Parte General del Derecho Penal Internacional: Bases para una Elaboracion Dogmatica* (Uruguay, Konrad-Adenauer-Stiftung, 2005) 175–9 [hereinafter Ambos, *La Parte General del Derecho Penal Internacional*]. Common law authors usually use the term 'co-principals' or 'joint principals'. Except for Australia, participants in a joint criminal enterprise are considered accessories to the crime as opposed to co-principals or joint principals. See JC Smith and B Hogan, *Criminal Law* (11th edn, London, Butterworths, 2005) 168–9 [hereinafter Smith and Hogan]; P Gillies, *Criminal Law* (4th edn, North Ryde, LBC Information Services, 1997) 155 [hereinafter Gillies].

[2] *Lubanga* Case (Pre-Trial Chamber I Decision on the Confirmation of Charges) ICC-01/04-01/06 (29 Jan 2007) para 326 [hereinafter *Lubanga Case* Confirmation of Charges]. See also *Katanga and*

The concept of co-perpetration is an open concept that can be resorted to regardless of whether one embraces the formal-objective approach, the subjective approach or the material-objective approach to the distinction between perpetration (principal liability) and participation (accessorial liability). Nevertheless, in any given system of criminal justice, the open concept of co-perpetration is given a specific content through certain definitional criteria. As ICC Pre-Trial Chamber I has pointed out:

> The definitional criterion of the concept of co-perpetration is linked to the distinguishing criterion between principals and accessories to a crime where a criminal offence is committed by a plurality of persons.[3]

In other words, when a crime is committed by a plurality of persons acting pursuant to a common plan, principals to the crime as a whole will only be those who carry out an objective element of the crime, if a formal-objective approach to the notion of perpetration (and thus to the distinction between perpetration and participation) is adopted.[4] However, if a subjective approach is chosen, principals to the crime as a whole will be all those who make their contributions (regardless of their importance) with the intent to have the crime as their own deed.[5] Finally, if a material-objective approach is chosen, principals to the crime will only be those who make an essential contribution for the completion of the crime in the sense that without it the crime would not have been committed.[6]

As seen in Chapter 2, a subjective approach to the notion of perpetration (and thus to the distinction between perpetration and participation) is inherent to the notion of joint criminal enterprise or the common purpose doctrine.[7] According to this notion, when a crime is committed by a plurality of persons acting in furtherance of a common criminal plan, principals to the crime are all those who make their contributions (regardless of their significance), sharing the aim to have the crimes included in the common plan committed.[8]

In turn, co-perpetration based on joint control of the crime, as a manifestation of the broader notion of control of the crime, is rooted in a material-objective approach to the notion of perpetration (and thus to the distinction between

---

Ngudjolo Case (Pre-Trial Chamber I Decision on the Confirmation of Charges) ICC-01/04-01/07 (1 Oct 2008) para 520 [*Katanga and Ngudjolo Case* Confirmation of Charges].

[3] *Lubanga Case* Confirmation of Charges (*Ibid*), at para 327.

[4] E Mezger, *Tratado de Derecho Penal Vol II* (Madrid, Editorial Revista de Derecho Privado, 1957) 339–40; A Gimbernat Ordeig, *Autor y Complice en Derecho Penal* (Madrid, Universidad de Madrid, 1966) 19–22 [hereinafter Gimbernat Ordeig]; JM Zugaldia Espinar (ed), *Derecho Penal: Parte General* (Valencia, Tirant lo Blanch, 2002) 733–4 [hereinafter Zugaldia Espinar].

[5] Fletcher (Above n 1), at 657–9; C Roxin, *Autoria y Dominio del Hecho en Derecho Penal* (6th edn, Madrid, Marcial Pons, 1998) 71 [hereinafter Roxin, Autoria]; Gimbernat Ordeig (*Ibid*), at 42–4; Zugaldia Espinar (*Ibid*), at 732–3.

[6] Munoz Conde and Garcia Aran (Above n 1), at 448–9; Roxin, Autoria (*Ibid*), at 58; Gimbernat Ordeig (*Ibid*), at 115–17; Zugaldia Espinar (*Ibid*), at 734–5. See Ch 2, s VI and s VII.B.

[7] *Ibid.*

[8] *Ibid.*

perpetration and participation).[9] According to co-perpetration based on joint control, when a crime is committed by a plurality of persons acting in furtherance of a common criminal plan, principals to the crime are only those who share the control of the crime (and are aware of it) as a result of the key role that their contributions play in the execution of the common plan.[10]

As joint criminal enterprise and joint control of the crime are two competing definitional criteria of the concept of co-perpetration, they will be dealt with in separate chapters. As a result, co-perpetration based on joint criminal enterprise is the subject of this chapter, whereas co-perpetration based on joint control is the subject of the next chapter.

II Three Forms of Co-perpetration Based on Joint Criminal Enterprise

The ICTY Appeals Judgment in the *Tadic* case not only defined the notion of co-perpetration based on joint criminal enterprise, but it also distinguished three different variants of this notion.[11] Subsequent case law of the *Ad hoc* Tribunals has usually referred to them as 'the basic form of JCE, the systemic form of JCE and the extended form of JCE'.[12]

The basic and systemic forms of joint criminal enterprise are applicable to the so-called 'core crimes' of the enterprise, which are those that are an integral part of the common criminal plan because their commission is its ultimate goal or the means to achieve it.[13] The systemic form of joint criminal enterprise is a subcategory of the basic form, and is only applicable when the common criminal plan

---

[9] See Ch 2, s VI and Ch 5, s I.

[10] *Ibid.*

[11] *Prosecutor v Kvocka et al* (Appeals Chamber Judgment) ICTY-98-30/1-A (28 Feb 2005) paras 79–82 [hereinafter *Kvocka Case* Appeals Judgment] referring to the *Prosecutor v Tadic* (Appeals Chamber Judgment) ICTY-94-1-A (15 Jul 1999) paras 195–226 [hereinafter *Tadic Case* Appeals Judgment]. See also *Prosecutor v Krnojelac* (Appeals Chamber Judgment) ICTY-97-25-A (17 Sep 2003) paras 83–4 [hereinafter *Krnojelac Case* Appeals Judgment]; *Prosecutor v Vasiljevic* (Appeals Chamber Judgment) ICTY-98-32-A (25 Feb 2004) para 96 [hereinafter *Vasiljevic Case* Appeals Judgment]; *Prosecutor v Stakic* (Appeals Chamber Judgment) ICTY-97-24-A (22 Mar 2006) para 64 [hereinafter *Stakic Case* Appeals Judgment]; *Prosecutor v Brdanin* (Appeals Chamber Judgment) ICTY-99-36-A (3 April 2007) para 364 [hereinafter *Brdanin Case* Appeals Judgment]; *Prosecutor v Krajisnik* (Judgment) ICTY-00-39-T (27 Sep 2006) paras 79–81 [hereinafter *Krajisnik Case* Trial Judgment].

[12] V Haan, 'The Development of the Concept of Joint Criminal Enterprise at the International Criminal Tribunal for the Former Yugoslavia' (2005) 5 *International Criminal Law Review* 170 [hereinafter Haan]. See also *Kvocka Case* Appeals Judgment (*Ibid*), at paras 82–3.

[13] As a result, once the Trial Chamber finds that it has been proven beyond reasonable doubt that the crimes charged in the indictment have been committed, the question arises as to 'whether one or more of these crimes was not part of the common objective of the JCE (JCE form 1) but rather was a natural and foreseeable consequence of the implementation of the JCE's common objective (JCE form 3) or fell outside the JCE altogether'. See *Krajisnik Case* Trial Judgment (Above n 11), at para 1096.

consists of setting up and/or furthering an organised system of ill-treatment (such as a concentration camp or a detention camp) to commit the crimes.[14]

The extended form of joint criminal enterprise is only applicable to the so-called 'foreseeable' crimes, that is to say, those crimes (i) committed beyond the scope of the common criminal plan because they are not an integral part of it; but (ii) are, nevertheless, a natural and foreseeable consequence of its implementation.[15]

A 'foreseeable' crime may become a 'core' crime of the enterprise over time. As the ICTY Trial Judgment in the *Krajisnik* case explained it:

> An expansion of the criminal means of the objective is proven when leading members of the JCE are informed of new types of crime committed pursuant to the implementation of the common objective, take no effective measures to prevent recurrence of such crimes, and persist in the implementation of the common objective of the JCE. Where this holds, JCE members are shown to have accepted the expansion of means, since implementation of the common objective can no longer be understood to be limited to commission of the original crimes. With acceptance of the actual commission of new types of crime and continued contribution to the objective, comes intent, meaning that subsequent commission of such crimes by the JCE will give rise to liability under JCE form 1.[16]

---

[14] As *Prosecutor v Krnojelac* (Judgment) ICTY-97-25-T (15 Mar 2002) para 78 [hereinafter *Krnojelac Case* Trial Judgment] affirmed: 'The Trial Chamber is satisfied that the only basis for the distinction between these two categories made by the *Tadic* Appeals Chamber is the subject matter with which those cases dealt, namely concentration camps during World War II'. See also *Tadic Case* Appeals Judgment (Above n 11), at paras 202, 203, 228; *Krnojelac Case* Appeals Judgment (Above n 11), at para 89; *Vasiljevic Case* Appeals Judgment (Above n 11), at para 98; *Kvocka Case* Appeals Judgment (Above n 11), at para 82; *Krajisnik Case* Trial Judgment (*Ibid*), at para 80; Haan (Above n 12), at 186.

[15] Its application has been considered particularly apposite to cases in which the common criminal plan is to forcibly remove at gunpoint members of one ethnicity from their town, village or region (to effect 'ethnic cleansing') with the consequence that, in the course of doing so, one or more of the victims is shot and killed. While murder may not have been explicitly acknowledged to be part of the common plan, it was nevertheless foreseeable that the forcible removal of civilians at gunpoint could very well result in the death of one or more of those civilians. See *Vasiljevic Case* Appeals Judgment (*Ibid*), at para 99; *Prosecutor v Kordic* (Judgment) ICTY-95-14/2-T (26 Feb 2001) para 396 [hereinafter *Kordic Case* Trial Judgment]; *Tadic Case* Appeals Judgment (*Ibid*), at paras 204, 220, 228; *Krnojelac Case* Appeals Judgment (*Ibid*), at para 32; *Kvocka Case* Appeals Judgment (*Ibid*), at para 83; *Stakic Case* Appeals Judgment (Above n 11), at para 65; *Prosecutor v Blaskic* (Appeals Chamber Judgment) ICTY-95-14-A (29 Jul 2004) para 33 [hereinafter *Blaskic Case* Appeals Judgment]; *Krajisnik Case* Trial Judgment (*Ibid*), at para 81; Haan (Above n 12), at 191–2.

[16] *Krajisnik Case* Trial Judgment (*Ibid*), at para 1098. According to the Trial Chamber, the Bosnian Serb leadership did not discontinue its discriminatory forced displacement programme in light of the increasing number and range of crimes being reported. On the contrary, it persisted with its territorial conquests and demographic re-compositions. As a result, whereas in the early stages of the Bosnian-Serb campaign the common criminal plan of the JCE was discriminatory deportation and forced transfer, soon thereafter it became clear to the members of the JCE, including the defendant, that the implementation of the common criminal plan involved, as a matter of fact, the commission of an expanded set of crimes. For the Trial Chamber, acceptance of this greater range of criminal means, coupled with persistence in implementation, signalled an intention to pursue the common criminal plan through these new means. As a result, these crimes became core crimes of the joint criminal enterprise during the course of the indictment period (this phenomenon was described by the Trial Chamber with the expression 'redefine the criminal means of the JCE's common objective'). See *Krajisnik Case* Trial Judgment, at paras 1100–18, 1124.

These cases must be distinguished from those other cases in which there are several joint criminal enterprises running simultaneously. In relation to this second group of cases, the ICTY Trial Judgment in the *Kvocka* case introduced the notion of 'subsidiary joint criminal enterprises'.[17] According to this notion, a joint criminal enterprise exists whenever two or more persons participate in a common criminal endeavour (no matter whether it consists of the robbing of a bank by two persons or the systematic slaughter of millions by thousands of persons during a vast criminal regime),[18] and within a broad joint criminal enterprise (such as the persecution of the non-Serb population in the territory of the Serb Republic of Bosnia and Herzegovina) there might be other subsidiary joint criminal enterprises (such as the Omarska detention camp) running simultaneously.[19] As a result:

> [W]ere the entire Nazi regime to be considered a joint criminal enterprise, that would not preclude a finding that Dachau Concentration Camp functioned as a subsidiary of the larger joint criminal enterprise, despite the fact that it was established with the intent to further the larger criminal enterprise. Within some subsidiaries of the larger criminal enterprise, the criminal purpose may be more particularized: one subset may be established for purposes of forced labour, another for purposes of systematic rape for forced impregnation, another for purposes of extermination, etc.[20]

Furthermore, there is a third group of cases in which several joint criminal enterprises run successively. For instance, the ICTY Trial Judgment in the *Krstic* case found the existence of an initial joint criminal enterprise to persecute the Bosnian-Muslim population of the Srebrenica enclave, which over time turned into a second joint criminal enterprise whose goal was the destruction of the Bosnian-Muslim male population of Srebrenica.[21]

III Elements of Co-perpetration Based on Joint Criminal Enterprise

A Objective Elements

All three forms of co-perpetration based on joint criminal enterprise have in common the following three objective elements: (i) plurality of persons; (ii) existence

---

[17] The notion of 'subsidiary joint criminal enterprises' has been used by some writers to solve the problem of whether a joint criminal enterprise must include the persons who physically carry out the objective elements. See K Gustafson, 'The Requirements of an "Express Agreement" for Joint Criminal Enteprise Liability: A Critique of Brdanin' (2007) 5 *Journal of International Criminal Justice* 150–58 [hereinafter Gustafson].

[18] *Prosecutor v Kvocka et al* (Trial Judgment) ICTY-98-30/1-T (2 Nov 2001) para 307 [hereinafter *Kvocka Case* Trial Judgment].

[19] *Ibid*.

[20] *Ibid*.

[21] *Prosecutor v Krstic* (Trial Judgment) ICTY-98-33-T (2 Aug 2001) para 621 [hereinafter *Krstic Case* Trial Judgment].

of a common plan, design or purpose which amounts to or involves the commission of a crime; and (iii) contribution to further the common criminal plan.[22]

i Plurality of Persons

Co-perpetration based on joint criminal enterprise requires the involvement of two or more persons in the commission of the crime. They need not be organised in a military, political or administrative structure. Indeed, they need not have a previous relationship. Moreover, they need not be personally identified; it is sufficient if there is evidence demonstrating that a group of individuals, whose identities could be established, at least, by reference to their category as a group, furthered a common plan.[23] The question arises as to whether the persons who physically carry out the objective elements of the crime must also be part of the joint criminal enterprise. As seen below, the answer to this question is affirmative for the traditional notion of joint criminal enterprise (a theory of co-perpetration *stricto sensu*),[24] whereas it is negative for the notion of joint criminal enterprise at the leadership level (a theory of indirect co-perpetration).[25]

ii Existence of a Common Plan, Design or Purpose, which Amounts to or Involves the Commission of a Crime

The common criminal plan comes into being as a result of an arrangement or understanding amounting to an agreement between two or more persons, which either aims at the commission of a crime or sees the commission of a crime as the means to achieve its ultimate goal.[26] There is no necessity for this common criminal plan to have been previously arranged or formulated because it may materialise extemporaneously.[27] The arrangement or understanding need not be express,

---

[22] *Tadic Case* Appeals Judgment (Above n 11), at para 227; *Krnojelac Case* Appeals Judgment (Above n 11), at para 31; *Vasiljevic Case* Appeals Judgment (Above n 11), at para 100; *Kvocka Case* Appeals Judgment (Above n 11), at para 96; *Stakic Case* Appeals Judgment (Above n 11), at para 64; *Brdanin Case* Appeals Judgment (Above n 11), at para 364.

[23] *Tadic Case* Appeals Judgment (*Ibid*), at para 227; *Krnojelac Case* Appeals Judgment (*Ibid*), at para 31; *Vasiljevic Case* Appeals Judgment (*Ibid*), at para 100; *Kvocka Case* Appeals Judgment (*Ibid*), at para 81; *Stakic Case* Appeals Judgment (*Ibid*), at para 64; *Brdanin Case* Appeals Judgment (*Ibid*), at para 364; *Krajisnik Case* Trial Judgment (Above n 11), at para 883. On the issue of identification by reference to a group, see *Prosecutor v Limaj* (Judgment on Sentencing Appeal) ICTY-03-66-A (27 Sep 2007) para 102 [hereinafter *Limaj Case* Appeals Judgment].

[24] See Ch 4, s IV.A.

[25] See Ch 4, s V.B.

[26] *Tadic Case* Appeals Judgment (Above n 11), at para 227; *Krnojelac Case* Appeals Judgment (Above n 11), at para 31; *Vasiljevic Case* Appeals Judgment (Above n 11), at para 100; *Kvocka Case* Appeals Judgment (Above n 11), at para 81; *Stakic Case* Appeals Judgment (Above n 11), at para 64; *Brdanin Case* Appeals Judgment (Above n 11), at para 364; *Prosecutor v Simic* (Judgment) ICTY-95-9-T (17 Oct 2003) para 158 [hereinafter *Simic Case* Trial Judgment]; *Krajisnik Case* Trial Judgment (Above n 11), at para 883.

[27] *Ibid.*

and it may be inferred from all the circumstances, including from the fact that a plurality of persons acts in unison to put into effect a common criminal plan. Indeed, the fact that two or more persons are participating together in the commission of a particular crime may itself establish an unspoken understanding or arrangement amounting to an agreement formed between them to commit that particular criminal act.[28]

For instance, in the *Furundzija* case, the defendant, a local commander of an HVO unit, interrogated the victim (a Bosnian Muslim female who was naked throughout the whole interrogation process) to obtain information valuable to the HVO, while another member of his unit assaulted and raped her.[29] When the Defence argued that there was no proof of an agreement between the defendant and the other member of his unit involved in the interrogation process to torture the victim, the Appeals Chamber explained:

> The Appeals Chamber agrees with the Prosecutor's submission that the events in this case should not be artificially divided between the Large Room and the Pantry, as the process was a continuum and should be assessed in its entirety. Once the abuses started and continued successively in two rooms, the interrogation did not cease. There was no need for evidence proving the existence of a prior agreement between the Appellant and Accused B to divide the interrogation into the questioning by the Appellant and physical abuse by Accused B. The way the events in this case developed precludes any reasonable doubt that the Appellant and Accused B knew what they were doing to Witness A and for what purpose they were treating her in that manner; that they had a common purpose may be readily inferred from all the circumstances, including (1) the interrogation of Witness A by the Appellant in both the Large Room while she was in a state of nudity, and the Pantry where she was sexually assaulted in the Appellant's presence; and (2) the acts of sexual assault committed by Accused B on Witness A in both rooms, as charged in the Amended Indictment. Where the act of one accused contributes to the purpose of the other, and both acted simultaneously, in the same place and within full view of each other, over a prolonged period of time, the argument that there was no common purpose is plainly unsustainable.[30]

If the common criminal plan, design or purpose achieves an institutional structure, it becomes a 'system of ill-treatment' or a 'system of repression'.[31] There are two main characteristics of such a system: (i) the existence of an institution or an organisation with comparable structure;[32] and (ii) the fact that either the ultimate

---

[28] *Tadic Case* Appeals Judgment (*Ibid*), at para 227; *Prosecutor v Furundzija* (Appeals Chamber Judgment) ICTY-95-17/1-A (21 Jul 2000) para 114 [hereinafter *Furundzija Case* Appeals Judgment]; *Krnojelac Case* Appeals Judgment (*Ibid*), at para 97; *Vasiljevic Case* Appeals Judgment (*Ibid*), at para 109; *Prosecutor v Vasiljevic* (Judgment) ICTY-98-32-T (29 Nov 2002) para 66 [hereinafter *Vasiljevic Case* Trial Judgment]; *Simic Case* Trial Judgment (*Ibid*), at para 158.

[29] *Prosecutor v Furundzija* (Judgment) ICTY-95-17/1-T (10 Dec 1998) paras 264–7 [hereinafter *Furundzija Case* Trial Judgment]; *Furundzija Case* Appeals Judgment (*Ibid*), at para 120.

[30] *Furundzija Case* Appeals Judgment (*Ibid*), at para 120.

[31] Normally, a concentration or detention camp, but also a children's home or a hospital could qualify as a system of ill-treatment under certain conditions. See *Tadic Case* Appeals Judgment (Above n 11), at para 203.

[32] *Kvocka Case* Trial Judgment (Above n 18), at para 300.

goal of the institution or the means relied on by the institution are criminal. To prove the existence of this second characteristic, the *Kvocka* Trial Judgment relied on evidence of the large scale and systematic use of violence against the inmates of the institution.[33]

Some writers have affirmed that:

> Once a prison camp has been characterized as an 'institution of ill-treatment', its shape and character automatically defines the scope of the JCE. All crimes committed within the borders of the institution are assumed to be part of the common enterprise to persecute the inhabitants of the institution.[34]

However, in the author's view, this equation is not automatic. On the contrary, the ICTY Trial Judgment in the *Kvocka* case, in spite of finding that crimes committed at the Omarska detention camp were primarily committed as part of a systemic form of joint criminal enterprise,[35] did not exclude the possibility of an extended form of joint criminal enterprise in relation to any crime (including sexual violence) that could be a natural and foreseeable consequence.[36] In this regard, the ICTY Appeals Chamber in this case, made the following observation:

> The Appeals Chamber notes, however, that the Trial Chamber did not hold any of the Appellants responsible for crimes beyond the common purpose of the joint criminal enterprise. Nonetheless, the Appeals Chamber wishes to affirm that an accused may be responsible for crimes committed beyond the common purpose of the systemic joint criminal enterprise, if they were a natural and foreseeable consequence thereof.[37]

Furthermore, in the *Krnojelac* case, the ICTY Appeals Chamber pointed out that the Prosecution should have pleaded a systemic form of joint criminal enterprise among the camp warden, the camp staff and the military personnel involved in the KP Dom prison facility, in which the common criminal plan should not have covered all crimes committed within the KP Dom. According to the ICTY Appeals Chamber, in defining the common criminal plan, the most appropriate approach was to limit the core crimes of the enterprise to those which, in light of the

---

[33] The Omarska camp was considered to function as a joint criminal enterprise, which intended to persecute and subjugate non-Serb detainees through crimes such as murder, torture, and rape and by various means, such as mental and physical violence and inhumane conditions of detention. The crimes committed in Omarska consisted of a broad mixture of serious abuses committed intentionally, maliciously, selectively, and in some instances sadistically against the non-Serbs detained in the camp. They could only have been committed by a plurality of persons, as the establishment, organisation, and functioning of the camp required the participation of many individuals playing a variety of roles and performing different functions of greater or lesser degrees of importance See *Kvocka Case* Trial Judgment, at para 320.

[34] Haan (Above n 12), at 187.

[35] *Kvocka Case* Trial Judgment (Above n 18), at para 268; *Kvocka Case* Appeals Judgment (Above n 11), at para 84.

[36] *Kvocka Case* Trial Judgment (*Ibid*), at paras 326–7; *Kvocka Case* Appeals Judgment (*Ibid*), at para 85.

[37] *Kvocka Case* Appeals Judgment (*Ibid*), at para 86.

context and evidence, could be considered as common to all offenders beyond all reasonable doubt.[38] As the ICTY Appeals Chamber explained:

> The search for the common denominator in its evidence should have led the Prosecution to define the common purpose of the participants in the system in place at the KP Dom from April 1992 to August 1993 as limited only to the acts which sought to further the unlawful imprisonment at the KP Dom of the mainly Muslim, non-Serb civilians on discriminatory grounds related to their origin and to subject them to inhumane living conditions and ill-treatment in breach of their fundamental rights.[39]

The question arises as to whether, in addition to a common criminal plan, the notion of joint criminal enterprise also requires a specific agreement between the defendant and the physical perpetrators to commit the core crimes of the enterprise. This issue has arisen in two different scenarios. First, it has arisen in the context of a systemic form of joint criminal enterprise, in which the common criminal plan, design or purpose has achieved an institutional structure. In the *Krnojelac* case, the Trial Chamber required proof of a specific agreement for each type of crime committed at the KP Dom between the defendant (the warden of the KP Dom prison facility) and the physical perpetrators (the staff of the KP Dom and certain military personnel).[40] However, the ICTY Appeals Chamber rejected this approach. Since a system of ill-treatment, which sought to subject non-Serb detainees to inhumane living conditions and ill-treatment on discriminatory grounds, was in place at the KP Dom, the ICTY Appeals Chamber considered it sufficient to examine whether the defendant knew of this system and agreed to it, without it being necessary to establish that he had entered into an agreement with the physical perpetrators.[41] In other words, for the ICTY Appeals Chamber:

> [I]t is less important to prove that there was a more or less formal agreement between all participants than to prove their involvement in the system.[42]

Second, it has also arisen in the context of the notion of 'joint criminal enterprise at the leadership level', where the physical perpetrators of the core crimes of the enterprise are not part of it because membership in the enterprise is limited to a core group of senior political and military leaders who use them as tools to have the crimes committed. As seen below in further detail, the ICTY Appeal Judgment in the *Brdanin* case has held that no specific agreement between the defendant and

---

[38] *Krnojelac Case* Appeals Judgment (Above n 11), at para 120. For this reason, the author considers that it is not correct to affirm that the *Krnojelac Case* Appeals Judgment stands for the position that once a prison camp has been qualified as an institution of ill-treatment, all crimes committed within the borders of the institution are assumed to be part of the joint criminal enterprise to persecute the inhabitants of the institution. Compare Haan (Above n 12), at 187.

[39] *Krnojelac Case* Appeals Judgment (*Ibid*), at para 118.

[40] *Krnojelac Case* Trial Judgment (Above n 14), at paras 170, 187.

[41] *Krnojelac Case* Appeals Judgment (Above n 11), at para 97. See also *Kvocka Case* Appeals Judgment (Above n 11), at para 118.

[42] *Krnojelac Case* Appeals Judgment (*Ibid*), at para 96.

the physical perpetrators to commit the core crimes of the enterprise is required in this context.[43]

iii Contribution to Further the Common Criminal Plan

To incur criminal liability as a co-perpetrator for participating in a joint criminal enterprise, it is necessary to contribute to the implementation of the common criminal plan. This can take place through a variety of roles as long as the participation takes the form of assistance in, or contribution to, the execution of the common plan.[44] One way of participating in the enterprise is by physically carrying out the objective elements of the crime.[45] However, there are also other means through which an individual can participate.[46] Indeed, a participant in a joint criminal enterprise does not even need to be present at the time the objective elements of the crime are carried out by the physical perpetrators, and he can make his contribution not only through actions but also through omissions.[47]

Whether a person is criminally liable as a principal (co-perpetrator) for his participation in a joint criminal enterprise in relation to crimes committed outside his presence is a factual issue to be decided in light of the evidence.[48] Hence, no automatic exclusion of principal liability is warranted in relation to those crimes committed prior to the defendant's arrival to, or after his departure from, a detention camp, or during his absences from the camp.[49]

The question arises as to the necessary level of contribution to the implementation of the common criminal plan. In principle, the ICTY Appeal Judgment in the *Stakic* case held that one of the main elements to distinguish the notion of co-perpetration based on joint criminal enterprise (which gives rise to principal liability) from the notion of aiding and abetting (which gives rise to accessorial liability) is that:

> The aidor and abettor carries out acts specifically directed to assist, encourage or lend moral support to the perpetration of a certain specific crime (murder, extermination,

---

[43] *Brdanin Case* Appeals Judgment (Above n 11), at para 418.

[44] *Tadic Case* Appeals Judgment (Above n 11), at para 227; *Krnojelac Case* Appeals Judgment (Above n 11), at para 31; *Vasiljevic Case* Appeals Judgment (Above n 11), at para 100; *Kvocka Case* Appeals Judgment (Above n 11), at paras 97–98; *Stakic Case* Appeals Judgment (Above n 11), at para 64; *Brdanin Case* Appeals Judgment (*Ibid*), at para 364; *Krajisnik Case* Trial Judgment (Above n 11), at para 883.

[45] *Ibid.*

[46] *Tadic Case* Appeals Judgment (*Ibid*), at para 192; *Krnojelac Case* Appeals Judgment (*Ibid*), at para 81; *Kvocka Case* Appeals Judgment (*Ibid*), at para 112.

[47] *Kvocka Case* Appeals Judgment (*Ibid*), at paras 112, 187; *Prosecutor v Mpambara* (Judgment) ICTR-01-65-T (11 Sep 2006) para 24; Haan (Above n 12), at 137.

[48] *Kvocka Case* Appeals Judgment (*Ibid*), at para 113.

[49] *Ibid* at para 114. The *Kvocka Case* Trial Judgment excluded the defendants' criminal responsibility for crimes committed prior to their arrival at the camp and after their departure from the camp. This ruling was not overturned by the Appeals Chamber because it was considered a factual finding based on the evidence brought by the Prosecution at trial that the Prosecution had chosen not to appeal.

rape, torture, wanton destruction of civilian property, etc.), and this support has a substantial effect upon the perpetration of the crime. By contrast, in the case of acting in pursuance of a common purpose or design, it is sufficient for the participant to perform acts that in some way are directed to the furthering of the common plan or purpose.[50]

In the view of the author, the low level of contribution required by the ICTY Appeals Chamber in the *Tadic* case is consistent with the subjective approach to the distinction between perpetration and participation that is inherent to the notion of joint criminal enterprise—it is the state of mind with which the contribution is made, and not the significance of the contribution, that marks the distinction between principals and accessories to the crime. This has been formulated as follows by the ICTY Appeals Chamber in the *Ojdanic* JCE Appeals Decision:

> [I]nsofar as a participant shares the purpose of the joint criminal enterprise (as he or she must do) as opposed to merely knowing about it, he or she cannot be regarded a mere aidor and abettor to the crime which is contemplated.[51]

Hence, while a certain level of contribution to the implementation of the common criminal plan is required, it does not need to be significant or substantial[52] because:

> The seriousness of what is done by a participant in a joint criminal enterprise who was not the principal offender is significantly greater than what is done by one who merely aids and abets the principal offender. That is because a person who merely aids and abets the principal offender need only be aware of the intent with which the crime was committed by the principal offender, whereas the participant in a joint criminal enterprise with the principal offender must share that intent.[53]

However, in the context of a systemic form of joint criminal enterprise in the Omarska detention camp, the ICTY Trial Judgment in the *Kvocka* case stressed that not everyone working in a detention camp where conditions are abusive becomes automatically liable as a co-perpetrator for his participation in a joint criminal enterprise.[54] On the contrary, the contribution must be 'significant', meaning by that:

---

[50] *Tadic Case* Appeals Judgment (Above n 11), at para 229.

[51] *Prosecutor v Milutinovic* (Decision on Dragoljub Ojdanic's Motion Challenging Jurisdiction—Joint Criminal Enterprise) ICTY-99-37-AR72 (21 May 2003) para 20 [hereinafter *Ojdanic* JCE Appeals Decision].

[52] See also Gustafson (Above n 17), at 141. Nevertheless, AM Danner and JS Martinez, 'Guilty Associations: Joint Criminal Enterprise, Command Responsibility and the Development of International Criminal Law' (2005) 93 *California Law Review* 150–51 [hereinafter Danner and Martinez] emphasise the need for the interpretation of the notion of joint criminal enterprise as requiring a significant level of contribution to the implementation of the common criminal plan. Likewise, JD Ohlin, 'Three Conceptual Problems with the Doctrine of Joint Criminal Enterprise' (2007) 5 *Journal of International Criminal Justice* 89 [hereinafter Ohlin] proposes to require a 'substantial and indispensable contribution' before criminal liability is invoked for participation in a joint criminal enterprise under ('Rome Statute of the International Criminal Court' UN Diplomatic Conference of Plenipotentiaries on the Establishment of an International Criminal Court (Rome 15 Jun–17 Jul 1998) (17 Jul 1998) UN Doc A/Conf. 183/9 [hereinafter RS]) art 25(3)(d) RS.

[53] *Krnojelac Case* Trial Judgment (Above n 14), at para 75.

[54] *Kvocka Case* Trial Judgment (Above n 18), at paras 308–309.

[A]n act or omission that makes an enterprise efficient or effective; eg a participation that enables the system to run more smoothly or without disruption.[55]

Furthermore, in the same case, the Trial Chamber distinguished between mid and low level actors and persons with authority. In relation to the former, it emphasised that 'participation would need to be assessed on a case by case basis'.[56] With regard to persons with authority, it stressed that:

It may be that a person with significant authority or influence who knowingly fails to complain or protest automatically provides substantial assistance or support to criminal activity by their approving silence, particularly if present at the scene of criminal activity. In most situations, the [. . .] co-perpetrator would not be someone readily replaceable, such that any 'body' could fill his place.[57]

The ICTY Trial Judgment in the *Simic* case extended to all forms of joint criminal enterprise the requirement that the level of contribution be 'significant' in the sense of making an enterprise 'efficient or effective'.[58] Moreover, given his minor role at the municipal level, the Trial Chamber did not convict Miroslav Tadic as a participant in the joint criminal enterprise to persecute the non-Serb population of the municipality of Bosanski Samac (BiH). As the Trial Chamber explained:

The Trial Chamber is not satisfied that there is sufficient evidence that Miroslav Tadic participated in the persecution of non-Serb prisoners through unlawful arrest and detention. While there is evidence that he was present at the detention facilities in Bosanski Samac, and had knowledge of their existence and conditions, he rarely entered the facilities, and visited these sites only in his role of conducting exchanges. Unlike Blagoje Simic, he did not hold a leading position in the Crisis Staff. His position as member of the Exchange Commission, did not afford him authority or influence over the arrest and detention of non-Serb civilians, nor did it require that he attend all meetings of the Crisis Staff. There is no evidence that he was contacted to make any decisions on the arrest or detention of non-Serbs.[59]

Nevertheless, the ICTY Appeals Judgment in the *Kvocka* case rejected the Trial Chamber's conclusion that the contribution to the implementation of the common criminal plan must be 'significant' or 'substantial'. In doing so, it gave the following reasons:

The Appeals Chamber notes that, in general, there is no specific legal requirement that the accused make a substantial contribution to the joint criminal enterprise. However, there may be specific cases which require, as an exception to the general rule, a substantial contribution of the accused to determine whether he participated in the joint criminal enterprise. In practice, the significance of the accused's contribution will be relevant to demonstrating that the accused shared the intent to pursue the common purpose.[60]

---

[55] *Ibid* at para 309.
[56] *Ibid.*
[57] *Ibid.*
[58] *Simic Case* Trial Judgment (Above n 26), at para 159.
[59] *Simic Case* Trial Judgment (*Ibid*), at para 998.
[60] *Kvocka Case* Appeals Judgment (Above n 11), at para 97.

Furthermore, the ICTY Appeals Chamber also made clear that the contribution does not need to amount to a *condition sine qua non* for the commission of the crimes,[61] and that participation in a joint criminal enterprise is not dependant on whether the defendant is or is not easily replaceable.[62]

In light of these findings, the ICTY Appeal Judgment in the *Kvocka* case addressed also the question of whether a person who does not have a superior position over the physical perpetrators because he lacks authority (power to prevent and punish) over them, would automatically also lack the necessary authority to make the required level of contribution to become a participant in a joint criminal enterprise.[63] It concluded that co-perpetration based on joint criminal enterprise and superior responsibility are 'distinct categories of individual criminal responsibility'[64] (each of them with specific legal requirements), and that the former does not require any showing of superior-subordinate relationship between the defendant and the physical perpetrators.[65]

Subsequently, the *Vasiljevic* Trial[66] and Appeal[67] Judgments, the *Brdanin* Trial Judgment[68] and the *Krajisnik* Trial Judgment[69] have followed the approach taken by the ICTY Appeals Chamber in the *Kvocka* case. As a result, they have held that, as a matter of law, the contribution to the implementation of the common criminal plan need not be necessary or substantial.

The recent ICTY Appeal Judgment in the *Brdanin* case has affirmed that:

[A]lthough the contribution need not be necessary or substantial, it should at least be a significant contribution to the crimes for which the accused is to be found responsible.[70]

Accordingly, it seems prima facie that the ICTY Appeals Chamber has brought back the 'significant contribution' requirement. However, if one looks more carefully, one realises that this finding is accompanied by a footnote quoting the following excerpt from paragraph 97 of the *Kvocka* Appeal Judgment:

In practice, the significance of the accused's contribution will be relevant to demonstrating that the accused shared the intent to pursue the common purpose.

As a result, the author considers that (i) the conclusion of the ICTY Appeals Chamber in the *Brdanin* case is an evidentiary one, according to which, when the intent of the defendant is to be inferred from his level of contribution, this must

---

[61] *Ibid* at para 98.

[62] *Ibid.*

[63] *Ibid* at para 104. Although the question arouse in the context of a systemic form of joint criminal enterprise at the Omarska camp, the answer provided by the ICTY Appeals Chamber was general and thus applicable to all forms of joint criminal enterprise.

[64] *Kvocka Case* Appeals Judgment (*Ibid*), at para 104; *Blaskic Case* Appeals Judgment (Above n 15), at para 91.

[65] *Kvocka Case* Appeals Judgment (*Ibid*), at para 104.

[66] *Vasiljevic Case* Trial Judgment (Above n 28), at para 67.

[67] *Vasiljevic Case* Appeals Judgment (Above n 11), at para 100.

[68] *Prosecutor v Brdanin* (Judgment) ICTY-99-36-T (1 Sep 2004) para 263 [hereinafter *Brdanin Case* Trial Judgment].

[69] *Krajisnik Case* Trial Judgment (Above n 11), at para 883.

[70] *Brdanin Case* Appeals Judgment (Above n 11), at para 430.

be 'significant'; and (ii) that the requisite level of contribution to the implementation of the common criminal plan remains fairly low.

Finally, the question has also arisen as to whether the required level of contribution to the implementation of the common criminal plan (particularly in a systemic form of joint criminal enterprise within a detention camp) can be inferred from the position of authority over the physical perpetrators.[71] In answering this question, the ICTY Appeals Chamber highlighted in the *Kvocka* case that the Trial Chamber did not err in its discussion of post WW II concentration camp cases which:

> [S]eemingly establish a rebuttable presumption that holding an executive, administrative, or protective role in a camp constitutes general participation in the crimes committed therein.[72]

It further stated that a de jure or de facto position of authority within a detention camp, as well as employment within the camp, are some of the 'contextual factors' to be assessed (and thus relevant evidence) in determining whether the level of contribution raises to the level of participating in enforcing or perpetuating the common criminal purpose of the system.[73]

B Subjective Elements

The subjective elements of the notion of co-perpetration based on joint criminal enterprise differ according to the form of joint criminal enterprise under consideration:[74] (i) the basic form of joint criminal enterprise requires that 'all of co-perpetrators possess the same intent to effect the common purpose';[75] (ii) the systemic form only requires personal knowledge of the organised system of

---

[71] *Kvocka Case* Appeals Judgment (Above n 11), at para 100. The issue was raised by Miroslav Kvocka (Omarska detention camp deputy commander) and Dragoljub Prcac (administrative aide to the Omarska camp commander) in the context of a systemic form of joint criminal enterprise at the Omarska camp.

[72] *Kvocka Case* Appeals Judgment (*Ibid*), at para 103; *Kvocka Case* Trial Judgment (Above n 18), at para 278.

[73] *Kvocka Case* Appeals Judgment (*Ibid*), at para 102. See also *Krnojelac Case* Appeals Judgment (Above n 11), at para 96.

[74] *Tadic Case* Appeals Judgment (Above n 11), at para 228; *Krnojelac Case* Appeals Judgment (*Ibid*), at para 32; *Vasiljevic Case* Appeals Judgment (Above n 11), at para 101; *Kvocka Case* Appeals Judgment (*Ibid*), at paras 82–3; *Stakic Case* Appeals Judgment (Above n 11), at para 65; *Brdanin Case* Appeals Judgment (Above n 11), at para 365.

[75] For instance, a plan formulated by the participants in a joint criminal enterprise to kill, where, although each of them may carry out a different role, each of them have the intent to kill. See *Vasiljevic Case* Appeals Judgment (*Ibid*), at para 97; *Tadic Case* Appeals Judgment (*Ibid*) at para 228; *Krnojelac Case* Appeals Judgment (*Ibid*), at para 84; *Kvocka Case* Appeals Judgment (*Ibid*), at para 82; *Stakic Case* Appeals Judgment (*Ibid*), at para 65; See also *Simic Case* Trial Judgment (Above n 26), at para 157; *Krajisnik Case* Trial Judgment (Above n 11), at para 79. See also A Bogdan, 'Individual Criminal Responsibility in the Execution of a "Joint Criminal Enterprise" in the Jurisprudence of the Ad hoc International Tribunal for the Former Yugoslavia' (2006) 6 *International Criminal Law Review* 82.

ill-treatment and intent to further the criminal purpose of such a system;[76] and (iii) the extended form of joint criminal enterprise requires the intent to participate in, and contribute to, the common criminal plan of the enterprise, the awareness that the foreseeable crimes might be committed in its implementation and the wilful taking of the risk by joining or continuing to participate in the enterprise.[77]

i Basic Form of Joint Criminal Enterprise

With regard to the basic form of joint criminal enterprise, the ICTY Appeal Chamber affirmed in the *Tadic* case that:

> [W]hat is required is the intent to perpetrate a certain crime (this being the shared intent on the part of all co-perpetrators).[78]

This language indicates that any participant in a basic form of joint criminal enterprise must specifically intend to cause the objective elements of the core crimes of the enterprise (*dolus directus* in the first degree)[79] insofar as they are the ultimate goal of the enterprise or the means through which the goal of the enterprise is to be achieved.[80] Furthermore, it also indicates that, in relation to those crimes (such as torture), which, in addition to the general subjective element, require an ulterior intent or *dolus specialis* (the physical or mental pain must be specifically inflicted for one of the forbidden purposes),[81] any participant in a

---

[76] *Tadic Case* Appeals Judgment (*Ibid*), at paras 202, 203, 228; *Krnojelac Case* Appeals Judgment (*Ibid*), at para 32; *Vasiljevic Case* Appeals Judgment (*Ibid*), at paras 98, 105; *Kvocka Case* Appeals Judgment (*Ibid*), at para 82; *Stakic Case* Appeals Judgment (*Ibid*), at para 65; *Simic Case* Trial Judgment (*Ibid*), at para 157; *Krajisnik Case* Trial Judgment (*Ibid*), at para 80. See also, Haan (Above n 12), at 189–90.

[77] *Tadic Case* Appeals Judgment (*Ibid*), at paras 204, 220, 228; *Vasiljevic Case* Appeals Judgment (*Ibid*), at para 99; *Kvocka Case* Appeals Judgment (*Ibid*), at para 83; *Stakic Case* Appeals Judgment (*Ibid*), at para 65; *Blaskic Case* Appeals Judgment (Above n 15), at para 33; *Krnojelac Case* Trial Judgment (Above n 14), at para 78; *Krajisnik Case* Trial Judgment (*Ibid*), at paras 881, 890. See also H Van der Wilt, 'Joint Criminal Enterprise: Possibilities and Limitations' (2007) 5 *Journal of International Criminal Justice* 96 [hereinafter Van der Wilt].

[78] *Tadic Case* Appeals Judgment (*Ibid*), at para 228; *Krnojelac Case* Appeals Judgment (Above n 11), at para 32, for similar language. See also *Vasiljevic Case* Appeals Judgment (*Ibid*), at para 101; *Kvocka Case* Appeals Judgment (*Ibid*), at para 82; *Stakic Case* Appeals Judgment (*Ibid*), at para 65; *Brdanin Case* Appeals Judgment (Above n 11), at para 365; *Simic Case* Trial Judgment (Above n 26), at para 158; *Krajisnik Case* Trial Judgment (*Ibid*), at paras 879, 883.

[79] The notion of *dolus directus* of the first degree was defined in the *Lubanga Case* Confirmation of Charges (Above n 2), at para 352, as follows: 'situations in which the suspect (i) knows that his or her actions or omissions will bring about the objective elements of the crime, and (ii) undertakes such actions or omissions with the concrete intent to bring about the objective elements of the crime (also known as dolus directus of the first degree)'.

[80] *Tadic Case* Appeals Judgment (Above n 11), at para 228; *Krnojelac Case* Appeals Judgment (Above n 11), at para 32; *Vasiljevic Case* Appeals Judgment (Above n 11), at para 101; *Kvocka Case* Appeals Judgment (Above n 11), at para 82; *Stakic Case* Appeals Judgment (Above n 11), at para 65; *Brdanin Case* Appeals Judgment (Above n 11), at para 365; *Simic Case* Trial Judgment (Above n 26), at para 158; *Krajisnik Case* Trial Judgment (Above n 11), at paras 879, 883.

[81] The subjective elements of a crime can be classified into: (i) a general subjective element consisting of the state of mind that must drive the execution of the objective elements of a crime; and (ii) additional subjective elements (usually referred to as ulterior intent or dolus specialis), which are

167

basic form of joint criminal enterprise must also act motivated by such an ulterior intent. As the Trial and Appeal Judgments in the *Furundzija* case have explained:

[T]o distinguish a co-perpetrator from an aidor or abettor, 'it is crucial to ascertain whether the individual who takes part in the torture process also *partakes of the purpose behind torture* (that is, acts with the intention of obtaining information or a confession, of punishing, intimidating, humiliating or coercing the victim or a third person, or of discriminating, on any ground, against the victim or a third person)'.[82]

The motives of the defendant are irrelevant for the purposes of assessing whether the defendant has the intent required by the core crimes of the joint criminal enterprise. In this regard, the *Tadic*,[83] *Jelisic*,[84] *Krnojelac*[85] and *Kvocka*[86] Appeal Judgments have highlighted the irrelevance and inscrutability of motives in criminal law. Hence, the lack of enthusiasm, satisfaction or initiative to perform the relevant contribution to the common criminal plan does not necessarily lead to the conclusion that the defendant did not have the intent required by the core crimes of the enterprise.[87]

In the absence of direct evidence, the intent of the defendant to commit the core crimes of the enterprise has often been inferred from his contribution to the implementation of the common criminal plan. For instance, the ICTY Trial Judgment in the *Kordic* case found that (i) from November 1991 through January 1994 there was a campaign of persecution against the Bosnian Muslim population of Central Bosnia;[88] (ii) the defendant Mario Cerkez, as commander of the Viteska Brigade, played his part in that campaign by commanding the troops involved in some of the incidents (attacks on Vitez, Stari Vitez and Donja Veceriska, which constituted a high point of the campaign of persecution); and (iii) 'as such he was a co-perpetrator; and that he had the necessary mens rea may be inferred, also in his case, from his part in the campaign'.[89] In this regard, the ICTY Appeals Chamber has recently affirmed in the *Brdanin* case that, when the defendant's intent is to be inferred from his level of contribution to the common criminal plan, it must be 'significant'.[90]

Moreover, in the *Krajisnik* case, the Trial Chamber held that in the absence of direct evidence as to the intent of the defendant to commit the core crimes of the

comprised of specific purposes that must motivate the commission of a crime. See *Lubanga Case* Confirmation of Charges (Above n 2), at paras 349–350. See also Smith and Hogan (Above n 1), at 112–13, in particular, the explanation of the notion of ulterior intent; Fletcher (Above n 1), at 575–6.

[82] *Furundzija Case* Trial Judgment (Above n 29), at para 257; *Furundzija Case* Appeals Judgment (Above n 28), at para 118.

[83] *Tadic Case* Appeals Judgment (Above n 11), at para 269.

[84] *Prosecutor v Jelisic* (Appeals Chamber Judgment) ICTY-95-10-A (5 July 2001) para 49.

[85] *Krnojelac Case* Appeals Judgment (Above n 11), at para 102.

[86] *Kvocka Case* Appeals Judgment (Above n 11), at para 106.

[87] *Krnojelac Case* Appeals Judgment (Above n 11), at para 100; *Kvocka Case* Appeals Judgment (*Ibid*), at para 106.

[88] *Kordic Case* Trial Judgment (Above n 15), at para 827.

[89] *Ibid* at para 831.

[90] *Brdanin Case* Appeals Judgment (Above n 11), at para 430.

enterprise, such intent can be inferred from his knowledge of the common criminal plan combined with his continued participation in the enterprise.[91] As a result, the Trial Chamber considered that the information received during the indictment period by the defendant Momcilo Krajisnik—who was the President of the Assembly of the self-proclaimed Serb Republic of Bosnia and Herzegovina, and one of the most influential members of its Presidency—was an important element to determine his criminal responsibility.[92] According to the Trial Chamber:

> [T]he Accused became aware of information—if not always its specifics, then at least in outline—on such matters reported to the Bosnian-Serb leadership, if not to him in particular, as the civilian detention, deportation or forced transfer, cruel or inhumane treatment, murder and extermination, and destruction of personal and cultural property of Muslims and Croats by Bosnian-Serb forces. Such inferences are made secure by the Chamber's finding that the Accused was no passive repository of information, but was eager to obtain information, indeed detailed information, about the unfolding events. He cultivated daily contact with expertly informed persons and was a focus of consultation for the administrators of the Bosnian-Serb provinces. The Chamber has no doubt that he and his closest associate, Radovan Karadzic, shared between themselves all important information about Bosnian-Serb affairs.[93]

The requirement that the intent to commit the core crimes of the enterprise (including any requisite ulterior intent or *dolus specialis*) must be shared by all co-perpetrators, that is to say by all participants in the joint criminal enterprise, has been recently restated as follows by the ICTY Appeals Chamber in the *Brdanin* case:

> The mens rea required for a finding of guilt differs according to the category of joint criminal enterprise liability under consideration. Where convictions under the first category of JCE are concerned, the accused must both intend the commission of the crime and intend to participate in a common plan aimed at its commission.[94]

The subjective requirement that all participants in a basic form of joint criminal enterprise must share the intent to commit the core crimes of the enterprise is closely related to the objective requirement of a common plan, design or purpose which aims at the commission of the core crimes of the enterprise (or which considers their commission as the means to achieve its ultimate goal), and that comes into being as a result of an arrangement, or an understanding amounting to an agreement, between the participants in the enterprise. In the view of the author these elements are the cornerstone of the notion of co-perpetration based on joint criminal enterprise because one can only attribute the contributions made by one participant in the joint criminal enterprise to the other participants in the enterprise if everyone acts in furtherance of a common plan, design or purpose with the intent to implement it. In this regard, Haan has pointed out that:

---

[91] *Krajisnik Case* Trial Judgment (Above n 11), at para 890.
[92] *Ibid.*
[93] *Ibid* at para 893.
[94] *Brdanin Case* Appeals Judgment (Above n 11), at para 365. See also *Prosecutor v Martic* (Appeals Chamber Judgment) ICTY-95-11-A (8 Oct 2008) para 82 [hereinafter *Martic Case* Appeals Judgment].

The meaning and significance of the requirement 'shared' remains unclear in most judgements, because there is a discrepancy between the theoretical interpretation and the practical application of the term 'shared intent' to the specific case. On a theoretical level, the Chambers unanimously take the view that the accused is to have shared with the person who *personally perpetrated the crime* the required state of mind. Consequently, this would mean that a person who did not personally commit a crime but who participated indirectly in the joint criminal enterprise can only be held liable for offences the direct perpetrators actually intended. For example, the (indirect) participant could be held liable for persecution as a co-perpetrator only if he himself and the direct perpetrators possessed the discriminatory intent. But it seems that only the *Krnojelac* Trial Chamber applied this prerequisite thoroughly and uncompromisingly. No other judgement dealing with the responsibility of persons indirectly involved in the crimes examined the state of mind of the direct perpetrators—which in most cases would have hardly have been possible given the high numbers of participants. If at all, the Chambers examined the state of mind of persons that acted on an equal or higher hierarchical level compared to the accused.[95]

The author considers that the problem highlighted by this writer is not related to the 'meaning and significance' of the so-called 'shared' requirement, but it is rather related to the fundamental question of whether the persons who physically carry out the objective elements of the core crimes of the enterprise must also be participants in the enterprise.[96]

Concerning the content of the 'shared' requirement, the case law of the *Ad hoc* Tribunals is clear in requiring that the aim of specifically causing the objective elements of the core crimes of the enterprise (along with any requisite ulterior intent or *dolus specialis* required by such crimes) must be shared by all co-perpetrators. Moreover, for the most part, this requirement has been applied scrupulously both in cases (such as *Furundzija* or *Vasiljevic*) where the physical perpetrators were found to be participants in the joint criminal enterprise, and in cases (such as *Kordic, Stakic, Krajisnik* or *Brdanin*) where the physical perpetrators were not considered participants in the enterprise.

Nevertheless, the author observes that in a few cases—which, as the *Simic* case, can be characterised as transitional cases between the application of the traditional notion of joint criminal enterprise and the application of the notion of joint criminal enterprise at the leadership level[97]—the defendants and the physical perpetrators were all considered to be part of the same joint criminal enterprise to commit the crimes charged in the indictment, and no analysis of the shared intent between the former and the latter was undertaken.[98]

[95] Haan (Above n 12), at 185.
[96] See Ch 4, s IV.A and s IV.C.i.
[97] See Ch 4, s IV.C.i.a.
[98] See Ch 4, s IV.C.i.

ii Systemic Form of Joint Criminal Enterprise

In relation to the systemic form of joint criminal enterprise, the ICTY Appeals Chamber stated in the *Tadic* case that:

> [P]ersonal knowledge of the system of ill-treatment is required (whether proved by express testimony or a matter of reasonable inference from the accused's position of authority), as well as the intent to further this common concerted system of ill-treatment.[99]

But, what did the ICTY Appeals Chamber mean when it referred to the intent to further a system of ill treatment? In the author's opinion, it meant the intent to commit the crimes that are the ultimate goal (or the means to achieve such goal) of the common criminal purpose, which is being implemented through the system of ill treatment.

This has been subsequently clarified by the ICTY Appeals Chamber in the *Kvocka*[100] and *Brdanin*[101] cases. In these cases, it has explicitly affirmed that the systemic form of joint criminal enterprise requires 'the intent to further the common purpose of the system'.[102] This confirms that there is no difference between the basic and the systemic forms of joint criminal enterprise in relation to the requirement that the defendant must have the intent (*dolus directus* in the first degree) to commit the crimes that are the ultimate goal (or the means to achieve such goal) of the common criminal plan, design or purpose.[103] In the case of a systemic form of joint criminal enterprise, where the common purpose is implemented through a system of ill treatment, this requirement is often encapsulated in the expression 'intent to further the system of ill treatment'.[104]

This interpretation is further supported by the fact that in the *Krnojelac* and *Kvocka* cases, the ICTY Appeals Chamber has held that when an ulterior intent crime is committed within a system of ill treatment, the defendant is only liable as

---

[99] *Tadic Case* Appeals Judgment (Above n 11), at para 228.

[100] *Kvocka Case* Appeals Judgment (Above n 11), at para 82.

[101] *Brdanin Case* Appeals Judgment (Above n 11), at para 365.

[102] *Ibid.* See also *Kvocka Case* Appeals Judgment (Above n 11), at para 82.

[103] *Vasiljevic Case* Trial Judgment (Above n 28), at para 68. This interpretation was hinted at, for the first time, by the *Krnojelac Case* Appeals Judgment (Above n 11), at paras 93–4. In this case, the Trial Chamber required the Prosecution to show that the defendant (the warden of the KP Dom prison facility) had the intent to commit each of the different types of crimes that were allegedly part of the system of ill treatment established at the KP Dom. The Prosecution appealed this finding and the ICTY Appeals Chamber found that: (i) the Prosecution had relied in the indictment on a joint criminal enterprise between the defendant, the staff at the KPDom and the military personnel that entered the KP Dom; (ii) the Prosecution had solely defined the common criminal purpose of the joint criminal enterprise at the KP Dom 'as the sum of the constituent acts charged, that is imprisonment, torture and beatings, killings, forced labour, inhumane conditions, deportation and expulsion'; and (iii) that the approach taken by the Trial Chamber, although corresponding more closely to the basic form of joint criminal enterprise than to the systemic one, did not amount to an error of law because 'the Prosecution did not provide a more suitable definition of common purpose when referring to the systemic form of joint criminal enterprise'.

[104] See Haan (Above n 12), at 189.

a co-perpetrator if he acted motivated by the requisite ulterior intent.[105] If the defendant did not have such an ulterior intent, he can only be held liable as an aidor and abettor whenever he makes a substantial contribution to the commission of the crime in the awareness that the physical perpetrators have the requisite ulterior intent.[106]

The ICTY Appeals Chamber in the *Krnojelac* case inferred the intent to commit the core crimes of the systemic joint criminal enterprise at the KP Dom from the defendant's duties as warden of the KP Dom, the period of time in which he exercised those duties, his knowledge of the system of ill-treatment in place, the crimes committed as part of the system, and their discriminatory nature.[107] Hence, a de jure or de facto position of authority within a detention camp, as well as employment within the camp, are some of the 'contextual factors' to be assessed (and thus relevant evidence) in determining knowledge and intent to further a system of ill-treatment.[108]

In this regard, the ICTY Trial Judgment in the *Kvocka* case also held that knowledge that a detention camp constitutes a system of ill treatment can be inferred from working at the camp during a certain period of time.[109] Furthermore, the intent to further the system may be also inferred from knowledge of the system and continued participation, if the participation is significant in position or effect.[110] As the Trial Chamber explained it:

> For example, an accused may play no role in establishing a joint criminal enterprise and arrive at the enterprise and participate in its functioning for a short period without knowledge of its criminal nature. Eventually, however, the criminal nature of the enterprise is learned, and thereafter participation in the enterprise is engaged in knowingly. Once the evidence indicates that a person who substantially assists the enterprise shares the goals of the enterprise, he becomes a co-perpetrator. For instance, an accountant hired to work for a film company that produces child pornography may initially manage accounts without awareness of the criminal nature of the company. Eventually, however, he comes to know that the company produces child pornography, which he knows to be illegal. If the accountant continues to work for the company despite this knowledge, he could be said to aid or abet the criminal enterprise. Even if it was also shown that the accountant detested child pornography, criminal liability would still attach. At some point, moreover, if the accountant continues to work at the company long enough and performs his job in a competent and efficient manner with only an occasional protest regarding the despicable goals of the company, it would be reasonable to infer that he shares the criminal intent of the enterprise and thus becomes a co-perpetrator.[111]

---

[105] *Krnojelac Case* Appeals Judgment (Above n 11), at para 111; *Kvocka Case* Appeals Judgment (Above n 11), at para 110, confirming the conclusions reached in this regard by the *Krnojelac Case* Trial Judgment (Above n 14), at para 487; *Kvocka Case* Trial Judgment (Above n 18), at para 288.

[106] *Kvocka Case* Appeals Judgment (*Ibid*), at para 110.

[107] *Krnojelac Case* Appeals Judgment (Above n 11), at para 111.

[108] *Ibid* at para 96. See also *Kvocka Case* Appeals Judgment (Above n 11), at para 102.

[109] *Kvocka Case* Appeals Judgment (*Ibid*), at para 284.

[110] *Ibid*.

[111] *Ibid* at paras 285–6.

As already seen above, the ICTY Appeals Chamber reversed the finding of the Trial Chamber in the *Kvocka* case that the contribution to the implementation of the common criminal plan must raise to the level of 'significant' or 'substantial'. Nevertheless, it highlighted that from an evidentiary perspective, the significance of the contribution is relevant to show intent to further the system of ill treatment.[112] In this regard, Haan has pointed out that:

> Again, on first view, the subjective requirement seems to be identical to that of the basic category of JCE. But there is one main difference between the two variants of JCE concerning the inference of the intent from the circumstances of the case. [] While the subjective elements of the first category of JCE—knowledge and the shared intent to commit the crime—might be inferred from all circumstances of a case, they could not be inferred automatically from the objective elements but only after a thorough examination of the circumstances of the specific case. [. . .] In contrast, in the case of second category of JCE, the accused's intent does not need to be established on a case by case basis but may be automatically inferred. The systematic character of the enterprise seems to justify a general assumption that a person who met the objective requirements of the JCE, i.e. who contributed significantly to the establishment or maintenance of the prison camp, also acted with knowledge of the criminal character of the institution and also intended all crimes that have been committed within the institution during the time he worked there.[113]

In the author's view, this statement is not completely accurate. First, as seen above, the level of contribution required for the basic and systemic forms of joint criminal enterprise is the same, and in no case needs to reach the level of 'significant' or 'substantial'. Hence, a lower level of contribution to the common criminal plan would suffice for the purpose of fulfilling the objective elements of co-perpetration based on joint criminal enterprise, but it would be insufficient to infer the defendant's intent to commit the core crimes of the enterprise (basic form) or to further the system of ill-treatment (systemic form). Nevertheless, once the defendant's intent to commit the core crimes of the enterprise, or to further the system of ill-treatment is proven, what is different between the basic and the systemic forms of joint criminal enterprise is the type of circumstances from which one can infer the existence of a 'shared' internet between the defendant and the other participants in the enterprise.

In this regard, it is important to highlight that in the basic and systemic forms of joint criminal enterprise, the requisite of 'shared intent' is normally inferred from the existence of an arrangement, or understanding amounting to an agreement, between all participants in the enterprise to commit the core crimes of the enterprise or to further the system of ill-treatment. However, the difference resides in that in the systemic form of joint criminal enterprise, where the common criminal plan or purpose has achieved an institutional structure, the arrangement, understanding or agreement between all participants in the enterprise is inherent

---

[112] *Ibid* at para 97.
[113] Haan (Above n 12), at 189.

to their acceptance of the system of ill-treatment as a whole, including its way of functioning and its results over time.

It is for this reason that the ICTY Appeals Chamber highlighted in the *Krnojelac* case that 'it is less important to prove that there was a more or less formal agreement between all participants than to prove their involvement in the system'.[114] It is also for this reason that, in the same case, the ICTY Appeals Chamber, while accepting that there is no difference between the basic and systemic forms of joint criminal enterprise in relation to the requirement that the defendant must have the intent (*dolus directus* in the first degree) to commit the crimes that are the ultimate goal (or the means to achieve such goal) of the common criminal plan or purpose, found inadequate the absence of any reference in the Trial Judgment to the concept of system of ill-treatment when determining whether the intent required by such crimes was shared by the defendant and the KP Dom guards and military personnel who physically committed the crimes.[115]

iii Extended Form of Joint Criminal Enterprise

a Advertent Recklessness as the Subjective Element of the Extended Form of Joint Criminal Enterprise

According to ICTY Appeal Judgment in the *Tadic* case, the extended form of joint criminal enterprise requires:

[T]he *intention* to participate in and further the criminal activity or the criminal purpose of a group and to contribute to the joint criminal enterprise or in any event to the commission of a crime by the group. In addition, responsibility for a crime other than the one agreed upon in the common plan arises only if, under the circumstances of the case, (i) it was *foreseeable* that such a crime might be perpetrated by one or other members of the group and (ii) the accused *willingly took that risk*.[116]

Hence, there is no extended form of joint criminal enterprise without the existence of a basic or systemic form of joint criminal enterprise in which the defendant participates. Only if the defendant is found to be a co-perpetrator of the core crimes of a basic or systemic enterprise, can one proceed to analyse whether the defendant might also be a co-perpetrator of those other crimes, which, despite falling outside the common criminal plan, are natural and foreseeable consequences of its implementation. As a result, only because General Krstic was found to be a participant in a basic form of joint criminal enterprise to ethnically cleanse the Srebrenica enclave by deporting and forcibly transferring the Bosnian Muslim population of the enclave, the Trial Chamber went on to analyse whether he was also liable pursuant to an extended joint criminal enterprise for the

---

[114] *Krnojelac Case* Appeals Judgment (Above n 11), at para 96.
[115] *Ibid* at para 90.
[116] *Tadic Case* Appeals Judgment (Above n 11), at para 228.

opportunistic killings, rapes, beatings and abuses committed against the Bosnian Muslims in Potocari when the deportation and forcible transfer operation was underway.[117]

The extended form of joint criminal enterprise also requires the defendant (i) to be aware that the commission of the foreseeable crimes is a possible consequence of the implementation of the common criminal plan, and (ii) to take voluntarily the risk by joining or continuing to participate in the enterprise.[118] From this perspective, the ICTY Appeals Chamber has recently highlighted in the *Martic* case:

> For the finding of responsibility under the third category of JCE, it is not sufficient that an accused created the conditions making the commission of a crime falling outside the common purpose possible; it is actually necessary that the occurrence of such crime was foreseeable to the accused and that he willingly took the risk that this crime might be committed.[119]

The ICTY Appeal Judgment in the *Stakic* case referred to this subjective element as *dolus eventualis* or *advertent recklessness*,[120] and held that the application of this subjective element to convict a person as a co-perpetrator of the foreseeable crimes of the enterprise does not violate the legality principle. According to the ICTY Appeals Chamber:

> In the *Ojdanic* Decision on Jurisdiction, the Appeals Chamber recognised the existence of joint criminal enterprise as a mode of liability in customary law existing as early as 1992 [. . .] A basis in customary law having been established, the Appeals Chamber in that case came to the conclusion that the notion of joint criminal enterprise did not violate the principle *nullem crimen sine lege*. As the concept of *dolus eventualis* (or 'advertent recklessness') is clearly 'required for the third form of joint criminal enterprise', the same conclusion is applicable in the instant case. As joint criminal enterprise does not violate the principle of legality, its individual component parts do not violate the principle either.[121]

The author considers that the *Stakic* Appeal Judgment's characterisation of the subjective element required by the extended form of joint criminal enterprise is not accurate. As seen above, ICC Pre-Trial Chamber I has explained that the notions of *dolus eventualis* and advertent recklessness are, by no means, similar because the former requires an individual to make peace, or reconcile oneself, with the idea that the crime will be committed, whereas advertent recklessness does not

---

[117] *Krstic Case* Trial Judgment (Above n 21), at para 616.
[118] *Tadic Case* Appeals Judgment (Above n 11), at paras 204, 220, 228; *Vasiljevic Case* Appeals Judgment (Above n 11), at paras 99–101; *Kvocka Case* Appeals Judgment (Above n 11), at para 83; *Stakic Case* Appeals Judgment (Above n 11), at para 65; *Blaskic Case* Appeals Judgment (Above n 15), at para 33; *Krnojelac Case* Trial Judgment (Above n 14), at para 78; *Krajisnik Case* Trial Judgment (Above n 11), at paras 881, 890; *Brdanin Case* Trial Judgment (Above n 68), at para 265. See also Van der Wilt (Above n 77), at 96.
[119] *Martic Case* Appeals Judgment (Above n 94), at para 83.
[120] *Stakic Case* Appeals Judgment (Above n 11), at paras 99–101.
[121] *Ibid* at paras 100–101.

require an individual to accept such a result (it only requires an individual to take a risk, regardless of whether or not he believes that the crime might indeed take place).[122] Furthermore, according to ICC Pre-Trial Chamber I and to the Trial Chamber in the *Stakic* case, in situations of *dolus eventualis* one can distinguish two types of scenarios:

> First, if the risk of bringing about the objective elements of the crime is substantial (that is, there is a risk of the substantial likelihood that "it will occur in the ordinary course of events") the fact that the suspect accepts the idea of bringing about the objective elements of the crime can be inferred from: (i) the awareness by the suspect of the substantial likelihood that his or her actions or omissions would result in the realisation of the objective elements of the crime; and (ii) the decision by the suspect to carry out his or her actions or omissions despite such awareness. Secondly, if the risk of bringing about the objective elements of the crime is low, the suspect must have clearly or expressly accepted the idea that such objective elements may result from his or her actions or omissions.[123]

As a result, the author considers that the extended form of joint criminal enterprise embraces an advertent recklessness standard—as opposed to a *dolus eventualis* standard. The reason is two-fold. First, the defendant need not be aware that there is a 'likelihood' or a 'substantial likelihood' (high level of risk) that the foreseeable crimes will be committed as a result of implementing the common criminal plan. He needs only to be aware that the commission of the foreseeable crimes is just a 'possible consequence' (low level of risk) of effecting the common criminal plan.[124] Second, in spite of the fact that the defendant only needs to be aware of the existence of a low level of risk, he is not required to 'clearly or expressly' accept the commission of the foreseeable crimes. On the contrary, it is sufficient if he takes the risk by joining or continuing to participate in the joint criminal enterprise.

This interpretation is supported by the ICTY Appeal Judgment in the *Blaskic* case, which made the following comments on the subjective elements required by the extended form of joint criminal enterprise:

> In relation to the responsibility for a crime other than that which was part of the common design, the lower standard of foreseeability—that is, an awareness that such a crime was a possible consequence of the execution of the enterprise—was applied by the Appeals Chamber. However, the extended form of joint criminal enterprise is a situation where the actor already possesses the intent to participate and further the common criminal purpose of a group. Hence, criminal responsibility may be imposed upon an actor

---

[122] See Ch 3, s I.C.ii. See also *Lubanga Case* Confirmation of Charges (Above n 2), at paras 352–5; Fletcher (Above n 1), at 443.

[123] *Lubanga Case* Confirmation of Charges (*Ibid*), at paras 352–353. In the same sense, see the definition of *dolus eventualis* provided in *Prosecutor v Stakic* (Judgment) ICTY-97-24-T (31 Jul 2003) para [hereinafter *Stakic Case* Trial Judgment]; See also Ch 3, s I.C.ii.

[124] According to *Karemera v Prosecutor* (Appeals Chamber Decision on Jurisdictional Appeals: Joint Criminal Enterprise) ICTR-98-44-AR72.5 (12 Apr 2006) para 14 [hereinafter *Karemera Case* Decision on Joint Criminal Enterprise], the fact that the defendant can only be held liable for crimes foreseen by him constitutes a sufficient safeguard against the fears of 'strict liability' for crimes committed by fellow participants in the enterprise that are structurally or geographically remote from the defendant.

for a crime falling outside the originally contemplated enterprise, even where he only knew that the perpetration of such a crime was merely a possible consequence, rather than substantially likely to occur, and nevertheless participated in the enterprise.[125]

In this regard, the ICTY Appeals Chamber has recently underscored in the *Martic* case:

> Turning to Martic's claim that the third category of JCE is controversial as it 'lowers the *mens rea* required for commission of the principal crime without affording any formal disminution in the sentence imposed', the Appeals Chamber recalls that it has already found that 'in practice, this approach may lead to some disparities, in that it offers no formal distinction between JCE members who make overwhelming large contributions and JCE members whose contributions, though significant, are not as great.' It is up to the trier of fact to consider the level of contribution—as well as the category of JCE under which responsibility attaches—when assessing the appropriate sentence, which shall reflect not only the intrinsic gravity of the crime, but also the personal criminal conduct of the convicted person and take into account any other relevant cricumstance.[126]

Absent direct evidence, the awareness of the possible commission of the foreseeable crimes can be inferred from a multiplicity of factors. For instance, the Trial Chamber in the *Krstic* case found that 'given the circumstances at the time the plan was formed, General *Krstic* must have been aware that an outbreak of these crimes would be inevitable given the lack of shelter, the density of the crowds, the vulnerable condition of the refugees, the presence of many regular and irregular military and paramilitary units in the area and the sheer lack of sufficient numbers of UN soldiers to provide protection'. In relation to the defendant's voluntary taking of risk, this has been consistently inferred from the fact that he joined or continued participating in the joint criminal enterprise despite being aware of the possible commission of the foreseeable crimes.[127]

b Application of the Extended Form of Joint Criminal Enterprise to Crimes that Require a Subjective Element more Stringent than Advertent Recklessness, Including Ulterior Intent Crimes such as Genocide

The question arises as to whether the extended form of joint criminal enterprise is applicable to crimes whose definition requires a more stringent general subjective element, such as *dolus directus* in the first degree (specifically aiming at causing the objective elements of the crime)[128] *dolus directus* in the second degree (acceptance

---

[125] *Blaskic Case* Appeals Judgment (Above n 15), at para 33.

[126] *Martic Case* Appeals Judgment (Above n 94), at para 84.

[127] *Krstic Case* Trial Judgment (Above n 21), at para 616. See also *Tadic Case* Appeals Judgment (Above n 11), at paras 204, 220, 228; *Vasiljevic Case* Appeals Judgment (Above n 11), at para 99; *Kvocka Case* Appeals Judgment (Above n 11), at para 83; *Stakic Case* Appeals Judgment (Above n 11), at para 65; *Blaskic Case* Appeals Judgment (Above n 15), at para 33; *Krnojelac Case* Trial Judgment (Above n 14), at para 78; *Krajisnik Case* Trial Judgment (Above n 11), at paras 881, 890. See also Van der Wilt (Above n 77), at 96.

[128] *Lubanga Case* Confirmation of Charges (Above n 2), at para 351.

of the occurrence of the objective elements of the crime as a necessary consequence of the achievement of one's main purpose)[129] or even *dolus eventualis*.[130]

This issue was raised on appeal by the Defence in the *Stakic* case. There, the
Defence argued that the extended form of joint criminal enterprise, as a theory of
co-perpetration that gives rise to principal liability, cannot be applied to crimes
which require a general subjective element that is more stringent than mere awareness of the possible commission of the crime and the voluntary taking of the
risk.[131] Otherwise, a theory of co-perpetration would be used to 'impermissibly
enlarge' the general subjective element provided for in the definition of such
crimes and that would constitute a violation of the principle of legality.[132] The
ICTY Appeals Chamber rejected the Defence's claim without addressing the sub-
stance of the Defence's allegations. It simply stated that, insofar as the notion of
joint criminal enterprise does not violate the principle of legality because it has
been found to be part of customary international law since 1992, its individual
components (including the subjective element of the extended form of joint criminal enterprise) do not violate the legality principle either.[133]

The question also arises as to whether the extended form of joint criminal enterprise is applicable to crimes that require, in addition to the general subjective element, an additional ulterior intent or *dolus specialis*. This question came up in the
Brdanin case in relation to the crime of genocide. The Trial Chamber held that the
extended form of joint criminal enterprise, as a theory of co-perpetration that
gives rise to principal liability, cannot be applied to ulterior intent crimes such as
genocide.[134] Otherwise, while the definition of genocide requires the perpetrator
(principal to the crime) to act with the ulterior intent to destroy in whole or in part
the group to which the victim belongs, the application of the extended form of
joint criminal enterprise to genocide would allow the defendant to be convicted as
a principal to genocide, even though he did not act with the requisite genocidal
intent.

In other words, the Trial Chamber found that if the extended form of joint
criminal enterprise was applicable to genocide, any defendant who participates in
a basic form of joint criminal enterprise to commit murder would become liable
as a co-perpetrator (principal) of genocide by merely: (i) being aware of the possibility that any other member of the enterprise could carry out the agreed upon
murder with a genocidal intent; and (ii) voluntarily taking the risk by joining or
continuing to participate in the enterprise despite such awareness.[135] As a result,

---

[129] *Lubanga Case* Confirmation of Charges (Above n 2), at para 352.

[130] In the author's view, as the general subjective element of the extended form of joint criminal
enterprise is advertent recklessness, the same issue arises in relation to crimes which, at the very least,
require *dolus eventualis*.

[131] *Stakic Case* Appeals Judgment (Above n 11), at para 99 referring to paras 274, 322, 336, 351 of
the Defence Appeals Brief and to para 116 of the Defence Reply Brief.

[132] *Ibid.*

[133] *Ibid* at paras 100–101.

[134] *Prosecutor v Brdanin* (Decision on Motion for Acquittal Pursuant to Rule 98bis) ICTY-99-36-
R77 (19 Mar 2004) para 30.

[135] *Ibid* at paras 55–7.

according to the Trial Chamber in the *Brdanin* case, a theory of co-perpetration would be used to impermissibly circumvent the genocidal intent requirement provided for in the definition of genocide.[136] The same conclusion was subsequently reached by the Trial Chamber in the *Stakic* case.[137]

Nevertheless, the ICTY Appeals Chamber disagreed with this conclusion because, in its view, it conflated the subjective elements of the crime (genocide) with the subjective elements of the mode of liability pleaded by the Prosecution (the extended form of joint criminal enterprise).[138] According to the Appeals Chamber:

> The third category of joint criminal enterprise liability is, as with other forms of criminal liability, such as command responsibility or aiding and abetting, not an element of a particular crime. It is a mode of liability through which an accused may be individually criminally responsible despite not being the direct perpetrator of the offence. An accused convicted of a crime under the third category of joint criminal enterprise need not be shown to have intended to commit the crime or even to have known with certainty that the crime was to be committed. Rather, it is sufficient that that accused entered into a joint criminal enterprise to commit a different crime with the awareness that the commission of that agreed upon crime made it reasonably foreseeable to him that the crime charged would be committed by other members of the joint criminal enterprise, and it was committed. [] For example, an accused who enters into a joint criminal enterprise to commit the crime of forcible transfer shares the intent of the direct perpetrators to commit that crime. However, if the Prosecution can establish that the direct perpetrator in fact committed a different crime, and that the accused was aware that the different crime was a natural and foreseeable consequence of the agreement to forcibly transfer, then the accused can be convicted of that different offence. Where that different crime is the crime of genocide, the Prosecution will be required to establish that it was reasonably foreseeable to the accused that an act specified in Article 4(2) would be committed and that it would be committed with genocidal intent. [] As a mode of liability, the third category of joint criminal enterprise is no different from other forms of criminal liability, which do not require proof of intent to commit a crime on the part of an accused before criminal liability can attach. Aiding and abetting, which requires knowledge on the part of the accused and substantial contribution with that knowledge, is but one example. Command responsibility liability, which requires the Prosecution to establish that a

---

[136] *Ibid* at para 57.

[137] According to the *Stakic Case* Trial Judgment (Above n 123), at para 530: 'According to this Trial Chamber, the application of a mode of liability cannot replace a core element of a crime. The Prosecution confuses modes of liability and the crimes themselves. Conflating the third variant of joint criminal enterprise and the crime of genocide would result in the *dolus specialis* being so watered down that it is extinguished. Thus, the Trial Chamber finds that in order to "commit" genocide, the elements of that crime, including the *dolus specialis* must be met. The notions of "escalation" to genocide, or genocide as a "natural and foreseeable consequence" of an enterprise not aimed specifically at genocide are not compatible with the definition of genocide under Article 4(3)(a)'. This conclusion is supported by Ambos, '*Joint Criminal Enterprise* and Command Responsibility' (2007) 5 *Journal of International Criminal Justice* 159, at 180 and 181 [hereinafter Ambos, *Joint Criminal Enterprise*].

[138] *Prosecutor v Brdanin* (Decision on Interlocutory Appeal) ICTY-99-36-A (19 March 2004) para 10 [hereinafter *Brdanin Case* Decision on the Application of the Extended Form of Joint Criminal Enterprise to the Crime of Genocide].

Commander knew or had the reason to know of the criminality of subordinates, is another.[139]

The author does not share the conclusions reached by the ICTY Appeals Chamber in the *Stakic* and *Brdanin* cases, and he is particularly concerned by the fact that the *Stakic* Appeal Judgment jumped to its conclusion without addressing, in depth, the substantive arguments underlying the Defence's claim. In the author's view, when a plurality of persons are involved in the commission of a crime, they can be qualified as perpetrators or principals to the crime (if their liability can be established independently of all the other parties to the crime), or as accessories or secondary parties (if their liability derives from the principal liability of the perpetrators).[140] The definition of a crime contains the mental state with which a person must act in order to 'commit' such crime (that is to say, in order to become a principal to the crime).[141] As a result, unless a defendant himself has the mental state required by the definition of the crime, he cannot be considered a principal.

In other words, if the definition of a crime requires that the objective elements of the crime be carried with the specific aim to cause such elements (*dolus directus* in the first degree), a defendant can only be considered a principal to that crime if he carries out his conduct aiming at causing its objective elements. Likewise, if the definition of genocide requires an ulterior intent to destroy in whole or in part the national, ethnical, racial or religious group to which the victim belongs, a defendant can only be considered a principal to genocide if he carries out his conduct for that specific purpose.[142]

---

[139] *Ibid* at paras 5–7. See also G Werle, 'Individual Criminal Responsibility in Article 25 ICC Statute' (2008) 7 *International Criminal law Review* 953–75. The subsequent ICTR Appeals Decision on the Application of Joint Criminal Enterprise to Genocide in the *Rwamakuba Case* did not explicitly deal with the question of whether the extended form of joint criminal enterprise can be applied to genocide. On the contrary, it dealt with the general issue of whether 'international customary law supports the application of joint criminal enterprise to the crime of genocide', and, in its analysis, the ICTR Appeals Chamber did not distinguish between the basic, the systemic and the extended forms of joint criminal enterprise. Hence, one could say that, by answering the said question in the affirmative, the ICTR Appeals Chamber, at best, implicitly endorsed the conclusion reached by the ICTY Appeals Chamber in the *Brdanin* case, that the extended form of joint criminal enterprise is also applicable to genocide. See *Rwamakuba v Prosecutor* (Appeals Chamber Decision on Interlocutory Appeal Regarding Application of Joint Criminal Enterprise to the Crime of Genocide) ICTR-98-44-AR72.4 (22 Oct 2004) paras 10, 14, 31 [hereinafter *Rwamakuba Case* Decision on the Application of Joint Criminal Enterprise to the Crime of Genocide].

[140] See Ch 2, s II and s III. See also Smith and Hogan (Above n 1), at 166; Fletcher (Above n 1), at 636.

[141] The mental state required for accessories differs from the mental state required for principals to the crime. As Gillies (Above n 1), at 158, explains: 'The principal's participation in crime is quite different, conceptually, to that of an accessory. The principal personally perpetrates the crime, whereas an accessory does not, and so at the level of physical conduct a distinction must be made. The mental state is likewise different, in a number of ways. Most obviously, the common law does not require that the accessory act with the intention that the crime be committed, while most crimes require that the principal have either intention in respect of the physical harm or at least the purpose that the act constituting or causing this harm take place. Further, accessorial liability being a common law doctrine, the accessory is required to have a guilty mind, even where the offence is not one of mens rea'. See also Smith and Hogan (Above n 1), at 179; Munoz Conde and Garcia Aran (Above n 1), at 455–7.

[142] Ambos, *Joint Criminal Enterprise* (Above n 137), at 180 and 181. See also Smith and Hogan (*Ibid*), at 179; Munoz Conde and Garcia Aran (*Ibid*), at 455–7.

If the defendant only knows that the physical perpetrator has the *dolus directus* in the first degree required by the crime in question, or the genocidal intent required by genocide, he cannot be considered a principal to such crimes. This does not mean that the defendant will be acquitted. On the contrary, he could still be held liable as an accessory to the crime for planning, ordering, instigating or aiding and abetting. For instance, if the defendant's assistance in the commission of a crime reaches the level of 'substantial', he will become an accessory to the crime as an aidor and abettor.

Now the question arises as to whether the extended form of joint criminal enterprise constitutes a theory of co-perpetration, which gives rise to principal liability, or is it, on the contrary, a theory of accessorial liability? Only in this second scenario could the extended form of joint criminal enterprise be applicable to genocide in cases where the defendant does not act with a genocidal intent, but is aware of the possibility that some of the other participants in the enterprise may do it.

In order to justify the application of the extended form of joint criminal enterprise to genocide, Van Sliedriegt has affirmed that it is a theory of accessorial liability to which the principles of derivative liability apply.[143] She reaches her conclusion in light of the following two premises: (i) the notion of joint criminal enterprise as elaborated by the case law of the *Ad hoc* Tribunals is rooted in the common purpose doctrine applied in common law jurisdictions and in post WW II cases; and (ii) common law jurisdictions and post WW II cases have never regarded the common purpose doctrine as a theory of co-perpetration giving rise to principal liability; quite the contrary, they considered it as a theory of accessorial liability.[144]

The author considers that there is ample evidence confirming the accuracy of Van Sliedregt's two premises[145]—indeed, one of the main problems caused by the insistence of the ICTY and the ICTR Appeals Chambers in resorting to post WW II case law in order to specify the content of the notion of joint criminal enterprise at the *Ad hoc* Tribunals is the fact that the common purpose doctrine in post WW II case law was not a theory of principal liability. Nevertheless, Van Sliedregt's reasoning fails because she does not take into consideration that the notion of joint criminal enterprise (regardless of its specific form) has evolved in the case law of the *Ad hoc* Tribunals to become a theory of co-perpetration or principal liability.[146]

As a result, insofar as in the case law of the *Ad hoc* Tribunals, the extended form of joint criminal enterprise also constitutes a theory of co-perpetration that gives rise to principal liability, it cannot be applied to convict those defendants who do not fulfil the subjective elements of the crimes charged in the indictment (including any requisite ulterior intent).

---

[143] E Van Sliedregt, 'Joint Criminal Enterprise as a Pathway to Convicting Individuals for Genocide' (2007) 5 *Journal of International Criminal Justice* 184 [hereinafter Van Sliedregt, *Joint Criminal Enterprise*].

[144] *Ibid* at 201–5.

[145] See Ch 2, s VII.C.ii and s VII.C.iv.

[146] See Ch 2, s VII.B.

IV Traditional Notion of Joint Criminal Enterprise

A Concept

When analysing in the previous section the elements of the three forms of joint criminal enterprise, we left unanswered the question of whether the persons who physically carry out the objective elements of the crime must be part of the joint criminal enterprise. This question is closely related to the determination of the participants in the enterprise, which is the cornerstone of the notion of joint criminal enterprise for the following reasons: (i) as in any other theory of co-perpetration, the notion of joint criminal enterprise is only applicable when the realisation of the objective elements of the crime is the result of the sum of the co-ordinated individual contributions of a plurality of persons;[147] and (ii) the principal liability of the defendant for the crimes committed during the implementation of the common criminal plan is only the result of attributing to him those contributions made by other participants in the enterprise.[148]

Hence, before holding a defendant criminally liable as a principal to a crime due to the consideration of the actions or omissions of the other participants in the enterprise as his own actions or omissions, it is essential to know (i) who those other participants in the enterprise are (and, in particular, those who physically carry out the objective elements of the crime), and (ii) whether they, together with the defendant, act in a coordinated manner (that is to say, in pursuance of a common criminal plan, design or purpose).

Based on these premises, Haan has highlighted that, 'on a theoretical level', the Chambers have unanimously taken the view that the persons who physically carry out the objective elements of the crimes must be part of the joint criminal enterprise.[149] For Cassese, to extend criminal liability to instances where there was no agreement or common plan between the perpetrators and those who participated in the common plan would seem to excessively broaden the notion'.[150] Likewise, Gustafson points out that the requirement that the physical perpetrators be part

---

[147] *Tadic Case* Appeals Judgment (Above n 11), at para 227; *Krnojelac Case* Appeals Judgment (Above n 11), at para 31; *Vasiljevic Case* Appeals Judgment (Above n 11), at para 100; *Kvocka Case* Appeals Judgment (Above n 11), at paras 81, 96; *Stakic Case* Appeals Judgment (Above n 11), at para 64; *Krajisnik Case* Trial Judgment (Above n 11), at para 883.

[148] *Tadic Case* Appeals Judgment (*Ibid*), at paras 190–92; *Krnojelac Case* Appeals Judgment (*Ibid*), at paras 30, 73; *Vasiljevic Case* Appeals Judgment (*Ibid*), at paras 95, 102, 111; *Blaskic Case* Appeals Judgment (Above n 15), at para 33; *Kvocka Case* Appeals Judgment (*Ibid*), at paras 79, 91; *Ojdanic* JCE Appeals Decision (Above n 51), at paras 20, 31; *Krajisnik Case* Trial Judgment (*Ibid*), at para 883. See also *Lubanga Case* Confirmation of Charges (Above n 2), at para 326.

[149] Haan (Above n 12), at 185.

[150] A Cassese, 'The Proper Limits of Individual Responsibility under the Doctrine of Joint Criminal Enteprise' (2007) 5 *Journal of International Criminal Justice* 126 [hereinafter Cassese].

of a joint criminal enterprise 'operates as a limit on the potential scope of JCE liability'.[151] Finally Van Sliedregt acknowledges that:

[I]n the Tribunal's case law there have been attempts to interpret the 'plan element' beyond its original understanding, i.e. an agreement between the 'physical' and a 'non-physical perpetrator'.[152]

Nevertheless, in her view:

The underlying rationale of the Trial Chamber's 'explicit agreement requirement' in *Brdanin* was to dismiss such an understanding of JCE[153]

The reason for this statement is that:

The common purpose links the physical perpetrator to the non-physical perpetrator and provides the basis for attributing individual criminal responsibility.[154]

The author does not agree with Haan in that the case law of the *Ad hoc* Tribunals has unanimously requested that the physical perpetrators be part, together with the defendant, of the joint criminal enterprise. On the contrary, in the author's view, one can distinguish two separate groups of cases: (i) those cases against low and mid level defendants who were present or close to the scene of the crime at the time the crimes were committed (Category A); and (ii) those other cases against mid and high level defendants who were far away from the scene of the crime at the relevant time (Category B).

When the notion of joint criminal enterprise has been applied to the first group of cases, the case law of the *Ad hoc* Tribunals has consistently required that the physical perpetrators and the defendant all be part of the same joint criminal enterprise—and, hence, that they all act pursuant to a common criminal plan and they all share the intent to commit the core crimes of the enterprise. These types of cases resemble those cases in which, at the national level, particularly in common law jurisdictions, the notion of joint criminal enterprise, or the common purpose doctrine, is usually resorted to.[155] It also resembles the type of post WW II cases reviewed by the ICTY Appeals Chamber in the *Tadic* case to declare the customary status of the notion of joint criminal enterprise.[156]

---

[151] Gustafson (Above n 17), at 142.

[152] Van Sliedregt, *Joint Criminal Enterprise* (Above n 143), at 200.

[153] *Ibid.*

[154] *Ibid.*

[155] Gillies (Above n 1), at 173–5; Smith and Hogan (Above n 1), at 190–93.

[156] The cases referred to in the *Tadic Case* Appeals Judgment (Above n 11), at paras 196–220, include (i) the *Georg Otto Sandrock et al* case (also known as the *Almelo Trial*), the *Jepsen and others* case, the *Schonfeld et al* case, the *Ponzano case*, the *Belsen* case, and the *Essen Lynching* case (also called the *Essen West* case), all tried before British Courts sitting in Germany; (ii) the *Einsatzgruppen* case, the *Dachau Concentration Camp* case, and the *Kurt Goebell et al* case (also called the *Borkum Island* case), all tried before US Courts sitting in Germany; (iii) the *Hoelzer et al* case tried before a Canadian Military Court; and (iv) the *D'Ottavio et al* case, the *Aratano et al* case, the *Tosani* case, the *Bonati et al* case, the *Peveri* case, the *Manneli* case, the *PM v Minafo* case, the *Montagnino* case, the *Solesio et al* case, the *Minapo el al* case and the *Antonino et al* case, all tried before Italian Courts.

Cases falling within Category A were the first brought before the *Ad hoc* Tribunals. As a result, their case law focused on this type of cases when elaborating on the elements of the notion of joint criminal enterprise. This led to require that the physical perpetrators and the defendant must all: (i) be part of the same enterprise; (ii) act pursuant to a common criminal plan; and (iii) share the intent to commit the core crimes of the enterprise. If the *Tadic* Appeal Judgment left any doubt on the existence of these requirements, the *Krnojelac* Appeal Judgment affirmed them in such a way as to eliminate any doubt.

In this regard, in the *Krnojelac* case, the Trial Chamber held that in order to establish the basic form of joint criminal enterprise, the Prosecution must show that:

> [E]ach of the persons charged and (if not one of those charged) the principal offender or offenders had a common state of mind, that which is required for that crime.[157]

The Prosecution appealed this legal finding because, in its view, this approach would render the notion of joint criminal enterprise useless in the context of state criminality. For instance, this notion could not be used in a context in which senior political and military leaders who, from a distant location, plan the widespread destruction of civilian buildings (hospitals and schools) in a particular area in order to demoralise the enemy without the soldiers responsible for carrying out the attacks sharing the objective in question or even knowing the nature of the relevant targets.[158] However, the ICTY Appeals Chamber rejected the Prosecution's argument for the following reasons:

> The Appeals Chamber finds that, apart from the specific case of the extended form of joint criminal enterprise, the very concept of joint criminal enterprise presupposes that its participants, other than the principal perpetrator(s) of the crimes committed, share the perpetrators' joint criminal intent. The Appeals Chamber notes that the Prosecution does not put forward any contrary arguments and does not show how this requirement contravenes the *Tadic* Appeals Judgement, as it alleges. The Appeals Chamber also notes that the example given by the Prosecution in support of its argument on this point appears more relevant to the planning of a crime under Article 7(1) of the Statute than to a joint criminal enterprise.[159]

This interpretation of the notion of joint criminal enterprise—whereby the defendant and the physical perpetrators must all be part of the same enterprise, act pursuant to a common criminal plan and share the intent required by the core crimes of the enterprise—is referred to in this book as 'the traditional notion of joint criminal enterprise'.

---

[157] *Krnojelac Case* Trial Judgment (Above n 14), at para 83.

[158] *Krnojelac Case* Appeals Judgment (Above n 11), at para 83.

[159] *Ibid*, at para 84. The requirements that the defendant and the physical perpetrators must all be part of the same enterprise, act pursuant to a common criminal plan or purpose and share the intent required by the core crimes of the enterprise have also been explicitly endorsed by the *Simic Case* Trial Judgment (Above n 26), at para 160, and the *Brdanin Case* Trial Judgment (Above n 68), at paras 262, 264, 344, 347. These two trial judgments are discussed in further detail in Ch 4, s IV.C.i.a and s V.B.

B Problems Posed by the Application of the Traditional Notion of Joint Criminal Enterprise to Low Level Defendants

The main problem presented by the traditional notion of joint criminal enterprise stems from the fact that, as the ICTY Appeals Chamber has explicitly held in the *Furundzija*[160] and *Vasiljevic*[161] cases, all participants in a joint criminal enterprise are 'equally liable' as principals (co-perpetrators) to the core crimes of the enterprise (and to the foreseeable crimes committed by any member of the enterprise in the implementation of the common criminal purpose), regardless of the part played by each of them in their commission. As a result, there has always been a concern in relation to the risk of an unacceptable extension of criminal liability for those low and mid level members of the enterprise who do not physically carry out the objective elements of the crime. This concern has been recently formulated as follows by the ICTY Appeals Chamber in the *Brdanin* case:

> In the Prosecution Response on JCE, however, the Prosecution does not 'identify each individual [on-the-ground] actor and put on proof of his intent'. Instead, it merely asserts that the JCE encompasses the vast category of (unnamed) Relevant Physical Perpetrators. A coherent application of such a notion could make each one of the RPPs, as members of the JCE, responsible for each one of the crimes that the Trial Chamber found were committed throughout the territory of the ARK during the Indictment period.[162]

This concern has even arisen in the context of the application of the traditional notion of joint criminal enterprise to the members of a platoon, who, acting in a concerted manner, torture a handful of prisoners with the shared intent of obtaining information about the positions of the enemy on the other side of the hill. Even in this limited scenario, a number of writers, such as Danner and Martinez, have advocated that only those who 'substantially' or 'significantly' contribute to the implementation of the common criminal purpose should be considered participants in the joint criminal enterprise and, hence, they should be the only ones held 'equally liable' as principals to the crimes.[163] In this regard, Cassese has pointed out that:

> By and large, all the dangers and misapprehension of the doctrine by international courts, feared by a number of commentators, have not materialized. Courts have tended to apply the notion in a wise and well-balanced manner, insisting, among other things, on the need that the contribution of participants in the JCE be 'substantial' for criminal liability to arise.[164]

---

[160] *Furundzija Case* Appeals Judgment (Above n 28), at paras 117–18.
[161] *Vasiljevic Case* Appeals Judgment (Above n 11), at para 111.
[162] *Brdanin Case* Appeals Judgment (Above n 11), at para 445.
[163] Danner and Martinez (Above n 52), at 150–51.
[164] Cassese (Above n 150), at 133.

However, as seen above,[165] the attempts by the Trial Chambers in the *Kvocka*[166] and *Simic*[167] cases have been reversed by the ICTY Appeals Chamber because, as a matter of law, the contribution to the implementation of the common criminal plan need not have been significant, substantial or necessary.[168]

i *The* Furundzija *Approach*

The *Furunzdija* case constitutes a singular attempt to restrict the criminal liability as principals to the crimes of low level defendants for their participation in a traditional joint criminal enterprise. The defendant, a local commander of an HVO unit, was convicted as a co-perpetrator, together with a second member of his unit involved in the interrogation process, for his participation in a basic form of joint criminal enterprise to torture the victim.[169] The Trial Chamber justified the conviction because the activities of both individuals were considered to be part of the same process, and therefore, the defendant had participated by virtue of his interrogation in an integral part of torture.[170] Nevertheless, the Trial Chamber did not convict the defendant as a participant in a basic form of joint criminal enterprise to sexually assault and rape the victim—it was the other member of his unit who sexually assaulted and raped the victim while the defendant interrogated her.[171] The defendant was only convicted for aiding and abetting because he did not carry out an integral part of the objective elements of such crime.[172] The ICTY Appeals Chamber confirmed the approach of the Trial Chamber that a defendant is only liable as a co-perpetrator for his participation in a basic form of joint criminal enterprise if he carries out an integral part of the objective elements of the crime charged in the indictment.[173]

The *Furundzija* approach has not been subsequently followed by the case law of the *Ad hoc* Tribunals. Indeed, in the view of the author, by limiting the criminal liability of those participating in a basic form of joint criminal enterprise in this

---

[165] See Ch 4, s III.A.iii.

[166] *Kvocka Case* Trial Judgment (Above n 18), at para 309.

[167] *Simic Case* Trial Judgment (Above n 26), at para 159.

[168] *Tadic Case* Appeals Judgment (Above n 11), at paras 227, 229; *Kvocka Case* Appeals Judgment (Above n 11), at para 97; *Vasiljevic Case* Appeals Judgment (Above n 11), at para 100; *Krajisnik Case* Trial Judgment (Above n 11), at para 883.

[169] *Furundzija Case* Trial Judgment (Above n 29), at para 267.

[170] *Ibid. See also Furundzija Case* Appeals Judgment (Above n 28), at para 118.

[171] During the first part of the defendant's interrogation of the victim in the 'large room', she was naked and the second member of his unit rubbed his knife on her inner thighs and threatened to cut out her private parts if she did not tell the truth about the activities of members of her family, her relationship with certain HVO soldiers and her alleged involvement with the ABiH. See *Furundzija Case* Trial Judgment (*Ibid*), at paras 264–5. During the second part of the defendant's interrogation of the victim in the 'pantry', she was still naked and the second member of his unit, after hitting her, assaulted and raped her before the defendant and an 'audience' of soldiers. As the interrogation intensified, so did the sexual assaults and the rape. See *Furundzija Case* Trial Judgment (*Ibid*), at para 266.

[172] *Ibid* at para 270.

[173] *Ibid* at para 257; see also *Furundzija Case* Appeals Judgment (Above n 28), at para 118.

way, the nature of this notion is altered. Such limitation turns the subjective approach to the concept of co-perpetration (which is based on the shared state of mind of the co-perpetrators and is inherent to the notion of joint criminal enterprise)[174] into a formal-objective approach (according to which, the relevant criterion is whether the defendant carries out any of the objective elements of the crime).[175]

ii *The* Vasiljevic *Approach*

The concern to limit the criminal liability as principals to the crimes of low level defendants for their participation in a traditional joint criminal enterprise has also appeared in broader contexts, such as the criminal activities of a paramilitary group against the local Muslim population of a municipality of BiH over a period of two months or a persecutorial campaign by local army units against the local Muslim population of a village in Central Bosnia over a period of more than a year.

In the *Vasiljevic* case, the defendant (an informant, but not a member of Milan Lukic's paramilitary group) was convicted as a co-perpetrator for his participation, together with Lukic and two unidentified members of his group, in a basic form of joint criminal enterprise to kill seven Bosnian Muslims in the Drina River Bank on 14 June 2007 (the defendant was directly involved in this incident).[176] Nevertheless, he was not considered a participant in the broader joint criminal enterprise by the members of the Milan Lukic's group to persecute the local Muslim population of the Visegrad municipality through a number of crimes committed in the weeks following the withdrawal of the JNA on 19 May 1992.[177]

The most relevant feature of this case is the Trial Chamber's narrow definition of the basic form of joint criminal enterprise in which the defendant participated insofar as it only included one isolated incident, particularly in light of the Trial Chamber's finding that the defendant shared with the members of Lukic's group the discriminatory intent to persecute on religious or political grounds the local Muslim population of the Visegrad municipality.

In the author's view, the narrow definition of the core crimes of the joint criminal enterprise in this case constitutes an attempt to limit the responsibility of low level participants in the enterprise (such as Mitar Vasiljevic, who was just one of the informants of the group) to those specific crimes in which they have a direct involvement. In order to achieve this goal, the Trial Chamber equated the

---

[174] See Ch 2, s V and Ch 5, sI.

[175] *Ibid.*

[176] The defendant personally participated in the implementation of the common criminal plan by (i) preventing the seven Muslim men from fleeing by pointing a gun at them while they were detained at the Vilina Vlas Hotel; (ii) escorting them to the bank of the Drina River and pointing a gun at them to prevent their escape; and (iii) standing behind the Muslim men with his gun together with the other three offenders shortly before the shooting started. See *Vasiljevic Case* Trial Judgment (Above n 28), at paras 206, 208, 209, 254.

[177] *Ibid* at paras 251–2.

defendant's lack of direct involvement in most crimes committed by Lukic's group (murders, physical assaults, sexual assaults, destruction of property and the like) with his lack of shared intent to commit such crimes (and this, in spite of the fact that the defendant was found to share the discriminatory intent to persecute the local Muslim population on religious or political grounds). If the Trial Chamber had taken a different approach by extending the core crimes of the joint criminal enterprise in which the defendant participated to all persecutory acts carried out by Lukic's group, then the defendant would have been convicted as a co-perpetrator of all the crimes, despite the fact that he was only directly involved in the Drina River Incident.

The approach of the Trial Chamber seems a cautious approach to the notion of co-perpetration based on joint criminal enterprise in relation to low level perpetrators. Moreover, even if the Prosecution would have relied, which it did not, on the extended form of joint criminal enterprise, it is very unlikely that the other persecutory acts committed by Lukic's group could have been considered as natural and foreseeable consequences of the killings that occurred in the Drina River Incident on 14 June 1992.

Nevertheless, the author considers that this approach has two main problems. First, it looks 'artificial' to say that Mitar Vasiljevic did not share the intent to commit the crimes carried out by Lukic's group when he (i) was aware of the crimes committed by the group, (ii) participated in the killings that occurred at the Drina River Incident on 14 June 1992, and (iii) shared the persecutory intent of Lukic's group when he transmitted relevant information to the group about local Muslims, who he knew were potential targets of the group.

Second, this approach leads to multiple joint criminal enterprises (each of them with different core crimes and participants) concerning the very same crimes. For instance, in the Drina River Incident, Milan Lukic, two unidentified members of his group and Mitar Vasiljevic were directly involved. As a result, the case against any of them would include their responsibility as co-perpetrators in the killings that took place in this incident. Nevertheless, as they all (except Vasiljevic) were directly involved in other persecutory acts against the local Muslim population of Visegrad, the Trial Chamber's approach would lead to having a different joint criminal enterprise in the case against each of them (with the Drina River Incident being a common core crime).

iii The Kupreskic Approach

In this case, Zoran Kupreskic (an HVO local commander in the Ahmici area since October 1992) and Mirjan Kupreskic (brother of Zoran and an HVO soldier in the Ahmici area since mid April 1993) were convicted by the Trial Chamber as co-perpetrators for their participation in a common criminal enterprise, carried out by the HVO from October 1992 until April 1993, to ethnically cleanse the village of Ahmici and its environs of its Bosnian Muslim inhabitants through their deliberate and systematic killing, their organised detention and expulsion and the comprehensive destruction of their homes and property.[178]

According to the ICTY Appeals Chamber, the Trial Chamber based the defendants' conviction for the period prior to 16 April 1993 on the alleged involvement of the defendants with the HVO without explaining what constituted the defendants' illegal conduct from October 1992 until 15 April 1993.[179] The ICTY Appeals Chamber held that there was nothing unlawful about the fact that Zoran and Mirjan Kupreskic were involved with the village guard at that time.[180] Furthermore, Zoran Kupreskic was found to have assumed responsibility for facilitating the safe return of Muslims after the events in October 1992, and for providing security and ensuring that there would be no problems regarding the return of the Bosnian Muslim population.[181]

As a result, the ICTY Appeals Chamber considered that no evidence indicated the participation of the defendants in the persecutory joint criminal enterprise prior to 16 April 1993, and reversed their conviction as co-perpetrators of the crime of persecution prior to such date because it was unreasonable.[182] In other words, in this case, the ICTY Appeals Chamber adopted the approach that no criminal responsibility arises for those crimes committed in execution of a common criminal plan prior to the moment in which the defendants start making their contribution.

C Problems Posed by the Application of the Traditional Notion of Joint Criminal Enterprise to Mid and High Ranking Political and Military Leaders

i First Approach to the Problem

Despite the concerns raised by the application of the traditional notion of joint criminal enterprise to low level defendants, the author considers that as long as the scope of the enterprise is not defined in a broad manner they are not insurmountable. Indeed, the main problems posed by the traditional notion of joint criminal enterprise arise when one tries to apply it to mid and high ranking political and military leaders who are structurally and geographically remote from the physical perpetrators.

---

[178] *Prosecutor v Kupreskic* (Judgment) ICTY-95-16 (14 Jan 2000) paras 480, 490 [hereinafter *Kupreskic Case* Trial Judgment]; *Prosecutor v Kupreskic* (Appeals Chamber Judgment) ICTY-95-16 (23 Oct 2001) paras 77, 243 [hereinafter *Kupreskic Case* Appeals Judgment].

[179] *Kupreskic Case* Appeals Judgment (*Ibid*), at para 243.

[180] *Ibid.*

[181] *Ibid.*

[182] *Ibid.* The ICTY Appeals Chamber also reversed the conviction of Zoran and Mirjian Kupreskic for the crime of persecution in relation to the 16 April 1993 HVO attack to the village of Ahmici. The reason for this reversal was the ambiguity with which the Prosecution had pleaded the crime in the indictment and during the proceedings before trial.

Two types of reasons explain this. First, in situations of large scale or systematic criminality, the higher the position of a political or military leader, the broader the criminal activities in which he has been involved are and, consequently, the higher the number of members of the joint criminal enterprise in which he has allegedly participated are as well. Second, the traditional notion of joint criminal enterprise requires the inclusion within the enterprise of: (i) the small group of senior political and military leaders who design and set into motion the common criminal plan; (ii) the mid level superiors who prepare its implementation; and (iii) the hundreds or thousands of low level followers who physically implement it.

As a result, the application of the traditional notion of joint criminal enterprise to mid and high ranking political and military leaders who are geographically and structurally remote from the physical perpetrators presupposes the existence of such broad joint criminal enterprises that they become a sort of a legal fiction that can hardly correspond to reality insofar as they require that all members of the enterprise: (i) act in furtherance of a common criminal plan; (ii) share the intent of committing the core crimes of the enterprise; and (iii) share any ulterior intent (*dolus specialis*) required by such core crimes. Furthermore, some writers expressed the concern that the application of the traditional notion of joint criminal enterprise in this kind of scenario may come close to a form of collective criminal liability.[183]

As the cases brought before the *Ad hoc* Tribunals started targeting mid and high ranking political and military leaders, the array of crimes covered by them has progressively broadened, and the above-mentioned problems became more and more apparent. At one point, even Del Ponte, former ICTY and ICTR Prosecutor, acknowledged these problems by stating that:

> [C]riminal liability of high ranking leaders who share the intent to commit a crime and jointly act to achieve it through various means, cannot be dependent on whether one of them actually physically commits the crime.[184]

The *Simic* case before the ICTY highlights the scope of these problems because they became even more evident as a result of the attempt by the Trial Chamber to obviate them.

a The Simic *Case: Prosecuting the President of the Crisis Staff of the Municipality of Bosanski Samac in BiH on a Traditional Joint Criminal Enterprise Basis*

In the *Simic* case, the defendant Blagoje Simic (president of the Crisis Staff, War Presidency and Municipal Assembly of the Bosanski Samac municipality in BiH) was convicted as a co-perpetrator for his participation in a basic form of joint

---

[183] Ambos, *Joint Criminal Enterprise* (Above n 137), at 167 and 168. See also M Elewa Badar, 'Just Convict Everyone!—Joint Perpetration from Tadic to Stakic and Back Again' (2006) 6 *International Criminal Law Review* 302 [hereinafter Badar].

[184] C Del Ponte, 'Investigation and Prosecution of Large-Scale Crimes at the International Level. The Experience of the ICTY' (2006) 4 *Journal of International Criminal Justice* 550–51.

criminal enterprise to (i) take over the vital facilities and institutions of the town of Bosanki Samac; and (ii) persecute the non-Serb civilian population of the municipality through acts of unlawful arrest, detention, confinement, cruel and inhumane treatment, deportation, forcible transfer, and the issuance of orders, policies and decisions that violated their fundamental rights.[185]

The Trial Chamber found that the joint criminal enterprise was put into effect from September 1991 to the end of 1993 and its participants were the members of the Crisis Staff of the municipality (including Blagoje Simic as its president), the Bosnian-Serb police of the municipality (including the Police Chief, Stevan Todorovic, who was also a member of the Crisis Staff), the Bosnian-Serb paramilitaries operating in the municipality, and the army units deployed in the municipality (the 17th Tactical Group of the JNA).[186] Moreover, according to the Trial Chamber, Blagoje Simic was the highest-ranking civilian in the municipality and presided over its Crisis Staff—which was responsible for the economy, humanitarian and medical care, information and propaganda, procurement of food supplies and communications,[187] and whose decisions and orders provided for the legal, political, and social framework in which the other participants of the joint criminal enterprise worked and from which they profited.[188] As a result, the defendant was found to be at the 'apex' of the joint criminal enterprise,[189] to know that his role and authority were essential for the accomplishment of the common persecutorial goal,[190] and to share with the other participants in the joint criminal enterprise (including the physical perpetrators) the intent to persecute the non-Serb population of the Bosanski Samac municipality.[191]

In this case, the Trial Chamber applied the traditional notion of joint criminal enterprise because the physical perpetrators were included among the participants in the enterprise.[192] As the Trial Chamber explained:

> To prove the basic form of joint criminal enterprise, the Prosecution must demonstrate that each of the persons charged, and (if not one of those charged) the principal offender or offenders, had a common state of mind, that which is required for that crime. As

---

[185] *Simic Case* Trial Judgment (Above n 26), at paras 987, 992, 1115; *Prosecutor v Simic* (Appeals Chamber Judgment) ICTY-95-9-A (28 Nov 2006) para 19 [hereinafter *Simic Case* Appeals Judgment]. The conviction was reversed in appeal because the ICTY Appeals Chamber found that the Prosecution had not properly pleaded the notion of co-perpetration based on joint criminal enterprise in the various amended indictments. See *Simic Case* Appeals Judgment (*Ibid*), at para 74. As a result, the ICTY Appeals Chamber partially substituted a conviction for aiding and abetting for a conviction as a co-perpetrator for participation in a basic form of joint criminal enterprise. See *Simic Case* Appeals Judgment (*Ibid*), at paras 189–91.

[186] *Simic Case* Trial Judgment (*Ibid*), at para 984; *Simic Case* Appeals Judgment (*Ibid*), at para 19.

[187] *Simic Case* Trial Judgment (*Ibid*), at para 992.

[188] *Ibid*.

[189] *Ibid*. See also *Simic Case* Appeals Judgment (Above n 185), at para 19.

[190] *Simic Case* Trial Judgment (*Ibid*), at para 992; *Simic Case* Appeals Judgment (Above n 184), at para 19.

[191] *Ibid*.

[192] Indeed, when defining the notion of joint criminal enterprise, the Trial Chamber required that the physical perpetrators also be part of the joint criminal enterprise. See *Simic Case* Trial Judgment (*Ibid*), at para 160.

compared with the requisite *mens rea* for aiding and abetting, '[t]he participant in the basic form of joint criminal enterprise must share with the person who physically carried out the crime the state of mind required for that crime; the person who merely aids and abets must be aware of the essential elements of the crime committed, including the state of mind of the person who physically carried it out, but he need not share that state of mind'.[193]

Nevertheless, when one analyses how the Trial Chamber dealt with the problems posed by the application of the traditional notion of joint criminal enterprise to mid level political leaders, such as the defendant, one notices that it did not address the question of the existence of a common criminal plan and a shared state of mind between (i) the mid and low level members of the civil police, paramilitary groups and army units deployed in Bosanski Samac who physically committed the crimes, and (ii) the political and military authorities of the municipality who planned and directed the commission of the crimes charged in the indictment.

The Trial Chamber started its analysis by highlighting that on a 'horizontal level', the participants in the joint criminal enterprise acted pursuant to a common plan to set up institutions and authorities to persecute the non Bosnian-Serb population of the municipality.[194] Nevertheless, the Trial Chamber was not satisfied that the existence of this common criminal plan could be 'vertically extended' to the political leadership of the Srpska Republic.[195]

Subsequently, in its analysis of the 'horizontal level', the Trial Chamber focused on the coordination and joint action among the authorities of the civil administration, civil police, army units and paramilitary groups deployed in the municipality.[196] Against this backdrop, the Trial Chamber reached the conclusion that the common goal to commit the acts of persecution could not have been achieved without the joint action of the police, paramilitaries and the 17th Tactical Group of the JNA and Crisis Staff—no participant could have achieved the common goal on their own.[197]

The Trial Chamber inferred the existence of a common criminal plan among the civil and military authorities of the municipality and the physical perpetrators from the mere fact that they were all acting in unison.[198] Furthermore, the Trial Chamber found that the defendant and all the other participants in the enterprise shared the intent to commit the crimes without explaining the evidentiary basis for such a finding.[199]

In author's view, the fact that the Trial Chamber preferred to disregard, as opposed to address, the problems posed by the application of the traditional notion of joint criminal enterprise in this case gave rise to important gaps in the Trial Judgment. However, the ICTY Appeals Chamber did not have the opportu-

---

[193] *Ibid.*
[194] *Ibid* at para 986.
[195] *Ibid* at para 985.
[196] *Ibid* at paras 988–91.
[197] *Ibid* at para 991.
[198] *Ibid* at para 987.
[199] *Ibid* at para 992.

nity to address them because it reversed the defendant's conviction for his participation in a basic form of joint criminal enterprise due to the Prosecution's failure to properly plead it in the various amended indictments.[200]

ii Solutions Proposed by Writers

a Increasing the Required Level of Contribution to the Common Criminal Plan

A number of different solutions have been proposed to address the problems presented by the traditional notion of joint criminal enterprise to senior political and military leaders. For Danner and Martinez the solution against what they called an 'over-expansive JCE doctrine' is to be found in an increase of the required level of contribution to the common criminal plan.[201] In other words, only those who substantially contribute to the joint criminal enterprise should be considered participants in the enterprise.

However, this approach has been explicitly rejected by the case law of the *Ad hoc* Tribunals.[202] Additionally, this approach does not take into account that the essence of the problem lies in the pretended existence of a common plan and a shared intent among individuals who do not know each other and have such different positions as the president of the Federation of Serbia and Montenegro and a private of the Bosnian Serb Army who was physically involved in the execution of thousands of Bosnian Serbs after the fall of Srebrenica.

b Unsuitability of the Notion of Joint Criminal Enterprise to Prosecute Senior Political and Military Leaders

According to Cassese, the notion of joint criminal enterprise may not be resorted to when the physical perpetrators of the crimes charged in the indictment are not part of the common criminal plan because extending criminal liability to those instances 'would seem to excessively broaden the notion'. Hence, when the application of the traditional notion of joint criminal enterprise to senior political and military leaders leads to 'vast criminal enterprises where the fellow participants may be structurally or geographically remote from the accused', the only solution is not to rely on any joint criminal enterprise theory.[203] This position has been expressly embraced in the ICTY Trial Judgment in the *Brdanin* case.[204]

---

[200] *Simic Case* Appeals Judgment (Above n 185), at para 74.
[201] Danner and Martinez (Above n 52), at 150–51.
[202] See Ch 4, s III.A.iii.
[203] Cassese (Above n 150), at 110, 126, 133.
[204] A O'Rourke, 'Joint Criminal Enterprise and Brdanin: Misguided Overcorrection' (2006) 47 *Harvard International Law Journal* 323, shows a total disagreement with this solution because in her view, the approach of the *Brdanin Case* Trial Judgment 'curtails JCE's ability to describe individual criminal responsibility'.

In this regard, in the *Brdanin* case, the Trial Chamber found the existence of a persecutorial campaign from October 1991 until the signature of the Dayton Agreement in 1995. The goal of this campaign was to forcibly remove the Bosnian Muslim and Bosnian Croat population from the territory of the autonomous region of Krajina ('the ARK').[205] The persecutorial campaign included killings, torture, physical violence, rapes, sexual assaults, constant humiliation and degradation, destruction of property and religious and cultural buildings, deportation, forcible transfer and denial of fundamental rights.[206]

The Prosecution charged the defendant Radoslav Brdanin (who was the president of the ARK Crisis Staff and the ARK War Presidency, and later became the Minister of Construction, Traffic and Utilities in the government of the Serbian Republic of Bosnia and Herzegovina) as a co-perpetrator in a basic form and, alternatively, in an extended form of joint criminal enterprise. The Prosecution also alleged that 'a great number' of persons participated in this enterprise, including 'other members of the ARK Crisis Staff, the leadership of the Serbian Republic and the SDS, including Radovan Karadzic, Momcilo Krajisnik and Biljana Plavsic, members of the Assembly of the Autonomous Region of Krajina and the Assembly's Executive Committee, the Serb Crisis staffs of the ARK municipalities, the army of the Republika Srpska, Serb paramilitary forces and others'.[207]

The Trial Chamber found that during the second half of 1991, the Bosnian Serb leadership created the Strategic Plan, which they knew could only be implemented by resorting to force and fear.[208] The Strategic Plan aimed at gaining control over the Serb-populated areas in BiH, linking them together and creating a separate Bosnian Serb State, from which most non-Serbs would be permanently removed.[209] Radoslav Brdanin, and many of the persons included in the joint criminal enterprise alleged by the Prosecution, adhered to this plan and furthered its implementation in the following months and until 1995.[210]

Nevertheless, the Trial Chamber found that none of the crimes had been physically committed by the defendant or by the members of the ARK Crisis Staff, the leadership of the Serbian Republic of BiH and the SDS, the members of the ARK Assembly and the Assembly's Executive Committee, or the members of the Serb Crisis Staffs of the ARK municipalities.[211] Indeed, according to the Trial Chamber, the crimes were physically committed by members of army units, Bosnian Serb police and Serb paramilitary groups deployed in the ARK territory, as well as by Bosnian Serb armed civilians and unidentified individuals.[212] In most cases, the

---

[205] *Brdanin Case* Trial Judgment (Above n 68), at para 1050.
[206] *Ibid.*
[207] *Prosecutor v Brdanin* (Sixth Amended Indictment) ICTY-99-36-T (9 Dec 2003) para 27(2).
[208] *Brdanin Case* Trial Judgment (Above n 68), at para 349.
[209] *Ibid.*
[210] *Ibid* at para 350.
[211] *Ibid* at para 345.
[212] *Ibid.*

physical perpetrators were not identified, and only the group to which they belonged was identified.[213]

In applying the traditional notion of joint criminal enterprise, as defined by the *Krnojelac* Appeal Judgment[214] and the *Simic* Trial Judgment,[215] the Trial Chamber highlighted that:

> In order to hold the Accused criminally responsible for the crimes charged in the Indictment pursuant to the first category of JCE, the Prosecution must, *inter alia*, establish that between the person physically committing a crime and the Accused, there was an understanding or an agreement to commit that particular crime. In order to hold him responsible pursuant to the third category of JCE, the Prosecution must prove that the Accused entered into an agreement with a person to commit a particular crime (in the present case the crimes of deportation and/or forcible transfer) and that this same person physically committed another crime, which was a natural and foreseeable consequence of the execution of the crime agreed upon. [. . .] The Trial Chamber in this context emphasises that for the purposes of establishing individual criminal responsibility pursuant to the theory of JCE it is not sufficient to prove an understanding or an agreement to commit a crime between the Accused and a person in charge or in control of a military or paramilitary unit committing a crime.[216]

In analysing whether the requisites of the traditional notion of joint criminal enterprise were met in the case against Radoslav Brdanin, the Trial Chamber found that many of the physical perpetrators also 'espoused' the Strategic Plan and furthered its implementation.[217] However, in spite of this finding, the Trial Chamber considered that:

> The mere espousal of the Strategic Plan by the Accused on the one hand and many of the Relevant Physical Perpetrators on the other hand is not equivalent to an arrangement between them to commit a concrete crime. Indeed, the Accused and the Relevant Physical Perpetrators could espouse the Strategic Plan and form a criminal intent to commit crimes with the aim of implementing the Strategic Plan *independently from each other* and without having an understanding or entering into any agreement between them to commit a crime. Moreover, the fact that the acts and conduct of an accused facilitated or contributed to the commission of a crime by another person and/or assisted in the formation of that person's criminal intent is not sufficient to establish beyond reasonable doubt that there was an understanding or an agreement between the two to commit that particular crime. An agreement between two persons to commit a crime requires a *mutual* understanding or arrangement with each other to commit a crime.[218]

According to the Trial Chamber, the goal of Brdanin's public speeches and the decisions of the ARK Crisis Staff (which could be considered as his own decisions) was to implement the Strategic Plan and facilitate the commission of the crimes.

---

[213] *Ibid.*
[214] *Krnojelac Case* Appeals Judgment (Above n 11), at paras 83–4.
[215] *Simic Case* Trial Judgment (Above n 26), at para 160.
[216] *Brdanin Case* Trial Judgment (Above n 68), at paras 262, 264, 344, 347.
[217] *Ibid* at para 350.
[218] *Ibid* at paras 351–2.

However, the Trial Chamber did not find direct evidence, nor could it make an inference, as to the existence of an understanding or agreement between the defendant and the physical perpetrators.[219] In its view, the physical perpetrators (most of whom had not been identified) could have acted in furtherance of the Strategic Plan but without entering into an agreement with Brdanin to commit the crimes, or could have carried out the crimes in furtherance of orders and instructions from their military or paramilitary superiors (in this scenario the superiors might have been the only ones intending to implement the Strategic Plan).[220] All in all, the Trial Chamber concluded that:

> JCE is not an appropriate mode of liability to describe the individual criminal responsibility of the Accused, given the extraordinarily broad nature of this case, where the Prosecution seeks to include within a JCE a person as structurally remote from the commission of the crimes charged in the Indictment as the Accused. Although JCE is applicable in relation to cases involving ethnic cleansing, as the Tadic Appeal Judgement recognises, it appears that, in providing for a definition of JCE, the Appeals Chamber had in mind a somewhat smaller enterprise than the one that is invoked in the present case. An examination of the cases tried before this Tribunal where JCE has been applied confirms this view.[221]

c Resorting to Subsidiary Joint Criminal Enterprises

Gustafson proposes to deal with the above-mentioned problems by resorting to the notion of 'subsidiary joint criminal enterprises' within a broader joint criminal enterprise.[222] According to her, in a situation such as the one in the *Brdanin* case, it will be possible to have 'two separate and inter-linked' joint criminal enterprises, as opposed to a single (all encompassing) one.[223] As she explains it:

> In this scenario, let us further suppose that the leader of this military or paramilitary unit had separately made an agreement with a high-level individual (eg with a political leader such as Brdanin) to commit the crimes that were then perpetrated by the unit operating as a JCE. If these crimes were committed by the unit pursuant to the agreement made between the unit leader and the political leader, then, since the nature of the unit leader's guilt for those crimes is equivalent to that of the principal perpetrators, what difference does it make whether or not the political leader has made an explicit agreement to commit the crimes with one or more of the physical perpetrators? The political leader has entered into a common plan with one of the co-perpetrators (the unit leader) to commit these crimes. If the other elements of JCE liability have been established as between the accused and the unit leader, then, in my view, the accused should be liable for the crimes on this basis [. . .] Under this model, the senior JCE (JCE I) would not contain a single principal perpetrator of the crimes charged; however, it would need to include at least

---

[219] *Ibid* at paras 353–4.
[220] *Ibid* at para 354.
[221] *Ibid* at para 355. See also T Blumenstock, 'The Judgment of the International Criminal Tribunal for the Former Yugoslavia in the *Brdanin Case*' (2005) 18 *Leiden Journal of International Law* 72–3.
[222] *Kvocka Case* Trial Judgment (Above n 18), at para 307. See also Ch 4, s 2.
[223] Gustafson (Above n 17), at 147.

one co-perpetrator of the subsidiary JCE (JCE 2). Under the principles of JCE liability, this co-perpetrator's criminal responsibility for the crimes is equivalent to that of the principal perpetrators. As such, an agreement to commit the crimes made between an accused and this co-perpetrator of JCE 2 should have the same status as a direct agreement between the accused and the principal perpetrator of JCE 2. Indeed, it is not difficult to envision scenarios in which an agreement between the accused and this non-physical co-perpetrator of JCE 2 could, practically speaking, be a far more efficient and effective method of putting the agreement into action than agreement between the accused and a principal perpetrator of JCE 2.[224]

In other words, according to Gustafson, the two key features of the notion of co-perpetration based on joint criminal enterprise are that each participant in the enterprise: (i) is attributed the contributions made by the other participants because they are carried out in furtherance of a common criminal plan with the shared intent to implement it; and (ii) is held liable as a principal to the crimes (co-perpetrator). Therefore, as long as the contribution of one of the participants in the joint criminal enterprise (the head of the paramilitary unit in the example given by Gustafson) is of such nature as to, by itself, make that person a principal to the core crimes of the enterprise, the rest of the participants in the enterprise (the senior political and military leaders with whom the head of the paramilitary unit agrees to commit the crimes) can be also held liable as principals because they all are attributed such contribution. As a result, as long as one person who is a principal to the crimes is a participant in the enterprise, there is no need for the physical perpetrators to be part of the enterprise.

The question then arises as to what type of contribution to the commission of the crimes is required for at least one member of the enterprise, who is not a physical perpetrator, to qualify as a principal to the crimes. As seen in previous chapters, this depends on the approach taken to the distinction between principal (perpetration) and accessorial (participation) liability.[225] According to the formal-objective approach, if an individual has not carried out an objective element of the crime, he cannot be a principal to the crime.[226] According to the approach based on the notion of control of the crime, only those persons who dominate the commission of the crime because they are in a position to decide whether the crime will be carried out and how it will be performed can be considered principals to the crimes.[227] Therefore, if an individual has not physically carried out the objective elements of the crime (control of the action), he must be an indirect perpetrator who commits the crime by using the physical perpetrator as a 'tool' who is controlled by his dominant will.[228] Finally, according to the subjective approach

---

[224] *Ibid.*

[225] See Ch 2, s V.

[226] *Ibid.*

[227] See Ch 2, s V and s VI.

[228] *Ibid.* The notion of co-perpetration based on joint control of the crime, which results from the essential tasks assigned to a person in the implementation of a common criminal plan, is not applicable in this context insofar as joint criminal enterprise and joint control are two competing theories of co-perpetration that cannot be jointly applied.

based on the traditional notion of joint criminal enterprise, all those persons who participate with the physical perpetrators in a joint criminal enterprise to commit a crime can be held liable as principals because the contributions of the physical perpetrators will be attributed to all of them.[229]

The solution put forward by Gustafson is based on this last approach to the distinction between principals and accessories. Hence, when a person (the head of a paramilitary group) has not physically carried out any of the objective elements of the crimes, he still becomes a principal to the said crimes by participating together with the physical perpetrators (the members of his paramilitary group) in a joint criminal enterprise to commit them. Furthermore, he can also simultaneously participate, together with the senior political and military leaders of his area of operations, in a second joint criminal enterprise, which aims at planning and securing the commission of such crimes. As a result of the participation of the head of the paramilitary group (who is a principal to the crimes) in this second enterprise (which is separate from, and interlinked with, the first one), the senior political and military leaders participating in it also become principals to the crimes, and this, in spite of the fact that the physical perpetrators are not part of this second enterprise (the head of the paramilitary group to which the physical perpetrators belong is the link between both enterprises).

According to Gustafson, the notion of 'subsidiary joint criminal enterprises' could be applied to the *Brdanin* case in the following manner:

> In my view, these factual findings by the Trial Chamber might have been sufficient to ground JCE liability for the accused if the Trial Chamber had not insisted on the existence of an explicit agreement between the accused and the principal perpetrators. Since the ARK Crisis Staff contained military and paramilitary leaders, if the evidence had been sufficient for the Trial Chamber to find that the military and paramilitary groups headed by these leaders perpetrated crimes in furtherance of the Strategic Plan in a manner that satisfied the requirements of JCE liability, this would have led to the conclusion that the leaders of these groups were co-perpetrators of the crimes, even absent evidence that they played a physical role in their commission. As such, these leaders could have served as the link that connected the accused to the perpetration of the crimes through the medium of a second senior JCE whose members would have included the accused along with these military and political leaders.[230]

The author considers Gustafson's approach to be the best fit with the choice made by the case law of the *Ad hoc* Tribunals to rely on a subjective approach to the distinction between principals ((co) perpetrators) and accessories (participants or secondary parties) to the crimes. As result, no matter the level of contribution to the implementation of the common criminal plan, principals to the crimes will be those who participate in a joint criminal enterprise together with: (i) the physical perpetrators; or (ii) a non-physical perpetrator who is considered a principal to the crimes because he participates in a subsidiary joint criminal enterprise with the physical perpetrators.

---

[229] See Ch 2, s V and s VI.
[230] Gustafson (Above n 17), at 147.

Nevertheless, in the view of the author, this approach is also problematic because, when it comes to prosecuting senior political and military leaders, it is likely to lead to a chain of inter-linked joint criminal enterprises. For instance, if one relies on this approach to prosecute Slobodan Milosevic for the campaign of persecution against the non-Serb population of the ARK which was physically carried out by Bosnian Serb military personnel and paramilitary units, one will need, at the very least, four levels of interlinked joint criminal enterprises: (i) the first between the physical perpetrators and the heads of their units; (ii) the second, between the members of the ARK Crisis Staff, including its president Radoslav Brdanin and the heads of the units to which the physical perpetrators belong; (iii) the third between Radoslav Brdanin and the political and military leadership of the Srpska Republic; and (iv) the fourth between a core group of the Bosnian Serb political and military leadership in Pale (Radovan Karadzic, Momcilo Krajisnik, Biljana Plavsic) and key members of the government of Serbia and of the Federation of Serbia and Montenegro, including its former president Slobodan Milosevic.

Logically, the requirements of each of these four interlinked joint criminal enterprises will have to be proven at trial by the Prosecution. Furthermore, if Slobodan Milosevic is to be charged with crimes committed in other parts of Bosnia and Herzegovina, such as in Srebrenica, Sarajevo, Prijedor, Foca or Visegrad, the participants in the lowest two levels of interlinked joint criminal enterprises will change—the physical perpetrators, the superiors of their units, and the local politicians involved in the commission of the crimes in these other areas of BiH will not be the same than those involved in the commission of the crimes in the ARK.

The author considers that, although Gustafson's approach is the best fit with the choice made by the case law of the *Ad hoc* Tribunals to rely on a subjective approach to the distinction between principals and accessories to the crime, the need for an indefinite number of interlinked joint criminal enterprises makes it unsuitable to prosecute senior political and military leaders. The essence of the problem lies in the fact that the notion of co-perpetration based on joint criminal enterprise, as any other theory of co-perpetration, is an appropriate tool to reflect horizontal relationships.[231] However, the idea of a group of people working together in furtherance of a common criminal plan is much less effective to reflect vertical or hierarchical relationships.[232] As a result, it does not adequately encapsulate situations in which (i) senior political and military leaders plan the crimes and set into motion the organisations that they direct to secure their commission; (ii) hundreds of mid level members of such organisations further prepare the commission of the crimes; and (iii) thousands of low level members physically commit the crimes throughout a territory as broad as the Srpska Republic during a period of four years.

---

[231] See Ch 3, s III.C.iv and Ch 5, s IV.A.
[232] *Ibid.*

It is from this perspective that the author shares the remarks of Cassese in the sense that when the application of the traditional notion of joint criminal enterprise to senior political and military leaders leads to 'vast criminal enterprises where the fellow participants may be structurally or geographically remote from the accused', the only solution is not to rely on any joint criminal enterprise theory.[233] However, in the author's view, one should go a step further and analyse what the value of the notion of co-perpetration based on joint criminal enterprise is to prosecute international crimes, if it cannot be applied to senior political and military leaders. In other words, has the case law of the *Ad hoc* Tribunals made the right choice when it opted for the subjective approach inherent to the notion of joint criminal enterprise in order to distinguish between principals ((co) perpetrators) and accessories (participants or secondary parties) to the crime?

d Requiring a High Degree of Solidarity among the Participants in the Enterprise and a High Degree of Control over the Physical Perpetrators

Van Sliedregt proposes to tackle the problems posed by the application of the traditional notion of joint criminal enterprise to senior political and military leaders from a different angle. She considers that the solution lies in requiring (i) a high degree of solidarity among those participating in the joint criminal enterprise, (ii) a high degree of control over those whose conduct generates collective responsibility, (iii) the voluntary acceptance of a certain role within the collective, and (iv) the power to distance oneself from the group by abandoning such a role.[234]

However, the author does not see how these adjustments are compatible with Van Sliedregt's claims (i) that it is the common criminal plan or purpose between the physical perpetrators and those other participants in the joint criminal enterprise who do not physically commit the crimes 'that provides the basis for attributing individual criminal responsibility',[235] and (ii) that by interpreting the notion of joint criminal enterprise in an expansive manner in order to include those who plan crimes at the senior level, such a notion is turning into 'a surrogate conspiracy concept'.[236]

Moreover, it is unclear how, as she argues, the ICTY Trial Judgment in the *Krajisnik* case supports her position. Indeed, as seen below in further detail,[237] this trial judgment departs from the traditional notion of joint criminal enterprise to embrace the notion of joint criminal enterprise at the leadership level, which leaves the physical perpetrators out of the enterprise, and only includes those political and military leaders who design the common criminal plan and direct its

---

[233] Cassese (Above n 150), at 110, 126, 133. It is also from this perspective that Ambos proposes to resort to the notions of indirect perpetration and command responsibility in the said situations. See Ambos, *Joint Criminal Enterprise* (Above n 137), at 179–83,

[234] E Van Sliedregt, *The Criminal Responsibility of Individuals for Violations of International Humanitarian Law* (The Hague, TMC Asser Press, 2003) 351 [hereinafter Van Sliedregt].

[235] *Ibid* at 200.

[236] *Ibid.*

[237] See Ch 4, s V.D.v.

implementation.[238] It is only in this context that the *Krajisnik* Trial Judgment requires that the participants in the enterprise 'must be shown to act together'.[239]

e Simultaneous Application of Co-perpetration based on Joint Criminal Enterprise and Co-perpetration based on Joint Control

Van Der Wilt's approach takes some of the elements of the approach proposed by Van Sliedregt, particularly those relating to the high degree of solidarity among those who act together pursuant to a common criminal plan and the high degree of control over the physical perpetrators.[240] Nevertheless, he reaches the conclusion that the traditional notion of joint criminal enterprise has serious limitations when it is applied to senior political and military leaders because:

> The strong element in the common purpose doctrine is that it assumes that members, by entering into a prior agreement, have proved to be psychologically capable and prepared to commit (those) crime. It suggests that they have incapacitated themselves from recoil and, therefore, have to blame themselves for their predicament. This is precisely the reason why a prior and explicit agreement is such a crucial element because it is the only link that binds the group members together [. . .] In larger groups with hierarchical distinctions and subdivisions such mutual understanding and explicit agreements are usually absent: in these cases the doctrine of JCE is of no avail.[241]

As a result, Van Der Wilt proposes to maintain the traditional notion of joint criminal enterprise for those cases in which it can be operative,[242] and to rely on the notion of 'functional perpetration' for the prosecution of senior political and military leaders.[243] According to him, this last notion is more suitable for these types of cases because:

> The concept of functional perpetration enables courts to disentangle complex structural relationships and to identify precisely each contribution to the repressive system. It recognizes that functionaries and their contributions are interrelated and may thus be helpful in obtaining the whole picture of system of criminality, which is arguably one of the major goals of international criminal law enforcement.[244]

In the author's view, Van Der Wilt's approach is to rely on the notion of control of the crime in those cases in which the traditional notion of joint criminal enterprise is of no avail, and, in particular, in the prosecution of senior political and military leaders. The author agrees with Van Der Wilt that the criminal liability of senior political and military leaders as principals to international crimes is best reflected by the different manifestations of the notion of control of the crime—that is to say, indirect perpetration (particular in its variant of OSP),

---

[238] *Krajisnik Case* Trial Judgment (Above n 11), at para 883.
[239] *Ibid* at para 884.
[240] Van der Wilt (Above n 77), at 103.
[241] *Ibid* at 107.
[242] *Ibid* at 107–108.
[243] *Ibid* at 104–106.
[244] *Ibid* at 106.

co-perpetration based on joint control, and indirect co-perpetration based on the joint application of OSP and joint control).[245]

Moreover, as seen in chapter 5 in further detail,[246] the author also notices that the approach suggested by Van Der Wilt has been expressly followed by the ICTY Trial Judgment in the *Stakic* case[247] (although such an approach was subsequently reversed in appeal)[248] and implicitly endorsed by the ICTY Appeal Judgment in the *Vasiljevic* case.[249]

However, in the author's view, the distinction between principals (perpetration) and accessories (participation) to crimes against humanity, war crimes and genocide cannot be based on different criteria depending on the factual scenario. This is precisely the result of Van Der Wilt's approach: relying on a subjective approach to such distinction whenever the traditional notion of joint criminal enterprise is applicable, whereas in other scenarios (and, in particular, when prosecuting senior political and military leaders) an approach based on the notion of control of the crime is resorted to.

V The Notion of Joint Criminal Enterprise at the Leadership Level

Regardless of the various approaches proposed by different writers, the case law of the *Ad hoc* Tribunals has addressed the problems posed by the application of the traditional notion of joint criminal enterprise to senior political and military leaders in a rather 'creative' manner. It has jointly applied the notions of co-perpetration based on joint criminal enterprise and indirect perpetration (one of the manifestations of the notion of control of the crime). As a result, it has departed from the traditional notion of joint criminal enterprise and has embraced the notion of 'joint criminal enterprise at the leadership level', which, in the author's view, constitutes a *sui generis* variant of 'indirect co-perpetration'.

A The *Rwamakuba* and *Karemera Cases* before the ICTR Appeals Chamber: Rejecting the Claim that the Notion of Joint Criminal Enterprise is Limited to Small Cases

In the *Rwamakuba* case, the Defence claimed that the application of the notion of joint criminal enterprise or the common purpose doctrine is limited to small cases. It argued that joint criminal enterprise, as applied in post WW II cases:

---

[245] See Ch 4, s V.E and Ch 5, s VI.D.
[246] See Ch 5, s V.B and s VI.C.
[247] *Stakic Case* Trial Judgment (Above n 123), at para 439. See also Ch 5, s VI.C.
[248] *Stakic Case* Appeals Judgment (Above n 11), at para 62.
[249] *Vasiljevic Case* Appeals Judgment (Above n 11), at paras 126–31. See also Ch 5, s V.B.

[W]as confined to crimes with great specificity in relation to the identity and the relationship as between co-perpetrators and victims to the extent that the cases dealt with specific incidents or situations.[250]

The ICTR Appeals Chamber rejected the Defence's claim because:

[T}he Justice Case shows that liability for participation in a criminal plan is as wide as the plan itself, even if the plan amounts to a nation wide government organized system of cruelty and injustice.[251]

Moreover, the ICTR Appeals Chamber also found that the language in the IMT Charter and in the indictment submitted to the IMT:

[H]ave much in common with the language used in the *Tadic* Appeals Judgement to describe the elements of a joint criminal enterprise.[252]

In the *Karemera* case, the Defence claimed that the ICTR lacked jurisdiction to hold a defendant liable under the extended form of joint criminal enterprise for crimes committed by fellow participants—particularly those structurally or geographically remote from the defendant—in enterprises of 'vast scope'.[253] The Defence argued that the application of the extended form of joint criminal enterprise to enterprises of 'vast scope' lacks support in customary international law and to permit it would be bad policy because it would turn the notion of joint criminal enterprise or the common purpose doctrine in a 'form of strict liability'[254] and produce 'unfair convictions'.[255]

The ICTR Appeals Chamber rejected the Defence's claim because (i) the extended form of joint criminal enterprise is firmly accepted in customary international law as shown by the *Tadic* Appeal Judgment;[256] (ii) the Defence had conceded that, as already stated by the ICTR Appeals Chamber in the *Rwamakuba* case, some post WW II cases involved vast criminal enterprises;[257] and (iii) the Defence's fear about establishing strict liability are unfounded insofar as the defendant can only be held liable for crimes foreseen by him.[258]

B The *Brdanin* Case: The Notion of Joint Criminal Enterprise at the Leadership Level Explicitly Embraced by the ICTY Appeals Chamber

The 3 April 2007 ICTY Appeal Judgment in the *Brdanin* case, following the ruling of the ICTR Appeals Chamber in the *Rwamakuba* case, held that the application

---

[250] *Rwamakuba Case* Decision on the Application of Joint Criminal Enterprise to the Crime of Genocide (Above n 139), at para 25.

[251] *Ibid.*

[252] *Ibid* at para 24.

[253] *Karemera Case* Decision on Joint Criminal Enterprise (Above n 124), at para 11.

[254] *Ibid* at para 14.

[255] *Ibid* at para 15.

[256] *Ibid* at para 13.

[257] *Ibid* at para 14.

[258] *Ibid.*

of the notion of joint criminal enterprise is not limited to small cases.[259] According to the ICTY Appeals Chamber, as long as a contribution to implement the common criminal plan is required, there is no risk that individuals structurally remote from the crimes be held guilty by 'mere association'.[260] Furthermore, the fact that there might be some problems in identifying the criminal object of the enterprise 'does not as such preclude the application of the JCE theory'.[261]

Although the ICTY Appeals Chamber shared the concern of the Trial Chamber, that it is not appropriate to hold a defendant liable where the link between him and the physical perpetrators is 'too tenuous',[262] it also found that the Trial Chamber erred in holding (i) that the physical perpetrators of the crimes must necessarily be part, together with the defendant, of the joint criminal enterprise, regardless of its scope; and (ii) that, in addition to the common criminal plan or purpose of the enterprise, an additional understanding or agreement must exist between the defendant and the physical perpetrators.[263] According to the ICTY Appeals Chamber, what matters in a basic form of joint criminal enterprise is not whether the person who physically carried out the objective elements of a particular crime is a participant in the enterprise, but rather whether the crime in question forms part of the common criminal plan or purpose.[264] Hence:

> In cases where the principal perpetrator of a particular crime is not a member of the JCE, this essential requirement may be inferred from various circumstances, including the fact that the accused or any other member of the JCE closely cooperated with the principal perpetrator in order to further the common criminal purpose. In this respect, when a member of the JCE uses a person outside the JCE to carry out the *actus reus* of a crime, the fact that the person in question knows of the existence of the JCE—without it being established that he or she shares the *mens rea* necessary to become a member of the JCE—may be a factor to be taken into account when determining whether the crime forms part of the common criminal purpose. However, this is not a *sine qua non* for imputing liability for the crime to that member of the JCE. When the accused, or any other member of the JCE, in order to further the common criminal purpose, uses persons who, in addition to (or instead of) carrying out the *actus reus* of the crimes forming part of the common purpose, commit crimes going beyond that purpose, the accused may be found responsible for such crimes provided that he participated in the common criminal purpose with the requisite intent and that, in the circumstances of the case, (i) it was foreseeable that such a crime might be perpetrated by one or more of the persons used by him (or by any other member of the JCE) in order to carry out the *actus reus* of the crimes forming part of the common purpose; and (ii) the accused willingly took that risk—that is the accused, with the awareness that such a crime was a possible consequence of the implementation of that enterprise, decided to participate in that enterprise.[265]

---

[259] *Brdanin Case* Appeals Judgment (Above n 11), at para 423.
[260] *Ibid* at para 424.
[261] *Ibid*.
[262] *Ibid* at para 418.
[263] *Ibid* at para 410.
[264] *Ibid*.
[265] *Ibid* at paras 410–11.

The ICTY Appeals Chamber reached this conclusion after examining a number of elements. First, it took notice of the Defence's caution against the temptation of creating a 'new concept of JCE' in order to prosecute senior political and military leaders.[266] Likewise, it took also notice of the following Prosecution's claims: (i) the fulfilment of the object and purpose of international criminal law requires the prosecution and punishment of those who commit international crimes as leaders, not only their subordinates, because 'high-level individuals directing the execution of crimes have a higher degree of responsibility than the physical perpetrators',[267] (ii) holding senior political and military leaders as principals (co-perpetrators) to international crimes is important because, 'even though other modes of liability may apply (ordering, planning, instigating and aiding and abetting), they do not necessarily always capture the true situation and the true culpability of the high-level offenders';[268] and (iii) the notion of joint criminal enterprise is an appropriate tool to achieve this goal because a joint criminal enterprise could exist 'entirely at a leadership level', so that the senior political and military leaders who participate in the enterprise use the physical perpetrators to secure the commission of the crimes.[269]

Second, the ICTY Appeals Chamber highlighted that, not only is the language of the ICTY Appeal Judgment in the *Tadic* case not clear as to whether the physical perpetrators must be also part of the joint criminal enterprise, but also, the factual scenario in that case involved a small group of individuals operating within one municipality and the physical perpetrators were 'clearly' participants in the joint criminal enterprise.[270] Furthermore, in most subsequent cases, not only is the same language than in Tadic used, but the enterprises were also small and the fact that some physical perpetrators may not have been part of it 'does not appear to have been much of an issue'.[271] Finally, the ICTY Appeals Chamber found that its conclusion was particularly supported by certain post WW II cases, and especially by the *Justice* and *RuSHA* cases.[272]

The ICTY Appeals Chamber also acknowledged that in order to hold a defendant criminally liable for the conduct of another person:

> [T]here must be a link between the accused and the crime as legal basis for the imputation of criminal liability.[273]

Concerning the nature of this link, it held:

> According to the Prosecution, this link is to be found in the fact that the members of the joint criminal enterprise use the principal perpetrators as 'tools' to carry out the crime.

---

[266] *Ibid* at para 371.
[267] *Ibid* at para 378. See also the Prosecution Appeal Brief in the *Brdanin Case*, paras 4.18, 4.25.
[268] *Brdanin Case* Appeals Judgment (*Ibid*), at para 367.
[269] *Ibid*.
[270] *Ibid* at para 406.
[271] *Ibid* at para 407. For this reason, according to the ICTY Appeals Chamber, the *Krnojelac Case* Appeals Judgment and the *Vasiljevic Case* Appeals Judgment did not conclusively resolve the question of whether the physical perpetrators must be part of the same joint criminal enterprise as the defendant.
[272] *Brdanin Case* Appeals Judgment (*Ibid*), at para 404.
[273] *Ibid* at para 413.

Considering the discussion of post-World War II cases and of the Tribunal's jurisprudence above, the Appeals Chamber finds that, to hold a member of a JCE responsible for crimes committed by non-members of the enterprise, it has to be shown that the crime can be imputed to one member of the joint criminal enterprise, and that this member—when using a principal perpetrator—acted in accordance with the common plan. The existence of this link is a matter to be assessed on a case-by-case basis.[274] [. . .]

In cases where the principal perpetrator shares that common criminal purpose of the JCE or, in other words, is a member of the JCE, and commits a crime in furtherance of the JCE, it is superfluous to require an additional agreement between that person and the accused to commit that particular crime. In cases where the person who carried out the *actus reus* of the crime is not a member of the JCE, the key issue remains that of ascertaining whether the crime in question forms part of the common criminal purpose. This is a matter of evidence.[275]

Despite these findings, the ICTY Appeals Chamber did not convict Radoslav Brdanin for any of the crimes charged in the indictment pursuant to the notion of joint criminal enterprise at the leadership level because (i) the parties agreed that they would proceed to argue their respective cases at trial in the understanding that the physical perpetrators had to be part of the joint criminal enterprise, and thus the Prosecution did not request the Appeals Chamber to convict the defendant as a participant in a joint criminal enterprise in which the physical perpetrators were not included;[276] and (ii) on the basis of the Trial Chamber's factual findings and the Prosecution Appeal Brief, the Appeals Chamber considered that:

[I]t appears that the fact that the RPPs [Relevant Physical Perpetrators] were used as mere "tools" by their superiors was, actually, the most likely explanation for what happened in the territory of the ARK during the indictment period.[277]

In conclusion, the *Brdanin* Appeal Judgment addressed the problems posed by the application of the traditional notion of joint criminal enterprise by limiting the participants in the enterprise to those senior political and military leaders who design the common criminal plan and direct their subordinates to implement it. This approach reduces the number of participants in enterprises, which aim at committing international crimes in a broad territory over an extended period of time. Furthermore, all participants in the enterprise are members of the political and military leadership and the relationship among them is more of a horizontal than of a hierarchical or vertical nature. Due to all these features, this type of joint criminal enterprise is referred to in this book as 'joint criminal enterprise at the leadership level'.

After the *Brdanin* Appeal Judgment, the notion of joint criminal enterprise at the leadership level has been embraced by the ICTY Trial Judgment in the *Martic* case. In the *Martic* case, the Trial Chamber formulated this notion as follows:

---

[274] *Brdanin Case* Appeals Judgment (*Ibid*), at paras 413–14.
[275] *Ibid* at para 418.
[276] *Ibid* at para 436.
[277] *Ibid* at para 448.

It is not required that the principal perpetrators of the crimes which are part of the common purpose be members of a JCE. An accused or another member of a JCE may use the principal perpetrators to carry out the *actus reus* of a crime. However, 'an essential requirement in order to impute to any accused member of the JCE liability for a crime committed by another person is that the crime in question *forms part of the common criminal purpose*'. This may be inferred, *inter alia*, from the fact that 'the accused or any other member of the JCE closely cooperated with the principal perpetrator in order to further the common criminal purpose'.[278]

C Do Post WW II Cases Really Support the Notion of Joint Criminal Enterprise at the Leadership Level?

The ICTR Appeal Decision on the Application of Joint Criminal Enterprise to Genocide in the *Rwamakuba* case and the ICTY Appeal Judgment in the *Brdanin* case have found that some post WW II cases, such as the *Justice* and the *RuSHA* cases under Control Council Law No 10, and even the *Nuremberg* Trial, support the notion of 'joint criminal enterprise at the leadership level'. In these cases, the defendants were found criminally liable 'on a basis equivalent to that of joint criminal enterprise' and the courts did not even discuss the physical perpetrators' state of mind or whether they adhered to, or knew of, the broader common criminal plan.[279] However, the author is concerned with the manner in which post WW II cases have been analysed in these decisions.

i The Justice *Case under Control Council Law No 10*

In order to explain the author's concerns with the manner in which post WW II cases have been analysed in the above-mentioned decisions, this section will follow the reasoning of the ICTR Appeals Chamber in the *Rwamakuba* case in relation to the *Justice* case tried by a US Military Tribunal under Control Council Law No 10 step by step—the ICTY Appeals Chamber in the *Brdanin* case subsequently relied on this reasoning.

In the *Justice* case, the main defendants were Ernst Lautz (Chief Public Prosecutor of the People's Court) and Oswald Rothaug (former Chief Justice of the Special Court in Nuremberg). The Prosecution alleged that they were criminally responsible for the following crimes:

---

[278] *Prosecutor v Martic* (Judgment) ICTY-95-11-T (12 Jun 2007) para 438. This finding has been quoted with approval by the *Martic* Case Appeals Judgment (Above n 94), at para 68.

[279] *Rwamakuba Case* Decision on the Application of Joint Criminal Enterprise to the Crime of Genocide (Above n 139), at paras 15–25; *Brdanin Case* Appeals Judgment (Above n 11), at paras 395–404.

German criminal laws, through a series of expansions and perversions by the Ministry of Justice, finally embraced passive defeatism, petty misdemeanors and trivial private utterances as treasonable for the purpose of exterminating Jews or other nationals of the occupied countries. Indictments, trials and convictions were transparent devices for a system of murderous extermination, and death became the routine penalty . . . Non-German nationals were convicted of and executed for 'high treason' allegedly committed against the Reich. The above-described proceedings resulted in the murder, torture, unlawful imprisonment, and ill treatment of thousands of persons [. . .] German criminal laws through a series of additions, expansions, and perversions by the defendants became a powerful weapon for the subjugation of the German people and for the extermination of certain nationals of the occupied countries. This program resulted in the murder, torture, illegal imprisonment, and ill treatment of thousands of Germans and nationals of occupied countries[280]

The US Military Tribunal found the existence of a pattern or plan of racial persecution to enforce the criminal laws against Poles and Jews.[281] They also found that Lautz (who had authorised numerous indictments charging a number of Poles, who were subsequently convicted and executed, with high treason for leaving their places of work and attempting to escape Germany by crossing the border into Switzerland) and Rothaug (who applied the cruel and discriminatory law against Poles and Jews) were criminally liable for war crimes and crimes against humanity despite the fact that they did not physically carry out the objective elements of any of these crimes.[282] Indeed, the physical perpetrators were the executioners who carried out the death sentences in execution of the orders of the court. The judgment did not discuss the state of mind of the physical perpetrators. It did not even discuss whether the physical perpetrators were aware that the death sentences formed part of a pattern or plan of racial persecution, which aimed at perverting the law for the purpose of exterminating Jews and other 'undesirables'.[283]

The ICTR Appeals Chamber started its analysis of the *Justice* case by highlighting that:

> Article II(2) of Control Council Law No. 10, which set out the various modes of criminal responsibility recognized in proceedings under that Law, provided that a person 'is deemed to have committed a crime' if he was: (*a*) a principal or (*b*) was an accessory to the commission of any such crime or ordered or abetted the same or (*c*) took a consenting part therein or (*d*) was connected with plans or enterprises involving its commission.

According to the ICTR Appeals Chamber, the structure of this section makes clear that the criminal responsibility of an accused who is 'connected with plans or

---

[280] *US v Altstoetter* (1947) in Trial of the Major War Criminals? before the International Military Tribunal under Control Council Law No 10, Vol III (US Government Printing Office, 1951) 954 [hereinafter *Justice Case* Trial Judgment]. *Justice Case* (Indictment) at paras 11, 23.

[281] *Justice Case* Trial Judgment (*Ibid*), at 1081.

[282] *Ibid* at 1155–6. See also *Prosecutor v Milutinovic* (Decision On Ojdanic's Motion Challenging Jurisdiction: Indirect Co-Perpetration, Separate Opinion of Judge Bonomy) ICTY-05-87-PT (22 Mar 2006) paras 18–22 [hereinafter *Milutinovic Case*, Decision on Indirect Co-Perpetration, Separate Opinion of Judge Bonomy].

[283] *Ibid.*

enterprises involving' commission of a crime differs conceptually from that of an accessory, one who ordered or abetted the commission of a crime, or one who took a consenting part in it, even though all are punished as having 'committed a crime'.[284]

Nevertheless, if one follows the logic of the ICTR Appeals Chamber, the structure of article II(2) of Control Council Law No 10 makes it clear that criminal responsibility for being 'connected with plans or enterprises involving its commission' under sub-paragraph (d) not only differs conceptually from that of an accessory under sub-paragraph (b), but, by the same token, it differs conceptually from the criminal responsibility of a principal to the crime pursuant to subparagraph (a). Furthermore, one should not forget that the notion of joint criminal enterprise has been elaborated by the case law of the *Ad hoc* Tribunals as a theory of principal liability.[285]

The ICTR Appeals Chamber in the *Rwamakuba* case continued its analysis by explaining that:

> The Tribunal noted that the defendants were accused of 'participating in carrying out a governmental plan and program for the persecution and extermination of Jews and Poles' and stated:
>
>> The overt acts of the several defendants must be seen and understood as deliberate contributions toward the effectuation of the policy of the Party and the State. The discriminatory laws themselves formed the subject matter of war crimes and crimes against humanity with which the defendants are charged. The material facts which must be proved in any case are (1) the fact of the great pattern or plan of racial persecution and extermination; and (2) specific conduct of the individual defendant in furtherance of the plan. This is but an application of general concepts of criminal law.[286]

In other words, the US Military Tribunal affirmed that criminal liability for 'being connected with plans or enterprises' would arise if the existence of a common criminal plan ('the fact of the great pattern or plan of racial persecution and extermination') and a specific contribution of the defendant in furtherance of it are proven. The author notes that the US Military Tribunal, in applying the statutory framework set in article II(2) of Control Council Law No 10, did not request proof of a common criminal plan and a shared intent between the defendant and the other participants in the enterprise. As a result, for the US Military Tribunal, the interaction between the defendant and the other participants in the enterprise was irrelevant.

However, as the ICTY Appeals Chamber has made clear in the *Vasiljevic* case, in the absence of either of these two requirements, the defendant cannot be found guilty as a participant in a joint criminal enterprise (principal to the crimes or co-perpetrator)—although he could still be held liable as an accessory to the crimes

---

[284] *Rwamakuba Case* Decision on the Application of Joint Criminal Enterprise to the Crime of Genocide (Above n 139), at para 18.

[285] See Ch 2, s VII.B.

[286] *Rwamakuba Case* Decision on the Application of Joint Criminal Enterprise to the Crime of Genocide (Above n 139), at para 19.

for aiding and abetting.[287] This is because the interaction between the defendant and the other participants in the enterprise is the cornerstone of the notion of co-perpetration based on joint criminal enterprise (as elaborated by the case law of the *Ad hoc* Tribunals) insofar as it justifies that the contributions made by the other participants in the enterprise be attributed to the defendant.

The ICTR Appeals Chamber in the *Rwamakuba* case referred subsequently to the US Military Tribunal's finding of the existence of a common plan or enterprise.[288] As the ICTR Appeals Chamber explained:

> After setting out the evidence of a plan to commit war crimes and crimes against humanity, the *Justice* tribunal summarized its task as follows:
>
> > The pattern and plan of racial persecution has been made clear. General knowledge of the broad outlines thereof in all its immensity has been brought home to the defendants. The remaining question is whether or not the evidence proves beyond a reasonable doubt in the case of the individual defendants that they each consciously participated in the plan or took a consenting part therein.
>
> The tribunal later stated that 'the essential elements to prove a defendant guilty under the indictment in this case are that a defendant had knowledge of an offense charged in the indictment and established by the evidence, and that he was connected with the commission of that offense'.[289]

Hence, the US Military Tribunal made clear that criminal liability for 'being connected with plans or enterprises' arises even though the defendant does not have the intent to commit the core crimes of the enterprise. He only needs to have 'knowledge' of the offence and be aware that 'he was connected with the commission of the offense'. A situation that, according to the case law of the *Ad hoc* Tribunals, would only give rise to accessorial liability (aiding and abetting) if the assistance has a substantial effect in the commission of some of the core crimes of the enterprise.[290]

As a result, one can conclude that the US Military Tribunal did not rely on any form of criminal liability that could be qualified as 'similar' or 'equivalent' to the notion of co-perpetration based on joint criminal enterprise as elaborated by the case law of the *Ad hoc* Tribunals. Indeed, the form of criminal liability resorted to by the US Military Tribunal in the *Justice* case does not even meet the requirements

---

[287] *Vasiljevic Case* Appeals Judgment (Above n 11), at paras 126–31.

[288] *Rwamakuba Case* Decision on the Application of Joint Criminal Enterprise to the Crime of Genocide (Above n 139), at para 20.

[289] *Ibid.*

[290] *Prosecutor v Bagilishema* (Judgment) ICTR-95-01A-T (7 Jun 2001) para 33 [hereinafter *Bagilishema Case* Trial Judgment]; *Prosecutor v Kajelijeli* (Judgment) ICTR-98-44A-T (1 Dec 2003) para 766 [hereinafter *Kajelijeli Case* Trial Judgment]; *Prosecutor v Kamuhanda* (Judgment) ICTR-95-54A-T (22 Jan 2004) para 597 [hereinafter *Kamuhanda Case* Trial Judgment]; *Furundzija Case* Trial Judgment (Above n 29), at para 249; *Prosecutor v Aleksovski* (Judgment) ICTY-95-14/1-T (25 Jun 1999) para 61 [hereinafter *Aleksovski Case* Trial Judgment]; *Prosecutor v Kunarac* (Judgment) ICTY-96-23-T and ICTY-96-23/1-T (22 Feb 2001) para 391 [hereinafter *Kunarac Case* Trial Judgment]; *Krnojelac Case* Trial Judgment (Above n 14), at para 88; *Prosecutor v Oric* (Judgment) ICTY-03-68-T (30 Jun 2006) para 282 [hereinanfter *Oric Case* Trial Judgment]. See also Ch 4, s VII.A.

for accessorial liability pursuant to the notion of aiding and abetting under articles 7(1) ICTYS and 6(1) ICTRS. According to these two provisions, when the intent of a defendant to commit the core crimes of a joint criminal enterprise is not proven, and he is only found to be aware of such offences, he must, at the very least, make a substantial contribution to the specific crimes in order to become an accessory; a simple 'connection with the offence' does not suffice for criminal liability to arise.

This is confirmed by the next excerpt of the *Justice* case quoted by the ICTR Appeals Chamber in the *Rwamakuba* case:

> In concluding its discussion of Lautz's criminal responsibility, the Justice tribunal stated:
>
>> We have cited a few cases, which are typical of the activities of the prosecution before the People's Court in innumerable cases. The captured documents, which are in evidence, establish that the defendant Lautz was criminally implicated in enforcing the law against Poles and Jews which we deem to be a part of the established governmental plan for the extermination of those races. He was an accessory to, and took a consenting part in, the crime of genocide.

In conclusion, the author considers that the form of criminal liability pursuant to which the defendants in the *Justice* case were convicted can, by no means, be considered as an 'equivalent basis' to the notion of co-perpetration based on joint criminal enterprise as elaborated by the case law of the *Ad hoc* Tribunals. Quite the contrary, both forms of criminal liability have fundamental differences in spite of the fact that, prima facie, the expression 'being connected with plans or enterprises involving the commission of crimes' may, to some extent, resemble the expression 'participation in a joint criminal enterprise'.

Hence, in the author's view, the only value that the *Justice* case has as a precedent is that:

(i) under a form of accessorial (as opposed to principal) liability, which article II(2) of Control Council Law No 10 refers to as 'being connected with plans or enterprises involving the commission of crimes', accessorial liability arises for a defendant who (a) carries out specific conduct in furtherance of a criminal plan designed by others; and (b) is aware of the criminal nature of the plan and of the fact that his conduct facilitates the commission of the offences which are part of the plan; and

(ii) for the purpose of this form of accessorial liability, (a) there is no need for an understanding or agreement between the defendant and the physical perpetrators to commit the crimes included in the common plan; and (b) it is irrelevant whether the defendant shares with the physical perpetrators the intent to commit such crimes.

The author believes that the inaccurate conclusion reached by the ICTR Appeals Chamber in the *Rwamakuba* case and the ICTY Appeals Chamber in the *Brdanin* case that post WW II cases support the notion of 'joint criminal enterprise at the leadership level' is due to a terminological confusion. Indeed, post WW II cases, such as the *Justice* and the *RuSHA* cases under Control Council Law No 10, and even the *Nuremberg* Trial, use language that prima facie resembles, to a certain extent, the language used to define the elements of the notion of co-perpetration based on joint criminal enterprise in the case law of the *Ad hoc* Tribunals. Evidence of this terminological confusion can be found in the following finding of the ICTR Appeals Chamber in the *Rwamakuba* case:

> The language used in the Charter of the International Military Tribunal, the indictment submitted to that tribunal, Control Council Law No. 10, and the indictment and judgement in the *Justice Case* have much in common with the language used in the *Tadic* Appeals Judgement to describe the elements of a joint criminal enterprise. The post-World War II materials do not always fit neatly into the so-called "three categories" of joint criminal enterprise discussed in *Tadic*, in part because the tribunals' judgements did not always dwell on the legal concepts of criminal responsibility, but simply concluded that, based on the evidence, the accused were "connected with," "concerned in," "inculpated in," or "implicated in" war crimes and crimes against humanity. Nonetheless, it is clear that the post-World War II judgements discussed above find criminal responsibility for genocidal acts that are physically committed by other persons with whom the accused are engaged in a common criminal purpose.[291]

ii Trials pursuant to the IMT and IMTFE Charters

As seen above in relation to the *Justice* case, when one carefully analyses the nature of the forms of liability used in these post WW II cases, one realises that they have nothing to do with the notion of co-perpetration based on joint criminal enterprise as elaborated by the case law of the *Ad hoc* Tribunals. A further example of this phenomenon is found if one carefully analyses the nature of the forms of criminal liability embraced by article 6(c) of the IMT Charter and included in the indictment presented by Chief Prosecutor Jackson before the IMT.

In spite of the fact that the ICTR Appeals Chamber in the *Rwamakuba* case found that the language used in the IMT Charter and in the indictment presented before the IMT has much in common with the language used in the *Tadic* Appeals Judgment to describe the elements of a joint criminal enterprise, it is important to highlight that:

(i)   the IMT and IMTFE Charters did not distinguish between principal and accessorial liability;[292]

(ii) the main provisions of the IMT and IMTFE Charters on the punishable forms of intervention in the commission of crimes (articles 6(c) IMT Charter and 5(c) IMTFE Charter) refer to 'participating in the formulation or execution of a common plan or conspiracy', thereby equating the concept of 'common plan' with the notion of 'conspiracy';

---

[291] *Rwamakuba Case* Decision on the Application of Joint Criminal Enterprise to the Crime of Genocide (Above n 139), at para 24.

[292] See also Ambos, *La Parte General del Derecho Penal Internacional* (Above n 1), at 75. See also Ch 2, s III.

(iii) for criminal liability to arise pursuant to the IMT and IMTFE Charters, there is no need to carry out any act in furtherance of a common criminal plan or purpose because participation in the formulation of a common plan or conspiracy suffices;

(iv) articles 6(c) IMT Charter and 5(c) IMTFE Charter distinguish, according to the nature of their contributions, up to four different types of individuals participating in a common plan or conspiracy: the leaders, the organisers, the instigators and the accomplices.[293]

As a result, the statutory framework of the IMT and IMTFE Charters has very little to do with the notion of co-perpetration based on joint criminal enterprise as elaborated by the case law of the *Ad hoc* Tribunals. This conclusion is based on the fact that this last notion: (i) is a theory of co-perpetration that gives rise to principal (as opposed to accessorial) liability;[294] (ii) has been explicitly distinguished from the notions of 'conspiracy' and 'membership in a criminal organisation';[295] (iii) always requires a contribution to the implementation of the common criminal plan or purpose;[296] and (iv) does not make distinctions among the participants in the enterprise in light of their different roles because they are all 'equally liable' as principals (co-perpetrators) to the crimes.[297]

Moreover, if as the ICTR Appeals Chamber in the *Rwamakuba* case has suggested,[298] one looks at counts three and four of the indictment filed by Chief Prosecutor Jackson before the IMT,[299] one realizes that the language is similar to that of article 6(c) of the IMT Charter, and it greatly resembles the 'conspiracy theory' that had been embraced a year before in the *Pinkerton* case (and which expanded, in an unprecedented manner, the notion of 'conspiracy' under US law).[300]

---

[293] According to these provisions, '[l]eaders, organizers, instigators and accomplices participating in the formulation or execution of a common plan or conspiracy to commit any of the foregoing crimes are responsible for all acts performed by any persons in execution of such plan'.

[294] See Ch 2, s VII.B.

[295] See Ch 2, s VI.

[296] See Ch 2, s VI and Ch 4, s III.A.iii.

[297] *Furundzija Case* Appeals Judgment (Above n 28), at paras 117–18; *Vasiljevic Case* Appeals Judgment (Above n 11), at para 111.

[298] *Rwamakuba Case* Decision on the Application of Joint Criminal Enterprise to the Crime of Genocide (Above n 139), at para 23.

[299] For instance, Count 3 of the indictment alleged that: 'The said War Crimes were committed by the defendants and by other persons for whose acts the defendants are responsible (under Article 6 of the Charter of the International Military Tribunal) as such other persons when committing the said War Crimes performed their acts in execution of a common plan and conspiracy to commit the said War Crimes, in the formulation and execution of which plan and conspiracy all the defendants participated as leaders, organizers, instigators, and accomplices'. See Indictment of the International Military Tribunal at Nuremberg, Count 3, Pt VIII, in Trial of the Major War Criminals before the International Military Tribunal under Control Council Law No 10, Vol I (US Government Printing Office, 1951) 43. Similar language appeared in Count 4 of the indictment, which charged crimes against humanity. See Indictment of the International Military Tribunal at Nuremberg, Count 4, Pt X, at 65.

[300] *Pinkerton v United States*, 328 US 640 (1946).

D The Notion of Joint Criminal Enterprise at the Leadership Level prior to its Explicit Endorsement by the ICTY Appeals Chamber in the *Brdanin* Case

Although, as seen in the previous section, post WW II cases did not rely on the notion of 'joint criminal enterprise at the leadership level', or on any other 'equivalent' basis, the author considers that several cases before the ICTY had applied this notion prior to its explicit endorsement by the ICTY Appeals Chamber in the *Brdanin* case.

i The Kordic *Case*

The defendant in this case, Dario Kordic, was the vice-president of the Croatian Community of Herzeg Bosnia (later Croatian Republic of Herzeg Bosnia) since its foundation on 18 November 1991. Although he occupied an important position in the Bosnian Croat leadership, the Trial Chamber found that he was not in the top echelon, insofar as he was answerable to the president, Mate Boban. Nevertheless, he was a political leader with 'tremendous influence and power' in Central Bosnia (the region from where he originally came from).[301] Indeed, according to the Trial Chamber, he was 'the political leader of the Bosnian Croats in Central Bosnia', with particular authority in the Lasva Valley.[302]

The Prosecution's case against Dario Kordic was based on the allegation that he, together with other persons holding positions of authority in the Croat and Bosnian Croat leadership, designed a common plan to persecute the Bosnian Muslim population of Central Bosnia through a variety of unlawful acts. According to the Prosecution, as 'an overall architect' of the joint criminal purpose, Dario Kordic contributed to it by planning, preparing, instigating and ordering it with the requisite intent.[303]

The Trial Chamber found that from November 1991 through January 1994, there was a campaign of persecution against the Bosnian Muslim population of Central Bosnia orchestrated from Zagreb, and conducted through the organs of the Croatian Community of Herzeg-Bosna and the HDZ-BiH.[304] The Bosnian Croat leadership had a common plan or design to conduct this campaign, whose purpose was the subjugation of the Bosnian Muslim population, and which included as core crimes unlawful attacks to towns and villages, killings, physical

---

[301] *Kordic Case* Trial Judgment (Above n 15), at para 838; *Prosecutor v Kordic* (Appeals Chamber Judgment) ICTY-95-14/2-A (17 December 2004) para 3 [hereinafter *Kordic Case* Appeals Judgment].

[302] *Kordic Case* Trial Judgment (*Ibid*), at para 829.

[303] *Ibid* at para 828, referring to paras 437–8 of the same Trial Judgment. See also *Prosecutor v Kordic* (First Amended Indictment) ICTY-95-14/2 (30 Sep 1998) paras 25, 28–29 [hereinafter *Kordic Case* First Amended Indictment].

[304] *Kordic Case* Trial Judgment (*Ibid*), at para 827.

assaults, detention, and destruction and plunder of property.[305] Moreover, according to the Trial Chamber, Dario Kordic, as a regional political leader:

> [L]ent himself enthusiastically to the common design of persecution by planning, preparing and ordering those parts of the campaign which fell within his sphere of authority. (It is to be inferred that he did so intending to advance the policy and sharing the discriminatory intent from his active participation in the campaign).[306]

As a result, the Trial Chamber convicted the defendant for the crime of persecution against the Bosnian Muslim population of Central Bosnia from November 1991 through January 1994.

In the author's view, Dario Kordic was convicted as a participant in a basic form of joint criminal enterprise in which the other participants were limited to the Bosnian Croat leadership (and perhaps the Croatian leadership as well). The persons who physically committed the persecutory acts against the Bosnian Muslim population of Central Bosnia were not included in the joint criminal enterprise (most likely because they were seen as mere tools used by the participants in the enterprise to secure the implementation of the campaign of persecution). Hence, the Trial Chamber implicitly applied the notion of joint criminal enterprise at the leadership level. Nevertheless, the Trial Chamber did not explain that it was departing from the traditional notion of joint criminal enterprise and did not give any reason why departing from this last notion was necessary in this case.[307]

---

[305] *Ibid.*

[306] *Ibid* at para 829.

[307] The Trial Chamber also made a distinction between: (i) Kordic's conviction for the crime of persecution as a participant in a joint criminal enterprise whose contribution consisted in planning, preparing and ordering those parts of the campaign which fell within his sphere of authority; and (ii) Kordic's conviction for the rest of the crimes that were part of the common criminal design (unlawful attacks on towns and villages, killings, injuries, unlawful detention and destruction and plunder of property). With regard to this last set of crimes, it seems that the Trial Chamber did not rely on the notion of co-perpetration based on joint criminal enterprise. Indeed, from the following excerpts of the Trial Judgment, it appears that the Trial Chamber relied on forms of accessorial liability such as planning, instigating or ordering: 'In relation to the crimes of unlawful destruction, wilful killing, inhuman treatment, detention and destruction, the Trial Chamber finds that in those cases where Kordic participated in the HVO attacks he intended to commit the crimes associated with them and did so. His role was as political leader and his responsibility under Article 7(1) was to plan, instigate and order the crimes'. See *Kordic Case* Trial Judgment (*Ibid*), at para 834. The author considers that this last excerpt misled the ICTY Appeals Chamber and caused it to inaccurately state that the notion of co-perpetration based on joint criminal enterprise had not been relied on by the Trial Chamber in relation to Dario Kordic. See *Kordic Case* Appeals Judgment (Above n 301), at para 6. Nevertheless, the language used by the Trial Chamber in convicting Dario Kordic for the crime of persecution (*Kordic Case* Trial Judgment (*Ibid*), at paras 827–9) clearly shows that he was convicted as a co-perpetrator for his participation, together with the Bosnian Croat leadership, in a joint criminal enterprise to persecute the Bosnian Muslim population of Central Bosnia. This conclusion is further supported by the fact that: (i) the Trial Chamber explicitly acknowledge that the extended form of joint criminal enterprise 'seem[ed] particularly apposite to the issues in this case (*Kordic Case* Trial Judgment (*Ibid*), at para 396); and (ii) Dario Kordic was acquitted for the abuse and inhuman treatment of the detained Muslims (including their use as hostages and human shields and for trench-digging) not only because he was not connected with the way the detention camps were run and the manner in which detainees were treated, but also because such crimes were not part of the common criminal plan or design. See *Kordic Case* Trial Judgment (*Ibid*), at para 802.

ii The Krstic *Case*

The defendant in this case, Radislav Krstic, was the Chief of Staff/Deputy Commander of the Drina Corps from October 1994 to 12 July 1995.[308] On 13 July 1995, he became the Commander of the Drina Corps,[309] which was the Brigade of the Serbian Bosnian Military (VRS). During this time, the Srebrenica enclave and its surrounding areas were under the responsibility of the Drina Corps.[310]

General Krstic was convicted as a co-perpetrator for his participation, together with 'the political and/or military leadership of the VRS', in two consecutive joint criminal enterprises against the Bosnian Muslim population of the Srebrenica enclave. The Trial Chamber defined the first enterprise as follows:

> The political and/or military leadership of the VRS formulated a plan to permanently remove the Bosnian Muslim population from Srebrenica, following the take-over of the enclave. From 11 through 13 July, this plan of what is colloquially referred to as 'ethnic cleansing' was realised mainly through the forcible transfer of the bulk of the civilian population out of Potocari, once the military aged men had been separated from the rest of the population. General Krstic was a key participant in the forcible transfer, working in close co-operation with other military officials of the VRS Main Staff and the Drina Corps. The *actus reus* requirements for joint criminal enterprise liability therefore have been met.[311]
>
> The Trial Chamber is not, however, convinced beyond reasonable doubt that the murders, rapes, beatings and abuses committed against the refugees at Potocari were also an agreed upon objective among the members of the joint criminal enterprise. However, there is no doubt that these crimes were natural and foreseeable consequences of the ethnic cleansing campaign.[312]

Subsequently, the Trial Chamber defined the second 'elevated' joint criminal enterprise of 'General Mladic and the VRS Main Staff Personnel' as follows:

> The Trial Chamber has made findings that, as of 13 July, the plan to ethnically cleanse the area of Srebrenica escalated to a far more insidious level that included killing all of the military aged Bosnian Muslim men of Srebrenica. A transfer of the men after screening for war criminals—the purported reason for their separation from the women, children and elderly at Potocari—to Bosnian Muslim held territory or to prisons to await a prisoner exchange was at some point considered an inadequate mode for assuring the ethnic cleansing of Srebrenica. Killing the men, in addition to forcibly transferring the women, children and elderly, became the object of the newly elevated joint criminal enterprise of General Mladic and VRS Main Staff personnel. The Trial Chamber concluded that this campaign to kill all the military aged men was conducted to guarantee that the Bosnian Muslim population would be permanently eradicated from Srebrenica and therefore constituted genocide.[313]

---

[308] *Krstic Case* Trial Judgment (Above n 21), at paras 328–32.
[309] *Ibid.*
[310] *Ibid* at paras 291–2, 296.
[311] *Ibid* at para 612.
[312] *Ibid* at para 617.
[313] *Ibid* at para 619.

General Krstic may not have devised the killing plan, or participated in the initial decision to escalate the objective of the criminal enterprise from forcible transfer to destruction of Srebrenica's Bosnian Muslim military-aged male community, but there can be no doubt that, from the point he learned of the widespread and systematic killings and became clearly involved in their perpetration, he shared the genocidal intent to kill the men. This cannot be gainsaid given his informed participation in the executions through the use of Drina Corps assets.[314]

These excerpts show that the Trial Chamber in the *Krstic* case did not rely on the traditional notion of joint criminal enterprise because the physical perpetrators were not participants in any of the two consecutive enterprises. According to the Trial Chamber, only the political and military leadership of the VRS, including its Commander-in-Chief and the members of the VRS Main Staff, participated in the two joint criminal enterprises. General Krstic was found to be a participant in both joint criminal enterprises because, as Commander of the Drina Corps, he worked in close coordination with the other VRS military superiors to implement the common criminal plan. As a result, when analysing whether General Krstic shared the intent to implement the core crimes with the other participants in the two consecutive enterprises, the Trial Chamber did not discuss the state of mind of the physical perpetrators.[315]

The approach taken by the Trial Chamber in the *Krstic* case has been explained as follows by Judge Iain Bonomy in his Separate Opinion to the ICTY Trial Decision on Indirect Co-perpetration in the *Milutinovic* case:

> The position of *Brdanin* is to be contrasted with the approach of the Trial Chamber in *Krstic*. There the Trial Chamber made no mention of a requirement that the physical perpetrator should be a member of the JCE. The Chamber then proceeded in paragraph 617 to find the accused guilty of inhumane acts and persecution as crimes against humanity for his participation in a JCE, formulated between him and other high-ranking Bosnian Serb political and military leaders, to forcibly transfer Muslim women, children, and elderly out of Potocari. In paragraph 645 the Chamber similarly found him guilty of genocide for his participation in a JCE, formulated among the same persons, with the object of killing all the military-aged Bosnian Muslim men of Srebrenica. In both instances the physical perpetrators appear to have been foot soldiers and other low-ranking members of the Drina Corps of the Bosnian Serb Army.[316]

Hence, in the author's view, the Trial Chamber implicitly applied the notion of joint criminal enterprise at the leadership level in the *Krstic* case. However, as in the *Kordic* case, it did not explain that it was departing from the traditional notion of joint criminal enterprise and did not give any reason why it was necessary to depart from this last notion.[317]

---

[314] *Ibid* at para 633.

[315] *Ibid* at paras 616, 617, 633.

[316] *Milutinovic Case*, Decision on Indirect Co-Perpetration, Separate Opinion of Judge Bonomy (Above n 282), at para 11.

[317] The question of whether the physical perpetrators had to be part of the two consecutive joint criminal enterprises was not subsequently raised in appeal.

iii The Stakic Case

In the *Stakic* case, the Prosecution alleged that Milomir Stakic (the president of the Crisis Staff and War Presidency of Prijedor municipality, and the highest civil authority in the municipality since the Bosnian Serb take over at the end of April 1992)[318] was a participant in a joint criminal enterprise to persecute the non-Bosnian-Serb population of the municipality. According to the Prosecution:

> Numerous individuals participated in this joint criminal enterprise, including Milomir STAKIC, Milan KOVACEVIC, Simo DRLJACA, other members of the Prijedor Crisis Staff, members of the Assembly of the Serbian People in Prijedor Municipality and Assembly's Executive Committee, Radoslav BRDANIN, General Momir TALIC and Stojan ZUPLJANIN, other members of the ARK Crisis Staff, the leadership of the Serbian republic and the SDS, including Radovan KARADZIC, Momcilo KRAJISNIK and Biljana PLAVSIC, members of the Assembly of the ARK and the Assembly's Executive Committee, the Serb Crisis staffs of the ARK municipalities, members of the VRS, Serb and Bosnian Serb paramilitary forces and others.[319]

The Trial Chamber applied the notion of control of the crime ('co-perpetratorship') to overcome the problems posed by the application of the traditional notion of joint criminal enterprise to political and military leaders.[320]

However, the ICTY Appeals Chamber reversed the Trial Chamber's approach because:

> This mode of liability, as defined and applied by the Trial Chamber, does not have support in customary international law or in the settled jurisprudence of this Tribunal, which is binding on the Trial Chambers.[321]

It then entered a conviction pursuant to the notion of joint criminal enterprise on the basis of the factual findings of the Trial Chamber.[322]

---

[318] *Stakic Case* Trial Judgment (Above n 123), at paras 822–3; *Stakic Case* Appeals Judgment (Above n 11), at para 75.

[319] *Prosecutor v Stakic* (First Amended Indictment) ICTY-97-24-I (23 Jun 1998) para 27.

[320] See Ch 5, s VI.C.

[321] *Stakic Case* Appeals Judgment (Above n 11), at para 62.

[322] *Ibid* at paras 64–104. The ICTY Appeals Chamber proceeded in this manner, *propio motu*, insofar as neither party had appealed the application of the notion of control of the crime by the Trial Chamber. It did so despite the following concerns of the Prosecution: 'While clearly stating that joint criminal liability could be found to attach based on the findings at trial, the Prosecution expressed its concerns that (1) neither party had challenged the mode of liability in the Trial Judgment and any answer in the hearing would be in the abstract; (2) the question should not be decided by the Appeals Chamber except after full briefing and argumentation by the parties; (3) the Trial Chamber itself did not analyse the evidence on a joint criminal enterprise theory; and (4) any such analysis would require a review of the entire record'. See *Stakic Case* Appeals Judgment (*Ibid*), at para 61. The ICTY Appeals Chamber justified this way of proceeding for the following reasons: 'The question of whether the mode of liability developed and applied by the Trial Chamber is within the jurisdiction of this Tribunal is an issue of general importance warranting the scrutiny of the Appeals Chamber *propio motu*. The introduction of new modes of liability into the jurisprudence of the Tribunal may generate uncertainty, if not confusion, in the determination of the law by parties to cases before the Tribunal as well as in the application of the law by Trial Chambers. To avoid such uncertainty and ensure respect for the values of consistency and coherence in the application of the law, the Appeals Chamber must intervene to assess whether the mode of liability applied by the Trial Chamber is consistent with the jurisprudence of this Tribunal'. See *Stakic Case* Appeals Judgment (*Ibid*), at para 59.

The Trial Chamber found that the co-perpetrators of the crimes (those who shared control over the crimes charged in the indictment) were those political and military leaders who headed the three organised structures of power (the civil administration, the civil police and the army) that existed in the Prijedor municipality in the Spring and Summer of 1992. None of the physical perpetrators (mid and low level members of the civil administration, civil police and army) were included among the co-perpetrators because they did not have any control over the crimes as they were used as 'tools' by their superiors to have the crimes committed.[323]

Nevertheless, the ICTY Appeals Chamber relied on this finding to hold that:

> The Trial Chamber's findings demonstrate that there was a plurality of persons that acted together in the implementation of a common goal. This group included the leaders of political bodies, the army, and the police who held power in the Municipality of Prijedor.[324]

The ICTY Appeals Chamber also held that (i) the common goal identified by the Trial Chamber (which consisted of a discriminatory campaign carried out between 30 April and 30 August 1992 to ethnically cleanse the Prijedor municipality of its non-Bosnian Serb population so as to secure Serbian control) amounted to a common purpose within the meaning of the Tribunal's joint criminal enterprise doctrine,[325] and that (ii) persecuting, deporting, and forcibly transferring such population were the core crimes of the enterprise[326] (whereas murder and extermination were natural and foreseeable consequences of its implementation).[327] Furthermore, according to the ICTY Appeals Chamber, the Trial Chamber's findings concerning Stakic's coordinating role between the civil administration, the civil police and the army, and the fact that he directed the civil administration to carry out a part of the common plan, clearly showed that Stakic played an important role in the implementation of the common purpose.[328]

For the ICTY Appeals Chamber, the existence of a shared intent among the participants in the joint criminal enterprise was shown by the following findings of the Trial Chamber:[329]

(i)   'Evidence supports the finding that the civilian authorities, the police and the military co-operated on the same level within the municipality of Prijedor in order to achieve their aforementioned common goals at any cost'.[330]

---

[323] As the Trial Chamber explained, the co-perpetrators were only 'the authorities of the self-proclaimed Assembly of the Serbian People in Prijedor Municipality, the SDS, the Prijedor Crisis Staff, the Territorial Defence and the police and military. In particular, Dr. Stakic acted together with the Police Chief, Simo Drljaca, prominent members of the military such as Colonel Vladimir Arsic and Major Radmilo Zeljaja [sic], the president of the Executive Committee of Prijedor Municipality, Dr. Milan Kovacevic, and the Commander both of the Municipal Territorial Defence Staff and the Trnopolje camp, Slobodan Kuruzovic'. See *Stakic Case* Trial Judgment (Above n 123), at para 469. See also *Stakic Case* Appeals Judgment (*Ibid*), at para 68.

[324] *Stakic Case* Appeals Judgment (*Ibid*), at para 69.

[325] *Ibid* at para 73.

[326] *Ibid* at para 78.

[327] *Ibid* at para 92.

[328] *Ibid* at paras 75–6.

[329] *Ibid* at paras 80–83.

[330] *Stakic Case* Trial Judgment (Above n 123), at para 364.

(ii)   There was an 'agreement amongst members of the Crisis Staff to use armed force against civilians and to establish the Omarska, Keraterm and Trnopolje camps';[331] and 'the Crisis Staff, presided over by Dr. Stakic, was responsible for establishing the Omarska, Keraterm and Trnopolje camps, and, as discussed before, there was a coordinated cooperation between the Crisis Staff, later the War Presidency, and members of the police and the army in operating these camps'."[332]

(iii) 'The evidence shows that Dr. Stakic as the leading figure in the municipal government, worked together with the Police Chief, Simo Drljaca, the highest ranking man in the military, Colonel Vladimir Arsic, and the President of the Executive Board, Dr. Milan Kovacevic to implement the SDS-initiated plan to consolidate Serb authority and power within the municipality'.[333]

(iv)   'Dr. Stakic knew that his role and authority as the leading politician in Prijedor was essential for the accomplishment of the common goal. He was aware that he could frustrate the objective of achieving a Serbian municipality by using his powers to hold to account those responsible for crimes, by protecting or assisting non-Serbs or by stepping down from his superior positions'.[334]

Finally, the ICTY Appeals Chamber also held that the findings of the Trial Chamber showed that Stakic (i) had the intent required by the core crimes of the enterprise (persecution, deportation and forcible transfer), including the requisite discriminatory intent for the crime of persecution;[335] and (ii) foresaw the likelihood of the commission of murder and extermination and reconciled himself with such a result.[336]

In the author's view, the ICTY Appeals Chamber used ambiguous language, which did not permit the reader to identify, with certainty, the participants in the joint criminal enterprise. In this regard, when the ICTY Appeals Chamber referred to a group of individuals which 'included the leaders of political bodies, the army, and the police who held power in the Municipality of Prijedor', it gave the impression that the said leaders were not the only participants in the enterprise and that the physical perpetrators might have also been included in the enterprise.

If this were the case, the ICTY Appeals Chamber, in trying to apply the traditional notion of joint criminal enterprise, would have held that the findings of the Trial Chamber permitted to extend the group of co-perpetrators (participants in the joint criminal enterprise) to the physical perpetrators. However, the Appeals Chamber did not explain how the findings of the Trial Chamber met the requirements of the traditional notion of joint criminal enterprise that all participants in

---

[331] *Ibid* at para 477.
[332] *Ibid* at para 377.
[333] *Ibid* at para 593.
[334] *Ibid* at para 498.
[335] *Stakic Case* Appeals Judgment (Above n 11), at para 83.
[336] *Stakic Case* Trial Judgment (Above n 123), at paras 93–7.

the enterprise (and not only those who were part of Stakic's inner circle): (i) acted in furtherance of a common criminal plan or purpose; and (ii) shared the intent required by the core crimes of the enterprise (including any requisite ulterior intent or *dolus specialis*).

In the author's view, the ICTY Appeals Chamber could not have provided such an explanation because the main reason why the Trial Chamber relied on the notion of control of the crime was to limit the group of co-perpetrators to those senior leaders of the civil administration, civil police and army who shared control over the crimes committed in the Prijedor municipality.[337] This was the only solution that the Trial Chamber found to overcome the problems posed by the application of the traditional notion of joint criminal enterprise to the defendant (the highest civilian authority in the Prijedor municipality).[338] As a result, the Trial Chamber repeatedly used the expression 'perpetrator behind the direct perpetrator/actor' to indicate that the state of mind of the physical perpetrators was irrelevant, because their superiors used them as 'tools' to have the crimes committed.[339]

Moreover, if one reviews the findings of the Trial Chamber concerning the members of the group of co-perpetrators and their shared intent, one realises that they all refer to a very limited group of persons who were at the top of the civil administration, the civil police and the army in Prijedor municipality in mid 1992.[340] For instance, at paragraphs 364, 477 and 479 of the *Stakic* Trial Judgment, one can read:

> Evidence supports the finding that the civilian authorities, the police and the military co-operated on the same level within the municipality of Prijedor in order to achieve their aforementioned common goals at any cost.[341]
>
> The creation of an atmosphere of fear in Prijedor Municipality culminated in the agreement amongst members of the Crisis Staff to use armed force against civilians and to establish the Omarska, Keraterm and Trnopolje camps. The order to set up the Omarska camp on 31 May 1992, signed by Simo Drljaca, was issued 'in accordance with the Decision of the Crisis Staff' presided over by Dr. Stakic. The Trial Chamber finds no reason to doubt Dr. Stakic's own statement in a television interview that '[Omarska, Keraterm, and Trnopolje were] a necessity in the given moment' and his confirmation that these camps 'were formed according to a decision of [his] civilian authorities in Prijedor'.[342]
>
> Throughout the period immediately after the takeover, Dr. Stakic, in co-operation with the Chief of Police, Simo Drljaca, and the most senior military figure in Prijedor,

[337] Compare H Olasolo and A Perez Cepeda, 'The Notion of Control of the Crime in the Jurisprudence of the ICTY: The Stakic Case' (2004) 4 *International Criminal Law Review* 508–511 [hereinafter Olasolo and Perez Cepeda].

[338] H Olasolo, 'Reflections on the Treatment of the Notions of Control of the Crime and Joint Criminal Enterprise in the Stakic Appeal Judgment' (2007) 7 *International Criminal Law Review* 148–9.

[339] *Stakic Case* Trial Judgment (Above n 123), at paras 741, 743, 774. See also Olasolo and Perez Cepeda (Above n 337), at 513–15.

[340] See *Stakic Case* Trial Judgment (*Ibid*), at paras 364, 377, 469, 477, 498, 593. See also *Stakic Case* Appeals Judgment (Above n 11), at paras 68, 69, 80–83; Olasolo and Perez Cepeda (*Ibid*), at 517–18.

[341] *Stakic Case* Trial Judgment (*Ibid*), at para 364.

[342] *Ibid* at para 477.

Colonel Vladimir Arsic, worked to strengthen and unify the military forces under Serb control. The response to the incidents at Hambarine and Kozarac in late May 1992 heralded the first in a series of measures taken by the Crisis Staff, in cooperation with the military and the police, to rid the municipality of non-Serbs.[343]

The language used in paragraphs 64 to 104 of the ICTY *Stakic* Appeal Judgment can also be interpreted to mean that the individuals participating in the joint criminal enterprise were only those political and military leaders who were at the top of the civil administration, the civil police and the army in Prijedor municipality. Indeed, in the *Krajisnik* case, the Prosecution claimed that the *Stakic* Appeal Judgment convicted the defendant on the basis of a joint criminal enterprise, which did not include the physical perpetrators, because they were used by the co-perpetrators as tools in securing the commission of the crimes.[344] As the Prosecution explained:

> The *Stakic* Appeal Judgement implicitly confirms that a JCE may be comprised of participants at the leadership level who use the principal perpetrators of the crimes as their 'instruments'.[345]

If the interpretation of the Prosecution is correct, then the ICTY Appeals Chamber in the *Stakic* case would have implicitly applied the notion of joint criminal enterprise at the leadership level without explaining the 'cogent reasons in the interest of justice' requiring to depart from the traditional notion of joint criminal enterprise. However, more importantly, the ICTY Appeals Chamber would have implicitly applied the notion of indirect perpetration (which is one of the main manifestations of the notion of control of the crime and a key component of the notion of joint criminal enterprise at the leadership level) after having summarily dismissed in the same judgement the application of the notion of control of the crime, and its possible customary status, before the ICTY.[346]

iv The Milutinovic Case

In the *Milutinovic* case, the Defence made a jurisdictional motion before the Trial Chamber challenging inter alia the Prosecution's allegation in the Amended Indictment that a defendant may be held liable for his participation in a joint criminal enterprise in which the physical perpetrators do not participate.[347] The Trial Chamber declined to take a decision on the issue raised by the Defence for the following reasons:

> In other words, he accepts that the Tribunal has jurisdiction to find an accused guilty of the commission of a crime as the result of his participation in a JCE. His challenge is a

---

[343] *Ibid* at para 479.
[344] *Krajisnik Case* Trial Judgment (Above n 11), at para 875.
[345] *Ibid.*
[346] *Stakic Case* Appeals Judgment (Above n 11), at para 62.
[347] *Prosecutor v Milutinovic* (Decision On Ojdanic's Motion Challenging Jurisdiction: Indirect Co-Perpetration) ICTY-05-87-PT (22 Mar 2006) paras 10–11.

much narrower one, and amounts to no more than a claim that the concept of JCE does not extend to circumstances in which the commission of a crime is said to have been effected through the hands of others whose *mens rea* is not explored and determined, and who are not shown to be participants in the JCE. In the Trial Chamber's view, that question does not raise the issue of the Tribunal's jurisdiction over the activities of a JCE, but instead relates to the contours of JCE responsibility. Like challenges relating to the contours of a substantive crime, challenges concerning the contours of a form of responsibility are matters to be addressed at trial. The question at trial in relation to Ojdanic and each of his co-Accused—all of whom are alleged to be participants in the JCE—will be whether it is proved that each committed crimes through participation in the JCE. The Trial Chamber will have to decide, applying the law to the evidence in the case, whether JCE liability has been established for each Accused.[348]

In his Separate Opinion, Judge Bonomy stated that no binding decision of the ICTY Appeals Chamber would prevent a participant in a joint criminal enterprise from being found guilty as a co-perpetrator for the crimes physically committed by other persons:

[W]ho simply act as an instrument of the JCE, and who are not shown to be participants in the JCE.[349]

Hence, according to Judge Bonomy, the application of the notion of joint criminal enterprise at the leadership level would not be inconsistent with the previous case law of the ICTY.[350]

v *The* Krajisnik *Case*

In the *Krajisnik* case, the defendant Momcilo Krajisnik—the president of the Assembly of the self-proclaimed Srpska Republic and one of the key members (number two) of its Presidency[351]—was held liable as a co-perpetrator for his participation in a basic form of joint criminal enterprise to ethnically recompose the territories under the control of the Bosnian Serbs by expelling and thereby drastically reducing the proportion of Bosnian Muslims and Bosnian Croats living in the Srpska Republic (which included approximately two thirds of BiH).[352] According to the Trial Chamber, the defendant held 'a central position' in the joint criminal enterprise and was one of 'the driving forces behind it'.[353] His 'overall contribution' to the implementation of the common criminal plan was (i) to help establish and perpetuate the SDS and the structures of the Srpska Republic that

---

[348] *Ibid* at para 23.
[349] *Milutinovic Case*, Decision on Indirect Co-Perpetration, Separate Opinion of Judge Bonomy (Above n 282), at para 13.
[350] *Ibid.*
[351] *Krajisnik Case* Trial Judgment (Above n 11), at para 1085.
[352] *Ibid* at para 1090.
[353] *Ibid* at para 119.

were instrumental to the commission of the crimes; and (ii) to deploy his political skills both locally and internationally to facilitate its implementation.[354]

The Prosecution alleged that the following persons participated, together with the defendant, in the joint criminal enterprise:

Each participant, by acts or omissions, contributed to achieving the objective of the enterprise. Momcilo Krajisnik and Biljana Plavsic worked in concert with other members of the joint criminal enterprise, including Radovan Karadzic and Nikola Koljevic. Other members of the joint criminal enterprise included: Slobodan Milosevic, Zeljko Raznatovic (aka 'Arkan'), General Ratko Mladic, General Momir Talic, Radoslav Brdanin, and other members of the Bosnian Serb leadership at the Republic, regional and municipal levels; members of the SDS leadership at the Republic, regional and munici-pal levels; members of the Yugoslav People's Army ('JNA'), the Yugoslav Army ('VJ'), the army of the Serbian Republic of Bosnia and Herzegovina, later the army of the Republika Srpska ('VRS'), the Bosnian Serb Territorial Defence ('TO'), the Bosnian Serb police ('MUP'), and members of Serbian and Bosnian Serb paramilitary forces and volunteer units and military and political figures from the (Socialist) Federal Republic of Yugoslavia, the Republic of Serbia and the Republic of Montenegro.[355]

---

[354] *Krajisnik Case* Trial Judgment (Above n 11), at para 1120. Furthermore, he also contributed to the implementation of the common criminal plan in the following manners:

    (i)   Formulating, initiating, promoting, participating in, and/or encouraging the development and implementation of SDS and Bosnian Serb governmental policies intended to advance the objective of the joint criminal enterprise;

    (ii) Participating in the establishment, support or maintenance of SDS and Bosnian Serb gov-ernment bodies at the Republic, regional, municipal, and local levels, including Crisis Staffs, War Presidencies, War Commissions ("Bosnian Serb Political and Governmental Organs") and the VRS, TO, and the MUP ("Bosnian Serb Forces") through which [he] could implement the objective of the joint criminal enterprise; although Momcilo Krajisnik was found not to have been involved in the establishment of the SDS party and the TO;

    (iii) Supporting, encouraging, facilitating or participating in the dissemination of information to Bosnian Serbs that they were in jeopardy of oppression at the hands of Bosnian Muslims and Bosnian Croats, that territories on which Bosnian Muslims and Bosnian Croats resided were Bosnian Serb land, or that was otherwise intended to engender in Bosnian Serbs fear and hatred of Bosnian Muslims and Bosnian Croats or to otherwise win support for and participation in achieving the objective of the joint criminal enterprise;

    (iv) Directing, instigating, encouraging and authorizing the Bosnian Serb Political and Governmental Organs and the Bosnian Serb Forces to carry out acts in order to further the objective of the joint criminal enterprise;

    (v) Aiding or abetting or instigating the commission of further crimes by failing to investigate, to follow up on investigations [. . .] for crimes committed against Bosnian Muslims, Bosnian Croats or other non-Serbs throughout the period described in this indictment; and

    (vi) Engaging in, supporting or facilitating efforts directed at representatives of the inter-national community, non-governmental organizations and the public denying or provid-ing misleading information about crimes against Bosnian Muslims, Bosnian Croats or other non-Serbs of Bosnia and Herzegovina and about the role that Bosnian Serb Forces had played in those crimes'. See *Krajisnik Case* Trial Judgment (*Ibid*), at para 1121.

[355] *Prosecutor v Krajisnik* (Consolidated Amended Indictment) ICTY-00-39 (7 Mar 2002) para 7. See also *Krajisnik Case* Trial Judgment (*Ibid*), at para 1079.

Nevertheless, in its Final Trial Brief, the Prosecution highlighted:

Should the Trial Chamber find that the members of the JCE consisted only of a core group (such as Krajisnik, Karadzic, Plavsic, Koljevic, Mladic, Mico Stanisic and Mandic), liability still attaches to Krajisnik for participation in that JCE, as the physical perpetrators of the crimes were acting as instruments of that JCE. Similarly, insofar as any crimes were committed by local Bosnian Serbs who were not members of the JCE, those Serbs were acting as instruments under the direction of participants in the JCE.[356]

The Trial Chamber started its analysis of the Prosecution's case by dismissing the Defence's argument that the notion of joint criminal enterprise was not applicable in this case due to (i) the size and scope of the case and (ii) the fact that the defendant was structurally remote from the scene of the crimes when they were committed. According to the Trial Chamber:

The Appeals Chamber has never suggested that JCE liability can arise only from participation in enterprises of small size or scope. Far from being inappropriate, JCE is well suited to cases such as the present one, in which numerous persons are all said to be concerned with the commission of a large number of crimes.[357]

Moreover, citing the above-mentioned Separate Opinion of Judge Iain Bonomy in the *Milutinovic* Case,[358] the Trial Chamber explicitly endorsed the notion of joint criminal enterprise at the leadership level by stating:

A JCE may exist even if none or only some of the principal perpetrators are part of it, because, for example, they are not aware of the JCE or its objective and are procured by members of the JCE to commit crimes which further that objective.[359]

In relation to the first two elements of JCE liability, it is the common objective that begins to transform a plurality of persons into a group or enterprise, as this plurality has in common the particular objective. It is evident, however, that a common objective alone is not always sufficient to determine a group, as different and independent groups may happen to share identical objectives. Rather, it is the interaction or cooperation among persons— their joint action—in addition to their common objective, that makes those persons a group. The persons in a criminal enterprise must be shown to act together, or in concert with each other, in the implementation of a common objective, if they are to share responsibility for the crimes committed through the JCE. A concern expressed by the Trial Chamber in *Brdanin* about the issue of alleged JCE participants acting independently of each other, is sufficiently addressed by the requirement that joint action among members of a criminal enterprise is proven.[360]

---

[356] Prosecution Final Trial Brief in the *Krajisnik Case*, para 3. See also *Krajisnik Case* Trial Judgment (*Ibid*), at para 1080.

[357] *Krajisnik Case* Trial Judgment (*Ibid*), at para 873.

[358] See Ch 5, s V.D.iv.

[359] *Krajisnik Case* Trial Judgment (Above n 11), at para 883.

[360] *Ibid*. On this last point, the Trial Chamber held: 'The Prosecution was invited by the Chamber to comment on the kinds of evidence which would distinguish perpetrators of crimes acting as part of a JCE from persons not part of that JCE but who were committing similar crimes. The Prosecution listed some distinguishing factors: Whether the perpetrator was a member of, or associated with, any organised bodies connected to the JCE; whether the crimes committed were consistent with the pattern of similar crimes by JCE members against similar kinds of victims; whether the perpetrator acted

In light of these findings, the Trial Chamber held that the participants of the joint criminal enterprise in which the defendant also participated included, first and foremost, a Pale based Bosnian-Serb leadership component comprised of inter alia Momcilo Krajisnik, Radovan Karadzic, Biljana Plavsic, Nikola Koljevic, Momcilo Mandic, Velibor Ostojic, Mico Stanisic and, as of 12 May 1992, General Ratko Mladic. Moreover, the rank and file members of the joint criminal enterprise consisted of local politicians, military and police commanders, paramilitary leaders, and others, which were based in the regions and municipalities of the Srpska Republic and maintained close links with Pale.[361] The Trial Chamber did not include the physical perpetrators among the participants in the joint criminal enterprise because they were 'tools' or 'instruments' used by the political and military leaders who participated in the enterprise to secure the commission of the crimes.

In conclusion, the author considers that the Trial Chamber in the *Krajisnik* case explicitly endorsed the notion of joint criminal enterprise at the leadership level and applied it. However, due to the inclusion of local politicians, local commanders and local leaders of paramilitary groups (the so-called 'rank and file' members of the enterprise), the degree of solidarity among the participants in the enterprise was lower than usual, and the relationships among them were not only horizontal but also hierarchical. As a result, in spite of departing from the traditional notion of joint criminal enterprise, the Trial Chamber could not identify all participants in the enterprise. As the Trial Chamber explained:

> It was a vast criminal enterprise, and, like any vast criminal enterprise, its membership was not static. The members of the JCE participated in different ways, in different geographical areas, with the shared intent to secure the objective of forcibly removing non-Serbs from the targeted territory across great parts of Bosnia and Herzegovina.[362]

at the same time as members of the JCE, or as persons who were tools or instruments of the JCE; whether the perpetrator's act advanced the objective of the JCE; whether the perpetrator's act was ratified implicitly or explicitly by members of the JCE; whether the perpetrator acted in cooperation or conjunction with members of the JCE at any relevant time; whether any meaningful effort was made to punish the act by any member of the JCE in a position to do so; whether similar acts were punished by JCE members in a position to do so; whether members of the JCE or those who were tools of the JCE continued to affiliate with the perpetrators after the act; finally—and this is a non-exhaustive list— whether the acts were performed in the context of a systematic attack, including one of relatively low intensity over a long period. The Chamber accepts the submissions in the previous paragraph, which essentially identify indicia (from an indefinite range of such indicia) concerning connections or relationships among persons working together in the implementation of a common objective. A person not in the JCE may share the general objective of the group but not be linked with the operations of the group. Crimes committed by such a person are of course not attributable to the group. On the other hand, links forged in pursuit of a common objective transform individuals into members of a criminal enterprise. These persons rely on each other's contributions, as well as on acts of persons who are not members of the JCE but who have been procured to commit crimes, to achieve criminal objectives on a scale which they could not have attained alone'. See *Krajisnik Case* Trial Judgment (*Ibid*), at paras 1081–2.

[361] *Ibid* at para 1087.
[362] *Ibid* at para 1123.

For the Trial Chamber this was not a problem because:

What is necessary is to be convinced that the defendant was sufficiently connected and concerned with persons who committed crimes pursuant to the common objective in various capacities, or who procured other persons to do so.[363]

Nevertheless, the author considers that this last finding of the Trial Chamber overlooks the requirements of the common criminal plan and shared intent among <u>all</u> participants in the enterprise, and brings back some of the ambiguous language (such as 'being connected and concerned with') contained in the statutory framework of post WW II cases. Indeed, the essence of the problem lies in the fact that the Trial Chamber, despite embracing the notion of joint criminal enterprise at the leadership level, did not apply it in its entirely because it included as participants in the enterprise, hundreds of local political, military and paramilitary leaders. This, in addition to decreasing the level of solidarity among the participants in the enterprise, brought back the problem of the existence of a common criminal plan and a shared intent among all those participating in the enterprise.

E Conclusion: The Struggle for Making the Best of a Bad Choice

As seen above, the ICTY Appeals Judgments in the *Stakic* and *Brdanin* cases, and the ICTY Trial Judgments in the *Kordic*, *Krstic*, *Krajisnik* and *Martic* cases have resorted to the notion of joint criminal enterprise at the leadership level to overcome the problems posed by the traditional notion of joint criminal enterprise in relation to senior political and military leaders. Moreover, the ICTR Appeals Chamber in the *Rwamakuba* and *Karemera* cases has also left the door open for its application.

The question arises as to how the notion of joint criminal enterprise at the leadership level deals with the problem addressed by Gustafson through a chain of separate and interlinked joint criminal enterprises.[364] In other words, if the exclusion of the physical perpetrators from the joint criminal enterprise requires that, at least, one of the participants in the enterprise (participant A) is a principal to the crimes, what type of contribution to the commission of the crimes is required for participant A to become a principal to the crimes?

The notion of joint criminal enterprise at the leadership level solves this problem by relying on the notion of indirect perpetration, according to which a political or military leader who does not physically carry out the objective elements of the crimes becomes an indirect perpetrator (and hence a principal to the crimes) if he uses the physical perpetrators (usually his subordinates) as 'instruments' or 'tools' to have the crimes committed.[365]

---

[363] *Ibid* at para 1086.
[364] See Ch 4, s IV.C.ii.c.
[365] See Ch 2, s VI and Ch 3, s III.A.

Hence, the problem addressed by Gustafson through a chain of separate and interlinked joint criminal enterprises, is solved by the notion of joint criminal enterprise at the leadership level by requiring that, at least, one of the senior political or military leaders participating in the enterprise uses his authority over the physical perpetrators to secure the commission of the crimes.[366]

In the author's view, the notion of joint criminal enterprise at the leadership level results in a higher degree of solidarity among the members of the enterprise as requested by Van Sliedregt,[367] and makes the existence of a common criminal plan and a shared intent among all participants in the enterprise more realistic. Furthermore, if senior political and military leaders are in control of organised structures of power (such as the army, the military police or the civil police) and use them to have the crimes committed, then the state of mind of the physical perpetrators becomes wholly irrelevant.[368]

As the group of participants in a joint criminal enterprise at the leadership level is limited to the senior political and military leadership, it adequately reflects the horizontal relationship among its members. Logically, the smaller the core group of senior political and military leaders included in the enterprise is, and the more horizontal their relationship is, the higher the degree of solidarity among them will be; and, accordingly, the better their criminal liability will be reflected by a theory of co-perpetration as the notion of joint criminal enterprise at the leadership level. For this reason, the author considers that the proper application of this notion requires that those mid-level superiors, who prepare logistically and operationally the physical commission of the crimes, be left out of the enterprise together with the physical perpetrators.

Concerning its nature, the notion of joint criminal enterprise at the leadership level is a *sui generis* variant of the concept of indirect co-perpetration because it results from the joint application of (i) co-perpetration based on joint criminal enterprise and (ii) OSP as a variant of indirect perpetration.

It is important not to confuse the notion of joint criminal enterprise at the leadership level with the notion of 'co-perpetratorship' (which is the expression used by the *Stakic* Trial Judgment to refer to the notion of indirect co-perpetration based on the joint application of joint control and OSP).[369] The main difference between both types of indirect co-perpetration is that 'co-perpetratorship' is the result of combining two manifestations of the very same notion of control of the crime (co-perpetration based on joint control and OSP) while the notion of joint criminal enterprise at the leadership level conflates two competing approaches to the distinction between principals and accessories to the crime: the subjective approach which is inherent to the notion of joint criminal enterprise, and the approach based on the notion of control of the crime which is at the roots of OSP.

---

[366] See Ch 3, s III.C.i.
[367] See Ch 4, s IV.C.ii.d.
[368] See Ch 3, s III.C.
[369] See Ch 5, s VI.A.

As a result, the question arises as to what is the controlling criterion to consider in determining whether a participant in a joint criminal enterprise at the leadership level is a principal to the crime; or, to put it in a different way, where does the essence of the wrongdoing of a participant in this type of enterprise lie? Is the essence of the wrongdoing the fact that he shares the intent to implement the common criminal plan with the other senior political and military leaders participating in the enterprise? Is the essence of the wrongdoing the fact that he shares the ultimate control over the commission of the crimes with the other senior political and military leaders participating in the enterprise? Is it both?

In jointly applying two competing approaches to the distinction between principals and accessories, the notion of joint criminal enterprise at the leadership level constitutes a hybrid in which the state of mind of the participants in the enterprise and their control over crime are equally important. From this perspective, this notion departs from the subjective approach to the distinction between principals and accessories, which is inherent to the traditional notion of joint criminal enterprise. Nevertheless, it does not go as far as to completely switch from a subjective approach to an approach solely based on the notion of control of the crime.

In the author's view, the notion of joint criminal enterprise at the leadership level is the result of (i) the lack of the necessary foresight by the early case law of the *Ad hoc* Tribunals when dealing with smaller cases to choose the approach to the distinction between principal and accessorial liability that best fits the nature of international crimes; and (ii) the attempt of the subsequent case law of the *Ad hoc* Tribunals to make the best of a bad choice once the problems posed by the application of the traditional notion of joint criminal enterprise to senior political and military leaders became evident. And this, in spite of the efforts of the ICTY and ICTR Appeals Chambers to circumvent this situation by arguing that the traces of a joint criminal enterprise at the leadership level can be found in a few post WW II cases, and in the *Justice* and the *RuSHA* cases in particular.[370]

The author considers that there are a number of reasons that supports this conclusion. First, as seen in Chapter 2, none of the approaches to the distinction between principal and accessorial liability has today reached the level of customary status in international law.[371]

Second, senior political and military leaders usually dominate the commission of international crimes in the sense that they decide whether the crimes will be carried out and how they will be performed. This is not an automatic consequence of their position of authority; quite the contrary, this is the result of the fact that they mastermind such crimes and use their position of authority to secure their commission by their subordinates (who are usually used as 'tools' by them). It is for this reason, and not just because of the state of mind, that (i) the criminal liabilty of senior political and military leaders can be established independently of all other parties to the crime; and (ii) senior political and military leaders bear a

---

[370] See Ch 4, s V.a and s V.b.
[371] See Ch 2, s VII.D.

higher degree of culpability.[372] As a result, they are to be considered principals, as opposed to mere accessories, to the crimes. Obviously, this is best achieved when the controlling criterion to distinguish between principal and accessorial liability is the notion of control of the crime.

Third, as Ambos, Van Der Wilt and other writers have explained, the notion of control of the crime (particular in its manifestations of OSP, co-perpetration based on joint control, and indirect co-perpetration) provides adequate tools to reflect (i) the 'vertical relationship' between senior political and military leaders and physical perpetrators (usually subordinates who are used by the former as 'tools' to secure the commission of the crimes); and (ii) the 'horizontal relation-ship' among those senior political and military leaders who work together in a coordinated fashion to plan and direct the execution of genocide, crimes against humanity and war crimes.[373]

Fourth, the notion of control of the crime is, by no means, a new creation of national or international criminal law. On the contrary, there are numerous prece-dents of application of this notion at the national and international levels, which show that the different manifestations of this notion can be also applied to distin-guish between principals and accessories to the crimes in smaller cases.[374]

Fifth, as the level of contribution required by the notion of joint criminal enterprise is fairly low, and it is not a relevant factor in determining whether senior political and military leaders are participants in the enterprise, the definition of the crimes becomes wholly irrelevant for the purpose of distinguishing between principal and accessorial liability. Additionally, the safeguards provided for by such definition in this regard are lost.[375]

Sixth, the traditional notion of joint criminal enterprise requires that senior political and military leaders who design and set into motion the common criminal plan, mid level superiors who logistically and operationally prepare its implementation and low level subordinates or followers who physically commit the crimes, all be a part of an all encompassing joint criminal enterprise. As a result, this notion is not suitable to reflect the criminal liability of senior political and military leaders because it can hardly correspond to a reality that individuals who are geographically and structurally remote (i) act in furtherance of the common criminal plan; (ii) share the intent of committing the core crimes of the enterprise; and (iii) share any ulterior intent (*dolus specialis*) required by such crimes.[376] Even writers, such as Cassese, who strongly favour the application of the traditional notion of joint criminal enterprise, acknowledge its limitations.[377]

---

[372] See Ch 2, s VII.C.iii.

[373] See Ch 4, s IV.C.ii.e.

[374] See Ch 2, s VII.C and s VII.E.

[375] See Ch 2, s V.

[376] See Ch 4, s IV.C.i.

[377] Cassese (Above n 150), at 110, 126, 133. See also Ch 4, s IV.C.ii.b. Some writers have also alleged that the application of the traditional notion of joint criminal enterprise to senior political and military leaders becomes close to a form of collective criminal liability. See Badar (Above n 183), at 302.

Seventh, the problems posed by the application of the traditional notion of joint criminal enterprise to senior political and military leaders cannot be solved in a manner that is consistent with the subjective approach to the distinction between principal and accessorial liability, which is inherent to the traditional notion of joint criminal enterprise. The best attempt, which is the recourse to separate and interlinked subsidiary joint criminal enterprises proposed by Gustafson, is also unsuitable to be applied to senior political and military leaders because it leads to an indefinite chain of separate and interlinked enterprises.[378] Other attempts, such as the proposal of Danner and Martinez to require a 'substantial' or 'significant' level of contribution to the implementation of the common criminal plan fail because they do not address the problems relating to the interrelation between the senior political leaders, who mastermind the crimes, and the physical perpetrators.[379] In turn, one can see in Van Sliedregt's approach traces of the notion of control of the crime.[380]

Finally, in order to overcome the problems posed by the application of the traditional notion of joint criminal enterprise to senior political and military leaders, it is necessary to depart from this notion. The notion of joint criminal enterprise at the leadership level resorted to by the case law of the *Ad hoc* Tribunals[381] is a 'mermaid' that has the body of the notion of co-perpetration based on joint criminal enterprise and the tail of the notion of control of the crime. As a result, it departs from the subjective approach to the distinction between principal and accessorial liability without fully embracing the approach to such a distinction based on the notion of control of the crime. This conflates two competing approaches to the distinction between principal and accessorial liability, and creates uncertainty as to which is the controlling criterion to distinguish between principals and accessories to the crime. Furthermore, the case law of the *Ad hoc* Tribunal has drawn the contours of the notion of co-perpetration based on joint criminal enterprise at the leadership level from a few post WW II cases, which applied forms of accessorial liability, that have little to do with such notion of principal liability.[382]

VI Pleading Co-perpetration Based on Joint Criminal Enterprise

A Applicable Principles

One of the most controversial issues relating to the notion of co-perpetration based on joint criminal enterprise is the specificity with which the Prosecution

[378] See Ch 4, s IV.C.ii.c.
[379] See Ch 4, s IV.C.ii.a.
[380] See Ch 4, s IV.C.ii.d.
[381] Although the *Stakic Case* Trial Judgment (Above n 123) (see Ch 5, s VI.C) and the *Vasiljevic Case* Appeals Judgment (Above n 11) (see Ch 5, s V.B) have chosen to apply the notion of control of the crime.
[382] See Ch 4, s V.C.i and s V.C.ii.

must plead a joint criminal enterprise in the indictment. Undoubtedly, the main problem identified by the case law of the *Ad hoc* Tribunals in the indictments filed by the Prosecution is the absence of explicit pleading of the extended form of joint criminal enterprise—that is to say, the allegation that the defendant was criminally liable as a co-perpetrator for crimes which were not part of the common criminal plan but were nevertheless a natural and foreseeable consequence of its implementation. Furthermore, the level of specificity which is required to plead the personal, temporal and territorial scope of the enterprise and the defendant's contribution to its implementation has also been dealt with extensively by the case law of the *Ad hoc* Tribunals.

The general principles on the specificity with which the Prosecution must plead its case are contained in the following provisions:

(i)   articles 18(4) ICTYS and 17(4) ICTRS, which provide that the indictment must set out 'a concise statement of the facts and the crime or crimes with which the accused is charged';

(ii)   rules 47(C) ICTY RPE and 47(C) ICTR RPE, which provide that the indictment shall set out not only the name and particulars of the suspect but also 'a concise statement of the facts of the case'; and

(iii) articles 21(2), (4) (a) and (4)(b) ICTYS and 20(2), (4)(a) and (4)(b) ICTRS, according to which the obligation of the Prosecution to set out a concise statement of the facts of the case must be interpreted in light of the rights of the accused to a fair hearing in the determination of the charges against him, and in particular the rights to be informed of the nature and cause of the charges against him and to have adequate time and facilities for the preparation of his defence.

The Prosecution has repeatedly claimed (i) that these provisions do not require for the specific mode of the defendant's liability to be set out in the indictment; and (ii) that failure to do so cannot render the indictment null and void.[383] Nevertheless, according to the case law of the *Ad hoc* Tribunals, these provisions impose upon the Prosecution the obligation to plead in the indictment the specific mode or modes of liability for which the defendant is being charged.[384] Furthermore, unless the Prosecution intends to rely on all heads of responsibility provided for in article 7(1) ICTYS or 6(1) ICTRS, it has been systematically

---

[383] See *Krnojelac Case* Appeals Judgment (Above n 11), at para 126.

[384] *Semanza v Prosecutor* (Appeals Chamber Judgment) ICTR-97-20-A (20 May 2005) para 357 [hereinafter *Semanza Case* Appeals Judgment]; *Prosecutor v Ntakirutimana* (Appeals Chamber Judgment) ICTR-96-10-A (13 Dec 2004) para 473 [hereinafter *Ntakirutimana Case* Appeals Judgment]; *Prosecutor v Aleksovski* (Appeals Chamber Judgment) ICTY-95-14/1-A (24 Mar 2000) para 171, fn 319 [hereinafter *Aleksovski* Appeals Judgment]; *Blaskic Case* Appeals Judgment (Above n 15), at para 215; *Kvocka Case* Appeals Judgment (Above n 11), at para 29; *Simic Case* Appeals Judgment (Above n 185), at para 21; See also *Prosecutor v Brdanin* (Decision on Form of Further Amended Indictment and Prosecution Application to Amend) ICTY-99-36-T (26 Jun 2001) para 10 [hereinafter *Brdanin Case*, Decision on Form of Further Amended Indictment]; See also *Prosecutor v Krnojelac* (Decision on Preliminary Motion on Form of the Amended Indictment) ICTY-97-25-T (11 Feb 2000) para 60.

discouraged from the practice of merely restating such provisions due to the ambiguity that it causes.[385] In other words, the Prosecution must only plead in the indictment the forms of liability on which it intends to rely.[386]

Moreover, for each mode of liability alleged in the indictment, the Prosecution must state the material facts—as opposed to the evidence by which such facts are to be proven—which are relevant to it, so that the defendant is clearly informed of the charges against him and may prepare his defence; otherwise the indictment would be defective.[387] In this regard, although the Prosecution may rely additionally, or alternatively, in one or more legal theories of criminal liability of the defendant, this can only be done on condition that it is done clearly, early enough and, in any event, allowing enough time to enable the accused to know what exactly he is accused of and to enable him to prepare his defence accordingly'.[388]

The material character of a particular fact depends on the nature of the Prosecution's case (it cannot be determined in abstract).[389] The nature of the defendant's alleged criminal conduct constitutes a 'decisive factor' in determining the degree of specificity required from the Prosecution.[390] For instance, if the Prosecution claims that the defendant personally committed the criminal acts, the Prosecution will have to plead in detail the identity of the victims, the time and place of the events and the means by which the acts were committed. However, in cases where the scale of the alleged crimes is massive (which usually corresponds to cases against senior political and military leaders who did not physically commit the crimes), requiring a high degree of specificity in relation to the identity of the victims and the dates of the commission of the crimes may be impracticable.[391] This is the situation if the Prosecution claims that a defendant planned and set into motion a campaign of unlawful attacks on civilians that took place over a

---

[385] *Semanza Case* Appeals Judgment (*Ibid*), at para. 357; *Ntakirutimana Case* Appeals Judgment (*Ibid*), at para 473; *Blaskic Case* Appeals Judgment (*Ibid*), at para 228; *Krnojelac Case* Appeals Judgment (Above n 11), at para 138; *Kvocka Case* Appeals Judgment (*Ibid*), at para 29; *Simic Case* Appeals Judgment (*Ibid*), at para 21.

[386] *Simic Case* Appeals Judgment (*Ibid*), at para 21; *Kvocka Case* Appeals Judgment (*Ibid*), at para 41.

[387] *Kvocka Case* Appeals Judgment (*Ibid*), at paras 29, 41; *Simic Case* Appeals Judgment (*Ibid*), at para 21; *Furundzija Case* Appeals Judgment (Above n 28), at para 147; *Kupreskic Case* Appeals Judgment (Above n 178), at para 165; *Krnojelac Case* Appeals Judgment (Above n 11), at para 131; *Kordic Case* Appeals Judgment (Above n 301), at para 142; *Prosecutor v Ruzindana* (Appeals Chamber Judgment) ICTR-95-1-A (1 Jun 2001) para 303.

[388] *Krnojelac Case* Appeals Judgment (*Ibid*), at para 115. As the ICTY Appeals Chamber has explained: 'It would contravene the rights of the defence if the Trial Chamber, seized of a valid shifting indictment where the Prosecution has not stated the theory or theories it considered most likely to establish the accused's responsibility within accepted time-limits, chose a theory not expressly pleaded by the Prosecution'. See *Krnojelac Case* Appeals Judgment (*Ibid*), at para 117.

[389] *Kvocka Case* Appeals Judgment (Above n 11), at para 28.

[390] See *Kupreskic Case* Appeals Judgment (Above n 178), at paras 89–114; *Krnojelac Case* Appeals Judgment (Above n 11), at para 132; *Kvocka Case* Appeals Judgment (*Ibid*), at para 28. Failure to do so results in the indictment being unacceptably vague since such an omission would impact negatively on the ability of the accused to prepare his defence. See *Kupreskic Case* Appeals Judgment (Above n 178), at para 98.

[391] See *Kupreskic Case* Appeals Judgment (*Ibid*), at para 92; *Krnojelac Case* Appeals Judgment (*Ibid*), at para 132; *Kvocka Case* Appeals Judgment (*Ibid*), at para 28.

prolonged period of time and resulted in a large number of killings and forcible transfers. Nevertheless, as this information is valuable for the preparation of the Defence's case, the Prosecution should provide it whenever it is in its possession.[392]

In relation to the specificity with which the notion of co-perpetration based on joint criminal enterprise must be pleaded in an indictment, the ICTY Appeals Chamber has recently held in the *Simic* case that:

> When the Prosecution charges the 'commission' of one of the crimes under the Statute within the meaning of Article 7(1), it must specify whether the said term is to be understood as meaning physical commission by the accused or participation in a joint criminal enterprise, or both. It is not enough for the generic language of an indictment to 'encompass' the possibility that joint criminal enterprise is being charged. The Appeals Chamber reiterates that joint criminal enterprise must be specifically pleaded in an indictment. [. . .] Also, if the Prosecution relies on this specific mode of liability, it must plead the following material facts: the nature and purpose of the enterprise, the period over which the enterprise is said to have existed, the identity of the participants in the enterprise, and the nature of the accused's participation in the enterprise. In order for an accused charged with joint criminal enterprise to fully understand the acts he is allegedly responsible for, the indictment should also clearly indicate which form of joint criminal enterprise is being alleged. The Appeals Chamber considers that failure to specifically plead joint criminal enterprise in the indictment in a case where the Prosecution intends to rely on this mode of liability will result in a defective indictment.[393]

Hence, the Prosecution must specify in the indictment whether the core crimes of the joint criminal enterprise include all crimes for which the defendant is charged or only some of them. In this last situation, the Prosecution must explain under which form of liability the defendant is allegedly liable for those crimes

---

[392] See *Kupreskic Case* Appeals Judgment (*Ibid*), at para 92; *Krnojelac Case* Appeals Judgment (*Ibid*), at para 132; *Kvocka Case* Appeals Judgment (*Ibid*), at para 28.

[393] *Simic Case* Appeals Judgment (Above n 185), at para 22. See also *Gacumbitsi v Prosecutor* (Appeals Chamber Judgment) ICTR-2001-64-A (7 Jul 2006) paras 163, 167 [hereinafter *Gacumbitsi Case* Appeals Judgment]; *Prosecutor v Ntagerura* (Appeals Chamber Judgment) ICTR-99-46-A (7 Jul 2006) paras 24, 28 [hereinafter *Ntagerura Case* Appeals Judgment]; *Krnojelac Case* Appeals Judgment (*Ibid*), at paras 116–17; *Kvocka Case* Appeals Judgment (*Ibid*), at paras 28, 42; See also *Stakic Case* Appeals Judgment (Above n 11), at para 66; *Brdanin Case*, Decision on Form of Further Amended Indictment (Above n 384), at para 33. It is important to highlight that the *Tadic Case* Appeals Judgment (Above n 11), at paras 230–32, found the defendant liable under the extended form of joint criminal enterprise for the killing of five men from the village of Jaskici, even though neither this form of joint criminal enterprise nor any other was explicitly pleaded in the indictment. Indeed, *Prosecutor v Tadic* (Second Amended Indictment) ICTY-94-1-I (14 Dec 1995) paras 4–12 makes only a general reference to art 7(1) ICTYS without specifying any mode of liability provided for in that provision. In the *Furundzija* case, although the indictment did not refer to co-perpetration based on joint criminal enterprise nor to any other theory of co-perpetration as to the charge of torture, the Prosecution pleaded at trial that liability pursuant to art 7(1) of the Statute can be established by showing that the defendant had the intent to participate in the crime, that his acts contributed to its commission and that such contribution did not necessarily require participation in the physical commission of the crime. On this basis, the Trial Chamber convicted the defendant as a co-perpetrator for his participation in a joint criminal enterprise to commit acts of torture. In neither of these two cases the Defence raised the issue of lack of notice before the Trial Chamber or the Appeals Chamber.

falling outside of the common criminal plan.[394] As a result, if the Prosecution intends to rely on the extended form of joint criminal enterprise, it must indicate it explicitly in the indictment, and it must also specify what are the foreseeable crimes that resulted from the implementation of the common criminal plan.[395]

An indictment which fails to plead with sufficient detail the essential elements of the Prosecution case, including the material facts underlying any joint criminal enterprise in which the defendant is alleged to have participated, has a material defect.[396]

A defective indictment can be cured in some instances if the Defence is compensated by the Prosecution for the failure of the indictment to give proper notice of the charges.[397] This requires providing the defendant with timely, clear and consistent information that resolves any ambiguity or clarifies the vagueness of the indictment.[398] This can be done by amending the indictment or by requesting clarification from the Prosecution in a Pre-Trial Conference.[399] It can also be done through the Prosecution Pre-Trial Brief[400] or even through the Prosecution's opening statement.[401] In this regard, the ICTY Appeals Judgment has held in the *Simic* case that in considering whether the defendant has been given proper notice:

[394] *Gacumbitsi Case* Appeals Judgment (*Ibid*), at paras 163, 167; *Ntagerura* Case Appeals Judgment (*Ibid*), at paras 24, 28; *Krnojelac Case* Appeals Judgment (*Ibid*), at paras 116–17; *Kvocka Case* Appeals Judgment (*Ibid*), at paras 28,42; *Stakic Case* Appeals Judgment (*Ibid*), at para 66; *Simic Case* Appeals Judgment (*Ibid*), at para 22; *Brdanin Case*, Decision on Form of Further Amended Indictment (Above n 384), at para 33.

[395] *Ibid.*

[396] *Ibid.* See also *Kupreskic Case* Appeals Judgment (Above n 178), at para 114; *Krnojelac Case* Appeals Judgment (*Ibid*), at paras 116–17, 132.

[397] *Gacumbitsi Case* Appeals Judgment (*Ibid*), at para 163; *Ntagerura Case* Appeals Judgment (*Ibid*), at para 29; *Kupreskic Case* Appeals Judgment (*Ibid*), at para 114; *Kordic Case* Appeals Judgment (Above n 301), at para 142; *Prosecutor v Mladen Naletilic and Vinko Martinovic* (Appeals Chamber Judgment) ICTY-98-34-A (3 May 2006) para 26 [hereinafter *Tuta and Stela* Appeals Judgment]; *Kvocka Case* Appeals Judgment (*Ibid*), at para 34; *Simic Case* Appeals Judgment (*Ibid*), at para 24.

[398] *Ibid.*

[399] For instance, the indictment against Mitar Vasiljevic stated that the defendant 'acted in concert' with Milan Lukic, Sredoje Lukic and other unknown individuals with respect to acts of extermination, persecution, murder, inhumane acts and violence to life and person. It was at the Pre-Trial Conference on 20 July 2001 where the Trial Chamber, in order to avoid any confusion, asked the Prosecution what it meant by the expression 'in concert'. The Prosecution pointed out that such expression meant that the defendant did not act alone and did not commit the crimes by himself. Furthermore, at this Pre-Trial Conference, the Prosecution acknowledged that it was relying on a basic form of joint criminal enterprise. Moreover, when asked, the Prosecution expressly denied any intention to rely on an extended form of joint criminal enterprise. As a result, the Trial and Appeal Chambers only took into consideration the basic form of joint criminal enterprise. See *Vasiljevic Case* Trial Judgment (Above n 28), at para 63; *Vasiljevic Case* Appeals Judgment (Above n 11), at para 106.

[400] As the Appeals Chamber in the *Krnojelac Case* Appeals Judgment (Above n 11), at para 138, has held:'It is preferable for an indictment alleging the accused's responsibility as a participant in a joint criminal enterprise also to refer to the particular form (basic or extended) of joint criminal enterprise envisaged. However, this does not, in principle, prevent the Prosecution from pleading elsewhere than in the indictment—for instance in a pre-trial brief—the legal theory which it believes best demonstrates that the crime or crimes alleged are imputable to the accused in law in the light of the facts alleged. This option is, however, limited by the need to guarantee the accused a fair trial'. See also *Kordic Case* Appeals Judgment (Above n 301), at para 142.

[401] *Kupreskic Case* Appeals Judgment (Above n 178), at paras 117–18; *Blaskic Case* Appeals Judgment (Above n 15), at para 242; *Kordic Case* Appeals Judgment (*Ibid*), at para 169; *Kvocka Case* Appeals Judgment (Above n 11), at paras 44–7, 50; *Simic Case* Appeals Judgment (Above n 185), at para 24.

[T]he timing of the communications, the importance of the information to the ability of the accused to prepare his defence and the impact of the newly disclosed material facts on the Prosecution's case are relevant. The Appeals Chamber recalls that the mere service of witness statements or of potential exhibits by the Prosecution pursuant to the disclosure requirements of the Rules does not, however, suffice to inform the Defence of material facts that the Prosecution intends to prove at trial. Finally, an accused's submissions at trial, for example the motion for judgement of acquittal, the final trial brief or the closing arguments, may in some instances assist in assessing to what extent the accused was put on notice of the Prosecution's case and was able to respond to the Prosecution's allegations.[402]

There are some cases in which other measures can solve the problem, such as excluding certain evidence for not being within the scope of the indictment,[403] or even granting an adjournment where evidence at trial turns out differently than expected.[404]

Nevertheless, it is important to highlight that, given the factual and legal complexities normally associated with the crimes and the forms of liability within the jurisdiction of the *Ad hoc* Tribunals, curing a defective indictment is only possible in 'a limited category of cases'.[405] When a defective indictment cannot be cured, it causes a prejudice to the defendant, violates his right to a fair trial and warrants the reversal of a conviction, unless it is shown that the defect was harmless because the ability of the defendant to prepare his defence was not materially impaired.[406] In

---

[402] *Simic Case* Appeals Judgment (*Ibid*), at para 24. See also *Ntakirutimana Case* Appeals Judgment (Above n 384), at para 27; *Kupreskic Case* Appeals Judgment (*Ibid*), at paras 119–21; *Kordic Case* Appeals Judgment (*Ibid*), at para 148; *Tuta and Stela* Appeals Judgment (Above n 397), at para 27; *Kvocka Case* Appeals Judgment (*Ibid*), at paras 52–3; *Brdanin Case,* Decision on Form of Further Amended Indictment (Above n 384), at para 62.

[403] *Kupreskic Case* Appeals Judgment (*Ibid*), at para 92.

[404] *Ibid.*

[405] For instance, in the *Krnojelac* case, the ICTY Appeals Chamber confirmed the decision of the Trial Chamber not to apply the extended form of joint criminal enterprise because (i) in the its Decision on the Form of the Second Amended Indictment the Trial Chamber had interpreted that the expressions 'acted pursuant to a joint criminal enterprise with guards and soldiers' (in relation to the crime of persecution) and 'in concert with others' (in relation to the acts of torture, beatings and enslavement) corresponded to the basic form of joint criminal enterprise; and (ii) the Prosecution had not sought, after such decision and before filing its Pre-Trial Brief, to amend the indictment to make clear that it also intended to rely on the extensive form of joint criminal enterprise. The ICTY Appeals Chamber confirmed the approach of the Trial Chamber because the Prosecution's approach had created ambiguity on whether or not the extended form of joint criminal enterprise was being relied on. And this, despite the fact that: (i) the Prosecution relied on the extended form of joint criminal enterprise in its Pre-Trial Brief and in its opening statement, (ii) the Defence did not claim at trial that the failure of the indictment to make reference to an extended form of joint criminal enterprise had impaired his defence, and (iii) the Defence, in its Final Trial Brief, explicitly addressed all forms of joint criminal enterprise. See *Krnojelac Case* Trial Judgment (Above n 14), at paras 84–6; *Krnojelac Case* Appeals Judgment (Above n 11), at paras 135–44. See also *Ntakirutimana Case* Appeals Judgment (Above n 384), at para 472; *Kupreskic Case* Appeals Judgment (*Ibid*), at para 114; *Simic Case* Appeals Judgment (Above n 185), at para 23.

[406] *Ntagerura Case* Appeals Judgment (Above n 393), at para 30; *Ntakirutimana Case* Appeals Judgment (*Ibid*), at para 58; *Kupreskic Case* Appeals Judgment (*Ibid*), at paras 114, 122; *Krnojelac Case* Appeals Judgment (*Ibid*), at para 132; *Kordic Case* Appeals Judgment (Above n 301), at para 142; *Kvocka Case* Appeals Judgment (Above n 11), at para 35; *Simic Case* Appeals Judgment (*Ibid*), at para 24.

this situation, the question arises as to which party has the burden of proof: the Prosecution to show that the defect was harmless or the Defence to show that the defendant's ability to prepare his defence was materially impaired by the defect. As the ICTR Appeals Chamber has explained in the *Niyitegeka* case:

> In general, 'a party should not be permitted to refrain from making an objection to a matter which was apparent during the course of the trial, and to raise it only in the event of an adverse finding against that party'. Failure to object in the Trial Chamber will usually result in the Appeals Chamber disregarding the argument on grounds of waiver. [. . .] The importance of the accused's right to be informed of the charges against him under Article 20(4)(a) of the Statute and the possibility of serious prejudice to the accused if material facts crucial to the Prosecution are communicated for the first time at trial suggest that the waiver doctrine should not entirely foreclose an accused from raising an indictment defect for the first time on appeal. Where, in such circumstances, there is a resulting defect in the indictment, an accused person who fails to object at trial has the burden of proving on appeal that his ability to prepare his case was materially impaired. Where, however, the accused person objected at trial, the burden is on the Prosecution to prove on appeal that the accused's ability to prepare his defence was not materially impaired. All of this is of course subject to the inherent jurisdiction of the Appeals Chamber to do justice in the case.[407]

B Application of the Principles on Pleading Co-perpetration Based on Joint Criminal Enterprise by the Case Law of the *Ad hoc* Tribunals

Before concluding this section, it is important to show how the ICTR and ICTY Appeals Chambers have applied the above-mentioned principles on pleading co-perpetration based on joint criminal enterprise to different factual scenarios. The cases discussed have been divided into four groups: (i) those cases in which the indictment was found not to be defective; (ii) those cases in which the pleading was found to be defective but the material defect was subsequently cured; (iii) those cases in which the defective indictment was not subsequently cured; and (iv) the *Krnojelac* case, in which the ICTY Appeals Chamber provided for detailed guidance on how to plead co-perpetration based on joint criminal enterprise.

---

[407] *Niyitegeka v Prosecutor* (Appeals Chamber Judgment) ICTR-96-14-A (9 Jul 2004) paras 199–200 quoted by the *Gacumbitsi Case* Appeals Judgment (Above n 393), at para 52. See also *Prosecutor v Kayishema* (Appeals Chamber Judgment) ICTR-95-1-A (1 Jun 2001) para 91; *Ntagerura Case* Appeals Judgment (*Ibid*), at para 31; *Simic Case* Appeals Judgment (*Ibid*), at para 25. The question of waiver has also been dealt with from the perspective of the Prosecution. For instance, in the *Ntakirutimana* case, the ICTR Appeals Chamber, after noticing that the Prosecution Closing Brief only alleged that Elizaphah Ntakirutimana was an aidor and abettor to the Mugonero massacre, concluded that 'the Prosecution has waived the right to allege on appeal that the Trial Chamber erred in omitting to consider joint criminal enterprise liability when determining his criminal responsibility with respect to the events under the Mugonero Indictment'. See *Ntakirutimana Case* Appeals Judgment (*Ibid*), at para 477.

i Cases of Non-Defective Indictment

a The Stakic Case

In the *Stakic* case, the ICTY Appeals Chamber found that the Fourth Amended Indictment met the requirement that the specific form of joint criminal enterprise on which the Prosecution intends to rely be explicitly pleaded.[408] According to the ICTY Appeals Chamber, the Indictment's allegations made it clear that the Prosecution intended to rely on the basic and extended forms of joint criminal enterprise.[409] On the one hand, paragraph 26 of the Fourth Amended Indictment plainly alleged the basic form of joint criminal enterprise by stating that the purpose of the joint criminal enterprise was to cause a campaign of persecutions that encompassed the crimes alleged in counts 1 through 8 of the Indictment.[410] On the other hand, paragraphs 28 and 29 of the Fourth Amended Indictment pleaded the extended form of joint criminal enterprise by using the following language, which is similar to the language normally used to describe its elements:[411]

> Alternatively, the accused is individually responsible for the crimes enumerated in Counts 1 to 8 on the basis that these crimes were natural and foreseeable consequences of the execution of the common purpose of the joint criminal enterprise and Milomir STAKIC was aware that these crimes were the possible consequence of the execution of the joint criminal enterprise. Despite his awareness of the possible consequences, Milomir STAKIC knowingly and wilfully participated in the joint criminal enterprise. On this basis, he bears individual criminal responsibility for these crimes under Article 7(1) in addition to his responsibility under the same article for having planned, instigated, ordered or otherwise aided and abetted in the planning, preparation, or execution of these crimes.[412]

b The Simba Case

In the *Simba* case before the ICTR, the Trial Chamber dismissed the Defence's claim that the Prosecution had failed to plead the necessary material facts in relation to a joint criminal enterprise theory, that is to say, the participants, the

---

[408] *Stakic Case* Appeals Judgment (Above n 11), at para 66.

[409] *Ibid.*

[410] *Ibid. Prosecutor v Stakic* (Fourth Amended Indictment) ICTY-97-24-PT (10 Apr 2002) para 26 [hereinafter *Stakic Case* Fourth Amended Indictment] alleged as follows: 'Milomir STAKIC participated in the joint criminal enterprise, in his roles as set out in paragraph 22 above. The purpose of the joint criminal enterprise was the permanent forcible removal of Bosnian Muslim and Bosnian Croat inhabitants from the territory of the planned Serbian state, including a campaign of persecutions through the commission of the crimes alleged in Counts 1 to 8 of the Indictment. The accused Milomir STAKIC, and the other members of the joint criminal enterprise, each shared the state of mind required for the commission of each of these offences, more particularly, each, was aware that his or her conduct occurred in the context of an armed conflict and was part of a widespread or systematic attack directed against a civilian population.'

[411] *Stakic Case* Appeals Judgment (Above n 11), at para 66.

[412] *Stakic Case* Fourth Amended Indictment (Above n 410), at paras 28–9.

common criminal purpose, the timeframe and the nature of the defendant's con-tribution.[413] According to the Trial Chamber, the Indictment, together with the Prosecution's Pre-Trial Brief, made it clear: (i) that the common criminal purpose was to kill Tutsi at Kibeho Parish, Murambi Technical School, Cyanika Parish, and Kaduha Parish;[414] (ii) that the time frame of the joint criminal enterprise was from 6 April until 17 July 1994;[415] and (iii) that the defendant's contribution was to plan the massacres, to distribute weapons and to order and instigate the commission of the massacres.[416] Finally, in relation to the participants, the Trial Chamber, after noticing that the indictment named certain non-physical perpetrators with whom Simba planned and prepared the attacks (such as Prefect Bucyibaruta, Captain Sebuhura, and Bourgmestre Semakwavu),[417] held:

> In most cases, the participants who physically perpetrated the crimes are identified in each section of the Indictment dealing with a particular massacre site by broad category, such as *Interahamwe* or gendarmes, and then further identified with geographic and temporal details. In the context of this case and given the nature of the attacks, the Chamber is not satisfied that the Prosecution could have provided more specific identi-fication. The Indictment alleges Simba's interactions with the attackers in such a way as to reflect concerted action. In addition, paragraph 58 of the Indictment affirms that the attackers are participants when it pleads the *mens rea* for the basic form of joint criminal enterprise by stating that Simba shared the same intent to commit the pleaded crimes with 'all other individuals involved in the crimes perpetrated'. Moreover, the Prosecution Pre-Trial Brief and opening statement also confirm that the named individ-uals as well as the attackers should be considered as participants in the joint criminal enterprise.[418]

ii Cases of Defective Indictments Subsequently Cured

a The Kordic Case

In the *Kordic* case, the Prosecution contended that the First Amended Indictment pleaded with sufficient detail the defendant's criminal liability for his participation in a joint criminal enterprise to persecute the Bosnian Muslim population of Central Bosnia in 1992 and 1993. According to the Prosecution, the First Amended Indictment made clear (i) that the defendant, together with other per-sons holding positions of authority, designed the common criminal plan; (ii) that the defendant's contribution consisted in planning, preparing, instigating and ordering its implementation; and (iii) that, as an 'overall architect' of the plan, he

---

[413] *Prosecutor v Simba* (Judgment) ICTR-01-76-T (13 Dec 2005) paras 391–6 [hereinafter *Simba Case* Trial Judgment].

[414] *Ibid* at para 394.

[415] *Ibid* at para 395.

[416] *Ibid* at paras 395–6.

[417] See *Prosecutor v Simba* (Amended Indictment) ICTR-01-76-1 (10 May 2004) para 14. See also *Simbo Case* Trial Judgment (*Ibid*), at para 402.

[418] *Simba Case* Trial Judgment (*Ibid*), at para 393.

shared the intent to commit the crimes encompassed by the common criminal plan and intended to contribute to its implementation.[419]

The ICTY Appeals Chamber disagreed with the Prosecution and found that the indictment did not explicitly plead the participation of Dario Kordic in a joint criminal enterprise to persecute the Bosnian Muslim population of Central Bosnia in 1992 and 1993[420] because it only alleged that:

> Dario Kordic was a definite integral and important figure in the whole campaign, and had power, authority and responsibility to direct, control and shape its policies and execution, and to prevent, limit or punish crimes, violations or abuses which occurred or were carried out in the campaign. He publicly advocated the campaign's goals and encouraged and instigated the ethnic hatred, strife and distrust which served its ends.[421]

As a result, the question arouse as to:

> [W]hether the ambiguity resulting from unspecific allegations as to Kordic's liability was clarified by the Prosecution in its post-Indictment communications, and, if so, whether this gave Kordic sufficient and timely notice about it.[422]

The ICTY Appeals Chamber found that the Prosecution Pre-Trial Brief explicitly pleaded the alleged criminal liability of Kordic as a co-perpetrator for his participation in a joint criminal enterprise.[423] Furthermore, it also found that the Prosecution Pre-Trial Brief described in detail the manner in which the defendant allegedly participated in such an enterprise by planning, ordering and instigating the persecution of the Bosnian Muslim population of Central Bosnia.[424] Hence, any material defect relating to modes of liability in the Indictment was cured.

Moreover, in the same case, the ICTY Appeals Chamber found that the meeting between Bosnian Croat civilians and HVO military leaders on 15 April 1993 was a key part of the Prosecution's case against Dario Kordic for the crimes committed in the Lasva Valley on or around 16 April 1993, and that it therefore constituted a material fact that should have been pleaded in the First Amended Indictment.[425] However, according to the Appeals Chamber, the defendant was not prejudiced by this omission because he was able to effectively contest the fact in question by inter alia calling three witnesses on the matter.[426]

---

[419] *Kordic Case* Appeals Judgment (Above n 301), at para 138.
[420] *Ibid* at para 137.
[421] *Kordic Case* First Amended Indictment (Above n 303), at para 25.
[422] *Kordic Case* Appeals Judgment (Above n 301), at para 139.
[423] *Ibid* at para 140.
[424] *Ibid.*
[425] *Ibid* at paras 144, 147.
[426] *Ibid* at para 148.

b The Kvocka Case

In the *Kvocka* case, the Trial Chamber convicted the defendants as co-perpetrators of the crimes charged in the indictment for their participation in a systemic form of joint criminal enterprise at the Omarska detention camp. On appeal, the ICTY Appeals Chamber found the indictment to be defective because it failed to make any specific mention to the very notion of joint criminal enterprise, to the form of joint criminal enterprise on which the Prosecution intended to rely and to the material facts of the enterprise, such as the common criminal plan or purpose, the identities of the participants and the nature of the contribution of the accused.[427] Nevertheless, the ICTY Appeals Chamber considered that the defective indictment was cured because the Prosecution provided the defendants with timely, clear and consistent information on the fact that it was relying on a joint criminal enterprise theory, on the form of enterprise on which it was relying and on the material facts underlying such an enterprise.[428] The ICTY Appeals Chamber came to this conclusion after noting that:

(i) the Prosecution Pre-Trial Brief of 9 April 1999 mentioned the common purpose doctrine in broad terms, although it does not specify that the Prosecution intended to rely on it;[429]

(ii) the Updated Version of Prosecution Pre-Trial Brief of 14 February 2000 specifically pleaded the requisite elements of joint criminal enterprise, setting out the alleged common purpose, the plurality of participants, and the nature of the participation in the enterprise of each defendant. Furthermore, it described the basic, systemic and extended forms of joint criminal enterprise, and indicated which form of enterprise was alleged in relation to each defendant;[430]

(iii) in its opening statement of 28 February 2000, the Prosecution focused on joint criminal enterprise;[431]

(iv) in its further opening statement of 2 May 2000, the Prosecution addressed defendant Prcac's participation in a joint criminal enterprise together with the other co-defendants;[432]

---

[427] *Kvocka Case* Appeals Judgment (Above n 11), at para 42. The final version of *Prosecutor v Kvocka et al* (Amended Indictment) ICTY-98-30/1 (26 Oct 2000) para 16 alleged that: 'Miroslav KVOCKA, Dragoljub PRCAC, Milojica KOS, Mladjo RADIC and Zoran ZIGIC are individually responsible for the crimes charged against them in this indictment, pursuant to Article 7(1) of the Statute of the Tribunal. As defined by Article 7(1), individual criminal responsibility includes planning, instigating, ordering, committing or otherwise aiding and abetting in the planning, preparation or execution of any acts or omissions set forth below. The term "participation", as used in the Counts hereunder is intended to incorporate any and all forms of individual criminal responsibility as set forth in Article 7(1)'.

[428] *Kvocka Case* Appeals Judgment (*Ibid*), at para 43.

[429] *Ibid* at para 44.

[430] *Ibid* at para 45.

[431] *Ibid* at para 46.

[432] *Ibid* at para 47.

(v)   in the oral argument held on 13 October 2000 (at the time of the Prosecution's case at trial), the Prosecution reiterated its focus on joint criminal enterprise;[433]

(vi) in the Trial Chamber Decision on Defence Motions for Acquittal of 15 December 2000, the Trial Chamber explicitly considered whether a conviction could be entered pursuant to the notion of joint criminal enterprise;[434]

(vii) the submissions of the defendants at trial further demonstrated that they were on notice of the Prosecution's reliance on joint criminal enterprise during the trial proceedings;[435] and

(viii) in their final trial briefs and closing arguments, the defendants advanced legal and factual arguments relating to joint criminal enterprise;[436]

iii Cases of Non-Cured Defective Indictments

a The Ntakirutimana Case

In the *Ntakirutimana* case, the ICTR Appeals Chamber confirmed the approach of the Trial Chamber not to apply the notion of co-perpetration based on joint criminal enterprise because the Indictments and the Prosecution Pre-Trial Brief were too ambiguous to put the defendants on notice that they were charged with participation in a basic form of joint criminal enterprise to commit genocide against Tutsis in the Mugonero and Bisesero massacres.[437] The ICTR Appeals Chamber reached this conclusion in light of the following findings:

(i)   the Indictments did not contain any explicit reference to the expressions joint criminal enterprise, common plan or common purpose, or 'even to the fact that it intended to charge the Accused for co-perpetration of genocide, *i.e.*, not only for physically committing genocide but also for assisting those who physically committed it while sharing the same genocidal intent';[438]

(ii) as the Indictments charged the defendants for planning genocide, instigating genocide, aiding and abetting genocide, complicity in genocide and conspiracy to commit genocide,[439] it was not obvious that the alleged acts of participation of the defendants in the Mugonero and Bisesero massacres were also intended to be material facts of a joint criminal enterprise allegation;[440]

---

[433] *Kvocka Case* Appeals Judgment (*Ibid*), at para 48.

[434] *Ibid* at para 49.

[435] *Ibid* at para 52.

[436] *Ibid* at para 53.

[437] *Ntakirutimana Case* Appeals Judgment (Above n 384), at paras 448, 483–4.

[438] *Ibid* at para 479.

[439] In relation to Gerard Ntakirutimana: separating Tutsi patients from non-Tutsi patients, procuring of arms for the attacks, searching Tutsi survivors and conveying attackers. With regard to Elizaphan Ntakirutimana: refusing to protect Tutsis after receiving Pastor Sehibe's letter, searching for Tutsi survivors, conveying attackers to the killing sites, being present at killing sites, pursuing survivors and inciting attackers to perpetrate killings. *Ntakirutimana Case* Appeals Judgment (*Ibid*), at para 479.

[440] *Ibid* at para 481.

(iii) the Prosecution Pre-Trial Brief contained one reference to joint criminal enterprise, but it appeared in the section entitled 'Requisite *Mens Rea* under Article 6(1)', and it was merely used as an example to illustrate the submission that all modes of liability under article 6(1) ICTRS can be carried out with direct intent or with *dolus eventualis*;[441] and

(iv) the Prosecution Closing Brief merely repeated the explicit reference to joint criminal enterprise contained in the Prosecution Pre-Trial Brief.[442]

b *The* Kupreskic *Case*

In the *Kupreskic* case, the ICTY Appeals Chamber reversed a conviction for participation in a basic form of joint criminal enterprise due to material defects in the manner in which the Prosecution pleaded it. In this case, Zoran and Mirjan Kupreskic were convicted by the Trial Chamber as co-perpetrators for their participation in a common plan implemented by the HVO, from October 1992 until April 1993, to ethnically cleanse the village of Ahmici and its environs through the organised detention and expulsion of Bosnian Muslim civilians, their deliberate and systematic killing and the destruction of their homes and property.[443]

Nevertheless, according to the ICTY Appeals Chamber, the First Amended Indictment contained no detailed information about the manner in which Zoran and Mirjan Kupreskic had participated in the implementation of the common criminal plan.[444] This was particularly grave in light of two circumstances. First, the case against them prior to 16 April 1993 was exclusively based on the fact that they had been involved with the HVO (mainly by being members of the village guard, which per se could not be considered an unlawful act).[445] Second, the main case against them was 'dramatically' transformed because the First Amended Indictment alleged their integral involvement in the preparation, planning, organisation and implementation of the attack on Ahmici on 16 April 1993, and at trial the Prosecution limited its allegations to: (i) their presence as HVO members in Ahmici on 16 April 1993; (ii) their participation in the attack on the house of Suhret Ahmih (which was not even mentioned in the First Amended Indictment) and (iii) their participation in the attack on the house of Witness KL (which was found not proven by the Trial Chamber).[446] Under these circumstances, the allegations relating to the alleged participation of the defendants in the attack on the house of Suhret Ahmih were clearly material to the

---

[441] *Ibid* at para 479.

[442] *Ibid.*

[443] *Kupreskic Case* Trial Judgment (Above n 178), at paras 480, 490; *Kupreskic Case* Appeals Judgment (Above n 178), at paras 77, 243.

[444] *Kupreskic Case* Appeals Judgment (*Ibid*), at para 95.

[445] *Ibid* at para 243.

[446] *Ibid* at paras 93, 99.

Prosecution's case because the conviction on the count of persecution was critically dependent upon it.[447]

The ICTY Appeals Chamber also found that the information given to the defendants in the Prosecution Pre-Trial Brief did not cure this material defect because it only contained a short section stating that the defendants 'joined in the attack' on several houses 'participating in at least a half a dozen murders', without mentioning which particular houses they attacked or which murders they participated in.[448] Furthermore, the Prosecution's opening statement made no reference whatsoever to the attack on Suhret Ahmic's house or to Zoran and Mirjan Kupreskic's involvement in that event. [449] It was only at trial that the Prosecution informed the defendants that the allegation pertaining to the attack on Suhret Ahmic's house was relevant to the count of persecution.[450] Moreover, even the day before the last day of the trial, there was an exchange between the Trial Chamber and the parties due to the uncertainty as to whether the Trial Chamber was going to consider the evidence relating to this attack as relevant to the count of persecution.[451] As a result, the ICTY Appeals Chamber concluded that the defendants were not informed with sufficient detail of the charges against them so as to cure the defects in the First Amended Indictment, which infringed upon their ability to prepare their defence.[452]

As to the proper remedy, the ICTY Appeals Chamber decided to reverse the conviction and not to remand the matter for retrial due to the additional problems found in the evidence supporting several factual findings of the Trial Chamber. Nevertheless, it did not foreclose the door to have the matter remanded for retrial in other circumstances. As the ICTY Appeals Chamber explained:

> Having upheld the objections of Zoran and Mirjan Kupreskic based on the vagueness of the Amended Indictment, the question arises as to whether the appropriate remedy is to remand the matter for retrial. The Appeals Chamber might understandably be reluctant to allow a defect in the form of the indictment to determine finally the outcome of a case in which there is strong evidence pointing towards the guilt of the accused. However, additionally, Zoran and Mirjan Kupreskic have raised a number of objections regarding the factual findings made by the Trial Chamber. If accepted, these complaints would

---

[447] *Kupreskic Case* Appeals Judgment (*Ibid*), at para 99. The Prosecution explained, prior to and during trial, that evidence relating to the attack on Suhret Ahmic's house (Witness H) came into its possession late in the day and that it was anxious not to delay the commencement of the trial by amending again the already once amended indictment. However, the ICTY Appeals Chamber held that 'the goal of expediency should never be allowed to over-ride the fundamental rights of the accused to a fair trial. If expediency was a priority for the Prosecution, it should have proceeded to trial without the evidence of Witness H'. See *Kupreskic Case* Appeals Judgment (*Ibid*), at para 100.

[448] *Ibid* at para 117.

[449] *Ibid* at para 118.

[450] *Ibid* at para 119.

[451] *Ibid.*

[452] *Ibid* at para 121. The Appeals Chamber also took into consideration the fact that the alleged participation of the defendants on the attack to Suhret Ahmic house was solely based on the evidence of witness H, which was disclosed to the Defence only a week prior to the commencement of the trial and pursuant to an order of the Trial Chamber.

fatally undermine the evidentiary basis for the convictions of these two Defendants, rendering the question of a retrial moot.[453]

c The Simic Case

In the *Simic* case, the defendant Blagoje Simic was convicted as a co-perpetrator for his participation in a basic form of joint criminal enterprise. However, the ICTY Appeals Chamber reversed this conviction (and entered a conviction for aiding and abetting) because it found a material defect in the pleading by the Prosecution of the joint criminal enterprise theory, which had not been cured and had materially impaired the defendant's ability to prepare his defence at trial.

The ICTY Appeals Chamber started its analysis by highlighting that, although the expression 'joint criminal enterprise' was not contained in any of the various versions of the indictment against Blagoje Simic, this did not in and of itself make the indictment defective because the question is not whether a particular expression has been used but whether the defendants have been 'meaningfully' informed of the nature of the charges.[454]

When analysing the different versions of the indictment, it found that the Second Amended Indictment of 11 December 1998 used the expression 'along with various individuals' in the Background Section and the expression 'together with other[s]' in Count 1 (persecutions).[455] Nevertheless, according to the ICTY Appeals Chamber, this was 'grossly insufficient to imply an allegation of joint criminal enterprise' even if it was read together with the reference to the ethnic cleansing plan of the Serb authorities.[456]

With regard to the Third Amended Indictment, it found that it: (i) added the expressions 'common purpose' and 'in furtherance of the campaign' in the Factual Allegations Section; and (ii) replaced the expression 'together with other[s]' with the expression 'acting in concert together' in Count 1 (persecutions).[457] According to the Appeals Chamber, the addition of the expression 'common purpose' in the Factual Allegations Section did not meet the pleading requirements for a joint criminal enterprise allegation, and this, in spite of the fact that the expression 'common purpose' had been previously used interchangeably with the expression 'joint criminal enterprise'.[458] Furthermore, the use of the expression 'acting in concert together' in Count 1 (persecutions):

> [D]id not *per se* serve to dispel this vagueness, given the absence of a direct equivalence in meaning between those terms and 'joint criminal enterprise'.[459]

---

[453] *Ibid* at para 125.
[454] *Simic Case* Appeals Judgment (Above n 185), at para 32.
[455] *Ibid* at para 34.
[456] *Ibid.*
[457] *Ibid* at para 37.
[458] *Ibid* at para 39.
[459] *Ibid.*

The ICTY Appeals Chamber also found that even if the different sections of the Third Amended Indictment were read together, that was not sufficient in the instant case because the Prosecution had obtained the authorisation of the Trial Chamber to file the Third Amended Indictment after assuring the Chamber that the only change relevant to the defendant was the withdrawal of his alleged criminal liability under the doctrine of command responsibility (article 7(3) ICTYS).[460]

The Fourth Amended Indictment was filed on 9 January 2002, three months after the commencement of the trial, and included, for the first time, the expression 'acting in concert with others' in the paragraphs charging each of the defendants individually.[461] Nevertheless, the ICTY Appeals Chamber found that these amendments did not clarify that the Prosecution was relying on a joint criminal enterprise theory because (i) the Third Amended Indictment had not put the defendants on notice that they were charged under a joint criminal enterprise theory; and (ii) the Trial Chamber only authorised the Fourth Amended Indictment because it did not include any new charge.[462] Finally, the Firth Amended Indictment of 30 May 2002 only removed the charges against one of the defendants who had plead guilty during the trial.[463]

The ICTY Appeals Chamber held that the defective indictment had not been cured because:

(i)   the Prosecution Pre-Trial Brief merely stated that the indictment had put the defendants on notice that any of the theories of criminal liability under article 7(1) ICTYS could be applicable, and that, if the evidence showed that there was a 'prearranged agreement scheme or plan', they could be held liable under any of such theories.[464]

(ii)   no mention of joint criminal enterprise was made at the Pre-Trial Conference;[465]

(iii)   the Prosecution's opening statement was not 'any more specific' than its Pre-Trial Brief.[466]

(iv)   the fact that the Prosecution justified the relevance of the evidence of former co-defendant Stevan Todorovic due to the fact that the defendants 'acted in concert together, and with other Serb civilian and military officials' did not necessarily lead to the conclusion that it would be used to prove a joint criminal enterprise theory—one could have also considered that it was going to be used to prove other allegations of the indictments, such as the widespread nature of the attack against the civilian population or the international character of the armed conflict.[467]

---

[460] *Simic Case* Appeals Judgment (Above n 184), at para 39.
[461] *Ibid* at para 42.
[462] *Ibid* at paras 43–4.
[463] *Ibid* at para 45.
[464] *Ibid* at para 52.
[465] *Ibid* at para 53.
[466] *Ibid* at para 54.
[467] *Ibid* at para 55.

(v)   only at the end of the Prosecution's case, in its Rule 98bis Response, did the Prosecution give clear notice of its reliance on a joint criminal enterprise theory. Nevertheless, for the Appeals Chamber, 'this cannot be considered timely'.[468]

The ICTY Appeals Chamber also found that the defective indictment materially impaired the defendant's ability to prepare his defence because, although he could not have selected the Prosecution's witnesses, he was not afforded the possibility of conducting cross-examinations on the Prosecution's joint criminal enterprise theory.[469] As the ICTY Appeals Chamber explained:

> Had the Appellant known that he was defending himself against an allegation of participation in a joint criminal enterprise, he could have crafted his cross-examinations eliciting information from the Prosecution witnesses on this specific issue, and tried to demonstrate that the requirements for this mode of liability were not met.[470]
>
> The Appeals Chamber is of the view that recalling witnesses at that juncture—only a month and a half before the start of the Defence case—would have been impracticable for the Defence. It would also have been necessary for the Appellant to conduct new investigations and contact new witnesses to redefine an appropriate line of defence. Being given notice so late in the course of the proceedings would not, in any event, have enabled the Appellant to mount a proper defence with respect to joint criminal enterprise.[471]

iv Guidelines from the ICTY Appeals Chamber in the Krnojelac Case

In the *Krnojelac* case, the ICTY Appeals Chamber gave a number of guidelines on how to plead a joint criminal enterprise theory in light of the factual findings of the Trial Chamber. In that case, the crimes—which included unlawful imprisonment, inhumane conditions (lack of food, water, blankets or access to health care), cruel treatment (beatings), torture, forced labour, deportation and persecution—were mostly committed within the KPDom prison facility, and the defendant, Milorad Krnojelac, was the camp warden. The camp had become a system of ill-treatment which worked because the participants in such a system—that is to say the camp staff (including the camp warden) and the military personnel present at the camp—were aware that (i) the KPDom had stopped operating as an ordinary prison; and (ii) had become a system for subjecting the non-Serb civilian detainees to inhumane conditions and ill-treatment on discriminatory grounds related to their origin.[472]

According to the ICTY Appeals Chamber, the Prosecution should have pleaded a systemic form of joint criminal enterprise among the camp warden, the camp staff and the military personnel involved in the KPDom prison facility. The

---

[468] *Ibid* at para 56.
[469] *Ibid* at para 67.
[470] *Ibid*.
[471] *Ibid* at para 68.
[472] *Krnojelac Case* Appeals Judgment (Above n 11), at para 118.

common criminal purpose of the enterprise should not have included, however, all crimes committed within the KPDom. On the contrary, for the ICTY Appeals Chamber, the most appropriate approach would have been to limit the common criminal purpose of the enterprise to only those crimes, which, in light of the context and the evidence, could be considered as common to all offenders, beyond a reasonable doubt.[473] As the Appeals Chamber explained:

> The search for the common denominator in its evidence should have led the Prosecution to define the common purpose of the participants in the system in place at the KP Dom from April 1992 to August 1993 as limited only to the acts which sought to further the unlawful imprisonment at the KP Dom of the mainly Muslim, non-Serb civilians on discriminatory grounds related to their origin and to subject them to inhumane living conditions and ill-treatment in breach of their fundamental rights.[474]

In relation to those crimes which were not part of the common criminal purpose of the KPDom system, the ICTY Appeals Chamber highlighted that the Prosecution should have explicitly pleaded the theory under which the defendant incurred criminal liability.[475] For instance, the extended form of joint criminal enterprise could have been applicable with regard to those crimes committed within the KPDom, which, despite going beyond the common criminal purpose, were a natural and foreseeable consequence of its implementation (such as the killings of non-Serb detainees).[476]

According to the ICTY Appeals Chamber, there were other crimes (such as forced labour) that, despite having been committed within the KPDom, only implicated some of the participants in the systemic form of joint criminal enterprise at the KPDom, and could not be seen as a natural and foreseeable consequence of the implementation of the common criminal purpose. With regard to these crimes, the Appeals Chamber found that it would have been appropriate to plead a basic form of joint criminal enterprise with a limited number of participants and without any reference to the notion of a system of ill treatment.[477]

Finally, the ICTY Appeals Chamber underscored that there were certain crimes (such as unlawful imprisonment and deportation) which were partially committed outside the KPDom and fit into a broader criminal purpose. As the ICTY Appeals Chamber explained:

---

[473] *Krnojelac Case* Appeals Judgment (Above n 11), at para 120. For this reason, the author considers that it is not correct to affirm that the *Krnojelac Case* Appeals Judgment stands for the position that once a prison camp is found to be an institution of ill treatment, all crimes committed within its borders are assumed to be part of the common criminal purpose to persecute the inhabitants of the institution. Compare Haan (Above n 12), at 187.

[474] *Krnojelac Case* Appeals Judgment (*Ibid*), at para 118.

[475] *Ibid* at para 120.

[476] *Ibid* at para 121.

[477] *Ibid* at para 122. Pleading aiding and abetting in relation to these crimes would be appropriate if the defendant did not share the intent to commit them (for instance to impose forced labour on the non-Serb detainees at the KP Dom), but was nevertheless aware of the co-perpetrators' intent and lent them support which had a significant effect on the commission of the crimes.

It is undeniable that the decision arbitrarily to arrest the region's male, non-Serb civilians, imprison them at the KP Dom and then deport them from the region, or even physically eliminate some of them, must be linked to the criminal purpose of ethnically cleansing the Foca region pursued by some of its military and civilian authorities. This does not necessarily mean that all the co-perpetrators responsible for the living conditions and ill-treatment inflicted upon the non-Serb detainees at the KP Dom intended to take part in the ethnic cleansing of the region or were even aware of it at the time that they were physically committing the crimes and/or furthering the system in place.[478]

Concerning these crimes, the ICTY Appeals Chamber considered that, if they were part of the common criminal purpose shared by all participants in the system of ill-treatment (such as the unlawful imprisonment of non-Serb males at the KP Dom), it would have been appropriate for the Prosecution to plead these crimes as being included within the systemic form of joint criminal enterprise—although the Prosecution should have made it clear that some of the co-perpetrators (such as those civilian and military authorities who ordered the arbitrary arrests and detention of non-Serb males at the KP Dom) were persons outside the system in place at the camp.[479] If, on the contrary, these crimes were part of the common criminal purpose shared by only some of the participants in the system and some persons outside the system (such as the deportation or transfer of some of the non-Serb detainees at the KP Dom), the ICTY Appeals Chamber held that it would have been appropriate to plead a first category of joint criminal enterprise in which only those who shared the common purpose to commit such crimes would have been included, and without any reference to the notion of a system of ill-treatment.[480]

C Final Remarks

Most of the indictments filed during the early years of the *Ad hoc* Tribunals did not contain any reference to the notion of co-perpetration based on joint criminal enterprise because such a notion was not explicitly provided for in articles 7(1) ICTYS and 6(1) ICTRS and had not yet been endorsed by the case law of the *Ad hoc* Tribunals.

In several cases, by the time the defendants were transferred to the seat of the *Ad hoc* Tribunals, or by the time the trial started, the notion of co-perpetration based on joint criminal enterprise had been embraced by the case law, and the Prosecution sought to rely on it. As a result, requests to amend the indictments, pre-trial briefs, opening statements and even responses to Defence's motions for acquittal at the end of the Prosecution's case and closing briefs, were tools usually resorted to by the Prosecution to give notice to the Defence that it intended to rely on a theory of joint criminal enterprise.

---

[478] *Ibid* at para 119.

[479] *Ibid* at para 123.

[480] *Ibid*. Pleading aiding and abetting in relation to these crimes would be appropriate if the defendant did not share the intent to commit these crimes (for instance to transfer outside the Foca region of some of the non Serbs detained at the KP Dom), but he was nevertheless aware of the co-perpetrators' intent and lent them support which had a significant effect on the commission of the crimes.

Defence's counsels opposed the attempts by the Prosecution to rely on the notion of co-perpetration based on joint criminal enterprise when the Prosecution had not explicitly referred to it in the indictments.

Over time, those problems relating to the proper pleading of the notion of co-perpetration based on joint criminal enterprise reached the Appeals Chambers of the *Ad hoc* Tribunals. As a result, since 2003, those issues relating to the specificity with which the material facts of the notion of co-perpetration based on joint criminal enterprise must be pleaded, including the form of enterprise, the content of the common criminal plan, the period of time over which the enterprise existed, the identity of the participants in the enterprise, and the nature of the defendant's contribution to the enterprise, were progressively settled. In settling these matters, the ICTY and ICTR Appeals Chamber have progressively endorsed a higher degree of specificity in pleading the notion of co-perpetration based on joint criminal enterprise.

At the same time, the notion of joint criminal enterprise at the leadership level started to emerge in the case law of the *Ad hoc* Tribunals. This notion is characterised by limiting the group of participants in the enterprise to a core group of senior political and military leaders who design the common criminal plan and set it into motion. It permits the Prosecution to better identify the participants in the enterprise, to describe with more specificity the interrelation between the defendant and the other participants in the enterprise, and to single out with more clarity the specific contribution of the defendant to the implementation of the common criminal plan.

Unfortunately, these developments in the Ad hoc Tribunal's case law have, for the most part, come at a time in which the investigations at the *Ad hoc* Tribunals are concluding and the last indictments are being filed. Nevertheless, the determination of the identity of the co-perpetrators, the content of the common criminal plan, the time and place in which the plan is implemented and the defendant's contribution to its execution are all material facts of any theory of co-perpetration.

As a result, the author considers that the case law of the *Ad hoc* Tribunals on this matter will play an important role, pursuant to article 21(1)(b) RS, in the determination by the ICC of the level of specificity required for pleading forms of liability (and, in particular, the notion of co-perpetration based on joint control of the crime under article 25(3)(a) RS) in the Prosecution's charging documents.

In this regard, PTC I, in its recent 25 June 2008 decision in the *Katanga and Ngujolo* Case,[481] has held in relation to the pleading of the notion of co-perpetration based on joint control of the crime that:

---

[481] *Katanga and Ngudjolo Case* (Pre-Trial Chamber I Decision on the Three Defence's Requests Regarding the Prosecution's Amended Charging Document) ICC-01/04-01/07 (25 Jun 2008), at paras 23 to 27.

(i)   the Prosecution Amended Charging Document specifies the names of the two individuals, Germain Katanga and Mathieu Ngudjolo Chui, who, according to the Prosecution, are the only co-perpetrators of the crimes insofar as they were the only members of the common plan whose role and contribution gave them control over the commission of the crimes;

(ii)   the Prosecution is not required to identify every single member of the common plan who is not considered to be a co-perpetrator of the relevant crimes due to the lesser importance of his or her role and contribution;

(iii)   the Prosecution Amended Charging Document sufficiently specifies:

    a. the roles and contributions played by the suspects Germain Katanga and Mathieu Ngudjolo Chui in the common plan;
    b. the roles and contributions of other members of the common plan who cannot be considered as co-perpetrators due to the lesser importance of their roles and contributions;

(iv)   in a case in which the Prosecution alleges that the crimes were committed in the implementation, by two organised armed groups, of a common plan to carry out a coordinated indiscriminate attack, and in which the suspects are allegedly the highest commanders of the said groups, there is no need to specify in the Prosecution's Amended Charging Document to which of the two relevant groups the physical perpetrators of each of the relevant crimes belonged.

It is important to underline that PTC I reached these findings despite the fact that it had previously stated in the same decision that:

> The Single Judge also recalls that, as this Chamber has already held in the Decision on the confirmation of the charges in the Lubanga case, there are significant differences between the notions of co-perpetration based on joint control of the crime embraced by article 25(3)(a) of the Statute and the notion of co-perpetration based on joint criminal enterprise endorsed by the ICTY and ICTR case law.
>
> As a result, the Single Judge considers that the case law of the ad hoc Tribunals on the pleading of the different elements of the notion of coperpetration based on joint criminal enterprise in an indictment before the ad hoc Tribunals is not directly applicable to the pleading before this Court of the notion of co-perpetration based on functional control in the Prosecution's Charging Document.[482]

---

[482] *Ibid*, at paras 17 and 18.

VII Distinguishing between the Notion of Co-perpetration Based on Joint Criminal Enterprise and Aiding and Abetting as a Form of Accessorial Liability

A Objective and Subjective Elements of Aiding and Abetting as a Form of Accessorial Liability

Articles 25(3)(c) RS, 7(1) ICTYS and 6(1) ICTRS explicitly provide for aiding and abetting as a form accessorial liability. The ICTR and the ICTY Appeals Chambers have affirmed that aiding and abetting consists of actions or omissions 'specifically directed to assist, encourage, or lend moral support to the perpetration of a certain specific crime'.[483] The contribution can consist of physical, psychological, verbal or instrumental assistance or support, and must have a 'substantial effect' in the commission of the specific crime to which it is directed.[484]

---

[483] *Ntagerura Case* Appeals Judgment (Above n 393), at para 370; *Blaskic Case* Appeals Judgment (Above n 15), at paras 45–6; *Vasiljevic Case* Appeals Judgment (Above n 11), at para 102; *Simic Case* Appeals Judgment (Above n 185), at para 85; *Prosecutor v Blagojevic* (Appeals Chamber Judgment) ICTY-02-60-A (9 May 2007) para 127 [hereinafter *Blagojevic Case* Appeals Judgment].

[484] *Ibid.* See also *Bagilishema Case* Trial Judgment (Above n 290), at para 33; *Kajelijeli Case* Trial Judgment (Above n 290), at para 766; *Kamuhanda Case* Trial Judgment (Above n 290), at para 597; *Furundzija Case* Trial Judgment (Above n 29), at para 249; *Aleksovski Case* Trial Judgment (Above n 290), at para 61; *Kunarac Case* Trial Judgment (Above n 290), at para 391; *Krnojelac Case* Trial Judgment (Above n 14), at para 88; *Oric Case* Trial Judgment (Above n 290), at para 282. See also A Clapham 'On Complicity' in M Henzelin and R Roth (eds), *Le droit penal a l'epreuve de l'internationalisation* (Paris, LGDJ, 2002) 253; G Werle, *Tratado de Derecho Penal Internacional* (Valencia, Tirant lo Blanch, 2005) 222; J Rikhof, 'Complicity in International Criminal Law and Canadian Refugee Law. A Comparison' (2006) 4 *Journal of International Criminal Justice* 706 [hereinafter Rikhof]. Different approaches have been taken by national laws with regard to the level of the contribution required for an act of assistance to give rise to criminal liability. In accordance with Australian law, '[t]he most marginal act of assistance or encouragement will, it appears, amount to an act of complicity'. See Gillies (Above n 1), at 157. This author uses *Clarkson* [1971] 3 All ER 344 as an example where the defendant was convicted for mute spectatorship that amounted to an encouragement of the physical perpetrator. Furthermore, as Gillies (*Ibid*), at 157, highlights, 'the accessory's act need not be an effective one'. Similarly, in France, acts of assistance to the commission of a crime that are indirect, or even ineffective, give rise to criminal liability. See F Desportes and F Le Gunehec, *Droit Penal General* (12th edn, Paris, Economica, 2005) 420. Therefore, the person who, with the required mental state, provides the means to commit the crime becomes an accomplice, irrespective of whether the means provided assist, in fact, the perpetrator in the commission of the crime. See Judgment of the Cour de Cassation, Chambre Criminelle Dalloz (17 May 1962). In the United States, different approaches have been taken. On the one hand, in *State v Tazwell*, 30 La.Ann 884 (1878), the defendant was convicted as an accessory to the fact for providing specific material aid, which was not finally used in the commission of the offence. Similarly, in *State v Doody*, 434 A.2d 523 (1981), the defendant was convicted as an accessory to the fact for encouraging the killing by promising the perpetrator to make a car available for that purpose, though it turned out that the defendant's assistance was not needed. In addition, Model Penal Code §2.06(3)(a)(ii) makes criminal all attempted assistance on the ground that 'attempted complicity ought to be criminal and to distinguish it from effective complicity appears unnecessary where the crime has been committed'. See Model Penal Code §2.06, comment at p 314 (1985). On the other hand, other courts have stated that 'the assistance given . . . need not contribute to the criminal result in the sense that but for it the result would not have ensued. It is quite sufficient if it facilitated a

A number of different types of contribution have been considered sufficient to meet the 'substantial effect' standard of the case law of the *Ad hoc* Tribunals. For instance, the ICTY Appeal Judgment in the *Blagojevic* case has held that this standard is met when a military superior permits the use of resources under his or her control, including personnel, to facilitate the commission of the crime.[485] In the *Vasiljevic* case, the ICTY Appeals Chamber held that preventing the victims from escaping on the way to the Drina River bank and during the shooting had a substantial effect upon the perpetration of the crime[486]—it dismissed the Defence's claim that Vasiljevic had not substantially facilitated the commission of the crime because Milan Lukic and the other two shooters had been able to detain the victims (seven Muslim men) on the hill of Bikavac, and the risk of resistance from the victims was higher there than subsequently on the way to the Drina River bank and during the shooting.[487]

In the *Akayesu* case, the failure of the defendant (who was a *bourgmestre*) to maintain law and order in his commune, together with his failure to oppose killings and serious bodily or mental harm, aggravated by the fact that he was present in a number of occasions at the scene of the crime, was considered sufficient to meet the 'substantial effect' standard.[488] Supplying the weapons used for the commission of the crimes[489]or watching how the physical perpetrators committed the crimes without taking any action to prevent them,[490] are also contributions that the *Ad hoc* Tribunals have found to meet the 'sufficient effect' standard in a number of cases.

result that would have transpired without it. It is quite enough if the aid merely renders it easier for the principal actor to accomplish the end intended by him and the aidor and abetter, though in all human probability the end would have been attained without it'. See *State ex rel Attorney General v Talley*, 102 Ala 25 (1894), cited by WR LaFave and AW Scott, *Substantive Criminal Law* (St Paul, West Publishers, 1986) 578. In England and Wales, ineffective acts of assistance or moral encouragement do not give rise to criminal liability. For an act of assistance to the commission of a crime to give rise to criminal liability, it has to enable the perpetrator to commit the offence easily, earlier or with greater safety. See Smith and Hogan (Above n 1), at 172–3. In addition, for an act of moral encouragement to give rise to criminal liability, the perpetrator must, at least, be aware that he has the moral encouragement or the approval of the abettor to commit the crime. See *Wilcox v Jeffery* [1951] 1 All ER 464. In Spain, acts of assistance or moral encouragement are only punishable if they are useful for the commission of the crime in the sense that they significantly facilitate the performance of its objective elements. Hence, acts of assistance or moral encouragement, which have a minimal effect (or no effect) on the commission of the crime, do not give rise to criminal liability. See G Quintero Olivares, *Manual de Derecho Penal: Parte General* (3rd edn, Pamplona, Aranzadi, 2002) 637. See also Judgment of the Criminal Chamber of the Supreme Court of 27 Sep 2002.

[485] *Blagojevic Case* Appeals Judgment (Above n 483), at para 137. See also *Prosecutor v Krstic* (Appeals Chamber Judgment) ICTY-98-33-A (19 Apr 2004) paras 137–8, 144 [hereinafter *Krstic Case* Appeals Judgment].

[486] *Vasiljevic Case* Appeals Judgment (Above n 11), at para 134.

[487] *Ibid* at para 133.

[488] *Prosecutor v Akayesu* (Judgment) ICTR-96-4-T (2 Sep 1998) paras 705–705. See also A Cassese, *International Criminal Law* (Oxford, Oxford University Press 2003) 189.

[489] *Prosecutor v Tadic* (Judgment) ICTY-94-1 (7 May 1997) paras 680, 684 [hereinafter *Tadic Case* Trial Judgment].

[490] See also *Prosecutor v Delalic et al* (Judgment) ICTY-96-21-T (16 Nov 1998) paras 842 [hereinafter *Celebici Case* Trial Judgment]; *Furundzija Case* Trial Judgment (Above n 29), at paras 266–70. See also WA Schabas, 'The International Criminal Tribunal for the former Yugoslavia 1997–1999' in A Klip and G Sluiter, *Annotated Leading Cases of International Criminal Tribunals* (Vol 3, Oxford, Hart Publishing, 2001) 753.

The assistance can take place before, during or after the commission of the crime,[491] and does not require any previous plan or agreement between those senior political or military leaders who provide the assistance and the physical perpetrators.[492] Even assistance that is provided after the completion of the crime can be given *proprio motu* in the absence of any previous agreement with the physical perpetrators. This is the case of a military superior who, after being informed of a massacre carried out by some of his subordinates, decide to protect them by (i) burying the corpses in different graves in the countryside; and (ii) disguising the massacre as a lawful military operation against enemy civilians unlawfully taking an active part in the hostilities.

The contribution can be remote both in time and place from when and where the crimes are committed.[493] In this regard, the ICTY Trial Judgment in the *Oric* case has held that:

> [T]here is no reason why it should be treated differently from instigation which, as previously acknowledged, can be indirect. Accordingly, aiding and abetting should not be limited to direct contributions, as long as the effect of facilitating the crime is the same, irrespective of whether produced directly or by way of indirect means or intermediaries, provided, of course, that the final result is covered by the participant's corresponding intent.[494]

A senior political or military leader may be held liable for contributing to an individual crime committed by a single perpetrator or for contributing to all crimes committed by a plurality of persons involved in a joint criminal enterprise.[495] As a result:

> The requirement that an aidor and abettor must make a substantial contribution to the crime in order to be held responsible applies whether the accused is assisting in a crime committed by an individual or in crimes committed by a plurality of persons.[496]

In the context of a crime committed by several co-perpetrators in a joint criminal enterprise, the ICTY Appeals Chamber has held that:

> [T}he aidor and abettor is always an accessory to these co-perpetrators, although the co-perpetrators may not even know of the aidor and abettor's contribution.[497]

The ICTY Trial Judgment in the *Kvocka* case introduced the notion of aiding and abetting a joint criminal enterprise.[498] According to the Trial Chamber:

---

[491] *Ntagerura Case* Appeals Judgment (Above n 393), at para 372; *Blaskic Case* Appeals Judgment (Above n 15), at para 48; *Simic Case* Appeals Judgment (Above n 184), at para 85; *Blagojevic Case* Appeals Judgment (Above n 483), at para 127.

[492] *Tadic Case* Trial Judgment (Above n 489), at para 677; *Celebici Case* Trial Judgment (Above n 490), at paras 327–8. As Fletcher (Above n 1), at 645, has pointed out, assistance after the commission of the crime aims at ensuring impunity or profit to the physical perpetrators rather than contributing to the commission of a crime that has already been completed.

[493] *Oric Case* Trial Judgment (Above n 290), at para 285; *Prosecutor v Strugar* (Judgment) ICTY-01-42-T (31 Jan 2005) para 349.

[494] *Oric Case* Trial Judgment (*Ibid*), at para 285.

[495] *Kvocka Case* Appeals Judgment (Above n 11), at para 90.

[496] *Ibid.*

[497] *Vasiljevic Case* Appeals Judgment (Above n 11), at para 102.

[498] *Kvocka Case* Trial Judgment (Above n 18), at paras 284–7.

An accused may play no role in establishing a joint criminal enterprise and arrive at the enterprise and participate in its functioning for a short period without knowledge of its criminal nature. Eventually, however, the criminal nature of the enterprise is learned, and thereafter participation in the enterprise is engaged in knowingly. Depending on the level and nature of participation, the accused is either an aidor and abettor or a co-perpetrator of the criminal enterprise. Once the evidence indicates that a person who substantially assists the enterprise shares the goals of the enterprise, he becomes a co-perpetrator.[499]

The ICTY Trial Judgment in the *Simic* case also endorsed the notion of aiding and abetting a joint criminal enterprise when it held that:

A joint criminal enterprise may be aided and abetted, where it is demonstrated that the aidor and abettor knew the shared intent of the participants in the joint criminal enterprise.[500]

Nevertheless, the ICTY Appeals Chamber rejected this notion because:

[J]oint criminal enterprise is simply a means of committing a crime; it is not a crime in itself. Therefore, it would be inaccurate to refer to aiding and abetting a joint criminal enterprise. The aidor and abettor assists the principal perpetrator or perpetrators in committing the crime.[501]

The ICTY Trial Judgment in the *Krajisnik* case has also rejected the claim that the notion of aiding and abetting a joint criminal enterprise is a form of criminal responsibility under the ICTYS or under customary international law.[502] As a result:

[A] person's conduct either meets the conditions of JCE membership, as set out above, in which case he or she is characterized as a co-perpetrator, or the conduct fails the threshold, in which case there is no JCE responsibility.[503]

Concerning the subjective elements, the ICTR and ICTY Appeals Chambers have repeatedly stated that aiding and abetting requires knowledge: (i) that one's conduct substantially assists the execution by the physical perpetrators of the objective elements of the specific crime; (ii) that the physical perpetrators act with the state of mind required by the crime in question; and (iii) that the physical perpetrators' actions are motivated by any requisite ulterior intent or *dolus specialis*.[504]

Therefore, although some early case law of the *Ad hoc* Tribunals implied that a 'substantial likelihood' standard would be more appropriate than a 'knowledge'

---

[499] *Ibid* at para 285.
[500] *Simic Case* Trial Judgment (Above n 26), at para 160.
[501] *Kvocka Case* Appeals Judgment (Above n 11), at para 91.
[502] *Krajisnik Case* Trial Judgment (Above n 11), at para 86.
[503] *Ibid.*
[504] *Ntagerura Case* Appeals Judgment (Above n 393), at para 370; *Blaskic Case* Appeals Judgment (Above n 15), at para 46; *Vasiljevic Case* Appeals Judgment (Above n 11), at para 102; *Krstic Case* Appeals Judgment (Above n 485), at paras 140–41; *Simic Case* Appeals Judgment (Above n 185), at para 86; *Blagojevic Case* Appeals Judgment (Above n 483), at para 127; See also K Kittichaisaree, *International Criminal Law* (Oxford, Oxford University Press, 2001) 245.

requirement, the latest case law of the ICTR and ICTY Appeals Chambers has made clear that aiding and abetting requires a 'knowledge' standard according to which the senior political or military leader providing the assistance must be certain, or almost certain, that his actions or omission will substantially assist in the commission of a specific crime.[505] As a consequence, the mental requirement for aiding and abetting is higher than the 'awareness of substantial likelihood standard' required for planning,[506] instigating[507] and ordering.[508] In this regard, it is important to highlight that article 25(3)(c) RS establishes an even higher mental element for aiding and abetting, according to which the relevant senior political or military leader must make his contribution 'for the purpose of facilitating the commission of the crime'. In other words, he must act with *dolus directus* of the first degree because he must provide his assistance aiming at facilitating the commission of the crime.[509]

Senior political and military leaders who substantially assist in the commission of a crime do not need to act motivated by any ulterior intent or *dolus specialis* required by the crime in question.[510] Senior political and military leaders only need to know that the physical perpetrators' actions are motivated by such ulterior intent.[511] Therefore, if senior political and military leaders substantially assisting

---

[505] *Ntagerura Case* Appeals Judgment (Above n 392), at para 370.

[506] See Ch 3, s III.D.i.

[507] See Ch 3, s III.D.ii.

[508] See Ch 3, s III.D.iii.

[509] As K Ambos, 'Article 25. Individual Criminal Responsibility' in O Triffterer (ed), *Commentary on the Rome Statute of the International Criminal Court* (Baden-Baden, Nomos, 1999) 483 has pointed out: 'This concept introduces a subjective threshold which goes beyond the ordinary mens rea requirement within the meaning of article 30'. Concurring A Eser, 'Individual Criminal Responsibility' in A Cassese, P Gaeta, and JRWD Jones (eds), *The Rome Statute of the International Criminal Court: A Commentary* (Oxford, Oxford University Press, 2002) 801; Van Sliedregt (Above n 234), at 93.

[510] *Ntagerura Case* Appeals Judgment (Above n 394), at para 370; *Blaskic Case* Appeals Judgment (Above n 15), at para 46; *Vasiljevic Case* Appeals Judgment (Above n 11), at para 102; *Krstic Case* Appeals Judgment (Above n 485), at paras 140–1; *Simic Case* Appeals Judgment (Above n 185), at para 86; *Blagojevic Case* Appeals Judgment (Above n 483), at para 127. See also R Dixon, *Archbold International Criminal Courts: Practice, Procedure and Evidence* (London, Sweet and Maxwell, 2003) § 10–15.

[511] Nevertheless, the ICTR and the ICTY Appeals Chamber have based on this 'knowledge' requirement the distinction between aiding and abetting genocide under arts 6(1) ICTRS and 7(1) ICTYS and 'complicity to commit genocide' under arts 2(3)(e) ICTRS and 4(3)(e) ICTYS. According to the Appeals Chambers of the *Ad hoc* Tribunals, complicity encompasses a broader range of conduct than aiding and abetting. However, 'complicity to commit genocide' requires that the assistance for the commission of the underlying acts of genocide be motivated by the ulterior intent to destroy in whole or in part the targeted group. Hence, for conduct other than aiding and abetting that falls under the broader category of complicity to give rise to criminal liability, it is necessary that the relevant senior political or military leader acted motivated by a genocidal intent. See *Ntakirutimana Case* Appeals Judgment (Above n 384), at paras 500–1. See also *Krstic Case* Appeals Judgment (*Ibid*), at paras 140–42; *Prosecutor v Blagojevic* (Judgment) ICTY-02-60-T (17 Jan 2005) paras 678–80; *Prosecutor v Milosevic* (Decision on Motion for Judgment for Acquittal) ICTY-02-54-T (14 Jun 2004) paras 290–97. Before the ICTR and ICTY Appeals Chamber 'settled' this issue, the *Prosecutor v Semanza* (Judgment) ICTR-97-20-T (15 May 2003) paras 394–5 and the *Stakic Case* Trial Judgment (Above n 123), at paras 531–4 had held that: (i) there is no material distinction between 'complicity to commit genocide' under arts 2(3)(e) ICTRS and 4(3)(e) ICTYS and aiding and abetting under arts 6(1)

the commission of a crime do not need to fulfil the subjective elements of the crime, they cannot be considered principals to the crime (and the state of mind of the physical perpetrators becomes relevant to the determination of the existence of the crime to which such leaders are accessories). In this regard, the notion of aiding and abetting, like the notions of planning, instigating and ordering, as forms of accessorial or derivate liability, differ from the notions of indirect perpetration and co-perpetration (regardless of whether it is based on joint criminal enterprise or on joint control of the crime), which, as forms of principal liability, require the fulfilment of all subjective elements of the offences in question (including any requisite ulterior intent).[512]

However, the senior political or military leader providing the assistance does not need to know who the specific physical perpetrators are and who the specific victims will be. As a result, if a camp commander leaves the gate of a detention camp open for the sole purpose of letting unknown non-staff members enter the camp and mistreat some unidentified prisoners, he will be criminally liable for aiding and abetting as long as he is aware that, by leaving the gate of the detention camp open, he is substantially facilitating the mistreatment of prisoners by non-staff members.

The requisite mental element applies equally to aiding and abetting a crime committed by an individual or by a plurality of persons.[513] As a result, if a senior political or military leader is aware that his assistance is facilitating the commission of a single crime by a single person, he will only be liable for aiding and abetting such crime.[514] This applies regardless of whether the physical perpetrator is part of a joint criminal enterprise involving the commission of further crimes.[515] If, on the contrary, a senior political or military leader is aware that his assistance is facilitating the commission of all crimes committed by a plurality of persons involved in a joint criminal enterprise, he will liable for aiding and abetting all such crimes.

As a result, as the ICTY Appeals Chamber has held in the *Kvocka* case, whether a senior military or political leader is held responsible for assisting an individual

---

ICTRS and 7(1) ICTYS; and (ii) the subjective elements for 'complicity to commit genocide' mirrors those of aiding and abetting and other forms of accomplice liability in arts 6(1) ICTRS and 7(1) ICTYS. See WA Schabas, *Genocide in International Law* (Cambridge, Cambridge University Press, 2001) 285–303; A Reggio, 'Aiding and Abetting in International Criminal Law: The Responsibility of Corporate Agents and Business for "Trading with the Enemy" of Mankind' (2005) 5 *International Criminal Law* Review 641–2; A Greenwalt, 'Rethinking Genocidal Intent: The Case for a Knowledge-Based Interpretation' (1999) 99 *Columbia Journal Law Review* 2282; C Eboe-Osuji, ' "Complicity in Genocide" versus "Aiding and Abetting Genocide" ' (2005) 3 *Journal of International Criminal Justice* 71–2, 80–81; A Obote-Odora, 'Complicity in Genocide as Understood through the ICTR Experience' (2002) 2 *International Criminal Law Review* 375; Rikhof (Above n 484), at 705; K Gallagher, 'The Second Srebrenica Trial: Prosecutor v Vidoje Blagojevic and Dragan Jokic' (2005) 18 *Leiden Journal of International Law* 537.

[512] See Ch 3, s III.C.ii and Ch 5, s III.B.
[513] *Kvocka Case* Appeals Judgment (Above n 11), at para 90.
[514] *Ibid.*
[515] *Ibid.*

crime committed by a single person, or for assisting in all crimes committed by a plurality of persons involved in a joint criminal enterprise, depends on the effect of his assistance and on the extent of his knowledge.[516] Moreover, if a senior political or military leader:

> [K]nows that his assistance is supporting the crimes of a group of persons involved in a joint criminal enterprise and shares that intent, then he may be found criminally responsible for the crimes committed in furtherance of that common purpose as a co-perpetrator.[517]

B Co-perpetration Based on Joint Criminal Enterprise versus Aiding and Abetting

The ICTY Appeals Judgment in the *Tadic* case used the following four criteria to distinguish between co-perpetration based on joint criminal enterprise, which gives rise to principal liability, and aiding and abetting as a form of accessorial liability:

(i) the aidor and abettor is always an accessory to a crime perpetrated by another person, the principal.

(ii) in the case of aiding and abetting no proof is required of the existence of a common concerted plan, let alone of the pre-existence of such a plan. No plan or agreement is required: indeed, the principal may not even know about the accomplice's contribution.

(iii) the aidor and abettor carries out acts specifically directed to assist, encourage or lend moral support to the perpetration of a certain specific crime (murder, extermination, rape, torture, wanton destruction of civilian property, etc), and this support has a substantial effect upon the perpetration of the crime. By contrast, in the case of acting in pursuance of a common purpose or design, it is sufficient for the participant to perform acts that in some way are directed to the furthering of the common plan or purpose.

(iv) in the case of aiding and abetting, the requisite mental element is knowledge that the acts performed by the aidor and abettor assist the commission of a specific crime by the principal. By contrast, in the case of common purpose or design more is required (ie, either intent to perpetrate the crime or intent to pursue the common criminal design plus foresight that those crimes outside the criminal common purpose were likely to be committed), as stated above.[518]

The *Ojdanic* JCE Appeals Decision clarified the different nature of co-perpetration based on joint criminal enterprise and aiding and abetting. According to the ICTY Appeals Chamber:

---

[516] *Ibid*, at para 90.
[517] *Ibid*.
[518] *Tadic Case* Appeals Judgment (Above n 11), at para 229.

Insofar as a participant shares the purpose of the joint criminal enterprise (as he or she must do) as opposed to merely knowing about it, he or she cannot be regarded as a mere aidor and abettor to the crime which is contemplated. The Appeals Chamber therefore regards joint criminal enterprise as a form of 'commission' pursuant to Article 7(1) of the Statute.[519]

The ICTY Appeals Judgment in the *Vasiljevic* case has elaborated on the criteria for the distinction between co-perpetration based on joint criminal enterprise and aiding and abetting. According to this Judgment, both notions have a different nature because:

Participation in a joint criminal enterprise is a form of 'commission' under Article 7(1) of the Statute. The participant therein is liable as a co-perpetrator of the crime(s). Aiding and abetting the commission of a crime is usually considered to incur a lesser degree of individual criminal responsibility than committing a crime.[520]

Furthermore, in the *Vasiljevic* case, the ICTY Appeals Chamber also held that co-perpetration based on joint criminal enterprise and aiding and abetting have different objective and subjective elements. Concerning the objective elements:

The aidor and abettor carries out acts specifically directed to assist, encourage or lend moral support to the perpetration of a certain specific crime (murder, extermination, rape, torture, wanton destruction of civilian property, etc.), and this support has a substantial effect upon the perpetration of the crime. By contrast, it is sufficient for a participant in a joint criminal enterprise to perform acts that in some way are directed to the furtherance of the common design.[521]

With regard to the subjective elements:

In the case of aiding and abetting, the requisite mental element is knowledge that the acts performed by the aidor and abettor assist the commission of the specific crime of the principal. By contrast, in the case of participation in a joint criminal enterprise, i.e. as a co-perpetrator, the requisite *mens rea* is intent to pursue a common purpose.[522]

Finally, the ICTY Trial Judgment in the *Krajisnik* case has recently restated the main differences in the objective and subjective elements of co-perpetration based on joint criminal enterprise and aiding and abetting:

Actus reus: The aidor and abettor carries out acts specifically directed to assist, encourage, or lend moral support to the perpetration of a certain *specific* crime (murder, etc.), and this support has a substantial effect upon the perpetration of that crime. By contrast, in the case of action pursuant to a common criminal objective, it is sufficient for the participant to perform acts which in some way are directed to the furtherance of the common objective through the commission of crimes.[523]

---

[519] *Ojdanic* JCE Appeals Decision (Above n 51), at para 20.
[520] *Vasiljevic Case* Appeals Judgment (Above n 11), at para 102.
[521] *Ibid.*
[522] *Ibid.*
[523] *Krajisnik Case* Trial Judgment (Above n 11), at para 885.

Mens rea: In the case of aiding and abetting, the requisite mental element is knowledge that the acts performed by the aidor and abettor assist the commission of a specific crime by the principal. By contrast, in the case of co-perpetration as part of a JCE, intent to achieve the criminal objective is required.[524]

As one can see in the above-mentioned excerpts, the required level of contribution is higher for aiding and abetting (which gives rise to accesorial liability) than for participating in a joint criminal enterprise (which gives rise to principal liability as a co-perpetrator).

This is explained by the fact that the notion of co-perpetration based on joint criminal enterprise is based on a subjective approach to the distinction between principal and accessorial liability, according to which such a distinction depends on the state of mind with which the contribution to the crime is made. As a result, the lower level of contribution required by co-perpetration based on joint criminal enterprise is 'compensated' by a more stringent subjective element. Indeed, while aiding and abetting requires a 'knowledge' standard, co-perpetration based on joint criminal enterprise requires to aim at the achievement of the common criminal plan or purpose (*dolus directus* in the first degree). Nevertheless, this answer is not wholly satisfactory because it allows for central players in the commission of the crimes to be qualified as mere accessories, whereas those who play a limited role could be held liable as principals to the crimes.[525]

Moreover, the combination of a low level of contribution with a highly demanding subjective element does not exist in the extended form of joint criminal enterprise because, as the ICTY Appeals Chamber in the *Blaskic* case has explained:

> [C]riminal responsibility may be imposed upon an actor for a crime falling outside the originally contemplated enterprise, even where he only knew that the perpetration of such a crime was merely a possible consequence.[526]

Hence, the question arises as to why the extended form of joint criminal enterprise gives rise to principal liability (whereas aiding and abetting gives rise to accessorial liability) if both the objective and subjective requirements of aiding and abetting are more stringent? The ICTY Appeals Chamber in the *Blaskic* case has explained that this is only possible because:

> [T]he extended form of joint criminal enterprise is a situation where the actor already possesses the intent to participate and further the common criminal purpose of a group.[527]

In the author's view, this explanation is not convincing because a person cannot be held liable as a principal to a crime unless he acts with the state of mind

---

[524] *Krajisnik Case* Trial Judgment (Above n 11), at para 885.
[525] See Ambos, *Joint Criminal Enterprise* (Above n 137), at pp 170 and 171; Danner and Martinez (Above n 52), at 150–51; Ohlin (Above n 52), at 89. See also Ch 4, s III.A.iii.
[526] Blaskic Case Appeals Judgment (Above n 15), at para 33.
[527] Ibid.

required by the crime in question.[528] If he does not fulfil the subjective elements contained in the definition of the crime, he can, at best, be considered an accessory to the crime. Nevertheless, the case law of the *Ad hoc* Tribunals has repeatedly affirmed that the extended form of joint criminal enterprise gives rise to principal liability.[529]

VIII Final Remarks on the Relationship between the Notions of Co-Perpetration Based on Joint Criminal Enterprise, Aiding and Abetting and Superior Responsibility

As seen in previous sections, the notions of co-perpetration based on joint criminal enterprise, aiding and abetting and superior responsibility have a very different nature. Co-perpetration based on joint criminal enterprise is a theory of co-perpetration, according to which, when a crime is committed by a plurality of persons acting in furtherance of a common criminal plan, principals to the crime are all those who make their contributions (regardless of their significance) sharing the aim to have the crimes included in the common plan committed.[530]Aiding and abetting is a form of accessorial or derivate liability, according to which, all those who, without intending the commission of a crime, are aware that their conduct substantially assists in its commission, become accessories to the crime.[531] Superior responsibility is an offence of mere omission, according to which, criminal liability does not arise for subordinates' crimes, but for breaches of the duty imposed by international law on superiors to take the necessary and reasonable measures at their disposal to prevent and punish subordinates' offences once such duties have been triggered.[532] Nevertheless, in the context of article 28 RS, superior responsibility for failures to prevent is a form of accessorial liability, according to which, superiors are accessories to those crimes committed by their subordinates due to the effect that their failures to prevent have in the commission of such crimes.[533]

---

[528] This problem has been highlighted by Ohlin (Above n 52), at 83. As he points out, '[t]his is precisely the problem with the concept of foreseeability in joint criminal enterprise. All members of the conspiracy are treated equally, and the militia member who assumed the risk of joining the enterprise is charged with the same crime as the militia member who decided on his own to torture civilians. The distinction between the two participants is obliterated'.

For this reason Ambos, *Joint Criminal Enterprise* (Above n 137), at 168, states that the extended form of joint criminal enterprise amounts, indeed, to a form of aiding and abetting.

[529] See Ch 2, s VII.B and Ch 4, s III.B.iii.

[530] See Ch 2, s VI and Ch 4, s I.

[531] See Ch 4, s VII.A.

[532] See Ch 3, s II.B.ii.e.

[533] *Ibid.*

In the author's view, when assessing whether any of these three notions is applicable in any given case, one has to put particular attention to the state of mind of the relevant senior political or military leader. In this regard, it is important to keep in mind that, depending on the circumstances of the case, superiors' failures to prevent or punish subordinates' crimes could give rise to criminal liability under the notions of co-perpetration based on joint criminal enterprise, aiding and abetting and superior responsibility as long as the relevant senior political or military leaders fulfil the subjective elements required by these three notions.

As a result, one will have to undertake the type of analysis carried out by the Trial Chamber in the *Krnojelac* case with regard to the crime of persecution:

> The Prosecution alleges that the Accused incurred criminal responsibility under Article 7(1) as a participant in a joint criminal enterprise with guards and soldiers to persecute the Muslim and other male non-Serb civilian detainees. To attach criminal responsibility to the Accused for the joint criminal enterprise of persecution, the Prosecution must prove that there was an agreement between himself and the other participants to persecute the Muslim and other non-Serb civilian male detainees by way of the underlying crimes found to have been committed, and that the principal offenders and the Accused shared the intent required for each of the underlying crimes and the intent to discriminate in their commission [. . .]. To find the Accused guilty of aiding and abetting the persecution of the non-Serb detainees, the Prosecution must establish that the Accused had knowledge that the principal offenders intended to commit the underlying crimes and that by their acts they intended to discriminate against the non-Serb detainees, and that, with that knowledge, he made a substantial contribution to the commission of the discriminatory acts by the principal offenders. [. . .] To establish the Accused's responsibility as a superior, the Prosecution must demonstrate that the Accused knew of the commission of the underlying offence, that he knew that that offence was being committed on discriminatory grounds, or had information in his possession sufficient to put him on notice as to the commission of the underlying offence and its commission on discriminatory grounds, and that he failed to prevent or punish his subordinates for the commission of the underlying offence on discriminatory grounds.[534]

When the notions of co-perpetration based on joint criminal enterprise, aiding and abetting and superior responsibility are all applicable in a case, the author considers that one should look at their respective nature in order to determine the manner in which they should be applied. In this regard, the author considers that, although the case law of the *Ad hoc* Tribunals has not been consistent on this matter, theories of principal liability, such as co-perpetration based on joint criminal enterprise, must have preference over forms of accessorial or derivative liability, such as aiding and abetting (or superior responsibility for failures to prevent in the context of art. 28 RS). Furthermore, when in a case, no theory of principal liability is applicable, but there is more than one form of accessorial or derivative liability that can be applied, the form of accessorial liability that better suits the role played by the relevant senior political or military leader must be chosen. Finally, when a senior political or military leader has incurred an offence of mere omission

---

[534] *Krnojelac Case* Trial Judgment (Above n 14), at paras 487–8, 493.

for his failure to prevent or punish (superior responsibility), and has also participated as a principal, or as an accessory, in the commission of the crimes by his subordinates, he should be convicted for both offences. Subsequently, the rules on
concursus delictorum should be applied in determining the appropriate sentence.

5

Co-perpetration Based on
Joint Control of the Crime

I The Notion of Joint Control of the Crime

The notion of control of the crime includes, in addition to those cases of 'control of the action', and 'control of the will', those other cases of co-perpetration based on joint (functional) control of the crime.[1] As ICC Pre-Trial Chamber I has explained in the *Lubanga* and *Katanga and Ngudjolo* cases, the notion of co-perpetration based on joint control of the crime:

> [I]s rooted in the principle of the division of essential tasks for the purpose of committing a crime between two or more persons acting in a concerted manner [. . .] Although none of the participants has overall control over the offence because they all depend on one another for its commission, they all share control because each of them could frustrate the commission of the crime by not carrying out his or her task.[2]

In accordance with the notion of co-perpetration based on joint control, the contribution of several people to the commission of a crime amounts to the co-performance on the basis of the principle of division of tasks. As a result, the sum of the individual contributions considered as a whole amount to the completion of the objective elements of the crime. The control of each co-perpetrator over the crime is based on the division of functions without which it would be impossible to complete the objective elements of the crime. The co-perpetrators can only implement the common plan in as much as they act jointly, and each co-perpetrator may disrupt the implementation of the common plan by withholding

---

[1] C Roxin, *Täterschaft und Tatherrschaft* (7th edn, Berlin, Gruyter, 2000) 451 [hereinafter Roxin]. See also *Lubanga Case* (Pre-Trial Chamber I Decision on the Confirmation of Charges) ICC-01/04-01/06 (29 Jan 2007) para 332 [hereinafter *Lubanga Case* Confirmation of Charges]; *Katanga and Ngudjolo Case* (Pre-Trial Chamber I Decision on the Confirmation of Charges) ICC-01/04-01/07 (1 Oct 2008) para 488 [*Katanga and Ngudjolo Case* Confirmation of Charges].

[2] *Lubanga Case* Confirmation of Charges (*Ibid*), at para 342; *Katanga and Ngudjolo Case* Confirmation of Charges (*Ibid*), at paras 521 and 525. See also Roxin (*Ibid*), at 451; HH Jescheck and T Weigend, *Lehrbuch des Strafrechts* (5th edn, Berlin, Duncker and Humblot, 1996) 674 [hereinafter Jescheck and Weigend]; H Otto, *Strafrecht Allgemeiner Teil* (6th edn, 2000) No 57 (gemeinsames Innehaben der *Tatherrschaft*) [hereinafter Otto]; A Perez Cepeda, *La responsabilidad de los administradores de sociedades: criterios de atribucion* (Barcelona, Cedecs Editorial, 1997) 417 [hereinafter Perez Cepeda].

his contribution to the crime. This key position of each co-perpetrator is the basis of their shared control of the crime.[3]

The key element of co-perpetration based on joint control is that, due to the division of the essential functions for the commission of the crime, none of the co-perpetrators alone controls the execution of the crime, but all of the co-perpetrators share control. Therefore, they depend on one another, and only if all of them carry out their contributions in a co-ordinated manner, will the objective elements of the crime be completed. For instance, beatings will only occur if one person holds the victim while a second person, acting in co-ordination with the first one, inflicts the beatings upon the victim. Likewise, an old mosque would only be destroyed if an observation officer communicates to the artillery squad the necessary corrections for the next round.

As a result, any co-perpetrator has the power to disrupt the performance of the objective elements of the crime. The value of the observation officer's corrections is null if the artillery squad stops the shelling. Likewise, should the observation officer fail to communicate his corrections to the artillery squad, the latter could continue shelling the old mosque for a week without hitting it. Thus, one can conclude that each co-perpetrator controls more than his part of the crime, but, at the same time, he only directs the commission of the crime jointly with the other co-perpetrators. In this sense, joint control of the crime is inherent to the essential function of each co-perpetrator in the implementation of the overall common plan.[4]

Therefore, when a crime is committed by a plurality of persons, in principle, co-perpetrators (and hence principals to the crime) are only those persons who make a contribution which is essential for the performance of the objective elements of the crime because, without it, such a performance would be disrupted. There can be, however, many additional tasks which are performed at the preparatory and execution stages and which are not essential for the performance of the objective elements of the crime. Encouraging the beater while he is beating the victim, confirming to the artillery squad that it can use the anticipated ammunition, or advising the artillery squad not to stop the shelling of the old mosque are just some examples of these types of tasks. According to the notion of co-perpetration based on joint control, performing such functions, even if it is in a coordinated manner

---

[3] *Lubanga Case* Confirmation of Charges (*Ibid*), at paras 342 and 347; *Katanga and Ngudjolo Case* Confirmation of Charges (*Ibid*), at para 525; See also Roxin (*Ibid*), at 451; S Mir Puig, *Derecho Penal: Parte General* (6th edn, Barcelona, Edisofer Libros Juridicos, 2002) 385 [hereinafter Mir Puig]; F Munoz Conde and M Garcia Aran, *Derecho Penal: Parte General* (5th edn, Valencia, Tirant lo Blanch, 2002) 452–3 [hereinafter Munoz Conde and Garcia Aran].

[4] *Lubanga Case* Confirmation of Charges (*Ibid*), at paras 332 (iii), 342 and 347; *Katanga and Ngudjolo Case* Confirmation of Charges (*Ibid*), at paras 488, 521 and 525. See also Roxin (*Ibid*), at 451; K Kuhl, *Strafrecht Allgemeiner Teil* (4th edn, Munich, Vahlen Franz GMBH, 2002) No 99 [hereinafter Kuhl]; H Trondle and T Fischer, *Strafgesetzbuch Kommentar* (51st edn, Munich, 2003) § 25 No 6; J Wessels and W Beulke, *Strafrecht Allgemeiner Teil* (31st edn, Heidelberg, Muller, 2001) No 526 [hereinafter Wessels and Beulke];.

with the co-perpetrators in furtherance of a common plan, will only give rise to accessorial liability.[5]

II The Treatment of the Notions of Joint Control of the Crime and Joint Criminal Enterprise in the Rome Statute

As explained above, article 25(3)(a) RS, when referring to the person who 'commits such a crime, whether as an individual, jointly with another or through another person', adopts an approach to the distinction between principals and accessories to the crime based on the notion of control of the crime.[6] In this context, ICC Pre Trial Chamber I has stated in its Decision on the Confirmation of the Charges in the *Lubanga* case:

> The concept of co-perpetration embodied in article 25 (3) (a) of the Statute by the reference to the commission of a crime "jointly with (...) another person" must cohere with the choice of the concept of control over the crime as a criterion for distinguishing between principals and accessories. [...] Hence as stated in its *Decision to Issue a Warrant of Arrest*, the Chamber considers that the concept of co-perpetration embodied in article 25 (3)(a) of the Statute coincides with that of joint control over the crime by reason of the essential nature of the various contributions to the commission of the crime.[7]

---

[5] *Lubanga Case* Confirmation of Charges (*Ibid*), at para 347; *Katanga and Ngudjolo Case* Confirmation of Charges (*Ibid*), at para 525. See also Roxin (*Ibid*), at para 541; Munoz Conde and Garcia Aran (Above n 3), at 452–3; Kuhl (*Ibid*), at No 103, No 112; Wessels and Beulke (*Ibid*), at No 528;

[6] See Ch 2, s VII.C.i. See also *Lubanga Case* Confirmation of Charges (*Ibid*), at paras 333–8.

[7] *Lubanga Case* Confirmation of Charges (Above n 1),at paras 340–1. This decision confirms the *Lubanga Case* (Pre-Trial Chamber I Decision on Prosecution's Application for Warrant of Arrest) ICC-01/04-01/06 (10 Feb 2006) para 96 [*Lubanga Case* Warrant of Arrest], in which ICC Pre-Trial Chamber I had already stated that the notion of co-perpetration based on joint control of the crime was embraced by ('Rome Statute of the International Criminal Court' UN Diplomatic Conference of Plenipotentiaries on the Establishment of an International Criminal Court (Rome 15 Jun–17 Jul 1998) (17 Jul 1998) UN Doc A/Conf. 183/9 [hereinafter RS]) art 25(3)(a) RS and could be applicable to Thomas Lubanga Dyilo's alleged role in the commission of the crimes set out in the Prosecution's Application for a Warrant of Arrest. See also *Katanga and Ngudjolo Case* Confirmation of Charges (Above n 1), at para 488 (a), 520 and 521; K Ambos, 'Article 25. Individual Criminal Responsibility' in O Triffterer (ed), *Commentary on the Rome Statute of the International Criminal Court* (Baden-Baden, Nomos, 1999) 479 [hereinafter Ambos, *Article 25*]; JM Gomez Benitez, 'Elementos Comunes de los Crimenes contra la Humanidad en el Estatuto de la Corte Penal Internacional' (2002) 42 *Actualidad Penal* 1121–38. The notion of co-perpetration based on joint control of the crime is by no means a new notion. On the contrary, besides its application in *Prosecutor v Stakic* (Judgment) ICTY-97-24-T (31 Jul 2003) [hereinafter *Stakic Case* Trial Judgment], it has been regularly applied, as pointed out by *Gacumbitsi v Prosecutor* (Appeals Chamber Judgment, Separate Opinion of Judge Schomburg on the Criminal Responsibility of the Appellant for Committing Genocide) ICTR-2001-64-A (7 Jul 2006) para 30, in a number of national jurisdictions, such as Argentina, Colombia, France, Germany, Spain and Switzerland. In Argentina, see Judgment of the Camara Nacional en lo Criminal y Correccional Federal de la Capital Federal, 'Sala 1a' (31 Oct 1988). For Colombia, see art 29.2 of the Penal Code of Colombia ('Son coautores los que, mediando un acuerdo comun, actuan con division del trabajo criminal atendiendo la importancia del aporte'). French jurisprudence also relies on the importance of the

Hence, in those cases in which a plurality of persons are involved in the commission of a crime, only those who share the control of the crime as a result of the essential character of their contributions to its commission are considered to be co-perpetrators. The rationale behind this notion is that those individuals in charge of essential tasks can 'frustrate' the implementation of the common plan by not carrying out their contributions and, therefore, each of them retains joint control over the commission of the crime.[8]

As a result, the RS has rejected the formal-objective approach to the notion of co-perpetration, according to which, when the crime is committed by a plurality of persons, co-perpetrators are only those who carry out an objective element of the crime—thus, for this approach, anyone who does not carry out an objective element of the crime is not a co-perpetrator, no matter how important his contribution to the implementation of the common plan might be.[9] Likewise, the RS has rejected the subjective approach to the notion of co-perpetration, according to which, when the crime is committed by a plurality of persons, anyone who makes a contribution with the aim to implement the common criminal purpose is a co-perpetrator, regardless of the nature and scope of his contribution.[10]

---

role played during the commission of the crime. See Cour de Cassation, Chambre Criminelle Dalloz (25 Jan 1962) Bulletin Criminel No 68; H Angevin and A Chavanne, *Editions du Juris-Classeur Penal* (Paris, LexisNexis, 1998) Complicite: art 121–6 et 121–7. German jurisprudence has also occasionally embraced the notion of co-perpetration based on joint control. See Entscheidungen des Bundesgerichtshofs in Strafsachen 37 p 291, 38 p 319; Bundesgerichtshof, Strafverteidiger (1994) 241. Joint control has also been applied by the Spanish Supreme Court. See Judgment of the Spanish Supreme Court of 13 Dec 2002. Finally, the Swiss Supreme Court has also applied this notion. See Entscheidungen des Schweizerischen Bundesgerichts 118 IV 399, 120 IV 142; Entscheidungen des Schweizerischen Bundesgerichts 120 IV 272. Moreover, many legal writers, including the majority of German and Spanish writers, have accepted it. See Roxin (Above n 1), at 294; G Jakobs, *Strafrecht Allgemeiner Teil* (2nd edn, Berlin, Gruyter, 1991) para 21/35, fn 86 [hereinafter Jakobs] (he uses a different terminology, but following the distinction between control of the act, functional control and control of the will); Jescheck and Weigend (Above n 2), at 674; Kuhl (Above n 4), at No 99; K Lackner and K Kuhl, *Strafgesetzbuch mit Erlauterungen* (24th edn, Munich, CH Beck, 2001) § 25, No 11 [hereinafter Lackner and Kuhl]; F Haft, *Strafrecht Allgemeiner Teil* (7th edn, Munich, 1996) 199; R Maurach, KH Gossel and H Zipf, *Strafrecht Allgemeiner Teil, Teil II* (6th edn, Munich, 1984) 49/4; Wessels and Beulke (Above n 4), at No 528; V Krey, *Strafrecht Allgemeiner Teil* (Vol 2, Munich, 2002) No 165; Mir Puig (Above n 3), at 385; Munoz Conde and Garcia Aran (Above n 3), at 453–4; Perez Cepeda (Above n 2), at 417; J Cerezo Mir, *Problemas Fundamentales del Derecho Penal* (Madrid, Tecnos, 1982) 339; E Bacigalupo, 'La Distincion entre Autoria y Participacion en la Jurisprudencia de los Tribunales y el Nuevo Codigo Penal Aleman' in J Anton Oneca, *Estudios Penales: Libro Homenaje Al Prof J. Anton Oneca* (Salamanca, Ediciones Universidad de Salamanca, 1982) 30; E Bacigalupo, *Principios del Derecho Espanol II: El hecho Punible* (Madrid, 1985) 135; JM Gomez Benitez, 'El dominio del hecho en la autoria (validez y limites)' (1984) *Anuario de Derecho Penal y de las Ciencias Penales* 104; G Quintero Olivares, *Manual de Derecho Penal: Parte General* (3rd edn, Pamplona, Aranzadi, 2002) 605.

   [8] *Lubanga Case* Confirmation of Charges (Above n 1), at paras 342 and 347; *Katanga and Ngudjolo Case* Confirmation of Charges (Above n 1), at para 525. See also C Roxin, *Autoria y Dominio del Hecho en Derecho Penal* (6th edn, Madrid, Marcial Pons, 1998) 303–33; H Olasolo and A Perez Cepeda, 'The Notion of Control of the Crime in the Jurisprudence of the ICTY: The Stakic Case' (2004) 4 *International Criminal Law Review* 497–506 [hereinafter Olasolo and Perez Cepeda].

   [9] *Lubanga Case* Confirmation of Charges *(Ibid)*, at para 333; *Katanga and Ngudjolo Case* Confirmation of Charges *(Ibid)*, at para 482.

   [10] *Lubanga Case* Confirmation of Charges *(Ibid)*, at para 334; *Katanga and Ngudjolo Case* Confirmation of Charges *(Ibid)*, at para 483.

Moreover, when a crime is committed by a plurality of persons, all those who, despite making a contribution, do not share control, can only be criminally liable as accessories to the crime.[11] In this regard, articles 25(3)(b) to (d) RS provide for a number of forms of accessorial (as opposed to principal) liability. First, according to article 25(3)(b) RS, a senior political or military leader who 'orders, solicits or induces' the commission of a crime within the jurisdiction of the Court will be criminally liable as an accessory to the crime. 'Ordering' (or 'inducing' in those cases in which senior political and military leaders do not resort to their position of authority to prompt the physical perpetrators to commit the crimes) will be particularly applicable in those cases in which, due to the small size of those organisations used by senior political and military leaders to secure the commission of the crimes, they do not qualify as organised structures of power and, thus, the notion of indirect perpetration in its variant of OSP is not applicable.[12]

Second, as provided for in article 25(3)(c) RS, accessorial liability arises for any political or military leader who, for the purpose of facilitating the commission of a crime within the jurisdiction of the Court:

> [A]ids, abets or otherwise assists in its commission or its attempted commission, including providing the means for its commission.

As already explained, ICTR and ICTY case law has held that aiding and abetting the commission of a crime only gives rise to criminal liability if the assistance has a substantial effect on the commission of the crime or on the consolidation of its effects.[13] In the view of author, this interpretation is also applicable in relation to sub-paragraph (c) of article 25(3) RS because sub-paragraph (d) of the same provision deals explicitly with the criminal liability of those individuals who 'in any other way contributes' to the commission of the crime.[14]

---

[11] *Lubanga Case* Warrant of Arrest (Above n 7), at para 78; *Lubanga Case* Confirmation of Charges (*Ibid*) at para 320; *Katanga and Ngudjolo Case* Confirmation of Charges (*Ibid*), at paras 485 and 486.

[12] See Ch 3, s III.D.i. See also Roxin (Above n 1), at 245.

[13] *Prosecutor v Ntagerura* (Appeals Chamber Judgment) ICTR-99-46-A (7 Jul 2006) para 370 [hereinafter *Ntagerura Case* Appeals Judgment]; *Prosecutor v Blaskic* (Appeals Chamber Judgment) ICTY-95-14-A (29 Jul 2004) paras 45–6 [hereinafter *Blaskic Case* Appeals Judgment]; *Prosecutor v Vasiljevic* (Appeals Chamber Judgment) ICTY-98-32-A (25 Feb 2004) para 102 [hereinafter *Vasiljevic Case* Appeals Judgment]; *Prosecutor v Simic* (Appeals Chamber Judgment) ICTY-95-9-A (28 Nov 2006) para 85 [hereinafter *Simic Case* Appeals Judgment]; *Prosecutor v Blagojevic* (Appeals Chamber Judgment) ICTY-02-60-A (9 May 2007) para 127 [hereinafter *Blagojevic Case* Appeals Judgment]; *Prosecutor v Bagilishema* (Judgment) ICTR-95-01A-T (7 Jun 2001) para 33 [hereinafter *Bagilishema Case* Trial Judgment]; *Prosecutor v Kajelijeli* (Judgment) ICTR-98-44A-T (1 Dec 2003) para 766 [hereinafter *Kajelijeli Case* Trial Judgment]; *Prosecutor v Kamuhanda* (Judgment) ICTR-95-54A-T (22 Jan 2004) para 597 [hereinafter *Kamuhanda Case* Trial Judgment]; *Prosecutor v Furundzija* (Judgment) ICTY-95-17/1-T (10 Dec 1998) para 249 [hereinafter *Furundzija Case* Trial Judgment]; *Prosecutor v Aleksovski* (Judgment) ICTY-95-14/1-T (25 Jun 1999) para 61 [hereinafter *Aleksovski Case* Trial Judgment]; *Prosecutor v Kunarac* (Judgment) ICTY-96-23-T and ICTY-96-23/1-T (22 Feb 2001) para 391 [hereinafter *Kunarac Case* Trial Judgment]; *Prosecutor v Krnojelac* (Judgment) ICTY-97-25-T (15 Mar 2002) para 88 [hereinafter *Krnojelac Case* Trial Judgment]; *Prosecutor v Oric* (Judgment) ICTY-03-68-T (30 Jun 2006) para 282 [herianfter *Oric Case* Trial Judgment].

[14] See also Ambos, *Article 25* (Above n 7), at 481, 484.

Third, as provided for in article 25(3)(d) RS, accessorial liability arises for any political or military leader who 'in any other way contributes' to the commission of a crime within the jurisdiction of the ICC by a group of persons acting with a common purpose. As ICC Pre-Trial Chamber I has explicitly pointed out in relation to this provision:

> [A]rticle 25 (3) (d) of the Statute provides for a residual form of accessory liability which makes it possible to criminalise those contributions to a crime which cannot be characterised as ordering, soliciting, inducing, aiding, abetting or assisting within the meaning of article 25 (3) (b) or article 25 (3) (c) of the Statute, by reason of the state of mind in which the contributions were made.[15]

This interpretation is also supported by the two subjective elements provided for in article 25(3)(d) RS. On the one hand, the contribution of senior political and military leaders to the commission of the crime must be 'intentional'. As Fletcher and Ohlin have explained, this only means that:

> [A]ll that has to be intentional is the act of doing something that constitutes a contribution, eg selling gas to those who are driving to the scene of the intended massacre.[16]

On the other hand, senior political and military leaders must carry out their intentional acts of contribution (i) 'with the aim of furthering the criminal activity or criminal purpose of the group, where such activity or purpose involves the commission of a crime within the jurisdiction of the Court', or (ii) 'in the knowledge of the intention of the group to commit the crime'. Hence, article 25(3)(d) RS, unlike the notion of joint criminal enterprise or the common purpose doctrine in the case law of the *Ad hoc* Tribunals, does not require for the relevant senior political and military leaders to share the common criminal purpose of the group. On the contrary, article 25(3)(d) RS only requires senior political and military leaders to be aware of the common criminal purpose. As Fletcher and Ohlin have highlighted:

> The culpability nexus between the contribution and the ultimate criminal harm is left vague. The contributor might have the aim of furthering the plan (Article 25 (3)(d) (i)) or simply have the knowledge of the group's intention (Article 25(3)(d)(ii)), i.e., if the gas station attendant knows of the group's criminal objective, he is guilty for 'intentionally' selling them gas. In the final analysis, the knowledge requirement would be sufficient because no one could have the aim of furthering the group objective without having knowledge of that purpose.[17]

Hence, article 25(3)(d) RS is not only limited to those contributions to a crime which cannot be characterised as ordering, soliciting, inducing, aiding, abetting or assisting within the meaning of article 25 (3) (b) or article 25 (3) (c) of the

---

[15] *Lubanga Case* Confirmation of Charges (Above n 1), at para 337. See also *Katanga and Ngudjolo Case* Confirmation of Charges (Above n 1), at para 483.

[16] GP Fletcher and D Ohlin, 'Reclaiming Fundamental Principles of Criminal Law in the Darfur Case' (2005) 3 *Journal of International Criminal Justice* 549 [hereinafter Fletcher and Ohlin].

[17] *Ibid.*

Statute[18], it also does not require the accused to fulfil the mental elements of the crimes in question, including any requisite ulterior intent. For this reason, even if article 25(3)(d) RS resembles in certain ways the notion of joint criminal enterprise in the case law of the *Ad hoc* Tribunals, it cannot be considered as a notion of co-perpetration giving rise to principal liability. Indeed, in choosing a subjective approach to the concept of co-perpetration, the case law of the *Ad hoc* Tribunals has emphasised that, for principal liability to arise pursuant to the notion of joint criminal enterprise, any participant in the enterprise must share the common criminal purpose and, therefore, act motivated by any ulterior intent required by any of the core crimes of the enterprise.[19]

Moreover, while article 25(3)(c) RS requires that in order for accessorial liability to arise as a result of aiding, abetting or assisting in the commission of a crime, the assistance be carried out 'for the purpose of facilitating the commission of such a crime'; article 25(3)(d) RS does not include such a requirement. Thus, pursuant to article 25(3)(d) RS, as is also the case with the notion of aiding and abetting in the case law of the *Ad hoc* Tribunals,[20] criminal liability arises for acts which are carried out without the aim to facilitate the physical perpetrators in the commission of the crimes, but in the knowledge that they will be of assistance to them in their commission.

Under these circumstances, one can only conclude that article 25(3)(d) RS provides, within the system of RS, for a residual form of accessorial or derivative liability,[21] according to which criminal liability arises for those non-substantial contributions of senior political and military leaders which are carried out with, at least, the knowledge that such contributions facilitate the implementation of their common criminal purpose.[22] Furthermore, the author considers that this residual form of accessorial liability is the only mode of liability under article 25(3) RS,

---

[18] *Lubanga Case* Confirmation of Charges (Above n 1), at para 337.

[19] *Ntagerura Case* Appeals Judgment (Above n 13), at para 370; *Blaskic Case* Appeals Judgment (Above n 13), at paras 45–46; *Vasiljevic Case* Appeals Judgment (Above n 13), at para 102; *Simic Case* Appeals Judgment (Above n 13), at para 85; *Blagojevic Case* Appeals Judgment (Above n 13), at para 127; *Bagilishema Case* Trial Judgment (Above n 13), at para 33; *Kajelijeli Case* Trial Judgment (Above n 13), at para 766; *Kamuhanda Case* Trial Judgment (Above n 13), at para 597; *Furundzija Case* Trial Judgment (Above n 13), at para 249; *Aleksovski Case* Trial Judgment (Above n 13), at para 61; *Kunarac Case* Trial Judgment (Above n 13), at para 391; *Krnojelac Case* Trial Judgment (Above n 13), at para 88; *Oric Case* Trial Judgment (Above n 13), at para 282. Moreover, as the *Furundzija Case* Trial Judgment, at para 257, and *Prosecutor v Furundzija* (Appeals Chamber Judgment) ICTY-95-17/1-A (21 Jul 2000) para 118 [hereinafter *Furundzija Case* Appeals Judgment] have expressly stated, to distinguish a co-perpetrator (a participant in a joint criminal enterprise) from an aidor or abettor, 'it is crucial to ascertain whether the individual who takes part in the torture process also *partakes of the purpose behind torture*'. See also Ch 4, s III.B.i and s VII.B.

[20] *Ntagerura Case* Appeals Judgment (*Ibid*), at para 370; *Blaskic Case* Appeals Judgment (*Ibid*), at para 46; *Vasiljevic Case* Appeals Judgment (*Ibid*), at para 102; *Prosecutor v Krstic* (Appeals Chamber Judgment) ICTY-98-33-A (19 Apr 2004) paras 140–1; *Simic Case* Appeals Judgment (*Ibid*), at para 86; *Blagojevic Case* Appeals Judgment (*Ibid*), at para 327. See also K Kittichaisaree, *International Criminal Law* (Oxford, Oxford University Press, 2001) 245. See also Ch 4, s VII.A.

[21] *Lubanga Case* Confirmation of Charges (Above n 1), at para 337; *Katanga and Ngudjolo Case* Confirmation of Charges (Above n 1), at para 483.

[22] Ambos, *Article 25* (Above n 7), at 484–5.

which resembles, to a certain extent, the notion of joint criminal enterprise or the common purpose doctrine, which, as seen above, has been configured as a theory of co-perpetration by the case law of the *Ad hoc* Tribunals.[23]

As ICC Pre-Trial Chamber I has highlighted,[24] this marks an important difference between the RS—where the distinction between principal and accessorial liability is based on the notion of control of the crime and, consequently, the preferred theory of co-perpetration is that of the joint control of the crime—and the case law of the *Ad hoc* Tribunals, which has consistently endorsed a subjective approach to the distinction between principal and accessorial liability and has opted for the notion of joint criminal enterprise as the preferred theory of co-perpetration.[25]

In addition, it is important to underscore that, according to articles 25(3)(b) and (d) RS, senior political and military leaders participating in the commission of a crime by other persons will be criminally liable as accessories to the crime as soon as the execution stage is reached, regardless of whether the objective elements of the crime are finally completed. This marks an additional difference between the RS and the case law of the *Ad hoc* Tribunals, according to which planning, instigating, ordering and aiding and abetting only give rise to criminal liability if the crimes have been completed.[26]

---

[23] The same conclusion was reached by *Lubanga Case* Confirmation of Charges (Above n 1), at para 335. In this regard, as Fletcher and Ohlin (Above n 16), at 549, have affirmed that art 25(3)(d) RS differs from the notion of joint criminal enterprise in that: (i) it requires a lower subjective element (awareness of the common criminal plan as opposed to sharing it); and (ii) it does not provide for criminal liability for 'foreseeable crimes'. However, in the view of the author, the main difference is that, according to the case of the *Ad hoc* Tribunals, the notion of joint criminal enterprise gives rise to principal liability (co-perpetration), whereas art 25(3)(d) RS contains a residual form of accessorial or derivative liability. See also the analysis of K Ambos, 'Joint Criminal Enterprise and Command Responsibility' (2007) 5 *Journal of International Criminal Justice* 159, at 172 and 173 [hereinafter Ambos, *Joint Criminal Enterprise*], in which he concludes that 'the only form of participation comparable with JCE II or III is that of collective responsibility as laid forth in Article 25(3)(d) ICC Statute.'

[24] *Lubanga Case* Confirmation of Charges (*Ibid*), at para 338; *Katanga and Ngudjolo Case* Confirmation of Charges (Above n 1), at paras 506–508.

[25] *Lubanga Case* Confirmation of Charges (*Ibid*), at paras 329, 335, 337, 338, 341; *Prosecutor v Tadic* (Appeals Chamber Judgment) ICTY-94-1-A (15 Jul 1999) paras 227–8 [hereinafter *Tadic Case* Appeals Judgment]; *Furundzija Case* Appeals Judgment (Above n 19), at para 118; *Prosecutor v Kupreskic* (Appeals Chamber Judgment) ICTY-95-16 (23 Oct 2001) para 772; See also *Prosecutor v Delalic et al* (Appeals Chamber Judgment) ICTY-96-21-A (20 Feb 2001) paras 365–6; *Prosecutor v Krnojelac* (Appeals Chamber Judgment) ICTY-97-25-A (17 Sep 2003) para 29 [hereinafter *Krnojelac Case* Appeals Judgment]; *Prosecutor v Kordic* (Judgment) ICTY-95-14/2-T (26 Feb 2001) para 397 [hereinafter *Kordic Case* Trial Judgment]; *Prosecutor v Krstic* (Trial Judgment) ICTY-98-33-T (2 Aug 2001) para 601; *Prosecutor v Kvocka et al* (Trial Judgment) ICTY-98-30/1-T (2 Nov 2001) paras 265 [hereinafter *Kvocka Case* Trial Judgment]; *Krnojelac Case* Trial Judgment (Above n 13), at para 81; *Prosecutor v Vasiljevic* (Judgment) ICTY-98-32-T (29 Nov 2002) para 65 [hereinafter *Vasiljevic Case* Trial Judgment]; *Stakic Case* Trial Judgment (Above n 7), at para 431; *Prosecutor v Simic* (Judgment) ICTY-95-9-T (17 Oct 2003) para 149 [hereinafter *Simic Case* Trial Judgment]; *Prosecutor v Milutinovic* (Decision on Dragoljub Ojdanic's Motion Challenging Jurisdiction—Joint Criminal Enterprise) ICTY-99-37-AR72 (21 May 2003) para 20; See also Olasolo and Perez Cepeda (Above n 8), at 476–8, fn 6.

[26] See Ch 2, s IV.

III Elements of the Notion of Joint Control of the Crime

In order for a senior political or military leader to be criminally responsible as a co-perpetrator under the notion of joint control of the crime, the following two objective elements must be fulfilled: (i) the relevant leader must be part of an agreement or common plan between two or more persons;[27] and (ii) the relevant leader and his fellow co-perpetrators must carry out in a coordinated manner their essential contributions resulting in the realisation of the objective elements of the crime (joint commission of the crime).[28] As seen below, writers, however, have often shown disagreement regarding the scope of the common agreement or plan and of the essential contribution.

Moreover, it will also be necessary that the following three subjective elements be fulfilled: (i) the relevant leader must fulfil the subjective elements of the crime in question, including any requisite ulterior intent or *dolus specialis*;[29] (ii) the relevant leader and the other co-perpetrators must all be mutually aware and mutually accept that implementing their common plan may result in the realisation of the objective elements of the crime;[30] and (iii) the relevant leader must be aware of the factual circumstances enabling him to jointly control the crime.[31]

A Objective Elements

i Common Agreement or Common Plan

The need for a common agreement or a common plan is inherent to the very concept of co-perpetration, according to which a senior political or military leader is considered as a principal to the crime as a whole despite the fact that he has not carried out all the elements of such crime. This is only possible because the contributions made by the other co-perpetrators are attributed to him insofar as they

---

[27] *Lubanga Case* Confirmation of Charges (Above n 1), at paras 343–5; *Katanga and Ngudjolo Case* Confirmation of Charges (Above n 1), at paras 522–3. See also *Stakic Case* Trial Judgment (Above n 7), at paras 470–77, which, as seen below in Ch 5, s VI.C.ii.b and s VI.C.ii.c, divided this element into the following two sub-elements: (i) common goal; and (ii) agreement or silent consent.

[28] *Lubanga Case* Confirmation of Charges (*Ibid*), at para 346–8; *Katanga and Ngudjolo Case* Confirmation of Charges (*Ibid*), at paras 524–5. See also *Stakic Case* Trial Judgment (*Ibid*), at paras 478-91, which, as seen below in Ch 5, s VI.C.ii.d and s VI.C.ii.e, divided this element into the following two sub-elements: (i) coordinated co-operation; and (ii) joint control over criminal conduct.

[29] *Lubanga Case* Confirmation of Charges (*Ibid*), at paras 349–60. See also *Stakic Case* Trial Judgment (*Ibid*), at para 495, which refers to this element as '*mens rea* for the specific crime charged'.

[30] *Lubanga Case* Confirmation of Charges (*Ibid*), at paras 361–5. See also *Stakic Case* Trial Judgment (*Ibid*), at para 496, which refers to this element as 'mutual awareness of substantial likelihood that crimes would occur'.

[31] *Lubanga Case* Confirmation of Charges (*Ibid*), at paras 366–7. See also *Stakic Case* Trial Judgment (*Ibid*), at paras 397–8, which refers to this element as 'Dr. Stakic's awareness of the importance of his own role'.

are made in a coordinated manner in the implementation of a common plan. Accordingly:

> [P]articipation in the commission of a crime without co-ordination with one's co-perpetrators falls outside the scope of co-perpetration within the meaning of article 25 (3) (a) of the Statute.[32]

An agreement (common plan) is necessary because the co-perpetrators are inter-dependent and, in order to act in a co-ordinated fashion, they need to have reached an agreement to execute the crime together. A senior political or military leader who makes a contribution without having agreed upon this with the other co-perpetrators lacks awareness of the inter-dependent relationship among them and, hence, cannot be a co-perpetrator because he cannot be attributed the contributions made by them.[33] Such a leader could, at best, be an accessory to the crime.

The agreement among the co-perpetrators needs to contain 'an element of criminality'.[34] However, it does not need to be specifically directed at the commission of a crime.[35] On the contrary, it can be directed to attain a legal goal (i.e., securing political control of a given municipality in Bosnia and Herzegovina), and include a criminal element that will be triggered under certain conditions (the co-perpetrators were aware that, due to the opposition of the other side in the targeted municipality, a campaign of persecution against them might be needed in order to secure political control of the municipality).[36] In this last scenario, it suffices:

(i) [t]hat the co-perpetrators have agreed (a) to start the implementation of the common plan to achieve a non-criminal goal, and (b) to only commit the crime if certain conditions are met; and

(ii) that the co-perpetrators (a) are mutually aware of the probability that implementing the common plan (which is specifically directed at the achievement of a non-criminal goal) will result in the commission of the crime, and (b) mutually accept such an outcome.[37]

This marks an important difference with the notion of joint criminal enterprise because according to this notion, it is not sufficient if the common plan has an element of criminality that will only be triggered under certain conditions. On the contrary, the notion of joint criminal enterprise requires that either the ultimate goal of the implementation of the common plan or the means to achieve it be

---

[32] *Lubanga Case* Confirmation of Charges (*Ibid*), at para 343; *Katanga and Ngudjolo Case* Confirmation of Charges (Above n 1), at para 522.

[33] Perez Cepeda (Above n 2), at 417; Mir Puig (Above n 3), at 385–6; Kuhl (Above n 4), at § 20 No 106.

[34] *Lubanga Case* Confirmation of Charges (Above n 1), at para 344. See also *Stakie* Case Trial Judgment (Above n 7), at paras 470–477.

[35] Olasolo and Perez Cepeda (Above n 8), at 501.

[36] Another example would be if the co-perpetrators agree to only carry out the criminal conduct if any of them are detected and followed. See Entscheidungen des Bundesgerichtshofs in Strafsachen 11, p 268.

[37] *Lubanga Case* Confirmation of Charges (Above n 1), at para 344. See also *Stakie* Case Trial Judgment (Above n 7), at para 496.

criminal. In other words, for a common criminal purpose to exist, the common plan must necessarily involve the commission of a crime.[38]

Some writers, including Jakobs, don't even require a common agreement in the sense of meeting of the minds.[39] For him, the unilateral decision of adaptation,[40] through which one person links his contribution with the actions of another person (both being considered co-perpetrators), can be sufficient. However, most writers argue that co-perpetration based on joint control of the crime requires at least an implicit agreement among the co-perpetrators. There has to be a meeting of the minds regarding the common plan in the sense that each participant wants to carry it out with the others as equal partners.[41]

In the author's view, the criterion of the joint commission of the crime as a result of the co-ordinated sum of contributions constitutes the material basis for the reciprocal attribution to a co-perpetrator of the actions carried out by the other co-perpetrators. On the one hand, the contributions of all co-perpetrators, which taken in an isolated manner would not be sufficient to complete the objective elements of the crime, must all together complete the offence. On the other hand, the completion of the objective elements of the crime in this way is only possible through a connection between all co-perpetrators that is reflected by a division of functions and a co-ordinated addition of the efforts of each co-perpetrator. This makes the concurrence of the will of each co-perpetrator an inevitable requirement, which does not necessarily have to take the form of an explicit agreement (silent consent may suffice).[42] In addition, the existence of such an agreement may be inferred from the co-ordinated action of the co-perpetrators.[43]

---

[38] *Tadic Case* Appeals Judgment (Above n 25), at para 227; *Krnojelac Case* Appeals Judgment (Above n 25), at para 31; *Vasiljevic Case* Appeals Judgment (Above n 13), at para 100; *Prosecutor v Kvocka et al* (Appeals Chamber Judgment) ICTY-98-30/1-A (28 Feb 2005) paras 81, 96 [hereinafter *Kvocka Case* Appeals Judgment]; *Prosecutor v Stakic* (Appeals Chamber Judgment) ICTY-97-24-A (22 Mar 2006) para 64 [hereinafter *Stakic Case* Appeals Judgment]; *Prosecutor v Brdanin* (Appeals Chamber Judgment) ICTY-99-36-A (3 Apr 2007) para 364 [hereinafter *Brdanin Case* Appeals Judgment]; *Simic Case* Trial Judgment (Above n 25), at para 158; *Prosecutor v Krajisnik* (Judgment) ICTY-00-39-T (27 Sep 2006) para 883 [hereinafter *Krajisnik Case* Trial Judgment]; See also Ch 4, s III.A.ii.

[39] Jakobs (Above n 7), at para 21/43; HH Lesch, *Zeitschrift fur die gesamte Strafrechtswissenschaft* 105 (1993) p 292; FJ Vicente Remesal, E Penaranda Ramos, F Lavilla Baldo, M Diaz y Garcia Conlledo, JM Silva Sanchez, C Suarez Gonzalez, J Mira Benavent, and JL Gonzalez Cussac, 'Autoria y Participacion en Determinados Supuestos de Vigilancia: Comentarios a la STS de 21 de febrero de 1989' (1992) 27 *Poder Judicial* 195 [hereinafter Vicente Remesal et al].

[40] The term originally used by Jakobs (Above n 7) to refer to this notion is 'Einpassungsentschluss'.

[41] Entscheidungen des Bundesgerichtshofs in Strafsachen 37, p 292; M Diaz y Garcia Conlledo, *La Autoria en Derecho Penal* (Barcelona, Universidad de Leon, 1991) 653 [hereinafter Diaz y Garcia Conlledo]; S Cramer and G Heine in Schonke and Schroder (eds), *Kommentar zum Strafgesetzbuch* (26th edn, Munich, CH Beck, 2001) § 25, No 66; Kuhl (Above n 4), at 104; Jescheck and Weigend (Above n 2), at 678.

[42] *Lubanga Case* Confirmation of Charges (Above n 1), at para 345; *Katanga and Ngudjolo Case* Confirmation of Charges (Above I), at para 523.

[43] *Lubanga Case* Confirmation of Charges (Above n 1), at para 345; *Katanga and Ngudjolo Case* Confirmation of Charges (Above n 1), at para 523.

Co-perpetration based on joint control may also be applied to 'subsequent co-perpetrators' who join the common plan once the realisation of the objective elements of the crime have already started.[44] This is applicable in particular to:

(i) Continuous crimes, understood as cases in which the common plan encompasses the commission of a plurality of crimes of a similar nature, which are treated as if all of them would constitute one continuous crime—for instance, despite the fact that, every time a child under the age of 15 was used by the UPC/FPLC to actively participate in hostilities, a war crime was completed, ICC Pre-Trial Chamber I decided to treat as a continuous war crime all instances of use by the UPC/FPLC of children under the age of 15 years to participate actively in hostilities[45]; and

(ii) Permanent crimes, understood as cases in which the common plan encompasses an offence of a continuing nature—this is the case of the crime of enlisting or conscripting children under the age of 15 years because it continues to be committed as long as the children remain in the armed forces, and thus it only ceases to be committed when the children leave such forces or reach the age of 15.[46]

Senior political or military leaders who join the common plan at the execution stage will only be 'subsequent co-perpetrators' if, due to the essential character of the functions that are assigned to them, they share control over the continuing realisation of the objective elements of the crime with the original co-perpetrators. In addition, they are criminally liable as co-perpetrators only for that part of the execution of the common plan over which they have joint control. Hence, they are not criminally liable as co-perpetrators for those crimes already completed before they joined the common plan.[47] Though, depending on the circumstances, they could be held responsible as accessories to such crimes.[48]

---

[44] U Kindhauser, *Strafgesetzbuch, Lehr-und Praxiskommentar* (Portland, Nomos, 2002) § 25 No 50 [hereinafter Kindhauser]; Jescheck and Weigend (Above n 2), at 678; Roxin (Above n 1), at 289; Lackner and Kuhl (Above n 7), at § 25, No 12. See also *Lubanga Case* Warrant of Arrest (Above n 7), at para 105; *Lubanga Case* Confirmation of Charges (*Ibid*), at para 248, fn 321.

[45] *Lubanga Case* Warrant of Arrest (*Ibid*), at 105; *Lubanga Case* Confirmation of Charges (*Ibid*), at para 248, fn 321.

[46] As pointed out in the *Lubanga Case* Confirmation of Charges (*Ibid*), at para 248, offences of a continuing nature are referred to in some systems as 'permanent crimes' and in other as 'continuous crimes'.

[47] Kindhauser (Above n 44), at § 25 No 50; Jescheck and Weigend (Above n 2), at 678; Roxin (Above n 1), at 289; Lackner and Kuhl (Above n 7), at § 25, No 12.

[48] For instance, if the conduct of senior political and military leaders after the completion of these crimes substantially assists to secure the impunity of the physical perpetrators, they could be held liable for aiding and abetting pursuant to art 25(3)(c) RS, art 7(1) ICTYS and art 6(1) ICTRS. See *Ntagerura Case* Appeals Judgment (Above n 13), at para 372; *Blaskic Case* Appeals Judgment (Above n 13), at 48; *Simic Case* Appeals Judgment (Above n 13), at para 85; *Blagojevic Case* Appeals Judgment (Above n 13), at para 127; GP Fletcher, *Rethinking Criminal Law* (2nd edn, Oxford, Oxford University Press, 2000) 645; *United States v Oswald Pohl et al* (1947–48) in United Nations War Crimes Commission, Law Reports of Trial of War Criminals, Vol V, 53; See also Ch 4, s VII.A. Furthermore, even in cases in which the ex post facto assistance of senior political and military leaders does not reach the level of a substantial contribution, they could still be held liable pursuant to art 25(3)(d) RS. See Ch 5, s II. Moreover, if

ii Essential Contribution

A senior political or military leader has no joint control over the crime unless he is assigned an essential function in the implementation of the common plan. Only then would he be in a position of frustrating the implementation of the common plan by not carrying out his contribution.[49] This is a key difference with the notion of joint criminal enterprise, according to which the contribution to the implementation of the common criminal purpose need not be significant or substantial.[50] As a result, minor contributions may be sufficient to hold senior political and military leaders liable as co-perpetrators for their participation in a joint criminal enterprise as long as they share the common criminal purpose.[51]

For some writers, the statement that the co-perpetrators have a joint control of the crime does not hide the fact that each co-perpetrator is only in control of his own contribution, which he carries out consciously and freely, and that he, at best, has a 'negative control' over the contributions of the other co-perpetrators because he may only interrupt the implementation of the common plan by withholding his contribution.[52]

Furthermore, for some writers, joint control of the crime requires the performance of an essential function at the execution stage.[53] Political and military leaders who make their contributions at the planning or preparatory stages do not have joint control of the crime because, once they have made their contribution, the

the physical perpetrators of the crimes already completed are their own subordinates, senior political or military leaders could be held liable pursuant to art 28 RS, art 7(3) ICTYS and art 6(3) ICTRS for failures of their duty to punish. See *Blaskic Case* Appeals Judgment, at 72; *Prosecutor v Blaskic* (Judgment) ICTY-95-14-T (3 Mar 2000) para 355 [hereinafter *Blaskic Case* Trial Judgment]; *Kordic Case* Trial Judgment (Above n 25), at para 446; *Kvocka Case* Trial Judgment (Above n 25), at para 316; *Prosecutor v Halilovic* (Judgment) ICTY-01-48-T (16 Nov 2005) para 100; *Prosecutor v Hadzihasanovic* (Judgment) ICTY-01-47-T (15 Mar 2006) paras 173–4. See also Ch 3, s II.B.ii.

[49] *Lubanga Case* Confirmation of Charges (Above n 1), at para 347; *Katanga and Ngudjolo Case* Confirmation of Charges (Above 1), at para 525

[50] *Tadic Case* Appeals Judgment (Above n 25), at para 228; *Krnojelac Case* Appeals Judgment (Above n 25), at para 84; *Kvocka Case* Appeals Judgment (Above n 38), at para 82; *Vasiljevic Case* Appeals Judgment (Above n 13), at para 97; *Stakic Case* Trial Judgment (Above n 7), at para 65; *Brdanin Case* Appeals Judgment (Above n 38), at para 365; *Simic Case* Trial Judgment (Above n 25), at para 157; *Krajisnik Case* Trial Judgment (Above n 38), at para 79. Concurring A Bogdan, 'Individual Criminal Responsibility in the Execution of a "Joint Criminal Enterprise" in the Jurisprudence of the *Ad hoc* International Tribunal for the Former Yugoslavia' (2006) 6 *International Criminal Law Review* 82. See also Ch 4, s VII.B.

[51] K Gustafson, 'The Requirements of an "Express Agreement" for Joint Criminal Enteprise Liability: A Critique of Brdanin' (2007) 5 *Journal of International Criminal Justice* 141; AM Danner and JS Martinez, 'Guilty Associations: Joint Criminal Enterprise, Command Responsibility and the Development of International Criminal Law' (2005) 93 *California Law Review* 150–51; JD Ohlin, 'Three Conceptual Problems with the Doctrine of Joint Criminal Enterprise' (2007) 5 *Journal of International Criminal Justice* 89 [hereinafter Ohlin] have highlighted the need for the interpretation of the notion of joint criminal enterprise as requiring a significant level of contribution.

[52] Diaz y Garcia Conlledo (Above n 41), at 669; A Gimbernat Ordeig, *Autor y Complice en Derecho Penal* (Madrid, Universidad de Madrid, 1966) 147 [hereinafter Gimbernat Ordeig]; Vicente Remesal et al (Above n 39), at 197–9.

[53] Mir Puig (Above n 3), at 385; Roxin (Above n 1), at 294; RD Herzberg, *Taterschaft und Teilnahme* (Munich, Beck, 1977) 65; H Kohler, *Strafrecht Allgemeiner Teil* (Berlin, 1997) 518.

execution of the objective elements of the crime is out of their hands[54]. In fact, in these cases, the execution of the objective elements of the crime only depends on the will of those who carry them out as long as they act consciously and freely.

For instance, the senior political leader who informs a paramilitary group about the location of a group of civilians of the targeted ethnic group does not share control of the commission of the crime with the members of the paramilitary group. Once he has communicated the relevant information, he is 'out of the game', and, thus leaves the actual performance of the objective elements of the crime in the hands of the paramilitary group. As a result, the senior political leader who passed the information has no control, and thus, cannot be said to share control of the crime with the members of the paramilitary group.

But, what would happen if the informant, instead of a senior political leader, is one of the high-ranking members of the paramilitary group who has been assigned such a task as a result of a previous division of the functions to be carried out at the planning, preparatory and execution stages among the members of the paramilitary group? And, what would happen if the performance of the informant's task is considered to be a necessary pre-requisite to go ahead with the execution of the objective elements of the crime?

According to Roxin,[55] the above-mentioned high-ranking member of the paramilitary group who acts as an informant cannot be a co-perpetrator. He justifies this approach on two main reasons: (i) the informant does not share any control of the actual commission of the crime (once he has communicated his information, he leaves the actual commission of the crime up to the other members of the paramilitary group); and (ii) the performance of the objective elements of a crime may depend on many events, and if any participant in any such event were to be a co-perpetrator, the notion of co-perpetration based on joint control of the crime would be extremely broad, and the notion of aiding and abetting would almost be an empty notion.

In addition, the fact that a political or military leader plays a substantial role in the preparatory phase (ie in reaching the agreement to commit the crime) cannot make up for the lack of an essential function at the execution stage. Joint control can only be attained by the objective relevance of the function carried out at the execution stage and the awareness of such relevance. Political and military leaders who participate only at the preparatory stage can never be co-perpetrators even if they carry out their tasks with a view to implement the common plan.[56]

However, at the same time, Roxin states that a rigid distinction between the preparatory and execution stages is not possible. In his view, such a distinction should be undertaken on the basis of a set of guidelines (not fixed criteria) that

---

[54] For these writers, the military commander of a unit, the head of a paramilitary group or the boss of a gang, who do not participate in the execution of the crime, would, in general, not be considered as co-perpetrators. However, in those cases in which they direct or secure the execution of the crime, they could be considered co-perpetrators even if they are not present. See Roxin (*Ibid*), at 299.

[55] *Ibid* at 294.

[56] *Ibid* at 294 and 299.

need to take into consideration the facts of the case. These guidelines should be based on the notion of the 'unitary sense of the action'. As a result, events which are necessary for, directly linked to, or immediately before the carrying out of the objective elements of the crime, are part of the execution phase.

Numerous authors do not share Roxin's view that only contributions at the execution stage may give joint control of the crime.[57] In this regard, Gimbernat Ordeig has affirmed that this approach is contradictory because if the key element of the notion of joint control of the crime is the power to disrupt the plan by withholding one's contribution, it would seem that those persons who carry out essential contributions at the preparatory stage also have this power and therefore, would also have functional control of the crime.[58] Others, such as Munoz Conde, Jescheck, Weigend and Kuhl have pointed out that the requirement of a contribution at the execution stage can be waived because the contribution of any senior political or military leader in the crime for the purposes of determining whether or not he has functional control of the crime must be assessed from the overall perspective of the implementation of the common plan.[59] And, from this perspective, playing a key role at the preparatory stage suffices to have joint control of the crime.[60] Thus, the key element is not the intervention at the execution stage but the joint control of the crime, which can exist despite the fact that the contribution does not, *stricto sensu*, consist of executive acts.[61]

In the author's view, there are several reasons which support the view that co-perpetration based on joint control of the crime does not necessarily require that the contribution is made at the execution stage. First, from the perspective of the diversity of the criminal phenomenon, there is conduct that, despite the fact that it is not directly executive, is directly and immediately linked to the execution of the objective elements of the crime and the consequent harm on the societal value protected by international criminal law. Therefore, it should be considered an integral part of the commission of the crime.

Second, it is true that some writers see the notion of co-perpetration as a kind of conspiracy which is put in practice. Hence, they distinguish co-perpetration from conspiracy in that co-perpetration requires, besides the meeting of the minds, a subsequent contribution at the execution stage. However, it is also true

---

[57] See inter alia H Welzel, 'Studien zum System des Strafrechts' 58 (1939) *ZSTW* 551; Jescheck and T Weigend (Above n 2) 680; Kuhl (Above n 4), at No 111; K Ambos, *La Parte General del Derecho Penal Internacional: Bases para una Elaboracion Dogmatica* (Uruguay, Konrad-Adenauer-Stiftung, 2005) 192; Diaz y Garcia Conlledo (Above n 41), at 672.

[58] Gimbernat Ordeig (Above n 52), at 149.

[59] F Munoz Conde, '¿Dominio de la Voluntad en virtud de Aparatos Organizados en Organizaciones no Desvinculadas del Derecho?' (2000) 6 *Revista Penal* 113 [hereinafter Munoz Conde, *Dominio de la Voluntad*];Jescheck and Weigend (Above n 2), at 680; Kuhl (Above n 4), at No 111.

[60] *Ibid.* See also Kindhauser (Above n 44), at § 25 No 38. According to German case law, a contribution in the preparatory phase is sufficient, because they follow a more subjective approach of distinguishing between perpetrators and aidors and abettors.

[61] F Munoz Conde, 'Problemas de Autoria y Participacion en la Criminalidad Organizada' in C Ferre Olive and E Anarte Borrallo (eds), *Delincuencia Organizada: Aspectos Penales, Procesales y Criminologicos* (Universidad de Huelva, 1999) 67 [hereinafter Munoz Conde].

that the distinction between the preparatory and the execution stages is a difficult one when the crime is committed by an individual alone, and it becomes far more complicated when the crime is committed by the co-ordinated action of a plurality of persons.[62] In fact, even Roxin, aware of this problem, adopts quite a flexible approach to the distinction between the preparatory and execution stages.

Third, those who require a contribution at the execution stage don't seem to take into consideration that the objective elements of the crime may be comprised of more than one action.[63]

Fourth, article 25(3)(a) RS does not expressly require, *strictu sensu*, a contribution at the execution stage from the co-perpetrators, because it is simply referring to the commission of the crime 'joint with others'.[64] In this regard, ICC Pre Trial Chamber I has emphasised in the *Lubanga* and *Katanga and Ngudjolo* cases that:

> [A]lthough some authors have linked the essential character of a task—and hence the ability to exercise joint control over the crime—to its performance at the execution stage of the crime, the Statute does not contain any such restriction. Designing the attack, supplying weapons, and ammunitions, exercising the power to move the previously recruited and trained troops to the fields; and/or coordinating and monitoring the activities of those troops, may constitute contributions that must be considered essential regardless of when are they exercised (before or during the execution stage of the crime).[65]

It must be highlighted that this conclusion has been reached despite the fact that, according to article 25(3)(f) RS, the execution stage starts by carrying out any action or omission that constitutes a 'substantial step' for the execution of the objective elements of the crime—this constitutes a broad interpretation of the doctrine of unity of action between the execution of the objective elements of the crime and the performance of those other acts which immediately prepare for the execution.[66]

Finally, there are a number of national criminal laws, such as article 28(1) of the Spanish Penal Code[67] or article 29 of the Colombian Penal Code,[68] which, as

---

[62] F Munoz Conde, 'Problemas de Autoria y Participacion en la Criminalidad Organizada' in C Ferre Olive and E Anarte Borrallo (eds), *Delincuencia Organizada: Aspectos Penales, Procesales y Criminologicos* (Universidad de Huelva, 1999) 67 [hereinafter Munoz Conde].

[63] Vicente Remesal et al (Above n 39), at 204; E Bacigalupo, 'Notas sobre el fundamento de la coautoria en el Derecho Penal' (1993) 31 *Poder Judicial* 31–40.

[64] See A Eser, 'Individual Criminal Responsibility' in A Cassese, P Gaeta, and JRWD Jones (eds), *The Rome Statute of the International Criminal Court: A Commentary* (Oxford, Oxford University Press, 2002) 793–4 [hereinafter Eser]; Ambos, *Article 25* (Above n 7), at 478–80.

[65] *Katanga and Ngudjolo Case* Confirmation of Charges (Above 1), at para 526. See also *Lubanga Case* Confirmation of Charges (Above n 1), at para 348.

[66] See Ch 2, s IV.

[67] Art 28(1) of the Spanish Penal Code provides that: '*Son autores quienes realizan el hecho por si solos, conjuntamente o por medio de otro del que se sirven como instrumento*' (Perpetrators are those who commit the crime by themselves, jointly with others, or through another person whom they use as a tool; translation by the author); See F Munoz Conde, *El delito de alzamiento de bienes* (2nd edn, Barcelona, Libreria Bosch, 1999) 178. For some writers, the problem of this solution in Spanish law consists of the impossibility of distinguishing between co-perpetration and necessary cooperation if the requirement of the co-perpetrators' contribution at the execution stage is eliminated. See J Lopez Barja de Quiroga, *Autoria y Participacion* (Madrid, Akal, 1996) 81.

[68] Art 29 of the Colombian Criminal Code establishes: '*Son coautores los que, mediando un acuerdo comun, actuan con division del trabajo criminal atendiendo la importancia del aporte*' (Those persons

article 25(3)(a) RS, only refer to the joint commission of the crime ('*realizan el hecho [. . .] conjuntamente*'), without requiring any contribution at the execution stage.

B Subjective Elements

Co-perpetration based on joint control requires first and foremost that senior political and military leaders carry out their essential contributions with the subjective elements required by the crimes in question, including any requisite ulterior intent or *dolus specialis*.[69]

As seen above, ICC Pre Trial Chamber I has interpreted the 'intent and knowledge' requirement of article 30 RS as embracing the notion of *dolus* as a general subjective element of the crimes provided for in RS.[70] Despite the element of uncertainty recently introduced by the *Katanga and Ngudjolo Case* Confirmation of the Charges in relation to *dolus eventualis*, this includes, in principle, *dolus directus* in the first degree, *dolus directus* in the second degree and *dolus eventualis*.[71] Hence, unless otherwise provided for in the definition of the crimes in question, senior political and military leaders must carry out their contributions: (i) aiming at the commission of the crimes included in the common plan, (ii) being certain that the crimes will take place as a result of implementing the common plan, or, at the very least, (iii) being aware of the risk that the crimes will take place as a result of executing the common plan and accepting such a result.[72] Moreover, in cases of high level of risk—such as, when crimes will occur in the ordinary course of events or there is a substantial likelihood that crimes will occur—the acceptance of the occurrence of the crimes may be inferred from the fact that senior political and military leaders carry out their contribution in spite of their awareness of the high level of risk.[73]

As discussed in previous sections, the case law of the *Ad hoc* Tribunals has progressively moved towards a common general subjective element which is applicable to most crimes within their jurisdiction.[74] This standard is comprised

who, on the basis of a common plan, act in accordance with the principle of division of tasks for the performance of the crime are co-perpetrators depending on the importance of their contributions. Translation by the author).

[69] *Lubanga Case* Confirmation of Charges (Above n 1), at para 349; *Stakic Case* Trial Judgment (Above n 7), at para 495. In relation to the subjective elements of the crimes provided for in the RS, the ICTYS and the ICTRS, see Ch 3, s I.C.ii and s I.C.iii.

[70] *Lubanga Case* Confirmation of Charges (*Ibid*), at paras 351–2. See also Ch 3, s I.C.ii.

[71] *Ibid*. See also JL Rodriguez-Villasante y Prieto, 'Los Principios Generales del Derecho Penal en el Estatuto de Roma de la Corte Penal Internacional' (Jan-Jun 2000) 75 *Revista Espanola de Derecho Militar* 417; DK Piragoff, 'Article 30: Mental Element' in O Triffterer (ed), *Commentary on the Rome Statute of the International Criminal Court* (Baden-Baden, Nomos, 1999) 534. Compare E Van Sliedregt, *The Criminal Responsibility of Individuals for Violations of International Humanitarian Law* (The Hague, TMC Asser Press, 2003) 87 [hereinafter Van Sliedregt].

[72] *Lubanga Case* Confirmation of Charges (*Ibid*), at para 353.

[73] *Lubanga Case* Confirmation of Charges (*Ibid*), at paras 353–4. See also *Stakic Case* Trial Judgment (Above n 7), at para 487.

[74] See Ch 3, s I.C.iii.

of: (i) the awareness of the substantial likelihood that one's conduct will generate the objective elements of the crime, and (ii) the acceptance of such risk, which is considered to be implicit in the decision to proceed with one's conduct in spite of knowing the likely consequences of it.[75]

Co-perpetration based on functional control requires two additional subjective elements.[76] In relation to the first one, ICC Pre Trial Chamber I has held in the *Lubanga* case that:

> The suspect and the other co-perpetrators (a) must all be mutually aware of the risk that implementing their common plan may result in the realisation of the objective elements of the crime, and (b) must all mutually accept such a result by reconciling themselves with it or consenting to it.[77]

This is a key element of the notion of co-perpetration based on joint control because senior political and military leaders, who have not themselves carried out all the objective elements of the crime, can be attributed the contributions made by the other co-perpetrators only if all of them carry out their contributions to the implementation of the common plan having mutually accepted the likely result that this will bring about the commission of the crime. As ICC Pre-Trial Chamber I has explained:

> [I]t is precisely the co-perpetrators' mutual awareness and acceptance of this result which justifies (a) that the contributions made by the others may be attributed to each of them, including the suspect, and (b) that they be held criminally responsible as principals of the whole crime.[78]

The ICTY Trial Judgement in the *Stakic* case has defined this subjective element as 'mutual awareness of the substantial likelihood that crimes would occur',[79] in the understanding that, in cases of a high level of risk, there is no need for the co-perpetrators' explicit mutual acceptance of the crimes because this is inferred from their decision to carry out their respective contributions to the common plan in spite of their awareness of the high level of risk.[80]

---

[75] This standard was initially proposed by the Prosecution in the Kordic case. See *Kordic Case* Trial Judgment (Above n 25), at para 375, referring to paras 40–41 of Annex IV of the Prosecution Closing Brief. See also Ch 3, s I.C.iii.

[76] *Lubanga Case* Confirmation of Charges (Above n 1), at para 361.

[77] *Ibid.*

[78] *Ibid* at para 362.

[79] *Stakic Case* Trial Judgment (Above n 7), at para 496.

[80] See the definition of *dolus eventualis* given by the *Stakic Case* Trial Judgment (*Ibid*), at para 487. See also Ch 3, s I.C.iii. In this regard, ICC Pre-Trial Chamber I has distinguished two different scenarios in the *Lubanga* case. In the first scenario, the level of risk of bringing about the objective elements of the crime as a result of implementing the common plan is high (substantial likelihood standard). In these cases, the co-perpetrators' mutual acceptance of the occurrence of the crime can be inferred from (i) their mutual awareness of the substantial likelihood that the implementation of the common plan will bring about the objective elements of the crime, and (ii) their decision to implement the common plan despite such awareness. In the second scenario, the level of risk of bringing about the objective elements of the crime as result of executing the common plan is low. In these cases, all co-perpetrators 'must have clearly or expressly accepted the idea that implementing the common plan would result in the realisation of the objective elements of the crime'. See *Lubanga Case* Confirmation of Charges (Above n 1), at paras 353–4.

As a result, all co-perpetrators must, at the very least, share a *dolus eventualis* with regard to the realisation of the objective elements of the crimes as a result of implementing the common plan. Furthermore, if one takes into account that, as held by ICC Pre-Trial Chamber I in the *Lubanga* case,[81] *dolus eventualis* is also part of the 'intent and knowledge' requirement provided for in article 30 RS (and thus applicable as general subjective element to the crimes contained in RS), and that the 'awareness of the substantial likelihood' standard (which is applicable as general subjective element to most crimes within the jurisdiction of the *Ad hoc* Tribunals) can also fulfill, as seen in chapter 3, the requirements of *dolus eventualis*, one can only draw one conclusion. This is that co-perpetration based on joint control requires, as a general rule, that senior political and military leaders, in order to become principals to the crimes, carry out their essential contributions to the common plan sharing with the other co-perpetrators a *dolus eventualis* with regard to the realisation of the objective elements of the crimes as a result of implementing the common plan.

Logically, if the definition of the crimes in question explicitly requires (i) a general subjective element which is more stringent than a *dolus eventualis* standard (i.e. *dolus directus* in the first or *dolus directus* in the second degree), or (ii) an ulterior intent or *dolus specialis*, the relevant senior political or military leader will also have to fulfil it.[82]

This marks a key difference with the notion of joint criminal enterprise, which requires that all participants in the enterprise share the aim to commit the core crimes of the enterprise.[83] In other words, the notion of joint criminal enterprise requires that all participants in the enterprise share a *dolus directus* in the first degree with regard to the core crimes of the enterprise, regardless of whether the crimes in question require, in principle, a less stringent subjective element. In addition, if the core crimes of the enterprise require an ulterior intent or *dolus specialis*, all participants in the enterprise must also share such an ulterior intent. By requiring this stringent subjective element, the notion of joint criminal enterprise 'compensates' for the low level of contribution that is required from a senior political or military leader to become a participant in the enterprise (and thus a principal to the crimes).[84]

Furthermore, the notions of joint criminal enterprise and joint control of the crime also differ in the treatment of those crimes which are not part of the common plan. Co-perpetration based on joint control does not distinguish between core and foreseeable crimes and requires a shared *dolus eventualis* standard in relation to any crime committed as a result of the implementation of the common

---

[81] *Lubanga Case* Confirmation of Charges (*Ibid*), at paras 352–5.

[82] *Ibid*, at para 349. See also *Stakic Case* Trial Judgment (Above n 7), at para 495.

[83] *Tadic Case* Appeals Judgment (Above n 25), at para 228; *Krnojelac Case* Appeals Judgment (Above n 25), at para 32; *Vasiljevic Case* Appeals Judgment (Above n 13), at para 101; *Kvocka Case* Appeals Judgment (Above n 38), at para 82; *Stakic Case* Appeals Judgment (Above n 38), at para 65; *Brdanin Case* Appeals Judgment (Above n 38), at para 365; *Simic Case* Trial Judgment (Above n 25), at para 158; *Krajisnik Case* Trial Judgment (Above n 38), at paras 879, 883. See also Ch 4, s III.B.i.

[84] See Ch 4, s III.B.i and s VII.B.

plan. In turn, the notion of joint criminal enterprise distinguishes between core and foreseeable crimes, and in relation to the latter, only requires a standard which, as the ICTY Appeals Chamber has highlighted in the *Blaskic* case, is less stringent than a *dolus eventualis* standard, and which consists of the mere acceptance of the possibility that the foreseeable crimes might be committed in the execution of the common plan.[85]

Moreover, according to co-perpetration based on joint control, if the definition of any of the crimes committed as a result of the implementation of the common plan requires an ulterior intent or *dolus specialis*, the relevant senior political or military leader will have to act motivated by such ulterior intent in order to be considered a principal (co-perpetrator) to the crime.[86] In turn, the extended form of joint criminal enterprise only requires awareness of the mere possibility that the participant in the enterprise who commits the foreseeable crime may be acting with the requisite ulterior intent.[87]

The last subjective element required by co-perpetration based on joint control consists of the awareness of the relevant senior political or military leader of the factual circumstances enabling him to jointly control the crime.[88] According to ICC Pre-Trial Chamber I in the *Lubanga* and *Katanga and Ngudjolo* cases this element requires the senior political or military leader to be aware:

(i)   that his or her role is essential to the implementation of the common plan, and hence in the commission of the crime, and

(ii) that he or she can—by reason of the essential nature of his or her task—frustrate the implementation of the common plan, and hence the commission of the crime, by refusing to perform the task assigned to him or her.[89]

This element is alien to the notion of joint criminal enterprise because according to this notion, the level of control of a senior political or military leader over the commission of the crime, and his awareness of the factual circumstances giving rise to such level of control, are irrelevant.

---

[85] *Blaskic Case* Appeals Judgment (Above n 13), at 33. See also Ch 4, s III.B.iii.a.

[86] *Lubanga Case* Confirmation of Charges (Above n 1), at para 349; *Stakic Case* Trial Judgment (Above n 7), at para 495.

[87] *Prosecutor v Brdanin* (Decision on Interlocutory Appeal) ICTY-99-36-A (19 Mar 2004) paras 5–7. See also Ch 4, s III.B.iii.a.

[88] *Lubanga Case* Confirmation of Charges (Above n 1), at para 366; *Stakic Case* Trial Judgment (Above n 7), at paras 397–8.

[89] *Lubanga Case* Confirmation of Charges (*Ibid*), at para 367. See also *Stakic Case* Trial Judgment (*Ibid*), at paras 397–8, under the heading 'Dr. Stakic's awareness of the importance of his own role'; *Katanga and Ngudjolo Case* Confirmation of the Charges (Above n 1), at paras. 538–9.

IV Cases of Co-perpetration Based on Joint Control of the Crime versus Cases of Indirect Perpetration

A Unsuitability of Co-perpetration Based on Joint Control to Deal with Hierarchical Relationships within Organised Structures of Power

A number of writers consider that the joint action of senior political and military leaders and their subordinates must be treated as a case of co-perpetration based on joint control because, as subordinates act consciously and freely, superiors and subordinates share the control of the crime.[90] These writers use co-perpetration based on joint control, instead of indirect perpetration in its variant of OSP, for the very same purpose of attributing criminal liability as principals to the crime to those senior political and military leaders who design and control its commission. In their view, indirect perpetration is not applicable in cases of fully liable physical perpetrators[91] because, according to the principle of responsibility,[92] indirect perpetration cannot be extended to situations where the 'tool' is responsible for its behaviour.[93]

Those writers favouring the application of OSP have put forth three main reasons against the use of co-perpetration based on joint control to hold senior political and military leaders liable for the crimes committed by their subordinates in an organised structure of power: (i) lack of common agreement or common plan (there is no common decision to jointly commit the crime); (ii) lack of a joint commission of the crime; (iii) different structure (OSP is structured vertically in the sense that orders given by the members at the top of the organisation are transmitted down to the lowest ranks, while co-perpetration based on joint control is structured horizontally in the sense of co-ordinated equivalent and simultaneous contributions).[94]

In this regard, one cannot obviate the fact that, in principle, one could say that the requisite of the common agreement or common plan could be met by the mere acceptance by subordinates of the plan designed by their senior political and military leaders. Furthermore, the fact that the superiors' contribution is normally carried out at the preparation stage when they transmit their orders, does not

---

[90] See Jakobs (Above n 7), at 21/103; Jescheck and Weigend (Above n 2), at 670; Otto (Above n 2), at No 57; A Perez Cepeda, 'Criminalidad en la Empresa: Problemas de Autoria y Participacion' (2002) 9 *Revista Penal* 106–21 [Perez Cepeda, *Criminalidad en la Empresa*].

[91] Jescheck and Weigend (*Ibid*), at 670.

[92] The term originally used is 'Verantwortungsprinzip'.

[93] Jescheck and Weigend (Above n 2), at 664.

[94] C Roxin, 'Problemas de Autoria y Participacion en la Criminalidad Organizada' in C Ferre Olive and E Anarte Borrallo (eds), *Delincuencia Organizada: Aspectos Penales, Procesales y Criminologicos* (Universidad de Huelva, 1999) 194 [hereinafter Roxin, *Problemas de Autoria*]. See also C Roxin, *Strafrecht Allgemeiner Teil* (Vol II, Munich, Beck Juristischer Verlag, 2003) § 25, No 120–23 [hereinafter Roxin, *Strafrecht Allgemeiner Teil*].

exclude per se the application of co-perpetration based on joint control because an essential contribution at the preparatory stage may suffice.

However, in the final analysis, co-perpetration based on joint control requires the joint commission of the crime, and, thus, the common decision to jointly commit the crime will normally be an important factor.[95] In addition, not just any level of co-ordination is sufficient because the common agreement or common plan is the basis for the reciprocal attribution to the co-perpetrators of the objective elements of the crime physically carried out by the other co-perpetrators. More importantly, the explanation that the notion of co-perpetration based on joint control (which has a horizontal structure) cannot adequately reflect the vertical or hierarchical relationships among political and military leaders and their subordinates within organised structures of power, and the fact that a notion such as OSP (which has a vertical structure) is likely to better reflect such relationships is, in the author's opinion, compelling.[96]

B Application of Co-perpetration Based on Joint Control of the Crime to Offences Committed through Organisations Which Do Not Qualify as Organised Structures of Power

The distinction between indirect perpetration in its variant of OSP and co-perpetration based on joint control is particularly relevant in the context of economic crimes committed through companies when the physical perpetrators are fully liable for the crimes. Companies, in addition to having usually fewer members, are characterised because their hierarchical structure is not as rigid as it can be in the armed forces, military police, intelligence services and certain organised armed groups and paramilitary groups.[97] Hence, given the impossibility of applying OSP to crimes committed through companies, the question arises as to whether the members of the board of directors and those subordinates who physically implement the common criminal plan can be considered as co-perpetrators because they share the control of the crime.

The same question arises concerning crimes in which it is not possible to apply OSP because they are committed through organisations, which, for a variety of reasons, do not qualify as organised structures of power. This is the case in relation to crimes committed by senior political and military leaders through some paramilitary groups or intelligence units whose members are not interchangeable because of their small size (unless automatic compliance with their orders is secured via alternative means, such as intensive, strict and violent training regimes).[98] If one follows Roxin's approach, this is also the case if crimes are com-

---

[95] Roxin, *Strafrecht Allgemeiner Teil* (*Ibid*), at § 25 No 107.
[96] Entscheidungen des Bundesgerichtshofs in Strafsachen 40, p 237.
[97] See *Katanga and Ngudjolo Case* Confirmation of the Charges (Above n 1), at paras 515–518. See also Ch 3, s III.C.iii.
[98] See Ch 3, s III.C.ii and s III.D.i.

mitted by senior political and military leaders through certain military or police units which usually act in accordance with the law, so that their members cannot be said to be replaceable for the purposes of carrying out illegal activities.[99] As a result, the reasons given by writers in favour for and against the application of the notion of co-perpetration based on joint control to crimes committed through companies are, to an important extent, also valid in relation to crimes committed by senior political and military leaders through small paramilitary groups, intelligence units and some military and police units.

The application of co-perpetration based on joint control to crimes committed through companies has been defended by a number of writers in order to avoid the consideration of the members of the board of directors as mere accessories to those crimes committed by their subordinates—particularly in light of the fact that the members of the board of directors are usually the individuals planning the crimes, adopting the decision to commit the crimes and assigning the tasks to implement the criminal plan to their subordinates in the company[100]. Furthermore, the consideration of the members of the board of directors as mere accessories presents an additional problem concerning those crimes that can only be committed by a special category of individuals (such as civil servants or military personnel). In these cases, if those subordinates who physically carry out the objective elements of the crime do not have such status, and the members of the board of directors who have such status are not considered principals to the crime, one will have to conclude that there is no crime. As a result, the members of the board of directors who have the required status will not be criminally liable either.[101]

According to these writers, when crimes are committed through companies, the key elements are the existence of a common plan subscribed by all co-perpetrators and the fact that that all of them share control of the crime as a result of the key tasks assigned to them. The contribution of all co-perpetrators does not need to take place at the execution stage of the crime—indeed the members of the board of directors would normally make their contribution during the phase of design and adoption of the common criminal plan. As a result, the joint control of the members of the board of directors is: (i) positive while the criminal plan is being devised and discussed because they can prevent its approval; and (ii) negative while the plan is being implemented because they can disrupt its implementation by instructing subordinates to stop its execution.[102]

Roxin[103] and Perez Cepeda[104] have criticised this approach for the following reasons. First, there is no joint decision to commit the crime, because the decision is taken by the members of the board of directors and they, directly or through

---

[99] See Ch 3, s III.C.ii and s III.C.iv.

[100] Munoz Conde (Above n 61), at 67; JM Silva Sanchez, 'Responsabilidad Penal de las Empresas y de sus Organos en Derecho Espanol' in *Fundamentos del sistema europeo de derecho penal. Libro homenaje a Claus Roxin* (Barcelona, JM Bosch, 1995) 369 [hereinafter Silva Sanchez].

[101] Munoz Conde (*Ibid*), at 67.

[102] Munoz Conde (*Ibid*), at 67.

[103] Roxin, *Problemas de Autoria* (Above n 94), at 194.

[104] Perez Cepeda, *Criminalidad en la Empresa* (Above n 90), at 106–21.

intermediaries, instruct the subordinate physical perpetrators to commit the crimes. Second, there is no joint execution of the common criminal plan, because, once the members of the board of directors adopt the common criminal plan, they normally stop their involvement—only one, or a few of them, are usually given the task to properly instruct subordinates on the implementation of the common criminal plan. Moreover, after the instructions are given, even the involvement of the latter stops insofar as they merely oversee the execution of the common criminal plan by their subordinates and report back to the other members of board of directors.

These problems are less acute when the members of the board of directors agree to carry out the crimes and ask one of the members of the board (normally the one in charge of the relevant area) to physically implement the criminal plan, and the requested member, who has also participated in the decision-making process, freely and knowingly accepts and personally carries out the requested task. In this scenario, in which the physical perpetrator is a member of the board of directors who participates in the decision-making process to commit the crimes, one can talk about a joint decision among all co-perpetrators (the members of the board of directors) and a horizontal relationship among them. Thus, the main problem will be confined to the lack of joint implementation of the common criminal plan because, while all co-perpetrators participate in the decision making process where the criminal plan is devised and approved, only one or a few members of the board of directors are assigned to physically implement it. This problem is only insurmountable if one adopts the approach that co-perpetration based on joint control requires that the shared control of each co-perpetrator be derived from an essential contribution at the stage of execution of the crime.[105] Nevertheless, such an approach has been explicitly rejected by ICC Pre-Trial Chamber I Decision on the Confirmation of the Charges in the *Lubanga* case.[106]

Hence, in the author's view, co-perpetration based on joint control would be applicable if the physical implementation of the common criminal plan was assigned to one of the members of the board of directors—or to one of the senior political or military leaders—who participated in the design and approval of the common criminal plan. In this scenario, where there is a joint agreement and a horizontal relationship between all co-perpetrators, the fact that some of them do not make any important contribution at the execution stage and have joint control only because they could call for the suspension of the implementation of the common criminal plan, does not prevent the application of the notion of co-perpetration based on joint control.

More difficulties arise from the other scenario in which the members of the board of directors devise and approve the common criminal plan and, subsequently, instruct (directly or through an intermediary) their subordinates, who

---

[105] This approach is favoured by Roxin (Above n 1), at 299.

[106] *Lubanga Case* Confirmation of Charges (Above n 1), at para 348; Gimbernat Ordeig (Above n 52), at 149; Munoz Conde, *Dominio de la Voluntad* (Above n 59), at 113; Jescheck and Weigend (Above n 2), at 680; Kuhl (Above n 4), at No 111; Kindhauser (Above n 44), at § 25 No 38.

have not participated in the decision making process, to physically implement it. This second scenario also takes place when the members of the board of directors ask one of them (normally the one in charge of the relevant area) to assume the direction of the implementation of the common criminal plan, and the requested member, who has also participated in the decision-making process, freely and knowingly accepts to issue the relevant instructions, to oversee the execution of the common criminal plan and to report back to the board of directors.

In these cases, even if one considers that the joint execution of the deed is not a requirement of the notion of co-perpetration based on joint control, it is evident that: (i) the subordinate physical perpetrators have not participated in the decision making process together with the members of the board of directors (lack of common agreement) and (ii) the relationship between those alleged co-perpetrators who are members of the board of directors and direct the commission of the crimes, and those other alleged co-perpetrators who are further down in the hierarchical structure of the company and physically carry out the objective elements of the crimes is of a vertical (as opposed to horizontal) nature. Indeed, the alleged co-perpetrators do not normally decide anything together and there is no division of functions or tasks because what usually happens is that the members of the board of directors send instructions which are then implemented by their subordinates in the company.

In this regard, those writers who defend the applicability of co-perpetration based on joint control to crimes committed through companies—as well as to those crimes committed by senior political and military leaders through small paramilitary groups, intelligence units and some police and military units—consider that, although the subordinate physical perpetrators do not participate in the decision making process, the requirement of the joint agreement is met if the subordinates freely and knowingly accept the criminal plan as devised and approved by the members of the board of directors (or the relevant senior political and military leaders).[107]

However, in the author's opinion, this does not solve the problems posed by this second scenario in relation to: (i) the lack of participation of the subordinate physical perpetrators together with the members of the board of directors (or the relevant senior political or military leaders) in the decision making process; (ii) the vertical or hierarchical relationship between both groups of alleged co-perpetrators; (iii) the lack of division of functions or tasks between both groups of alleged co-perpetrators and (iv) the lack of a joint implementation of the common criminal plan because of the absence of any contribution of the members of the board of directors (or relevant senior political and military leaders) after the instructions to implement the plan has been passed on to the subordinate physical perpetrators or the intermediaries.

As a result, the author considers that in this second scenario, in which the members of the board of directors (or the relevant senior political and military leaders) devise and approve the common criminal plan, and subsequently instruct, either

---

[107] Munoz Conde (Above n 61), at 67; Silva Sanchez (Above n 100), at 369.

directly or through an intermediary, to implement it to subordinates who have not participated in the decision making process, the notion of co-perpetration based on joint control is not adequate. In this scenario, it is the author's view, that the members of the board of directors, or the relevant senior political and military leaders, could only be held liable as accessories for ordering (or even instigating) those crimes freely and knowingly committed by their subordinates in furtherance of their instructions.[108]

As a result, in those instances in which co-perpetration based on joint control is not applicable, this may lead to impunity if the crimes in question can only be committed by a specific category of individuals (such as civil servants or military personnel) to which the subordinate physical perpetrators do not belong.[109] This is the consequence of: (i) the unsuitability of the notion of co-perpetration based on joint control to deal with vertical or hierarchical relationships, where the common plan is not the result of a joint decision making process and there is no consensual division of functions or tasks; and (ii) the special features of the internal structure of companies and other organisations, such as small paramilitary groups, intelligence units or even some military and police units, which prevent them from being qualified as organised structures of power, thus making the notion of OSP inapplicable, either by itself (indirect perpetration) or in combination with joint control (indirect co-perpetration).[110]

Nevertheless, if one takes into account the definitions of the crimes provided for in the RS, ICTYS and ICTRS, one realises that this negative effect is almost non-existent in relation to genocide, crimes against humanity and war crimes. Moreover, the nature of these crimes is such that senior political and military leaders often carry them out through organisations which are comprised of interchangeable mid and low-level ranks because they (i) are of a larger size; (ii) are organised into a rigid hierarchy; and (iii) act outside the law not just in isolated instances. Therefore, in most cases in which indirect perpetration in its

---

[108] See also Perez Cepeda, *Criminalidad en la Empresa* (Above n 90), at 106–21; Gimbernat Ordeig (Above n 52), at 149; See also Ch 3, s III.C.iv, s III.D.i and s III.D.ii.

[109] For Perez Cepeda, *Criminalidad en la Empresa* (*Ibid*), at paras 106–21, whenever there are intermediaries (mid-level ranks within the company, paramilitary group, intelligence unit, military or police unit) between the board of directors, or the top political and military leaders, and the subordinate physical perpetrators, ordering or instigation are not applicable. As a result, only the intermediaries who are in direct contact with the subordinate physical perpetrators can be criminally liable for ordering or instigating, whereas the members of the board of directors (or the senior political and military leaders) could only be criminally liable if it can be shown that they aided and abetted the commission of the crimes. However, even if this holds true with regard to art 28 of the Spanish Criminal Code, which explicitly requires to directly prompt the physical perpetrators to carry out the crimes, this is not valid for 'ordering' and 'instigating' under art 25(3)(b) RS, art 7(1) ICTYS and art 6(1) ICTRS. See *Blaskic Case* Trial Judgment (Above n 48), at paras 274, 282; *Prosecutor v Brdanin* (Judgment) ICTY-99-36-T (1 Sep 2004) para 270. This approach is also supported by the ILC, 'Report of the International Law Commission on the Work of its 48th Session' (6 May–26 Jul 1996) UN Doc A/51/10, Draft Code of Crimes against Peace and Security of Mankind, art 2(1)(b), commentary para 14. See also Ambos, *Article 25* (Above n 7), at 480; Van Sliedregt (Above n 71), at 83; Eser (Above n 64), at 220. See also Ch 3, s III.D.i and s III.D.ii.

[110] See Ch 3, s III.C.ii and s III.C.iv.

variant of OSP and co-perpetration based on joint control cannot be applied in isolation, they could be jointly applied to hold senior political and military leaders criminal liable as indirect co-perpetrators (principals) of the crimes.

V Applications of the Notion of Co-perpetration Based on Joint Control

A The *Lubanga Case* before the ICC

i *Preliminary Remarks: Unsuitability of Indirect Perpetration in its Variant of OSP*

The best example to date of the application at the international level of the notion of co-perpetration based on joint control is ICC Pre-Trial Chamber I Decision on the confirmation of the charges in the *Lubanga* case. The case against Thomas Lubanga Dyilo deals with events which took place in the context of the armed conflict that occurred in the territory of Ituri (district of the *Orientale* Province in the Democratic Republic of the Congo) between 1 July 2002 and 31 December 2003.[111] ICC Pre-Trial Chamber I found that in this armed conflict, in addition to the army of the Republic of Uganda (Ugandan People Defence Forces, UPDF), a number of organised armed groups were involved, including *l'Union des Patriotes Congolais/Rassemblement pour la Paix* (UPC/RP) and its military wing *les Forces Patriotiques pour la Liberation du Congo* (FPLC), *le Partit pour l'Unite et la Sauvegarde de'l Integrite du Congo (PUSIC)* and *le Front National Integrationniste* (FNI).[112] In this context, the FPLC implemented a policy of enlistment and recruitment of young persons, which also involved children under the age of 15.[113] Furthermore, upon completing their training, the new, young FPLC recruits, including those under the age of 15, were used to actively participate in hostilities.[114]

According to ICC Pre-Trial Chamber I, from early September 2002 until the end of 2003, Lubanga, in addition to serving as de jure President of the UPC/RP:

> [H]ad de facto ultimate control over the adoption and implementation of UPC/RP policies, and only received technical advice from the movement's National Secretaries.[115]

---

[111] *Lubanga Case* Confirmation of Charges (Above n 1), at paras 167–237, in particular paras 220, 236, 237.

[112] The armed conflict was of an international character until the moment the UPDF withdrew from the territory of Ituri on 2 June 2003, and of a non-international character afterwards. See *Lubanga Case* Confirmation of Charges (*Ibid*), at paras 220, 236, 237.

[113] *Lubanga Case* Confirmation of Charges (*Ibid*), at paras 249, 253, 254, 258.

[114] *Ibid* at paras 266–7.

[115] *Ibid* at para 368.

Furthermore, according to ICC Pre-Trial Chamber 1, from the creation of the FPLC as the military wing of the UPC/RP in early September 2002 to the end of 2003, Lubanga served as de jure commander-in-chief of the FPLC, was briefed about the FPLC military operations and about the situation in the FPLC military training camps, and de facto regularly performed the duties associated to such a position.[116] Nevertheless, as a result of the various internal crises which took place in late 2002 and early 2003 within the FPLC, important divisions arose among its military officers.[117] This made Lubanga work more closely with some of the military officers. As a result, Lubanga had "in the main, but not on a permanent basis" the final say over the adoption of FPLC policies and over the implementation by the FPLC of those policies adopted either by UPC/RP or the FPLC.[118]

ICC Pre-Trial Chamber I also held that, as a consequence of these internal disputes, the level of de facto control exercised by Lubanga within the FPLC was lower than that exercised within the UPC/RP—as shown by the fact that members the FPLC General Staff, and in particular the FPLC Chief of Staff 'ordered the launching of military operations without consulting with Thomas Lubanga Dyil'.[119] This is likely the reason why ICC Pre-Trial Chamber I disregarded the application of the notion of indirect perpetration in its variant of OSP in this case. Indeed, in the absence of a clear vertical relationship between the defendant and some of the FPLC high-ranking officers who were apparently involved in the commission of the crimes, the latter could not be considered as interchangeable FPLC members under the control of the defendant. As a result, ICC Pre Trial Chamber I did not even analyse whether the FPLC complied with the requisites to be qualified as an organised structure of power comprised of interchangeable members.[120]

ii Application of the Objective Elements of Co-perpetration Based on Joint Control

a Common Agreement or Common Plan

According to ICC Pre-Trial Chamber I, when the FPLC was established in early September 2002, there was a common agreement among (i) Lubanga; (ii) the highest-ranking officials of the UPC/RP in charge of defence and security (the UPC/RP Deputy National Secretary for Defence and the UPC/RP Chief of

---

[116] *Ibid* at para 373.

[117] *Ibid* at para 375(a)–(b).

[118] *Ibid* at paras 375(c)–376.

[119] *Ibid* at para 374.

[120] This in spite of the fact that, in the *Lubanga Case* Warrant of Arrest (Above n 7), at para 9, ICC Pre-Trial Chamber I had held that 'there are reasonable grounds to believe that, given the hierarchical alleged relationship between Mr Thomas Lubanga Dyilo and the other members of the UPC and FPLC, the concept of indirect perpetration which, along with that of co-perpetration based on joint control of the crime referred to in the Prosecution's Application, is provided in article 25 (3) (a) of the Statute, could be applicable to Mr Thomas Lubanga Dyilo's alleged role in the commission of the crimes set out in the Prosecution's Application'.

Security); (iii) the highest-ranking officers of the FPLC (the FPLC Chief of Staff and the FPLC Deputy Chief of Staff for Military Operations); and (iv) other FPLC senior commanders.[121] All of these individuals knew each other and had worked with each other well before the creation of the FPLC.[122]

ICC Pre-Trial Chamber I found that the common agreement or common plan, which was implemented from early September 2002 until the end of 2003, aimed at furthering the UPC/RP and FPLC war effort by: (i) recruiting, voluntarily or forcibly, young persons into the FPLC; (ii) subjecting them to military training; and (iii) using them to actively participate in military operations and as body-guards to protect military objectives. The agreement did not specifically aim at the commission of a crime. However, it contained an element of criminality because, in spite of the fact that it did not specifically target children under the age of 15 (it targeted young recruits in general), its implementation entailed the objective risk that it would involve such children.[123]

b Essential Contribution

According to ICC Pre-Trial Chamber I, the defendant and the other members of the common plan implemented it in a coordinated manner.[124] The latter had a more direct responsibility in relation to voluntarily and forcibly recruiting young persons, providing them military training and weapons, assigning them to military units or as bodyguards and ordering them into combat.[125] In turn, the defendant (prior to being placed under detention in Kinshasa from 13 August 2003 until the end of 2003) played a coordinating role as a result of his direct and ongoing contacts with the other members of the common plan and his provision of the necessary financial resources.[126]

Furthermore, as held by ICC Pre-Trial Chamber 1, Lubanga contributed to the implementation of the common plan in several other ways, such as by (i) inspecting several FPLC military training camps to encourage and prepare the new FPLC young recruits to participate in hostilities; (ii) encouraging Hema families to contribute to the UPC/RP and FPLC war effort through inter alia the provision of young recruits for the FPLC; and (iii) using children under the age of 15 as his bodyguards.[127]

As a result, ICC Pre-Trial Chamber I found that Lubanga's role was essential because he was the only individual in the position to solve the financial and logistical problems encountered during the implementation of the common plan.[128] It

---

[121] *Lubanga Case* Confirmation of Charges (Above n 1), at para 377 (i).
[122] *Ibid* at para 378.
[123] *Ibid* at para 377.
[124] *Ibid* at paras 397–8.
[125] *Ibid* at para 383(i).
[126] *Ibid* at para 383(ii).
[127] *Ibid* at paras 383(ii)–(iii).
[128] *Ibid* at para 398.

was this role that gave him the power to frustrate the implementation of the common plan by refusing to perform his functions.[129]

iii Application of the Subjective Elements of Co-perpetration Based on Joint Control

ICC Pre-Trial Chamber I held that from the beginning of September 2002 until 13 August 2003, Lubanga and the other members of the common plan all shared the awareness that in the ordinary course of events the implementation of the common plan would involve the voluntary and forcible recruitment of children under the age of 15 in the ranks of the FPLC and the use of such children to participate actively in military operations and as bodyguards to protect military objectives.[130] They all also shared the acceptance of this result by reconciling themselves with it or condoning it.[131]

Moreover, according to ICC Pre-Trial Chamber 1, during this time, Lubanga was aware of (i) the specific role that he played within the UPC/RP and the FPLC; (ii) his coordinating role in the implementation of the common plan in furtherance of the UPC/RP and FPLC war efforts; (iii) the essential nature of his role; and (iv) his ability to frustrate the implementation of the common plan by refusing to play it.[132]

As a result, ICC Pre-Trial Chamber I affirmatively answered the question as to whether the notion of co-perpetration based on joint control of the crime could be applicable to the *Lubanga* case. Additionally, it confirmed the charges against Thomas Lubanga Dyilo because there was sufficient evidence establishing substantial grounds to believe that he held joint control over the crimes and was criminally liable as a co-perpetrator under article 25 (3)(a) RS.[133]

iv Final Remarks

In the author's opinion, the application of the notion of co-perpetration based on joint control in the *Lubanga* case presented two main difficulties: (i) the identification of the members of the common plan; and (ii) the fact that the common plan was not specifically directed at the commission of any crime.

Concerning the first issue, the author opines that determining the identity of the members of the common plan is the cornerstone and most difficult question of any application of the notion of co-perpetration based on joint control. On the one hand, joint control, as any other form of co-perpetration, requires that those

---

[129] *Ibid.*
[130] *Ibid* at paras 404(i)–408.
[131] *Ibid* at paras 404(ii)–408.
[132] *Ibid* at para 409.
[133] *Ibid* at para 410.

persons who physically carried out the objective elements of the crime be among the co-perpetrators. Hence, they must have participated in the decision making process to commit the crime and divide the tasks for the implementation of the common plan.

On the other hand, the further one goes down the chain of command to try to include among the co-perpetrators mid and low level members of the relevant organisation, the more difficult it is to explain (i) how the latter participated in the decision making process together with the senior political and military leaders at the top of the organisation; and (ii) how the division of tasks can be qualified as consensual in a scenario where mid and low level members of the organisation merely execute the instructions that are sent further down the chain of command by the senior political and military leaders who are at the top of the organisation.

Indeed, as seen above,[134] the notion of co-perpetration based on joint control is not suitable to deal with those situations in which the common plan is designed by senior political and military leaders, and it is, subsequently, implemented by their subordinates acting upon their orders (vertical or hierarchical relationships between the masterminds and the executioners). In these situations, one has to resort to the notion of indirect co-perpetration, which is comprised of a combined application of OSP and joint control. However, in the *Lubanga* case, due to the multiple internal disputes within the FPLC, it is doubtful whether the notion of indirect co-perpetration, as used by the ICTY Trial Judgement in the *Stakic* case, could have been applied.

The explicit inclusion among the members of the common plan of 'other FPLC senior commanders' is prima facie problematic because it is not clear how far down the FPLC chain of command this expression might go. Nevertheless, in the author's view, the fact that ICC Pre-Trial Chamber I referred to the FPLC Commander in charge of the South-East Sector (just one level below the highest-FPLC-ranking officers) as an example of who those other FPLC senior commanders could be, reduces, to an important extent, the scope of the problem. In this regard, it is important to highlight that the notion of co-perpetration based on joint control is suitable to the *Lubanga* case because the defendant and the highest-FPLC-ranking officers not only designed the common plan, but they also participated in its physical implementation. As a result, ICC Pre-Trial Chamber I was able to limit the group of co-perpetrators to a small group of top UPC/RP leaders and FPLC high-ranking officers, who were not in a strict hierarchical relationship.

In relation to the second issue, the fact that the common plan to further the UPC/RP and FPLC war effort by voluntarily or forcibly recruiting young people into the FPLC, and by using them to actively participate in hostilities, did not specifically target children under the age of 15, would have prevented the application of the notion of joint criminal enterprise or the common purpose doctrine as

---

[134] See Ch 5, s IV.A and s IV.B.

elaborated by the case law of the *Ad hoc* Tribunals.[135] The reason for this is that this notion constitutes a subjective approach to the concept of co-perpetration which gives priority to the mental state of the alleged co-perpetrators over their objective contribution to the implementation of the common plan. Therefore, it requires that they all agree on a common plan, which is specifically directed at the commission of the core crime(s) of the enterprise.[136]

This marks an important difference with the notion of co-perpetration based on joint control, which only requires that the common plan has an 'element of criminality' because the cornerstone of this notion is the joint control that each co-perpetrator has as a result of the essential function that each of them performs in the implementation of the common plan. Hence, the fact that the common plan did not specifically target children under the age of 15 did not prevent the application of co-perpetration based on joint control as long as its implementation entailed the objective risk that it would involve such children.

B The *Vasiljevic* Case before the ICTY: Co-perpetration Based on Control of the Crime under the Formal Label of Joint Criminal Enterprise

i *Preliminary Remarks: Distinguishing between the* Vasiljevic *and the* Stakic *Cases*

The *Vasiljevic* case is unique in that the ICTY Appeals Chamber attempted (i) to move away from the subjective approach to the distinction between principals and accessories to the crime, which is inherent to the notion of joint criminal enterprise as developed by the case law of the *Ad hoc* Tribunals, and (ii) to resort to the notion of control of the crime as a controlling criterion to distinguish between principals and accessories.

Its uniqueness derives from the fact that the ICTY Appeals Chamber carried out this exercise: (i) in an small case against a low level perpetrator, which did not pose any of the problems identified for the application of the traditional notion of joint criminal enterprise to senior political and military leaders; (ii) in an implicit manner (through the back door) by conditioning any factual finding on the

---

[135] *Tadic Case* Appeals Judgment (Above n 25), at para 227; *Krnojelac Case* Appeals Judgment (Above n 25), at para 31; *Vasiljevic Case* Appeals Judgment (Above n 13), at para 100; *Kvocka Case* Appeals Judgment (Above n 38), at paras 81, 96; *Stakic Case* Appeals Judgment (Above n 38), at para 64; *Brdanin Case* Appeals Judgment (Above n 38), at para 364; *Simic Case* Trial Judgment (Above n 25), at para 158; *Krajisnik Case* Trial Judgment (Above n 38), at para 883. See also Ch 4, s III.A.ii and Ch 5, s III.A.i.

[136] *Tadic Case* Appeals Judgment (*Ibid*), at para 228; *Krnojelac Case* Appeals Judgment (*Ibid*), at para 32; *Vasiljevic Case* Appeals Judgment (*Ibid*), at para 101; *Kvocka Case* Appeals Judgment (*Ibid*), at para 82; *Stakic Case* Appeals Judgment (*Ibid*), at para 65; *Brdanin Case* Appeals Judgment (*Ibid*), at para 365; *Simic Case* Trial Judgment (*Ibid*), at para 158; *Krajisnik Case* Trial Judgment (*Ibid*), at paras 879, 883. See also Ch 4, s III.B.i, s VII.B and Ch 5, s III.B.

defendant's intent to kill the victims to his actual degree of control over the killings; and (iii) maintaining the formal label 'joint criminal enterprise' or 'common purpose doctrine' to refer to a wholly different notion, that is to say the notion of co-perpetration based on joint control.

The *Vasiljevic* case is distinguishable from the *Stakic* case because in the *Stakic* case, ICTY Trial Chamber II applied the notion of co-perpetration based on joint control in order to overcome the problems posed by the application of the traditional notion of joint criminal enterprise to senior political and military leaders.

ii Findings of the Trial Chamber

According to the factual findings of the Trial Chamber (which were not reversed by the ICTY Appeals Chamber) on the afternoon of 7 June 1992, Milan Lukic— the head of a particularly violent and feared group of Serb paramilitaries which in the course of a few weeks in May and June 1992 committed numerous crimes (such as murders, physical and sexual assaults and looting and destruction of property) against the local Muslim population of the municipality of Visegrad in Southeast BiH[137]—and two other unidentified members of his group, forcibly detained seven Muslim male civilians and took them to a house near the Bikavac Hotel in the town of Visegrad.[138] Soon afterwards, they brought the seven Muslim men in two cars to the Vilina Vlas Hotel (the headquarters of the paramilitary group led by Milan Lukic which had been previously used to detain Muslim civilians).[139] At the Vilina Vlas Hotel, the seven Muslim men waited into the reception area, where the defendant Mitar Vasiljevic (a local Serb, with strong family ties with Milan Lukic, who acted as an informant for the latter's group)[140] was standing with an automatic weapon near the hotel counter.[141] The seven men were guarded by one of the unidentified armed men, who was pointing a rifle at them, preventing any of them from leaving the lobby of the hotel, while Milan Lukic started searching for some keys.[142] As Milan Lukic could not find the keys he was looking for, he ordered the Muslim men to go back to the cars, whereupon the seven Muslim men, Milan Lukic, the defendant and the two unidentified men entered the two cars and drove away.[143]

The Trial Chamber found that, once they reached Sase, instead of continuing towards Visegrad, the cars turned right towards Visegradska Zupa, stopping about one kilometre later.[144] Then the seven Muslim men were instructed to get out of

---

[137] *Vasiljevic Case* Trial Judgment (Above n 25), at para 46.

[138] *Ibid* at para 99.

[139] *Ibid.*

[140] Mitar Vasiljevic was *kumovi*—a strong, Serbian family bond—with Milan Lukic. Furthermore, he was Milan Lukic's best man at his wedding in 1995 or 1996, and since 1998, he had been the godfather of Milan Lukic's child. See *Vasiljevic Case* Trial Judgment (*Ibid*), at paras 46, 75, 95, 251, 252.

[141] *Ibid* at para 100.

[142] *Ibid* at para 100.

[143] *Ibid* at para 102.

[144] *Ibid* at para 104.

the cars and ordered by Milan Lukic to walk through a field towards the bank of the Drina River, which was about 100 metres away.[145] The defendant willingly accompanied Milan Lukic and his group with the seven Muslim men to the Drina River.[146] Lukic, the defendant and the other two unidentified men pointed their guns,[147] which had their safety catches off, at the Muslim men as they walked and told them that they would be killed if they tried to escape.[148] When they reached the bank of the river, the seven Muslim men were lined up facing the river, and Milan Lukic, the defendant and the other two unidentified men lined up approximately five to six metres behind the Muslim men.[149] All four armed men stood behind the seven Muslims, including the defendant.[150] Some of the Muslim men begged for their lives and their pleas were ignored.[151] Following a brief discussion on the manner in which to shoot them, two sequences of gunshots were fired at the seven Muslim men.[152] Subsequently, two of the armed men approached the river and fired more gunshots towards the Muslim men lying in the water.[153] Satisfied that all seven Muslim men were dead (although two of them managed to survive), the four armed men walked back to the cars and drove away.[154]

According to the Trial Chamber, the evidence did not permit to establish that (i) the defendant pointed his weapon at the seven Muslim men while he stood behind them with the other three armed men just before the shooting, (ii) that he fired his weapon at the same time as the other three men did, or (iii) that he personally killed any of the victims.[155] Nevertheless, the Trial Chamber convicted Vasiljevic as a co-perpetrator of the crimes based on his participation (together with Milan Lukic and the other two unidentified members of this group) in a basic form of joint criminal enterprise to kill the seven Muslim men.[156]

For the Trial Chamber, there was an understanding amounting to an agreement, which materialised at the time the defendant left the Vilina Vlas Hotel, or at the time the cars stopped near Sase (at the latest), between the defendant, Milan Lukic and the two unidentified members of his group to kill the seven Muslim men.[157] Furthermore, the murders and attempted murders were discriminatory acts because they were committed solely because the victims were Muslims, and the defendant, Milan Lukic and the two unidentified members of his group acted with the requisite discriminatory intent.[158] Moreover, the defendant personally

---

[145] *Ibid.*
[146] *Ibid* at para 107.
[147] *Ibid* at para 108.
[148] *Ibid* at para 104.
[149] *Ibid* at para 109.
[150] *Ibid* at para 110.
[151] *Ibid* at para 111.
[152] *Ibid.*
[153] *Ibid.*
[154] *Ibid.*
[155] *Ibid* at para 206; *Vasiljevic Case* Appeals Judgment (Above n 13), at para 129.
[156] *Vasiljevic Case* Trial Judgment (*Ibid*), at paras 210, 211, 238, 239.
[157] *Ibid* at para 208.
[158] *Ibid* at para 254.

participated in the implementation of the common criminal purpose by (i) preventing the seven Muslim men from fleeing by pointing a gun at them while they
were detained at the Vilina Vlas Hotel; (ii) escorting them to the bank of the Drina
River and pointing a gun at them to prevent their escape; and (iii) standing behind
the Muslim men with his gun together with the other three offenders shortly
before the shooting started.[159]

iii ICTY Appeals Chamber's Reversal of Vasiljevic's Conviction as a Co-perpetrator for His Participation in a Joint Criminal Enterprise

The ICTY Appeals Chamber reversed Vasiljevic's conviction as a co-perpetrator
for his participation in the joint criminal enterprise to kill the seven Muslim men,
and entered a conviction for aiding and abetting.[160]

According to the majority of the ICTY Appeals Chamber, it was not possible to
infer from the Trial Chamber's factual findings that the defendant shared the
intent to kill the seven Muslim men with Milan Lukic and the other two unidentified members of his group.[161] The Majority held that it was only at the time the
two cars were parked in Sase, and not before, that Vasiljevic learnt that the seven
Muslim men were going to be killed.[162] Hence, the fact that the defendant assisted
to prevent the seven Muslim men from fleeing at the Vilina Vlas Hotel was not
decisive as to whether he shared the intent to kill them.[163]

Furthermore, the Majority held that the actions of Mitar Vasiljevic from the
moment the cars were parked in Sase show that he did not act 'at the same level of
authority or with the same degree of control' over the killings as the other three
actors.[164] In this regard, the Majority found that the evidence did not show that
the defendant (i) pointed his gun at the seven Muslim men while they were lining
up facing the Drina River, (ii) fired his weapon at the same time as the other three
shooters, or (iii) personally killed any of the victims.[165] Moreover, according to the
two survivors, no one around Milan Lukic could have influenced him not to carry
out the killings.[166] As a result, the actions of Vasiljevic were ambiguous as to
whether or not he intended that the seven Muslim men be killed.[167]

Judge Shahabuddeen disagreed with the Majority. In his dissenting opinion, he
explained that even if Vasiljevic only learnt that the seven Muslim men were going
to be killed after parking the cars at Sase, the shortness of time which elapsed
between the arrival at Sase and the shooting on the bank of the Drina River is not
decisive to determine whether Vasiljevic shared the intent to kill them—according

---

[159] *Ibid* at para 209.
[160] *Vasiljevic Case* Appeals Judgment (Above n 13), at para 131.
[161] *Ibid.*
[162] *Ibid* at para 128.
[163] *Ibid* at para 126.
[164] *Ibid* at para 129.
[165] *Ibid.*
[166] *Ibid* at paras 129, 131.
[167] *Ibid* at para 131.

to him, what is decisive is the evidence of what happened during that time.[168] According to Judge Shahabuddeen, the *Vasiljevic* case can be distinguished from the *Djajic* case before the Supreme Court of Bavaria[169] because in Djajic, the only function of the defendant was to guard the victims to ensure that they were killed by others, while Vasiljevic not only guarded the victims but he also took his position with the killers when they drew up in a line at the time of the shooting.[170] By doing so, he demonstrated his willingness to participate in the act of killing rather than his indifference as to whether such an act was or was not going to be finally carried out.[171]

Judge Shahabuddeen explained how in common law jurisdictions,[172] the evidentiary difficulties to establish that a particular member of a firing party actually pulled his trigger, or kill any of the victims, are usually solved by resorting to the notion of joint criminal enterprise, so that as long as it is shown that he was a participant in the enterprise, he is convicted as a co-perpetrator of the ensuing crime even if it is not shown that he took part in the actual killing.[173] In these cases, it is considered that the persons who actually pull the trigger or kill the victims are acting pursuant to an understanding to which the defendant is also an active party, so that in carrying out the crime, the actual shooters carry out not only their own will but also the will of the defendant under such understanding.[174] Hence:

> The focus is not on whether he had power to prevent them from acting as they did; the focus is on whether, even if he could not prevent them from acting as they did, he could have withheld his will and thereby prevented their act from being regarded as having

---

[168] *Prosecutor v Vasiljevic* (Appeals Chamber Judgment, Separate and Dissenting Opinion of Judge Shahabuddeen) ICTY-98-32-A (25 Feb 2004) para17 [hereinafter *Vasiljevic Case* Appeals Judgment, Separate and Dissenting Opinion of Judge Shahabuddeen].

[169] *Prosecution v Djajic* (Judgment) 3 St 20/96 (23 May 1997) Supreme Court of Bavaria. In this case, 14 Muslim captives were made to line up on a bridge with their backs to the railing. Opposite to them, some soldiers and military police lined up pointing their weapons at them. Some additional Serbian guards, including the defendant, formed a semicircle behind them, holding their weapons with both hands in front of their chests to prevent the Muslims from fleeing. The 14 Muslim captives were shot dead by the soldiers and military police. There was no proof that the killing was done by the guards, including the defendant. The Supreme Court of Bavaria held that Djajic was an aidor and abettor, but not a co-perpetrator. There were no sure indications of the defendant's intent to participate in the killings. Indeed, he hung back somewhat when the group of Muslims and the guards walked onto the bridge. Furthermore, his participation in the incident was slight because, even though by standing up in the semi-circle of the guards, he objectively reduced the chance of escaping of the defenceless victims, he did not have any control over the killings. See *Vasiljevic Case* Appeals Judgment, Separate and Dissenting Opinion of Judge Shahabuddeen (Above n 168), at paras 36–40.

[170] *Vasiljevic Case* Appeals Judgment, Separate and Dissenting Opinion of Judge Shahabuddeen (Above n 168), at para 40.

[171] *Ibid.*

[172] See *R v Salmon* (1880) 6 QBD79; *R v Swindall* and Osborne (1846) 2 C & K 230; *Du Cros v Lambourne* [1907] 1 KB 40. It is different if all that can be proven is that one of the persons committed the crime, and there is no proof that they all shared a common intent to commit it or that there is no criminal legal nexus among them.

[173] *Vasiljevic Case* Appeals Judgment, Separate and Dissenting Opinion of Judge Shahabuddeen (Above n 168), at para 27.

[174] *Ibid* at para 32.

been done pursuant to his own will also [. . .] In sum, even if Lukic's personality was the dominant one, it does not follow that the appellant had no will of his own. [. . .] The appellant exercised his will when he joined the joint criminal enterprise led by Lukic, whom he had previously known. Under the joint criminal enterprise, his colleagues were acting pursuant to his will, as well as their own, when they committed the crime; thereupon, the crime became his crime also.[175]

iv Final Remarks

In the author's view, the *Vasiljevic* case falls within the category of 'mob' cases, in which a plurality of persons acting in unison commit the crime, but it is not possible to identify who pulled the trigger. In these cases, the intent to kill of each member of the 'mob' is inferred from the manner in which they participate together with the others in the course of action that leads to the death or serious injury of the victims, regardless of their degree of control over the crime. As Judge Shahabudeen rightly pointed out, given the actions taken by Vasiljevic after parking near Sase, the application of the notion of joint criminal enterprise as it is usually applied in 'mob' cases, would have led to the conviction of Vasiljevic as a participant in the joint criminal enterprise to kill the seven Muslim men.[176]

However, the Majority decided to make any factual finding of the defendant's intent to kill dependant on his actual degree of control over the killings. As a result, the Majority would have found that Vasiljevic had the intent to kill the seven Muslim men only if he had had a certain level of authority or degree of control over the crime.

In the view of the author, the Majority altered the nature of the notion of joint criminal enterprise as elaborated by the case law of the *Ad hoc* Tribunals. As seen above, according to this notion, the controlling criteria to distinguish between principals and accessories to the crime is the state of mind (shared intent) with which the different contributions to the common criminal plan are made[177]—this is also explicitly acknowledged by the Majority.[178] However, if the Appeals Chamber conditions any factual finding that a person involved in the commission of the crime shares the common criminal purpose to his level of authority or degree of control over the crime, it is his authority or degree of control over the offence that becomes the key criterion to distinguish between principals and accessories.

---

[175] *Ibid* at para 32, 34.
[176] *Ibid* at paras 34, 40.
[177] *Tadic Case* Appeals Judgment (Above n 25), at para 228; *Krnojelac Case* Appeals Judgment (Above n 25), at para 84; *Kvocka Case* Appeals Judgment (Above n 38), at paras 89–90; *Stakic Case* Appeals Judgment (Above n 38), at para 65; *Brdanin Case* Appeals Judgment (Above n 38), at para 365; *Simic Case* Trial Judgment (Above n 25), at para 158; *Krajisnik Case* Trial Judgment (Above n 38), at paras 879, 883. See also Ch 2, s VII and Ch 5, s III.B.
[178] *Vasiljevic Case* Appeals Judgment (Above n 13), at para 100.

The author does not dispute the fact that a number of reasons might justify the adoption of the notion of control of the crime as the key criterion to distinguish between principals and accessories to the crime, and that these reasons may become more evident in the context of cases against senior political and military leaders—although the wisdom of changing the approach to the distinction between principals and accessories at this stage of work of the *Ad hoc* Tribunals is debatable.

Nevertheless, the author considers that if the ICTY Appeals Chamber wishes to change the controlling criterion to the distinction between principals and accessories, and consequently the preferred approach to the concept of co-perpetration, it should say so explicitly, and it should explain what are 'the cogent reasons that in the interest of justice' require such a change.

VI Joint Application of the Notions of OSP and Joint Control: Indirect Co-perpetration

A Preliminary Remarks: Distinguishing the Notion of Indirect Co-perpetration Based on the Joint Application of OSP and Joint Control from the Notion of Joint Criminal Enterprise at the Leadership Level

In the *Juntas* trial[179] and in the *German Border* case,[180] the courts applied the notion of indirect perpetration in its variant of OSP to convict the senior political and military leaders accused. They were convicted for the crimes committed by their subordinates because they acted within one organised structure of power that they controlled and knew that their orders would be implemented by their subordinates, although they did not know who would implement them. However, in both cases, the courts failed to address the relationship between the several senior political and military leaders accused. The courts failed to do so even though such senior political and military leaders were at the same level within the collective governmental body to which they belonged: the three consecutive military Juntas (*Juntas Militares*) which governed Argentina from 1976 to 1983 in the *Juntas* trial and the National Defence Council (*Nationaler Verteidigungsrat*) responsible for the defence and security in East Germany in the *German Border* case.

As a result, the 31 July 2003 ICTY Trial Judgement in the *Stakic* case constitutes the first example at the international level of how the two main manifestations of the notion of control of the crime (indirect perpetration in its variant of OSP and co-perpetration based on joint control) can be jointly applied to overcome the

---

[179] See Ch 3, s III.C.iii.a.
[180] See Ch 3, s III.C.iii.b.

shortcomings inherent to the separate application of any of them.[181] It shows those situations in which the joint application of these two manifestations of the notion of control of the crime can take place.[182]

The Trial Chamber in the *Stakic* case used the expression 'co-perpetratorship' to refer to the joint application of OSP and joint control. Subsequently, the Trial Chamber in the *Milutinovic* case used the expression 'indirect co-perpetration', which had been originally proposed by the Prosecution.[183] As the Prosecution explained, it:

---

[181] Paras 741–4, 774, 818, 822 and 826 of the *Stakic* case Trial Judgment (Above n 7) show that what the Trial Chamber referred to as 'co-perpetratorship' consists of the combined application of the notions of indirect perpetration in its variant of OSP and co-perpetration based on joint control. See the explanation by Olasolo and Perez Cepeda (Above n 8), at 512–14.,

[182] In its findings on the applicable law concerning the modes of liability under art 7(1) ICTYS, the *Stakic Case* Trial Judgment (*Ibid*), at para 439, held that the notion of indirect perpetration was included within the term 'committing': 'The accused must have participated, physically or otherwise directly or indirectly, in the material elements of the crime charged through positive acts or, based on a duty to act, omissions, whether individually or jointly with others'. Though the Trial Chamber did not explicitly define the notion of indirect perpetration, it added a footnote to its definition of the term 'committing' explaining that:'Indirect participation in German Law (Mittelbare Taterschaft) or "the perpetrator behind the perpetrator"; terms normally used in the context of white collar crime or other forms of organised crime'. See *Stakic Case* Trial Judgment, at para 439, fn 942. Furthermore, the Trial Chamber referred at para 741 to the variant of indirect perpetration in which the crime is committed through an organised structure of power (OSP), which it subsequently applied: 'The Trial Chamber deliberately used both terms [perpetrator behind the] "perpetrator" and [perpetrator behind the] "actor" because it is immaterial for the assessment of the intention of the indirect perpetrator whether the actor had a discriminatory intent; the actor may be used as an innocent tool only'.

The *Stakic* Case Trial Judgment (*Ibid*) also emphasised, at para 438, that 'joint criminal enterprise is only one of several possible interpretations of the term "commission" under Article 7(1) of the Statute and [. . .] other definitions of co-perpetration must equally be taken into account. Furthermore, a more direct reference to "commission" in its traditional sense should be given priority before considering responsibility under the judicial term "joint criminal enterprise"'. Subsequently, the Trial Chamber, after repeatedly citing at para 440 the section on co-perpetration based on joint control of the crime contained in Roxin (Above n 1), at 440, 442, gave the following definition of co-perpetration based on joint control of the crime: 'For co-perpetration it suffices that there was an explicit agreement or silent consent to reach a common goal by coordinated co-operation and joint control over the criminal conduct. For this kind of co-perpetration it is typical, but not mandatory, that one perpetrator possesses skills or authority, which the other perpetrator does not. These can be described as shared acts which, when brought together, achieve the shared goal based on the same degree of control over the execution of the common acts'. (Objective Requirements) 'The accused must also have acted in the awareness of the substantial likelihood that punishable conduct would occur as a consequence of coordinated co-operation based on the same degree of control over the execution of common acts. Furthermore, the accused must be aware that his role is essential for the achievement of the common plan'. (Subjective Requirements).

Finally, although the Trial Chamber did not mention it explicitly, it implicitly declared, at para 439, that the joint application of indirect perpetration in its variant of OSP and co-perpetration based on joint control was also included in the definition of the term 'committing' under art 7(1) ICTYS: 'The accused must have participated, physically or otherwise directly or *indirectly*, in the material elements of the crime charged through positive acts or, based on a duty to act, omissions, whether individually or *jointly with others*'. Further, the *Stakic Case* Trial Judgment (*Ibid*), at para 468 stated the essential elements of the joint application of indirect perpetration in its variant of OSP and co-perpetration based on joint control.

[183] *Prosecutor v Milutinovic* (Decision On Ojdanic's Motion Challenging Jurisdiction: Indirect Co-Perpetration) ICTY-05-87-PT (22 Mar 2006) para 25 [hereinafter *Milutinovic Case*, Decision on Indirect Co-Perpetration].

[U]sed the term 'indirect co-perpetration' in the Proposed Amended Joinder Indictment 'to describe the form of indirect co-perpetration based on joint control as applied in Stakic'.[184]

The author considers that the expression 'indirect co-perpetration' better suits the nature of the combined application of a form of indirect perpetration (OSP) and a theory of co-perpetration (joint control).

Furthermore, it is important to highlight that one should not confuse this notion, which is the result of the joint application of two manifestations of the notion of control of the crime (OSP and joint control), with the notion of joint criminal enterprise at the leadership level. As seen above, this last notion is a *sui generis* variant of indirect co-perpetration, which results from the combined application of (i) joint criminal enterprise as a theory of co-perpetration, and (ii) OSP as a form of indirect perpetration.[185] It conflates two competing approaches to the distinction between principals and accessories to the crime: the subjective approach inherent to the notion of co-perpetration based on joint criminal enterprise and the approach based on the notion of control of the crime.[186]

One should be careful when relying on the ICTY Trial Judgement in the *Stakic* case because the ICTY Appeals Chamber overturned the joint application of OSP and joint control insofar as it considered that the notion of control of the crime was not part of customary international law at the time the events included in the indictment against Milomir Stakic took place in the spring and summer of 1992.[187]

Moreover, one should also keep in mind that, prior to the issuance of the Appeal Judgement in the *Stakic* case, the Trial Chamber in the *Milutinovic* case was seized with the specific question of whether the joint application of OSP and joint control (indirect co-perpetration) had achieved customary status in 1992. The Trial Chamber denied such customary status and prevented the application of the notion of 'indirect co-perpetration' in the *Milutinovic* case[188] because:

> [E]ven if Roxin or other authorities did provide clear evidence that the very specific definition of co-perpetration in paragraphs 440 and 442 of *Stakic* exists in German or other national law, such evidence would not support a conclusion that there is state practice and *opinio juris* demonstrating the existence of the *Stakic* definition in customary international law. Neither *Stakic* nor the Prosecution has cited any authority that convincingly establishes state practice or *opinio juris* for the *Stakic* definition.[189]

---

[184] *Ibid* at para 7. In this case, the Prosecution argued that 'indirect co-perpetration as a form of responsibility is either part of customary international law or is a general principle of law, and further argues that an accused can be held liable under this theory of liability "if he has an agreement with others, plays a key role in the agreement and one or more participants used others to carry out crimes"'.

[185] See Ch 4, s V.B and s V.F.

[186] See Ch 4, s V.F.

[187] *Stakic Case* Appeals Judgment (Above n 38), at para 62.

[188] *Milutinovic Case*, Decision on Indirect Co-Perpetration (Above n 183), at paras 40–41.

[189] *Ibid* at para 40.

Subsequently, the joint application of OSP and joint control (indirect co-perpetration) has been relied upon by ICC Pre-Trial Chambers I and III in the Katanga and Ngudjolo[190] and Bemba cases.[191] Nevertheless, it is important to emphasise that the notion of indirect co-perpetration was not relied upon by the *Lubanga Case* Confirmation of the Charges insofar as the charges against Thomas Lubanga were confirmed on the sole basis of the notion of co-perpetration based on joint control of the crime. This was only possible because the defendant and the highest-FPLC-ranking officers not only designed the common plan but they also participated in its physical implementation. Moreover, due to the multiple internal disputes within the FPLC, it is doubtful whether the notion of OSP could, in any way, have been applied in the *Lubanga* case.

In the *Katanga and Ngudjolo* case, ICC Pre-Trial Chamber I explained at length the reasons why the joint application of OSP and joint control (indirect co-perpetration) was permitted under article 25(3)(a) RS. According to ICC Pre-Trial Chamber I:

First, the Chamber recalls that the Defence for Germain Katanga submitted that, while article 25(3)(a) of the Statute provides, respectively, for 'co-perpetration' and 'indirect perpetration', it does not incorporate a combined notion of 'indirect co-perpetration' because article 25(3)(a) of the Statute states, '[. . .] jointly with another or through another person', and not, 'jointly with another *and* through another person' (emphasis added). [] The Chamber notes that article 25(3)(a) uses the connective 'or', a disjunction (or alternation). Two meanings can be attributed to the word 'or'—one known as weak or inclusive and the other strong or exclusive. An inclusive disjunction has the sense of 'either one or the other, and possibly both' whereas an exclusive disjunction has the sense of 'either one or the other, but not both'. Therefore, to interpret the disjunction in article 25(3)(a) of the Statute as either 'inclusive' or 'exclusive' is possible from a strict textualist interpretation. In the view of the Chamber, basing a person's criminal responsibility upon the joint commission of a crime through one or more persons is therefore a mode of liability 'in accordance with the Statute'. [] The Chamber finds that there are no legal grounds for limiting the joint commission of the crime solely to cases in which the perpetrators execute a portion of the crime by exercising direct control over it. Rather, through a combination of individual responsibility for committing crimes through other persons together with the mutual attribution among the co-perpetrators at the senior level, a mode of liability arises which allows the Court to assess the blameworthiness of 'senior leaders' adequately. [] An individual who has no control over the person through whom the crime would be committed cannot be said to commit the crime by means of that other person. However, if he acts jointly with another individual—one who controls the person used as an instrument—these crimes can be attributed to him on the basis of mutual attribution. Although the importance of this notion to the present case will be further clarified below, it must be kept in mind that, due to ethnical loyalties within the respective organisations led by Germain Katanga (FRPI) and

---

[190] Katanga *and Ngudjolo Case* Confirmation of Charges (*Above n 1*), at paras 540–582.
[191] *Bemba Case* (Pre-Trial Chamber III Decision on the Prosecutor's Application for a Warrant of Arrest against Jean-Pierre Bemba Gombo) ICC-01/05-01/08-14-TEn (10 Jun 2008) paras 69–84 [hereinafter *Bemba Case* Warrant of Arrest].

Mathieu Ngudjolo Chui (FNI), some members of these organisations accepted orders only from leaders of their own ethnicity.[192]

ICC Pre-Trial Chamber I also explained in the *Katanga and Ngudjolo* case the reasons why the fact that the ICTY Appeals Chamber had found in the *Stakic* case that the joint application of OSP and joint control (indirect co-perpetration) was not part of customary international law in 1992 did not prevent its application before the International Criminal Court. As ICC Pre-Trial Chamber I pointed out:

> This doctrine has also been applied in international criminal law in the jurisprudence of the international tribunals. In The Prosecutor v. Milomir Stakic Judgement, Trial Chamber II of the ICTY relied on the liability theory of coperpetration of a crime through another person as a way to avoid the inconsistencies of applying the so-called 'Joint Criminal Enterprise' theory of criminal liability to senior leaders and commanders. [] As noted by the Defence for Germain Katanga, the Trial Chamber's Judgement was overturned on appeal. However, the reasoning of the ICTY Appeals Chamber's Judgement is of utmost importance to an understanding of why the impugned decision does not obviate its validity as a mode of liability under the Rome Statute. [] The Appeals Chamber rejected this mode of liability by stating that it did not form part of customary international law. However, under article 21(l)(a) of the Statute, the first source of applicable law is the Statute. Principles and rules of international law constitute a secondary source applicable only when the statutory material fails to prescribe a legal solution. Therefore, and since the Rome Statute expressly provides for this specific mode of liability, the question as to whether customary law admits or discards the 'joint commission through another person' is not relevant for this Court. This is a good example of the need not to transfer the ad hoc tribunals' case law mechanically to the system of the Court.[193]

B Objective and Subjective Elements of the Notion of Indirect Co-Perpetration Based on the Joint Application of OSP and Joint Control

The notion of indirect co-perpetration based on the joint application of OSP and joint control requires the simultaneous fulfilment of the objective and subjective elements of OSP and joint control. As seen above, from an objective perspective, OSP requires the existence of an organised structure of power, or part thereof, characterised by the interchangeable character of its members, to which the physical perpetrators belong.[194] Further, OSP also requires that the senior political or

---

[192] *Katanga and Ngudjolo Case* Confirmation of Charges (Above n 1), at paras 490–93

[193] *Ibid,* at paras 506–508.

[194] See Ch 3, s III.C.ii. Due to the fact that, in order to ascertain the criminal responsibility of the senior political and military leaders at the top of the organisation, it is not necessary to previously determine whether the persons who physically carried out the objective elements of the crimes are criminally liable, the *Stakic Case* Trial Judgment (Above n 7) used the expression 'direct perpetrator(s)/actor(s)' to cover both plausible scenarios (the expression 'direct perpetrator(s)' refers to those situations where they are criminally liable, and the expression 'direct actor(s)' refers to those other situations where they are not criminally liable).

military leader at the top of such organised structure of power controls it (position of authority) and uses it to secure the execution of the objective elements of the crime.[195]

In turn, co-perpetration based on joint control requires an agreement or common plan among the co-perpetrators, which, although it does not need to be specifically directed at the commission of a crime, must contain an 'element of criminality'.[196] Moreover, each co-perpetrator needs to make an essential contribution to the implementation of the common plan, and all co-perpetrators need to act in a co-ordinated manner.[197] Only then will each of them be in a position of frustrating the implementation of the common plan by refusing to play his role.[198]

From a subjective perspective, OSP and joint control require that the relevant senior or political leader fulfils the subjective elements of the offence in question, including any requisite ulterior intent or *dolus specialis*.[199] OSP also requires that the relevant leader be aware of his position of authority within the organised structure of power (or part thereof) that he controls,[200] whereas according to functional control, such a leader must be aware of his ability to frustrate the implementation of the common plan as a result of the essential tasks assigned to him.[201]

Furthermore, co-perpetration based on joint control requires an additional subjective element comprised of the fact that all co-perpetrators must share a *dolus eventualis* with regard to the realisation of the objective elements of the crime as a result of implementing the common plan.[202] Finally, it is important to highlight that according to OSP, whether the physical perpetrators meet all subjective elements of the crime is irrelevant for the purpose of ascertaining the criminal liability of the senior political or military leader at the top of the organisation.[203]

C The Application of Indirect Co-perpetration based on OSP and Joint Control in the *Stakic* Case before the ICTY

i The Situation in the Stakic Case

The *Stakic* case refers to events that took place in the Municipality of Prijedor (Bosnia and Herzegovina) in the spring and summer of 1992. Three organised structures of power existed at that time: (i) the civil administration of Prijedor, which was under the direction of the Prijedor Municipal Assembly/Crisis Staff/War Presidency headed by the defendant Miroslav Stakic, who was also the

---

[195] See Ch 3, s III.C.ii.
[196] See Ch 5, s III.A.i.
[197] See Ch 5, s III.A.ii.
[198] *Ibid.*
[199] See Ch 3, s III.C.ii and Ch 5, s III.B.
[200] See Ch 3, s III.C.ii.
[201] See Ch 5, s III.B.
[202] See Ch 5, s III.B.
[203] See Ch 3, s III.C.i and s III.C.ii.

major of Prijedor; (ii) the civil police of Prijedor; and (iii) the military units posted in Prijedor (mainly the JNA/VRS Garrison and the Territorial Defence of Prijedor).[204]

The Trial Chamber found that the political and military leaders at the top of each of structure were in control of their respective organised structures of power. These leaders knew that their orders would be implemented by their subordinates, and that they had the power to stop the commission of crimes by their subordinates at any time. As a result, mid and low level members of these three organised structures of power, including the physical perpetrators of the crimes, were interchangeable, and the political and military leaders at the top of the organisations had control of the will regarding their subordinates and ultimately they had control over the crimes.[205]

According to the Trial Chamber, the core crime committed in the Municipality of Prijedor was a campaign of persecution against its non-Bosnian Serb population, which included mass murders, torture, physical violence, rapes and sexual assaults, constant humiliation and degradation, destruction and looting of residential and commercial properties, destruction of religious and cultural buildings, mass deportations and denial of fundamental rights.[206] Such a campaign—which took place, to an important extent, inside camps and detention centres, and during military operations against the civilian population—could be only carried out through the joint action of all three organised structures of power existing in Prijedor in 1992.[207]

For this reason, Stakic and the heads of the civil police and army divided the essential tasks for the implementation of the campaign of persecution among themselves. As a result, they were dependent on one another to execute it, and any of them could have frustrated the implementation of the persecutorial campaign by refusing to play his essential role. The civil administration headed by Stakic was mainly in charge of providing logistics and financial assistance to the civil police and the army.[208] Furthermore, Stakic coordinated the cooperation among all three organised structures of power.[209] Although the members of the civil administration did not physically carry out the objective elements of the crime, the civil police and the army could not have implemented the campaign of persecution by themselves.[210]

---

[204] The Trial Chamber stated that, in general, the associates of Stakic included the authorities of the self-proclaimed Assembly of the Serbian People in the Prijedor Municipality, the SDS, the Prijedor Crisis Staff, the Territorial Defence, the police and the military. In particular Stakic acted together with: (a) the chief of Police (Simo Drljaca); (b) the military commanders of the military units posted in Prijedor (Colonel Vladimir Arsic and Major Radmilo Zeljaja); (c) the president of the Executive Committee of the Prijedor Municipality (Dr Milan Kovacevic); and (d) the commander both of the Municipal Territorial Defence Staff and the Trnopolje camp (Slobodan Kuruzovic). See *Stakic Case* Trial Judgment (Above n 7), at para 469.

[205] *Ibid* at paras 86–101, 469–8.

[206] *Ibid* at paras 818–26.

[207] *Ibid* at para 490.

[208] *Ibid* at para 482, 486.

[209] *Ibid* at para 482.

[210] *Ibid* at para 490. The only exception was the crime of deportation, in the physical execution of which members of the civil administration participated under the orders of Stakic. See *Ibid* at para 712.

The situation in the *Stakic* case differed in several respects from the situation in the *Juntas* trial and the *German Border* case. First, in the *Juntas* trial and the *German Border* case, the organisations controlled by the senior political and military leaders brought to trial had the capability to commit the crimes without resorting to any external assistance. Second, in the *Stakic* case, unlike in the *Juntas* trial and the *German Border* case, the physical perpetrators of the crimes did not belong to the organised structure of power controlled by the defendant, but to the other two organised structures of power existing in 1992 in Prijedor (the civil police and the army). Hence, the Trial Chamber could not base Stakic's criminal liability on the notion of indirect perpetration in its variant of OSP.[211]

At the same time, in addition to designing the persecutorial campaign against the non-Serb population of the Prijedor, the main contribution of Stakic and the heads of the civil police and army to the implementation of such a campaign was to instruct their respective subordinates to carry out the tasks respectively assigned to the civil administration, the civil police and the army. Therefore, the physical perpetrators of the crimes were low-level members of the civil police and army acting upon instructions of their superiors, and assisted by low-level members of the civil administration acting pursuant to Stakic's instructions. As a result, the Trial Chamber could not base Stakic's criminal liability on the notion of co-perpetration based on joint control because (i) the physical perpetrators of the crimes did not participate in any decision making process together with Stakic and the heads of the civil police and army; and (ii) there was no consensual division of tasks. In other words, the notion of co-perpetration based on joint control was unsuitable given the hierarchical relationship between the physical perpetrators and the political and military leaders who designed the campaign of persecution and put it on motion through the use of the organised structures of power that they controlled.

As a result, the Trial Chamber in the *Stakic* case decided to rely on the concept of indirect co-perpetration by combining the application of OSP and joint control. It did so in order to adequately reflect the horizontal relationship among Stakic and the heads of the civil police and army, and the vertical relationship among them and their subordinates who physically carried out the objective elements of the crimes. Hence, Stakic, the highest political authority in the Municipality of Prijedor,[212] was convicted for his essential contribution in the implementation of the common plan agreed upon by the highest political, military and police authorities of Prijedor, which aimed at directing the civil administration, the civil police and the army in a coordinated manner to secure the execution of a campaign of persecution against the non-Serb population of Prijedor in the spring and summer of 1992. Moreover, the Trial Chamber also took into account the co-ordinating role Stakic played among the three organisations.[213]

---

[211] See Ch 3, s III.C.i and Ch 5, s VI.C.i.
[212] *Stakic Case* Trial Judgment (Above n 7), at paras 493–4.
[213] *Ibid* at para 482.

ii Application of the Objective Elements of Indirect Co-perpetration Based on OSP and Joint Control

In combining the application of OSP and joint control, the Trial Chamber put forward the following five objective elements: (i) co-perpetrators, (ii) common goal, (iii) agreement or silent consent, (iv) coordinated co-operation, (v) joint control over criminal conduct, and (vi) Dr Stakic's authority.

a Co-perpetrators

Under the heading 'co-perpetrators',[214] the Trial Chamber listed 'the associates of the [a]ccused'.[215] By doing so, the Trial Chamber first addressed the key question in any theory of co-perpetration: who are the co-perpetrators? Nevertheless, this paragraph cannot be considered an objective element of the notion of indirect co-perpetration because one has to refer to the other co-perpetrators only for the purposes of attributing the objective elements of the crime to the defendant, despite the fact that he did not personally fulfil them. Therefore, this paragraph can be considered to be an introduction to the objective elements rather than to constitute an element itself.

b Common Goal

The Trial Chamber divided the requirement of a common agreement or common plan into two sub-elements: 'common goal' and 'agreement or silent consent'.[216] The common goal is described as the objective of consolidating Serbian control in the municipality of Prijedor, which had a majority Muslim population, and to establish a Serb-dominated and Serb-controlled territory at the municipal level.[217] This common goal refers to the overall aim of the campaign. The common goal is more global than the common plan, because it is neither limited to the criminal plan, nor to the co-perpetrators.

c Agreement or Silent Consent

The Trial Chamber distinguished the common goal from subsequent agreements directed at progressively implementing it. Indeed, while the common goal

---

[214] *Ibid* at para 469.

[215] *Ibid.* This list included the authorities of the self-proclaimed Assembly of the Serbian People in the Municipality of Prijedor, the Prijedor Crisis Staff, the Territorial Defence, the civil police and the army. In particular, Stakic acted together with the chief of the police, the commanders of the military units posted in Prijedor, the president of the Executive Committee of the Municipality of Prijedor and the commander of the Municipal Territorial Defence staff and the Trnopolje camp.

[216] *Stakic Case* Trial Judgment (*Ibid*), at paras 470–77.

[217] *Ibid* at para 470.

describes the aim in a more abstract way, the agreement or silent consent also refers to the common agreement or common plan required by joint control and specifies how the common goal shall be reached.[218] Under the heading 'agreement or silent consent', the Trial Chamber found that, after months of planning, on 29 April 1992, the final decision was agreed upon to take over power in the municipality of Prijedor.[219] After the take-over, Stakic and other SDS leaders assumed positions in the municipal government,[220] legally elected Muslim and Croat politicians were forcibly removed,[221] the Serb leadership sought to achieve a state of readiness for war in the municipality of Prijedor,[222] restrictions were imposed[223] and a propaganda campaign was undertaken.[224] The creation of an atmosphere of fear in the municipality of Prijedor finally culminated in the agreement among the members of the Crisis Staff to use armed force against the civilians and to establish the Omarska, Keraterm and Trnoplje camps.[225]

d Coordinated Cooperation

This element refers to the essential contribution of each co-perpetrator during the joint implementation of the common plan. However, the Trial Chamber, as it did with the common plan, also divided this element of joint control into two sub-elements: 'co-ordinated co-operation'[226] and 'joint control over the criminal conduct'.[227] Under the heading 'co-ordinated co-operation', the Trial Chamber described how the take-over of the municipality of Prijedor was carried out through close co-ordinated cooperation among the Bosnian-Serb civilian authorities, the army, the Territorial Defence forces and the civil police,[228] which resulted in the joint commission of the crimes. It described the contribution of the civil administration, headed by Stakic, to the commission of the crimes by providing logistical and financial assistance to the army and the civil police, by providing oversight of the security in the camps and by adopting decisions prolonging the detention of non-Serb citizens of Prijedor. Moreover, it explained how Stakic himself, through his positions as president of the Prijedor Municipal Crisis Staff and the Prijedor Municipal People's (National) Defence Council, facilitated the co-ordination among the civil police, the army and the civilian authorities.[229]

---

[218] See Ch 5, s III.A.i.
[219] *Stakic Case* Trial Judgment (Above n 7), at para 472.
[220] *Ibid* at para 473.
[221] *Ibid.*
[222] *Ibid* at para 474.
[223] *Ibid* at para 475.
[224] *Ibid* at para 476.
[225] *Ibid* at para 477.
[226] *Stakic Case* Trial Judgment (Above n 7), at para 478.
[227] *Ibid* at para 490.
[228] *Ibid* at para 478.
[229] *Ibid* at para 482.

As Stakic made his contribution, for the most part, through the civil administration (the organised structure of power that he controlled), the Trial Chamber, under the heading 'co-ordinated co-operation', also implicitly referred to the following objective elements of OSP: (i) the existence of three organised structures of power (civil administration, civil police and army) in the Municipality of Prijedor in the spring and summer of 1992, which were directed in a concerted manner to secure the commission of the crimes, and to which the physical perpetrators belonged; and (ii) how the defendant directed the civil administration to carry out the essential tasks assigned to it for the implementation of the common plan.

In this regard, the Trial Chamber, despite not using the expression 'organised structure of power', explained in detail the structure of the main governmental bodies of the civil administration and the Serb para-municipal bodies in Prijedor prior to the Serb take-over on the 30 April 1992.[230] It also referred to the structure, composition and functions of the main governmental bodies of the civil administration of the Municipality after the Serb take-over: Prijedor Municipality People's Defence Council (National Defence Council) and Prijedor Crisis Staff (later War Presidency).[231] Furthermore, it addressed the position of the defendant within the above-mentioned bodies.[232]

The Trial Chamber adopted a broad approach to the issue of the interchangeability of the members of the civil administration by referring to those decisions which were taken by the various bodies of the civil administration and highlighting the fact that such decisions were subsequently systematically implemented by the municipal staff. [233] In this way, the Trial Chamber implicitly ascertained the existence of an organised structure of power within which Stakic operated. Moreover, the Trial Chamber did not elaborate in detail upon the civil police and the army—the organised structures of power controlled by the defendant's co-perpetrators and to which the physical perpetrators belonged. Nevertheless, when listing the co-perpetrators,[234] it referred to their top positions in organisations, which are usually characterised by their hierarchical structure and the replaceable character of their members.

The Trial Chamber emphasised the fact that, even though the objective elements of the crimes were not physically carried out by mid and low members of

---

[230] *Ibid* at paras 44–66.

[231] *Ibid* at paras 86–101.

[232] *Ibid* at paras 93–9.

[233] For instance, the Trial Chamber found at para 377 of the *Stakic* Case Trial Judgment (Ibid) that the 'Crisis Staff participated by overseeing security there, taking decisions on the continuing detention of Prijedor citizens, providing transport and the necessary fuel for the transfer of prisoners between the various camps and from the camps to non-Serb controlled territory, as well as coordinating the provision of food for the detainees'. However, there is no detailed discussion on how the municipality staff implemented the decisions of the Crisis Staff. On the other hand, the Trial Chamber stated at para 482 that 'the Crisis Staff set up the Logistics Base at Cirkin Polje which provided meals for police at checkpoints and guards at the camps, fuel for transporting detainees to and between camps, and ammunition for the police and army'.

[234] *Stakic Case* Trial Judgment (*Ibid*), at para 469.

the civil administration, they substantially contributed to their commission. In this regard, although the Trial Chamber did not explicitly discuss whether the persons who directly provided financial and logistical assistance or oversight of security in the camps were members of the civil administration, it inferred such membership from the fact that decisions were adopted by the main bodies of the civil administration and were subsequently implemented by persons other than members of the police, the army or the local Territorial Defence forces.

Finally, the Trial Chamber inferred the use by Stakic of the civil administration to secure the commission of the crimes from his role in actively directing the civil administration at (i) providing logistical and financial support for the police and the army,[235] and (ii) providing support for the detention facilities[236] and the deportations[237]—in addition to his co-ordinating role.[238]

e Joint Control over Criminal Conduct

This element refers to the joint control of the crime held by Stakic and by his fellow co-perpetrators as a result of the essential role played by them in the implementation of the common plan. In this regard, the Trial Chamber emphasised that none of the Bosnian-Serb political or military leaders of the municipality of Prijedor could have achieved the common goal on his own, although each of them could have individually frustrated the plan by refusing to play his part or by reporting the crimes.[239] Such a wide-scale, complex and brutal persecutory campaign could never have been achieved without the essential contribution of the leading politicians in the municipality of Prijedor, such as Stakic.[240] Indeed, had the civil administration led by Stakic not participated, the common plan would have been frustrated.[241] Furthermore, Stakic could have frustrated the objective of achieving a Serbian municipality by using his powers to hold accountable those responsible for the crimes, by protecting or assisting non-Serbs or by stepping down from his leadership position.[242]

f Dr Stakic's Authority

The inclusion of this element among the objective requirements of indirect co-perpetration is due to the fact that the combined application of the OSP and joint

---

[235] *Ibid* at para 483.

[236] *Ibid* at para 377–401.

[237] *Ibid* at para 402–408.

[238] In addition to heading the civil administration, Stakic himself, through his position as president of the Crisis Staff and the National Defence Council, facilitated the coordination between the civil police, the army and the civil administration. See *Ibid* at para 482.

[239] *Stakic Case* Trial Judgment (*Ibid*), at para 490.

[240] *Ibid* at para 906.

[241] *Ibid* at para 490.

[242] *Ibid* at para 498.

control results in two control requirements: (a) the control by the relevant senior political or military leader of an organised structure of power (or part thereof) as a result of his position of authority; and (b) the joint control of the crime by such a leader as a result of the essential functions assigned to his organisation. The Trial Chamber deals with this second requisite under the heading 'joint control over the criminal conduct'. Hence, under the heading 'Dr Stakic authority', the Trial Chamber looked at the level of control exercised by Stakic over the civil administration of Prijedor. This is the only objective requirement of OSP explicitly referred to in the judgement. The rest, as has already been pointed out, are only referred to implicitly.

In analysing the level of control held by Stakic over the civil administration, the Trial Chamber did not require that his position of authority be based on a de jure superior-subordinate relationship. It started by mentioning the positions held de jure by Stakic as President of the Assembly of the Serbian People in Prijedor, President of the Municipal Assembly, President of the Prijedor Municipal People's (National) Defence Council and President of the Prijedor Crisis Staff. Nevertheless, it subsequently found that Stakic was the leading political figure in Prijedor in 1992[243] and that there was neither de facto nor de jure authority, nor any individual who would be above Stakic in Prijedor.[244] The Trial Chamber put particular emphasis on the fact that Stakic had special responsibility for events in Prijedor and had also the power to change their course;[245] and it noted the cumulative effect of Stakic's functions as a superior in the central bodies of the Municipality in the sense of article 7(3) of the Statute.[246]

iii Application of the Subjective Elements of Indirect Co-perpetration Based on OSP and Joint Control

In combining the application of OSP and joint control, the Trial Chamber in the *Stakic* case put forward the following three subjective requirements: (a) '*mens rea* for the specific crime charged';[247] (b) 'mutual awareness of the substantial likelihood that crimes would occur';[248] and (c) 'Dr. Stakic's awareness of the importance of his own role'.[249]

---

[243] *Ibid* at para 492.

[244] *Ibid* at para 493.

[245] *Ibid* at para 494.

[246] *Ibid* at para 494. According to art 7(3) ICTYS, '[t]he fact that any of the acts referred to in Articles 2 to 5 of the present Statute were committed by a subordinate does not relieve his superior of criminal responsibility if he knew or had reason to know that the subordinate was about to commit such acts or had done so and the superior failed to take the necessary and reasonable measures to prevent such acts or to punish the perpetrators thereof'.

[247] *Stakic Case* Trial Judgment (*Ibid*), at para 495.

[248] *Ibid* at para 496.

[249] *Ibid* at para 497.

a Mens Rea for the Specific Crime Charged

Insofar as the requirement that the defendant must fulfil all subjective elements of the crime in question, including any *dolus specialis* or ulterior intent, is common to OSP and joint control, the Trial Chamber analysed it in relation to any of the crimes with which Stakic had been charged.[250]

b Mutual Awareness of Substantial Likelihood that Crimes Would Occur

Under this heading, the Trial Chamber discussed that the co-perpetrators acted in the awareness that crimes would likely occur as a consequence of their pursuit of the common goal.[251] This subjective requirement is a key element of the notion of co-perpetration based on joint control.[252] The *Stakic* Trial Judgement stated that the co-perpetrators consented to the removal of Muslims from Prijedor by whatever means necessary and either accepted the likely consequence that crimes would occur or actively participated in their commission.[253] It seems that the *Stakic* Trial Judgement required the subjective equivalent of the common goal and agreement or silent consent. In addition, in this subjective element, it is made clear that the common goal needs to have a criminal element.

c Dr Stakic's Awareness of the Importance of his Own Role

Under this heading, the Trial Chamber first implicitly ascertained Stakic's awareness of his control over the will of the members of the civil administration of Prijedor as a result of his position of authority and their interchangeable character.[254] Subsequently, it discussed Stakic's awareness that his role was essential for the implementation of the common plan, and that he could have frustrated it by not directing the civil administration (the organised structure of power controlled by him) to make the necessary contribution to the implementation of the common plan.[255] In particular, the Trial Chamber explicitly affirmed that Stakic was aware that his role and authority as the leading politician in Prijedor was essential for the accomplishment of the common goal. As the Trial Chamber put it, he was aware that he could frustrate the objective of achieving a Serbian municipality by

---

[250] In the findings on the applicable law, the Trial Chamber affirmed, under the heading '*Mens rea for the specific crime charged*' (*Stakic Case* Trial Judgment (*Ibid*), at para 495), that the specific subjective elements required for each offence charged will be considered separately in the section dealing with that offence. For instance, when dealing with the specific offences of murder and persecution, the Trial Chamber underscored, at paras 587, 818, that while *dolus eventualis* suffices to establish the crime of murder under art 3 of the Statute, the crime of persecution also requires a discriminatory intent.

[251] *Stakic Case* Trial Judgment (*Ibid*), at para 496.

[252] *Ibid.*

[253] *Ibid.*

[254] *Stakic Case* Trial Judgment (*Ibid*), at paras 497–8.

[255] *Ibid* at paras 498.

using his powers to hold those responsible for the crimes accountable, by protecting or assisting non-Serbs or by stepping down from his leadership position.[256] Finally, the Trial Chamber also affirmed that the joint application of OSP and joint control did not require the Chamber to ascertain whether the physical perpetrators met all subjective elements of the crimes in order to decide upon the criminal liability of the senior political leader on trial.[257]

D The Application of Indirect Co-perpetration Based on OSP and Joint Control in the *Bemba* Case before the ICC

After the joint application of indirect perpetration in its variant of OSP and co-perpetration based on joint control (indirect co-perpetration) in the *Stakic* case before the ICTY, ICC Pre-Trial Chambers I and III have recently relied on the notion of indirect co-perpetration in the cases against Germain Katanga, Mathieu Ngudjolo Chui and Jean-Pierre Bemba.

The *Bemba* case is still in its preliminary phase. The main decision issued so far by ICC Pre-Trial Chamber III in relation to this case is the *Bemba Case* Warrant of Arrest. According to this decision, the case concerns war crimes and crimes against humanity (wilful killings, torture, rapes, outrages upon personal dignity and pillage) allegedly committed against the civilian population of the Southern part of the Central African Republic ('CAR') between 25 October 2002 and 15 March 2003.[258]

As the *Bemba Case* Warrant of Arrest pointed out, the crimes were allegedly the result of the implementation of a common plan between Angel-Felix Patasse, former CAR president, and Jean Pierre Bemba, the *de iure* and *de facto* president and commander in-chief of the *Mouvement pour la Liberation du Congo* ('MLC')[259]. The common plan consisted of:

(i) Jean Pierre Bemba's deployment of an important part of the MLC in the CAR territory to provide military support to Angel-Felix Patasse in the conflict in which the latter was engaged against the armed forces loyal to current CAR president Francois Bozize[260]; and

(ii) Angel-Felix Patasse's strategic and logistical support to Jean Pierre Bemba against the current DRC president Joseph Kabila.

---

[256] *Ibid.*

[257] *Ibid* at para 743, where the Trial Chamber held: 'In cases of indirect perpetratorship, proof is required only of the general discriminatory intent of the indirect perpetrator in relation to the attack committed by the direct perpetrators/actors. Even if the direct perpetrator/actor did not act with a discriminatory intent this, as such, does not exclude the fact that the same act may be considered part of a discriminatory attack if only the indirect perpetrator had the discriminatory intent'.

[258] Bemba *Case* Warrant of Arrest (Above n 191), at paras 45 and 68.

[259] *Ibid*, at paras 69–72.

[260] *Ibid.*

As the *Bemba Case* Warrant of Arrest highlighted, according to the common plan, MLC forces, once in CAR territory, would act jointly and in a coordinated manner with CAR forces still loyal to Angel-Felix Patasse (mainly the Presidential Security Unit) in order to stop the offensive of Francois Bozize's forces.[261]

According to ICC Pre-Trial Chamber III, the common plan was not aimed at the commission of the crimes. Moreover, the commission of crimes was not the necessary result of the implementation of the common plan. The commission of the crimes was thus not an integral part of the common plan.[262]

Nevertheless, as the *Bemba Case* Warrant of Arrest pointed out, the commission of the crimes was a likely outcome of the implementation of the common plan, given the numerous acts of violence against the civilian population (murders, thefts, destruction of property and rapes) that the MLC forces that were about to be deployed in CAR territory had carried out in recent military campaigns in several parts of the DRC[263]. Therefore, the common plan had an 'element of criminality' within the meaning of the *Lubanga Case* Confirmation of Charges.[264]

Furthermore, according to the *Bemba Case* Warrant of Arrest, Angel-Felix Patasse and Jean Pierre Bemba did not implement the common plan with the aim of having the crimes committed or even with the awareness that its implementation would necessarily bring about the commission of the crimes. On the contrary, for ICC Pre-Trial Chamber III, Angel-Felix Patasse and Jean Pierre Bemba acted with shared *dolus eventualis* because they (i) were merely aware of the fact that the commission of crimes against the civilian population of Southern CAR was a likely outcome of the implementation of the common plan; and (ii) had mutually accepted this likely outcome.[265]

As the *Bemba Case* Warrant of Arrest pointed out, Angel-Felix Patasse and Jean Pierre Bemba did not carry out any of the objective elements of the crimes directly.[266] As a result, unlike in the *Lubanga* case, the notion of co-perpetration based on joint control was not applicable, because neither member of the common plan had made a contribution by way of directly committing the crimes. Instead, they had each made their contribution to the common plan by using their subordinates in the armed groups that they controlled *de iure* and *de facto*.

Furthermore, according to ICC Pre-Trial Chamber III, the physical perpetrators were allegedly members of the MLC, of which Jean-Pierre Bemba was the *de iure* and *de facto* leader. This could have, in principle, made it possible to consider Jean-Pierre Bemba as an indirect perpetrator, who committed the crimes through his subordinates. However, the *Bemba Case* Warrant of Arrest highlighted that the evidence presented by the Prosecution showed reasonable grounds to believe that the crimes were committed as a result of Jean Pierre Bemba and Angel Felix

---

[261] *Ibid*, at paras 74–6.
[262] *Ibid*, at paras 72–4 and 82.
[263] *Ibid*, at para 80.
[264] *Lubanga Case* Confirmation of Charges (Above n 1), at para 377.
[265] *Bemba Case* Warrant of Arrest (Above n 191), at paras 82–3.
[266] *Ibid* at paras. 80–2.

Patasse's *coordinated* efforts to implement their common plan.[267] In the final analysis, the commission of the crimes was possible due to the coordinated action of their respective subordinates in order to stop Francois Bozize's attempted *coup d' etat*.

In conclusion, although ICC Pre-Trial Chamber III did not state it expressly, Jean-Pierre Bemba was considered an indirect co-perpetrator of the crimes, who, with full awareness of the essential nature of his functions in the implementation of the common plan, carried them out via the organised armed group (the MLC) that he controlled *de jure* and *de facto*[268].

E The Application of Indirect Co-perpetration Based on OSP and Joint Control in the *Katanga and Ngudjolo* Case before the ICC

i The Situation in the Katanga and Ngudjolo *Case*

ICC Pre-Trial Chamber III's initial approach to the notion of indirect co-perpetration has been recently developed by ICC Pre-Trial Chamber I in the *Katanga and Ngudjolo Case* Confirmation of Charges. This case, as the *Lubanga* case, refers to events occurred during the armed conflict that took place in the Ituri District (DRC) in the second half of 2002 and in 2003. The suspects were the two ex commanders in-chief of the Ngiti (FRPI) and Lendu (FNI) armed groups, who fought, with the support of the UPDF, against the provisional government of Ituri, which at that time was controlled by the main Hema political movement (UPC/RP) and its military branch (FPLC).[269]

According to the *Katanga and Ngudjolo Case* Confirmation of Charges, the only two members of the common plan were Germain Katanga (FRPI ex-commander in-chief) and Mathieu Ngujolo Chui (FNI ex-commander in-chief),[270] who had already closely worked together in the past.[271] They both agreed to launch a joint attack on 24 February 2003 against the village of Bogoro, which at that time had an undeniable military value derived from its strategic location at the crossroads between the Bunia-Beni[272] and the Kasenyi-Mongwalu[273] roads.[274]

According to ICC Pre-Trial Chamber I, the common plan had two main objectives. On the one hand, obtaining the control of Bogoro, which was an important

---

[267] *Ibid* at paras 73, 74 and 81.

[268] *Ibid* at paras 52–5 (on the MLC hierarchical structure), 75–81 (on the essential nature of Jean Pierre Bemba's contribution to the implementation of the common plan) and 83 (on the Jean Pierre Bemba's awareness of his leadership position within the MLC, as well as his essential role in the execution of the common plan).

[269] *Katanga and Ngudjolo Case* Confirmation of Charges (*Above n 1*), at pp. 71–5.

[270] *Ibid*, at paras 548–53.

[271] *Ibid*, at para 552.

[272] Bunia and Beni are respectively the capitals of the Ituri District and North Kivu Province.

[273] Kasenyi is the most important village in the Congolese side of Lake Albert, whereas one of the most important gold mines of the Great Lakes region is located in Mongwalu.

[274] *Katanga and Ngudjolo Case* Confirmation of Charges (*Above n 1*), at paras 275–83 and 548.

military objective, given its strategic value.[275] On the other hand, securing that such control would be subsequently maintained through the destruction of the civilian population of Bogoro, which, to a large extent, belonged to the Hema ethnic group and supported the FPLC forces defending the village.[276] As a result, the *Katanga and Ngudjolo Case* Confirmation of Charges found that the common plan was integrally criminal because it specifically aimed at attacking the civilian population of Bogoro.[277]

According to ICC Pre-Trial Chamber I, apart from the active use of children in hostilities, Germain Katanga and Mathieu Ngudjolo Chui did not directly commit any of the crimes that occurred during the attack on Bogoro. On the contrary, once the launch of the attack was agreed upon, their role was to ensure: (i) coordination in its implementation by discussing the details of the attack with those commanders in charge of leading the troops in the field; (ii) the supply of the necessary weapons; (iii) the deployment of their respective forces; and (iv) the issuance to the field commanders of the order to launch the attack against Bogoro.[278] As a result, both suspects carried out their contribution *via* the organised armed groups that they controlled *de jure* and *de facto*,[279] and which, in the view of ICC Pre-Trial Chamber I, complied with the requirements of hierarchical organisation and replaceability of their members as required by OSP.[280]

Moreover, as ICC Pre-Trial Chamber I pointed out, Germain Katanga and Mathieu Ngudjolo Chui belonged to different ethnic groups (Ngiti and Lendu) and had control over organised armed groups with a different ethnic composition.[281] As a consequence:

> [t]he distinction between the Ngitis and the Lendus made it unlikely for combatants to comply with the orders of a leader who was not of the same ethnicity.[282]

The success of the attack was, therefore, dependant on the joint and coordinated action between Germain Katanga and Mathieu Ngudjolo Chui because their respective subordinates would not execute orders given by the other (essential coordinated contributions giving rise to joint control over the crime).[283]

Under these circumstances, the notion of OSP could hardly be applied because it was not possible to identify to which specific armed group the direct perpetrators of each crime belonged. Furthermore, the notion of co-perpetration based on

---

[275] *Ibid*, at paras 273 and 275.

[276] *Ibid*, at paras 273, 275 and 548–9.

[277] As will be seen below, this difference is going to play a fundamental role in the manner in which ICC Pre-Trial Chamber I dealt with the subjective elements in the *Katanga and Ngudjolo* case confirmation of charges.

[278] *Katanga and Ngudjolo Case* Confirmation of Charges (*Above n 1*), at paras 555–61.

[279] *Ibid*, at paras 540–1.

[280] *Ibid*, at paras 543–7.

[281] The FRPI were mainly comprised of members of the Ngiti ethnic group to which Germain Katanga belonged. In turn, the FNI was main comprised of members of the Lendu ethnic group to which Mathieu Ngudjolo Chui belonged.

[282] *Katanga and Ngudjolo Case* Confirmation of Charges (*Above n 1*), at para 519.

[283] *Ibid*, at para 560.

joint control of the crime could not be applied either because neither member of the common plan had directly committed the crimes that took place during the attack on Bogoro—indeed, according to ICC Pre-Trial Chamber 1, the evidence brought before it did not show that Germain Kalonga and Mathieu Ngudjolo Chui entered Bogoro prior to the conclusion of the attack. As a result, ICC Pre-Trial Chamber 1 applied the notion of indirect co-perpetration based on OSP and joint control.

ii Application of the Objective Elements of Indirect Co-perpetration Based on OSP and Joint Control

In combining the application of OSP and joint control, ICC Pre-Trial Chamber put forward the following five objective elements of the notion of indirect co-perpetration: (a) Germain Katanga and Mathieu Ngudjolo Chui had control over the organisation; (b) both organisations—FNI and FRPI—were hierarchically organised; (c) compliance with Germain Katanga and Mathieu Ngudjolo Chui's orders was ensured; (d) Germain Katanga and Mathieu Ngudjolo Chui agreed on common plans; and (e) coordinated essential contribution by each co-perpetrator resulting in the realisation of the objective elements of the crime.[284]

a Germain Katanga and Mathieu Ngudjolo Chui Had Control over the Organisation;

As required by OSP, ICC Pre-Trial Chamber I analysed under this heading the *de iure* and *de facto* position of authority that the two suspects had within their respective armed groups at the time crimes were committed. According to ICC Pre-Trial Chamber I, from the beginning of 2003 until their integration into the armed forces of the DRC at the end of 2004:

> Germain Katanga: (i) served as de jure supreme commander of the FRPI; and (ii) had de facto ultimate control over FRPI commanders who sought his orders for obtaining or distributing weapons, and ammunitions and was the person to whom other commanders reported.[285]

> Mathieu Ngudjolo Chui: (i) served as de jure supreme commander of the FNI; and (ii) had de facto ultimate control over FNI commanders, who sought his orders for obtaining or distributing weapons and ammunitions; and was the person to whom other commanders reported.[286]

---

[284] *Ibid*, at paras 540–61.
[285] *Ibid*, at para. 540.
[286] *Ibid*, at para. 541.

b Both organisations—FNI and FRPI—were hierarchically organised

In this subsection ICC Pre-Trial Chamber I analysed the structure of the armed groups, the FRPI and the FNI, led by the two suspects. As required by OSP, ICC Pre Trial Chamber I gave particular attention to whether the relevant armed groups were organised into a hierarchy. It concluded that:

[T]he FRPI, over which Germain Katanga had the command, was a hierarchically organised group. This is shown in particular by the fact that:

i.   the FRPI was organised into camps within the Irumu territory, in the Walendu Bindi collectivite and that each of these camps had a commander;

ii. Germain Katanga was the commander of the Aveba camp which served as the headquarters of the FRPI;

iii. the FRPI was a military structured organisation divided into sectors, battalions and companies;

iv. FRPI commanders had the ability to communicate with each other through hand-held short-range radios; there was also a phonie at Germain Katanga's headquarters in Aveba; Germain Katanga notably used these assets to give his orders;

v.   Germain Katanga, in his powers as a superior leader, had the ability to jail and adjudicate—for instance, he executed 12 FRPI soldiers for creating troubles at Lake Albert, And punished an Ngiti soldier for raping an Ngiti woman.[287]

[T]he FNI, over which Mathieu Ngudjolo Chui had the command, was a hierarchically organised group. This is shown in particular by the fact that:

i.   the FNI was organised into camps within the Ezekere groupement and that each of these camps had a commander;

ii. Mathieu Ngudjolo Chui was the commander of the Zumbe camp that served as the central camp in the Ezekere groupement;

iii. the FNI was a military structured organisation divided into sectors, battalions, companies, platoons and sections;

iv. FNI commanders had the ability to communicate with each other through two way radios (Motorola); Mathieu Ngudjolo Chui used a phonie and even appointed a phonic operator; and it is notably through these assets that Mathieu Ngudjolo Chui gave his orders;

v.   Mathieu Ngudjolo Chui, in his power as a superior leader, had the ability to jail and adjudicate. For instance, he punished an FNI soldier for sexually enslaving a Lendu woman.[288]

c Compliance with Germain Katanga ana Mathieu Ngudjolo Chui's Orders Was 'Ensured'

In this subsection ICC Pre-Trial Chamber I analysed whether the internal composition of the organised armed groups headed by the two suspects was such as to

---

[287] *Ibid*, at para 543.
[288] *Ibid*, at para 544.

ensure automatic compliance with their orders. As required by OSP, ICC Pre-Trial Chamber I paid particular attention to the size of the groups and the repleaceability of their members. It also analysed whether alternative means to ensure compliance with the suspects' orders,—the severe and violent training of their new young recruits—had been resorted to. After its analysis, ICC Pre-Trial Chamber I concluded as follows:

> [T]he FNI and the FRPI were large organisations each providing its leaders with an extensive supply of soldiers. In this regard, the Chamber has taken into consideration the statement of Witness 250 according to which four battalions of the FRPI, hence a total of approximately 1,000 soldiers, took part in the attack against Bogoro village, whereas one battalion and half of the FNI, hence a total of approximately 375 soldiers, took part in the attack against Bogoro village.[289]
>
> [O]ne of the main characteristics of the militias like the ones led by Germain Katanga and Mathieu Ngudjolo Chui is the interchangeability of the lowest level soldiers, which ensure that the orders given by the highest commanders, if not complied with by one soldier, will be complied with by another one.[290]
>
> At the same time, because the soldiers were young, were subjected to a brutal military training regime and had allegiance to the military leaders of their ethnic groups, they were likely to comply with the orders of those leaders almost automatically, without asking any questions.[291]

d Germain Katanga and Mathieu Ngudjolo Chui Agreed on Common Plan

In this subsection, ICC Pre-Trial Chamber I analysed whether the suspects were members of a common plan to attack the village of Bogoro. As required by the notion of co-perpetration based on joint control, ICC Pre-Trial Chamber I placed particular emphasis on (i) the determination of who were the members of the common plan; and (ii) whether such a common plan was inherently criminal or contained an element of criminality within the meaning of the *Lubanga Case* Confirmation of Charges. It concluded as follows:

> Germain Katanga and Mathieu Ngudjolo Chui agreed on a common plan to 'wipe out' Bogoro [] by directing the attack against the civilian population, killing and murdering the predominantely Hema population and destroying their properties.[292]

According to ICC Pre-Trial Chamber I, although the evidence was insufficient to show that the common plan also entailed a specific instruction for the soldiers to pillage the village of Bogoro or to rape or sexually enslave civilian women, there was sufficient evidence to establish that 'in the ordinary course of events, implementation of the common plan would inevitably result in: (i) the pillaging of the village of Bogoro village; and (ii) the rape or sexual enslavement of civilian women.[293]

---

[289] *Katanga and Ngudjolo Case* Confirmation of Charges (*Above n 1*), at para 545.
[290] *Ibid*, at para 546.
[291] *Ibid*, at para 547.
[292] *Ibid*, at paras 548–9.
[293] *Ibid*, at paras 550–1.

e Coordinated Essential Contribution by Each Co-perpetrator Resulting in the Realisation of the Objective Elements of the Crime

ICC Pre-Trial Chamber I analysed in this subsection whether the functions assigned to Germain Katanga and Mathieu Ngudjolo Chui were essential for the implementation of their common plan, and whether they carried out such functions in a coordinated manner. This constitutes the core requisite of the notion of co-perpetration based on functional control as defined in the *Lubanga Case* Confirmation of Charges. However, unlike in the *Lubanga* case, the analysis focused more on the role played by the suspects to ensure that their subordinates directly implemented their common plan to attack the village of Bogoro and its civilian population. As a result of this analysis, ICC Pre-Trial Chamber I made the following findings:

[F]rom the meeting in Aveba to the day of the attack against the village of Bogoro on 24 February 2003:

i. after agreeing on the plan, Germain Katanga and Mathieu Ngudjolo Chui had direct responsibility for its implementation, which included:

   a. ordering the militias to 'wipe out' Bogoro village;
   b. the distribution of the plan of the attack to FRPI and FNI commanders; and
   c. the distribution of weapons and ammunitions.

ii. Germain Katanga played an overall coordinating role in the implementation of the common plan, in particular, by:

   a. having direct and ongoing contacts with the other participants in the implementation of the common plan;
   b. personally travelling to Beni to obtain weapons and ammunitions;
   c. distributing the weapons and ammunitions not only to the FRPI commanders, but also to the FNI; and
   d. organising the meeting at his Aveba camp where the attack against Bogoro village was planned.

iii. Germain Katanga personally performed other tasks in the implementation of the common plan, in particular, by encouraging the soldiers under his command through military parades in his presence during which songs with hate-filled lyrics were sung.

iv. Mathieu Ngudjolo Chui played an overall coordinating role in the implementation of the common plan, in particular, by:

   a. having direct and ongoing contacts with the other participants in the implementation of the common plan;
   b. travelling to Beni to obtain weapons and ammunitions;
   c. sending Commander Boba Boba on his behalf to the meeting at Aveba Camp, and staying in contact with him through a phonie;
   d. obtaining weapons and ammunitions as part of the outcome of the meeting at Aveba camp; and
   e. distributing the weapons and ammunitions to FNI camps.

v. Mathieu Ngudjolo Chui personally performed other tasks in the implementation of the common plan, in particular, by encouraging the soldiers under his command through military parades in his presence during which songs with hate-filled lyrics were sung.[294]

[T]he attack was planned in early 2003 and that the implementation of the common plan started on the eve of the attack on Bogoro village [. . .] the day before the attack, Germain Katanga and Mathieu Ngudjolo Chui, followed by their respective battalion commanders:

i. met in specific camps for parades, briefing, and singing, notably in Ladile and Lagura;
ii. deployed to different points around the village of Bogoro and prepared for the attack; and
iii. at around 5 a.m. on 24 February 2003, the battalion commanders and soldiers under Germain Katanga and Mathieu Ngudjolo Chui entered the village of Bogoro and attacked the inhabitants.[295]

[J]ust before or during the attack:

i. Germain Katanga was present in the surroundings of the village of Bogoro and gave his last instructions to the soldiers before they entered Bogoro;
ii. Mathieu Ngudjolo Chui was on p/ionfe/Motorola communication with Commander KUTE and was giving instructions throughout the attack[296];

[S]oon after the attack against the village of Bogoro, Germain Katanga and Mathieu Ngudjolo Chui celebrated the common plan's having been carried out, in particular, by:

i. meeting at the centre of the village, near the institute/UPC barracks; and
ii. congratulating other commanders.[297]

[Moreover] Germain Katanga and Mathieu Ngudjolo Chui:

iii. took no punitive action against the other commanders or soldiers under their command for the killings;
iv. in any event congratulated the other commanders around them;
v. ordered the burial of the bodies of the civilians, in order to hide the number of victims.[298]

In conclusion, ICC Pre Trial Chamber I held that:

[. . .] FRPI soldiers would obey only orders issued by FRPI commanders and that, similarly, FNI soldiers would obey only orders issued by FNI commanders. Therefore, the fact that Germain Katanga and Mathieu Ngudjolo Chui were the highest commanders of the Ngiti and Lendu combatants, respectively, corroborates the finding that without their agreement on the common plan and their participation in its the implementation, the crimes would not have been committed as planned.[299]

---

[294] *Ibid*, at para. 555.
[295] *Ibid*, at para. 556.
[296] *Ibid*, at para. 557.
[297] *Ibid*, at para. 558.
[298] *Ibid*, at para. 559.
[299] *Ibid*, at para. 560.

iii Application of the Subjective Elements of Indirect Co-perpetration Based on OSP and Joint Control

In combining the application of OSP and joint control, ICC Pre-Trial Chamber I put forward the following two subjective elements of the notion of indirect co-perpetration: (i) the suspects were aware of the factual circumstances enabling them to exercise joint control over the crimes through another person; and (ii) the suspects were mutually aware and mutually accepted that the implementation of the common plan would result in the realisation of the crimes.[300]

a The Suspects Were Aware of the Factual Circumstances Enabling Them to Exercise Joint Control over the Crimes through Another Person

Under this subsection, ICC Pre-Trial Chamber I analysed whether Germain Katanga and Mathieu Ngudjolo Chui were respectively aware of (i) the essential tasks assigned to each of them for the implementation of the common plan (joint control); and (ii) their *de facto* control over the armed groups that they respectively used to perform such tasks (OSP). According to ICC Pre-Trial Chamber I:

Germain Katanga and Mathieu Ngudjolo Chui:

i. as the highest commanders of the organisations, were aware of the specific role that they played within the FRPI and FNI, respectively;
ii. were aware of the hierarchically organised character of their respective organisations;
iii. were aware of the circumstances allowing automatic compliance with the orders due to:
   a. the size of the organisations, composed mainly of low level and interchangeable soldiers;
   b. the brutal training undergone by the soldiers, specially children under the age of fifteen years; and
   c. the allegiance of the soldiers to the military leaders of their ethnic groups.[301]

[Furthermore] Germain Katanga and Mathieu Ngudjolo Chui:

i intentionally agreed on the plan to 'wipe out' Bogoro and commanded their respective troops to attack Bogoro village;
ii were aware of their coordinating role in the implementation of the common plan;
iii were aware of the essential nature of their coordinating role in the implementation of the common plan and their ability to frustrate the implementation of the plan by refusing to activate a mechanism leading to the soldiers' almost automatic compliance with the orders.[302]

---

[300] *Ibid*, at paras 562–72.
[301] *Ibid*, at para. 562.
[302] *Ibid*, at para. 563.

b The Suspects Were Mutually Aware and Mutually Accepted that the Implementation of the Common Plan Would Result in the Realisation of the Crimes

Under this subsection, ICC Pre-Trial Chamber I, after having identified who the members of the common plan were, analysed whether they all shared the awareness and acceptance that the crimes would be committed as a result of the implementation of the common plan. According to ICC Pre-Trial Chamber I, this is the core subjective element of the notion of co-perpetration based on joint control because it is the basis for the mutual attribution to each member of the common plan of the contributions made by the other members.[303]

Furthermore, ICC Pre-Trial Chamber I also analysed in this subsection whether Germain Katanga and Matheiu Ngudjolo Chui fulfilled all the mental elements required by the definition of the crimes (this requirement is common to OSP and joint control).[304]

As a result, of its analysis, ICC Pre-Trial Chamber I found as follows:

[F]rom the Aveba meeting in early 2003 to the day of the attack on 24 February 2003, Germain Katanga and Mathieu Ngudjolo Chui, as part of the common plan to 'wipe out' Bogoro, intended:

    a. to carry out the attack against the civilian population of the Bogoro village;

    b. to carry out the killings or murder of the civilian population of Bogoro village; and

    c. to destroy properties.[305]

[Moreover] from the Aveba meeting in early 2003 to the day of the attack on 24 February 2003, Germain Katanga and Mathieu Ngudjolo Chui knew that, as a consequence of the common plan, pillaging would occur in the ordinary course of the events.[306]

The majority of ICC Pre-Trial Chamber I also found in relation to crimes of sexual violence that:

[F]rom the Aveba meeting in early 2003 to the day of the attack on 24 February 2003, Germain Katanga and Mathieu Ngudjolo Chui knew that, as a consequence of the common plan, rape and sexual slavery of women and girls would occur in the ordinary course of the events. [] When they planned, ordered and monitored the attack on Bogoro and on other villages inhabited mainly by Hema population, the suspects knew that rape and sexual slavery would be committed in the ordinary course of the events.[307]

Finally, with regard to the war crimes of inhuman treatment and outrages upon personal dignity, ICC Pre-Trial Chamber I held as follows:

Although the evidence is sufficient to establish substantial grounds to believe that FNI/FRPI members committed the war crimes of inhuman treatment, including against

---

[303] *Ibid*, at paras 533–37.
[304] *Ibid*, at paras 527–32.
[305] *Ibid*, at para. 565.
[306] *Ibid*, at para. 566.
[307] *Ibid*, at paras 567–69.

Witness 268, and outrages upon personal dignity, including against Witness 287, in the view of the Chamber, the Prosecution brought no evidence showing that the commission of such crimes was intended by the Germain Katanga and Mathieu Ngudjolo Chui as part of the common plan to 'wipe out' Bogoro village [] Moreover, in the view of the Chamber, the Prosecution has not brought sufficient evidence to establish substantial grounds to believe that, as a result or part of the implementation of the common plan, these facts would occur in the ordinary course of events. Instead, they appear to be crimes intended and committed incidentally by the soldiers, during and in the aftermath of the attack on Bogoro village, without a link to the suspects' mental element.[308]

iv Final Remarks

The *Katanga and Ngudjolo* case before the ICC constitutes to date the best example of the application at the international level of the notion of indirect co-perpetration based on OSP and joint control. Just like ICTY Trial Chamber II in the *Stakic* case, ICC Pre-Trial Chamber I resorted to this notion in a situation in which there was a common plan among a small group of senior political and military leaders who had *de facto* control over different organisations/armed groups organised hierarchically and comprised of interchangeable members. Moreover, as in the *Stakic* case, once the functions for the implementation of the common plan were divided, the senior leaders who were part of the common plan carried them out in a coordinated manner *via* the organisations that they controlled. As a result, the crimes were committed physically by their subordinates during the implementation of the common plan.[309]

The *Katanga and Ngudjolo* Case Confirmation of Charges elaborates with particular clarity on the objective and subjective elements of indirect co-perpetration based on OSP and joint control. Nevertheless, it does not address in detail the following two issues:

(i) whether indirect co-perpetration requires that, at the very minimum, the crimes be a necessary outcome of the implementation of the common plan; or whether it is sufficient if the crimes are a likely consequence of such implementation; and

(ii) whether indirect co-perpetration requires that all members of the common plan be aware and mutually accept that the crimes will be a necessary outcome of the implementation of the common plan; or, whether, it is sufficient if the members of the common plan (a) are aware that the implementation of the common plan will likely bring about the commission of the crimes; and (b) mutually accept such a likely outcome.

This can be explained by the fact that the Majority of ICC Pre-Trial Chamber I found that there was sufficient evidence before it showing substantial grounds to believe that all crimes included in the Prosecution Amended Charging Document

---

[308] *Ibid*, at paras 570–1.
[309] The objective elements of the notion of indirect co-perpetration are set out at paras 495–526 of the *Katanga and Ngudjolo* Case Confirmation of Charges (*Ibid*).

were the ultimate goal or the necessary outcome of the implementation of the common plan. As a result, although some footnotes in the *Katanga and Ngudjolo Case* Confirmation of Charges showed that the Majority of ICC Pre-Trial Chamber I favoured the approach taken in the *Lubanga Case* Confirmation of Charges,[310] it found it unnecessary to elaborate in detail on the question of whether, as the *Lubanga* Case Confirmation of Charges had held, the *notion of dolus eventualis* is included within the general subjective element provided for in article 30 RS.[311]

F Final Remarks: Indirect co-perpetration Based on the Joint Application of OSP and Joint Control as a Fourth Manifestation of the Notion of Control of the Crime

Indirect co-perpetration based on the joint application of OSP and joint control constitutes a fourth manifestation of the notion of control of the crime, which is applicable to two types of scenarios:

(i) When several political and military leaders who have joint control over one organised structure of power jointly use it to secure the commission of the crimes—this is the factual situation in the *German Border* case, where the National Defence Council, which was the organ responsible for defence and security in East Germany, was comprised of several members (however the German Federal Supreme Court failed to address the horizontal relationship between the members of the Council and only applied the notion of OSP);[312]

---

[310] *Ibid*, at para 251, fn. 329. See also *Katanga and Ngudjolo Case* Confirmation of Charges, (Partially Dissenting Opinion of Judge Anita Usascka) ICC-01/04-01/07 (1 Oct 2008) para 12, fn 10.

[311] *Katanga and Ngudjolo Case* Confirmation of Charges (*Ibid*), at para 531. See also *Katanga and Ngudjolo Case* (Pre-Trial Chamber I Decision on the Applications for Leave to Appeal the Decision on the Admission of the Evidence of Witnesses 132 and 287 and on the Leave to Appeal on the Decision on the Confirmation of Charges) ICC-01/04-01/07 (24 Oct 2008) pp 15–16 [hereinafter *Katanga and Ngudjolo Case* Leave to Appeal]. At pp 15 and 16 of this last decision, ICC Pre-Trial Chamber I held, in relation to the third issue for which leave to appeal was requested by the Defence for Germain Katanga, that:

[T]he Defence for Germain Katanga raises no concern in relation to:

(i) the Chamber's distinction between (a) the notion of dolus directus of the second degree (the suspect carries out his action or omission despite being aware that the commission of the crime is its necessary outcome); and (b) the notion of dolus eventualis (the suspect carries out his action or omission in the awareness that the commission of the crime is its likely outcome and accepting such an outcome);

(ii) the Chamber's approach not to entertain the question of whether or not the notion of dolus eventualis is part of the general subjective element provided for in article 30 of the Statute.

[312] *Entscheidungen des Bundesgerichtshofs in Strafsachen* 40, p 218. The German Federal Supreme Court found all three accused guilty of homicide as indirect perpetrators pursuant to the notion of OSP. But the Federal Court did not treat the relationship among the different defendants. Due to the fact that they acted jointly in the National Defence Council, one could have considered them as indirect co-perpetrators because they jointly controlled the decisions of the Council.

(ii) When several political and military leaders, who are each of them in control of one organised structure of power (or a part thereof) direct their different organisations to implement in a coordinated manner a common criminal plan[313]—this is the factual scenario in the *Stakic* Case Trial Judgement, the *Bemba* Case Arrest Warrant and the *Katanga* and *Ngudjolo* Case Confirmation of Charges. In the *Juntas* trial, where each Military Junta was comprised of the Commanders-in-Chief of the Argentinean army, navy and air forces, there were three different organised structures of power (the army, the navy and the air forces). However, unlike in the *Stakic* case, the Federal Court of Appeals considered that such organisations did not act in a co-ordinated manner in the commission of the crimes. As a result, their respective Commanders-in-Chief were only convicted as indirect perpetrators for the crimes committed by their own subordinates.[314]

From a theoretical point of view, there is no difficulty in accepting the notion of indirect co-perpetration based on the joint application of OSP and joint control because the notions of OSP and joint control are both based on the same overall idea: those senior political and military leaders who control the commission of the crimes by planning them and controlling the means and tools through which the criminal activities are carried out ought to be considered principals, and not mere accessories to the crimes.

In this regard, it is important to highlight that this control can either result from the control of the action as such (direct perpetrator) or from the control of the will of the person used as a tool to physically commit the crime (indirect perpetrator). Furthermore, there are cases in which a plurality of persons shares a joint control over the offence as a whole as a result of their essential contributions to the implementation of a common plan (co-perpetrators). Moreover, if it is possible for several direct co-perpetrators to share the control of the crime in this way, there is no

---

[313] One could imagine a third scenario where not all co-perpetrators control one organised structure of power. In this scenario, those co-perpetrators who do not control any organised structure of power would co-ordinate the implementation of the common criminal plan by those other co-perpetrators who use their organised structures of power to have the crimes committed.

[314] One of the most important issues in the *Juntas* Trial was whether the Commanders-in-Chief of the three branches of the armed forces were criminally responsible as individuals, or collectively responsible as members of a governing junta. The Prosecution argued that each member of the three juntas was collectively responsible for all acts committed by any of the three organisations (army, navy, and air force). That would have made the Commander-in-Chief of the air force equally responsible for the crimes committed by those who acted under the command of the army and navy. The Federal Court of Appeals rejected this argument, accepting the Defence's argument that the Commanders-in-Chief of the separate services remained autonomous, not subject to any general orders of the Junta as a whole. As the Federal Court of Appeals put it:

'It has been established in these proceedings that the orders in question did not originate with the Military Junta, but that each of the defendants retained the exclusive and effective command of his respective force. Accordingly, the charges brought by the prosecutor against a commander for crimes committed by subordinates belonging to another force must be rejected'. See Judgment of the Federal Appeals Court (9 Dec 1985) p 29, 804. See also the analysis by MA Sancinetti, *Derechos Humanos en la Argentina Postdictatorial* (Buenos Aires, Hammurabi, 1988).

reason why it should not be possible for several senior political and military leaders to share the control of the crime when they use in a concerted manner their respective organised structures to secure the implementation of the common plan (indirect co-perpetrators).

The notion of indirect co-perpetration is also justified from the perspective that when one deals with situations, that constitute the gravest examples of crimes committed through organised structures of power, it is essential to reinforce the preventive function of international criminal law by directing the intervention at those centres of power where the decisions to carry out the most egregious crimes against the international community as a whole are taken.

Further, resorting to the notion of indirect co-perpetration in order to properly reflect both the horizontal and vertical relationships which brought about the commission of the crimes, also shows sensitivity to the problem that the more exceptions are allowed to the distinction between the notions of perpetration (principal liability) and participation (accessorial or derivative liability), the more the conceptual analysis of international criminal law is damaged, and the higher the risk of losing a key instrument for the protection of the fundamental principles on which international criminal law is founded.[315]

In fact, the concepts of perpetration and participation (and the categories of principals and accessories to the crime) should not depend on the factual circumstances of a given case which are not contained in the law, nor should they be defined so as to encompass all such factual circumstances in such a broad way that their material content is so diffused that it is no longer possible to distinguish between the general rule and exceptions. It is from this perspective that the notion of joint criminal enterprise at the leadership level is particularly problematic insofar as it conflates two competing approaches to the distinction between the notions of perpetration and participation—the subjective approach which is inherent to the notion of joint criminal enterprise, and the approach based on the notion of control of the crime which is at the root of OSP—and creates uncertainty as to which is the controlling criterion to distinguish between the notions of perpetration (principal liability) and participation (accessorial or derivative liability).[316]

---

[315] S Bottke, 'Criminalidad Economica y Derecho Criminal Economico en la Republica Federal de Alemania' (1999) 4 *Revista Penal* 24.
[316] See Ch 4, s V.F.

Epilogue: Future Developments of International Criminal Law in relation to the Responsibility of Superiors for International Crimes

PROF DR KAI AMBOS [1]

Hector Olasolo asked me to write a short epilogue regarding possible future developments in the area covered by the topic of his book. I accepted this kind invitation since I consider the question of the responsibility of superiors for international crimes to be of utmost importance for the future development of International Criminal Law (hereinafter 'ICL'), with a view to holding these persons accountable and thus strengthening the deterrent effect of ICL.

As I tried to explain elsewhere[2] the **core aspect** of the increasingly relevant general part of ICL is the question of **attribution or imputation** (*imputatio, Zurechnung, imputación*), ie, the link or connection between a certain criminal result[3] and a person. One can say that, as a rule, establishing such a link becomes more difficult the more tenuous the relationship between the respective person and that result becomes. Thus, while from a theoretical perspective it is quite simple to link the material perpetrator (the killer) to the result (death of his victim) brought about by his actions, it is not so simple to attribute this result to other persons who have only indirectly contributed to it (the persons behind the scenes, the man in the background etc).[4] This is not a particularity of ICL but a general problem of imputation in criminal law. Everybody easily recognises that there is a (factual and normative) difference between the person who kills, attacks, steals etc and the person who causes someone to do so by ordering, instigating etc or the person who (only) lends assistance to these acts.

---

[1] Chair for Criminal Law, Criminal Procedure, Comparative Law and International Criminal Law, Georg August Universität Göttingen. Head of the Department for Foreign and International Criminal Law of the Institute for Crimianl Law and Criminal Justice of the Georg August Universität Göttingen.

[2] 'Remarks on the General Part of International Criminal Law', 4 *Journal of Int Criminal Justice* (JICJ) 2006, 660 et seq.

[3] I limit myself here to result crimes since only these have a clear causality requirement.

[4] Michael Bohlander employs in his recent translation of the German Criminal Code (The German Criminal Code—A Modern English Translation (Hart Publishing, Oxford/Portland, 2008), § 84) the term 'hinterman' referring to other words borrowed from German into English terminology, such as 'hinterland', which suggest that English native-speakers will be familiar with the connotations of the prefix 'hinter-' and be able to adapt it to new combinations.

One may prefer, in a so-called unitary **model of participation** (*Einheit-stätermodell*), to give decisive weight to these differences only at the sentencing stage and not, as in a so called differentiated or participation model (*Differen-zierungs* or *Beteiligungsmodell*), at the level of imputation. One may also, as article 25(3) of the ICC Statute does, distinguish between the forms and functions of participation by explicitly mentioning them without, however, attaching material consequences to these distinctions with a view to the classification of the participants and the sentences (so called functional unitary system of participation, *funktionelles Einheitstätermodell*).[5] The question of what model to follow is basically a policy decision and it is neither productive nor innovative to turn it into a question of principle between the 'civil law' and the 'common law' approach. Criminal law doctrine in common law jurisdictions, especially in England, has moved to the centre of academic attention over the last years[6]. The common problems of the general part are being discussed at a high theoretical level, and maybe not surprisingly with the same or similar outcomes, both in common law and civil law jurisdictions.[7] In any case, the determination of the responsibility of senior leaders for international crimes is not predicated on the preference for one or the other model of participation. If we can agree, as a kind of minimum common denominator, that mere causation does not suffice to impute a criminal result to a person, be it as direct or indirect perpetration, we have to develop more sophisticated (normative) forms of imputation and these are not, in principle, dependent on the chosen model of participation. Clearly, things become more complicated in ICL due to its well known **particularities of imputation.** First of all, the relationship between the system (criminality) and the individual (criminal) is not always clear. While there seems to be consensus that ICL is concerned with macro-crime in the sense of Herbert Jäger's fundamental study[8] and that domestic criminal law is, normally, concerned with ordinary and individual crime, the boundaries between the system and the individual level are blurred. While criminal law, at whatever level and in whatever form, always goes after the individual perpetrator, it is clear that ICL cannot do without investigating and understanding the political, social, economic and cultural framework (the 'context') and background of the crimes (the 'crime base') and thus goes well beyond the establishment of mere individual responsibility. This is all the more true if we take into account that current practice in ICL concentrates increasingly, as a matter of law or fact, on the top

---

[5] See further on the models, Ch 2, s II in this volume with a preference for a differentiated model.

[6] There is a legion of recent books on criminal law doctrine which impressively demonstrate the high level of common law discourse on classical general part issues, see eg RA Duff, *Answering for crime: responsibility and liability in the Criminal Law* (Oxford, Hart, 2007); S Shute,AP Simester, *Criminal Law Theory* (Oxford, OUP, 2002); S Shute,J Gardner,J Horder (eds), *Action and value in criminal law* (Oxford, OUP, 2003).

[7] One could quote almost any notorious general part issue, see eg for the treatment of the battered woman who kills her (sleeping) tormenter or the so called issue of an unknown justification, K Ambos, 'Toward a universal system of crime: comments of George Fletcher's Grammar of Criminal Law', 28 *Cardozo Law Review* (2007), 2647, at 2660–61 and 2663–4 with further references.

[8] H Jäger, *Makrokriminalität. Studien zur Kriminologie kollektiver Gewalt* (Frankfurt am Main: Suhrkamp 1989).

or high level perpetrators and leaves the mid or low level perpetrators to the domestic jurisdictions.[9] The focus on those most responsible necessarily leads to an inquiry into the criminal structures they represent. In this sense, it seems clear that the system and individual levels are not mutually exclusive but rather complement each other; a one-sided focus on one or the other would not fully take into account the complexities of macro-crime. For the analysis of individual criminal responsibility this means that one should focus on the rules of imputation or attribution for the top perpetrators, the intellectual masterminds, the 'men in the background', ie, the people running the criminal organisation or enterprise responsible for the atrocities.

In the **collective or systemic level** of international macro-crimes, the collective and organisational context in which these crimes take place makes it difficult to identify and isolate the individual contributions of those who are the 'human element' in these contexts. If mass crimes, such as genocide, persecution and forced deportation, are committed, the first task of investigators and analysts is to disentangle persons, events, acts and context. They must identify and delimitate criminal events and results and bring them together with persons, acting normally in a collective setting. The importance of this **operation of individualisation** with the subsequent determination of the accused's role, function and position in the criminal organisation and the weight of his individual contributions cannot be overestimated. It is, on a micro-level, the prerequisite of a just and fair distribution of responsibilities taking into account each actor's individual culpability, ie, it is the prerequisite of modern (normative) imputation. It almost necessarily focuses on those most responsible, who are able to control and dominate the collective action with full responsibility. On a macro level it is the prerequisite of a criminal justice system which rests on the fundamental principles of criminal law, in particular the principles of legality and culpability (moral blameworthiness).[10]

The future of this system lies with the **International Criminal Court**. This is good news since all *ad hoc* Tribunals—from Nuremberg to the Hague—have suffered from a congenital defect, ie their essentially backward-looking and limited jurisdiction, thereby violating the principles of *nullum crimen sine lege* and of equality. While this old model may be characterised as an '*ex post facto ad hoc imposition*', the ICC model represents a '*prospective universal system*'. It breaks with the old *ad hoc* model in many respects. So far, the ICC case law has shown

---

[9] Cf ICC, Office of the Prosecutor ('OTP'), *Paper on some policy issues before the Office of the Prosecutor* (The Hague, Sep 2003) <www.icc-cpi.int/library/organs/otp/030905_Policy_Paper.pdf>, p 3, 7 ('focus (. . .) on those who bear the greatest responsibility); more recently OTP, *Fourth Report of the Prosecutor of the International Criminal Court*, to the Security Council pursuant to UNSC 1593 (2005), (The Hague, 14.12.2006) <www.icc-cpi.int/library/organs/otp/OTP_ReportUNSC4-Darfur_English.pdf>, p 4. For Pre-Trial Chamber I this *ratione personae* limitation is also ensured by the gravity threshold of art 17(1)(d) (Situation in the DRC in the case of the Prosecutor v Thomas Lubanga Dyilo. Decision concerning PTC I's Decision of 10 Feb 2006 and the Incorporation of Documents into the Record of the Case against Mr Thomas Lubanga Dyilo, ICC-01/04-01/06, 24 Feb 2006, para 50: 'intended to ensure that the Court initiates cases only against the most senior leaders of being the most responsible').

[10] Cf Ambos (Above n 2), at 669 et seq.

quite clearly that the ICC, while taking into account the jurisprudence of the ICTY and ICTR, does not feel bound or even guided by it.[11] This does not mean that there are no areas where it may be worthwhile and/or reasonable to follow settled ICTY/ICTR practice,[12] but the ICC is free not to do so and should to that effect be guided by its own law. I call this the ***tabula rasa*** (clean slate) **principle.**

In the context of this book it is worthwhile mentioning the new **emerging law of participation** as an expression of this *tabula rasa* principle. This law follows, as analysed in detail in this book, the differentiated model and the theory of control or domination of the act (*Tatherrschaft*).[13] The ICC has in particular dissociated itself from the ICTY's approach to co-perpetration. While the ICTY *Stakic* Appeals Chamber—quite surprisingly[14]—held that co-perpetration 'does not have support in customary international law or in the settled jurisprudence of this tribunal'[15] the ICC's Pre Trial Chamber I has, in the *Lubanga* confirmation decision, correctly stated:

> The concept of co-perpetration based on joint control over the crime is rooted in the principle of the division of essential tasks for the purpose of committing a crime between two or more persons acting in a concerted manner. Hence, although none of the participants has overall control over the offence because they all depend on one another for its commission, they all share control because each of them could frustrate the commission of the crime by not carrying out his or her task.[16]

Taking into account this jurisprudential tendency, it seems quite clear that the future of imputation in ICL lies in the **further elaboration of the control/ domination of the act** theory. The theory defended in the last chapter of this book, ie, the indirect perpetration of top level co-perpetrators, is one possible elaboration of this theory.[17] Admittedly, from the perspective of, for example, German or

---

[11] Similarly C Kreß, 'Claus Roxins Lehre von der Organisationsherrschaft und das Völkerstrafrecht', 153 *Goltdammer's Archiv für Strafrecht* (2006) 304, at 307.

[12] Eg, as to the principles and criteria with regard to pleading co-perpetration based on JCE (see Ch 4, s IV in this volume).

[13] Olasolo and PTC I in *Lubanga* use 'control of the act', but literally 'Herrschaft' means domination; therefore, a more accurate translation would be 'domination of the act'.

[14] This is surprising since the joint criminal enterprise liability is based on co-perpetration; it is, in fact, in its basic form (JCE I) co-perpetration and in its extended form (JCE III) an extension of co-perpetration for acts going beyond the original agreement (enterprise) in order to impute these (excessive) acts to all members of the enterprise (see K Ambos, 'Joint Criminal Enterprise and Command Responsibility', 5 *JICJ* [2007] 159, at 159–61, 167 et seq.).

[15] *Prosecutor v. Stakic*, Case No IT-97-24-A, Appeal Judgement 22.03.2006, para 62. For a critical analysis of this judgement see M Badar ' "Just convict everyone!"—Joint perpetration: From Tadic to Stakic and back again',6 *International Criminal Law Review* (2006), 293; crit also Ambos (*Ibid*), at 170 with fn 79.

[16] *Le Procureur v Lubanga*, La Chambre Préliminaire I, Situation en RD Congo, Décision sur la confirmation des charges, 29.1.2007 [ICC-01/04-01/06-803], para 342 quoting *Prosecutor v. Stakic*, Trial Judgement 31 Jul 2003 (IT-97-24), para 440 (English translation by the Court).

[17] Olasolo calls this 'indirect co-perpetration based on OSP and joint control' (Ch 5) and sees a clear conceptual difference to 'horizontal joint criminal enterprise at the leadership level' (analysed in detail in Ch 4, s V). I think the author overstates this difference since in both cases senior leaders work together as co-perpetrators (horizontal relationship, element of joint control) and commit crimes through other persons and thus are indirect perpetrators (vertical relationship, *Organisationsherrschaft*).

Spanish criminal law doctrine, these constructions are nothing new but still the challenge for international and comparative criminal lawyers is to make them fit into the system of ICL. As to the doctrine of control/domination of the act **by virtue of a hierarchical organisation** (shorter: domination by virtue of an organisation, '*Organisationsherrschaft*') I tried to explain elsewhere how this theory must be understood and construed to serve as a convincing form of imputation in ICL.[18] As to the remaining forms of imputation, ie joint criminal enterprise ('JCE') and command responsibility, one must distinguish as follows: **Command responsibility** will certainly continue to serve as an important instrument of imputation for a superior's failure at providing adequate supervision given its explicit and detailed codification in article 28 ICC Statute.[19] As to **joint criminal enterprise** one must further distinguish between JCE I on the one hand, and JCE II and III on the other. JCE I understood as mere co-perpetration can be subsumed under article 25(3)(a) ICC Statute ('jointly with another'),[20] JCE II and III constitute new and autonomous (systemic) concepts of imputation without an explicit basis in written international criminal law[21] and, in addition, conflict with the principle of culpability.[22]

Ultimately, the doctrine of *Organisationsherrschaft* confirms what has been identified as the **underlying rationales** of JCE and also command responsibility. First of all, the traditional system of individual attribution of responsibility, as applied for ordinary criminality characterised by the individual commission of distinct crimes, must be adapted to the needs of ICL aiming at the development of a *mixed system of individual-collective responsibility* in which the criminal enterprise or organisation as a whole serves as the entity upon which attribution of criminal responsibility is based. The doctrine has called this a *Zurechnungsprinzip Gesamttat*,[23] ie a principle or theory of attribution according to which the 'global act' (the criminal enterprise) constitutes the central object of attribution. In a way, such a doctrine brings together all the theories discussed in this paper and proves the central point of the JCE doctrine, ie to take the *criminal enterprise as the starting point of attribution* in international criminal law. Secondly, all the doctrines discussed here have the common aim of attributing the individual crimes committed within the framework of the system, organisation or enterprise to its *leadership*, or 'masterminds', leaving the destiny of low level executors and mid level officials in the hands of the national criminal justice systems. Last but not

---

[18] See K Ambos, 'Command responsibility and Organisationsherrschaft', in: A Nollkaemper, H van der Wilt (eds), *System Criminality in International Law* (Cambridge, CUP, 2008), IV. For a comparison with JCE and command responsibility see Ambos (Above n 14), at 181 et seq.

[19] See for my view most recently Ambos (Above n 14), at 161–2, 176 et seq.

[20] Ambos, (Above n 14), at 170–71.

[21] *Ibid*, at 172–3.

[22] *Ibid*, at 173 et seq.

[23] On this new concept of attribution for collective criminality see the fundamental work of F Dencker, *Kausalität und Gesamttat* (Berlin, Duncker und Humblot, 1996), 125 et seq, 152 et seq, 229, 253 et seq and *passim*. The concept was further elaborated by H Vest, *Genozid durch organisatorische Machtapparate* (Baden-Baden, Nomos, 2002), at 214 et seq, 236 et seq, 303, 304 et seq, 359 et seq.

least, the criminal responsibility of leaders presupposes a kind of (*normative*) control over the acts imputed to them and a mental state linking them to these acts, thereby complying with the principle of *culpability*.

Prof Dr Kai Ambos
Göttingen
29 June 2008

BIBLIOGRAPHY

Akehurst M, 'Custom as a Source of International Law' (1974) 47 *British Yearbook of International Law* 1.

Ambos K, *Dominio del Hecho por Dominio de la Voluntad en virtud de Aparatos Organizados de Poder* (Bogota, Universidad Externado de Colombia, 1998).

—— 'Article 25. Individual Criminal Responsibility' in O Triffterer (ed), *Commentary on the Rome Statute of the International Criminal Court* (Baden-Baden, Nomos, 1999).

—— Der Allgemeine Teil des Volkerstrafrechts: Ansatze einer Dogmatisierung (Berlin, Duncker und Humblot, 2002).

—— 'Superior Responsibility' in A Cassese, P Gaeta, and JRWD Jones (eds.), *The Rome Statute of the International Criminal Court: A Commentary* (Oxford, Oxford University Press, 2002).

—— *La Parte General del Derecho Penal Internacional: Bases para una Elaboracion Dogmatica* (Uruguay, Konrad-Adenauer-Stiftung, 2005).

—'Nulla Poena Sine Lege in International Criminal Law' in R Haveman and O Olusanya (eds), *Sentencing and Sanctioning in Supranational Criminal Law* (Antwerp, Intersentia, 2006).

—— 'Joint Criminal Enterprise and Command Responsibility' (2007) 5 *Journal of International Criminal Justice* 159.

—— (ed.) Imputacion de Crimenes de los Subordinados al Dirigente: Un Estudio Comparado (Bogotá, Temis 2008).

Ambos K and Grammer C, 'Dominio del Hecho por Organizacion. La Responsabilidad de la Conduccion Militar Argentina por la Muerte de Elisabeth Kasemann' (2003) 12 *Revista Penal* 27.

Angevin H and Chavanne A, *Editions du Juris-Classeur Penal* (Paris, LexisNexis, 1998).

Ashworth A, *Principles of Criminal Law* (3rd edn, Oxford, Oxford University Press, 1999).

Bacigalupo E, 'La Distincion entre Autoria y Participacion en la Jurisprudencia de los Tribunales y el Nuevo Codigo Penal Aleman' in R Nuñez Barbero (ed.), *Estudios Penales: Libro Homenaje Al Prof J. Anton Oneca* (Salamanca, Ediciones Universidad de Salamanca, 1982).

—— *Principios del Derecho Espanol II: El hecho Punible* (Madrid, 1985) 135.

—— 'Notas sobre el fundamento de la coautoria en el Derecho Penal' (1993) 31 *Poder Judicial* 31.

Bantekas I, 'The Contemporary Law of Superior Responsibility' (1999) 93 *American Journal of International Law* 575.

Bantekos I and Nash S, International Criminal Law (3rd edition, Routledge-Cavendish 2007).

Barret RP and Little RP, 'Lessons of Yugoslav Rape Trials: A Role for Conspiracy Law in International Criminal Tribunals' (2003) 88 *Minnessotta Law Review* 30.

Bassiouni MC, 'The United Nations Commission of Experts Established pursuant to Security Council Resolution 780' (1994) 88 *American Journal of International Law* 784.

Bassiouni MC, *International Criminal Law: A Draft International Criminal Code* (2nd edn, Ardsley, New York, Transnational Publishers, 1999).
—— *Introduction to International Criminal Law* (Ardsley, New York, Transnational Publishers, 2003).
Bloy R, *Die Beteiligungsform als Zurechnungstypus im Strafrecht* (Berlin, Duncker and Humblot, 1985).
Blumenstock T, 'The Judgement of the International Criminal Tribunal for the Former Yugoslavia in the Brdanin Case' (2005) 18 *Leiden Journal of International Law* 65.
Boas G, Bischoff DL and Reid NL, *International Criminal Law Practitioner Library: Forms of Responsibility in International Criminal Law* (Cambridge, Cambridge University Press 2008).
Boelaert-Suominen S, 'Prosecuting Superiors for Crimes Committed by Subordinates: A Discussion of the First Significant Case Law' (2001) 41 *Virginia Journal of International Law* 747.
Bogdan A, 'Individual Criminal Responsibility in the Execution of a "Joint Criminal Enterprise" in the Jurisprudence of the *ad hoc* International Tribunal for the Former Yugoslavia' (2006) 6 *International Criminal Law Review* 63.
Bohlander M, *The German Criminal Code: A Modern Translation* (Oxford, Hart Publishing 2008).
Bottke S, 'Criminalidad Economica y Derecho Criminal Economico en la Republica Federal de Alemania' (1999) 4 *Revista Penal* 25.
Brady H and Goy B, Current Developments at the Ad Hoc International Criminal Tribunals (2008) 6 *Journal of International Criminal Justice* 569.
Brownlie I, *Principles of Public International Law* (5th edn, Oxford, Oxford University Press, 1998).
Bruno A, *Direito Penal, Vol II* (3rd edn, Rio de Janeiro, Forense, 1967).
Bueno Arus F, 'Perspectivas de la Teoria General del Delito en el Estatuto de Roma de la Corte Penal Internacional de 17 de Julio de 1998' in FJ Quel Lopez (ed), *Creacion de una Jurisdiccion Penal Internacional, Coleccion Escuela Diplomatica* (4th edn, Madrid, 2000).
Bustos Ramirez J, *Obras Completas, Vol. I. Derecho Penal: Parte General* (Lima, ARA Editores EIRL, 2004).
Carnero Rojo E and Lagos Polas F, 'The Strugar Case before the International Criminal Tribunal for the Former Yugoslavia' (2005) 2 *Journal of International Law of Peace and Armed Conflict* 140.
Cassese A, *International Criminal Law* (Oxford, Oxford University Press 2003; 2nd edn 2008).
—— 'The Proper Limits of Individual Responsibility under the Doctrine of Joint Criminal Enteprise' (2007) 5 *Journal of International Criminal Justice* 110.
Cerezo Mir J, *Problemas Fundamentales del Derecho Penal* (Madrid, Tecnos, 1982).
Clapham A, 'On Complicity' in M Henzelin and R Roth (eds), *Le droit penal a l'epreuve de l'internationalisation* (Paris, LGDJ, 2002).
Cornils and Greve V, *Das Danische Strafgesetz-Straffeloven*, Zweisprachige Ausgabe (2nd edn, Friburg, Max-Planck-Institut, 2001).
Cramer S and Heine G in Schonke and Schroder (eds), *Kommentar zum Strafgesetzbuch* (26th edn, Munich, CH Beck, 2001).
Cramer S and Sternberg-Lieben in Schonke and Schroder (eds), *Kommentar zum Strafgesetzbuch* (26th edn, Munich, CH Beck, 2001).

Cryer R, Friman H, Robinson D and Wilmshurst E, *Introduction to International Criminal Law and Procedure: Principles, Procedures, Institutions* (Cambridge, Cambridge University Press 2007).

Cuello Calon E, *Derecho Penal* (9th edn, Barcelona, Libreria Bosch, 1926).

Damaska M, 'The Shadow Side of Command Responsibility' (2001) 49 *The American Journal of Comparative Law* 455.

Danner AM and Martinez JS, 'Guilty Associations: Joint Criminal Enterprise, Command Responsibility and the Development of International Criminal Law' (2005) 93 *California Law Review* 75.

Del Ponte C, 'Investigation and Prosecution of Large-Scale Crimes at the International Level. The Experience of the ICTY' (2006) 4 *Journal of International Criminal Justice* 539.

Dell'Andro R, *La fattispecie plurisoggettiva in diritto penale* (Milan, Giuffre, 1957).

Della Morte G, 'De-Mediatizing the Media Case: Elements of a Critical Approach' (2005) 3 1019.

Delmas-Marty M and Spencer SR, *European Criminal Procedures* (Cambridge, Cambridge University Press 2005).

Desportes F and Le Gunehec F, *Droit Penal General* (12th edn, Paris, Economica, 2005).

Diaz M y Garcia Conlledo, *La Autoria en Derecho Penal* (Barcelona, Universidad de Leon, 1991).

Dixon R, Archbold International Criminal Courts: Practice, Procedure and Evidence (London, Sweet and Maxwell, 2003).

Dressler J, *Understanding Criminal Law* (2nd edn, Albany, Lexis Publishing, 1995).

Duttwiler M, 'Liability for Omissions in International Criminal Law' (2006) 6 *International Criminal Law Review* 1.

Eboe-Osuji E, '"Complicity in Genocide" versus "Aiding and Abetting Genocide"' (2005) 3 *Journal of International Criminal Justice* 56.

Eckhardt WG, 'Command Criminal Responsibility: A Plea for a Workable Standard' (1982) 97 *Military Law Review* 1.

Elewa Badar M, 'Just Convict Everyone!—Joint Perpetration from Tadic to Stakic and Back Again' (2006) 6 *International Criminal Law Review* 302.

Eser A, 'Individual Criminal Responsibility' in A Cassese, P Gaeta, and JRWD Jones (eds), *The Rome Statute of the International Criminal Court: A Commentary* (Oxford, Oxford University Press, 2002).

—— 'Mental Element, Mistake of Fact and Mistake of Law' in A Cassese, P Gaeta, and JRWD Jones (eds), *The Rome Statute of the International Criminal Court: A Commentary* (Oxford, Oxford University Press, 2002).

Faraldo Cabana P, *Responsabilidad Penal del Dirigente en Estructuras Jerarquicas* (Valencia, Tirant lo Blanch, 2004).

Fenrick WJ, 'Article 28. Responsibility of Commanders and Other Superiors' in O Triffterer (ed), *Commentary on the Rome Statute of the International Criminal Court* (Baden-Baden, Nomos, 1999).

Fichtelberg A, 'Conspiracy and International Criminal Justice' (2006) 17 *Criminal Law Forum* 149.

Figueiredo Dias J, 'Autoria y Participacion en el Dominio de la Criminalidad Organizada: El Dominio de la Organizacion' in C Ferre Olive and E Anarte Borrallo (eds), *Delincuencia Organizada: Aspectos Penales, Procesales y Criminologicos* (Universidad de Huelva, 1999).

Fisse B, *Howard's Criminal Law* (5th edn, Sydney, Law Book Company Limited, 1990).

Fletcher GP, 'Is Conspiracy Unique to the Common Law?' (1995) 43 *American Journal of Comparative Law* 171.

—— *Basic Concepts of Criminal Law* (New York/Oxford, Oxford University Press, 1998).

—— *Rethinking Criminal Law* (2nd edn, Oxford, Oxford University Press, 2000).

—— 'The Handam Case and Conspiracy as a War Crime. A new Beginning for International Law in the US' (2006) 4 *Journal of International Criminal Justice* 442.

Fletcher GP and Ohlin D, 'Reclaiming Fundamental Principles of Criminal Law in the Darfur Case' (2005) 3 *Journal of International Criminal Justice* 539.

Fontan Balestra C, *Tratado de Derecho Penal: Parte General* (Albany, Lexis Publishing, 1995).

Gallagher G, 'The Second Srebrenica Trial: Prosecutor v. Vidoje Blagojevic and Dragan Jokic' (2005) 18 *Leiden Journal of International Law* 523.

Gil y Gil A, 'El Caso Espanol', in K Ambos (ed), *Imputacion de Crimenes de Subordinados al Dirigente: Un Estudia Comparado* (Bogotá, Temis 2008) 87.

Gilles P, *Criminal Law* (4th edn, North Ryde, LBC Information Services, 1997).

Gimbernat Ordeig A, *Autor y Complice en Derecho Penal* (Madrid, Universidad de Madrid, 1966).

Gomez Benitez JM, 'El Dominio del Hecho en la Autoria (validez y limites)' (1984) *Anuario de Derecho Penal y de las Ciencias Penales* 104.

—— Elementos Comunes de los Crimenes contra la Humanidad en el Estatuto de la Corte Penal Internacional (2002) 42 *Actualidad Penal* 1121.

Green LC, 'Superior Orders and Command Responsibility' (1989) 27 *Canadian Yearbook of International Law* 167.

Greenwalt A, 'Rethinking Genocidal Intent: The Case for a Knowledge-Based Interpretation' (1999) 99 *Columbia Journal Law Review* 2259.

Gustafson K, 'The Requirements of an "Express Agreement" for Joint Criminal Enteprise Liability: A Critique of Brdanin' (2007) 5 *Journal of International Criminal Justice* 134.

Haan V, 'The Development of the Concept of Joint Criminal Enterprise at the International Criminal Tribunal for the Former Yugoslavia'(2005) 5 *International Criminal Law Review* 175.

Haft F, *Strafrecht Allgemeiner Teil* (7th edn, Munich, 1996).

Hamdorf K, *Beteiligungsmodelle im Strafrecht: Ein Vergleich von Teilnahme—und Einheitstatersystemen in Skandinavien, Osterreich und Deutschland* (Friburg, Max-Planck-Institut, 2002).

—— 'The Concept of a Joint Criminal Enterprise and Domestic Modes of Liability for Parties to a Crime: A Comparison of German and English Law' (2007) 1 *Journal of International Criminal Justice* 210.

Hamilton VL and Kelman H, *Crimes of Obedience: Towards a Social Psychology of Authority and Responsibility* (Binghamton, Yale University Press, 1989).

Heine G, Taterschaft und Teilnahme in staatlichen Machtapparaten (2000) *JZ* 920.

Hernandez Plasencia JL, *La Autoria Mediata en Derecho Penal* (Granada, Comares, 1996).

Herzberg RD, *Taterschaft und Teilnahme* (Munich, Beck, 1977).

Hinek S, 'The Judgement of the International Criminal Tribunal for the Former Yugoslavia in Prosecutor v. Pavle Strugar' (2006) 19 *Leiden Journal of International Law* 477.

Hoyer S in HJ Rudolphi, H Eckard and E Samson, *Systematischer Kommentar zum Strafgesetzbuch* (Munich, Luchterhand Fachb, 2003).

Jackson J, Langer M and Tillers P, Crime, Procedure and Evidence in a Comparative and International Context: Essays in Honour of Professor Mirjan Damarska (Oxford, Hart Publishing 2008).

Jakobs G, *Strafrecht Allgemeiner Teil* (2nd edn, Berlin, Gruyter, 1991).

Jescheck HH and Weigend T, *Lehrbuch des Strafrechts* (5th edn, Berlin, Duncker and Humblot, 1996).

Jia BB, 'The Doctrine of Command Responsibility: Current Problems' (2000) 3 *Yearbook of International Humanitarian Law* 131.

Kadish SH, 'Complicity, Cause and Blame: A Study in the Interpretation of Doctrine' (1985) 73 *California Law Review* 337.

Kang Y and Wu T, 'Criminal Liability for the Actions of Subordinates: The Doctrine of Command Responsibility and its Analogues in United States Law' (1997) 38 *Harvard International Law Journal* 272.

Keijzer N and Van Sliedregt E, 'Commentary to Blaskic Judgement' in A Klip and G Sluiter, *Annotated Leading Cases of International Criminal Tribunals* (Vol 4, Oxford, Hart Publishing, 2001).

Keith KMF, 'The Mens Rea of Superior Responsibility as Developed by ICTY Jurisprudence' (2001) 14 *Leiden Journal of International Law* 617.

Kienapfel D, *Erscheinungsformen der Einheitstaterschaft* in Strafrechtsdogmatik und Kriminalpolitik (Cologne, Muller-Dietz, 1971).

Kindhauser U, *Strafgesetzbuch, Lehr- und Praxiskommentar* (Portland, Nomos, 2002).

Kittichaisaree K, *International Criminal Law* (Oxford, Oxford University Press, 2001).

Kohler H, *Strafrecht Allgemeiner Teil* (Berlin, 1997).

Krey V, *Strafrecht Allgemeiner Teil* (Vol 2, Munich, 2002).

Kugler I, 'Two Concepts of Omission' (2003) 14 *Criminal Law Forum* 421.

Kuhl K, *Strafrecht Allgemeiner Teil* (4th edn, Munich, Vahlen Franz GMBH, 2002).

Kuper W, *Mittelbare Taterschaft, Verbotsirrtum des Tatmittlers und Verantwortungsprinzip* in Juristenzeitung (1989).

Kupper G, 'Zur Abgrenzung der Taterschaftsformen' (1998) 3 *Goldammer's Archiv* 519.

Lackner K and Kuhl K, *Strafgesetzbuch mit Erlauterungen* (24th edn, Munich, CH Beck, 2001).

LaFave WR and Scott AW, *Substantive Criminal Law* (St Paul, West Publishers, 1986).

Lamb S, 'Nullum Crimen sine Lege' in A Cassese, P Gaeta, and JRWD Jones (eds.), *The Rome Statute of the International Criminal Court: A Commentary* (Oxford, Oxford University Press, 2002).

Landrum BD, 'The Yamashita War Crimes Trial: Command Responsibility Then and Now' (1995) 149 *Military Law Review* 293.

Lesch HH, Zeitschrift fur die Gesamte Strafrechtswissenschaft 105 (1993).

Lippman MR, 'The Evolution and Scope of Command Responsibility' (2000) 13 *Leiden Journal of International Law* 157.

Lopez Barja de Quiroga J, *Autoria y Participacion* (Madrid, Akal, 1996).

Lopez Peregrin MJ, *La Complicidad en el Delito* (Valencia, Tirant Lo Branch, 1997).

Magalhaes Noronha E, *Direito Penal, Vol 1: Introducao e Parte Geral* (37th Edition, Saraiva, Sao Paulo, 2003).

Malarino E, 'El Caso Argentino', in K Ambos (ed), Imputacioǹ dé Crimenes de Subordinados al Dirigente: Un Estudio Comparado (Bogotá, Temis 2008) 37.

Maurach R, Gossel KH and Zipf H, *Strafrecht Allgemeiner Teil, Teil II* (6th edn, Munich, 1984).

Meloni C, 'Command Responsibility: Mode of Liability for the Crimes of Subordinates or Separate Offence of the Superior?' (2007) 5 *Journal of International Criminal Justice* 619.

Mezger E, *Tratado de Derecho Penal* Vol II (Madrid, Editorial Revista de Derecho Privado, 1957).

Mir Puig S, *Derecho Penal: Parte General* (6th edn, Barcelona, Edisofer Libros Juridicos, 2002).

Moore M, *Act and Crime: The Philosophy of Action and its Implications for Criminal Law* (Oxford, Oxford University Press, 1993).

Morris V and Scharf MP, *The International Criminal Tribunals for Rwanda* (Ardsley, New York, Transnational Publishers, 1998).

Munoz Conde F, *El Delito de Alzamiento de Bienes* (2nd edn, Barcelona, Libreria Bosch, 1999).

—— 'Problemas de Autoria y Participacion en la Criminalidad Organizada' in C Ferre Olive and E Anarte Borrallo (eds), *Delincuencia Organizada: Aspectos Penales, Procesales y Criminologicos* (Universidad de Huelva, 1999).

—— '¿Dominio de la Voluntad en virtud de Aparatos Organizados en Organizaciones no Desvinculadas del Derecho?' (2000) 6 *Revista Penal* 104.

—— '¿Como Imputar a Titulo de Autores a las Personas que sin Realizar Acciones Ejecutivas, Deciden la Realizacion de un Delito en el Ambito de la Delincuencia Economica Empresarial?' in Donna (dir), *Revista de Derecho Penal* (9th edn, Buenos Aires, 2002).

Munoz Conde F and Garcia Aran M, *Derecho Penal: Parte General* (5th edn, Valencia, Tirant lo Blanch, 2002).

Nybondas M, 'Civilian Superior Responsibility in the Kordic Case' (2003) 50 *Netherlands International Law Review* 59.

Obote-Odora A, 'Conspiracy to Commit Genocide: Prosecutor v Jean Kambanda and Prosecutor v Alfred Musema' (2001) 8 *Murdoch University Electronic Journal of Law.*

—— 'Complicity in Genocide as Understood through the ICTR Experience' (2002) 2 *International Criminal Law Review* 375.

O'Brien E, 'The Nuremberg Principles, Command Responsibility and the Defence of Captain Rockwood' (1985) 149 *Minnessotta Law Review* 275.

Ohlin JD, 'Three Conceptual Problems with the Doctrine of Joint Criminal Enterprise' (2007) 5 *Journal of International Criminal Justice* 69.

Olasolo H, *The Triggering Procedure of the International Criminal Court* (Leiden, Brill, 2005).

—— 'A Note on the Evolution of the Principle of Legality in International Criminal Law' (2007) 2 *Criminal Law Forum* 301.

—— 'Reflections on the Treatment of the Notions of Control of the Crime and Joint Criminal Enterprise in the Stakic Appeal Judgement' (2007) 7 *International Criminal Law Review* 143.

—— *Unlawful Attacks in Combat Operations* (Leiden, Brill, 2007).

Olasolo H and Perez Cepeda A, 'The Notion of Control of the Crime in the Jurisprudence of the ICTY: The Stakic Case' (2004) 4 *International Criminal Law Review* 474.

O'Rourke A, 'Joint Criminal Enterprise and Brdanin: Misguided Overcorrection' (2006) 47 *Harvard International Law Journal* 323.

Otto H, *Strafrecht Allgemeiner Teil* (6th edn, 2000).

Pagliaro A, *Principi di Diritto Penale: Parte Generale* (8th edn, Milan Giuffre, 2003).

Paliero CE, 'Grunderfordernisse des Allgemeinen Teils fur ein europaisches Sanktionenrecht. Landesbericht Italien' (1998) 100 *ZSTW* 438.

Parks WH, 'Command Responsibility for War Crimes' (1973) 62 *Military Law Review* 1.

Perez Cepeda A, *La Responsabilidad de los Administradores de Sociedades: Criterios de Atribucion* (Barcelona, Cedecs Editorial, 1997). 'Criminalidad en la Empresa: Problemas de Autoria y Participacion' (2002) 9 *Revista Penal* 106.

Piragoff DK, 'Article 30: Mental Element' in O Triffterer (ed), *Commentary on the Rome Statute of the International Criminal Court* (Baden-Baden, Nomos, 1999).

Politoff S, Matus JP and Ramirez MC, *Lecciones de Derecho Penal Chileno: Parte General* (Santiago de Chile, Editorial Juridica de Chile, 2003).

Pradel J, *Droit Penale Compare* (Paris, Dalloz, 2002).

Quintero Olivares G, *Manual de Derecho Penal: Parte General* (3rd edn, Pamplona, Aranzadi, 2002).

Ransiek A, *Unternehmensstrafrecht. Strafrecht, Verfassungsrecht, Regelungsalternativen* (Munich, Muller Jur Vlg CF, 1996).

Rassat ML, *Droit Penal General* (2nd edn, Paris, Presses Universitaires France, 1999).

Reed A, Fitzpatrick B and Seago P, *Criminal Law* (Andover, Sweet and Maxwell Publishing, 1999).

Reggio A, 'Aiding and Abetting in International Criminal Law: The Responsibility of Corporate Agents and Business for "Trading with the Enemy" of Mankind' (2005) 5 *International Criminal Law Review* 623.

Renzikowski J, *Restriktiver Taterbegriff und Fahrlassige Beteiligung* (Tubingen, Mohr Siebeck, 1997).

Rikhof J, 'Complicity in International Criminal Law and Canadian Refugee Law. A Comparison' (2006) 4 Journal of International Criminal Justice 702.

Robinson PH, 'Criminal Liability for Omissions: A Brief Summary and Critique of the Law of the United States' (1984) 55 *Revue Internationale de Droit Penal* 633.

Rodriguez Mourullo G, *Comentarios al Codigo Penal* (Civitas Ediciones, 1997).

Rodriguez-Villasante y Prieto JL, 'Los Principios Generales del Derecho Penal en el Estatuto de Roma de la Corte Penal Internacional' (January-June 2000) 75 *Revista Espanola de Derecho Militar* 381.

Rogall K, 'Bewaltigung von Systemkriminalitat' in C Roxin and G Widmaier (eds), *50 Jahre Bundesgerichtshof, Festgabe aus der Wissenschaft, Band IV* (Munich, 2000).

Rotsch T, 'Die Rechtsfigur des Taters hinter dem Tater bei der Begehung von Straftaten im Rahmen organisatorischer Machtapparate und ihre Ubertragbarkeit auf wirtschaftliche Organisationsstrukturen' (1998) *Neue Zeitschrift fur Strafrecht* 495.

—— 'Tatherrschaft Kraft Organisationsherrschaft' (2000) 112 *Zeitschrift fir die gesamte Strafrechtswissenschaft* 518.

Roxin C, *La Responsabilidad de los Administradores de Sociedades: Criterios de Atribucion* (Barcelona, Cedecs Editorial, 1997).

—— *Autoria y Dominio del Hecho en Derecho Penal*, (6th edn, Madrid,Marcial Pons, 1998).

—— 'Problemas de Autoria y Participacion en la Criminalidad Organizada' in C Ferre Olive and E Anarte Borrallo (eds), *Delincuencia Organizada: Aspectos Penales, Procesales y Criminologicos* (Universidad de Huelva, 1999).

—— *Taterschaft und Tatherrschaft* (7th edn, Berlin, Gruyter, 2000).

—— *Strafrecht Allgemeiner Teil* (Vol II, Munich, Beck Juristischer Verlag, 2003).

Rush P and Yeah S, *Criminal Law Sourcebook* (Sydney, Butterworths, 2000).

Sadat LN, *The International Criminal Court, and the Transformation of International Law* (Ardsley, New York, Transnational Publishers, 2002).

Saland P, 'International Criminal Law Principles' in RS Lee (ed), *The International Criminal Court: The Making of the Rome Statute* (The Hague, Kluwer, 1999).

Sancinetti MA, *Derechos Humanos en la Argentina Postdictatorial* (Buenos Aires, Hammurabi, 1988).

Sancinetti MA and Ferrante M, *El Derecho Penal en la Proteccion de los Derechos Humanos, La Proteccion de los Derechos Humanos mediante el Derecho Penal en las Transiciones Democraticas* (Buenos Aires, Hammurabi, 1999).

Sandoz Y, Swinarski C, and Zimmermann B, (eds), *ICRC Commentary on the Additional Protocols of 8 June 1977* (Geneva, Martinus Nijhoff Publishers, 1987).

Schabas WA, 'General Principles of Criminal Law in the International Criminal Court Statute, Part III' (1998) 6 *European Journal of Crime, Criminal Law and Criminal Justice* 417.

—— *Genocide in International Law* (Cambridge, Cambridge University Press, 2001).

—— 'The International Criminal Tribunal for the former Yugoslavia 1997–1999' in A Klip and G Sluiter, *Annotated Leading Cases of International Criminal Tribunals* (Vol 3, Oxford, Hart Publishing, 2001).

—— *An Introduction to the International Criminal Court* (2nd edn, Cambridge, Cambridge University Press, 2004).

Schlosser J, *Mittelbare Individuelle Verantwortlichkeit im Volkerstrafrecht* (Berlin, 2004).

Schroeder FC, *Der Tater hinter dem Tater: Ein Beitrag zur Lehre von der mittelbaren Taterschaft* (Berlin, Duncker and Humblot, 1965).

Silva Sanchez J, *El Nuevo Codigo Penal: Cinco Cuestiones Fundamentales* (Barcelona, 1997).

—— 'Responsabilidad Penal de las Empresas y de sus Organos en Derecho Espanol' in *Fundamentos del Sistema Europeo de Derecho Penal. Libro homenaje a Claus Roxin* (Barcelona, JM Bosch, 1995).

Simons KW, 'Rethinking Mental States' (1992) 72 *Boston University Law Review* 486.

Smith JC and Hogan B, *Criminal Law* (11th edn, London, Butterworths, 2005).

Snyman CR, *Criminal Law* (Durban, Butterworths, 1995).

Taylor T, *The Anatomy of the Nuremberg Trials: A Personal Memoir* (Boston, Little Brown and Company, 1992).

Thompson B, *The Criminal Law of Sierra Leone* (Lanham, University Press of America, 1999).

Tinta MF, 'Commanders on Trial: The Blaskic Case and the Doctrine of Command Responsibility' (2000) 47 *Netherlands International Law Review* 293.

Trechsel S and Noll P, *Schweizerisches Strafrecht, Allgemeiner Teil I, Allgemeine Voraussetzungen der Strafbarkeit* (5th edn, Zurich, Schulthess, 1998).

Tremeear's Criminal Code, Statutes of Canada Annotated (2003, Carswell).

Triffterer O, *Die Osterreichische Beteiligungslehre: Eine Regelung Zwischen Einheitstater und Teilnahmesystem?* (Vienna, 1983).

—— (ed), Commentary on the Rome Statute of the International Criminal Court (Baden-Baden, Nomos 1999; 2nd edition 2008).

—— 'Article 10' in O Triffterer (ed), *Commentary on the Rome Statute of the International Criminal Court* (Baden-Baden, Nomos, 1999).

—— 'Article 33: Superior Orders and Prescription of Law' in O Triffterer (ed), *Commentary on the Rome Statute of the International Criminal Court* (Baden-Baden, Nomos, 1999).

—— 'Causality, A Separate Element of the Doctrine of Superior Responsibility as Expressed in Article 28 Rome Statute?' (2002) 15 *Leiden Journal of International Law* 179.

Trondle H and Fischer T, *Strafgesetzbuch Kommentar* (51st edn, Munich, 2003).

Van Der Wilt H, 'Joint Criminal Enterprise: Possibilities and Limitations' (2007) 5 *Journal of International Criminal Justice* 96.

Van Schaack B and Slye RC, *International Criminal Law and Its Enforcement: Cases and Materials* (West Conshohocken, Foundation Press 2007).

Van Sliedregt E, 'Joint Criminal Enterprise as a Pathway to Convicting Individuals for Genocide' (2007) 5 *Journal of International Criminal Justice* 184.

—— *The Criminal Responsibility of Individuals for Violations of International Humanitarian Law* (The Hague, TMC Asser Press, 2003).

Velasquez F, *Manual de Derecho Penal: Parte General* (2nd edn, Bogota, Comlibros, 2004).

Vest H, 'Humanitatsverbrechen—Herausforderung fur das Individualstrafrecht?' (2001) 113 *Zeitschrift fir die gesamte Strafrechtswissenschaft* 457.

Vetter GR, 'Command Responsibility of Non-Military Superiors in the ICC' (2000) 25 *Yale Journal of International Law* 89.

Vicente Remesal FJ, Penaranda Ramos E, Lavilla Baldo F, Diaz M y Garcia Conlledo, Silva Sanchez JM, Suarez Gonzalez C, Mira Benavent J, and Gonzalez Cussac JL, 'Autoria y Participacion en Determinados Supuestos de Vigilancia: Comentarios a la STS de 21 de febrero de 1989' (1992) 27 *Poder Judicial* 189.

Vives Anton T, *Libertad de Prensa y Responsabilidad Penal (La regulacion de la autoria en los delitos cometidos por medio de la imprenta)* (Madrid, 1977).

Von Hebel H and Robinson D, 'Crimes within the Jurisdiction of the Court' in RS Lee (ed), *The International Criminal Court: The Making of the Rome Statute* (The Hague, Kluwer, 1999).

Waller L and Williams C, *Criminal Law Text and Cases* (Sydney, Butterworths, 2001).

Weigend E, *Das Polnische* Strafgesetzbuch/Kodeks Karny. Zweisprachige Ausgabe (Freiburg, Max-Planck-Institut, 1998) 43.

—— 'Intent, Mistake of Law, and Co-perpetration in the Lubanga Decision on Confirmation of Charges (2008) 6 *Journal of International Criminal Justice* 471.

Welzel H, 'Studien zum System des Strafrechts' 58 (1939) *ZSTW* 491.

Werle G, *Principles of International Criminal Law* (Cambridge, TMC Asser Press, 2005).

—— *Tratado de Derecho Penal Internacional* (Valencia, Tirant lo Blanch, 2005).

—— 'Individual Criminal Responsibility in Article 25 ICC Statute' (2008) 7 *International Criminal law Review* 953.

Wessels J and Beulke W, *Strafrecht Allgemeiner Teil* (31st edn, Heidelberg, Muller, 2001).

Williamson JA, 'Command Responsibility in the Case Law of the International Criminal Tribunal for Rwanda' (2003) 13 *Criminal Law Forum* 365.

Winograd J, 'Federal Criminal Conspiracy' (2004) 41 *American Criminal Law Review* 611.

Zaffaroni ER, *Manual de Derecho Penal: Parte General* (6th edn, Buenos Aires, Editor SA, 2003).

Zahar A, 'Command Responsibility for Civilian Superiors for Genocide' (2001) 14 *Leiden Journal of International Law* 613.

—— 'The ICTR's Media Judgement and the Reinvention of Direct and Public Incitement to Commit Genocide' (2005) 16 *Criminal Law Forum* 33.

Zahar A and Sluiter G, *International Criminal Law: A Critical Introduction* (Oxford, Oxford University Press, 2007).

Zoll A, 'Alleinhandeln und Zusammenwirken aus Polnischer Sicht' in K Cornils, A Eser and B Huber (eds), *Einzelverantwortung und Mitverantwortung im Strafrecht* (Friburg, Max-Planck-Institut, 1998).

Zugaldia Espinar JM, (ed), *Derecho Penal: Parte General* (Valencia, Tirant lo Blanch, 2002).

INDEX